I0129406

The 2015 Hampton Reader

SELECTED ESSAYS AND ANALYSES FROM THE HAMPTON INSTITUTE: A WORKING-CLASS THINK TANK

Hampton Institute Press

HAMPTON

www.hamptoninstitution.org

ISBN: **0991313615**
ISBN-13: 978-0991313617

CONTENTS

Criminal Justice

The National Securitization of Traditional Criminal Justice

Dr. Jason Michael Williams

In the post-911 era, traditional criminal justice processes have become nearly ancient. For example, according to some scholars within criminology/criminal justice, the administration of justice presently finds itself at a strange crossroad (Wacquant, 2009; Garland, 2001; Braithewaite, 2000; Simon, 2007). This crossroad has been linked to several paradigmatic shifts that have been occurring within the crime control complex that has governed the administration of justice since the 1980s. Some believe this shift is the consequence of late modernity (Garland, 2001; Monahan, 2006) and others blame neo-liberalism (Brown, 2010), and the changing currents within the social, political, and cultural contexts. Birthed from this discourse are crimes of late modernity. These crimes consist of terrorism, cyber- crime, and other crimes categorized under the umbrella of national security.

What is of essential importance is the context in which the mechanisms of punishment and crime control has changed. For example, traditionally, rights afforded to U.S. citizens via the Constitution were off limits and could never be challenged or taken away under any circumstances; however, today, because of various laws and powers of the Executive Branch of government, U.S. citizens are at a greater risk of being punished and surveilled by the government. A

2

good indicator of this reality is the current debates on the Obama Administration and the National Security Administration's (NSA) spying program. The ACLU has taken measures to combat the intrusive qualities of the NSA's spying program.

According to the ACLU, the U.S. government does not seem to have a concrete purpose for collecting data on its citizens; it simply alleges that, by doing so, it makes it easier for intelligence officials to identify trends and possible leads later. This shifting in the administration of justice implicates a minority report-effect wherein law enforcement has become involved in the business of preemptive-law enforcement. This shift is a process whereby the government investigates to prevent crime but under a dogmatic notion that everyone is possibly guilty before committing the crime. This logic is abundantly counterproductive to the usual processes of law enforcement. However, the biggest question regarding this discourse is why this is happening and what are some critical elements that may need to be contextualized for a better understanding on what is occurring.

In the post-911 era, the crime control model of administering justice has been placed on steroids. Packer (1968) describes the crime control model as a process in which justice is swift and based on just deserts. There is very little room for improvement of the individual under this model, for justice is at best an assembly line and crime is never-ending and unfixable. The crime control model operates off the presumption of guilt, which is congruent to the way in which the system operates today under preemptive-law enforcement. Large quantities of cases are brought into adjudication and convicts are swiftly assigned punishment. In fact, many cases are never brought to court due to the continuous movement of the system and the large amounts of persons being charged daily. According to the Bureau of Justice Assistance, 90-95% of defendants on both the federal and state levels never reach the trail stage due to plea bargains, which have more striking cons to them than pros. Timothy Lynch of the CATO Institute has written a compelling article that focused on government's response to one's option/right to a trial by jury, thus alleging that government retaliates against those defendants who are apathetic to pleas.

On the other hand, Packer describes the due process model as a more egalitarian approach to administering justice. Under this model, the humanity of the victim and perpetrator is recognized, and there is no loss of Constitutional rights for either side. The due process model understands that error can occur within the fact-finding process and makes strides toward making sure that such errors are avoided and considered; thus, it tries to maintain the integrity of justice.

However, the impact that all the above has on modern day criminal justice is one of the most important questions that must be answered. Since 911, social control has become more punitive. Government can now surveil people in ways never done before. Techno-surveillance has become a very attractive tool in modern-day spying. More strikingly, state and local law enforcement agencies are starting to impersonate federal protocol. For example, many states now have counter-terrorism units, cyber-crime units, and departments of homeland security and emergency management. These advents are indicative of a dual police state (federal and state), or a system in which surveillance reigns supreme 24/7 and within all spaces of governance.

Another critical element to process is the extent to which the private sector has increasingly become involved in the administration of justice. Because the post-911 era brings with it a hyper-punitive platform of administering justice, mass incarceration has become a huge phenomenon and profitable idea to many in the private sector. Some scholars have looked at private prisons and the reentry industry as two of the main beneficiaries of mass incarceration (Thompkins, 2010; Wacquant, 2010; Hallett, 2006; Price, 2006), alleging that private prisons and reentry organizations profit off modern-day punishment and surveillance. For example, Thompkins (2010) explains that, many times, ex-prisoners are recommitted back to prison because of their inability to prioritize their need to work alongside attending counseling sessions with reentry organizations. As a result of not attending mandated counseling sessions because of simple scheduling concerns, many ex-prisoners are sent back to prison to repeat the never-ending cycle of surveillance; meanwhile, reentry organizations and prisons continue to profit off their misery and endless captivity.

The private market found its transformational niche in criminal justice after 911. As a result of 911, intelligence became the key focus within crime control. The government wanted to prevent another attack from happening, which gave the intelligence community an opportunity of a lifetime; however, much of what it was and can do requires the voluntary submission of many civil liberties from the citizenry. This new focus would later become known as the intelligence industrialization complex. Under this complex, intelligence is outsourced to private entities to conduct the usual tasks of intelligence gathering and assessment that would be done by government agencies. However, due to neo-liberal logic, this task has been handed over to private industry under the ludicrous assumption that the private sector is free of error and more efficient. Sadly, most are unaware of the effects this has caused on the local levels of law enforcement. It has turned ordinary citizens into criminal suspects. Preemptive-law enforcement has become part of the daily routine within traditional criminal justice. For example, occurrences of police brutality have been met with extreme protests within the last decade. Civil protests have become occasions for law enforcement to test their counter-terrorism exercises on apparent non-threatening citizens, and policies like stop and frisk have become legitimated under the mantras of "get tough" and "crime control."

Under what appears to be a national security-criminal justice, even law-abiding citizens are suspected criminals, and much of this "suspicion" has racial implications behind them. For example, a report by the Public Advocate, analyzing 2012 NYC stop and frisk data, found the following:

1. **The likelihood a stop of an African American New Yorker yielded a weapon was half that of white New Yorkers stopped.** The NYPD uncovered a weapon in one out every 49 stops of white New Yorkers. By contrast, it took the Department 71 stops of Latinos and 93 stops of African Americans to find a weapon.

2. **The likelihood a stop of African American New Yorker yielded contraband was one-third less than that of white New Yorkers stopped.** The NYPD uncovered contraband in one out every 43 stops of white New Yorkers. By contrast, it took the Department 57 stops of Latinos and 61 stops of African Americans to find contraband.

3. **Despite the overall reduction in stops, the proportion involving black and Latino New Yorkers has remained unchanged.** They continue to constitute 84 percent of all stops, despite comprising only 54 percent of the general population. And the innocence rates remain at the same level as 2011 - at nearly 89 percent.

The above findings are grounds for new theorization on the impact of national security and its impact on localized crime. Localized crime under national security-criminal justice has become just as punitive and totalitarian as crimes on the federal level regarding national security. Furthermore, this new formation of administering justice as noticed above seems to have a disparate impact on racial-minorities. The disparate impact has more to do with labeling and stereotypes than any genuine threat. Furthermore, immigration is another "crime issue" in which to contextualize under national security-criminal justice. Immigration, of course, has racial implications behind it as well due to the assortment of pejoratives used against Spanish-speaking persons who are automatically alleged to be "illegals."

What is most important about this new system of social control is the extent to which it has hyper-punitized the traditional system of criminal justice. The same justifying arguments used by the Bush and Obama Administrations have been used by local government officials concerning, for example, stop and frisk and Mayor Bloomberg. Much of this justifying rhetoric is believed by many due to the unwavering presence of totalitarianism. Most people do not care to know whether or not a certain law or practice is just, especially when the law or practice does not affect them. This is the case with stop and frisk, whereas most Caucasians in NYC are not particularly concerned about stop and frisk because their Mayor and flawed police statistics tells them minorities are to blame for rampant crime and, therefore, *minorities* will be the targets of stop and frisk. However, funny enough, this narrative works notwithstanding the facts as reported by the Public Advocate as well as prior data that had long depicted that the myth of the dangerous minority could not be further from truth.

By framing certain criminal acts under national security, the traditional methodology of responding to crime becomes obsolete. Instead, adjudication is very swift and harsh, and justified by a zero tolerance ideology. There is very little room for fact-finding, which takes away the scrutiny that usually comes with traditional trials. Nonetheless, what is especially intriguing is the extent to which some traditionally domestic issues have suddenly become part of national security discussions, and many of those issues are tied to politically powerless groups. For example, in NYC at one time, there were talks regarding the labeling of street gangs as terrorists. Another issue would be immigration and the extent to which republicans/conservatives believe immigration to be pertinent to national security. Both of the aforementioned issues have racially-anchored implications hidden in the subtext. Therefore, policy implemented in those areas can only lead to disparate treatment onto those selected groups hidden in the subtext (Monahan, 2010).

Moreover, the state will argue the need for such precautionary measures in the name of risk management, which is the quintessential logic behind preemptive-law enforcement and post-modern surveillance. This logic is also legitimated through the use of fear as a tool of galvanizing support for the new form of social control-national security-criminal justice. As the traditional system of criminal justice becomes more like that of national security, citizens can expect harsher policy and penal control. Sadly, much is not being done to on behalf of researchers and government regarding an exploration on the extent to which the powerless will be as always innocent victims in this paradigmatic shifting (see, e.g., Haggerty & Samatas, 2010; Manahan, 2006).

With the ongoing and aggressive warehousing of undocumented persons and citizens in private detention facilities, and the continued expression of racial disparities in the criminal justice system, time can only tell whether or not the American people will tap into a greater consciousness that will catapult the system into a more egalitarian reality. However, in order for such a revolution to happen, the essentialist concept of hyper-individualism must cease to exist. Furthermore, justice itself must be re-conceptualized to fit the post-911 context (see, e.g., Hudson, 2009) to make brainstorming on this matter efficient. People must begin to sympathize with others, they must begin to see beyond the context of the self and discover the interconnectedness between those who are not suspected criminals (predominantly Caucasian) and those under indefinite surveillance (predominantly people of color). Otherwise, national security-criminal justice will continue to turn the U.S into a police state that will eventually impact everyone - even those who may not be targets of this vicious system at the present time. The national securitization of traditional criminal justice is partly due to society's inability to understand issues of late modernity, and so instead of evaluating the issues logically so that a proper response can be applied society responds in the only way in which it knows. It responds via the institution of usually racist, xenophobic, sexist, and classist, campaigns against the "other/issue," which routinely gets entangled into the criminal justice system, because punishment and social control is of course the only option in America.

Works Cited

Braithwaite, J. (2000). The New Regulatory State And The Transformation Of Criminology. *British Journal of Criminology 40:2*, 222-238.

Brown, D. (2011). Neoliberalism as a criminological subject. *Australian & New Zealand Journal of Criminology 44:1*, 129-142.

Garland, D. (2001). *The Culture of Control Crime Control and Social Order In Contemporary Society.*Chicago : The University of Chicago Press.

Haggerty, K. D., & Samatas, M. (2010). *Surveillance and democracy.* New York : Routledge .

Hallett, M. A. (2006). *Private prisons in America : a critical race perspective.* Urbana : University of Illinois Press.

Hudson, B. (2009). Justice in a Time of Terror. *British Journal of Criminology*, 702-717.

Monahan, T. (2006). The Surveillance Curriculum: Risk Management and Social Control in the Neoliberal School. In T. Monahan, *Surveillance And Security Technological Politics And Power In Everyday Life* (pp. 109-124). NY: Routledge .

Monahan, T. (2010). Surveillance as governance: social inequality and the pursuit of democratic surveillance. In K. D. Haggerty, & M. Samatas, *Surveillance and Democracy* (pp. 91-110). NY: Routledge

Packer, H. L. (1968). *The limits of the criminal sanction.* Stanford : Stanford University Press .

Price, B. (2006). *Merchandizing prisoners: who really pays for prison privatization?* Westport: Praeger.

Simon, J. (2007). *Governing through crime: how the war on crime transformed American democracy and created a culture of fear.* New York: Oxford University Press.

Thompkins, D. E. (2010). The expanding prisoner reentry industry. *Dialectical Anthropology 34:4*, 589-604.
Wacquant, L. (2009). *Punishing the Poor: The Neoliberal Government of Social Insecurity.* Durham: Duke University Press.

Wacquant, L. (2010). Prisoner reentry as myth and ceremony. *Dialect Anthropology 34:*, 605-620.

The System Isn't Broken, It Was Designed That Way

A Critical Analysis of Historical Racial Disadvantage in the Criminal Justice System

Dr. Chenelle A. Jones

Contemporary ideologies concerning the structure of the criminal justice system often purports that the system is somehow broken and in dire need of repair from the institutionalized racism that continues to permeate the system. However, to make this assertion of "brokenness" is to also make the assumption that the system was void of any racialized erroneous features at its genesis. This resounding fallacy concerning the structural makeup of the criminal justice system is exasperating because historical trends in justice administration have shown that the criminal justice system is not broken, it was designed that way. The criminal justice system was created in such a way to disadvantage, subdue, and control certain minority groups, namely African Americans. Trends in every facet of criminal justice research concerning police, courts and corrections, provide evidence that the criminal justice system is doing exactly what it was designed to do - marginalize and control minority populations. Although African Americans comprise 13% of the U.S. population, they account for 29% of arrests, 38% of prisoners in state and federal facilities, 42% of death penalty cases, and 37% of executions (Snell, 2011). Research continues to highlight the racial disparities that infiltrate the criminal justice system. While often the recipient of differential treatment, subjective laws, and more punitive sentences, African Americans experience the wrath of the criminal justice system when they are the offenders of crimes. However, when African Americans are victimized by crimes, their victimization is often disregarded and/or addressed with futile effort. Higginbotham (1996) noted these racialized differences in the administration of justice after an extensive review of punishment for crimes committed by both White Americans and African Americans from 1630 to 1865. He found that White Americans tend to ascribe little justice to African Americans while White Americans were indifferent to their own criminality (Higginbotham, 1996). Hawkins (1996) used the phrase "black life is cheap" to describe the devaluation of African American life and their inability to be afforded justice when victimized.

The devalued status of African Americans and their disparate treatment concerning offending and victimization as identified by both Higginbotham and Hawkins, predates the Antebellum period. Even the U.S. Constitution once considered African Americans only 3/5th of a person. So, the notion that the disparities in the criminal justice system are the result of a "broken" system is to overlook and disregard the historical context from which the system was designed. The criminal justice system has been used as a means to perpetuate racial inequalities since its inception. It is a social institution that is vulnerable to numerous external influences and therefore the belief that it is "broken" and somehow in need of repair, is to display a misguided understanding of the macro and micro level contextual factors that affect the criminal justice system and its historical role in race relations. The system is operationally and structurally unsound. There is a need to reconsider the very essence and mechanisms of the criminal justice system. There is a need to reconsider the external influences such as racism, classism, and sexism that influence the system. There is also a need to reconsider the economic and political institutions that control the system. The system is not just "broken" and in need of repair, the system was never right from its establishment.

The criminal justice system is a reflection of society. African Americans have a historical reputation of marginalization and denigration in the United States that reputation is paralleled in the criminal justice system. During the slavery era, African Americans were considered chattel. They were deemed inferior to Whites and forced into slave labor to support the southern economy. Attempts to escape or revolt prompted Whites to use slave patrollers and pass "slave codes" which embraced criminal law and regulated almost every aspect of slave life (Gabbidon and Greene, 2012). These laws were only applicable to African Americans and their violations resulted in harsh punishment because they threatened the very institution of slavery and challenged the status quo. This disparate application of law and the unequal distribution of criminal penalties perpetuated the ideology of White supremacy and Black inferiority. As a result of being birthed from this ideology, the criminal justice system still harbors structural glitches that disadvantage African Americans. Therefore, the assertion that the system is "broken" is an inaccurate assessment; the system was never right from the beginning.

The enforcement of slave codes provides one example of disparate treatment in criminal justice. Laws regulating the slave trade provide another. The slave trade consisted of the abduction, trade, and sell of Africans into slavery, often involving long passages across the Atlantic Ocean. W.E.B. Du Bois found that even after the death penalty was instituted in America for trading slaves, very few Whites were convicted, let alone executed for slave trading (Du Bois 1891). He found that many White Americans believed the punishment of death was too severe a punishment to impose on someone engaging in the slave trade, therefore, White offenders were often found not guilty of the offense. This early form of White crime in America was allowed to persist, particularly due to White supremacy, the devaluation of African American lives, and the economic benefits of the institution of slavery (Du Bois, 1891). Again, historical race relations served as a key component in criminal justice disparities concerning application of the law and imposition of punishments.

Even after 1863 when the Emancipation Proclamation granted freedom to slaves, laws were passed to regulate the lives of African Americans. These laws, commonly known as "Black Codes", penalized African Americans for offenses such as vagrancy and prevented them from testifying against White Americans, serving on juries, and voting. These disparate laws were then enforced by criminal justice practitioners such as the police. Violators were often tried in court by all-White juries, found guilty, and punished by being made to work in the convict-leasing system (Du Bois, 1901). From the beginning, the criminal justice system granted very little justice to African Americans, but if African Americans committed crimes, they endured biased and prejudicial juries who often found them guilty and imposed strict punishments. Conversely, if White Americans committed crimes against African Americans such as rape and/or lynching, rarely were they convicted and made to endure any punitive consequences.

In Southern Horrors: Lynch Law in All Its Phases (1892), Ida B. Wells notes the injustices experienced by African Americans within the criminal justice system. While conducting a broad study of lynchings in America, she found that African Americans were often shot, hanged, or burned to death for minor offenses such as testifying in court, disrespecting Whites, and failing to repay debts. Most of the lynching cases against black men were for rape, even when there was evidence of a consensual relationship. In 1892, Wells found that 66% of the reported 241 lynchings had African American victims. She also found that most White offenders who conducted the lynchings were not convicted of any crime (Wells, 1892). The exclusion of African Americans from testifying in court and the blatant acceptance of White crimes against African Americans without penalty, speaks to the devalued status of African Americans in society and the criminal justice system. It also illuminates the ideology of White supremacy that overtly governed almost every aspect of life then and continues to exist, although covertly now.

The injustices experienced by African Americans within the criminal justice system not only existed in slave codes, black codes, and lynchings, Jim Crow laws further criminalized the mundane behavior of African Americans and subjected them to disparate treatment within the criminal justice system. Jim Crow laws were legal statutes that perpetuated segregation and prevented African Americans from schools, parks, restaurants, theatres, buses, trains, etc. that were designated for White Americans. Violation of these discriminatory laws, which were enforced by law enforcement officials working for their respective criminal justice agencies, carried severe penalties for African Americans. This often led to the increased criminalization of African Americans. Sutherland (1947) noted that African Americans were arrested, convicted, and committed to prisons at a rate of almost three times that of White Americans. Sutherland's findings reveal that even years after its origin, the criminal justice system continued to be used as a means of social control to maintain the social hierarchy of White superiority and black inferiority. This supports the assertion that the system was never broken, it was designed to marginalize African Americans and in doing that, it was very successful.

Building on the idea that the criminal justice system consistently devalues African American life, Johnson (1941) developed a Hierarchy of Homicide Seriousness in which he describes racially disparate perceptions of crime (See Figure 1). Hawkins (1983) further expanded on Johnson's model to include "stranger", "friend", and "acquaintance". Both models highlight the historical devalued status of African Americans in the criminal justice system by noting that crimes are considered "most serious" when there is a White victim and Black offender. These crimes disrupt the established social hierarchy and indicate that African Americans are somehow behaving incongruently with their position in society. As a result, the punishments for these crimes are often very harsh. Crimes in which there is an African American victim and White offender are considered "least serious" because these crimes align with the established social order. African Americans are perceived as inferior to White Americans, therefore their victimization is often overlooked. This model of disparate treatment concerning the victimization of White and African Americans is evidenced in the administration of justice quite frequently.

Figure 1: Johnson's Hierarchy of Homicide Seriousness

Rating	Offense
Most Serious	Negro versus White, White versus White
Least Serious	Negro versus Negro, White versus Negro

Source: Johnson, G. B. (1941). The Negro and Crime. The American Annals of the American Academy of Political and Social Science. 217:93-104.

The Scottsboro Boys is one case that supports Johnson's (1941) model of racially disparate perceptions of crime. The Scottsboro Boys were several African American boys who rode on a train with a group of White boys and two White girls. While they were on the train a fight erupted. Although the White boys were removed from the train, the two White girls who remained on the train claimed they were raped by the African American boys. As a result of their devalued status in society and the belief of White superiority, the African American boys were presumed guilty before the case even began. This was further evidenced by the lynch mob that formed immediately following the girl's claims. The African American boys were granted a trial, however they were tried by an all-White jury, denied legal counsel, found guilty of the crime and sentenced to death. It was later revealed that the girls lied, however the Scottsboro Boys had already served a combined 104 years in prison by that time (Walker, Spohn, & DeLone, 2004). For Scottsboro boys, the criminal justice system was the very mechanism used to steal the boy's liberties and ensure their punishment for crimes they did not commit by denying them a fair trial and any protection under the law.

The case of Emmitt Till is another example of the criminal justice system devaluing the life of African Americans. While accused of whistling at a White girl, Emmitt Till was kidnapped, beat beyond recognition, and shot in the head. His offenders were tried for murder. The case was decided by an all-White, all-male jury because women and African Americans were not permitted to sit on juries. The jury acquitted the offenders of all charges and a few months later, they confessed to the crime. Like the Scottsboro case, the case of Emmitt Till demonstrates the inability of the criminal justice system to provide justice to African Americans.

The Scottsboro Boys and the case of Emmett Till are just a few of many examples in which the lives of African Americans are devalued by the criminal justice system. During the civil rights era, White law enforcement officials frequently used clubs, tear gas, dogs, and hoses on African Americans without penalty (Gabbidon and Greene, 2012). Thus proving that the very institution that should have provided protection to African Americans, was the primary source of harm to African Americans. So the idea that the criminal justice system is "broken" is incorrect. Since its inception, African Americans were granted very little justice in the criminal justice system. It was designed that way and continues to operate that way.

The cases of Rodney King, Sean Bell, Oscar Grant, and Lorenzo Collins are just a few contemporary examples of the continued perceptions of the devalued life of African Americans in the criminal justice system. Each of these cases involved an African American victim and a police offender. For these cases, the police offender was either acquitted of all charges or convicted of a much lesser charge. Further solidifying the belief that the lives of African Americans are not valued in the criminal justice system.

Most recently, the verdict in the case of Trayvon Martin reaffirmed the devalued status of African American life. The unarmed, 17-year old boy was racially profiled, shot and killed by an overzealous neighborhood watchman named George Zimmerman who claimed self-defense. The offender's acquittal of all charges, by a predominately White jury, speaks to the historical denigration of African American life in both American society and the criminal justice system. It also reveals the implicit institutionalized racism, birthed from the racialized ideologies of the Antebellum period, which continue to manifest itself within the criminal justice system. The posthumous vilification of Trayvon Martin during the trial and the subsequent verdict parallels a historical trend of injustice afforded to African Americans within the criminal justice system. Furthermore, the verdict contradicts the notion that the system is broken, conversely, it affirms the system is operating the way it was designed to function, which is to suppress, subdue, and socially control African Americans. The system is not broken, it was never right in the first place, and until a substantive systematic change occurs, the criminal justice system will continue to be used by privileged Whites as a means to marginalize African Americans.

Works Cited

Du Bois, W.E.B. (1891). Enforcement of the Slave Trade Laws (American Historical Association, Annual Report). Washington, D.C.: Government Printing Office.

Du Bois, W.E.B. (1901). The Spawn of Slavery: The Convict Lease System in the South. Missionary Review of the World, 14, 737-745.

Du Bois, W.E.B. (1904). The Suppression of the African Slave-Trade to the United States of America, 1638-1870. Longmans, Green, and Company.

Gabbidon, S.L., & Greene, H.T. (2012). Race and Crime (3rd edition). Thousand Oaks, CA: Sage Publications.

Greene, H.T., & Gabbidon, S.L. (2011) (eds.). Race and Crime: A Text/Reader. Thousand Oaks, CA: Sage Publications.

Hawkins, D.F. (1893). Black and White Homicide Differentials: Alternatives to an Inadequate Theory. Criminal Justice and Behavior, 10, 407-440.

Hawkins, D. F. (1987). Devalued Lives and Racial Stereotypes: Ideological Barriers to the Prevention of Family Violence Among Blacks. In R.L. Hampton (Ed.), Violence in the Black Family. 189-205.

Higginbotham, A.L. (1996). Shades of Freedom: Racial Politics and the Presumptions of the American Legal Process. Oxford, UK: Oxford University Press.

Johnson, G. B. (1941). The Negro and Crime. The American Annals of the American Academy of Political and Social Science. 217:93-104.

Snell, T. L. (2013). Capital Punishment, 2011 Statistical Tables. Bureau of Justice Statistics. Retrieved from: http://www.bjs.gov/content/pub/pdf/cp11st.pdf.
Sutherland, E.H. (1947). Principles in Criminology (4th ed.). Philadelphia: Lippincott.

Walker, S., Spohn, C., & DeLone, M. (2004). The Color of Justice: Race, Ethnicity, and Crime in America. (3rd ed.), Belmont, CA.: Thompson Learning.

Wells, Ida B. (1892). Southern Horrors: Lynch Law in All Its Phases. New York Age Print. New York.

Martin Luther King, Jr. and the Definition of Justice

Dr. Jason Michael Williams

As many commemorate the life of Martin Luther King, Jr., I cannot help but to ask how he might define justice in late-modernity. Forty-six years after his death, America still has not dealt with its issue of racialized social control. America continues to be the leading nation regarding incarceration rates, especially of minority and oppressed groups. The current state of the country is not only a scolding denunciation to that which King stood for, but it dictates the fact that America continues to be the land where minorities are seemingly unable to receive due process-a terrible picture of fact for a nation that prides itself as the moral compass of the world.

On his supposed birthday (January 20th), many people, especially Americans, routinely take to social media and television and exclaim their respect and gratefulness for this great leader; however, few of them mention the rate at which Black males, in particular, are continuously sought and destroyed by the American justice system. On this day, the agents of punditry fail miserably to apply King's dream to contemporary realities of oppression and repression. Politicians assume the role of blindness against the numbers of mass incarceration, which are ever so readily available for their viewing. And some educators, both within criminal justice and outside, fail to use mass incarceration as a pedagogical tool in conjunction with teaching and understanding King's call for social justice.

The US' problem with mass incarceration is one that continues to bear its hypocritical soul. Time and time again, the US demands from others what it cannot do for its own. How can the government stand as the world's foremost arbiter of humanitarianism when members of its own society have long been the target of inhumane treatment at the hands of government itself? Moreover, while the US government assumes this role, members of the oppressed are sold the adage of self-responsibility in hopes that somehow the issues that plague the undesirables will simply and magically go away. Not only is this farce consciously known by many in America, but it is also a well-known fact throughout the world.

Despite the status quo's mentioning of there being a fair justice system, reports from all corners continue to display the utter opposite. For example, The Sentencing Project produced a chilling info-graphic depicting the likelihood of imprisonment over the lifespan (see, fig 1.). This data shows that men are more likely to be arrested than women, which is consistent with much of the gender-based literature regarding criminality. However, when looking at the racial differences, the data shows that, when it comes to both men and women, members of minority groups are more likely to be arrested than their white counterparts. In fact, Black males take the lead followed by Latino males and this is also reflected in the female data. A critical consultation with this data suggests that minorities, for whatever reason, are being arrested at rates much higher than their white-counterparts. Not only is this disparity a modern national disgrace, but it should be noted that such practices have historical roots.

One controversial offense that is included within the aforementioned rates of incarceration is that of drug violations. For example, the Bureau of Justice Statistics (BJS) released a report entitled, "Prisoners in 2012, Trends in Admissions and Releases, 1991-2012" and within this report are numbers gathered from the states regarding commitments to prison based on offense. It has long been empirically shown that Whites and Blacks tend to use drugs at equal rates, yet imprisonment rates defy the logic found in the empirical literature (see, e.g., Alexander, 2009; Tonry,

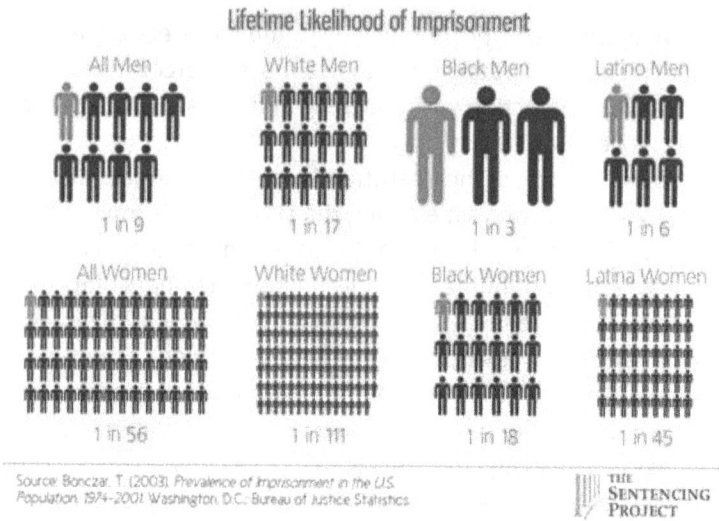

Lifetime Likelihood of Imprisonment

All Men	White Men	Black Men	Latino Men
1 in 9	1 in 17	1 in 3	1 in 6

All Women	White Women	Black Women	Latina Women
1 in 56	1 in 111	1 in 18	1 in 45

Source: Bonczar, T. (2003) *Prevalence of Imprisonment in the U.S. Population 1974-2001* Washington, D.C.: Bureau of Justice Statistics

THE SENTENCING PROJECT

Fig. 1.

2010). For example, in 1991, the BJS report mentioned above showed that Blacks accounted for approximately 39% of drug related offenses while Whites accounted for 19% of those offenses. It should be noted that Hispanics are not included within these figures.

In 2001, however, a category for Hispanic is accessible. The numbers in this year show that Blacks account for approximately 37% of drug offenses, Hispanics 36%, and Whites 23%. In 2006, drug offenses for Blacks were at 35%, Hispanics approximately 30%, and Whites approximately 24%. Lastly, in 2011, Blacks were recorded for 24% of drug offenses, Hispanics approximately 26%, and Whites 23%. Clearly, throughout the years there have been minor decreases in drug-related prison commitments; however, even with the decreases a disparity remained. Therefore, such disparity forces society to answer for the tactics and strategies used in drug enforcement, especially when empirical data continues to show that there are no real differences between the races regarding drug use.

It is also profoundly important to mention that when most people are released from prison they face major *de jure* and *de facto* discrimination. This atrocity is presented in a ground breaking book entitled, "But They All Come Back: Facing the Challenges of Prisoner Reentry" by Jeremy Travis. The most crude form of ex-con discrimination is the banning of drug offenders from receiving federal funding for education. This is one legal consequence that hurts minority groups the most being that they are least likely to afford college without the help of federal funding. Moreover, in a society where education is considered the great equalizer, those whom most need it are by law locked out of the dream of earning degrees-a paper that could, in fact, reduce recidivism. As a result of the *de jure* and *de facto*discrimination, most ex-cons are recommitted to the prison. This is especially inhumane when these violations include those whom were originally arrested for non-violent offenses, like drugs.

The BJS report cited above displays numbers regarding parole violations for those originally convicted of drug offenses. For example, in 1991 Blacks accounted for 33% of those violated under parole while Whites sat at approximately 18%. Those numbers also include Hispanics. In 2001, the violations were as follow, 42% of Blacks, 36% of Hispanics, and 29% of Whites. Moving into 2006 the counts were 39% Black, 30% Hispanic, and approximately 27% White. In 2011, there were 31% Blacks violated, approximately 25% Hispanic, and 23% White. Once again, here, we see a variation between the races that begs for contextualization. It should be noted that much of the scholarly literature is helpful toward understanding those percentages. Much of the disparity has to do with bias and differential treatmentwithin the administration of justice (Walker, 2012), differential employment and housing opportunities(Visher & Farrell, 2005) and lack of social bonds (ibid) and self-actualization after being released.

What is more important to recognize here is the fact that ex-cons are instantly denied their right to self-actualization and determination. This is accomplished by the many forms of *de jure* and *de facto*discrimination they face upon release. Also, such discrimination can be viewed in the aggregate or locally. When controlling for race, the differences are astoundingly similar to the conditions of Jim Crow for Black males (Alexander, 2009). In addition, Black females are steadily becoming the newest victim of mass incarceration. Not only does this aid in the destruction of the Black family but it destroy whole communities (Clear, 2007). Such maltreatment is validated by law and custom (see, e.g. Browne-Marshall, 2013) that is to say that, society has found it to be "ok" or "normal" for Black bodies to be treated as penal caricatures numb to the pains of imprisonment and maltreatment. Sadly, that societal feeling may have credence considering the historical context by which Blacks have long been the target of social undesirableness. Blacks know all too well how to prepare for an unjust traffic stop, or how to prepare for an unjust verdict, whether it is in the context of Zimmerman or Mehserle. Nevertheless, these experiences are no different from the extrajudicial lynching of their forebearers and the undemocratic nature of Southern law enforcement during the Jim Crow era. To put it simple, Blacks have long had to experience the wrath of state-sponsored terror democratically disguised as "justice".

If King was brought back to life today how might he define justice? He will probably look at the above numbers, which are only an *inch* of the problem, and bow his head in shame. He would denounce what little progress has been made and cry that more *could* have been done. He would shame political leaders for their utter abandonment of those who cannot help themselves against the power of a state preoccupied with white supremacy and plutocratic interests. He will possibly shame society for falling for a two-faced friendship with neoliberalism. He would remind us that, in relationships, all parties must sacrifice and give, but sadly neoliberalism has only robbed society - not give to it. He would encourage us to revert to a mechanical society, or a society in which people care for their neighbor and the suffering of others. King would remind us that the definition of justice as it stands today is not of its origin. In fact, he would probably define justice as:

1. The dehumanization of minority bodies disguised as justice.
2. The practice of disposing human bodies as worthless and undesirable.
3. The utter obsolescence of an ideology that cares for those who cannot do for themselves.
4. The destruction of Black youth as a *consequence* of the enslavement of their parents.
5. The refusal to recognize the LGBTQ community as human beings deserving of their pursuit to happiness and prosperity and protection from the U.S. Constitution.
6. The refusal to recognize women as the sole authority of their bodies, lives, and as equal partners to men.
7. The *radical opposite* of due process and fairness for all.

King would have to admit that the dream since his death has been continuously deferred-by design! He would have to investigate the beneficiary of this deferral and confront that entity head-on. As people celebrate King's accomplishments they should try to ask themselves one simple question, how might King define justice in light of today's issues of oppression and repression? Because although most like to bask themselves in his accomplishments, it is time for individuals to begin to ask themselves how might *they* make King's dream a reality, as opposed to an idea that is cherished each year without any forthright action or critical consultation. Lastly, King would remind us to read and study his letter from a Birmingham jail, for the cure for our social decay is not so far away!

Extended Bibliography

Agozino, B. (2003). *Counter-colonial criminology : a critique of imperialist reason.* London: Pluto Press.

Alexander, M. (2010). *The new Jim Crow : Mass incarceration in the age of colorblindness. .* New York City: New Press .

Browne-Marshall, G. J. (2013). *Race, law, and American society : 1607-present.* NY: Routledge .

Clear, T. (2007). *Imprisoning communities : how mass incarceration makes disadvantaged neighborhoods worse.* NY: Oxford .

Georges-Abeyie, D. (1989). Race, ethnicity, and the spatial dynamic: Toward a realistic study of black crime, crime victimization, and criminal justice processing. *Social Justice 16*, 35-64.

Hudson, B. (1993). Racism and criminology: Concepts and controversies. In D. Cook, & B. Hudson,*Racism & Criminology* (pp. 1-27). London: Sage .

Simon, J. (2007). *Governing through crime: How the war on crime transformed American democracy and created a culture of fear. .* New York City: Oxford Univerity Press.

Staples, R. (1975). White racism, black crime, and American justice: An application of the colonial model. *Phylon 36*, 14-22.

Tatum, B. (1994). The colonial model as a theoretical explanation of crime and delinquency . In A. T. Sulton, *African American Perspectives on: Crime Causation, Criminal Justice Administration, and Crime Prevention* (p. 33.52). Woburn: Butterworth-Heinemann .

Tonry, M. (1995). *Malign Neglect: Race Crime and Punishment in America.* New York: Oxford University Press. .

Tonry, M. (2010). *Punishing race: A continuing American dilemma.* New York City: Oxford University Press .

Visher, C., & Ferrell, J. (2005). *Chicago Communities and Prisoner Reentry*. D.C: Urban Institute .

Wacquant, L. (2009). *Punishing the poor: The neo-liberal government of social insecurity.* Durham: Duke University .

Walker, S. (2012). *The Color of Justice: Race, Ethnicity, and Crime in America.* Belmont: Wadsworth .

Race and the American Judicial System

A Critical Analysis

Sean Wilson

The constitutional guarantee of equal protection in courtrooms and the practice of allowing prosecutors to use peremptory challenges have resulted in tension between citizens and legal figures. The right to a jury trial is a hallmark of the American criminal justice system. However, the fairness of the American criminal justice has recently been called into question. The Sixth Amendment of the Constitution guarantees the right to a trial by an impartial jury of one's peers; however, several different court procedures have prevented this constitutional guarantee from becoming a reality. The "trial by jury" standard has been believed to mean that jurors should be reflective of the community in which the defendant lives. However, within the past few centuries, courts throughout the nation, especially southern courts, have made sure that African-Americans who were charged with crimes were subject to jury trials that consisted of all-white juries.

As a result, legal lynchings against black defendants became common practice within the American judicial system. White jurors have often engaged in jury nullification when white defendants are charged for crimes committed against black victims. The well-known trials of the killers of Medgar Evers and Emmet Till, and more recently Trayvon Martin, highlight injustices committed by biased white jurors who some believe ignored the facts, and instead focused on extra-legal factors to make a decision. As a product of these incidences, the process of finding justice in courts has changed substantially but there are still tools used by the judicial system for invidious race and gender discrimination. The peremptory challenge is a tool used by both prosecutors and defense attorneys to eliminate unfavorable candidates from severing as a juror. This article critically examines the history, use, and effects of peremptory challenges and suggest solutions to what Hoffman (1997:847) describes as "the last tool of Jim Crow" (as cited in, Rose, 1999, p. 696).

The Evolution of Trial by Jury in America

The notion of a trial by jury originated from English common law and dates as far back as King Henry II's idea of a self-informing jury. A self-informing jury is a jury that consists of individuals who are members of the community who are familiar with parties involved in the trial and had some knowledge of the dispute between parties. The right to a jury trial was eventually brought to America by the English colonists to serve as a tool against oppression and a symbol of freedom (Weddle, 2013). The right of a defendant to have a trial by jury is written in Article III of the constitution and the Sixth and Seventh Amendments, which grant defendants the right to trails by an impartial jury in all criminal prosecutions and the right to have juries in common-law civil cases. In addition, the Sixth Amendment also requires that a jury that harbors bias against the defendant will not try defendants.

Although the constitution did not set forth any guidelines for impartiality, The Supreme Court ruled that an impartial jury is a jury that is impartial to issues that may arise in a given trial. Therefore, parties are allowed to question potential jurors during *voir dire*. Parties are also granted the opportunity to remove jurors who may hold biases against them by using challenges with or without cause. The hypocrisy of the Sixth Amendment and early American history is that not every citizen was able to serve on juries. Most states typically only allowed property-owning taxpaying white men to serve on juries. Jury qualifications were later loosened by the late 19th century, but the issue was not fully addressed until the Fourteenth Amendment was passed in 1868. The Fourteenth Amendment guarantees all citizens equal protection under the law, and it is used to make the Bill of Rights applicable to all states. The Fourteenth Amendment ensures that no state will implement laws that can infringe on the rights of citizens of the United States or deny persons equal protection of the laws. In addition, the Fourteenth Amendment also granted citizenship to emancipated African-Americans, and it gave congress the power to enforce the provisions of the Fourteenth Amendment against states that failed to provide equal protection of laws for all citizens. Thus, it became harder for states to bar citizens from serving on juries, though several states found ways to exclude citizens from serving on juries.

The Importance of Strauder v. West Virginia (1880)

The earliest case to touch on the racial makeup of the jury was *Strauder v. West Virginia* (1880). In*Strauder*, the Supreme Court held that the Equal Protection Clause of the Fourteenth Amendment of the Constitution prohibited the government from purposely prohibiting individuals from serving on juries based on race. The Supreme Court invalidated a West Virginia Statue that disqualified African-Americans from serving on juries and a conviction of an African-American man who was found guilty of murder by an all white jury was reversed. *Strauder* was reaffirmed by the Supreme Court repeatedly between 1860 and 1965, and several other state statutes that excluded African-Americans from jury service were invalidated (Burgess and Smith, 2011). The *Strauder* Court ruled that a defendant's right to a jury by their peers does not mean that the defendant is tried by their friends, but rather by people that share common characteristics with them. Common characteristics such as race, gender, and socio-economic status can help a juror empathize with the defendant, and such characteristics may be helpful when deciding guilt or innocence (Weddle, 2013).

In *Strauder*, the Supreme Court ruled that the denial of equal opportunity only applies when a member of the defendant's race is purposefully excluded from the jury venire. The Supreme Court also ruled that defendants are not guaranteed to have a jury that is wholly or partially comprised of members of the defendant's race. Although the decision in *Strauder* attempted to eliminate discriminatory elimination of African-American jurors during jury selection, states were able to circumvent *Strauder's* requirements by implementing racially neutral eligibility requirements for jury selection. For example, southern states were able to keep African-Americans off juries by excluding them from voting lists and requiring that potential jurors are educated property owners, such requirements often excluded African-Americans from serving on juries.

Swain v. Alabama (1965)

In 1965, the issue of racial discrimination in the jury selection process reared its head again when the Supreme Court heard the case of Swain v. Alabama, which involved a Black man being indicted for raping a white girl. The prosecutor used his peremptory challenges to eliminate six Black jurors. Swain was convicted, and he later appealed his conviction by arguing that he was denied equal protection by the state's exercise of peremptory challenges to exclude blacks from the petit jury. The Alabama and the U.S. Supreme court sided with the prosecution. Browne-Marshall (2007) noted that the Supreme Court decided that in order for Swain to win his appeal, he had to prove that the removal of the jurors was based on purposeful discrimination, which is an extremely difficult standard to meet. The Supreme Court also found that the principle of *Strauder*, which held that the Equal Protection Clause forbids excluding people from jury service on the basis of race, applied to peremptory challenges in a limited sense (Burgress & Smith, 2011). As a result, the court placed a heavy burden on criminal defendants who sought to show a constitutional violation in their case.

In order for a defendant to prove that an Equal Protection Clause violation occurred the defendant must show that a systematic use of purposefully race-based peremptory challenges occurred over time; because the court felt that a low burden of proof would defeat the purpose of peremptory challenges (Burgess & Smith, 2011). Swain was not able to meet the courts burden although the prosecution had used six peremptory challenges to remove all of the African-American jurors from the jury. The defense attempt to introduced evidence that showed that no African-American person had served on a jury in that county since 1950 was unsuccessful. Three Supreme Court justices dissented on the grounds that the majority undermined the principle of *Strauder*, which subjected Swain to criticism throughout the years due to its extremely high burden of proof (Burgess & Smith, 2011).

Batson v. Kentucky (1986)

The Supreme Court revisited the issue of racially based peremptory challenges two decades after the Swain decision in *Batson v. Kentucky*. This case involved an African-American man who was charged with 2nd degree burglary and the possession of stolen goods. Four African-American jurors were struck by the prosecution, which resulted in an all-White jury. As a result, Batson's attorney sought to have the jury dismissed, by arguing that the removal of all of the black jurors denied Batson of his Fourteenth Amendment equal protection rights. The Supreme Court ruled in favor of Swain by finding that removing black jurors from the trial was a violation of the Fourteenth Amendment. As a result, the Supreme Court made it unconstitutional for attorneys to exclude jurors based on race or the belief that a juror cannot impartially rule on the case because of their race (Browne-Marshall, 2007). In addition, the Supreme Court also outlined three steps to determine if a peremptory challenge is based on a race-neutral explanation.

First, a *prima facie* case revealing discrimination must be established, and then the burden shifts to the side that made the challenge to give a race-neutral explanation. Finally, the court must decide if they will accept the challenge after an explanation is heard. Thus, the *Batson* court overturned Swain's burden of proof for showing a violation of the Equal Protection Clause in jury selection. A defendant can now solely rely on evidence of the prosecutor's use of peremptory challenges to remove prospective jurors of a defendant's race from a jury pool to argue that a Batson Violation occurred. Therefore, the defendant can now rely on circumstantial evidence from his trial to make a *prima facia* showing of racial discrimination. In order for the prosecution to give a successful race-neutral explanation, the prosecution's race-neutral explanation must contain legitimate reasons and be clear and reasonably specific (Gabbidon, Kowal, Jordan, Roberts, Vincenzi, 2008).

The design of the *Batson* procedure is to provide actual answers to suspicions that discrimination may have impacted the jury selection process. Justice Marshall, in dissent, noted that he feared that Batson did not go far enough, and he felt that the court should have abolished peremptory challenges altogether. Marshall also argued that it is extremely difficult to assess the motives of prosecutors, especially when a strike can be attributed to the prosecutor's unconscious bias, and where an explanation based on demeanor can be used to mask a prosecutor's racial bias. In addition, Justice Marshall predicted that the *Batson* framework would be ineffective in abolishing discriminatory use of peremptory challenges. Therefore, Batson has done little to address the impact that racial biases play on jury instructions. Batson critics have argued that *Batson* has done little to change the makeup of jurors and race plays an important role in jury selection, regardless of Supreme Court decisions (McGuffee, Garland, Eigenberg, 2007). Golash (1992) argues that Batson does more to enhance the appearance of fairness in the jury selection process rather than creating a racially unbiased method of seating a jury. Golash (1992) stated:

The widespread prosecutorial practice of striking all minority groups members from the jury was a public embarrassment to the judicial system. The requirement of offering such (non-racial) reasons may not stop the well-trained prosecutor from striking minorities from juries, but it will provide the occasion for him to offer an excuse for doing so (p.176).

Thus, prosecutors typically use slick strategies during jury selection to pick jurors that will support the state. As a result, prosecutors can work around Batson by providing race-neutral explanations for using peremptory challenges.

The Peremptory Challenge

During the venire process, potential jurors are sometimes questioned by the judge or by counsel. If the judge feels that a potential juror may harbor biases that may affect their ability to make an unbiased judgment during a trial, they can be dismissed for cause. Challenges for cause are unlimited and are used when a juror does not possess the qualifications to serve on a jury. Peremptory challenges give litigants the ability to remove potential jurors from a jury panel without a given reason or explanation. The Constitution does not specifically legitimize peremptory challenges, but they have always been used in the United States, and the Supreme Court acknowledged the importance of peremptory challenges under the Sixth Amendment when speaking on the importance of achieving an impartial jury. Preemptory challenges are different from challenges for cause because peremptory challenges are limited in number, and they are used when there is not enough evidence to remove a juror for cause.

Peremptory Challenge: Race-Neutral Explanations

In order for a peremptory challenge to be accepted by a judge counsel has to provide a race-neutral explanation as to why a juror was striked. Courts have continuously extended the acceptable range of race-neutral explanations, and accepted examples of race-neutral explanations include the juror's age, marital status, occupation, socio-economic status, demeanor, education, religion, and experience with the criminal justice system (Weddell, 2013). Moreover, the Supreme Court has held that counsel has the right to exercise a peremptory challenge based on silly reasons such as a potential juror having unkempt hair. The Supreme Court also has found that it is acceptable to exclude potential jurors who are bilingual. Thus, widespread discrimination remains in jury selection methods because attorneys can simply provide a race-neutral explanation for their use of a peremptory challenge; although their motives for removal of a potential juror may be racially based. Batson violations are extremely difficult to prove because most judges are willing to accept race-neutral reasons that counsel offer.

Peremptory challenges after *Batson*

The Supreme Court made it easier to win a race-based peremptory challenge case in *Johnson v. California* (2005). The court held that "permissible inferences of discrimination were sufficient to establish prima facie case of discrimination under *Batson*, shifting the burden to the state to adequately explain the racial exclusion by offering permissible race-neutral justification for the strikes" (*Johnson v. California* 2005). However, even with the *Batson* and *Johnson* rulings legal observers still believe that attorneys still use race-based peremptory challenges (Page, 2005). The debate regarding peremptory challenges features two sides, one side that argues for the eradication of peremptory challenges (Hoffman 1997; Marder, 2006), and another side that argues for the modification of peremptory challenges (Page,

2005; Stolz, 2007). Those who argue for the eradication of peremptory challenges argue that many peremptory challenges are being masked as being race-neutral when in reality they are racially based which violates *Batson*. However, those for the modification of preemptory challenges argue that African-Americans are incapable of neutrally deciding cases that have African-American defendants (Krauss & Schulman, 1997). Several legal and social scholars have examined the juror selection process and the social and psychological parts of the process in order to determine which side was more likely to use a peremptory challenge. Rose (1999) found, through the analysis of thirteen criminal trials in North Carolina that the most frequently used tool to excuse a juror was the peremptory challenge. In addition, Rose (1999) also found that blacks and whites were equally likely to be removed from the jury through peremptory challenges, but race did matter when identifying which side was likely to strike a juror. For example, African-Americans were more likely to be dismissed by the prosecution (81%), while the defense was more likely to dismiss white jurors (71%) (Rose, 1999).

Research by Clark, Boccaccini, Caillouet, and Chaplin (2007) found that young unemployed African-American males were more likely to be excused by the prosecution. A study conducted by Gabbidon et al. (2008), which studied the characteristics of race based peremptory challenges, found that black jurors are most likely to be removed from the jury through peremptory challenges, most likely due to the long history of the legal system not trusting Blacks to neutrally rule in cases. Young unemployed African-American males are not the only group affected by racist legal practices. Rose (1999) also found that some district attorneys also distrusted African-American female jurors, and some district attorneys even went as far as to target African-American female jurors for removal. There was even a well-known training tape in Philadelphia that was given to district attorneys that labeled African-American women as downtrodden and angry about their gender and race, which can result in them taking their frustration off on the state (Rose, 1999).

Some district attorneys throughout the nation feel that African-Americans are unable to be objective when serving on juries due to their animosities towards society. Gabbidon et al. (2008) also studied the results of race-based peremptory challenge litigation after the Johnson decision in 2005. The results found that when defendants challenge peremptory challenges they often lose their cases, and that federal courts often accept the prosecutions peremptory challenge explanations as race neutral. In addition, Gabbidon et al. (2008) also found that after the Johnson decision in 2005 the largest share of the peremptory challenge litigation occurred in 2006, most likely a product of the Johnson litigation. However, the results of the cases in 2006 were not any more successful than cases in prior years. For example, only 20% of the individuals who brought forth cases were successful in their appeal. Although this number is significant, Gabbidon et al. (2008) argues that it is still too early to make a clear assessment of the Johnson decision because it occurred so recently. Thus, the Batson and Johnson decisions have done little to address the impact that peremptory challenges have on the representation of African-American jurors in trials.

Jury Nullification as a Tool to Fight Peremptory Challenges

After the O.J Simpson trial and verdict of not guilty several legal scholars and legal commentators saw the deep racial rifts that infiltrate the justice system and legitimize the justice system in America. Some saw the Simpson verdict as a form of jury nullification, and one legal analyst even argued that African-American defense attorney Johnnie Cochran urged jurors towards jury nullification (Fukurai & Krooth, 2003). Jury nullification is the notion that jurors have the right to refuse to enforce unjust laws when laws have been unjustly enforced. With jury nullification, the jury can sidestep legal requirements by using their discretionary power to acquit a defendant contrary to the evidence or the law. Thus, the jury has the power to ignore the law and the evidence of a trial to make an independent judgment when embracing a more lenient approach to deciding a verdict. African-Americans have historically been wary of law enforcement and the judicial system due to years of harassment and oppression by law enforcement and the judicial system.

Therefore, it is not surprising that most African-Americans question the legitimacy of administering justice in America. Thus, in order to legitimize the justice system for African-Americans, African-Americans must become active participants within the justice system, which includes working within the system and participating in the justice system as jurors. However, with the increasing prevalence of racially based peremptory challenges used by prosecutors and even defense attorneys, African-American citizens continue to be barred from participating in the process of justice by serving on juries. African-American jurors should use their political function of serving on a jury to acquit a black defendant of a crime that may result in arbitrary enforcement of laws when granted the opportunity to serve on a jury, in order to curtail oppression that results from flawed criminal justice policies and practices. The Supreme Court ruled in Duncan v. Louisiana (1968) (391 U.S. 145, 1968) that the jury's fundamental role in criminal cases is to provide defense against arbitrary enforcement. The Supreme Court stated that:

A right to jury trial is granted to criminal defendants in order to prevent oppression by the government. Those who wrote our constitution knew from history and experience that it was necessary to protect against unfounded criminal charges brought to eliminate enemies and against judges too responsive to the voice of higher authority. Providing an accused with the right to be tried by a jury of his peers gave him an inestimable safeguard against the corrupt or overzealous prosecutor and against the compliant, biased or eccentric judge (391 U.S. 145, 1968).

Racially based jury nullification can be used as an effective tool to check the exercise of abusive state power, which can protect the interest of minority citizens. Paul Butler in his article "Racially-Based Jury Nullification: Black Power in the Criminal Justice System" (1995) argues that black jurors should be thoughtful about who they send to prison, and for the safety of the community murderers, rapists, and robbers should be convicted, but when black people are prosecuted for drug offenses and other victimless crimes, Butler recommended that jurors consider nullification (Butler, 1995). Butler believes that the African-American community can better address non-violent offenders than the racist criminal justice system and that it is the "moral responsibility of black jurors to emancipate black outlaws" (p. 679). Jury nullification is needed for African-American non-violent defendants because African-Americans are disproportionately incarcerated in America.

Minton and Golinelli (2014) found that, as of midyear 2013, African-American inmates accounted for 36% of the total jail population, although they only constituted for 13% of the general population. In addition to disproportionate incarceration rates African-Americans are also more likely to be punished more severely than similarly situated white defendants (Miller, 1996). Also, because most states bar felons from voting, African-Americans are less likely to serve on juries because many municipalities pull their jury pools from voting registries (Harrison & Beck, 2006). Thus, racial discrimination often occurs before a prosecutor may have to use a peremptory challenge to remove an African-American juror from the jury pool. Thus, it is crucial to take Butler's racially based jury nullification recommendations into consideration to ensure justice throughout the legal system for African-Americans. The criminal justice system is anti-rehabilitative; therefore, non-violent offenders should be subject to nullification because their community can rehabilitate such offenders.

There are many critics of Butler's racially based jury nullification framework who argue that implementing Butler's ideas would only further racism. Leipold (1996), for example, argues that the gains that have been made in society will be dismissed by Butler's recommendations and that individuals who are critical of the criminal justice system must be patient when waiting for solutions to racist criminal justice policies and practices. Leipold's critique is off base because many African-Americans continue to be subjected to disparate treatment and impact by the criminal justice system in America. African-Americans cannot afford to wait to address injustices in the criminal justice system because injustices will continue to grow. Legal segregation supposedly ended 49 years ago when the Civil Rights Act of 1964 was passed to end legal segregation and legal discrimination based on race. However, African-Americans continue to be oppressed by an inherently racist criminal justice system. Therefore, recommendations such as Butler's racially based jury nullification must be taken into consideration to address the disparate impact that preemptory challenges have on African-Americans.

Recommendations to Fight Un-Checked Peremptory Challenges

The Supreme Court should reevaluate the use of peremptory challenges and possibly adhere to the framework that was set in *Batson*. *Batson* determined that after an individual makes a case for purposeful discrimination, it is then up to the proponent of the strike to give a clear, neutral explanation to the strike that is related to a given case. However, since Batson, the Supreme Court has altered the *Batson* test and courts now allow proponents of challenges to offer any neutral explanation, no matter how far-fetched an explanation may be. Therefore, the use of peremptory challenges should be limited or perhaps even abolished. Representativeness of juries should also be improved in order to ensure that juries are diverse, which can inject a sense of fairness into the legal process. Massachusetts provides a framework for increasing diversity and representativeness by relying on a municipal census to pull jurors for jury duty rather than relying on voter registration lists (Weddle, 2013). Many underrepresented groups and less affluent people are less likely to be registered voters. Therefore, it is imperative that municipalities draw from official records rather than voter registration lists, because official records will represent a broader range of people. Simply pulling names from more comprehensive lists can increase jury diversity. Peremptory challenges are an issue because great discretion is afforded in the application of peremptory challenges. Simply put, *Batson* violations are far too hard to prove. Thus, the culture within the legal process should change because too many courts are willing to accept race-neutral explanations. Society must address the unchecked use of discriminatory peremptory challenges in order to ensure justice for all.

Institutional discrimination in the justice system should not be tolerated by society because the American criminal justice system prides itself in being a democratic system that serves to protect all citizens. However, due to the use of unchecked peremptory challenges and ineffective jury selection strategies, citizens from marginalized communities are often underrepresented during jury trails in America. The jury trial allows average citizens the opportunity to engage in justice and ensure that the state does not sidestep or abuse the law. Thus, improvements should be implemented during the jury selection process to ensure that individuals from diverse backgrounds are allowed to participate in the democratic process of serving on a jury to seek justice.

References

Browne-Marshall, G. (2007). *Race, Law, and American Society.* New York: Routledge .

Burgess, W. H. and Smith, D. G. (2011). The Proper Remedy For a Lack of Batson Findings: The Fall-Out From Snyder V. Louisiana. *The Journal of Criminal Law & Criminology*, 1-29.

Butler, P. (1995). Racially based jury nullification: Black power in the criminal justice system . *Yale Law Journal* , 677-725.

Clark, J., Boccaccini, M. T., Caillouet, B. and Chaplin, W. F. (2007). Five factor model personality traits, jury selection, and case outcomes in criminal and civil cases. *Criminal Justice and Behavior* , *34*, 641-660.

Fukurai, H. and Krooth, R. (2003). *Race in the Jury Box* . Albany: State University of New York Press.

Gabbidon, S. L., Kowal, L. K., Jordan, K. L., Roberts, J. L. and Vincenzi, N. (2008). Race-Based Peremptory Challenges: An Empirical Analysis of Litigation from the U.S. Court of Appeals, 2002-2006.*American Journal of Criminal Justice*, 59-68.

Golash, D. (1992). Race, fairness, and jury selection. *Behavioral Sciences and Law, 10* (2), 155-177.

Hoffman, M. B. (1997). Peremptory Challenges should be abolishes: A trial judge's perspective.*University of Chicago Law Review*, 809-871.

Krauss, E. and Schulman, M. (1997). The myth of black jury nullification: Racism dressed up in jurisprudential clothing. *Cornell Journal of Law and Public Policy, 64*, 809-871.*

Leipold, A. D. (1996). The dangers of race-based jury nullification: A response to Professor Butler.*UCLA Law Review*, 109-141.

Marder, N. S. (2006). Symposium: The jurisprudence of Justice Stevens: Panel I: Criminal justice: Justice Stevens, the peremptory challenge, and the jury. *Fordham Law Review, 74*, 1683-1730.

McGuffee, K., Garland, T. S., & Eigenberg, H. (2007). Is Jury Selection Fair? Perceptions of Race and the Jury Selection Process. *Criminal Justice Studies* , 445-468.

Miller, J. (1996). *Search and Destroy: African American males in the criminal justice system.* New York: Cambridge University Press.

Minton, T. D., & Golinelli, D. (2014). *Jail Inmates at Midyear 2013-Statistical Tables* . Washington D.C: U.S Department of Justice: Bureau of Justice Statistics .

Page, A. (2005). Batson's blind-spot: Unconscious stereotyping and the peremptory challenge. *Boston University Law Review, 85*, 155-263.

Rose, M. R. (1999). The Peremptory Challenge Accused of Race or Gender Discrimination? Some Data from One County. *Law and Human Behavior, 23* (6), 695-702.

Stolz, B. W. (2007). Rethinking the peremptory challenge: Letting Lawyers enforce the principles of Batson. *Texas Law Review, 85*, 1031-1057.

Weddle, H. (2013). A Jury of Whose Peers? Eliminating Racial Discrimination in Jury Selection Procedures. *Boston College Journal of Law & Social Justice* , 453-486.

Cases Cited
Batson v. Kentucky - 476 U.S. 79 (1986)
Duncan v. Louisiana - 391 U.S. 145 (1968)
Johnson v. California (04-6964) 545 U.S. 162 (2005)
Strauder v. West Virginia, 100 U.S. 303 (1879)
Swain v. Aalabama, 380 U.S. 202 (1965)

Social Control and "Otherness"

Dr. Jason Michael Williams

When looking at the consequences of the war on drugs, many politicians who voted toward its fruition presently look back and iterate expressions of sorrow. They claim to feel guilt and wish as if they had never voted for a policy that not only has obliterated Black community efficacy but a policy that has also broken up Black families like never seen since the days of slavery. Politicians of this order are the worst kind of politician because they can engage in political-malpractice while not being held accountable. However, the blame for much of this malpractice also falls upon the ignorance and profound silence of the masses that continually refuse to speak up in the face of such grave injustice, simply because this threat of injustice does not apply to them, or so they think.

The end-result of this problem, of course, is the death of people, communities, and the nation. Nevertheless, the consequences of this problem has failed to shock the majority into acting in a manner consistent with human dignity and the urgency necessary to combat this never-ending war against certain segments of society. The criminal justice system, for the most part, operates as a contemporary system of slavery. For example, slavery, before it was "officially" done away with, provided the majority with a system that kept them at the top, while also keeping Blacks at the bottom. After the Civil War, slavery had lost its footing in the south and the advent of Black Codes and Jim Crow took its place. However, it would not be too long before human dignity/rights would prevail again, thus canceling "separate but equal." However, now the majority was left with another problem, it was one of social control yet again. How could the majority control the masses contemporarily without appearing as if it is denying the "others" human dignity/rights? The answer to this question would come by way of the criminal justice system.

The criminal justice system, a supposedly democratic and impartial institution would later punish and control the "others" in the name of democracy and fairness. In fact, it was during the 1980s when the "war on drugs" in particular gained superior footing alongside the emergence of conservative criminology, which really catapulted the administration of justice away from the rehabilitative practices won in the 1960s-70s and toward a more punitive orientation. This shift within policy and academic criminology led to the grave disparities and injustices presently recognized in the system today.

Nonetheless, the outcome of this paradox accentuates that although Blacks are citizens of the U.S., by way of the criminal justice system they have subjective citizenship (this is reflected in disenfranchisement studies/stats). Blacks possess a citizenship that must be constantly validated (e.g., birthers), and at any time their citizenship can lose its benefits if they should ever come in contact with the criminal justice system, which is highly likely because of differential law enforcement and the occupation of Black communities by law enforcement. This partnership between the criminal justice system and racial demotion/subjugation is one that maintains white supremacy. Today, the criminal justice system serves as a democratic function in furthering white supremacy at the expense of minorities (mostly Blacks) and nobody speaks upon it because, theoretically, the processes that govern the administration of justice are based on the consensus model.

What further complicates this absurdity is the advent or notion of colorblindness-that, in fact, the U.S. presently operates in a reality that excludes race as a factor in any fashion. The use of colorblindness as a reality is, of course, an anecdotal expression of white conservation it is neither true nor achievable because colorblindness is the quintessential enemy of individualism. More important, an adaptation to colorblindness presents to society the same issue that colorblindness attempts to solve, a society in which people cannot be themselves.

Furthermore, many people wonder if a consciousness will ever arise out the U.S. regarding the issue of subjective citizenship by way of criminal sanctions, yet one must also wonder if it serves the best interests of the majority to rid it. Would the majority be willing to sacrifice and allow others to be themselves and participate in the greater American society without having to be someone else? Major contemporary implications regarding the criminal justice system as a tool of racial control would be the post-911 era and the super heightened surveillance complex that presently invades minority life. Although many (regardless of race/ethnicity) in the U.S. are now complainants against the strong surveillance state which now exists, they should be reminded that such a reality is nothing new to minority communities - yet the majority only sees such mechanisms as strange when they are the target. Until citizenship is conceptualized as an equal possession for all, the lives of certain sectors within society will continue to be micro-managed via the criminal justice system, "democratically" of course. However, those who have lived under auspices of validation and superiority for so long may soon need to rethink their position given the onslaught of the surveillance complex which is slowly but surely becoming racially indiscriminate in its processes. Now is the time to bind together as one despite these differences. Whether this is possible or not remains to be seen.

Ecology & Sustainability

DEPARTMENT

Restoring the Sacred Land

An Inquiry into the Origins and Implications of Land-Ownership

Jeriah Bowser

"The first person who, having enclosed a plot of land, took it into his head to say this is mine and found people simple enough to believe him was the true founder of civil society. What crimes, wars, murders, what miseries and horrors would the human race have been spared, had someone pulled up the stakes or filled in the ditch and cried out to his fellow men: "Do not listen to this imposter. You are lost if you forget that the fruits of the earth belong to all and the earth to no one!"

- Jean Jacques-Rousseau

    "Sold! To bidder number 70!" the large man in a white shirt jovially declared, as he successfully transferred the ownership of 22,500 acres of Southern Utah's gorgeous Redrock wilderness to a young man whom he assumed was a representative of the oil and gas industry. The assumed course of action would be for the representative to then set about drilling and extracting oil from the area- doing irreparable damage to one of the most unique and beautiful pieces of land in the world. Bidder 70 was not an oil baron; however, he was Tim DeChristopher, a 32-year old economics student who was *"interfering with an illegitimate auction that threatened his future."*[1] Once the BLM (Bureau of Land Management) authorities realized what he was up to, they removed him from the auction immediately, but the damage had been done. The auction had to be rescheduled for the next month,

44

which was just enough time for the U.S. Department of the Interior to investigate the auction and discover that Tim was right - the auction was being conducted with insufficient scientific and environmental review and, thus, all BLM parcels sold in that auction were cancelled.

Tim had successfully stopped an illegitimate auction and saved an incredible amount of land in Utah from destruction - actions which should have earned him a hero's status. Instead, he was indicted by the Federal government, given a grossly unfair and lengthy trial, and sentenced to 21 months in a Federal Penitentiary.[2]

What logic would drive a government to punish an individual who had tried to protect land from environmental destruction? How did the actions of this young, idealistic activist necessitate almost two years in prison?

To answer these questions, we need to look into the origins of land-ownership and how humans have engaged with the earth throughout history. We need to explore the concepts and implications of land-ownership: how can we pretend to own a planet which has existed for billions of years before humans and will exist for billions more years after the frail and imperious species of *homo-sapiens* has perished?

I encountered the land ownership dilemma recently while my partner and I were considering buying some land with which to set up a sustainable, off-the-grid home and farm. I have long held the opinion that the very principle of land ownership is false and those who participate in such a system are contributing to a destructive and immoral task. This idealism, however, was quickly dashed against the rocks of reality - the reality that unless I purchase a piece of land, I will forever be a serf to a landowner, forever paying "rent" to another person who "owns" the land I am living on. And even if I do manage to acquire a parcel of land, I will be forced to pay taxes to the government in which 'my' land is located in, or I will have 'my' land forcibly taken from me. There is simply nowhere to live for free, no public areas, no "commons" with which one can live simply and quietly without having to participate in industrial society.

Why not? Where did all the wild places go? When did humans gain the audacity to lay claim to portions of the earth? How did the myth of private ownership of land emerge?

To answer this question we need to go back in time, way back - back to the Neolithic revolution, approximately 12,000 years ago. The Neolithic revolution marked the end of an approximately 200,000 year period in which *homo-sapiens* were organized in small bands of nomadic hunter-gatherers. Up to this point, human development had been limited to simple tool-making, fire-making, and a very basic form of language. The dawn of the Neolithic age was perhaps the most decisive turning point in human history, as *homo-sapiens* moved away from their nomadic, hunter-gatherer lifestyles and began engaging in agricultural practices. This may not seem like much of a revolutionary shift until you understand the implications associated with the shift. Agriculture required people to abandon their nomadic lifestyles and settle down in one location, forming towns, cities, and nations. The vast amount of organization and labor required to feed a large, sedentary population necessitated the division of labor, which means that certain people now had specific "roles" or "jobs." No longer could you spend a leisurely day doing whatever you wanted, you now had to take part in a certain aspect of the agricultural process. This ultimately led to class divisions and the concepts of hierarchy and inequality, as the more powerful members of the community were given roles of overseeing and organizing, whilst the weaker members were relegated to the heavy, dirty labor. Gender specializations and the concept of Patriarchy emerged during this era as well, as women now were given certain tasks such as child-rearing, textile manufacturing, and food preparation, as opposed to their earlier status as equal members and contributors to the community. [3][4][5]

Humans weren't the only group affected by this transition, as the environment started to take a heavy hit with the intensive agricultural techniques that a sedentary population necessitated. This time period was marked with mass extinctions of plants and animals, as humans hunted animal populations to extinction and intensive agricultural practices eliminated many plant species. As intensive irrigation techniques were employed, water and top-soil depletion became a huge issue; as the land had never before been subjected to continuous, extensive usage without respite.[6]

The most fundamental and decisive shift during this time period, however, had nothing to do with the physical landscape or human organization. It was an idea. It was the introduction of a concept which was completely foreign to humanity for over 200,000 years - a concept which predicated the formation of Empires, Burger King, War, Politics, Banks, Levi jeans, and Slavery. It was the concept of private property; the idea that a particular thing, whether it be a bone tool, another human, a house, a plant, or a piece of land, could be owned by a particular human.

With the evolution of the concept of private property came the evolution of civilization, and it now became humanity's mission to 'enclose' or privatize every corner of the earth. Enclose we did. Empires rose, and empires fell, each giving birth to a new incarnation of civilization, and each expanding the reach of privatization to include more humans, animals, plants, natural resources, and land than the previous Empire. The social and environmental implications of this were extremely far-reaching and pervasive. Empires with lots of 'property' to protect necessitated armies to defend against 'others' who wanted more property as well, thus war was invented. Massive labor projects needed massive numbers of humans to carry out the labor, thus slavery became an integral part of expanding empires. Imperialistic culture was no place for women to be ruling or have any say in official matters, and large battles needed large numbers of young men to die for their nation, therefore women were further relegated and forced into the domestic roles of making babies and supporting the men in their conquests. As history progressed, the remaining indigenous peoples (those who had not tasted the forbidden fruit of civilization) quickly fell to the sword and slavers' whip. The advent of the monotheistic, organized religions of Judaism, Christianity, and Islam solidified the role of property and land as sanctioned by not only the rule of the elite, but now with the word of God himself (as evidenced in "*thou shalt not steal*" of the Hebraic book of Exodus and " *as for the thief, amputate their hands in recompense for what they committed as a punishment from Allah*" of the fifth chapter of the Qur'an). The formation of the nation-state and the rise of monarchy and feudalism in Europe, Asia, and the Middle East in the following centuries firmly placed land into the laps of Kings, Emperors, and Chieftains who all served the insatiable god of private property and militaristic expansion.

This was a fine and tidy system for those fortunate enough to have been born into the ruling class, and a system that flourished in Europe from the 9th to 17th centuries. For almost a thousand years, much of Europe was a Feudalistic society, an economic system in which individuals were loosely divided into two classes of people: Lords (landowners), and Serfs (non-landowners.) If you were a serf living on a lord's land, you would essentially be a renter, paying for the privilege of living on the lord's land with a percentage of your labor, the first form of rent. In return, you would receive a relative amount of protection from the lord's army and access to the "commons" which was essentially everything that the land provided: water, land to grow crops on, animals to hunt, and forests rich with food and timber. When the Enlightenment swept Europe during the fifteenth century, the concepts of Monarchy and Feudalism collapsed, and many of the lords began squabbling for the scraps of the empire. This left vast areas of unclaimed land which officially belonged to no-one and was "there for the taking." Mass populations of former serfs moved into these areas, attempting to create a simple, quiet lifestyle for themselves separate from war-hungry industrial machine which was beginning to dominate the European landscape. For the rising Mercantilist class, the predecessor of our modern Capitalist ruling class, this presented an enormous problem. How could you force people to work in a factory for twelve hours a day under miserable conditions when they could very easily move to the forests and live a much happier lifestyle away from the toxic factories and urban living conditions? The economic machine was losing its labor-base due to all this unclaimed land, so something had to be done. England passed a series of "land enclosure acts" between 1750 and 1860 which parceled out almost all of the public lands, which were known as the "commons," to landowners and nobles. Now, with no land to live on without paying exorbitant taxes to private landowners, the serfs were forced to move into industrial, urban centers and to provide the labor base for industry.[7][8]

This movement towards privatizing the land was quickly adopted by other European nations, and by the late 1800s almost the entire continent was "owned" by the ruling class. This concept was popularized and legitimized by the writings of Jean-Jacques Rousseau, Thomas Hobbes, and most notably John Locke, who argued that land has no inherent value in itself, and should be owned and exploited by those most willing and capable of producing from it. This view of the land has remained very popular amongst the ruling class ever since Locke published his words, as it advocates for complete extortion of the earth with no responsibility to maintain or preserve anything for future generations and fails to recognize that the Earth has any inherent value outside of its immediate commodification and consumption to humans.

The colonization of North America was a textbook example of this mentality. Many of the early explorers and settlers were thoroughly indoctrinated in Lockeian political theory, and upon setting foot in the "New World," immediately put his theory into action- pillaging, exploiting, and destroying the land as quickly as possible. Locke's argument that, " *as much land as a man tills, plants, improves, cultivates, and can use the product of, so much is his property... the improvement of labor makes the far greater part of the value [9]*" was the justification used to force indigenous peoples off of their land, as their low-impact, hunter-gatherer lifestyles did not constitute "improvement" in the eyes of the European settlers. The rapid economic expansion and industrialization of North America was largely due to the incredibly fertile and richly layered landscapes of this pristine continent untainted with notions of private ownership and industrialization, despite being inhabited with millions of Native Americans for thousands of years. Coupled with a large slave-labor base and the technological advances of the steam engine and industrialization, the land was thoroughly exploited at the highest level humanly possible, and continues to this day.

The cost of the North American land enclosure has been heavy. In less than 500 years, over four million square miles of land have been colonized, privatized, and commodified. Over 95% of the standing forests in the US are gone[10], the soils of the once-fertile breadbasket of the Midwest are extremely depleted[11], over 37% of the rivers in the US are declared "unusable" due to pollution and contamination[12], over 1,000 species of plants and animals have become extinct since European colonization of North America[13], and the largest genocide in history took the lives over 50 million indigenous people.[14] The rich and promising "land of opportunity" was apparently only an opportunity for a few, at the expense of many.

Given the vast amount of human suffering, inequality, and oppression that has been enacted on humanity since the concept of land-ownership was introduced to us and the continued social costs associated with it: famine caused by environmental degradation, wars, borders to protect, refugees, and economic disparity, it is not hard to see why many great thinkers in the past two centuries have looked back at the scope of history and rejected the human creation of private property. They hold that the concept of private property was a huge mistake, and that the survival of humanity will depend on our ability to cooperate and share, rather than the competition and greed that is indicative of our current capitalist culture.

Accepting that land ownership is immoral and illogical, what is one to do in a world where such a belief is not only commonplace, but heavily enforced with law and government? To answer this question, let's look at a similar dilemma that abolitionists faced in the early 1800s. As with any social movement, there were many facets to the resistance and many different tactics to fight the system of slavery. One method, led by

William Greenleaf Eliot, was to purchase slaves in the southern slave markets, transport them north, and then set them free in areas where they would have a relative degree of safety and liberty. Eliot's purchasing of slaves was criticized by many other abolitionists as legitimizing and funding the institution of slavery - as with every human purchased, another human would inevitably be transported from Africa to the American slave markets to replace her. He argued that "*in a society that trades flesh, one must pay the price to free men from the bonds which hold them.*"[15] Eliot and his followers freed over 300 humans from oppression through their controversial methods, and arguably saved many more lives when you realize that these freed men and women went on to start families and leave a legacy of freedom to their children and grandchildren. [16]

Whether or not you agree with his tactics, it is undeniable that many human lives were saved due to Eliot's and his followers actions. Let us also be very clear that the institution of slavery is in no way comparable to land-ownership, as the value of a human life is incomparable to a piece of land, or any sum of money or property for that matter. This is not an attempt to equate the evils or land-ownership with the evils of human-ownership, but merely an attempt to challenge the way we see the world around us, as only 140 years ago we were actively engaged in the slave-trade and were quite comfortable with the notion of trading a human life for a sum of dollars or acres. Lest you savor a moment of moral indignation and think those days are far behind us, know that in many ways we continue this deplorable trade today, in the form of sex-slavery, mass incarceration, and deplorable sweatshop-style factory working conditions around the world.

While respecting the differences between land-ownership and human-ownership, it is also important to also understand the similarities. The two concepts emerged at the same time and are based on the same ideological assumptions of hierarchy and domination. They both require an implied 'social contract' and the participation of the rest of one's community in the proliferation and implementation of the ownership, as it would be ridiculous and ineffective to attempt to take ownership of another human, object, or parcel of earth without your community's participation. To test this theory, simply live your life as if these implied social contracts did not exist for a day. You would undoubtedly be placed in jail or a mental hospital within hours, if not shot dead by the police or an enthusiastic civilian believer, supporter, and defender of private property. Both concepts of ownership have been tested, tried, and found wanting in light of the amount of death, extinction, suffering, and destruction that has been produced at the practical application of these ideas.

Due to this perspective and understanding, the old motto of the slave-abolitionists to "*abolish the ownership of humans by other humans*" has been taken a step further by the modern land-abolitionists as they boldly declare to "*abolish the ownership of humans, land, animals, and every other facet of the environment by humans.*" Maybe the first practical step towards creating a new world is undoing the very ideological assumptions that created this one and reversing the power of private property, especially land ownership.

"Noble idea!" one might reply, "But what is one to do in a world where land-ownership and all of the associated social ills are normalized, and seen by many as integral to our identities as humans? In a world of normalized land-slavery, how does one go about its abolition?" Let's go back to the tactics of the early abolitionists, who saw that one of the safest and sustainable methods of freeing slaves was to purchase them. Doesn't that make one a complicit participant in slavery? Yes, it does. Yet in a society where almost no other options were presented, where many slaves who ran away were found, caught, and brutally murdered, it was a convincing option. Likewise, in our current society where the entire land-base has been parceled out and privatized, and those who attempt to 'liberate it' will most likely be institutionalized or murdered (remember our earlier test of this theory), purchasing and holding land, though an intrinsically immoral task, may indeed be the most effective method of land-abolition.

What does it mean to be a 'land-abolitionist' as a land-owner? How can one use their economic power to free land and restore it to the commons? For those who are interested in these concepts and exploring what might be a code of responsible land ethics for those who reject the legitimacy of land-ownership, I believe a conversation is needed. In the spirit of Aldo Leopold, Edward Abbey, Wendell Berry, Paul B. Thompson, and Barbara Kingsolver, we need to have a conversation that outlines what 'restoring the sacred land' looks like and how concerned land-owners can participate in this voluntary agrarian revolution that not only seeks to preserve land, plants, and animals, but also allows humans to participate in their own liberation from the capitalist machine by living simply and frugally off of the land.

For those of us who are not landowners and don't have the economic means to purchase and then free land, there are still many actions we can participate in to help the land-abolitionist movement along. Squatting, eviction-resisting, and communal housing are some actions that people are engaging in that disrupt the slave-trade. Education is critical to this movement, as the more people are aware of this movement, the more sympathizers and supporters will emerge and begin reclaiming the earth for human, animal, and plant conservation purposes. Participating in or starting a land conservancy is a great way to preserve and reclaim land. Engaging in direct-action to protect land-grabs by government and corporate powers is another way that you can participate in this movement, as Tim DeChristopher so eloquently and nobly demonstrated in Utah a few years ago. Anytime you refuse to participate in the land-ownership system, by either not paying rent, by not leaving an eviction site, by educating yourself or others on the issues surrounding land-ownership, by stopping land-grabs through direct-action, or by sharing living spaces, you are throwing a small wrench into the machinery of capitalism.

Is the cry for land-abolition an unrealistic, utopian plea? Maybe, but not any more so than the plea of the slave-abolitionists who were fighting for and arguing against a system which had been an established truth for thousands of years and which was legitimized by both God and the State. Does the modern cry for land-freedom really seem that crazy when compared to the current logic of the Capitalistic class who "*intend that one day everything will be owned by somebody, and we're not just talking goods here. We're talking human rights, human services, and essential services for life. Education, public health, social assistance, pensions, housing. We're also talking about the survival of the planet....air and water...we want the whole universe, the whole of earth owned?*"[17] I seriously hope not, for our survival as a species may depend on our answer to that question.

References

[1] Quote from DeChristopher in "*Bidder 70*", a 2012 film
[2] "*Bidder 70*" - 2012 film

[3] "*First Farmers: The Origins of Agricultural Societies*" - Peter Bellwood (2004)

[4] "*Guns, germs and steel. A short history of everybody for the last 13,000 year*s" - Jared Diamond (1997)

[5] "*Evolution, Consequences and Future of Plant and Animal Domestication*" - Jared Diamond (2002)

[6] "*The Food Crisis in Prehistory: Overpopulation and the Origins of Agriculture*" - Mark Nathan Cohen (1977)

[7] http://www.thelandmagazine.org.uk/articles/short-history-enclosure-britain

[8] http://www.branchcollective.org/?ps_articles=ellen-rosenman-on-enclosure-acts-and-the-commons

[9] "*Second Treatise of Government*" - John Locke (1690)

[10] http://saveamericasforests.org/resources/Destruction.htm

[11] http://www.soils.wisc.edu/~barak/poster_gallery/minneapolis2000a/

[12] http://articles.latimes.com/1995-12-15/news/mn-14391_1_water-pollution

[13] http://www.biologicaldiversity.org/programs/biodiversity/elements_of_biodiversity/extinction_crisis/

[14] "*American Holocaust: The Conquest of the New World*" - David Stannard (1992)

[15] http://wulibraries.typepad.com/bears_repeating/2012/11/slavery-and-abolition.html

[16] "*William Greenleaf Eliot-Conservative Radical*" - Earl K. Holt III (1985)

[17] Michael Walker in an interview in "*The Corporation*", a 2003 film

Nihilism and Desperation in Place-Based Resistance

Mark Seis

One needs something to believe in, something for which one can have whole-hearted enthusiasm. One needs to feel that one's life has meaning, that one is needed in this world (Hannah Senesh rpt in Derrick Jensen 361).

One of the most daunting challenges of our time is to construct a collective vision for how humans should live in nature. The dominant culture continues to persist in the destruction of our planet. Global warming, population growth, peak oil, unrelenting fossil fuel consumption, species extinction, desertification, deforestation, oceanic contamination all continue relatively unabated despite some minimal mitigation efforts. Notwithstanding the ecological decline in just about every living system on the planet there remains substantial dominant cultural resistance to establishing a sustainable, collective vision for how humans should live in nature-witness Palin chanting, "drill baby drill!" at the 2008 republican convention and more recently the resistance to basic cap and trade legislation deemed too costly in times of economic recession/depression. Despite a growing number of voices to the contrary, the dominant culture is still guided by a belief that nature is, above all, a resource for human exploitation.

The struggles of activists to preserve the integrity of place against a dominant ideology of "nature as resource" can be interpreted as an attempt to generate and affirm human meaning in connection with non-human nature. Another way of interpreting activists' efforts to resist the destruction of place is as a struggle against nihilism: against the obliteration of the individual's ability to experience meaning and to engage physically, emotionally, and cognitively with the natural world.

I divide this paper into three sections examining the threat of cultural nihilism as it presents itself to environmental activists engaged in defense of place (specific political, legal and other actions taken to protect a place that is threatened.) In the first section, I sketch out a conception of cultural nihilism and the nihilist bind as it will pertain to my analysis of two different types of environmental texts. The second section explores cultural nihilism and individual place based resistance through communiqués from Earth Liberation Front (ELF) extracted from Jay Hasbrouck's dissertation "*Primitive Dissidents: Earth Liberation Front and the Making of a Radical Anthropology*." In the last section, I examine cultural nihilism and place based resistance from the perspective of Derrick Jensen's *End Game*.

I

Yet our anger is impotent; if all is relative, we really have no means by which to criticize and correct others, or to entrench our own "values"...Perhaps even more challenging, though less commonly addressed, is the concomitant lack of purpose that we all experience. That is, the absence of external authority that makes possible this relativistic freedom also removes any given end for the project of human existence (Neil Everden 7).

In this section, I am concerned with establishing a theoretical explanation for types of consciousness that propel radical environmentalists towards desperation in their defense of place. The dominant cultural perspective alluded to above has led many activists to experience a state of nihilism as I demonstrate in the following sections. For many environmental activists, meaningful experiences of place are frequently nullified by economic and political imperatives of resource exploitation. The unceasing transformation of the land bases which many individuals uniquely identify as dignified natural places is the source of desperation and a sense of nihilism that permeates the radical environmental movement.

The term nihilism first appeared in 1787, and then again in 1796 and 1797 (Carr), and became widely used in the 19th century. In the first half of the century nihilism was linked to the intellectual study of idealism, and in the latter half of the 19th century nihilism began to be associated with the nothingness that was created in 'God's death' as Nietzsche eloquently illustrated in his essay, "*The Madman.*"(Carr 15). Nihilism has been expressed in many ways; it has been described as " *a historical process, a psychological state, a philosophical position, a cultural condition, a sign of weakness, a sign of strength, as the danger of dangers, and as a divine way of thinking* " (Carr 27). Nihilism stems from the Latin nihil which means literally nothingness. According to the *Internet Encyclopedia of Philosophy* the Greek Skeptics were the first to argue against any foundations of certainty, truth claims were simply matters of opinion. The Skeptic position is linked to what is referred to in contemporary discourses as epistemological nihilism or what postmodernism refers to as anti-foundationalism. These positions simply hold that there is no way to claim something is knowledge or truth because there simply is no way to know for sure.

Other Philosophical categories of nihilism include alethiological nihilism which "*is the denial of the reality of truth*" (Carr 17). Ontological or metaphysical nihilism "*is the denial of an (independently existing) world, expressed in the claim, 'nothing is real'*" (Carr 18). Yet another philosophical category is ethical or moral nihilism." *An ethical or moral nihilist does not deny that people use moral or ethical terms; the claim is rather that these terms refer to nothing more than the bias or taste of the assertor* "(Carr 18). Existential nihilism denotes a belief that life has no intrinsic meaning and therefore is pointless and absurd. Political nihilism holds that the political, economic and social institutions of society are so corrupt that they need to be destroyed. This is the type of nihilism we see expressed in many modern environmentalists such as Derrick Jensen.

From this brief survey of usages, one can say that innuendos of nihilism as a problem confronting the truth of subjective experience have been around since the Greeks. Every 'thinking' human being has probably experienced some skepticism about truth claims. Is there really a God? Does our life really have universal meaning? A healthy individual skepticism is, without doubt, a good thing. But when does nihilism become debilitating and destructive to human dignity? Friedrich Nietzsche warned that the threat of nihilism *"uncanniest of all guests"* represented in the death of God would create a crisis in which *"everything lacks meaning" and hence "awakens the suspicion that all interpretations of the world are false"* (7). Nietzsche foreshadowed what has become the greatest challenge of post modernity, creating meaning in the absence of meaning but not in the absence of power.

Power is central to the study of culturally generated nihilism. Capitalist cultures represent a normalized set of objectives and behaviors which are solidified in state sanctioned legal codes and normalized in institutional behaviors. This type of cultural power creates a type of moral and ethical nihilism for the individual-witness the "just taking orders" defense. When power manifested through economic, political and social institutions negates individual moral and ethical action, individual nihilism becomes a permanent cultural condition. Postmodern culture places the individual into precarious and moral existence, where every individual is allowed to believe what they want to, but forced to live the way power dictates. Capitalist cultural imperatives render individual moral agency impotent, reducing ethical behavior to a series of personal decisions about consumption. Cultural power is manifested in the unquestioned acceptance of corporate and government exploitation of people and nature in the pursuit of profit. Individual nihilism exists when individual moral and ethical agency are relegated to the realm of individual consumer preferences.

Karen Carr suggests that the cheerful acquiescence of nihilism leads to the perpetuation of the status quo, a condition in which power alone determines what is ethical, moral and intellectually worthy of pursuing (140). In our postmodern corporate capitalist's culture, power exercised through economic, political, and social systems and institutions does appear to be the sole determinant of how moral, ethical and intellectual pursuits for us, as individuals, are determined. I may publicly oppose nuclear weapons, genetically modified organisms, clearcuts, mining, and oil and gas development on public lands, yet I will ultimately be silenced by the machinery of hegemonic power which will declare such positions impractical and even extreme. Despite my declared opposition, I still subsidize such activities through my tax dollars. I may choose not to pay taxes, but I will go to jail, becoming even more socially impotent. The psychological cost of this moral precariousness is what I refer to as the nihilist bind.

The nihilist bind occurs when existing social forces deny us human agency--the ability to act on values and interpret our own subjective experiences with others in an attempt to frame an alternative collective vision. This has been the experience of all indigenous and colonized people throughout history and now it is becoming the experience of all activists attempting to alter the course of political and economic power. Jack Forbes, in his book "*Columbus and other Cannibals,*" refers to this consuming of another's life by powerful people and cultures as a type of cannibalism. Forbes writes:

Cannibalism, as I define it, is the consuming of another's life for one's own private purpose or profit...Thus, the wealthy exploiter "eats" the flesh of oppressed workers, the wealthy matron "eats" the lives of her servants, the imperialist "eats" the flesh of the conquered, and so on (24- 25).

Using this logic, the economic and political imperatives of this culture are inherently cannibalistic of nature and people, and especially of people who resist these imperatives. This nihilistic situation, as Carr denotes in the title of her book, is anything but banal. What postmodern civilization is placing beyond our reach is agency--the ability to actualize our subjective values in discourse with others in creating authentic modes of existence. I can no more live in a world where the air I breathe is healthy, and the water I drink free of carcinogens than I can live in a culturally conscious world that works toward that end. In fact, working for such a world places me at odds with the political, economic, and social systems and institutions that prioritize commerce over people and nature.

The ultimate expression of this nihilistic impotence lies in the fact that in a postmodern world where all truth claims may be, like it or not, construed as on equal footing with all other truth claims, only a few individuals holding the reigns of economic and political power decide how we all will live. As atomized individuals we remain powerless, unable to act as moral agents with other moral agents in the production of our lives. Corporate capitalism and the hegemonic nature of nationalism have successfully robbed individuals of their moral and ethical agency, reducing individuals to masses generating the types of adaptations discussed by scholars like Fromm as "*automatons,*" or Mills as "*cheerful robots,*" and Marcuse as "*one dimensional men.*" Attempts by individuals to formulate alternative discourses in our postmodern world are immediately marginalized as special interest politics confined to lobbying, voting, commentary, and state approved protest. Hold your sign in the appropriate cage or offer your one minute, timed comment expressing your utter disgust with the Forest Service's endorsement to open another road-less area to oil and gas exploitation, mining, or logging. These prescribed modes of dissent are exercises in futility at best, humiliating and infuriating at worst.

We now turn to those who find such futile and ineffective prescriptions for ending environmental destruction as unacceptable, and hence, a source of desperation and individual nihilism. I will conduct my analysis guided by the following questions: 1) How do the activists convey the experience of a culturally generated condition of moral and ethical nihilism? 2) How do the activists convey the nihilist bind? and 3) How does engaging in defense of place mitigate the crisis of the nihilist bind? Let us now turn to the texts of the Earth Liberation Front (ELF) who are classified as domestic terrorists by the US Congress and FBI due to their repeated use of arson and sabotage as methods of resistance.

II

Time is running out-change must come, or eventually all will be lost. A belief in state sanctioned legal means of social change is a sign of faith in the legal system of that same state. We have absolutely no faith in the legal system of the state when it comes to protecting life, as it has repeatedly shown itself to care far more for the protection of commerce and profits than for its people and the natural environment (Elf Communiqué, January 1, 2003 claiming responsibility for destruction and damage of SUV's at Bob Ferrando Ford Lincoln Mercury in Erie, PA rpt in Jay Hasbrouck 2).

In this section I will be using select communiqués of ELF as they appear in Jay Hasbrouck's Dissertation " *Primitive Dissidents: Earth liberation Front And The Making Of A Radical Anthropology.*" Hasbrouck's focus is on examining " *key discourses surrounding the actions, ideology, and motivations of a self-described green anarchist network known as the Earth Liberation Front (ELF)"* (viii). I have chosen his dissertation because it is the most comprehensive body of radical environmentalist activists' communiqués that I have encountered. My project differs from his with respect to concepts and mode of analysis and scope. His is a dissertation, mine is an academic paper. In short, the communiqués he has acquired are an excellent, in-depth look into the radical environmental movement's philosophy and actions.

As the above epigraph indicates, desperation clearly underlies ELF's motives for damaging SUVs. The words *"time is running out-change must come, or eventually all will be lost"* (ELF rpt in Hasbrouck 2) express an end of the world crisis. The no *" faith in the legal system"* denotes the disingenuous nature of legal recourse as means to halting further destruction to people and the environment. In this case, SUVs were targeted because they represented the culture of over-consumption. This can be seen in how the ELF chooses their targets: the number one target of radical environmentalists' actions are housing developments and urban sprawl, followed by facilities conducting genetic engineering, followed by logging operations, and finally sport utility vehicles (Hasbrouck 22).

ELF's targets are specific and they are directed at the ideological heart of corporate capitalism. They are driven by a deep repulsion with the moral and ethical nature of postmodern corporate consumer capitalism, as this ELF communique illustrates.

...it is the same state structure, big business and consumer society that is directly responsible for the destruction of the planet for the sake of profit. When these entities have repeatedly demonstrated their prioritizing of monetary gain ahead of life, it is absolute foolishness to continue to ask them nicely for reform or revolution. Matters must be taken into the hands of the people who need to more and more step outside of this societal law to enforce natural law (rpt in Hasbrouck 2).

The appeal to natural law suggests that the ELF believes in higher laws, in this case they refer to "natural law." ELF members are obviously not nihilists in their beliefs; they believe in natural law on our planet and in the universe, and they believe in the inherent sacredness that all plants, animals, and facets of the natural world have. Hasbrouck demonstrates that most ELF members identify with the living philosophies outlined by green anarchists. Green anarchists reject civilization and its power relations in exchange for deinstitutionalized, "primitive" modes of subsistence or what is referred to as anarcho-primitivism (Hasbrouck 3-23). It is obvious that ELF believes in the wisdom of nature (natural law) and that humans should respect the integrity that is inherent to particular land bases. But ELF's beliefs are not shared by the status quo, and, in fact, are antithetical to the status quo. Take this ELF communiqué for instance:

Western civilization, with its throw away conveniences, its status symbols, and its unfathomable hoards of financial wealth, is unsustainable, and comes at a price. Its pathological decadence, fueled by brutality and oceans of bloodshed, is quickly devouring all life and undermining the very life support system we all need to survive. The quality of our air, water, and soil continues to decrease as more and more life forms on the planet suffer and die as a result. We are in the midst of a global environmental crisis that adversely effects and directly threatens every human, every animal, every plant, and every other life form on the face of the Earth (rpt in Hasbrouck 185).

It is clear that ELF rejects state organized corporate consumer capitalism, and it is not hard to see why. ELF rejects the disconnection that capitalism has from the natural world, as capitalism shows absolute preference for capital and profit, with no regard for the consequences that extracting such a profit costs. ELF questions the sanity of state-organized corporate capitalism's persistence in destroying its ecological base, and they daily witness the relentless violence committed against human and nonhuman life to perpetuate an unsustainable existence. ELF sees the legal system as disingenuous, and they perceive mainstream environmental groups as largely ineffective. In return, ELF is rejected by mainstream environmental groups for their emphasis on property destruction, among other ideological differences. An ELF communiqué response to a mainstream environmentalist group illustrates this friction:

Grassroots and mainstream organizations who have come out publicly against the actions of the ELF do so either due to economic reasons (they rely on donations from the public, members, or grants from charities or governmental or non-governmental organizations) and/or they have a firm belief and an exceptional amount of faith in the system of government in operation in their particular area. Either way this attitude demonstrates a clear misunderstanding and/or a great reluctance to accept the seriousness of the threats to life on this planet and to make a firm commitment to work to actually stop that destruction of life. All of us must remember that the movement to protect all life must not be a means of monetary gain for individuals and organizations but rather one that produces concrete results. (Anonymous rpt in Hasbrouck 201).

The ELF, along with many supporters, believe that many mainstream environmentalists are careerist and do not seek the abolition of industrial civilization but rather its regulation through technical solutions. In fact, leading environmental thinkers Michael Shellenberger and Ted Nordhaus in their article "*The Death of Environmentalism-Global Warming Politics in a Post-Environmental World*" noted that every environmental leader they had ever interviewed understood the immense urgency of global warming, but not one had a clear articulate vision for how to confront the problem. They contend that "*green groups are defining the problem so narrowly-so unecologically-that they have alienated potential allies and become just another special interest* " (Shellenberger and Nordhaus 21). ELF criticism of the mainstream environmental movement is shared by many mainstream environmentalists experiencing the nihilist bind from behind the walls of their non-profit 501c3s.

So what is a faceless, alienated, eco-conscious ELF to do? As Worldwatch scientist Erik Assadourian writes, the 2005 " *Millennium Ecosystem Assessment made it clear that nearly two thirds of ecosystem services have been degraded or are being used unsustainably, and indicators like the Ecological Footprint have demonstrated that human society has been living beyond its means since 1987* " (67). He goes on to note that we "*are now using the equivalent of 1.25 planets' worth of resources*" (Assadourian 66). Yet U.S. politicians and economists aggressively refute any large scale changes that would jeopardize business as usual. The March/April 2009 issue of *Multinational Monitor* indicates that the greenhouse gas industry lobby outnumbers health and environment by 8-to-1, with respect to trade and cap global warming legislation (Wedekind 4). The Center for Public Integrity is warning that it is going to be extremely difficult to get any meaningful greenhouse gas reduction legislation passed with this lobby effort. The law remains biased towards private interests and the mainstream environmentalists do not want to give-up their iPhones nor risk alienating their wealthy granters by speaking the truth and actually attempting to enact change on the system which is set up to protect the interests of corporations; not humans, animals, or the planet. Faced with this bleak reality it is understandable why one would feel rather nihilistic about change coming from within. In fact, we might conclude that the type of deep-rooted change needed to begin to address the current environmental catastrophe is beyond the imagination of either the state-organized corporate/consumer capitalism or the futile efforts of the environmental lobbying groups.

Does the full-scale conceptual awareness of the scope of our environmental problem produce a state of individual nihilism? For the ELF, the answer appears to be yes. The following communiqué followed an ELF action of "*vandalizing construction equipment and an attempted arson of four houses under construction...in Placer County, PA*" (rpt in Hasbrouck 186).

Psychologically speaking we are all on the verge of death, with no way out in sight. Suicide, alcoholism, and drug addiction are epidemic. Nearly everyone is on drugs be it Prozac, lithium, lattes, mochas, cigarettes, beer, pot, cocaine, or chocolate. The world we have is empty and boring us to death. WE are forced to sell our souls 8, 10, 12, 14 + hours a day 5, 6, even 7 days a week for more than half our lives, not to mention school before that, they have us work jobs we hate so we can buy shit we don't need...We are through with the lies (rpt in Hasbrouck 186)

It is also clear from this communiqué that many engaging in ELF activities do so out of a sense of reconciling the impotence created by the nihilist bind. As one anonymous ELF writes " *you can decide to be apathetic and complacent, and hope for it all to collapse, or, you can decide to take responsibility and fight to destroy this death machine...Either way you will have blood on your hands, it's just a matter of whose* " (Anonymous 2003a rpt in Hasbrouck 6). It would also seem from this statement that ELF has accepted the premise that one loses either way. Complacency will end life as we know it, leaving blood on our hands, and engaging in illegal property destruction could lead to blood on ELF hands and potential incarceration. Taking responsibility for what is happening is the ELF mantra. Take, for example, this communiqué:

There is absolutely no excuse for any one of us, out of greed, to knowingly allow this to continue. There is a direct relationship between our irresponsible over-consumption and the lust for luxury products, and the poverty and destruction of other people and the Natural world. By refusing to acknowledge this simple fact, supporting this paradigm with our excessive lifestyles, and failing to offer direct resistance, we make ourselves accomplices in the greatest crime ever committed (rpt in Hasbrouck 185).

The resolution of the nihilist bind for ELF participants is to engage in illegal property destruction, which is risking being classified as domestic terrorists and subjected to lengthy prison sentences. Their risks are rationalized by the alternative, which is being complicit in the destruction of the planet-a relegation of their agency they refuse to accept. Do ELF members really think they are going to bring down state-organized corporate/consumer capitalism with random acts of property destruction? This ELF communiqué offers some insight:

We are not so naïve as to believe that we would have stopped development in Twelve Bridges. Though we could have caused over 2 million in damages, it was still a fairly symbolic protest and the message should have still registered; that we are exceptionally serious, the necessity of new discussions and that all of the true eco-terrorists such as JTS should consider themselves forewarned (rpt in Hasbrouck 206).

There is little doubt ELF wants to encourage other like-minded individuals to engage an eco-sabotage, but they do not appear naïve about the overall impact of their work on the culture they wish to destroy. Their intentions are more than symbolic, however; they wish to instill fear in those that perpetuate the destruction of the planet out of greed; they also seek to reclaim the term eco-terrorist by turning the concept against those who terrorize the natural environment for self-serving ends. It is as the old saying goes "one person's freedom fighter is another's terrorist" except in this case it is one person's environmental liberator is another's eco-terrorist.

ELF creates, if nothing else, a discourse about the state of our environment. Legislatures are more apt to not see mainstream environmentalists as radical, making environmental groups' demands more palatable. Unfortunately, the deeper message that ELF seeks to convey, which is that life is sacred and not negotiable, will fall on deaf ears in backrooms where the natural environment is bartered as a commodity for consumption. The ELF identity alleviates for many individuals the sense of nihilism that plagues many people in our culture through acting on their fears and concerns about the health of our planet. One can speculate that ELF actions create a sense of power in what is otherwise a hopeless and powerless situation. There probably is a spark of excitement and empowerment in acting in defiance of the totalitarian culture that seeks to make us blind and dumb nihilists, numb enough to watch our future dissolve in front of our eyes.

On the other hand, law enforcement also finds a new sense of purpose. The US Legislature recently created new laws with increased public funding to expand police powers to seek out "eco-terrorists" with a vengeance. Law enforcement must feel righteous in knowing that private interests to exploit the natural environment have been preserved. The message is be clear: to resist is futile. After all, there is a normalized process in our country to create change.

III

Premise One: Civilization is not and can never be sustainable. This is especially true for industrial civilization (Derrick Jensen ix).
I advocate not allowing those in power to take resources by force, by law, by convention, or any other real or imagined means. Beyond not allowing, I advocate actively stopping them from doing so (Derrick Jensen 85).

Anyone who has read Derrick Jensen knows of his passion for the natural world and his lack of patience for western civilization and its apologists. Jensen's writing is fierce and leaves no aspect of western civilization unturned, be it state organized corporate/consumer capitalist society, science, technology, or any other form that violence against human and non-human life takes. Jensen's first book agent accused him of being a nihilist and that he should tone down his work. He writes, "*I felt vaguely insulted. I didn't know what a nihilist was, but I knew from her tone it must be a bad thing* " (Jensen 363). After researching the topic, Jensen decided he did not meet the first definition of nihilism; that is, he believed in truth, beauty and love. The second definition, however, that dealt with describing the current social order as being " *so destructive and irredeemable that it needs to be*

65

taken down to its core, and to have its core removed-fits me like a glove" (Jensen 363).

In his book, "*End Game,*" Jensen defends 20 constructed premises in over 890 pages of text. He exposes the violence of civilization as it has been committed against all life, human and nonhuman: from the genocide of Native Americans and Jews, to the genocide of the Buffalo and the passenger pigeon, to vivisection of animals, to factory farms, to domestic violence, to normalized rape in war, to factory fish trawlers, to genocidal statements made throughout US history by political and economic elites, Jensen unmasks the sickness that fuels a civilization bent on destroying the landbase. "*Civilization is incompatible with human and nonhuman freedoms, and in fact, with human and nonhuman life*" (Jensen 13). Jensen writes "*the story of civilization is the story of the reduction of the world's tapestry of stories to only one story, the best story. The real story, the most advanced story, the most developed story, the story of power and the glory that is western civilization* "(23). Civilization, for Jensen, is based on hegemonic control aimed at making one particular way of living the only way of living regardless of how destructive it may be. Jensen defers to Stanley Diamond's definition that "*civilization originates in conquest abroad and repression at home*" (rpt in Jensen 15). In order for civilization to thrive and continue to do relentless damage to all life and land, Jensen argues that the individual must pay a heavy psychological, sociological and spiritual toll with respect to truncated experiences and individual agency. Take, for example, this long passage offering a painful description of the process of normalizing cultural nihilism.

A high school student bags the groceries. She's been through the mill. Twelve years of it, not counting her home life, twelve years of sitting in rows wishing she were somewhere else, wishing she was free, wishing it was later in the day, later in the year, later in her life when at long last her time-her life-would be her own. Moment after moment she wishes this. She wishes it day after day, year after year, until-and this was the point all along-she ceases anymore to wish at all (except to wish her body looked like those in magazines, and to wish she had more money to buy things she hopes will for at least one sparkling moment of purchase take away the ache she never lets herself feel), until she has become subservient, docile, domestic. Until her will...has been broken...Until the last vestiges of the wildness and freedom that are her birthright-as they are the birthright of every animal, plant, river, piece of

*ground, breath of wind-have been worn or torn away. Free will at this
point becomes almost meaningless, because by now victims participate
of their own free will-having long since lost touch with what free will
might be...There is no longer any need for force, because the people-or
more precisely those who were once people-have been fully metabolized
into the system, have become self-regulating, self-policing. (Jensen 285).*

Most people can identify with some aspects of the drudgeries
outlined above in our long and tedious endeavor to learn docility and
acceptance of the fact that our life belongs to those in power. The clock
teaches us that large tracts of our life belong to others, starting with
school and ending with work. The leftover time you have is to live your
life according to prescribed consumer behaviors. Women should love to
shop after their enculturation and men should love to sit on their asses
drinking corporate brewed beer watching others perform shows and
games.

Jensen wrote *"End Game"* to appeal to those who feel a sense of rage
at what passes for their lives. He writes *"we are people who are tired of
living hollow lives guided by abstract moralities expressly created to
serve those in power, moralities divorced from physical realities,
including the land we love, including the land we rely on"* (Jensen 828).
He continually encourages the reader that our fate is not inevitable,
*"We are people who refuse to continue as slaves...We are people who
are ready to take back our own lives and to defend our lives and the lives
of those we love, including the land"* (Jensen 828). He wrote this tome to
encourage those experiencing the nihilist bind to stop being victims and
to stop relying on an abstract hope for things to get better.

Jensen exalts individual agency in defying and resisting the civilization
that is killing humans, nonhumans, and the environment. Jensen
exclaims that he is in love *"with salmon, with trees outside my window,
with baby lampreys living in sandy stream bottoms, with slender
salamander crawling through the duff"* (332). He entreats *"if you love
you act to defend your beloved...You do what it takes. If my love doesn't
cause me to protect those I love, it's not love. And if I don't act to protect
my landbase, I'm not fully human "* (Jensen 332). It is rage against the
insanity that is our lives and a passion to do something, anything about
it, which makes Jensen a motivational destroyer of nihilism. Jensen
encourages people to bring down civilization by *"liberating ourselves"*
and *" by driving the colonizers out of our own hearts and minds: seeing
civilization for what it is, seeing those in power for who and what they*

are, and seeing power for what it is " (252). But what exactly does Jensen mean by bringing down civilization?

Bringing down civilization is millions of different actions performed by millions of different people in millions of different places in millions of different circumstances. It is everything from bearing witness to beauty to bearing witness to suffering to bearing witness to joy. It is everything from comforting battered women to confronting politicians and CEOs. It is everything from filing lawsuits to blowing up dams. It is everything from growing one's own food to liberating animals in factory farms to destroying genetically engineered crops and physically stopping those who perpetuate genetic engineering...It is destroying the capacity of those in power to exploit those around them. In some circumstances this involves education. In some circumstances this involves undercutting their physical power, for example by destroying physical infrastructure through which they maintain their power. In some circumstances it involves assassination...(Jensen 252).

Most people are willing to go along with most of what Jensen says until he discusses the need to counter the forces of civilization with violence. Throughout the book Jensen engages and counters common pacifist arguments, using analogies such as self-defense which ends in killing a potential rapist, the many assassination attempts of Hitler, the Jews whose survival rate was greatly increased from resisting in the Warsaw Ghetto uprising, and a mother grizzly bear's defense of her young. Jensen is relentless in rebutting the essentialist pacifist position. He loses many potential sympathizers on these points even though he relentlessly reminds the reader of the endless violence that is committed against life daily by states and corporations. Jensen forces us to confront this fact frequently by asking us to consider why violence against life is normalized while violence against those who destroy life is unacceptable? Reading Jensen's books are like having an ice pick tapping against your forehead echoing tic-tock on the planetary clock. It is blow-by-blow reading where every indictment against our civilization is supported with a factual account of atrocity after atrocity. It is a real dilemma. The violence is real, and the costs are real, and our inaction is real. He goads us:

We have the best excuse in the world to not act. The momentum of civilization is fierce. The acculturation deep. Those in power will imprison

*us if we effectively resist. Or they will torture us. Or they will kill us.
There are so many of them, and they have weapons. They have the
law...Because of all of this; there really is nothing we can do. We may as
well admit that (Jensen 178).*

Then there is the guilt problem of our culpability in participating in
civilization, a tactic Jensen is quick to point out is designed to put the
onus on us and not those in power. Jensen's rebuttal is that we can be
forgiven for having to live in the world, "*because we did not create the
system, and because our choices have been systematically eliminated...*"
(178). We become culpable when we do not exercise our agency, when
we do not "*stop them with any means necessary. For not doing that we
are infinitely more culpable than most of us-myself definitely included-
will ever be able to comprehend*" (Jensen 178). This is the sheer power
of Jensen's relentless rant; we are responsible for what happens to life
on this planet. Yes, we use the technologies of this civilization, but we
did not create the system that has eliminated our choice. But our
knowledge of the destructive nature of these technologies demands
that we once again assert our choice, our volition to end our servitude
and complicity to the destruction of our land base. It will not happen
without exercising our agency, our birthright to feel and think as our
hearts and brains tell us.

How does Jensen respond to those who tell him that he is great at
tearing down civilization but ask him what is the alternative? To this
Jensen replies "*I do not provide alternatives because there is no need.
The alternatives already exist, and they have existed-and worked-for
thousands and tens of thousands of years* "(889). To many this is simply
a cop out. Ten thousand years ago there were not 7.1 billion people,
and you cannot just let them die by shutting down the machine. In
defense of Jensen (not that he needs it), the crisis of peak oil is
predicted to cause more than a billion deaths alone, not to mention all
the other crises that peak oil will create. One way or the other, we are
headed for planetary ecological collapse. The three words most often
uttered from the lips of most environmentalists are "*we are fucked.*" It
is not easy to go back into denial after reading almost 900 pages of
Jensen. He is absolutely right in saying that our culture is sick and
destructive and needs to be destroyed. I am less sanguine than Jensen
about the likelihood of 10,000 years of civilization sickness being wiped
out by the actions of even a million dedicated eco-warriors. The cultural
inertia of 10,000 years will need more than a human push. We are

destined to undergo collapse and it is going to be an unfathomable experience for those who will have to bear witness. Human and nonhuman life is going to be decimated as catastrophic collapse implies.

Does Jensen's prescriptions help aid the sense of nihilism that many acutely feel? As the old Emiliano Zapata quote says, "*it is better to die on your feet than to live on your knees.*" To this end, Jensen's anti-nihilism campaign is invaluable at least to those who still feel a sense of dignity and compassion for the living world. We must fight, but as Jensen himself admits he is not a killer. Nor am I, nor are most people. That is not to say that people do not care, but most people-myself included-do not think my going to jail for dismantling some apparatus of the machine is going to make much of a dent. I may feel like a martyr for the first day in jail, but after that I will just be in an even more restrictive cage, denied relationship with all that I love. There are many out there who would willingly give their lives-myself included--if we thought it would stop the rape, pillage, and genocide of our current culture. I attend many public meetings on environmental issues and listen to the depth of the sickness as it drones on out of the spokespeople that represent industry and our government. You could take one out, but there are going to be another 100 standing in line to take their place, and that can be said about every position of power in this society, all the way down to midlevel management. For this reason I know Jensen will continue to write, and I will continue to read and act. Embracing meaninglessness is not an option in a universe filled with life. To let those in power deny you access to life, is not now nor is it ever acceptable. It is our duty and responsibility to resist the culture of nihilism and for this I harbor a sense of gratitude toward Jensen and all who engage in the struggle against the nihilist bind.

Conclusion

When one accepts nihilism as 'just the way things are,' it ceases to be a potential weapon against corrupt and decaying modes of thought...The possibility of any kind of ethical, religious, or political transformation is de facto ruled out and the perpetuation of the status quo is covertly promoted. Any disagreements that do exist deteriorate, ultimately into contests of power (Carr 140).

The crisis of nihilism that pervades the environmental movement would be entertaining if the consequences from inaction were not so dire. At the core of this problem is a flawed way of living that simply is not sustainable. We are exceeding the carrying capacity of the earth, and its various ecological systems are beginning to collapse. This is a fact that no literate person can deny. The question remains: what are we going to do about it?

Given the unequal distribution of world resources, which has the richest 20 percent of the world's population consuming about 86 percent of all resources and the poorest 20 percent consuming less than 2 percent, the scope of the problem is beyond just political and economic solutions but requires a deeper look into moral and ethical agency. To believe that the political and economic systems of the richest 20 percent of the world's population are going to undergo a voluntary transformation to a sustainable life is to be uselessly idealistic. Change is not likely to come voluntarily from the top. We can all rest assured that change is coming, it is just a matter of whether change is going to be guided by moral and ethical agency or thrust upon us from natural forces. At this point, change will probably consist of natural catastrophes, social collapse, and the unleashing of human rage at being forced to live a meaningless existence for thousands of years.

The rage that is mounting in people all over the world at having their lives stolen from them is beginning to escalate-witness how governments all over the world are more frequently criminalizing dissent. We see this in the US where we now classify property damage with a political emphasis as an act of terrorism. Those in power are scared--as they should be. As the younger generations come of age realizing they have little in the way of any future, it is doubtful that they will be contented with false promises and choices. Humans can understand emptiness, but in almost all circumstance they reject it in favor of a meaningful existence, and when the culture cannot provide meaning they will create it. Nihilism is an unbearable condition and extremely dangerous when fueled by desperation. It is for this reason that we must fight nihilism in our personal and public lives, replacing resignation with passion, alienation with connection, and inaction with action.

Works Cited

Assadourian, Erik. "Global Economic Growth Continues at Expense of ecological Systems." *Vital Signs 2009* Washington D.C.: World Watch Institute 2009. 66-68.

Carr, Karen L. *The Banalization of Nihilism: Twentieth-Century Responses to Meaninglessness. Albany: State University of New York Press 1992.*

Everden, Neil. *The Social Creation of Nature.* Baltimore, Maryland: The John Hopkins University Press 1992.

Forbes, Jack. *Columbus and other Cannibals.* New York: Seven Stories Press 2008.

Hasbrouck, Jay. *Primitive Dissidents: Earth Liberation Front and the Making Of A Radical Anthropology.* A Dissertation Presented to the University of Southern California December 2005.

Internet Encyclopedia of Philosophy. www.iep.utm.edu/n/nihilism. May 4 , 2009.

Jensen, Derrick. *Endgame Volume 1: The Problem Of Civilization* . New York: Seven Stories Press 2006. 1-496.

Jensen, Derrick. *Endgame Volume 2: Resistance.* New York: Seven Stories Press 2006. 513-929.

Nietzsche, Friedrich. *The Will to Power.* New York: Vintage Books 1968.

Shellenberger, Michael, and Ted Nordhaus. "The Death of Environmentalism--Global Warming Politics in a Post-Environmental World." *In These Times* July 11, 2005. 21.

Wedekind, Jennifer. "The Greenhouse Gas Lobby." *Multinational Monitor March/April 2009. 4.*

To Wrench or Not to Wrench

A Brief History of Direct Action in the Environmental Movement and its Potential Consequences, Ethical Implications, and Effectiveness

Jeriah Bowser

It could be said that every major social movement is divided into two main groups: above-ground advocacy, awareness, and reform activities; and below-ground, direct-action activities. The environmental movement is no exception, and its long history in the United States is rife with acts of sabotage, vandalism, arson, and various other extra-legal activities. Among environmental circles and groups, there is perhaps no greater source of contention and debate than whether to engage in direct action or stick to the democratic process; and, indeed, the entire history of the movement could be charted on two different graphs. Noted environmental groups such as the Sierra Club, Greenpeace, and the Audubon Society, etc. have taken great care to distinguish themselves from the more direct action-oriented groups such as the Earth Liberation Front (ELF), the Animal Liberation Front (ALF), Earth First! (EF!), and the Sea Shepherds, sometimes even working directly against their action-oriented counterparts due to the "negative image" that potentially looms across the movement as a whole.

For individuals who are concerned with the earth and want to do their part in preserving and conserving the environment, a basic but thorough exploration of the ethical, legal, and practical implications of engaging in "monkeywrenching," or direct-action activities, is needed. In order to fully understand the nature of direct-action in the U.S. today, we must first take a look at the history of the environmental movement and how direct action, also known as monkeywrenching or ecotage, has shaped our understanding of environmental activism and the effectiveness of such actions.

It is hard to identify the beginning of the environmental movement in the U.S., as there have always been individuals who have cared for the natural world and, therefore, have sought to protect it from those who would profit off of its destruction. For the purposes of this essay, let us start with December 7, 1972, when Harrison Schmitt, one of three members aboard the Apollo 17 space craft, turns and looks through the porthole of his small craft and snaps the first full-view photo of the planet Earth. In artistic terms, it's nothing remarkable: a small, pale-blue circle with swirls of white obscuring most of the terrain, which are the brown and green hues of Southern Africa. In terms of mankind's relationship with the earth, it is a breathtaking and life-changing moment. To see our earth not as a vast resource-pile to consume and destroy but as a small, fragile blue dot is truly an awe-inspiring and perspective-changing moment, and a moment that changed how many people saw and related to our planet. Several books were published in the late 1960s and early 1970s that contributed to the rising awareness of environmentalism, most notable of which were "Silent Spring," "The Population Bomb," and "The Monkey Wrench Gang." Several national incidents also caused alarm and concern for what our technology was really capable of, with the burning of the Cuyahoga River in Cleveland, Ohio in 1969, and the catastrophic oil spill in Santa Barbara, California in 1969. On April 22, 1970, America celebrated its first Earth Day, with an unparalleled twenty million people taking to the streets, parks, and other public areas to advocate for ecological responsibility and awareness.

The first Earth Day was a critical point in the environmental movement - a moment that suggested it was ok to care about the earth without being labeled a "hippie," "radical," or "communist." With that cultural shift came the emergence of a new class of environmental advocates - the rich and famous who could afford $500-a -plate dinners to benefit endangered species, and who quickly formed the political allegiances and factions of the mainstream environmental movement. As could be expected, with the emergence of the affluent environmentalist came the alter-ego of the radical activist.

The first direct-action environmental group was Earth First! (EF)[1], founded in 1980 by several disgruntled members of other mainstream environmental groups who were disheartened by the hijacking of the movement by some of the main contributors to environmental destruction: politicians, ranch-owners, corporate CEO's, and oil barons. EF started slowly, engaging in "passive," non-violent, civil-disobedience actions such as tree sitting, blocking logging roads, and street protests. Before a decade had passed, however, they had evolved as a much more potent enemy to industrialization than anyone would have expected. Tree-spiking, or driving huge nails into trees in an area doomed to be clear-cut, in order to break the saw-blades and discourage logging companies from cutting down old-growth forests, became a widespread issue for logging companies, culminating in the injury of a mill worker in Northern California in 1987.[2] Billboarding - or burning, cutting down, or otherwise defacing billboards - was a popular tool of resistance in the Southwest for many years until it spread to California and the Pacific Northwest, eventually creating the Billboard Liberation Front in San Francisco, CA.[3] Arson slowly emerged as the preferred method of resistance, however, and was co-opted by other emerging environmental and animal rights groups- most notably the Earth Liberation Front (ELF)[4] and the Animal Liberation Front (ALF)[5] in the early 1990s.

Starting in 1995, environmental sabotage gained national attention with the arson of the Dutch Dairy Girl Factory in Eugene, OR, where two dairy trucks were destroyed with homemade incendiary devices, causing over $150,000 in damages. Less than a year later, two forest service ranger stations were torched in Detroit, OR and Oakridge, OR, causing over five million dollars in damage. The ELF claimed responsibility for these attacks and described them as protests against the corrupt and irresponsible way in which the forest service was managing the Oregon wild lands, particularly allowing timber companies to clear-cut protected forest areas. These attacks, while very damaging and concerning to the public and forestry industry, were only the beginning.

A horse slaughterhouse was burned in 1997 in Redmond, OR, which was followed quickly with a torching of two BLM horse-corrals in Burns, OR and Rock Springs, WY. The horse-corrals supplied healthy, wild horses caught on public lands to slaughterhouses in order to clear the lands for deforestation and sell the meat to unaware consumers. These three actions together caused over one and a half million dollars in damages, and the slaughterhouse was never rebuilt, potentially saving the lives of hundreds of wild horses.

1998 was an especially active year for environmental sabotage - starting with the arson of the USDA Animal and Plant Health Inspection Services Center and the USDA Animal Damage Control Office, both located in Olympia, WA. Less than three months later, the Redwood Coast Trucking Company in Arcata, CA was targeted due to its participation in logging activities. Although twelve trucks were targeted, only one actually burned. To cap the year off, ELF/ALF staged its biggest direct action ever by targeting the Vail Mountain Ski Facility in Vail, CO, which was built on one of the last natural habitats for the endangered Lynx in Colorado despite numerous protests and pleas to preserve the area. Two lodges, a ski patrol headquarters, and four chair-lifts were destroyed in a highly coordinated and executed attack that ended up costing over twelve million dollars in damages.

Numerous acts of environmental sabotage in the first years of the twenty-first century brought even more national attention and concern to environmental issues: the Superior Lumber Company arson in Glendale, OR, the Childers Meat Company arson in Eugene, OR, the Legend Ridge Mansion arson in Boulder CO, the Jefferson Poplar Farm arson in Clatskanie OR, the University of Washington Arson in Seattle WA, the Joe Romania SUV dealership arson in Eugene OR, and the San Diego Condominium Arsons in San Diego, CA, all contributed to the formation of the FBI's "Operation Backfire" in 2004, which aimed to uncover and prosecute members of various animal and environmental rights groups who had engaged in "eco-terrorism." Within two years, the FBI had indicted eighteen individuals in the case. Of those eighteen, thirteen received lengthy prison sentences, one committed suicide in jail, and several others were given plea-bargains in exchange for snitching on their companions. Not only did Operation Backfire put away many leaders and icons in the environmental/ animal-rights movement, but it also set a precedent in dealing with similar actions in the future - most notably the prosecutors' ability to label individuals who had engaged in nonviolent acts of civil disobedience as "terrorists," and thereby seeking punishments as severe as life sentences in prison.

Not only did this strike a blow to the activist community, but it also played a key role in influencing public opinion. In legal terms, it allowed for the adoption of new laws and policies to further enforce the power of Federal and Local Governments to treat nonviolent activists with the same crushing force that had formerly been reserved for violent extremists. Astonishingly, the FBI currently considers ELF, EF, and ALF, "*A more serious threat to domestic security than Al-Qaeda,*" despite these organizations having killed or injured not a single person, and despite the fact that almost all of the targets were subjected to lengthy, aboveground advocacy, protests, and pleas before the activists resorted to civil disobedience as a last resort (when democracy didn't work).[6] The tactics used by the FBI to bring down the ALF and ELF cells during Operation Backfire have been widely criticized and condemned by various human rights groups, government watchdog groups, and free-speech advocates all over the world. Gross invasions of privacy were considered "justifiable" in the light of "the considerable financial damage" inflicted on the logging, building, and agricultural industries; and, as a result, phones were tapped, emails were read, individuals were threatened and coerced into snitching out their friends, and undercover informants were sent to infiltrate and collect data on so-called "suspected terrorists," all without warrants or any form of government supervision.[7] The post-9/11 hysteria was unfortunately seen by corporations and government bodies as an opportunity to further their own interests. As such, by capitalizing on the fear and panic that is produced by any mention of the word "terrorism," the FBI was able to manipulate the public into seeing nonviolent acts of conscience as the actions of violent, thoughtless criminals.

Not only was Operation Backfire a gross violation of civil rights and judicial protocol, but it was largely ineffective and futile. The arrests and prosecutions of the ALF and ELF members did not stop or even slow down the movement. Both organizations, as well as many other direct-action environmental organizations, reported increasing membership, donations, and public support following the trial and subsequent media coverage. Several acts of monkeywrenching have occurred since then, albeit with more covert tactics. Many of the thirteen activists currently in prison are actively engaged in the struggle, writing newsletters and articles from their cells, giving interviews to reporters, and studying the works and writings of other activists who have been imprisoned throughout history for opposing destructive regimes - Martin Luther King Jr., Nelson Mandela, Mohandas Gandhi, Huey Newton, etc.

The debate and actions continue as to the fate of our planet. Many people hold the traditional view that the planet is here for our enjoyment and exploitation, and needs no consideration or protection. On the other side of the pond are the "deep ecologists" who argue that earth and all of her inhabitants are sacred and have inherent value, regardless of their purpose or value to humans. For those individuals whose daily interactions with the voracious appetite of industrial society and the unprecedented plundering of the earth's resources lead them to feel as though something needs to change, there are often few choices presented. For those individuals who sense the overall futility in buying a Prius, switching to reusable shopping bags, and voting for the Green Party; and who want to actually do something to protect the few remaining sacred, un-commodified places and creatures in the world, the democratic process seems like a carrot on a stick - a dangling distraction to buy "greener" things while the corporations continue to do whatever the hell they want and aren't held accountable for any of the consequences.

For these individuals, engaging in direct-action often feels like the only choice left. So, the question remains: Are direct-action activities effective or justifiable, and what are the potential consequences? Let's break this down a bit.

Let's start with effectiveness. Are direct-action, extra-legal activities an effective way to combat deforestation, tar-sands projects, fur-farms, or any other environmental destruction currently taking place? It entirely depends on what your goal is. In some instances, the direct threat to animals or forests has been effectively stopped, as in the burning of horse-slaughterhouses and corrals, the release of animals from fur-farms, and the tree-spiking of large tracts of forest land which are still standing today. In many others, however, burned buildings were simply rebuilt, new animals were bred and slaughtered, and new equipment was ordered with almost no substantial loss to the offending company due to insurance policies. One could argue that rampant direct action actually harms the earth - as arson releases huge amounts of carbon into the atmosphere and necessitates the production and purchasing of more materials.

If, however, the goal is to create public awareness and concern for issues that are below the radar, they will almost always achieve that - as the media loves a good "eco-terrorism" story. The problem lies in what type of publicity this person or group may receive. Even with the flagrantly biased and ignorant coverage given by the media, the message is ultimately presented to the public, and will probably gain much more attention than a petition or a march would have. A case in point would be the vandalism committed by the Black Bloc during the WTO protests in Seattle in 1999. In the days leading up to the conference, over 50,000 protesters from all over the world gathered in

Seattle to protest further economic exploitation, or "trade negotiations." For the first several days of massive organized protests and demonstrations, there was a total media blackout, as the media did not want to lend any credence to the demonstrators or give their concerns any legitimacy. Only when a few members of an anarchist militia known as the Black Bloc began destroying corporate store fronts for companies which had been proven guilty of international criminal behavior did the media give any attention to the protests; however, did so with reckless bias, erroneously claiming that protesters, "hurled Molotov cocktails at police" and committed "*random* acts of vandalism and destruction."[8] Overall, the image presented to the public was not one of 50,000 deeply concerned, educated individuals who gathered to protest what they saw as the destruction of the planet and its inhabitants, but one of a group of angry, ignorant criminals who just wanted an excuse to break stuff. Regretful? Perhaps. Yet when compared to the 2001 WTO protests in Doha, Qatar, which accrued no property damage and, therefore, absolutely no media coverage, it becomes clear that sometimes even negative media attention is better than none. Such groups will sometimes deploy a very specific plan, well-prepared media releases, and eloquent spokespeople in an attempt to increase *accurate* public awareness, and to combat the expected media butchery and portrayal of such actions as *mindlessly* "violent" and "extremist."

   Many groups aren't so inclined to perform major acts of direct-action which could warrant an FBI investigation, yet still engage in monkeywrenching. These folks view small acts of dissent as being much more effective than large-scale acts, and will engage in everything from passing out literature, pulling up survey stakes, cutting fences, gluing locks, putting sugar in gas tanks, and generally being a nuisance to ecological offenders and their subsidiaries. In terms of a long, drawn-out battle, small, everyday acts of resistance can have enormous and often decisive effects. The defeat of the Confederate states in the American Civil War is a great example of this phenomenon. Very early in the war there was a widespread crop failure which heavily affected the Southern states. As a result, many of the confederate soldiers, who were concerned about their families' farms and land, deserted the front lines, went home to their families, and resisted conscription for the rest of the war. This theme only gained momentum as the war progressed; until, by late 1865, almost a quarter of a million troops had deserted the fight and gone home to tend to their farms. There was no organized social movement of desertion, no union leader or revolutionary spokesman, no great essays or books calling for mass desertion - only the small actions of many, many individuals that added up to a major event which shaped the political landscape of the nation and the world in an untold number of ways. Those who subscribe to such an approach typically recommend the book, "Ecodefense: A Field Guide to Monkeywrenching," by Dave Foreman and Bill Haywood.

Moving on to the question of being justifiable. Is it morally feasible to break the law and employ property damage in order to further one's own personal convictions and beliefs? This question is much too big and multi-faceted to completely explore here, so I will provide a series of examples to challenge some widely-held beliefs about this:

Example one: The Boston Tea Party, a popular event that precipitated the American Revolution, has received much attention in recent years due to the formation of a large political body that derives its name from the event. To put it bluntly, the original Tea Party was a non-violent, direct-action that destroyed private property in order to make a political point. The State (the British Empire at the time) declared it an "act of tyranny and treason, which calls for swift and relentless suppression."[9] Yet it is widely hailed as an act of *patriotism* and *courage*, not one of *terrorism*, due to the fact that the "*terrorists*" (as per the British Empire) essentially won and got to write the history books. Similar acts of economic sabotage have taken place in almost every social movement throughout history: the British Luddites destruction of weavers to protest factory conditions, the burning of slave auction-houses and slave ships during the abolitionist movement in the U.S., the bombing of the Chancellor Exchequer David Lloyd George's villa in Surrey during the women's suffragist movement in Britain, the many acts of economic sabotage used to get the U.S. military out of Vietnam, South Africa's anti-apartheid groups, India's independence movement, the list goes on. Yet not a single one of these acts are labeled as *terrorism*, due to the fact that the actions were legitimized and seen as necessary in the retrospect of history.

Example two: "*The Earth is our mother. Whatever befalls the Earth befalls the sons and daughters of the earth. This we know. All things are connected by the blood which unites one family. All things are connected.* "Chief Seattle of the Duwamish people originally spoke these words, and they have been repeated by many activists and protesters who resonate with the feeling that the earth is a living entity which deserves respect and love, and who are willing to fight others who wish to hurt her. As one native Huron woman said while being arrested during protests against Canadian Tar Sands project, *"Wouldn't you do this too, if they were killing your mother?"* For individuals of this persuasion, it matters little whether a few men in fancy suits exchanged money to "buy" areas of land to destroy them. It matters very little that a bunch more men in slightly less fancy suits declare their actions "illegal" and subsequently imprison them. Ask yourself: would you employ property damage in order to save your mother?

Example three: "Property is theft!" and property acquired through coercion and extortion is doubly so. The concept of private property as a social construct has gained momentum and popularity through the past few centuries, and the arguments supporting this are very compelling when seen through the eyes of the social historian. The concept that private property precipitates economic disparity and is thus a crime has been argued by such varied theorists as Rousseau, Proudhon, Marx, Locke, Bakunin, and Kropotkin. A very basic explanation of this theory is outlined in Proudhon's book, "What is Property? Or, an Inquiry into the Principle of Right and Government." For those whom employ this train of thought and see the destruction of the earth as an illegitimate and immoral task, property destruction is not an immoral act. To them, the earth belongs to everyone; and, therefore, everyone has a right to say what should happen to it; and when a few men are profiting off of the pillaging of the earth, then it is not immoral to destroy the property with which they are destroying the earth with, as it never belonged to them in the first place.

We come to the final question, what are the potential consequences for engaging in direct action activities? Up until the culmination of the FBI's Operation Backfire, the consequences were relatively minor. Property destruction was seen as just that- property destruction and nothing more. If someone was caught monkeywrenching, they would probably receive a fine and maybe a few days in County Jail. In post-Operation Backfire times, however, the game has totally changed. Now, if someone is found guilty of engaging in acts of *economic sabotage*, they will most likely receive a lengthy prison sentence (depending on their willingness to "cooperate" or snitch) and are branded as a *"terrorist"* for the rest of their life. This seemingly draconian punishment has driven many activist groups underground, and has resulted in a wave of independently operated cells as well as a more covert approach to the ecological resistance movement. The consequences, if convicted of "eco-terrorism," are indeed severe.

Even with these incredibly punitive and brutal tactics used against activists by the Federal Government, the resistance continues, and is growing. In the years following Operation Backfire, fields of GMO crops have been torched [10], more horse-slaughterhouses have been destroyed [11], GMO tree plantations have been cut down [12], fur-farms have been raided and animals set free, and many other small but effective actions have done their part to slow the industrial machine down and defend the earth against its predators and profiteers. We are currently engaged in a period of history where capital is lord, and all who stand in the way of this lord will be driven under the wheels of "progress" and "industry." It is often hard to see the context for this current social movement, as watching the advance of economic destruction often feels overwhelming and unstoppable. One can only wonder what history will tell of those eco-warriors, those brave abolitionists of speciesism and ecocide, and those who dared to throw a monkey-wrench into the gears of capitalism in the name of the earth and all of her inhabitants. We must not wonder for too long, however, and neglect our duty to resist, to fight, to act.

References

[1] http://www.earthfirst.org/about.htm
[2] http://www.iww.org/history/library/Bari/TreeSpiking1
[3] http://www.billboardliberation.com/
[4] http://earth-liberation-front.com/
[5] http://www.animalliberationfront.com/
[6] http://www.fbi.gov/news/testimony/the-terrorist-threat-confronting-the-united-states
[7] "Green is the New Red" - Will Potter (2007)
[8] http://www.nytimes.com/2000/06/04/us/police-brace-for-protests-in-windsor-and-detroit.html
[9] "Redcoats and Rebels: The American Revolution through British Eyes"

- Christopher Hibbert (2002)

[10] http://www.oregonlive.com/pacific-northwest-news/index.ssf/2013/06/genetically_engineered_sugar_b.html
[11] http://www.huffingtonpost.com/2013/07/30/valley-meat-company-slaughterhouse_n_3676353.html
[12] http://www.huffingtonpost.com/2013/09/29/ecoterrorism-papayas-hawaii_n_4013292.html

Rejecting Dystopia

Sustainability in a Changing World

Jeriah Bowser

Have you noticed something odd about the movies Hollywood has been producing over the past year or so? If you have watched many previews, been exposed to many advertisements, or seen many new movies lately, I wonder if you are noticing the same thing that I am. Dystopian action movies. Dozens of them. As me and my partner were watching "The Hobbit" a few months ago, we sat through the trailers for six dystopian action movies in a row. Six movies being released that were essentially the same story - A small band of survivors dealing with the aftermath of some horrible disaster wrought upon the earth, whether that be through our own self-destruction, zombies, aliens, or robots.

I found this fascinating, as I tend to view media as an excellent assessment tool for our culture's collective consciousness, and this theme was very intense and blatant. What is the meaning of all these depressing apocalyptic movies in which our planet as we know it has been annihilated? Could it be that we somehow know the way we are living is unsustainable? Could it be that we are beginning to understand we are slowly but surely headed for destruction and disaster if we choose to maintain our lifestyles and blindly ignore the warning signs on the way down? Could it be that we are manufacturing our own dystopian future but don't have the courage to face this fact yet?

Yes. It could be.

If this is true and my intuition is correct, then this dystopian trend raises some serious questions in regards to how we are participating in this inevitability and what our responsibility is to the earth, to each other, and to future generations of humanoids.

Let's start with defining "sustainable." I would provide a definition of sustainability as any process or action that can be continuously implemented without negatively affecting or diminishing the resources that allow the process to work.

For example, let's say that I want to set up a lemonade stand in my neighborhood. For excellent lemonade, one needs excellent lemons - so I grow a lemon tree in my backyard. If I choose to take care of the lemon tree and the ecosystem that sustains it, then my lemon tree will continue producing lemons every year. Then it could be said that I am a sustainable lemon grower. If, however, I choose to not take care of my tree and let it become sick or diseased, then my tree will eventually either die or stop producing juicy lemons, and my burgeoning lemonade stand will come to a dismal end. For me to continue being successful as a lemonade producer, I need to closely guard and take care of my assets - my lemons. For us as a human race to continue being successful, we need to closely guard and take care of our assets - our planet Earth.

Generally speaking, Americans are horrible at this. The average American consumes 1,966.3 lbs. of food every year [1] and produces over a ton of solid waste (trash) per year.[2] Compare that to your average resident of West Africa, who consumes just under 400 lbs. of food a year and produces 30 lbs. of trash. As far as the collective impact of our lifestyles, America currently consumes 24% of the world's resources, and yet contains only 5% of the world's population. [3] Something is very wrong with those numbers.

For the purposes of this essay, I have broken the concept of sustainability down into three areas that we all need to understand our involvement and responsibility in, if we are to heed the call of our planet.

Finite Resources

Every time you consume or purchase something- anything- it doesn't matter what, you are taking something from the earth. When you are hungry, you eat - which is taking minerals, water, land usage, solar energy, plants, and probably an animal's life from the earth. When you need to go somewhere, you use your car - which uses gas, which comes from petroleum deposits buried in the ground in limited deposits. When you buy a phone, bookshelf, water-bottle, or pretty much any item, you are taking metals, petroleum-based plastics, and various textile plants from the earth- much of which exist in limited quantities in the ground. Your electronic gadgets and artificial lighting need electricity, which is primarily produced by burning coal, which is also found under the ground in limited deposits. To heat your house or bake your casserole, you need natural gas - which is, you guessed it, buried under the ground in limited deposits.

It's a great system we've worked out - finding weird liquid, gas, and metals in the ground, taking them out of the ground, and making them work for us to make our lives easier. A great system until we run out of them.

Some estimates are that we will run out of oil in about 50 years[4], coal in 150 years [5], and natural gas in 250 years.[6] What then? Although there has been an increased focus on so-called "renewable energy" sources and alternative energies, it is simply not profitable enough for corporations to seriously look into them now, when they are making trillions of dollars on oil, coal, and natural gas. Many alternative energy sources have problems of their own, as hydro-electric dams disrupt fish migratory patterns and destroy eco-systems, wind-farms are inefficient and kill large numbers of birds, and solar panels rely on rare and unsustainable metals. It seems the "perfect" alternative energy source is a long way off, yet this does not absolve us of responsibility to limit our usage of energy while we are working towards better ones.

Metals and precious metals are also finite, and subject to the same unrelenting laws of finite-ness. It is very hard to estimate how just how much of these materials we have left, but as we use more and more of them, we are reduced to using more destructive means and methods to retrieve them - deep sea mining disrupts fisheries and marine ecosystems, mountain-top strip mining leaches radioactive and toxic chemicals into groundwater and kills entire ecosystems, and more recently, companies have begun mining the polar ice caps for their resources.[7]

Water may seem like an odd contribution to this conversation because, as everyone knows, 70% of our planet is covered in water and there seems to be plenty of it. Why then do people talk about "conserving water" and "an impending water crisis"? Yes, water is plentiful on our planet, but potable (safe for human consumption) water is not plentiful, nor is water abundant in many areas of the planet where lots of people live. It may surprise you to know that almost all of the water that currently supplies America's "breadbasket" of the Midwest comes not from rain or rivers but from huge underground tables of water known collectively as the "Ogllala Aquifer." And when it's gone... it's gone.[8] Similar water aquifers exist on nearly every continent around the world, and several are either completely depleted or rapidly on their way. [9] It may also surprise you to know the harsh desert terrain that currently dominates the landscape between Southwest Colorado and the Gulf of Mexico once harbored a tropical paradise that followed the Colorado River on its journey south. John Powell's captivating description of his exploration of the river in 1869 describes lush forest canopies obliterating the sun and the cries of jaguars and tropical birds of paradise echoing off the dense vegetation. Today, the scene is a barren wasteland, with the once mighty river now miserably trickling out into the desert, coming to an abrupt end some 50 miles from the sea where it once freely flowed into. What changed between then and now? [10]Progress. Progress in the form of cities, dams, irrigation, man-made reservoirs and lakes, and little regard for the seemingly endless supply of the magical elixir of life known as water. Indeed, water is much more precious and finite than we may ever realize, and future generations just might have to realize it for us.

And then there are the potentially renewable resources of wood and plant-based textiles (bamboo, hemp, cotton, etc). I say "potentially renewable" because, although there does exist sustainable methods of growing these resources, they are rarely used. It is much easier/cheaper to chop down a standing forest than to plant a new one; and it is much easier/cheaper to use plastic and petroleum-based textiles than to produce plant-based textiles.

Consuming and contributing to the use of finite goods is such an integral part of our culture, it is virtually inescapable. No-one is innocent. I know of only one person in my entire life who is truly living "off of the land," and he is a lonely desert-wanderer who roams the badlands of the Southwest with only his burro for companionship and his plant friends for food and medicine. Not exactly the lifestyle many of us are willing or capable of leading.

However, it is also not something entirely abstract and out of our grasp. I believe there is a very loud and consistent message that is being broadcasted to the populace in regards to the environment, and it goes something like, " There is nothing you need to worry about, there is nothing you can do to affect any real change on the environment. Let the professionals handle it; we will enact our legislature and fund scientific studies and will let you know if there's anything you need to do. For now, just keep buying stuff. " This is a very harmful and destructive idea, and completely not true. For all their money, power, and intimidation, corporations are completely dependent on the consumer to sustain them. If everyone stopped buying gas tomorrow, there would simply be no more oil spills, no more vehicle carbon emissions, and no more corporate-sponsored wars. It would simply cease to exist. Of course, that will probably not happen, but I believe it is important to realize that it is fundamentally just that simple. Stop or slow the purchasing and using of products that are finite, and then we won't run out of them.

For the average consumer, this looks like choosing higher gas mileage vehicles or vehicles that use an alternative energy source such as bio-diesel or WVO (waste vegetable oil), carpooling or using public transportation whenever possible, riding your bike or walking wherever you can, researching alternative heating and cooking methods such as wood-burning fireplaces and ovens, being mindful about how much electricity you use around the house or generating your own through home solar panels, rigging a grey-water system in your home and reducing your water consumption as much as possible [11], replacing your water-thirsty lawn with a xeri-scaped yard that requires little to no water, avoiding products that have a planned obsolescence and purchasing those that that can be repaired, recycling and reusing products whenever possible, and intentionally buying goods that were sourced and manufactured close to your community, thereby lessening the amount of fuel spent on transporting your products around the world.

On a deeper, more interpersonal level, we can start recognizing and honoring the gifts that the earth gives us freely, imbuing a feeling of respect and interconnectedness for the great giver. Try saying a simple prayer or statement of gratitude every time you purchase or acquire a product, transitioning from an attitude of entitlement to one of gratitude and respect. Whenever appropriate or possible, initiate discussions with family and friends about their relationship with the earth and what they are giving back. Creating dialogue and intentional conversations about this topic may be one of the most revolutionary and healing things you can ever do for our planet.

Climate Change

Whether you choose to call it global warming, climate change, or just a temporary rise in the earth's temperature while we figure some stuff out, it is undeniable that we are definitely doing *something* to our biosphere. Excepting a few politicians who claim this is all simply a hoax to scare the populace into submission (and whose campaigns are largely funded by the main contributors to this phenomenon)[12] [13], the general consensus is that we are slowly but surely building a "blanket" of carbon dioxide and air pollution around our earth, thereby trapping the sun's rays in our atmosphere and raising the overall temperature of our atmosphere.[14] This is happening very slowly, yet the consequences could be astronomical. Hypothetically, the warmer the planet gets, the more the ice-caps melt, the higher the oceans rise, the more water shortages there will be, the more coastal flooding there will be, the more species will die out due to inability to adapt, and the smaller our ecosystem becomes- ultimately ending in a reverse ice-age that will not be hospitable to homo-sapiens. It is projected that in as little as 200 years, most of our earth will become inhabitable and hostile to human life.[15]

There are ways to remove carbon dioxide (CO_2) and pollutants from the atmosphere (removing the "blanket"), mainly through plant respiration, ocean surface absorption, and plankton photosynthesis. Only very recently has the equilibrium between the amount of CO_2 put into the atmosphere and the amount taken out by plants and the ocean been thrown out of alignment, with increasing levels of CO_2 output (human impact) and decreasing levels of CO_2 absorption (largely due to the incredible amount of deforestation taking place worldwide.)

How are we contributing to this and how can we stop it? Essentially, any time you burn a fossil fuel or release an air pollutant, you are adding CO_2 to the "blanket." Obviously this cannot be completely eliminated overnight, but there are many small things that we can do to mitigate the damage. Being conservative with the energy you use and being conscious of the products that you buy are the main ways that most people can make a difference - purchasing locally sourced and crafted goods will drastically reduce your impact.

Find creative solutions to everyday problems - build greenhouses out of plastic bottles, carpool or ride bicycles whenever possible, make recycling fun by creating games and incentives for kids and adults, always look for repurposed lumber and building materials before buying new materials, go "guerilla gardening"[16], and try to repair as many products as you can around your house as opposed to disposing and buying new products.

Educate yourself- research what is happening and form your own opinions on what is going on and what you need to do about it. Ultimately, you will probably not experience the effects of climate change in your lifetime, but your children and your children's children will. What type of world do you want them to live in? Are they worth a little research, a few intentionally purchased products, or a couple extra minutes spent on repairing or repurposing something?

Food

As I've mentioned in previous articles, food is a big deal - not only for our own health and well-being, but for the health of the entire planet. There are an incredible number of ways that the way we eat affects the world and the overall picture of sustainability, and I highly encourage you to do further research into this topic. For the purposes of this essay, I will attempt to illustrate a few ways that we can be intentional about and make an impact on the world with our diet choices.

If you are a meat eater, then there are a couple things you need to know about your dietary impact on the world and what you can do about it. Agricultural usage for the purpose of meat consumption contributes up to 14% of the total CO_2 emissions worldwide and takes a heavy toll on the earth in regards to water, land-use, soil-depletion, plant-usage, and waste production.[17] There are many ways that you can minimize your contribution to this, and some you might even enjoy! Try purchasing locally-raised meat, grass-fed beef, and organically raised meat whenever possible, as doing so reduces the amount of oil used on transporting your meat, minimizes the amount of GMO crops grown to feed the animals, and eliminates the production of harmful chemicals used in treating and medicating the animals. Chicken and wild game are by far the most "environmentally friendly" meats, as they contribute very little to greenhouse gas emissions, waste production, and water aquifer depletion. Consider going "Meatless Mondays"- eating a vegetarian diet for just one day a week. You will probably be pleasantly surprised at how good you feel and how much you actually enjoy some vegetarian food choices.

Genetically-Modified foods (GMO's) are a growing concern in America, with the notorious "Monsanto Protection Act" signed into law by Barack Obama in March earlier this year.[18] Aside from the potential health risks and consequences of eating genetically modified food, there is a huge environmental cost as well. GMO crops are designed to be completely plowed under and re-planted every year, which causes severe soil erosion and mineral depletion. The rise of the GMO mono-crop has proved disastrous to food production worldwide, as hundreds of strains and varieties of plants are being reduced to merely a handful of varieties that have survived the hybridization plague. [19] This makes crops significantly more susceptible to pests and diseases, as well as reducing the overall quality and flavor of food. Small-scale, organic, and sustainable farms are barely able to compete with the corporate lords of the GMO industry, and so unsustainable practices have become standard in the American food industry. Cross-hybridization of GMO crops with "normal" crops has become such an issue that over 40 countries around the world have banned the import and sale of GMO crops.[20] Unfortunately, as most of the corporations behind these inventions are firmly planted in our native soil, we have instituted no such safety measures of our own.

Ultimately, the biggest impact you can have on GMO's is self-education. Many food activists, myself included, have begun to increasingly emphasize the importance of education and public awareness on this extremely important issue. In the US, GMO foods are not regulated or labeled, and it is up to the consumer to do their own research on which of their favorite foods was created in a laboratory. Consider joining events like the annual "March against Monsanto," which aims to educate and unify individuals who are concerned with their food supply and want their children's food future to be in good hands.

The third major way that food impacts the environment is something that I have already mentioned - local vs. foreign foods. It is indeed a marvel of modern technology, globalization, and coordination that we can enjoy a dinner that was grown on dozens of farms across the globe. Most of our fruits come from California, Florida, or Central America. Your rice was probably grown in Southeast Asia, your beans in South America, your coffee in Africa, your tea in India, and your sugar in South or Central America.[21] Pretty incredible. The downside of all this food globalization is the transportation costs that everything incurs. Although that bunch of bananas only costs you $2.00, it costs the earth quite a lot more in the oil it took to ship it from Ecuador. This is probably the single biggest way that most people contribute to an unsustainable planet, and also the single biggest way that you can learn to live in harmony with the earth and maximize your influence on a better tomorrow.

Purchasing local foods whenever possible is a great way to start your journey towards food sustainability. This looks like shopping at farmers markets, joining a CSA or food co-op[22], growing and hunting your own food, raising your own chickens for eggs and meat, purchasing a milk-share with a local dairy farm[23], or helping out at a local community garden. Learning to eat seasonally is another incredibly fun and powerful way to live with the earth, instead of against it. [24] Even a small step taken towards food sustainability will create a ripple effect that will influence the world in more ways than you may ever know.

Collective, Creative Solutions

In researching for and writing this article, I came across and read many articles of similar content and merit, all essentially advocating for the same basic solutions - buy "green" products, use less energy, and eat organic, local food. That's fantastic advice for those who are in a socio-economic position to be able to implement those changes. But what about the working man who is barely making enough money to afford the lowest cost food he can find to feed his family with? What about the poor inner-city kids who have no exposure to environmental ethics and who can't tell the difference between a tomato and a radish? What about the single moms on food stamps who are simply trying to survive and save a little for their kids' college? I find no helpful or practical solutions for them, and that deeply saddens and disturbs me. Being environmentally conscious seems to be an ideology of privilege, and the rest of us are just supposed to live off of the scraps of capitalism and recycle a few soda cans.

If we seriously care about our future and the future of our planet, we need to find creative solutions to involve and include everyone in our struggle for sustainability. As members of the dominant culture, we need to recognize the privilege that we hold and intentionally leverage that for the collective struggle. We need to try to create opportunities for less-privileged individuals to experience and engage in sustainable practices. Holding on to any sense of superiority due to our purchasing or lifestyle choices is completely absurd and detrimental to the common good.

As socio-economic or racial minorities, we need to recognize that there are small things that we can do to work towards a better earth, and to focus on those things. We need to organize and find like-minded family members and friends and collectively work towards creative solutions for our problems. We need to reject the stereotypes and systems of oppression and apathy that are expected of us and fight for the bigger picture, because the earth belongs to all of us.

As members of humanity, we need to think very seriously whether we care about what kind of world we are leaving to our children, and then intentionally act on whatever conclusion we come to. We are entering a critical time in our Earth's story, and we are all participants in it, whether we like it or not. Every dollar that you spend, every meal you eat, every voice you listen to is creating a certain world. I only hope that I have inspired you to dream of a better one, and given you the courage to create it.

References

[1] http://www.livescience.com/18070-food-americans-eat-year-infographic.html
[2] http://public.wsu.edu/~mreed/380American%20Consumption.htm
[3] http://public.wsu.edu/~mreed/380American%20Consumption.htm
[4] http://www.eia.gov/tools/faqs/faq.cfm?id=38&t=6
[5] http://www.greenbang.com/how-much-coal-is-left_21367.html
[6] http://www.iea.org/aboutus/faqs/gas/
[7] http://blogs.ei.columbia.edu/2012/09/19/rare-earth-metals-will-we-have-enough/
[8] http://www.waterencyclopedia.com/Oc-Po/Ogallala-Aquifer.html
[9] http://green.blogs.nytimes.com/2012/08/13/stressed-aquifers-around-the-globe/?_r=0

[10] "Chasing Water"
documentary http://forgemotionpictures.com/films/chasing-water/
[11] http://greywateraction.org/greywater-recycling
[12] http://thinkprogress.org/tag/climate-change-deniers/?mobile=nc
[13] Clive Hamilton (2010). *Requiem for a Species: Why We Resist the Truth about Climate Change*. Allen & Unwin.
[14] http://www.nrdc.org/globalwarming/f101.asp
[15] http://www.aip.org/history/climate/impacts.htm
[16] http://www.guerrillagardening.org/
[17] http://www.treehugger.com/green-food/6-ways-agriculture-impacts-global-warming.html
[18] http://www.globalresearch.ca/monsanto-protection-act-signed-by-obama-gmo-bill-written-by-monsanto-signed-into-law/5329388
[19] http://www.greenfudge.org/2009/09/24/monocrop-farming-green-revolution-or-environmental-blunder-of-historic-proportions/
[20] http://www.organicconsumers.org/gefood/countrieswithbans.cfm
[21] http://www.fao.org/ag/agn/nutrition/urban_globalization_en.stm
[22] http://www.localharvest.org/csa/
[23] http://www.realmilk.com/real-milk-finder/
[24] http://www.naturalnews.com/035575_seasonal_food_diet_health.html

Education

Standardization as a Tool of Oppression

How the Education System Controls Thought and Serves as a Gatekeeper to the Ruling Elite

Kali Ma

The "ruling elite" is a tiny minority roughly comprised of the nation's top 1% income earners who own more wealth than the bottom 95% of the population *combined*.[1] Those who make up this ruling elite are wealthy, mostly white, individuals. They are overwhelmingly educated at the most prestigious elite institutions and are the leaders in all major fields within society.

In order for this tiny minority to rule over the majority, it needs mechanisms in place to keep the majority from overtaking its power. Our standardized education system serves as a vital gatekeeper to the ruling class and legitimizes their power and authority. Standardization - or the use of pre-determined measures to judge individuals - is essential to controlling thought and promoting a particular ideology to the exclusion of all other perspectives. Ideology in this context means a set of values, beliefs and ideas shared by a group of individuals that reflects their economic, political, and social interests. For an ideology to become dominant, it must be accepted by the majority and serve as a lens through which most individuals view society. The more people interpret the world through a particular perspective, the more power those who benefit from that perspective gain.

Standardization is vital to perpetuating the elite's ideology and serves to: 1) legitimize the rule of those in power; 2) train individuals to obey and defer to authority, as opposed to teaching them critical thinking skills; and 3) exclude competing perspectives and people that threaten the interests of the ruling class. The education system is particularly effective in meeting these objectives because it presents itself as a system of merit where students are rewarded in proportion to their efforts. However, when we examine the education system more closely, it becomes clear that its structure heavily favors affluent individuals and those most likely to further the elite's ideology.

Legitimizing the Ruling Elite - The Myth of Meritocracy

Central to the legitimization of those in power is the myth of meritocracy, which consists of two main assumptions: 1) that individuals succeed in proportion to their abilities, and 2) that those in leadership occupy their positions because they are the most intelligent and talented individuals in society. It also asserts that anyone can attain this elite status if they possess superior abilities and talents.

As a result of these assumptions, meritocracy advances the philosophy that certain individuals are "superior," which legitimizes the rule by the "superior" few over those perceived as "inferior." This separation into "inferiors" and "superiors" takes place in our education system, which constantly ranks students based on standardized criteria. "Inferior" are those who, through inherent or self-created deficiencies, do not meet the "standard" and are, therefore, deemed unqualified or unintelligent. In other words, their voices and perspectives are silenced in favor of those who meet or exceed the standard. Persons deemed "inferior" simply become the subjects of power and thereby outsource their decision-making to a tiny privileged elite.

The most talented and intellectually "superior" individuals usually go on to attend our nation's elite universities. Contrary to the claims of meritocracy, however, students who attend these elite institutions are not necessarily more intelligent or talented, but rather enjoy the advantages of their socio-economic privilege.

Meritocracy Myth Debunked: Elite Schools and the "Intergenerational Reproduction of Privilege"

Elite universities play an essential role in generating new members for the ruling class and legitimizing their governance over the majority. Analyzing the process that produces this ruling elite is key to revealing how an affluent, mostly white, minority still remains in power today. Instead of public schools, upper-class children attend exclusive private schools, expensive prep or boarding schools, and eventually enroll at our nation's elite universities. Throughout their lives, they are groomed to be society's leaders and are constantly reminded of their "superior destiny." As a result, they are confident about their abilities and view lower classes as subjects to be led, ruled, and guided.

The dichotomy between the upper class and everyone else becomes obvious when we examine elite institutions. According to a study, only 6.5% of Harvard students received federal financial aid in the form of Pell Grants, which are generally given to students in the bottom half of the income distribution.[2] This means that only about 6.5% of students from the bottom half of the income bracket were enrolled at Harvard during the 2008-2009 school year. Nearly three quarters of all students at elite colleges come from the top income quartile, while only 3 percent come from households in the bottom quartile. [3] The top 25% in terms of income are 25 times more likely to attend a "top tier" college than are those in the bottom 25%.[4]

Most high-achieving, low-income students outside of urban areas do not even apply to selective universities because of geographic and social barriers. [5] Many lack the basic information about "top-tier" institutions while others simply do not know anyone who attended a selective university, and likely, sense that they do not belong in these schools.[6]

Admission into elite universities heavily favors the privileged in several ways, including: preference given to family legacy students, those who can afford to pay full tuition, and students who receive high scores on standardized exams for which tutoring is essentially required and usually quite expensive.[7]"Legacy applicants" who had at least one parent graduate from an elite institution are up to 45% more likely to be admitted to that school.[8] On the other hand, a study revealed that during the admissions process, elite schools awarded *zero* points to low-income individuals for their socio-economic status, thus failing to acknowledge the obvious economic and social disadvantages those students had to overcome in order to achieve academic success. [9]

Clearly, privileged individuals have significant advantages when it comes to enrollment at our nation's "top tier" institutions. This, however, is not entirely the result of their own efforts as the myth of meritocracy would have us believe, but rather the socio-economic advantages tied to their affluent status. Notably, even members of the elite establishment have admitted that the system favors the wealthy: according to Anthony Carnevale - former Clinton administration appointee and current director of the Georgetown University Center on Education and the Workforce -"The education system is an increasingly powerful mechanism for the intergenerational reproduction of privilege."[10]

Standardization Teaches Unquestioning Obedience

Meritocracy also assumes that all individuals are equally situated and can therefore be properly judged by the same measures. Merit is determined by extensive use of standardized exams that evaluate students' aptitude and rank them based on criteria established by the power structure.

Most schools today do not encourage children to think critically or express themselves in their own way; instead, they teach students how to best restate what they have learned. Individuals who memorize well and are able to repeat certain facts most closely to the expected standard are considered intelligent and reward with good grades and high scores on exams. Creativity, thinking outside the box, raising questions that challenge the status quo, and engaging with the learning material in a lively manner is simply not tolerated. Very rarely are students rewarded for their own critical thinking and creativity. A system that expects students to memorize and copy a pre-determined standard does not teach critical thinking or the sharing of different ideas and perspectives - it teaches obedience.

Proponents of standardized testing claim that the exams have the ability to assess students' abilities and predict future success. Standardization teaches us early on that there is a prevailing, dominant measure by which all people can be legitimately judged. As a result, it effectively promotes only one type of assessment based on the values of the dominant ideology to the exclusion of all other measures and perspectives. In other words, students are taught to believe that only one particular set of skills is valuable and that there is only one type of "intelligence" worth expressing. Standardization is, in effect, an authoritarian mechanism that measures a student's compliance to a set of criteria or answers deemed "correct" by those in authority. There is no independent critical or analytical thinking involved, which is exactly the type of intelligence the ruling elite - who depend on an obedient and unquestioning populace - counts on.

The values the dominant ideology promotes directly and indirectly through standardization are: unquestioning obedience to authority; the importance of such obedience; the belief that only certain skills and types of intelligence are "superior"; and that those in authority are the most qualified to occupy positions of power. These values and beliefs provide great deference to authority and obviously benefit the ruling elite.

Standardized exam performance also has a considerable impact on one's future educational and life opportunities; thus, it is a highly effective mechanism for separating individuals into their respective socio-economic ranks. The fact that standardized exams produce results that disproportionately disenfranchise minorities and lower classes is key to eliminating competition and securing the power of the ruling elite.

Standardized Testing: A Mechanism for Exclusion

Keeping the ranks of power homogeneous is essential to promoting a particular ideology that benefits the ruling class. Different perspectives and "outsiders" are a direct threat unless, of course, they can be assimilated into the system and used to promote its agenda. The mechanisms by which individuals are excluded are mostly covert and appear under the cloak of meritocracy which asserts that the "best and the brightest" naturally succeed.

Exclusion Based on Economic Status, Race, and Ideology

Racial and economic inequalities are ongoing problems that have never been properly addressed. In fact, economic inequality, which disproportionately affects women and minorities, is worse today than it was during the Great Depression.[11] In addition to pure racism, sexism and classism, systemic exclusion of most minorities, women, and the poor also serves to eliminate competing political interests and exclude different perspectives that threaten the interests of the ruling class.

1. Socio-Economic Exclusion

Most universities, including elite institutions, still use standardized testing as an important factor in admissions. Test scores from the SAT show white, wealthy students consistently outperforming minorities and the economically disadvantaged by a wide margin. [12] The results imply that the most intelligent and successful individuals within our society are wealthy whites.

Based on these results we can either believe that: a) the tests are legitimate and that minorities and economically disadvantaged individuals are*inherently inferior* to white, wealthy students OR, b) that minorities and economically disadvantaged students are *not inherently inferior*, and that the tests are illegitimate as assessors of intelligence and predictors of future success. If we believe that the tests are legitimate and that students perform poorly because of financial disadvantages, then we must still reject this unfair assessment that disproportionally affects economically disadvantaged students.

According to Edwin Black, author of the <u>War Against the Weak</u>, standardized exams such as the SAT serve as "vehicles for cultural exclusion." [13] Research linking test performance to family income suggests that what these exams really measure are an individual's access to certain resources like test preparation classes, tutoring, and private school education. [14] A study recently found that a student's socio-economic background has a "considerable" impact on his or her secondary educational achievements, particularly in the United States.[15] Standardized testing exploits this disadvantage and efficiently keeps people in their respective socio-economic ranks.

With so much emphasis placed on standardized testing, it is the perfect tool to prevent individuals from rising above their economic statuses in a seemingly legitimate way. Generally speaking, unless a person is well-connected - which often comes with wealth and social status - they are unlikely to do much better economically than their parents.

By continuing to legitimize standardized exams, it seems that we as a society have accepted the belief - consciously or not - that wealthy (mostly white) individuals are inherently superior. Interestingly, the origins of standardized testing are grounded in this exact racist and classist belief.

2. Racial Exclusion

Standardized exams and I.Q. tests emerged in the early 1900s and were extensively promoted by the eugenics movement. [16] The premise of eugenics was that Nordic, upper class whites were inherently superior and more intelligent than other races.[17] In the 1920s, Carl Brigham, a psychologist and figure in the eugenics movement, developed the Scholastic Aptitude Test, or what is now referred to as the SAT.[18] Brigham believed that whites born in America were inherently superior and more intelligent than other races, including southern and eastern European immigrants, whom he deemed equally inferior.[19] Eugenics was widely accepted throughout America's leadership class and heavily financed by influential organizations like the Carnegie Institution and Rockefeller Foundation.[20] Over a period of about 60 years, eugenics led to the forcible sterilization of 60,000 Americans who were deemed "unfit" due to race, social status or other "defective" traits.[21]

Is it a coincidence, then, that privileged white students disproportionately outperform minorities and economically disadvantaged students on an exam created by a man who firmly believed in the superiority of white, upper class individuals? Do we honestly believe that privileged whites are inherently superior to everyone else? And what does it say about the ideology of our ruling elite when some of its most influential members like the Carnegie and Rockefeller families financed an overtly racist and classist movement that led to the forcible sterilization of 60,000 people?

It is no coincidence that standardized testing promotes a certain type of intelligence that happens to benefit white, upper class individuals. The classist and racist implications of standardized testing are evident in their origins and results. By shaping the perception that certain groups are naturally unintelligent, the system dehumanizes whole classes of people and effectively silences their voices. The results provide seemingly legitimate "proof" that minorities and the poor are inherently inferior and that they deserve to occupy a lower rank in society. In truth, however, our education system is a convenient excuse to justify the position of those in power while giving the appearance, through seemingly legitimate means, that this power was attained in a fair and just manner.

3. Ideological Exclusion

Discrimination based on race and class is an intersection of several issues: pure racism and classism as well as the elimination of competing ideologies and political interests that would - at the very least - significantly weaken the dominant ideology. The inclusion of diversity is a direct threat to the homogeneous make-up of the ruling elite, which depends on its ideology to sustain its power. Being part of the ruling elite is not just about wealth, race, and social status: it is just as much - if not more - about sharing particular ideological perspectives that advance the interests of the privileged class as a whole.

For instance, while affirmative action programs have been instrumental in providing educational opportunities for racial minorities, they have mostly helped upper class minority students.[22] The fact that these programs assist mostly privileged students further suggests that the system favors the wealthy. One reason for this is that upper class individuals share similar social and economic interests with those in power and are more likely to advance the dominant ideology because they themselves have benefited from the status quo. As a result, they are less likely to challenge existing conditions in any significant way and are not viewed as a direct threat to the system.

It is important to note that simply placing women, racial minorities, or economically disadvantaged people into positions of power does not guarantee a diversity of ideas or that our system will become any more just. We only need to look at our current leaders in various areas who, despite their minority statuses, dutifully serve the power structure. It is not about *who* embodies the dominant ideology, but rather *what* values and beliefs an individual actually represents. That is why standardization of education is such an effective tool - by imposing its own standards and values, the system shuts out all alternative perspectives that do not advance the interests of the ruling class.

"Success" within society most often reflects the extent to which a person obeys or furthers the interests of the power structure. This is true for individuals of *all* backgrounds and social classes. While some people from modest or minority backgrounds move up to the ranks of the privileged elite, they are few and far between and heavily underrepresented compared to their numbers within the population. Because success depends on obedience to the dominant ideology, there is a strong incentive to disregard one's own viewpoints and assimilate to the system's ideology. Obviously, not all individuals within society have identical perspectives; yet the system, nevertheless, compels most of us to suppress our unique experiences, observations, and impressions in order to prevent us from utilizing those perspectives to meaningfully challenge the status quo.

This repression is a direct consequence of standardization, which rewards obedience to authority and promotes a one-sided perspective to which all people are expected to assimilate. This is why the status quo is incredibly difficult to change: because we are induced and indoctrinated into a mindset that only benefits those in power and severely restricts our self-expression. Any perspectives or ideas that fall outside of the artificial norm are disregarded, and the people who express them often alienated or even punished.

The standardized education system is particularly effective in procuring conformity because it makes "success" dependant on obedience to the dominant ideology that represents the interests of the ruling elite.

Alternatives to Standardization

According to educators who support systemic reform, a student-centered approach to education would produce much more equitable results. [23] A more holistic model for educating students would, for instance: teach children leadership skills and social responsibility, encourage them to cooperate with their peers, challenge students to critically analyze current events, and teach them to construct well-reasoned arguments to defend their ideas.[24] This type of teaching style would actively engage students with each other and foster critical thinking that encourages various viewpoints to enter into awareness. Such lively engagement would undoubtedly reveal talents, strengths, and abilities that standardized tests are designed to disregard.

Eventually, assessment of students would become much more equitable, because each individual would express different skills and talents as opposed to being judged by a fixed, homogeneous standard. There would be no preference for one type of intelligence, which would make standardized testing irrelevant. Without standardization, the system would find it much more difficult to promote its homogeneous ideology, legitimize the rule by a tiny elite, and justify its obvious discrimination against the poor, minorities, and alternative perspectives that challenge its power.

The essential feature of standardization is that it presents information from the perspective of those in power. For instance, corporate textbooks bury important historical facts and recount events from the one-sided point of view of the ruling class - presidents, businessmen, diplomats, and generals - thereby silencing the voices of ordinary people.[25] Recognizing this disparity, the Zinn Education Project offers teaching materials to educators based on Howard Zinn's bestselling book A People's History of the United States. [26] The materials introduce students to a more a comprehensive and honest version of history viewed from the perspective of ordinary people. The lesson plans focus on the history of women, working class people, Native Americans, people of color, as well as historical figures who are often mischaracterized or ignored in traditional textbooks.

One teaching strategy promoted by the Zinn Education Project focuses on role-playing during which students imagine themselves as various individuals throughout history and contemplate the circumstances and realities those people faced.[27] This creative technique encourages students to directly engage with traditionally ignored viewpoints and offers an alternative to the homogeneous (and often misleading) version of history promoted by the power structure.

As these few examples illustrate, standardized education is not the only option. There are many practical alternatives that bring education to life and teach students the necessary analytical skills essential to understanding the world and viewing it in a more complex, accurate light.

Current Education System Is About Indoctrination

Conformity to a standard severely limits our possibilities and is a devastating waste of human potential that only benefits those in power. The eugenics roots of standardized testing reveal that these exams are not harmless assessment tools, but rather instruments of oppression.

When we analyze the outcomes our current system has produced, it becomes clear that its goals are not about educating students. The education system: disenfranchises the lower classes and racial minorities; makes academic success dependent on financial resources and obedience to the dominant ideology; imposes the same standards on all individuals, as opposed to cultivating their unique talents and abilities; silences different perspectives and expressions of intelligence; imposes standards that disproportionally benefit the privileged few; and teaches students *what* to think instead of *how* to critically analyze their environment.

These poor results are not a coincidence or even a result of widespread incompetence - the system is simply designed to fail. This failure only benefits the ruling elite who continuously remains in power, is never disenfranchised, never too poor to afford education, never "inferior" enough to occupy low-ranking positions in society, and whose perspectives are never excluded or silenced from the mainstream. The *actual* purpose of our education system is to indoctrinate individuals into the dominant ideology and eliminate perspectives and people that challenge it in any way. This exclusion is reflected in the homogeneous ranks of power, which overwhelmingly include wealthy, mostly white individuals who share similar political, social, and economic interests.

When power is concentrated in the hands of the few, it becomes easy to maneuver and manipulate. Mechanisms such as standardized testing are introduced by those in authority and are, therefore, effortlessly implemented into the system. We rarely, if ever, question the decisions of people in power because we have been taught to obey authority and defer to its "superior" judgment.

This is how a tiny 1% elite is able to rule over the majority without overt tyranny: by controlling thought, and in turn, behavior. The standardized education system is critical to achieving this objective and thus serves as a protector and gatekeeper to those in power.

References

[1] Andrew Gavin Marshall, "The Shocking Amount of Wealth and Power Held by 0.001% of the World Population," *AlterNet*, June 12, 2013, http://www.alternet.org/economy/global-power-elite-exposed

[2] David Leonhardt, "How Elite Colleges Still Aren't Diverse," *The New York Times*, March 29, 2011,http://economix.blogs.nytimes.com/2011/03/29/how-elite-colleges-still-arent-diverse/?smid=tw-nytimeseconomix&seid=auto

[3] Thomas B. Edsall. "The Reproduction of Privilege", *The New York Times*, March 12, 2012,http://campaignstops.blogs.nytimes.com/2012/03/12/the-reproduction-of-privilege/

[4] Jerome Karabel, "The New College Try," *The New York Times*, September 24, 2007,https://www.nytimes.com/2007/09/24/opinion/24karabel.html

[5] Josh Freedman, "Why American Colleges Are Becoming a Force for Inequality," *The Atlantic*, May 16, 2013, http://www.theatlantic.com/business/archive/2013/05/why-american-colleges-are-becoming-a-force-for-inequality/275923/

[6] Marisa Treviño, Study: Low-income, high-achieving students think prominent universities are out of their league," *NBCLatino*, March 20, 2013, http://nbclatino.com/2013/03/20/study-low-income-high-achieving-students-think-prominent-universities-are-out-of-their-league/

[7] Kristin Rawls, "4 Ways College Admissions Committees Stack the Deck in Favor of Already Privileged Applicants," *AlterNet*, November 12, 2012, http://www.alternet.org/education/4-ways-college-admissions-committees-stack-deck-favor-already-privileged-applicants

[8] Elyse Ashburn, "Legacy's Advantage May Be Greater Than Was

Thought," *The Chronicle of Higher Education*, January 5, 2011, https://chronicle.com/article/Legacys-Advantage-May-Be/125812/?sid=at&utm_source=at&utm_medium=en

[9] David Leonhardt, "How Elite Colleges Still Aren't Diverse," *The New York Times*, March 29, 2011,http://economix.blogs.nytimes.com/2011/03/29/how-elite-colleges-still-arent-diverse/?smid=tw-nytimeseconomix&seid=auto

[10] Thomas B. Edsall, "The Reproduction of Privilege," *The New York Times*, March 12, 2012,http://campaignstops.blogs.nytimes.com/2012/03/12/the-reproduction-of-privilege/

[11] Annie Lowrey, "Income Inequality May Take Toll on Growth," *The New York Times*, October 18, 2012, https://www.nytimes.com/2012/10/17/business/economy/income-inequality-may-take-toll-on-growth.html?_r=0

[12] Scott Jaschik, "New Evidence of Racial Bias on SAT," *Inside Higher Ed*, June 21, 2010,http://www.insidehighered.com/news/2010/06/21/sat

[13] Edwin Black, *War Against the Weak: Eugenics and America's Campaign to Create a Master Race,*(New York: Four Walls Eight Windows 2003), p. 85

[14] Sean F. Reardon, "No Rich Child Left Behind," *The New York Times*, April 27, 2013,http://opinionator.blogs.nytimes.com/2013/04/27/no-rich-child-left-behind/

[15] Organization for Economic Co-Operation and Development, *Economic Policy Reports: Going for Growth* (2010), p. 187 http://www.oecd.org/tax/public-finance/chapter%205%20gfg%202010.pdf ; *see also* Dan Froomkin, "Social Immobility: Climbing the Economic Ladder is Harder In The U.S. Than In Most European Countries," September 21, 2010, http://www.huffingtonpost.com/2010/03/17/social-immobility-climbin_n_501788.html

[16] Black, 78-83

[17] Black, xv

[18] Black, 78-83

[19] Black, 78-83

[20] Black, 40, 93-99

[21] Black, xv

[22] Richard D. Kahlenberg, "Why not an income-based affirmative action?" *The Washington Post*, November 8, 2012, http://articles.washingtonpost.com/2012-11-08/opinions/35503696_1_racial-preferences-race-neutral-methods-grutter

[23] Jesse Hagopian, "'Occupy Education' Debates the Gates Foundation (and Wins)," March 13, 2012,https://www.commondreams.org/view/2012/03/13-4

[24] Jesse Hagopian, "'Occupy Education' Debates the Gates Foundation (and Wins)," March 13, 2012,https://www.commondreams.org/view/2012/03/13-4

[25] Teaching A People's History: Zinn Education Project, "About the Zinn Education Project,"https://www.zinnedproject.org/about/, Accessed June 18, 2013

[26] Teaching A People's History: Zinn Education Project, "About the Zinn Education Project,"https://www.zinnedproject.org/about/, Accessed June 18, 2013

[27] Bill Bigelow, "A People's History, A People's Pedagogy," Zinn Education Project, https://www.zinnedproject.org/about/a-peoples-history-a-peoples-pedagogy/, Accessed June 18, 2013

The Undercurrents of Our Education System

Recognizing and Subverting Cognitive Disinformation

Anna Brix Thomsen

In his book, *Underground History of American Education[1]*, one of the most progressive yet unappreciated voices of pedagogy today, John Taylor Gatto, exposes the undercurrents that steer the direction of the education system. One of the most prominent examples is Gatto's critical analysis of assistant professor at Harvard University, Alexander Inglis's (1879 - 1924) book*Principles of Secondary Education.* In the book from 1918, Inglis lists the 6 primary functions of education. Gatto then takes these as his critical point of departure to show how these functions are as alive and kicking today as they were one hundred years ago. Gatto writes [2]:

Inglis breaks down the purpose - the actual purpose - of modem schooling into six basic functions, any one of which is enough to curl the hair of those innocent enough to believe the three traditional goals listed earlier:

1) **The *adjustive* or *adaptive* function**. Schools are to establish fixed habits of reaction to authority. This, of course, precludes critical judgment completely. It also pretty much destroys the idea that useful or interesting material should be taught, because you can't test for reflexive obedience until you know whether you can make kids learn, and do, foolish and boring things.

2) **The *integrating* function**. This might well be called "the conformity function," because its intention is to make children as alike as possible. People who conform are predictable, and this is of great use to those who wish to harness and manipulate a large labor force.

3) **The *diagnostic and directive* function**. School is meant to determine each student's proper social role. This is done by logging evidence mathematically and anecdotally on cumulative records. As in "your permanent record." Yes, you do have one.

4) **The *differentiating* function**. Once their social role has been "diagnosed," children are to be sorted by role and trained only so far as their destination in the social machine merits - and not one step further. So much for making kids their personal best.

5) **The *selective* function**. This refers not to human choice at all but to Darwin's theory of natural selection as applied to what he called "the favored races." In short, the idea is to help things along by consciously attempting to improve the breeding stock. Schools are meant to tag the unfit - with poor grades, remedial placement, and other punishments - clearly enough that their peers will accept them as inferior and effectively bar them from the reproductive sweepstakes. That's what all those little humiliations from first grade onward were intended to do: wash the dirt down the drain.

6) **The *propaedeutic* function**. The societal system implied by these rules will require an elite group of caretakers. To that end, a small fraction of the kids will quietly be taught how to manage this continuing project, how to watch over and control a population deliberately dumbed down and declawed in order that government might proceed unchallenged and corporations might never want for obedient labor."

As can be seen from Gatto's deduction of Ingles list of primary functions of education, the base premise of education is to maintain and manage the status quo of the market-oriented society and within that, the segregation of citizens into manageable consumer groups. As someone who teaches children on a daily basis and spends my days observing what happens behind the walls of the school system, I cannot but confirm the accuracy of this list and its practical implications.

Yet you will not find these six purposes in any school policy. Instead these policies are elegantly written with goals and principles that honor virtues such as 'equality', 'diversity', 'inclusion', 'democracy' and 'life-long learning'. These key words are used in schools all over the industrialized world to innocuously present the education system as a benevolent place. But like the U.N's declaration of human rights, it is nothing but a red herring.

Students know they must go to school to learn for the sake of learning but are taught from an early age to not ask questions. They learn through ethnocentric course material that their culture is superior to other cultures and that a word like 'terrorist' is a synonym for Arabic sounding names. In fact, the stark inversion between the apparent principles that schools are supposed to teach and the actuality of life for children in schools resembles George Orwell's double-*speak,* where words were reversed and twisted to coax the population into placated obedience. (When an entire society is built on living a lie, it has to be assiduous in its efforts to maintain the illusion that the lie is truth.) Most importantly: students are taught that there are no viable alternatives to the current societal structure and that any alternatives they may encounter are at best laughable and at worst disruptive and dangerous for the status quo.

For young students who were born with brains and bodies not yet washed with that sweet but toxic detergent that is the current education system, it is not as easy as simply drinking the cool-aid and getting on with their business. They are prompted to learn about the importance of 'democracy' in a system that is anything but democratic. They are told to accept and include each other on the playground while being bombarded with images and music that tell them they must compete and stand out to be good enough. Buying the newest toy, gadget or clothing item becomes a matter of social life or death for them. It is no walk in the park to exist in a constant state of cognitive dissonance.

The current system, where citizens become consumers whose lives are indebted to corporations, is 'perfect' from the perspective that a full measure of control is maintained while everyone is blissfully unaware of it as they are caught up in the 'neon lights' of entertainment or existing in a perpetual state of petrification, leaving no room to do anything but struggle to survive. It is an effective system because people are so disoriented by the sheer amount of cognitive disinformation fed to them on a daily basis. This begins by brutally breaking children down before they have even developed themselves, like breaking the wings of a baby bird only to have it gratefully accept a place in the cage because it would otherwise not have survived.

The fact that politicians, market economists, financial tycoons and policy-makers are operating with two different agendas when it comes to education is remarkably obvious. Imagine for a moment a society where everyone knew the actual purposes of schooling: We would not be able to claim to live in a democratic society. In fact, we would live in an openly fascistic and totalitarian society, not unlike Orwell's nightmare vision of *1984*. What happens in such societies is that the citizens eventually revolt. We saw it in the French revolution, the Russian revolution, in Chile, in Venezuela and in many other countries around the world, obviously never with an outcome that actually changed anything for the better - because we never changed the foundation of our education systems and thus ourselves as humanity in the process.

So what are the solutions?

In The Purpose of Schooling[3], John Taylor Gatto condenses the functions of education into the following five dogmas:

1. Truth comes from Authority

2. Intelligence is the ability to remember and repeat

3. Accurate memory and repetition are rewarded

4. Non-compliance is punished

5. Conform: intellectually and socially

As a solution to subverting the dumbing-down of our children and the subsequent destruction of our planet, let's have a look at reversing these dogmas into practical living principles that will teach children on a real and fundamental level to become adults who will take on the guardianship of this earth with humbleness and compassion.

1. In our search for truth in this world, all we seem to find is more lies. As such what is required is stop focusing on truth and within that teach children to live on a lie and to instead teach children the necessary deductive skills to asses information critically, equally and within common sense. To do that they obviously need to be able to read and write, eventually at such an advanced level that no literature or document is beyond their comprehension. Segregating people through language proficiency levels and the extent of vocabulary is one of the most effective ways to ensure the acceptance of inequality. Through this principle of teaching all children to asses information at an equal level, they will be encouraged to be sovereign and thus empowered in such a way that they can make decisions that are not only best for them, but for all living beings. But more importantly; they will be equal in their understanding of the world, which means that socially engineered disinformation will be prevented from being disseminated as truth.

2. Intelligence must be measured based on the degree to which it contributes with ensuring a world that is best for all. It is really as simple as that. There is nothing 'intelligent' about inventing technologies that has no other purpose than to destroy our habitat or to regurgitate theories for no other reason than infatuation with intellect.

3. Education ought to be self-rewarding in the sense that we as individuals should be able to evaluate ourselves and accordingly measure our development within a particular learning process, so as to see where improvement is possible. In the current system rewards and punishment are used interchangeably to create compliant and fearful people that spite and ridicule each other. Again, if we measure intelligence according to which it contributes to a world that is best for all, this will then also be the reward of each individual's efforts: to

contribute to the creation of a world that is best for all and so for oneself. That is real value.

4. The problem with compliance is that it relies on followers that are complying out of fear. They are never making self-willed decisions and as such they will not take responsibility as co-creators of a business or a society. Instead they are merely following the scripts that are placed before them, while making no independent effort to optimize production processes or working conditions. The result of this is a faulty system where truck drivers fall asleep at the wheel and where doctors accidently kill patients and where no one really puts any effort into anything they do, because after all: "I just work here." Furthermore, having people comply out of fear always proposes the risk that they will eventually revolt in some way or another or at least carry a deep-seated blame causing them to never fully commit or give the system their all. For this world to thrive it is imperative that we as human beings become responsible, not only for our own lives, but for the world as a whole. This is our home and if we do not take responsibility for it, no one will. When each stand responsible for themselves and for the whole, they will have an ownership in what they do and thus an interest in the success of all involved. The work of each individual will therefore become valuable in a completely new way where it will not be necessary to use fear to motivate people because each will understand their value and as such be self-motivated.

5. Forcing people to conform to a system that was built to be broken, as Richard Grove from Tragedy and Hope [4] puts it; simply creates nothing but broken people. Broken people makes broken world, which eventually will lead to the demise of all of us - with animals and nature standing on the frontlines as the cannon fodder. So instead of wanting children to *conform*, we must assist them to *transform*, so that when they grow up, they do not make the same mistakes we did. To do that we have to transform ourselves, because we obviously cannot teach children anything that we ourselves have not yet learned.

While John Taylor Gatto spent decades teaching children in remarkable and provocative ways, his books and articles and interviews are equally rich sources of informative education, that we as adults can utilize to transform ourselves and reverse the conformity that has already been long stuffed down our throats, stifling any and all authentic expression. There are many other authors and trail-blazers through which we can initiate the re-education process of ourselves to become sovereign human beings that can stand as solid examples for the children entering this world. But the responsibility is, and can only be, our own. What is so fortunate about this day and age is that all information is virtually accessible through the Internet. All that is then required are the development of critical skills of discernment to circumvent the cognitive disinformation - and actually get to the real information about what is happening in this world. We do that through expanding our vocabulary, through cross-referencing what we find with others and through relentlessly unveiling ourselves from seeing what is really going on.

In a way it is quite simple; we have to stop living the lie. But as someone once said, self-honesty is the most difficult thing in the world because it forces us to take responsibility for who we have become and within that we have to let go of the wonderful world of illusion that we've created through the lie. Whether we like it or not, we're together on this sinking ship we call an earth. *More* wanted *more* and we were willing to pay any price to get it, even risking the future of all mankind and the earth in the process. This is what, up until now, has been the 'evolution' of humanity. The question is: can we afford to keep lying to ourselves when the world is falling apart around us, and at what price?

References

[1] http://www.johntaylorgatto.com/underground/index.htm

[2] Ibid.

[3] http://www.wesjones.com/gatto1.htm

[4] http://www.tragedyandhope.com

Education as Pedagogy of Possibility

Shedding Dogma through Reciprocal Learning

David Fields and Colin Jenkins

Like a snake that sheds its skin periodically throughout its lifecycle, the human mind must develop and shed itself of intellectual skin. Its evolution is characterized by cyclical bouts of learning, reflecting and reconsidering; however, unlike the snake, which is genetically inclined to molting, the mind may not mature and regenerate without being subjected to antagonistic curiosity. This may only be accomplished through frequent and consistent mental cultivation, whereas knowledge is acquired, ideas are processed, and intellectual fruit is born. This process is cyclical in its need for reflection, but most importantly, it is evolutionary in its wanting to refine itself; and it is this constant pursuit of knowledge and validation that drives the mind to absorb substantial information and secrete insignificant data.

Human intellectualism is inherently anti-dogmatic in its need for constant reflection. This is not to say that substantive beliefs can't stand the test of time, but only that they cannot do so without being incessantly validated along the way. In spite of this, and throughout the course of history, humans have shown a tendency to submit to the crude nature of indoctrination in order to appease their subconscious desire for simplicity. And herein lies the fundamental paradox of the human race: intellectualism is naturally fluid, yet human nature is innately simplistic. We are all blessed with a mind that is essentially limitless, yet we are at the same time limited by our instinctive nature to simplify matters of complexity. And without adequate motivation, the means to confront complex issues become nothing more than a tragedy of unrealized potential.

The process of learning, whether in a formal setting or through private exploration of curiosities, is a key motivator and major catalyst in the development of intellectualism.

Critical Pedagogy and Collaborative Inquiry

Society is an immensely complex entity, the broad functioning of which cannot be captured by obscure models of positive and normative simplification. As such, it is pertinent to recognize that the art of teaching should informed by Aristotle's conviction humans, by nature, have a desire to have a complex canonical knowledge of the social world. In this sense, the social practice of education is to both encourage and equip learners with the requisite tools to express and satisfy this desire. Although this desire to know is innate, it is more-or-less shaped by social structure, which suggests that satisfying it cannot happen in isolation. With this in mind, the classroom should be a place of collaborative inquiry requiring the full participation of both students and the instructor.

The intention is to construct pedagogy of possibility, a philosophy of praxis that that attempts to build the social conditions for a reconstruction and reconstitution of social imagination. This requires an approach to teaching that does not incorporate a 'knowledge from above' perspective, which establishes a pernicious division between 'expert' and 'novice". Rather, through what C. Wright Mills defined as the sociological imagination (i.e. the linking of individual biographies to great historical events) it is necessary to instill a critical macro-structural historical orientation such that students are enabled to question what is take for granted in society, so that underlying barriers which stifle human potential are broken down.

How is this to be accomplished? Cognition requires a shift in perception such that the understanding of a concept moves beyond initial appearances. In order to concretize what might initially appear as vague and indistinct, it is quite crucial to place classroom inquiry on a foundational basis that is infused with shared understandings, wherein the "teacher" learns a bit about the background of the student body, but also brings them to the same point of entry. In this sense, any real and perceived social relations of domination and inferiority between the teacher and student, which oftentimes undermine the capacity for knowledge absorption, is systematically negated. It can be said that ideas are learned when students have rescued it from a haze of abstraction and made it concretely his or her own.

In this process of taking ownership of not only the product of knowledge, but also the process of learning, the student's former subservient state is transformed into a partnership with the instructor. "In this way," explains Paulo Freire, "the problem-posing educator constantly re-forms his reflections in the reflection of the students. The students - no longer docile listeners - are now critical co-investigators in dialogue with the teacher. The teacher presents the material to the students for their consideration, and re-considers her earlier considerations as the students express their own." [1] This reciprocal process is the essence of critical pedagogy.

Rejecting Authoritative Learning and Standardization

It is contended that the simplicity of relative assessments. e.g. testing, does not allow for the opportunity to learn what a student does or does not know, but, in the final instance, fosters rankism, which inevitably undermines the positive social welfare outcomes of collective learning. It is of much greater significance, thus, to enable students to own ideas with which they become familiar, such that they are encouraged to collectively share their thoughts in a way that intellectual conversation and critical examination is encouraged and maximized; this is the process by which new ideas and discoveries about the social world are engineered. Hence, the objective is to assure that misunderstandings are revealed and thus resolved, which otherwise would not be possible in a traditional classroom where collective student participation is neither promoted nor embraced. This approach is vital because it helps students develop the social consciousness necessary to understand and effectively participate in what we often colloquially define as the "real world", despite the consequences of inequality derived from the social locations of class, race, gender, etc.

The purpose of education is to strive to resolve the inherent problem of the relationship between abstract phenomena and concrete realization, not via a top-down general form of logic, but through a dialectical mechanism of motion and contradiction that elucidates the philosophical, metaphysical, epistemological, ephemeral, and ontological qualities that altogether condition the human lived experience. What is necessary is pedagogy of possibility that inculcates into the minds of students the necessary methodological lens and working concepts needed to construct critical assessments and arguments with respect to subject matter, which may, in the end, ideally, provide the effective solutions that challenge the nature of current world dynamics. The strategic goal is to transform the classroom into an arena that delves deep beneath surface meaning and received wisdom, such that percipience of the conditions that shape manifest social phenomena is holistically cultivated.

This pedagogical approach "enables teachers and students to become Subjects of the educational process by overcoming authoritarianism and an alienating intellectualism; it also enables people to overcome their false perception of reality." "No longer something to be described with deceptive words," the world "becomes the object of that transforming action by men and women which results in their humanization." [2]

Cultivating Ideas and Unlocking Potential

Even with a predisposition that governs mental potency, human intellectualism has spawned many wondrous ideas in an effort to broaden the scope of existentialism, societal living and human interaction. Throughout history, these ideas have been pushed and prodded in every direction, constantly changing and evolving through a series of metaphysical connections that flawlessly pass from one generation to the next. Those who are bold enough to push the envelope of ideology beyond accepted norms are the ultimate drivers of human civilization; for regardless of how such ideas may be embraced by the dominant culture, they are at the very least invaluable catalysts for the constant development of the human mind. And while these ideas may be abused or misinterpreted at times, they are ultimately defined by their transcendent immortality - always readily available and accessible for reconsideration through an ongoing process of learning. The suppleness that creates such durability also leads to a vulnerability that is characterized by our subjective nature, which is limiting in its penchant for simplifying complex matters. Since the human mind is built for the fundamental purpose of troubleshooting problems that, in the most basic sense, threaten our survival, analytical skills often become secondary to the primary function of simplification. The brain confronts matters in the most efficient manner possible; so much so that it often becomes counterintuitive to undergo analysis which extends beyond the simplest explanation, even if that explanation is suspect. It is in this inherent method where dogma is born. However, the process of edification has the power to overcome innate tendencies towards reductionism. If we are to present education as a "humanist and liberating praxis" which "posits as fundamental that the people subjected to domination must fight for their emancipation," then this predisposition towards apathy - which is intensified through systems of coercive, disconnected, and hierarchical instruction - must be challenged with pedagogy that is cooperative, critical, and collaborative. The shedding of dogma is a key development in this application.

John Dewey once warned that, "Any movement that acts in terms of an 'ism becomes so involved in reaction against other 'isms that it is unwittingly controlled by them." The result of this hyper-focus on opposing views creates ideas that are formed in reaction to other 'isms "instead of by a comprehensive, constructive survey of actual needs, problems and possibilities." Our "banking" system of education which focuses on the memorization of narratives and which "achieves neither true knowledge nor true culture," consequently shapes minds that are susceptible to such reactionary thought. Because of this, the broad stigmatization of "Socratic questioning" that stems from our utilitarian nature has made the simple act of thinking quasi-revolutionary in itself. The most obvious deterioration is related to an abandonment of critical thinking. Ironically, the arrival of a technologically-advanced, information-based society has paralleled a pedagogical culture that is enamored with the mundane nature and meaningless pursuit of encyclopedic knowledge. This corollary development is the result of a neoliberalized trifecta of corporate education models, standardization, and a total reliance on the narrative/lecture-based "banking" approach to schooling. Freire tells us:

"A careful analysis of the teacher-student relationship at any level, inside or outside the school, reveals its fundamentally narrative character. This relationship involves a narrating Subject (the teacher) and patient listening objects (the students). The contents, whether values or empirical dimensions of reality, tend in the process of being

narrated to become lifeless and petrified. Education is suffering from narration sickness." [3]

In a corporate-dominated society where human beings are only valuable in a dehumanized state (as workers and consumers), intellectualism has given way to task-mastering. Responsible thought has been replaced by a demand for quick and unrelenting decision-making. Critical thinking and thorough analysis are relegated as a sign of weakness in a society that rewards those who develop speedy conclusions, regardless of accuracy, truth or consequences. The state of our education system -increased privatization, the implementation of standardization and "common core" models, and a gradual rejection of humanities - reflects this. If education is to realize its fundamental role as "pedagogy of possibility," we must not only redirect our current path, but also steer it towards an increasingly critical and collaborative nature which empowers students through reciprocal interactions and ownership of the learning process.

Work Cited

[1] Paulo Freire. Pedagogy of the Oppressed. New York: Continuum Books, 1993. Accessed onhttp://www2.webster.edu/~corbetre/philosophy/education/freire/freire-2.html
[2] Ibid
[3] Ibid

Geopolitics

Engineering Empire

An Introduction to the Intellectuals and Institutions of American Imperialism

Andrew Gavin Marshall

Educating yourself about empire can be a challenging endeavor, especially since so much of the educational system is dedicated to avoiding the topic or justifying the actions of imperialism in the modern era. If one studies political science or economics, the subject might be discussed in a historical context, but rarely as a modern reality; media and government voices rarely speak on the subject, and even more rarely speak of it with direct and honest language. Instead, we exist in a society where institutions and individuals of power speak in coded language, using deceptive rhetoric with abstract meaning. We hear about 'democracy' and 'freedom' and 'security,' but so rarely about imperialism, domination, and exploitation.

The objective of this report is to provide an introduction to the institutional and social structure of American imperialism. The material is detailed, but should not be considered complete or even comprehensive; its purpose is to function as a resource or reference for those seeking to educate themselves about the modern imperial system. It's not an analysis of state policies or the effects of those policies, but rather, it is an examination of the institutions and individuals who advocate and implement imperial policies. What is revealed is a highly integrated and interconnected network of institutions and individuals - the foreign policy establishment - consisting of academics (so-called "experts" and "policy-oriented intellectuals") and prominent think tanks.

Think tanks bring together prominent academics, former top government officials, corporate executives, bankers, media representatives, foundation officials and other elites in an effort to establish consensus on issues of policy and strategy, to produce reports and recommendations for policy-makers, functioning as recruitment centers for those who are selected to key government positions where they have the ability to implement policies. Thus, think tanks function as the intellectual engines of empire: they establish consensus among elites, provide policy prescriptions, strategic recommendations, and the personnel required to implement imperial policies through government agencies.

Among the most prominent American and international think tanks are the Council on Foreign Relations (CFR), the Bilderberg meetings, the Trilateral Commission, the Center for Strategic and International Studies (CSIS), the Brookings Institution, the Carnegie Endowment for International Peace, and the Atlantic Council. These institutions tend to rely upon funding from major foundations (such as Rockefeller, Ford, Carnegie, etc.) as well as corporations and financial institutions, and even various government agencies. There is an extensive crossover in leadership and membership between these institutions, and between them and their funders.

Roughly focusing on the period from the early 1970s until today, what emerges from this research is a highly integrated network of foreign policy elites, with individuals like Henry Kissinger, Zbigniew Brzezinski, Brent Scowcroft, and Joseph Nye figuring prominently in sitting at the center of the American imperial establishment over the course of decades, with powerful corporate and financial patrons such as the Rockefeller family existing in the background of American power structures.

Meet the Engineers of Empire

Within the U.S. government, the National Security Council (NSC) functions as the main planning group, devising strategy and policies for the operation of American power in the world. The NSC coordinates

125

multiple other government agencies, bringing together the secretaries of the State and Defense Departments, the CIA, NSA, Joint Chiefs of Staff, and various other government bodies, with meetings directed by the National Security Adviser, who is generally one of the president's most trusted and influential advisers. In several administrations, the National Security Adviser became the most influential voice and policy-maker to do with foreign policy, such as during the Nixon administration (with Henry Kissinger) and the Carter administration (with Zbigniew Brzezinski).

While both of these individuals were top government officials in the 1970s, their influence has not declined in the decades since they held such positions. In fact, it could be argued that both of their influence (along with several other foreign policy elites) has increased with their time outside of government. In fact, in a January 2013 interview with *The Hill*, Brzezinski stated: "To be perfectly frank - and you may not believe me - I really wasn't at all conscious of the fact that the defeat of the Carter administration [in 1980] somehow or another affected significantly my own standing... I just kept doing my thing minus the Office of the National Security Adviser in the White House." [1]

David Rothkopf has written the official history of the National Security Council (NSC) in his book, *Running the World: The Inside Story of the National Security Council and the Architects of American Power*, published in 2005. Rothkopf writes from an insider's perspective, being a member of the Council on Foreign Relations, a visiting scholar at the Carnegie Endowment, he was Under Secretary of Commerce for International Trade Policy and Development in the Clinton administration, and is currently president and CEO of Garten Rothkopf, an international advisory firm, CEO of *Foreign Policy* magazine, previously CEO of Intellibridge Corporation, and was also a managing director at Kissinger Associates, an international advisory firm founded and run by Henry Kissinger. In his book on the NSC, Rothkopf noted that, "[e]very single national security advisor since Kissinger is, in fact, within two degrees of Kissinger," referring to the fact that they have all "worked with him as aides, on his staff, or directly with him in some capacity," or worked for someone in those categories (hence, within "two degrees").[2]

For example, General Brent Scowcroft, who was National Security Advisor (NSA) under Presidents Ford and George H.W. Bush, was Kissinger's Deputy National Security Advisor in the Nixon administration; Zbigniew Brzezinski, Carter's NSA, served on the faculty of Harvard with

Kissinger, also served with Kissinger on the President's Foreign Intelligence Advisory Board during the Reagan administration, both of them are also members (and were at times, board members) of the Council on Foreign Relations, as well as members of the Trilateral Commission, and they are both currently trustees of the Center for Strategic and International Studies (CSIS). Other NSA's with connections to Kissinger include: Richard Allen, NSA under Reagan, who worked for Kissinger in the Nixon administration; William P. Clark, NSA under Reagan, who worked for Kissinger's former aide, Alexander Haig at the State Department; Robert McFarlane, also NSA under Reagan, worked with Kissinger in the Nixon administration; John Poindexter, also NSA for Reagan, was McFarlane's deputy; Frank Carlucci, also NSA in the Reagan administration, worked for Kissinger in the Nixon administration; Colin Powell, NSA for Reagan (and Secretary of State for George W. Bush), worked for Carlucci as his deputy; Anthony Lake, Clinton's NSA, worked directly for Kissinger; Samuel Berger, also NSA for Clinton, was Lake's deputy; Condoleezza Rice, NSA for George W. Bush, worked on Scowcroft's NSC staff; and Stephen Hadley also worked for Kissinger directly.[3]

The foreign policy establishment consists of the top officials of the key government agencies concerned with managing foreign policy (State Department, Pentagon, CIA, NSC), drawing upon officials from within the think tank community, where they become well acquainted with corporate and financial elites, and thus, become familiar with the interests of this group of people. Upon leaving high office, these officials often return to leadership positions within the think tank community, join corporate boards, and/or establish their own international advisory firms where they charge hefty fees to provide corporations and banks with strategic advice and use of their international political contacts (which they acquired through their time in office). Further, these individuals also regularly appear in the media to provide commentary on international affairs as 'independent experts' and are routinely recruited to serve as 'outside' advisors to presidents and other high-level officials.

No less significant in assessing influence within the foreign policy establishment is the relative proximity - and relationships - individuals have with deeply entrenched power structures, notably financial and corporate dynasties. Arguably, both Kissinger and Brzezinski are two of the most influential individuals within the foreign policy elite networks. Certainly of no detriment to their careers was the fact that both cultivated close working and personal relationships with what can be said to be America's most powerful dynasty, the Rockefeller family.

Dynastic Influence on Foreign Policy

At first glance, this may appear to be a rather obscure addition to this report, but dynastic power in modern state-capitalist societies is largely overlooked, misunderstood, or denied altogether, much like the concept of 'empire' itself. The lack of discourse on this subject - or the relegation of it to fringe 'conspiratorial' views - is not reason enough to ignore it. Far from assigning a conspiratorial or 'omnipotent' view of power to dynastic elements, it is important to place them within a social and institutional analysis, to understand the complexities and functions of dynastic influence within modern society.

Dynastic power relies upon a complex network of relationships and interactions between institutions, individuals, and ideologies. Through most of human history - in most places in the world - power was wielded by relatively few people, and often concentrated among dynastic family structures, whether ancient Egypt, imperial Rome, ancient China, the Ottoman Empire or the European monarchs spreading their empires across the globe. With the rise of state-capitalist society, dynastic power shifted from the overtly political to the financial and economic spheres. Today's main dynasties are born of corporate or banking power, maintained through family lines and extended through family ties to individuals, institutions, and policy-makers. The Rockefellers are arguably the most influential dynasty in the United States, but comparable to the Rothschilds in France and the UK, the Wallenbergs in Sweden, the Agnellis in Italy, or the Desmarais family in Canada. These families are themselves connected through institutions such as the Bilderberg Group and the Trilateral Commission, among others. The power of a corporate-financial dynasty is not a given: it must be maintained, nurtured, and strengthened, otherwise it will be overcome or made obsolete.

The Rockefeller family has existed at the center of American power for over a century. Originating with the late 19th century 'Robber Baron' industrialists, the Rockefellers established an oil empire, and subsequently a banking empire. John D. Rockefeller, who had a personal fortune surpassing $1 billion in the first decade of the 20th century, also founded the University of Chicago, and through the creation and activities of the Rockefeller Foundation (founded in 1913), helped engineer higher education and the social sciences. The Rockefeller family - largely acting through various family foundations - were also pivotal in the founding and funding of several prominent think tanks, notably the Council on Foreign Relations, the Asia Society, Trilateral Commission, the Group of Thirty, and the Bilderberg Group, among many others.

The patriarch of the Rockefeller family today is David Rockefeller, now in his late 90s. To understand the influence wielded by unelected bankers and billionaires like Rockefeller, it would be useful to simply examine the positions he has held throughout his life. From 1969 until 1980, he was the chairman and CEO of Chase Manhattan Bank and from 1981 to 1999 he was the chairman of the International Advisory Committee of Chase Manhattan, at which time it merged with another big bank to become JPMorgan Chase, of Rockefeller served as a member of the International Advisory Council from 2000 to 2005. David Rockefeller was a founding member of the Bilderberg Group in 1954, at which he remains on the Steering Committee; he is the former chairman of Rockefeller Group, Inc. (from 1981-1995), Rockefeller Center Properties (1996-2001), and the Rockefeller Brothers Fund, at which he remains as an advisory trustee. He is chairman emeritus and life trustee of the Museum of Modern Art, and the founder of the David Rockefeller Fund and the International Executive Service Corps.

David Rockefeller was also the chairman of the Council on Foreign Relations from 1970 to 1985, of which he remains to this day as honorary chairman; is chairman emeritus of the board of trustees of the University of Chicago; honorary chairman, life trustee and chairman emeritus of the Rockefeller University Council, and is the former president of the Harvard Board of Overseers. He was co-founder of the Global Philanthropists Circle, is honorary chairman of the Committee Encouraging Corporate Philanthropy (CECP), and is an honorary director of the Peterson Institute for International Economics. David Rockefeller was also the co-founder (with Zbigniew Brzezinski) of the Trilateral Commission in 1973, where he served as North American Chairman until 1991, and has since remained as honorary chairman. He is also the founder and honorary chairman of the Americas Society and the Council of the Americas.

It should not come as a surprise, then, that upon David Rockefeller's 90th birthday celebration (held at the Council on Foreign Relations) in 2005, then-president of the World Bank, James Wolfensohn delivered a speech in which he stated that, "the person who had perhaps the greatest influence on my life professionally in this country, and I'm very happy to say personally there afterwards, is David Rockefeller, who first met me at the Harvard Business School in 1957 or '58." He went on to explain that in the early 20th century United States, "as we looked at the world, a family, the Rockefeller family, decided that the issues were not just national for the United States, were not just related to the rich countries. And where, extraordinarily and amazingly, David's grandfather set up the Rockefeller Foundation, the purpose of which was to take a global view." Wolfensohn continued:

So the Rockefeller family, in this last 100 years, has contributed in a way that is quite extraordinary to the development in that period and has given ample focus to the issues of development with which I have been associated. In fact, it's fair to say that there has been no other single family influence greater than the Rockefeller's in the whole issue of globalization and in the whole issue of addressing the questions which, in some ways, are still before us today. And for that David, we're deeply grateful to you and for your own contribution in carrying these forward in the way that you did. [4]

Wolfensohn of course would be in a position to know something about the influence of the Rockefeller family. Serving as president of the World Bank from 1995 to 2005, he has since founded his own private firm, Wolfensohn & Company, LLC., was been a longtime member of the Steering Committee of the Bilderberg Group, an honorary trustee of the Brookings Institution, a trustee of the Rockefeller Foundation, and is a member of the Council on Foreign Relations. Wolfensohn's father, Hyman, was employed by James Armand de Rothschild of the Rothschild banking dynasty (after whom James was named), and taught the young Wolfensohn how to "cultivate mentors, friends and contacts of influence."[5] In his autobiography of 2002, *Memoirs*, David Rockefeller himself wrote:

For more than a century ideological extremists at either end of the political spectrum have seized upon well-publicized incidents such as my encounter with Castro to attack the Rockefeller family for the inordinate influence they claim we wield over American political and economic institutions. Some even believe we are part of a secret cabal working against the best interests of the United States, characterizing my family

130

and me as 'internationalists' and of conspiring with others around the world to build a more integrated global political and economic structure--one world, if you will. If that's the charge, I stand guilty, and I am proud of it. [6]

In the United States, the Rockefeller family has maintained a network of influence through financial, corporate, educational, cultural, and political spheres. It serves as a logical extension of dynastic influence to cultivate relationships among the foreign policy elite of the U.S., notably the likes of Kissinger and Brzezinski.

Intellectuals, 'Experts,' and Imperialists *Par Excellence*: Kissinger and Brzezinski

Both Kissinger and Brzezinski served as professors at Harvard in the early 1950s, as well as both joining the Council on Foreign Relations around the same time, and both also attended meetings of the Bilderberg Group (two organizations which had Rockefellers in leadership positions). Kissinger was a director at the Rockefeller Brothers Fund from 1956 until 1958, and thereafter became an advisor to Nelson Rockefeller. Kissinger was even briefly brought into the Kennedy administration as an advisor to the State Department, while Brzezinski was an advisor to the Kennedy campaign, and was a member of President Johnson's Policy Planning Council in the State Department from 1966 to 1968. When Nixon became president in 1969, Kissinger became his National Security Advisor, and eventually also took over the role of Secretary of State.

In 1966, prior to entering the Nixon administration, Henry Kissinger wrote an article for the journal *Daedalus* in which he proclaimed the modern era as "the age of the expert," and went on to explain: "The expert has his constituency - those who have a vested interest in commonly held opinions; elaborating and defining its consensus at a high level has, after all, made him an expert." [7] In other words, the "expert" serves entrenched and established power structures and elites ("those who have a vested interest in commonly held opinions"), and the role of such an expert is to define and elaborate the "consensus" of elite interests. Thus, experts, as Henry Kissinger defines them, serve established elites.

In 1970, Brzezinski wrote a highly influential book, *Between Two Ages: America's Role in the Technetronic Era*, which attracted the interest of Chase Manhattan Chairman (and Chairman of the Council on Foreign Relations) David Rockefeller. The two men then worked together to create the Trilateral Commission, of which Kissinger became a member. Kissinger remained as National Security Advisor for President Ford, and when Jimmy Carter became President (after Brzezinski invited him into the Trilateral Commission), Brzezinski became his National Security Advisor, also bringing along dozens of other members of the Trilateral Commission into the administration's cabinet.

In a study published in the journal *Polity* in 1982, researchers described what amounted to modern Machiavellis who "whisper in the ears of princes," notably, prominent academic-turned policy-makers like Walt Rostow, Henry Kissinger, and Zbigniew Brzezinski. The researchers constructed a 'survey' in 1980 which was distributed to a sample of officials in the State Department, CIA, Department of Defense and the National Security Council (the four government agencies primarily tasked with managing foreign policy), designed to assess the views of those who implement foreign policy related to how they measure influence held by academics. They compared their results with a similar survey conducted in 1971, and found that in both surveys, academics such as George Kennan, Hans Morgenthau, Henry Kissinger, and Zbigniew Brzezinski were listed as among the members of the academic community who most influenced the thinking of those who took the survey. In the 1971 survey, George Kennan was listed as the most influential, followed by Hans Morgenthau, John K. Galbraith, Henry Kissinger, E.O. Reischauer and Zbigniew Brzezinski; in the 1980 survey, Henry Kissinger was listed as the most influential, followed by Hans Morgenthau, George Kennan, Zbigniew Brzezinski and Stanley Hoffmann. [8]

Of the fifteen most influential scholars in the 1980 survey, eleven received their highest degree from a major East Coast university, eight held a doctorate from Harvard, twelve were associated with major East Coast universities, while seven of them had previously taught at Harvard. More than half of the top fifteen scholars had previously held prominent government positions, eight were members of the Council on Foreign Relations, ten belonged to the American Academy of Arts and Sciences and eight belonged to the American Political Science Association. Influence tended to sway according to which of the four government agencies surveyed was being assessed, though for

Kissinger, Morgenthau and Brzezinski, they "were equally influential with each of the agencies surveyed." The two most influential academic journals cited by survey responses were *Foreign Affairs* (run by the Council on Foreign Relations), read by more than two-thirds of those who replied to the survey, and *Foreign Policy*, which was read by more than half of respondents. [9]

In a 1975 report by the Trilateral Commission on *The Crisis of Democracy*, co-authored by Samuel Huntington, a close associate and friend of Zbigniew Brzezinski, the role of intellectuals came into question, noting that with the plethora of social movements and protests that had emerged from the 1960s onwards, intellectuals were asserting their "disgust with the corruption, materialism, and inefficiency of democracy and with the subservience of democratic government to 'monopoly capitalism'." Thus, noted the report: "the advanced industrial societies have spawned a stratum of value-oriented intellectuals who often devote themselves to the derogation of leadership, the challenging of authority, and the unmasking and delegitimation of established institutions, their behavior contrasting with that of the also increasing numbers of technocratic policy-oriented intellectuals."[10] In other words, intellectuals were increasingly failing to serve as "experts" (as Henry Kissinger defined it), and were increasingly challenging authority and institutionalized power structures instead of serving them, unlike "technocratic and policy-oriented intellectuals."

The influence of "experts" and "technocratic policy-oriented intellectuals" like Kissinger and Brzezinski was not to dissipate going into the 1980s. Kissinger then joined the Center for Strategic and International Studies (CSIS), taught at Georgetown University, and in 1982, founded his own consulting firm, Kissinger Associates, co-founded and run with General Brent Scowcroft, who was the National Security Advisor for President Ford, after being Kissinger's deputy in the Nixon administration. Scowcroft is also a member of the Council on Foreign Relations, the Trilateral Commission, CSIS, and The Atlantic Council of the United States, which also includes Kissinger and Brzezinski among its leadership boards. Scowcroft also founded his own international advisory firm, the Scowcroft Group, and also served as National Security Advisor to President George H.W. Bush.

Kissinger Associates, which included not only Henry Kissinger and Brent Scowcroft, but also Lawrence Eagleburger, Kissinger's former aide in the Nixon administration, and Undersecretary of State for Political

Affairs in the Reagan administration, and briefly as Deputy Secretary of State in the George H.W. Bush administration. These three men, who led Kissinger Associates in the 1980s, made a great deal of money advising some of the world's leading corporations, including ITT, American Express, Coca-Cola, Volvo, Fiat, and Midland Bank, among others. Kissinger Associates charges corporate clients at least $200,000 for "offering geopolitical insight" and "advice," utilizing "their close relationships with foreign governments and their extensive knowledge of foreign affairs."[11]

While he was Chairman of Kissinger Associates, advising corporate clients, Henry Kissinger was also appointed to chair the National Bipartisan Commission on Central America by President Reagan from 1983 to 1985, commonly known as the Kissinger Commission, which provided the strategic framework for Reagan's terror war on Central America. As Kissinger himself noted in 1983, "If we cannot manage Central America... it will be impossible to convince threatened nations in the Persian Gulf and in other places that we know how to manage the global equilibrium." [12] In other words, if the United States could not control a small region south of its border, how can it be expected to run the world?

Between 1984 and 1990, Henry Kissinger was also appointed to Reagan's (and subsequently Bush Sr.'s) Foreign Intelligence Advisory Board, an organization that provides "advice" to the President on intelligence issues, which Brzezinski joined between 1987 and 1989. Brzezinski also served as a member of Reagan's Chemical Warfare Commission, and from 1987 to 1988, worked with Reagan's U.S. National Security Council-Defense Department Commission on Integrated Long-Term Strategy, alongside Henry Kissinger. The Commission's report, *Discriminate Deterrence*, issued in 1988, noted that the United States would have to establish new capabilities to deal with threats, particularly in the 'Third World,' noting that while conflicts in the 'Third World' "are obviously less threatening than any Soviet-American war would be," they still "have had and will have an adverse cumulative effect on U.S. access to critical regions," and if these effects cannot be managed, "it will gradually undermine America's ability to defend its interest in the most vital regions, such as the Persian Gulf, the Mediterranean and the Western Pacific."[13]

Over the following decade, the report noted, "the United States will need to be better prepared to deal with conflicts in the Third World" which would "require new kinds of planning." If the United States could not effectively counter the threats to U.S. interests and allies, notably, "if the warfare is of low intensity and protracted, and if they use guerrilla forces, paramilitary terrorist organizations, or armed subversives," or, in other words, revolutionary movements, then "we will surely lose the support of many Third World countries that want to believe the United States can protect its friends, not to mention its own interests." Most 'Third World' conflicts are termed "low intensity conflict," referring to "insurgencies, organized terrorism, [and] paramilitary crime," and therefore the United States would need to take these conflicts more seriously, noting that within such circumstances, "the enemy" is essentially "omnipresent," meaning that the enemy is the population itself, "and unlikely ever to surrender."[14]

From Cold War to New World Order: 'Containment' to 'Enlargement'

At the end of the Cold War, the American imperial community of intellectuals and think tanks engaged in a process that continues to the present day in attempting to outline a geostrategic vision for America's domination of the world. The Cold War had previously provided the cover for the American extension of hegemony around the world, under the premise of 'containing' the Soviet Union and the spread of 'Communism.' With the end of the Cold War came the end of the 'containment' policy of foreign policy. It was the task of 'experts' and 'policy-oriented intellectuals' to assess the present circumstances of American power in the world and to construct new strategic concepts for the extension and preservation of that power.

In 1990, George H.W. Bush's administration released the *National Security Strategy of the United States* in which the Cold War was officially acknowledged as little more than a rhetorical deception. The document referenced U.S. interventions in the Middle East, which were for decades justified on the basis of 'containing' the perceived threat of 'communism' and the Soviet Union. The report noted that, "even as East-West tensions diminish, American strategic concerns remain." Threats to America's "interests" in the region, such as "the security of Israel and moderate Arab states" - otherwise known as ruthless dictatorships - "as well as the free flow of oil - come from a variety of sources." Citing previous military interventions in the region, the report stated that they "were in response to threats to U.S. interests that could not be laid at the Kremlin's door." In other words, all the rhetoric of protecting the world from communism and the Soviet Union was little more than deception. As the *National Security Strategy* noted: "The necessity to defend our interests will continue." [15]

When Bush became president in 1989, he ordered his national security team - headed by Brent Scowcroft - to review national security policy. Bush and Scowcroft had long discussed - even before the Iraqi invasion of Kuwait - the notion that the U.S. will have to make its priority dealing with "Third World bullies" (a euphemism referring to U.S. puppet dictators who stop following orders). At the end of the Cold War, George Bush declared a 'new world order,' a term which was suggested to Bush by Brent Scowcroft during a discussion "about future foreign-policy crises." [16]

Separate from the official *National Security Strategy*, the internal assessment of national security policy commissioned by Bush was partly leaked to and reported in the media in 1991. As the *Los Angeles Times* commented, the review dispensed with "sentimental nonsense about democracy." [17] The *New York Times* quoted the review: "In cases where the U.S. confronts much weaker enemies, our challenge will be not simply to defeat them, but to defeat them decisively and rapidly... For small countries hostile to us, bleeding our forces in protracted or indecisive conflict or embarrassing us by inflicting damage on some conspicuous element of our forces may be victory enough, and could undercut political support for U.S. efforts against them." [18] In other words, the capacity to justify and undertake large-scale wars and ground invasions had deteriorated substantially, so it would be necessary to "decisively and rapidly" destroy "much weaker enemies."

Zbigniew Brzezinski was quite blunt in his assessment of the Cold War - of which he was a major strategic icon - when he wrote in a 1992 article for *Foreign Affairs*, the journal of the Council on Foreign Relations, that the U.S. strategic discourse of the Cold War as a battle between Communist totalitarianism and Western democracy was little more than rhetoric. In Brzezinski's own words: "The policy of liberation was a strategic sham, designed to a significant degree for domestic political reasons... the policy was basically rhetorical, at most tactical." [19] In other words, it was all a lie, carefully constructed to deceive the American population into accepting the actions of a powerful state in its attempts to dominate the world.

In 1992, the *New York Times* leaked a classified document compiled by top Pentagon officials (including Paul Wolfowitz and Dick Cheney) devising a strategy for America in the post-Cold War world. As the *Times* summarized, the Defense Policy Guidance document "asserts that America's political and military mission in the post-cold-war era will be to ensure that no rival superpower is allowed to emerge in Western Europe, Asia or the territories of the former Soviet Union." The document "makes the case for a world dominated by one superpower whose position can be perpetuated by constructive behavior and sufficient military might to deter any nation or group of nations from challenging American primacy." [20]

In the Clinton administration, prominent "policy-oriented intellectuals" filled key foreign policy positions, notably Madeleine Albright, first as ambassador to the UN and then as Secretary of State, and Anthony Lake as National Security Advisor. Anthony Lake was a staffer in Kissinger's National Security Council during the Nixon administration (though he resigned in protest following the 'secret' bombing of Cambodia). Lake was subsequently recruited into the Trilateral Commission, and was then appointed as policy planning director in Jimmy Carter's State Department under Secretary of State (and Trilateral Commission/Council on Foreign Relations member) Cyrus Vance. Richard Holbrooke and Warren Christopher were also brought into the Trilateral Commission, then to the Carter administration, and resurfaced in the Clinton administration. Holbrooke and Lake had even been college roommates for a time. Madeleine Albright had studied at Columbia University under Zbigniew Brzezinski, who was her dissertation advisor. When Brzezinski became National Security Adviser in the Carter administration, he brought in Albright as a special assistant. [21]

Anthony Lake was responsible for outlining the 'Clinton Doctrine,' which he elucidated in a 1993 speech at Johns Hopkins University, where he stated: "The successor to a doctrine of containment must be a strategy of enlargement - enlargement of the world's free community of market democracies." This strategy "must combine our broad goals of fostering democracy and markets with our more traditional geostrategic interests," noting that, "[o]ther American interests at times will require us to befriend and even defend non-democratic states for mutually beneficial reasons." [22] In other words, nothing has changed, save the rhetoric: the interest of American power is in "enlarging" America's economic and political domination of the world.

In 1997, Brzezinski published a book outlining his strategic vision for America's role in the world, entitled *The Grand Chessboard.* He wrote that "the chief geopolitical prize" for America was 'Eurasia,' referring to the connected landmass of Asia and Europe: "how America 'manages' Eurasia is critical. Eurasia is the globe's largest continent and is geopolitically axial. A power that dominates Eurasia would control two of the world's three most advanced and economically productive regions. A mere glance at the map also suggests that control over Eurasia would almost automatically entail African subordination."[23] The "twin interests" of the United States, wrote Brzezinski, were, "in the short-term preservation of its unique global power and in the long-run transformation of it into increasingly institutionalized global cooperation." Brzezinski then wrote:

To put it in a terminology that hearkens back to the more brutal age of ancient empires, the three grand imperatives of imperial geostrategy are to prevent collusion and maintain security dependence among the vassals, to keep tributaries pliant and protected, and to keep the barbarians from coming together.[24]

The officials from the George H.W. Bush administration who drafted the 1992 Defense Policy Guidance report spent the Clinton years in neoconservative think tanks, such as the Project for the New American Century (PNAC). Essentially using the 1992 document as a blueprint, the PNAC published a report in 2000 entitled *Rebuilding America's Defenses: Strategy, Forces, and Resources for a New Century*. In contrast to previous observations from strategists like Brzezinski and Scowcroft, the neocons were not opposed to implementing large-scale wars, declaring that, "the United States must retain sufficient forces able to rapidly deploy and win multiple simultaneous large-scale wars." The report stated that there was a "need to retain sufficient combat forces to fight and win, multiple, nearly simultaneous major theatre wars" and that "the Pentagon needs to begin to calculate the force necessary to protect, independently, US interests in Europe, East Asia and the Gulf at all times."[25]

Drafted by many of the neocons who would later lead the United States into the Iraq war (including Paul Wolfowitz), the report recommended that the United States establish a strong military presence in the Middle East: "the United States has for decades sought to play a more permanent role in Gulf regional security. While the unresolved conflict with Iraq provides the immediate justification, the need for a substantial American force presence in the Gulf transcends the issue of the regime of Saddam Hussein."[26]

When the Bush administration came to power in 2001, it brought in a host of neoconservatives to key foreign policy positions, including Paul Wolfowitz, Donald Rumsfeld and Dick Cheney. As one study noted, "among the 24 Bush appointees who have been most closely identified as neocons or as close to them, there are 27 links with conservative think tanks, 19 with their liberal counterparts and 20 with 'neocon' think tanks," as well as 11 connections with the Council on Foreign Relations.[27]

The 2002 U.S. National Security Strategy announced by the Bush administration, thereafter referred to as the "Bush doctrine," which included the usual rhetoric about democracy and freedom, and then established the principle of "preemptive war" and unilateral intervention for America's War of Terror, noting: "the United States will, if necessary, act preemptively. The United States will not use force in all cases to preempt emerging threats, nor should nations use preemption as a pretext for aggression. Yet in an age where the enemies of civilization openly and actively seek the world's most destructive technologies, the United States cannot remain idle while dangers gather."[28] The doctrine announced that the U.S. "will constantly strive to enlist the support of the international community, [but] we will not hesitate to act alone, if necessary, to exercise our right of self-defense by acting preemptively against terrorists."[29]

A fusion of neoconservative and traditional liberal internationalist "policy-oriented intellectuals" was facilitated in 2006 with the release of a report by the Princeton Project on National Security (PPNS), *Forging a World of Liberty Under Law: U.S. National Security in the 21st Century*, co-directed by G. John Ikenberry and Anne-Marie Slaughter. Ikenberry was a professor at Princeton and the Woodrow Wilson School of Public and International Affairs. He had previously served in the State Department Policy Planning staff in the administration of George H.W. Bush, was a senior associate at the Carnegie Endowment for International Peace, a senior fellow at the Brookings Institution, and a member of the Council on Foreign Relations. Anne-Marie Slaughter was Dean of the Woodrow Wilson School of Public and International Affairs, has served on the board of the Council on Foreign Relations, the New America Foundation, the National Endowment for Democracy, New American Security, the Truman Project, and the Center for Strategic and International Studies (CSIS), and has also served on the boards of McDonald's and Citigroup, as well as often being a State Department adviser.

While the Bush administration and the neoconservatives within it had articulated a single vision of a 'global war on terror,' the objective of the Princeton Project's report was to encourage the strategic acknowledgement of multiple, conflicting and complex threats to American power. Essentially, it was a project formed by prominent intellectual elites in reaction to the myopic and dangerous vision and actions projected by the Bush administration; a way to re-align strategic objectives based upon a more coherent analysis and articulation of the interests of power. One of its main critiques was against the notion of "unilateralism" advocated in the Bush Doctrine and enacted with the Iraq War. The aim of the report, in its own words, was to "set forth agreed premises or foundational principles to guide the development of specific national security strategies by successive administrations in coming decades."[30]

The Honourary Co-Chairs of the Project report were Anthony Lake, Clinton's former National Security Adviser, and George P. Shultz, former U.S. Secretary of Labor and Secretary of the Treasury in the Nixon administration, U.S. Secretary of State in the Reagan administration, president of Bechtel Corporation, and was on the International Advisory Council of JP Morgan Chase, a director of the Peterson Institute for International Economics, a member of the Hoover Institution, the Washington Institute for Near East Policy, and was on the boards of a number of corporations.

Among the co-sponsors of the project (apart from Princeton) were: the Brookings Institution, the Council on Foreign Relations, the Carnegie Endowment for International Peace, the Centre for International Governance Innovation, Oxford, Stanford, the German Marshall Fund, and the Hoover Institution, among others. Most financing for the Project came from the Woodrow Wilson School/Princeton, the Ford Foundation, and David M. Rubenstein, one of the world's richest billionaires, co-founder of the global private equity firm the Carlyle Group, on the boards of Duke University, the Brookings Institution, the Council on Foreign Relations, President of the Economic Club of Washington, and the International Business Council of the World Economic Forum. [31]

Among the "experts" who participated in the Project were: Henry Kissinger, Zbigniew Brzezinski, Eliot Cohen, Francis Fukuyama, Leslie Gelb, Richard Haas, Robert Kagan, Jessica Tuchman Matthews, Joseph S. Nye, James Steinberg, and Strobe Talbott, among many others. Among the participating institutions were: Princeton, Harvard, Yale, CSIS, the

Brookings Institution, Council on Foreign Relations, Carnegie Endowment, Federal Reserve Bank of New York, World Bank, the State Department, National Security Council, Citigroup, Ford Foundation, German Marshall Fund, Kissinger Associates, the Scowcroft Group, Cato Institute, Morgan Stanley, Carlyle Group. Among the participants in the Project were no less than 18 members of the Council on Foreign Relations, 10 members of the Brookings Institution, 6 members of the Carnegie Endowment for International Peace, and several representatives from foreign governments, including Canada, Australia, and Japan.[32]

The Road to "Hope" and "Change"

After leaving the Clinton administration, Madeleine Albright founded her own consulting firm in 2001, The Albright Group, since re-named the Albright Stonebridge Group, co-chaired by Albright and Clinton's second National Security Adviser Samuel Berger, advising multinational corporations around the world. Albright is also chair of Albright Capital Management LLC, an investment firm which focuses on 'emerging markets.' Albright is also on the board of directors of the Council on Foreign Relations, is a professor at Georgetown University School of Foreign Service, chairs the National Democratic Institute for International Affairs, the Pew Global Attitudes Project, and is president of the Truman Scholarship Foundation. She is also on the board of trustees of the Aspen Institute, a member of the Atlantic Council, and in 2009 was recruited by NATO Secretary-General Anders Fogh Rasmussen to chair the 'group of experts' tasked with drafting NATO's New Strategic Concept for the world.

Kissinger, Scowcroft, and Albright are not the only prominent "former" statespersons to have established consulting firms for large multinational conglomerates, as the far less known Brzezinski Group is also a relevant player, "a consulting firm that provides strategic insight and advice to commercial and government clients," headed by Zbig's son, Ian Brzezinski. Ian is a Senior Fellow at the Atlantic Council and also sits on its Strategic Advisors Group, having previously served as a principal at Booz Allen Hamilton, a major global consulting firm. Prior to that, Ian Brzezinski was Deputy Assistant Secretary of Defense for Europe and NATO Policy in the Bush administration, from 2001 to 2005, and had previously served for many years on Capitol Hill as a senior staff member in the Senate. Zbigniew Brzezinski's other son, Mark Brzezinski, is currently the U.S. Ambassador to Sweden, having previously been a corporate and securities associate at Hogan & Hartson LLP, after which he served in Bill Clinton's National Security Council from 1999 to 2001. Mark Brzezinski was also an advisor to Barack Obama during his first presidential campaign starting in 2007. Among other notable advisors to Obama during his presidential campaign were Susan Rice, a former Clinton administration State Department official (and protégé to Madeleine Albright), as well as Clinton's former National Security Advisor Anthony Lake. [33]

No less significant was the fact that Zbigniew Brzezinski himself was tapped as a foreign policy advisor to Obama during the presidential campaign. In August of 2007, Brzezinski publically endorsed Obama for president, stating that Obama "recognizes that the challenge is a new face, a new sense of direction, a new definition of America's role in the world." He added: "Obama is clearly more effective and has the upper hand. He has a sense of what is historically relevant and what is needed from the United States in relationship to the world."[34] Brzezinski was quickly tapped as a top foreign policy advisor to Obama, who delivered a speech on Iraq in which he referred to Brzezinski as "one of our most outstanding thinkers."[35] According to an Obama campaign spokesperson, Brzezinski was primarily brought on to advise Obama on matters related to Iraq. [36]

Thus, it would appear that Brzezinski may not have been exaggerating too much when he told the Congressional publication, *The Hill*, in January of 2013 that, "I really wasn't at all conscious of the fact that the defeat of the Carter administration somehow or another affected significantly my own standing... I just kept doing my thing minus the Office of the National Security Adviser in the White House." While Brzezinski had advised subsequent presidents Reagan and Bush Sr., and had close ties with key officials in the Clinton administration (notably his former student and NSC aide Madeleine Albright), he was "shut out of the George W. Bush White House" when it was dominated by the neoconservatives, whom he was heavily critical of, most especially in response to the Iraq War. [37]

In the first four years of the Obama administration, Brzezinski was much sought out for advice from Democrats and Republicans alike. On this, he stated: "It's more a case of being asked than pounding on the doors... But if I have something to say, I know enough people that I can get in touch with to put [my thoughts] into circulation." When Afghan

President Hamid Karzai visited Washington, D.C. in early 2013, Brzezinski was invited to a special dinner hosted by the Afghan puppet leader, of which he noted: "I have a standard joke that I am on the No. 2 or No. 3 must-visit list in this city... That is to say, if a foreign minister or an ambassador or some other senior dignitary doesn't get to see the President, the Secretary of State, the Secretary of Defense, the National Security Adviser, then I'm somewhere on that other list as a fallback."[38]

Today, Zbigniew Brzezinski is no small player on the global scene. Not only is he an occasional and unofficial adviser to politicians, but he remains in some of the main centers of strategic planning and power in the United States. Brzezinski's background is fairly well established, not least of all due to his role as National Security Adviser and his part in the creation of the Trilateral Commission with David Rockefeller in 1973. Brzezinski was also (and remains) a member of the Council on Foreign Relations, and was a director of the CFR from 1972 to 1977. Today, he is a member of the CFR with his son Mark Brzezinski and his daughter Mika Brzezinski, a media personality on CNBC. Brzezinski is a Counselor and Trustee of the Center for Strategic and International Studies (CSIS), and he is also co-Chair (with Carla A. Hills) of the Advisory Board of CSIS, composed of international and US business leaders and current and former government officials, including: Paul Desmarais Jr. (Power Corporation of Canada), Kenneth Duberstein (Duberstein Group), Dianne Feinstein (U.S. Senator), Timothy Keating (Boeing), Senator John McCain, Senator John D. Rockefeller IV, and top officials from Chevron, Procter & Gamble, Raytheon, Lockheed Martin, Exxon Mobil, Toyota, and United Technologies.[39]

And now we make our way to the Obama administration, the promised era of "hope" and "change;" or something like that. Under Obama, the two National Security Advisors thus far have been General James L. Jones and Tom Donilon. General Jones, who was Obama's NSA from 2009 to 2010, previously and is now once again a trustee with the Center for Strategic and International Studies (CSIS). Just prior to becoming National Security Advisor, Jones was president and CEO of the U.S. Chamber of Commerce's Institute for 21st Century Energy, after a career rising to 32nd commandant of the Marine Corps and commander of U.S. European Command. He was also on the boards of directors of Chevron and Boeing, resigning one month prior to taking up his post in the Obama administration.

Shortly after Jones first became National Security Advisor, he was speaking at a conference in February of 2009 at which he stated (with tongue-in-cheek), "As the most recent National Security Advisor of the United States, I take my daily orders from Dr. Kissinger, filtered down through General Brent Scowcroft and Sandy Berger... We have a chain of command in the National Security Council that exists today."[40] Although said in jest, there is a certain truth to this notion. Yet, Jones only served in the Obama administration from January 2009 to October of 2010, after which he returned to more familiar pastures.

Apart from returning as a trustee to CSIS, Jones is currently the chairman of the Brent Scowcroft Center on International Security and is on the board and executive committee of the Atlantic Council (he was previously chairman of the board of directors from 2007 to 2009). Jones is also on the board of the East-West Institute, and in 2011 served on the board of directors of the military contractor, General Dynamics. General Jones is also the president of his own international consulting firm, Jones Group International. The Group's website boasts "a unique and unrivaled experience with numerous foreign governments, advanced international relationships, and an understanding of the national security process to develop strategic plans to help clients succeed in challenging environments." A testimonial of Jones' skill was provided by Thomas Donohue, the president and CEO of the U.S. Chamber of Commerce: "Few leaders possess the wisdom, depth of experience, and knowledge of global and domestic economic and military affairs as General Jones."[41]

Obama's current NSA, Thomas E. Donilon, was previously deputy to General James Jones, and worked as former Assistant Secretary of State and chief of staff to Secretary of State Warren Christopher in Clinton's administration. From 1999 to 2005, he was a lobbyist exclusively for the housing mortgage company Fannie Mae (which helped create and pop the housing bubble and destroy the economy). Donilon's brother, Michael C. Donilon, is a counselor to Vice President Joseph Biden. Donilon's wife, Cathy Russell, is chief of staff to Biden's wife, Jill Biden. [42] Prior to joining the Obama administration, Thomas Donilon also served as a legal advisor to banks like Goldman Sachs and Citigroup. [43]

CSIS: The 'Brain' of the Obama Administration

While serving as national security advisor, Thomas Donilon spoke at the Center for Strategic and International Studies (CSIS) in November of 2012. He began his speech by stating that for roughly half a century, CSIS has been "the intellectual capital that has informed so many of our national security policies, including during the Obama administration... We've shared ideas and we've shared staff."[44]

Indeed, CSIS has been an exceptionally influential presence within the Obama administration. CSIS launched a Commission on 'Smart Power' in 2006, co-chaired by Joseph S. Nye, Jr. and Richard Armitage, with the final report delivered in 2008, designed to influence the next president of the United States on implementing "a smart power strategy." Joseph Nye is known for - among other things - developing the concept of what he calls "soft power" to describe gaining support through "attraction" rather than force. In the lead-up to the 2008 presidential elections, Nye stated that if Obama became president, it "would do more for America's soft power around the world than anything else we could do."[45]

Joseph Nye is the former Dean of the Kennedy School, former senior official in the Defense and State Departments, former Chair of the National Intelligence Council, and a highly influential political scientist who was rated in a 2008 poll of international relations scholars as "the most influential scholar in the field on American foreign policy," and was also named as one of the top 100 global thinkers in a 2011*Foreign Policy* report. Nye is also Chairman of the North American Group of the Trilateral Commission, is on the board of directors of the Council on Foreign Relations, a member of the board of trustees of the Center for Strategic and International Studies (CSIS), and a former director of the Institute for East-West Security Studies, the International Institute of Strategic Studies, and a former member of the advisory committee of the Institute of International Economics.

Richard Armitage, the other co-chair of the CSIS Commission on Smart Power, is the President of Armitage International, a global consulting firm, and was Deputy Secretary of State from 2001-2005 in the George W. Bush administration, Assistant Secretary of Defense for International Security Affairs in the Reagan administration, and is on the boards of ConocoPhillips, a major oil company, as well as ManTech International and Transcu Group, and of course, a trustee at CSIS.

In the Commission's final report, *A Smarter, More Secure America*, the term 'smart power' was defined as "complementing U.S. military and economic might with greater investments in soft power," recommending that the United States "reinvigorate the alliances, partnerships, and institutions that serve our interests," as well as increasing the role of "development in U.S. foreign policy" which would allow the United States to "align its own interests with the aspirations of people around the world." Another major area of concern was that of "[b]ringing foreign populations to our side," which depended upon "building long-term, people-to-people relationships, particularly among youth." Further, the report noted that "the benefits of free trade must be expanded" and that it was America's responsibility to "establish global consensus and develop innovative solutions" for issues such as energy security and climate change. [46]

The forward to the report was authored by CSIS president and CEO, John Hamre, who wrote: "We have all seen the poll numbers and know that much of the world today is not happy with American leadership," with even "traditional allies" beginning to question "American values and interests, wondering whether they are compatible with their own." Hamre spoke for the American imperial establishment: "We do not have to be loved, but we will never be able to accomplish our goals and keep Americans safe without mutual respect." What was needed, then, was to utilize their "moment of opportunity" in order "to strike off on a big idea that balances a wiser internationalism with the desire for protection at home." In world affairs, the center of gravity, wrote Hamre, "is shifting to Asia." Thus, "[a]s the only global superpower, we must manage multiple crises simultaneously while regional competitors can focus their attention and efforts." What is required is to strengthen "capable states, alliances, partnerships, and institutions." Military might, noted Hamre, while "typically the bedrock of a nation's power," remains "an inadequate basis for sustaining American power over time."[47]

In their summary of the report, Nye and Armitage wrote that the ultimate "goal of U.S. foreign policy should be to prolong and preserve American preeminence as an agent for good." The goal, of course, was to 'prolong and preserve American preeminence,' whereas the notion of being 'an agent for good' was little more than a rhetorical add-on, since for policy-oriented intellectuals like those at CSIS, American preeminence is inherently a 'good' thing, and therefore preserving American hegemony is - it is presumed - by definition, being 'an agent

146

for good.' Nye and Armitage suggested that the U.S. "should have higher ambitions than being popular," though acknowledging, "foreign opinion matters to U.S. decision-making," so long as it aligns with U.S. decisions, presumably. A "good reputation," they suggested, "brings acceptance for unpopular ventures." This was not to mark a turn away from using military force, as was explicitly acknowledged: "We will always have our enemies, and we cannot abandon our coercive tools." Using "soft power," however, was simply to *add* to America's arsenal of military and economic imperialism: "bolstering soft power makes America stronger."[48]

Power, they wrote, "is the ability to influence the behavior of others to get a desired outcome," noting the necessity of "hard power" - military and economic strength - but, while "[t]here is no other global power... American hard power does not always translate into influence." While technological advances "have made weapons more precise, they have also become more destructive, thereby increasing the political and social costs of using military force." Modern communications, they noted, "diminished the fog of war," which is to say that they have facilitated more effective communication and management in war-time, "but also heightened the atomized political consciousness," which is to say that it has allowed populations all over the world to gain access to information and communication outside the selectivity of traditional institutions of power.[49]

These trends "have made power less tangible and coercion less effective." The report noted: "Machiavelli said it was safer to be feared than to be loved. Today, in the global information age, it is better to be both." Thus, "soft power... is the ability to attract people to our side without coercion," making "legitimacy" the central concept of soft power. As such, if nations and people believe "American objectives to be legitimate, we are more likely to persuade them to follow our lead without using threats and bribes." Noting that America's "enemies" in the world are largely non-state actors and groups who "control no territory, hold few assets, and sprout new leaders for each one that is killed," victory becomes problematic: "Militaries are well suited to defeating states, but they are often poor instruments to fight ideas." Thus, victory in the modern world "depends on attracting foreign populations to our side," of which 'soft power' is a necessity. [50]

Despite various "military adventures in the Western hemisphere and in the Philippines" in the late nineteenth and early twentieth centuries, "the U.S. military has not been put in the service of building a colonial empire in the manner of European militaries," the report read, acknowledging quite plainly that while not a formal colonial empire, the United States was an imperial power nonetheless. Since World War II, "America has sought to promote rules and order in a world in which life continues to be nasty, brutish, and short for the majority of inhabitants." While "the appeal of Hollywood and American products can play a role in inspiring the dreams and desires of others," soft power is not merely cultural, but also promotes "political values" and "our somewhat reluctant participation and leadership in institutions that help shape the global agenda." However, a more "interconnected and tolerant world" is not something everyone is looking forward to, noted the authors: "ideas can be threatening to those who consider their way of life to be under siege by the West," which is to say, the rest of the world. Smart power, then, "is neither hard nor soft - it is the skillful combination of both," and "means developing an integrated strategy, resource base, and tool kit to achieve American objectives, drawing on both hard and soft power." [51]

Other members of the CSIS Commission on Smart Power included: Nancy Kassebaum Baker, former US Senator and member of the advisory board of the Partnership for a Secure America; General Charles G. Boyd, former president and CEO of the Business Executives for National Security, former director of the Council on Foreign Relations (CFR); as well as Maurice Greenberg, Thomas Pickering, David Rubenstein and Obama's newest Secretary of Defense, Chuck Hagel. It's quite apparent that members of the CSIS Commission and CSIS itself would be able to wield significant influence upon the Obama administration. Joseph Nye has even advised Hillary Clinton while she served as Secretary of State. [52] Perhaps then, we should not be surprised that at her Senate confirmation hearing in January of 2009, Clinton declared the era of "rigid ideology" in diplomacy to be at an end, and the foreign policy of "smart power" to be exercised, that she would make decisions based "on facts and evidence, not emotions or prejudice."[53]

Before the Senate Foreign Relations Committee, Clinton declared: "We must use what has been called smart power, the full range of tools at our disposal - diplomatic, economic, military, political, legal, and cultural - picking the right tool, or combination of tools, for each situation." She quoted the ancient Roman poet Terence, "in every endeavor, the seemly course for wise men is to try persuasion first," then added: "The same truth binds wise women as well."[54]

148

While Joseph Nye had coined the term "soft power" in the 1990s, Suzanne Nossel coined the term "smart power." Nossel was the chief operating officer of Human Rights Watch, former executive at media conglomerate Bertelsmann, and was a former deputy to UN Ambassador Richard Holbrooke in the Clinton administration. She coined the term "smart power" in a 2004 issue of *Foreign Affairs*, the journal of the Council on Foreign Relations, after which time Joseph Nye began using it, leading to the CSIS Commission on Smart Power. At the Senate hearing, Senator Jim Webb stated, "the phrase of the week is 'smart power'." Nossel commented on Clinton's Senate hearing: "Hillary was impressive... She didn't gloss over the difficulties, but at the same time she was fundamentally optimistic. She's saying that, by using all the tools of power in concert, the trajectory of American decline can be reversed. She'll make smart power cool."[55]

Following the first six months of the Obama administration, Hillary Clinton was to deliver a major foreign policy speech to the Council on Foreign Relations, where she would articulate "her own policy agenda," focusing on the strengthening of "smart power." One official involved in the speech planning process noted that it would include discussion on "U.S. relations with [and] management of the great powers in a way that gets more comprehensive." The speech was long in the making, and was being overseen by the director of the State Department's Policy Planning Council, Anne-Marie Slaughter. [56]

Slaughter was director of Policy Planning in the State Department from 2009 to 2011, where she was chief architect of the Quadrennial Diplomacy and Development Review, designed to better integrate development into U.S. foreign policy, with the first report having been released in 2010. She is also a professor of politics and international affairs at Princeton, was co-Chair of the Princeton Project on National Security, former Dean of the Woodrow Wilson School of Public and International Affairs, served on the boards of the Council on Foreign Relations (2003-2009), the New America Foundation, the National Endowment for Democracy, New American Security, the Truman Project, and formerly with CSIS, also having been on the boards of McDonald's and Citigroup. Slaughter is currently a member of the Aspen Strategy Group, the CFR, a member of the board of directors of the Atlantic Council, and has been named on *Foreign Policy*'s Top 100 Global Thinkers for the years 2009-2012.

In preparation for her speech at the Council on Foreign Relations, according to the *Washington Post*blog, Plum Line, Clinton "consulted" with a "surprisingly diverse" group of people, including: Henry Kissinger, George Schultz, Zbigniew Brzezinski, Paul Farmer, Joseph Nye, Francis Fukuyama, Brent Scowcroft, Strobe Talbott (president of the Brookings Institution), John Podesta, and Richard Lugar, as well as Defense Secretary Robert Gates, then-National Security Advisor General James Jones, and President Obama himself.[57]

When Clinton began speaking at the Council on Foreign Relations in Washington, D.C., she stated: "I am delighted to be here in these new headquarters. I have been often to, I guess, the mother ship in New York City, but it's good to have an outpost of the Council right here down the street from the State Department. We get a lot of advice from the Council, and so this will mean I won't have as far to go to be told what we should be doing and how we should think about the future." Many in the world do not trust America to lead, explained Clinton, "they view America as an unaccountable power, too quick to impose its will at the expense of their interests and our principles," but, Clinton was sure to note: "they are wrong." The question, of course, was "not whether our nation can or should lead, but how it will lead in the 21st century," in which "[r]igid ideologies and old formulas don't apply." Clinton claimed that "[l]iberty, democracy, justice and opportunity underlie our priorities," even though others "accuse us of using these ideals to justify actions that contradict their very meaning," suggesting that "we are too often condescending and imperialistic, seeking only to expand our power at the expense of others."[58]

These perceptions, explained Clinton, "have fed anti-Americanism, but they do not reflect who we are." America's strategy "must reflect the world as it is, not as it used to be," and therefore, "[i]t does not make sense to adapt a 19th century concert of powers, or a 20th century balance of power strategy." Clinton explained that the strategy would seek to tilt "the balance away from a multi-polar world and toward a multi-partner world," in which "our partnerships can become power coalitions to constrain and deter [the] negative actions" of those who do not share "our values and interests" and "actively seek to undermine our efforts." In order to construct "the architecture of global cooperation," Clinton recommended "smart power" as "the intelligent use of all means at our disposal, including our ability to convene and connect... our economic and military strength," as well as "the application of old-fashioned common sense in policymaking... a blend of principle and pragmatism." Noting that, "our global and regional institutions were built for a world that has been transformed," Clinton stated that "they too must be transformed and reformed," referencing the UN, World Bank, IMF, G20, OAS, ASEAN, and APEC, among others. This "global architecture of cooperation," said Clinton, "is the architecture of progress for America and all nations."[59]

Just in case you were thinking that the relationship between CSIS and the Obama administration was not strong enough, apparently both of them thought so too. CSIS wields notable influence within the Pentagon's Defense Policy Board, which is chaired by the president and CEO of CSIS, John Hamre. A former Deputy Defense Secretary in the Clinton administration, Hamre is a member of the Aspen Strategy Group, sits on the board of defense contractors such as ITT, SAIC, and the Oshkosh Corporation, as well as MITRE, a "not-for-profit" corporation which "manages federally funded research and development centers." The Defense Policy Board provides the Secretary of Defense, as well as the Deputy Secretary and Undersecretary of Defense "with independent, informed advice and opinion on matters of defense policy;" from outside 'experts' of course. [60]

Also on the board is Sam Nunn, the chairman of CSIS, co-chair and CEO of the Nuclear Threat Initiative (NTI), former U.S. Senator from 1972-1996, member of the Council on Foreign Relations, and currently on the boards of General Electric, the Coca-Cola Company, Hess Corporation, and was recently on the boards of Dell and Chevron. Other CSIS trustees and advisors who sit on the Defense Policy Board are Harold Brown, Henry Kissinger, James Schlesinger, Brent Scowcroft, General Jack Keane, and Chuck Hagel. [61]

Harold Brown was the Secretary of Defense in the Carter administration, honorary director of the Atlantic Council, member of the boards of Evergreen Oil and Philip Morris International, former partner at Warburg Pincus, director of the Altria Group, Trustee of RAND Corporation, and member of the Trilateral Commission and the Council on Foreign Relations. James Schlesinger was the former Defense Secretary in the Nixon and Ford administrations, Secretary of Energy in the Carter administration, was briefly director of the CIA, a senior advisor to Lehman Brothers, Kuhn, Loeb Inc., and was on George W. Bush's Homeland Security Advisory Council. He is currently chairman of the MITRE Corporation, a director of the Sandia National Corporation, a trustee of the Atlantic Council and is a board member of the Henry M. Jackson Foundation.

Brent Scowcroft, apart from being Kissinger's deputy in the Nixon administration, and the National Security Advisor in the Ford and Bush

Sr. administrations (as well as co-founder of Kissinger), is currently a member of the Council on Foreign Relations, the Trilateral Commission, the Atlantic Council, and founded his own international advisory firm, the Scowcroft Group. General Jack Keane, a senior advisor to CSIS, is the former Vice Chief of Staff of the US Army, current Chairman of the board for the Institute for the Study of War; Frank Miller, former Defense Department official in the Reagan, Bush Sr., and Clinton administrations, served on the National Security Council in the George W. Bush administration, joined the Cohen Group in 2005, currently a Principal at the Scowcroft Group, and serves on the U.S.-European Command Advisory Group, is a member of the Council on Foreign Relations, a Director of the Atlantic Council, and he serves on the board of EADS-North America (one of the world's leading defense contract corporations).

Kissinger's record has been well-established up until present day, though he has been a member of the Defense Policy Board since 2001, thus serving in an advisory capacity to the Pentagon for both the Bush and Obama administrations, continues to serve on the steering committee of the Bilderberg meetings, is a member of the Trilateral Commission and he is currently an advisor to the board of directors of American Express, on the advisory board of the RAND Center for Global Risk and Security, honorary chairman of the China-United States Exchange Foundation, the board of the International Rescue Committee, and is on the International Council of JPMorgan Chase.

Another member of the Policy Board who was a trustee of CSIS was Chuck Hagel, who is now Obama's Secretary of Defense. Prior to his new appointment, Hagel was a US Senator from 1997 to 2009, after which he was Chairman of the Atlantic Council, on the boards of Chevron, Zurich's Holding Company of America, Corsair Capital, Deutsche Bank America, MIC Industries, was an advisor to Gallup, member of the board of PBS, member of the Council on Foreign Relations, and was a member of the CSIS Commission on Smart Power. Hagel also served on Obama's Foreign Intelligence Advisory Board, an outside group of 'experts' providing strategic advice to the president on intelligence matters.

Other members of the Defense Policy Board (who are not affiliated with CSIS) are: J.D. Crouch, Deputy National Security Advisor in the George W. Bush administration, and is on the board of advisors of the Center for Security Policy; Richard Danzig, Secretary of the Navy in the Clinton administration, a campaign advisor to Obama, and is the current Chairman of the Center for a New American Security; Rudy de Leon, former Defense Department official in the Clinton administration, a Senior Vice President at the Center for American Progress, and is a former vice president at Boeing Corporation; John Nagl, president of the Center for a New American Security, and is a member of the Council on Foreign Relations; William Perry, former Secretary of Defense in the Clinton administration, who now sits on a number of corporate boards, a senior fellow at the Hoover Institution, on the board of the Nuclear Threat Initiative (NTI), and has served on the Carnegie Endowment; Sarah Sewall, former Deputy Assistant Secretary of Defense for Peacekeeping and Humanitarian Assistance in the Clinton administration, on the board of Oxfam America, and was a foreign policy advisor to Obama's election campaign; and Larry Welch, former Chief of Staff of the US Air Force in the Reagan administration. More recently added to the Defense Policy Board was none other than Madeleine Albright.

Imperialism without Imperialists?

   The 'discourse' of foreign affairs and international relations failing to adequately deal with the subject of empire is based upon a deeply flawed perception: that one cannot have an empire without imperialists, and the United States does not have imperialists, it has *strategists, experts,* and *policy-oriented intellectuals*. Does the United States, then, have an empire without *imperialists*? In the whole history of imperialism, that would be a unique situation.
   Empires do not happen by chance. Nations do not simply trip and stumble and fall into a state of imperialism. Empires are planned and directed, maintained and expanded. This report aimed to provide some introductory insight into the institutions and individuals who direct the American imperial system. The information - while dense - is far from comprehensive or complete; it is a sample of the complex network of imperialism that exists in present-day United States. Regardless of which president or political party is in office, this highly integrated network remains in power.
   This report, produced exclusively for the Hampton Institute, is to serve as a reference point for future discussion and analysis of 'geopolitics' and foreign policy issues. As an introduction to the institutions and individuals of empire, it can provide a framework for people to interpret foreign policy differently, to question those quoted

and interviewed in the media as 'experts,' to integrate their understanding of think tanks into contemporary politics and society, and to bring to the surface the names, organizations and ideas of society's ruling class.

It is time for more of what the Trilateral Commission dismissively referred to as "value-oriented intellectuals" - those who question and oppose authority - instead of more policy-oriented *imperialists*. The Geopolitics Division of the Hampton Institute aims to do just that: to provide an intellectual understanding and basis for opposing empire in the modern world.

Empires don't just happen; they are constructed. They can also be deconstructed and dismantled, but that doesn't just *happen* either. Opposing empire is not a passive act: it requires dedication and information, action and reaction. As relatively privileged individuals in western state-capitalist societies, we have both the *opportunity* and the *responsibility* to understand and oppose what our governments do abroad, how they treat the people of the world, how they engage with the world. It is *our* responsibility to do something, precisely because we have the *opportunity* to do so, unlike the majority of the world's population who live in abject poverty, under ruthless dictators that we arm and maintain, in countries we bomb and regions we dominate. We exist in the epicenter of empire, and thus: *we are the only ones capable of ending empire*.

Notes

[1] Julian Pecquet, "Brzezinski: Professor in the halls of power," The Hill's Global Affairs, 22 January 2013:
http://thehill.com/blogs/global-affairs/americas/278401-professor-in-the-halls-of-power

[2] David Rothkopf, *Running the World: The Inside Story of the National Security Council and the Architects of American Power* (Public Affairs, New York: 2005), page 19.

[3] David Rothkopf, *Running the World: The Inside Story of the National Security Council and the Architects of American Power* (Public Affairs, New York: 2005), pages 19-20.

[4] James D. Wolfensohn, Council on Foreign Relations Special Symposium in honor of David Rockefeller's 90th Birthday, The Council on Foreign Relations, 23 May 2005:http://www.cfr.org/world/council-foreign-relations-special-symposium-honor-david-rockefellers-90th-birthday/p8133

[5] Michael Stutchbury, The man who inherited the Rothschild legend, The Australian, 30 October 2010:http://www.theaustralian.com.au/news/features/the-man-who-inherited-the-rothschild-legend/story-e6frg6z6-1225945329773

[6] David Rockefeller, Memoirs (Random House, New York: 2002), pages 404 - 405.

[7] Henry A. Kissinger, "Domestic Structure and Foreign Policy," *Daedalus* (Vol. 95, No. 2, Conditions of World Order, Spring 1966), page 514.

[8] Sallie M. Hicks, Theodore A. Couloumbis and Eloise M. Forgette, "Influencing the Prince: A Role for Academicians?" *Polity* (Vol. 15, No. 2, Winter 1982), pages 288-289.

[9] Sallie M. Hicks, Theodore A. Couloumbis and Eloise M. Forgette, "Influencing the Prince: A Role for Academicians?" *Polity* (Vol. 15, No. 2, Winter 1982), pages 289-291.

[10] Michel J. Crozier, Samuel P. Huntington and Joji Watanuki, The Crisis of Democracy: Report on the Governability of Democracies to the Trilateral Commission (New York University Press, 1975), pages 6-7.

[11] Jeff Gerth and Sarah Bartlett, "Kissinger and Friends and Revolving Doors," *The New York Times*, 30 April 1989: http://www.nytimes.com/1989/04/30/us/kissinger-and-friends-and-revolving-doors.html?pagewanted=all&src=pm

[12] Edward Cuddy, "America's Cuban Obsession: A Case Study in Diplomacy and Psycho-History,"*The Americas* (Vol. 43, No. 2, October 1986), page 192.

[13] Fred Iklé and Albert Wohlstetter, *Discriminate Deterrence* (Report of the Commission on Integrated Long-Term Strategy), January 1988, page 13.

[14] Fred Iklé and Albert Wohlstetter, *Discriminate Deterrence* (Report of the Commission on Integrated Long-Term Strategy), January 1988, page 14.

[15] *National Security Strategy of the United States* (The White House, March 1990), page 13.

[16] The Daily Beast, "This Will Not Stand," Newsweek, 28 February 1991:
http://www.thedailybeast.com/newsweek/1991/02/28/this-will-not-stand.html

[17] George Black, "Forget Ideals; Just Give Us a Punching Bag: This time, fronting for oil princes, we couldn't invoke the old defense of democracy; fighting 'evil' sufficed," The Los Angeles Times, 3 March 1991:
http://articles.latimes.com/1991-03-03/opinion/op-338_1_cold-war

[18] Maureen Dowd, "WAR IN THE GULF: White House Memo; Bush Moves to Control War's Endgame," The New York Times, 23 February 1991:
http://www.nytimes.com/1991/02/23/world/war-in-the-gulf-white-house-memo-bush-moves-to-control-war-s-endgame.html?src=pm

[19] Zbigniew Brzezinski, "The Cold War and its Aftermath," *Foreign Affairs* (Vol. 71, No. 4, Fall 1992), page 37.

[20] Tyler, Patrick E. *U.S. Strategy Plan Calls for Insuring No Rivals Develop: A One Superpower World.* The New York Times: March 8, 1992.
http://work.colum.edu/~amiller/wolfowitz1992.htm

[21] David Rothkopf, *Running the World: The Inside Story of the National Security Council and the Architects of American Power* (Public Affairs, New York: 2005), pages 17-18, 162, 172-175.

[22] Anthony Lake, "From Containment to Enlargement," Remarks of Anthony Lake at Johns Hopkins University School of Advanced International Studies, Washington, D.C., 21 September 1993:http://www.fas.org/news/usa/1993/usa-930921.htm

[23] Zbigniew Brzezinski, *The Grand Chessboard: American Primacy and its Geostrategic Imperatives*(Basic Books, 1997), pages 30-31.

[24] Zbigniew Brzezinski, *The Grand Chessboard: American Primacy and its Geostrategic Imperatives*(Basic Books, 1997), page 40.

[25] *Rebuilding America's Defenses* (Project for the New American Century: September 2000), pages 6-8: http://www.newamericancentury.org/publicationsreports.htm

[26] *Rebuilding America's Defenses* (Project for the New American Century: September 2000), page 25:http://www.newamericancentury.org/publicationsreports.htm

[27] Inderjeet Parmar, "Foreign Policy Fusion: Liberal interventionists, conservative nationalists and neoconservatives - the new alliance dominating the US foreign policy establishment," *International Politics* (Vol. 46, No. 2/3, 2009), pages 178-179.

[28] U.S. NSS, "The National Security Strategy of the United States of America," The White House, September 2002, page 15.

[29] U.S. NSS, "The National Security Strategy of the United States of America," The White House, September 2002, page 6.

[30] Inderjeet Parmar, "Foreign Policy Fusion: Liberal Interventionists, Conservative Nationalists and Neoconservatives - the New alliance Dominating the US Foreign Policy Establishment," *International Politics* (Vol. 46, No. 2/3, 2009), pages 181-183.

[31] G. John Ikenberry and Anne-Marie Slaughter, *Forging a World of Liberty Under Law: U.S. National Security in the 21st Century - Final Report of the Princeton Project on National Security* (The Princeton project on National Security, The Woodrow Wilson School of Public and

International Affairs, Princeton University, 27 September 2006), pages 79-90.

[32] G. John Ikenberry and Anne-Marie Slaughter, *Forging a World of Liberty Under Law: U.S. National Security in the 21st Century - Final Report of the Princeton Project on National Security* (The Princeton project on National Security, The Woodrow Wilson School of Public and International Affairs, Princeton University, 27 September 2006), pages 79-90.

[33] The Daily Beast, "The Talent Primary," Newsweek, 15 September 2007:
http://www.thedailybeast.com/newsweek/2007/09/15/the-talent-primary.html

[34] "Brzezinski Backs Obama," The Washington Post, 25 August 2007:
http://www.washingtonpost.com/wp-dyn/content/article/2007/08/24/AR2007082402127.html

[35] Russell Berman, "Despite Criticism, Obama Stands By Adviser Brzezinski," The New York Sun, 13 September 2007:
http://www.nysun.com/national/despite-criticism-obama-stands-by-adviser/62534/

[36] Eli Lake, "Obama Adviser Leads Delegation to Damascus," The New York Sun, 12 February 2008:
http://www.nysun.com/foreign/obama-adviser-leads-delegation-to-damascus/71123/

[37] Julian Pecquet, "Brzezinski: Professor in the halls of power," The Hill's Global Affairs, 22 January 2013:
http://thehill.com/blogs/global-affairs/americas/278401-professor-in-the-halls-of-power

[38] Julian Pecquet, "Brzezinski: Professor in the halls of power," The Hill's Global Affairs, 22 January 2013:
http://thehill.com/blogs/global-affairs/americas/278401-professor-in-the-halls-of-power

[39] Annual Report 2011, Center for Strategic and International Studies, Strategic Insights and Bipartisan Policy Solutions, page 8.

[40] General James L. Jones, "Remarks by National Security Adviser Jones at 45th Munich Conference on Security Policy," The Council on Foreign Relations, 8 February 2009: http://www.cfr.org/defensehomeland-security/remarks-national-security-adviser-jones-45th-munich-conference-security-policy/p18515

[41] Company Profile, Jones Group International website, accessed 9 May 2013: http://www.jonesgroupinternational.com/company_profile.php

[42] WhoRunsGov, "Thomas Donilon," The Washington Post: http://www.washingtonpost.com/politics/thomas-donilon/gIQAEZrv6O_topic.html

[43] Matthew Mosk, "Tom Donilon's Revolving Door," ABC News - The Blotter, 10 October 2010:http://abcnews.go.com/Blotter/national-security-advisor-tom-donilon/story?id=11836229#.UYsp6IJU1Ox

[44] Tom Donlinon, "Remarks by National Security Advisor Tom Donilon -- As Prepared for Delivery," White House Office of the Press Secretary, 15 November 2012: http://www.whitehouse.gov/the-press-office/2012/11/15/remarks-national-security-advisor-tom-donilon-prepared-delivery

[45] James Traub, "Is (His) Biography (Our) Destiny?," The New York Times, 4 November 2007:http://www.nytimes.com/2007/11/04/magazine/04obama-t.html?pagewanted=all

[46] Richard Armitage and Joseph Nye, Jr., "CSIS Commission on Smart Power: A Smarter, More Secure America," Center for Strategic and International Studies, 2007: page 1.

[47] Richard Armitage and Joseph Nye, Jr., "CSIS Commission on Smart Power: A Smarter, More Secure America," Center for Strategic and International Studies, 2007: pages 3-4.

[48] Richard Armitage and Joseph Nye, Jr., "CSIS Commission on Smart Power: A Smarter, More Secure America," Center for Strategic and International Studies, 2007: pages 5-6.

[49] Richard Armitage and Joseph Nye, Jr., "CSIS Commission on Smart Power: A Smarter, More Secure America," Center for Strategic and International Studies, 2007: page 6.

[50] Richard Armitage and Joseph Nye, Jr., "CSIS Commission on Smart Power: A Smarter, More Secure America," Center for Strategic and International Studies, 2007: page 6.

[51] Richard Armitage and Joseph Nye, Jr., "CSIS Commission on Smart Power: A Smarter, More Secure America," Center for Strategic and International Studies, 2007: page 7.

[52] Thanassis Cambanis, "Meet the new power players," The Boston Globe, 4 September 2011:
http://www.boston.com/bostonglobe/ideas/articles/2011/09/04/meet_the_new_world_players/?page=full

[53] David Usborne, "Clinton announces dawn of 'smart power'," The Independent, 14 January 2009:
http://www.independent.co.uk/news/world/americas/clinton-announces-dawn-of-smart-power-1334256.html

[54] Hendrik Hetzberg, "Tool Kit: Smart Power," The New Yorker, 26 January 2009:
http://www.newyorker.com/talk/2009/01/26/090126ta_talk_hertzberg

[55] Hendrik Hetzberg, "Tool Kit: Smart Power," The New Yorker, 26 January 2009:
http://www.newyorker.com/talk/2009/01/26/090126ta_talk_hertzberg

[56] Ben Smith, "Hillary Clinton plans to reassert herself with high-profile speech," Politico, 14 July 2009:
http://www.politico.com/news/stories/0709/24893.html

[57] Originally posted at Slum Line, "Hillary Consulted Republicans, Neocons, And Liberals For Big Foreign Policy Speech," Future Majority, 14 July 2009:
http://www.futuremajority.com/node/8143

[58] Hillary Clinton, "Foreign Policy Address at the Council on Foreign Relations," U.S. Department of State, 15 July 2009:
http://www.state.gov/secretary/rm/2009a/july/126071.htm

[59] Hillary Clinton, "Foreign Policy Address at the Council on Foreign Relations," U.S. Department of State, 15 July 2009:
http://www.state.gov/secretary/rm/2009a/july/126071.htm

[60] Marcus Weisgerber, "U.S. Defense Policy Board Gets New Members," Defense News, 4 October 2011:
http://www.defensenews.com/article/20111004/DEFSECT04/11004030
4/U-S-Defense-Policy-Board-Gets-New-Members

[61] Marcus Weisgerber, "U.S. Defense Policy Board Gets New Members," Defense News, 4 October 2011:
http://www.defensenews.com/article/20111004/DEFSECT04/11004030
4/U-S-Defense-Policy-Board-Gets-New-Members

Dropping the Bomb

A Historiographical Review of the Most Destructive Decision in Human History

Derek A. Ide

The historiography of the atomic bomb can be roughly categorized into three camps: traditionalists, revisionists, and middle-ground "consensus" historians. [1] Traditionalists, also referred to as orthodox[2] historians and post-revisionists, studying the atomic bomb generally accept the view posited by the Truman administration and articulated most clearly in Henry Stimson's 1947 *Harper's Magazine* article.[3] In short, this argument assumes that the use of the atomic bombs against Japan was justifiable on military grounds in order to prevent a costly invasion of the Japanese home islands. Often attached to such analysis is the notion that insofar as the atomic bombs ended the war prior to an invasion and saved hundreds of thousands or millions of lives, the use of the atomic bombs was also a morally sound decision. There tends to be a remarkable level of homogeneity amongst the traditionalist arguments. Whereas they may emphasize certain facts or aspects of the debate, they tend to present strikingly similar arguments, with a few exceptions.

The revisionists, in contrast, tend to be far more heterogeneous. Revisionist historians are unconvinced by the official narrative, and tend to emphasize the alternatives to the atomic bomb not pursued by the Truman administration. Furthermore, most revisionists accept, on some level, the "atomic diplomacy" thesis articulated first by Gar Alperovitz in

1965. To one degree or another revisionists argue that the Truman administration purposefully chose not to pursue alternatives to ending the war and that post-war diplomatic concerns vis-à-vis the Soviet Union were germane to, and in some historian's view dictated, the use of the atomic bombs.

The third camp, the consensus historians, are those who J. Samuel Walker refers to as having "reached a broad, though hardly unanimous, consensus on some key issues surrounding the use of the bomb."[4] These include the fact that Truman and his advisers were aware of alternatives that seemed likely to end the war, that invasion would likely not have been necessary, and that the atomic bomb did not save hundreds of thousands or millions of lives. What distinguishes them from the traditionalists is the argument that the atomic bombs were not a military necessity. On the other hand, their rejection or hesitancy to incorporate atomic diplomacy into their analysis differentiates them from the revisionists.

Given the nature of the three camps, the organizational framework I have utilized includes three sections. The first section will deal with the debate between traditionalists and revisionists. It will focus on questions of atomic diplomacy, the Potsdam Conference, unconditional surrender, Soviet entry into the war, projected casualty figures, and certain key figures in the Truman administration, the Soviet Union, and Japan. The second section will examine the points of disagreement within the revisionist camp. Although revisionists all challenge the orthodox position, they are significantly less homogenous than the latter. The third section of the essay will explore the consensus historians and their disagreements with both the traditionalists and the revisionists. Given the level of unanimity amongst the traditionalist historians, it is unnecessary to dedicate a section exploring differences between them because with rare exceptions, which will be noted when appropriate, there is remarkably little disagreement. The essay will conclude with a brief analysis of the authors, such as Robert Newman and Paul Boyer, who have extended their chronological framework significantly beyond the actual use of the atomic bombs.

The Traditionalists vs. the Revisionists

The five monographs within the traditionalist camp that will be analyzed here are Robert James Maddox's*Weapons for Victory: The*

Hiroshima Decision (2004)[5], Robert P. Newman's*Truman and the Hiroshima Cult* (1995), Richard B. Frank's *Downfall: The End of the Imperial Japanese Empire* (1999), Paul D. Walker's*Truman's Dilemma: Invasion or the Bomb* (2003), and Wilson D. Miscamble's *The Most Controversial Decision: Truman, the Atomic Bombs, and the Defeat of Japan* (2011). On the other side of the debate are four revisionist historians, including Gar Alperovitz's *The Decision to Use the Atomic Bomb and the Architecture of an American Myth* (1995)[6], Martin J. Sherwin's *A World Destroyed: Hiroshima and Its Legacies* (2003),[7] Ronald Takaki's *Hiroshima: Why America Dropped the Atomic Bomb* (1995), and Tsuyoshi Hasegawa's *Racing the Enemy: Stalin, Truman, and the Surrender of Japan* (2005). The positions of the traditionalists and the revisionists regarding atomic diplomacy, the Potsdam Conference, Japanese surrender, the unconditional surrender policy, Soviet entry into the war, projected casualty figures, and key individuals[8] involved in the decision to use the bomb and Japanese surrender are fundamentally at odds.

The question of atomic diplomacy is what creates the fundamental divide between the two camps. Although there is great variation between revisionist and traditionalist positions on unconditional surrender, the role and race and racism, and other factors, most questions tend to be subsumed within and intricately bound up with atomic diplomacy. Since the revisionists first posited this thesis, it is appropriate to adumbrate their arguments. Objecting to the official narrative that "Truman simply had no choice except to use the atomic bomb," Alperovitz argues that Truman, significantly influenced by Byrnes, used the bomb as a form of "atomic diplomacy" to pursue post-war U.S. interests in both Europe and Asia. In essence, Alperovitz argues that the U.S. government "generally understood" that "Japan was defeated and preparing to surrender before the bomb was used." [9] According to Alperovitz there was a "quite general" notion amongst U.S. officials at Potsdam that the bomb would strengthen U.S. diplomacy vis-à-vis the Soviet Union. It was during this time that "a conscious decision not to encourage Soviet participation in the war" was undertaken. Attempts "to delay the Red Army's attack to the extent feasible" were meant to "limit Soviet political influence in Asia."[10] For Alperovitz atomic diplomacy is the crucial element in explaining the use of the bomb.

Martin Sherwin supplements Alperovitz's atomic diplomacy thesis by extending the importance of such diplomatic concerns backwards into the Roosevelt administration. Sherwin posits that the policies of the Roosevelt administration suggest "that the diplomatic value of the bomb began to shape his atomic energy policies as early as 1943."[11] Although Sherwin cites Roosevelt's elusive decision making process and sudden death as inhibitors to fully understanding his policy, he posits that Roosevelt "consistently opposed international control and acted in accordance with Churchill's monopolistic, anti-Soviet views."[12] Ronald Takaki, despite emphasizing the role of race and racism in the decision, also concedes that atomic diplomacy was indeed a factor. He notes the "incredible pressure" on Manhattan project scientists to complete the bombs prior to the Potsdam conference. Similarly, he explains how Truman purposefully postponed the conference to coincide with the bomb tests. Takaki maintains that two "schools of thought" dominated the thinking of U.S. officials, including the "quid-pro-quo" strategy, articulated by people like Henry Stimson,[13] and the "monopoly" strategy a la James Byrnes. [14] In Tsuyoshi Hasegawa's view, the Potsdam Proclamation was not a warning to Japan, but an attempt to justify the use of the bomb.

Hasegawa's argument aligns with Alperovitz's as well. He maintains that a "race" began at Potsdam between the United States and the Soviet Union when the Soviets set August 15 as their projected state of entry into the war. This "gave American policymakers a definite deadline to work for." [15]Thus, the timing of the Potsdam Proclamation was "integrally connected with the schedule for deployment of the atomic bombs."[16] The Truman administration desired to end the war via the atomic bombs in order to avoid Soviet entry and maintain hegemony in the Pacific in the post-war world. Therefore, the Truman-Byrnes commitment to unconditional surrender and the Potsdam declaration was simply a prelude to the use of the atomic bombs. Byrnes position was essentially: "if we insisted on unconditional surrender, we could justify dropping of the atomic bomb."[17] Concerned about the post-war political consequences of Soviet participation in the war, U.S. planners sought to bring about Japan's surrender before the Soviets could join. At best, Soviet participation in the war was an "insurance policy" in case the atomic tests failed.[18]

Thus, the revisionist position is quite clear. Officials in the United States were deeply concerned about post-war hegemony, particularly in the Pacific but in Europe as well, and saw the use of the atomic bomb against Japan as a way to contain the Soviet Union. Subsequently, any and all alternatives that could have ended the war, albeit not in time to prevent Soviet entry, were disregarded and not pursued. This conclusion is often premised on the fact that Japan was already defeated and near surrender. Alperovitz argues that "Japan was defeated and preparing to surrender before the atomic bomb was used. Though the question of timing was in dispute, it is also certain that this was general understood in the U.S. government at the time." [19] Hasegawa contends that the "Soviet entry into the war played a greater role than the atomic bombs in inducing Japan to surrender" and, as such, the Japanese would have quickly surrender upon Soviet entry even without the use of the atomic bombs.

It is on these grounds that the traditionalists most vehemently challenge the revisionists. Robert James Maddox challenged what he saw as "blatant revisionist distortions" in order to construct his argument that the single-most decisive factor in forcing the Japanese to surrender and preventing a costly land invasion of Japan was the use of the atomic bombs. Whereas Alperovitz maintained that the casualty figures for a land invasion were inflated as post-war justifications by the Truman administration, Maddox suggests that the half-a-million figure "cited by Truman, and even higher ones, were circulated within the upper echelons of government."[20] For Maddox bombs were utilized out of military necessity because the Japanese would not have surrendered without the atomic destruction of Hiroshima and Nagasaki. Indeed, according to Maddox the "very idea of surrender was alien to the Japanese samurai tradition."[21] Furthermore, ULTRA intercepts suggest surrender prior to an invasion was not even a serious option, let alone inevitable. Richard Frank goes even further, arguing that the conclusions the revisionist reach regarding the MAGIC are erroneous because they ignore the fact that Japanese peace feelers were completely "want of official sanction." [22] Thus, the "thesis that Japan was actively seeking to surrender in 1945, and that American policy makers knew this primarily from code breaking," is rejected by the traditionalists.[23]

Robert Newman concurs with this analysis, adding that most "Hiroshima cultists,"[24] including Gar Alperovitz, P. M. S. Blackett, Paul Boyer, the Smithsonian exhibit authors, and others who "swallow this conclusion of the [United States Strategic Bombing Survey][25] whole" are incorrect because the study itself was extremely flawed. [26] Information in the survey was purposefully distorted to support conclusions already arrived at a priori by Paul Nitze, and the testimony of most high-ranking Japanese officials "overwhelmingly indicated that Japan was not about to surrender before the bomb."[27] Thus, the "Truman bashers"[28] are incorrect to argue that the bomb changed no minds. In fact, according to Newman it "created a situation in which the peace party and the emperor could prevail." [29] Wilson Miscamble also views himself as "exploding permanently the myth of a Japan ready to surrender," a "myth" perpetuated by the United States Strategic Bombing Survey of 1946. [30]

Richard Frank furthers this argument by explaining that Japan's "fundamental policy," based on the *Ketsu-Go* defense plan, was a national resistance program intended to bloody the invading enemy enough to force political negotiations and ipso facto avoid unconditional surrender. Frank relies heavily upon the document produced by the Big Six entitled "The Fundamental Policy to Be Followed Henceforth in the Conduct of the War," which argued Japan "must fight to the finish and choose extinction before surrender."[31] In essence, Japan was "effectively locked on course for a fight to the last man, woman, and child."[32] Furthermore, Frank continues this theme, arguing that the goal was to "severely bloody the invaders" to the point of achieving political goals. Ultra documents, according to Frank, did much to "unmask their carefully wrought plans."[33] The forces on Kyushu far exceeded the 350,000 number given to Truman. Indeed, by November 1 Japanese strength would be 680,000, much closer to the 1:1 ration of American to Japanese soldiers that U.S. leaders desperately wanted to avoid. Paul Walker takes this argument to its logical extreme. He argues that due the 35 percent casualty rate of the Iwo Jima and Okinawa battles, as well as the "fanaticism of the Japanese military and their updated code of Bushido," casualties would have ranged from around 250,000 in the invasion of Kyushu alone, to over one million with the invasion of both Kyushu and Honshu.[34] Miscamble maintains that "retrospective castigations" like William D. Leahy's memoirs in 1950, which denounced the atomic bomb as a "modern type of barbarism not worthy of Christian man," can be dismissed since "no military officials counseled the president against using the weapons *prior* to Hiroshima."[35]Maddox concurs, explaining that despite the retroactive denunciations of the atomic bomb by top-ranking military officials, no military officials seriously attempted to guide Truman away from using the bomb prior to its deployment. The fact that the bomb was utilized out of military necessity dismisses the "gravest charge against Truman," namely that the atomic bomb was deployed "primary as a diplomatic weapon to intimidate the Soviet Union."[36]

The question of Soviet entry into the war preoccupies an important space in the discourse as well. Tsuyoshi Hasegawa maintains that "Soviet entry into the war played a greater role than the atomic bombs in inducing Japan to surrender."[37] Interestingly, Maddox claims the Soviets invaded Manchuria not to be "a good ally" but rather "to get in on the kill,"[38] an analysis Hasegawa would largely share. However, where the revisionists and the traditionalists differ, is that most traditionalists seriously downplay the role of Soviet entry into the war. In Frank's narrative, "Soviet intervention was a significant but not decisive reason for Japan's surrender... reinforcing but not fundamental."[39] Miscamble maintains that revisionist historians who emphasize Soviet entry in the war "distort history by overemphasizing" its importance.[40] According to Miscamble, Hasegawa's claim that Truman was disappointed at the Soviet entry into the war "are not substantiated by the historical evidence." [41]Paul Walker points out that when the emperor finally surrendered on August 15, 1945, the Russian invasion was not mentioned as a cause of surrender. Hasegawa counters this point by citing "another historic document" written by Sakomizu's [42] assistant and sanctioned by the emperor that was not issued until August 17. This rescript explained that if Japan continued fighting after the entrance of the Soviet Union into the war it would endanger "the very foundation of the empire's existence," [43]reinforcing Hasegawa's claim that Soviet intervention was key.

Perhaps the most creative defense of the use of the atomic bomb from the traditionalist camp is the moral one. One of the primary objectives of Wilson Miscamble is to "confront the question regarding the morality of the atomic bomb."[44] Miscamble suggests that for Byrnes and Truman "moral complexity or future diplomatic implications failed to complicate their straight forward thinking." If the atomic bomb "might save American lives" then it must be used, and this "remained, throughout, the essential motivation that guided the decision." [45] Whereas revisionists argue that Japan was defeated, he makes a stark distinction between defeat and surrender, explaining that the U.S. would have eventually won the war by "continued obliteration bombing of Japanese cities and infrastructure, a choking blockade, the terrible invasions... [and these] would have meant significantly greater Allied casualties and much higher Japanese civilian and military casualties."[46] Likewise, the abrupt end to the war also brought an end to Japanese brutality in other parts of Asia. Furthermore, "indiscriminate bombing had become the norm for the Anglo-American forces well before 1945," indicating that any "moral Rubicon" had already been crossed prior to Hiroshima.[47] Thus, the bomb was the "lesser of the evils available," and subsequently Miscamble pleas that in "future anniversaries of the dropping of the atomic bomb... one might hope for less moralizing condemnation of Truman's decision... Perhaps there might even be some empathy for the man who felt required to make the decision and who carried the burden of it."[48]

Robert Newman makes a slightly less sophisticated moral defense, proclaiming that neither "Hiroshima cultists nor professional moralists had even considered the possibility that Hiroshima and Nagasaki were *legitimate retribution* for the millions of deaths caused by Japan's fourteen-year rampage through China and the Pacific,"[49] an idea he apparently entertains. Newman suggests that the atomic bombs were moral actions taken in order to prevent greater evil. According to him the general arguments against Truman's choice to use the bomb come in four general varieties: first, atomic bombs are intrinsically evil and should not be used; second, their use violated the principle of noncombatant immunity; third, the bombs were used on invalid motives, including retribution, revenge, and reprisal; and fourth, no specific warning was given. To the first, Newman responds that "the case for immorality of today's overkill arsenals and war fighting doctrines is strong," but "to apply the same case retrospectively to 1945, however, is senseless."[50] To the second, Newman quotes Bamba Nobuya to suggest that the "Marxist interpretation of imperialistic war," namely that "the 'people' should have been innocent," is incorrect. The Japanese population did not just passively support imperialism, "on the contrary, most people competed to get front seats on the fascist bandwagon." [51] Thus, they were not noncombatants and to attack them was legitimate. To the third point Newman maintains that because the Japanese were involved in developing atomic weapons as well, even though U.S. leaders were not aware of this at the time, it retroactively justifies the decision. Since "upwards of 250,000 people...*would have died each month the Japanese Empire struggled in its death throes beyond July 1945*," and since the bomb had the ability to end the war early, it could not have been used for the wrong reasons.[52] To the last point, he responds that the shock value of the bomb was decisive in ending the war, and thus it would have been ineffective and prolonged the war to issue the warning.

Finally, the issue of culture and its relationship to policies of surrender are intricately bound up in the traditionalist narrative. For Paul Walker, a key element of the war was the "barbarism, savageness, and race hatred" of "an oriental enemy with a brutal heritage." [53] According to Walker, the Japanese in World War II "believed they were fighting in the proud traditions of their samurai ancestors."[54] This ideological reliance upon "a version of Bushido" meant that military schools taught "a perverted cult of death" which made "young Japanese men expendable numbers for the military's reckless and costly adventures." [55] Tracing Japanese history from the Forty Seven Ronin to the Meiji Restoration and beyond, Walker paints a picture of uniform brutality and aggression. This culminates in the period from 1894 to 1945, where "Japan was involved in almost constant warfare with her neighbors."[56] Since being a prisoner of war was "completely unacceptable, considered dishonorable or shameful, and contrary to the samurai code," the Japanese were essentially automatons that fought to the death. In contrast with U.S. imperialism, where "Filipinos had a positive image of America" and U.S. intervention in Vietnam "sorted itself out,"[57] Japanese imperialism was infinitely more brutal, according to Walker. This notion that the Japanese were imbued with fanaticism and the ideology of Bushido, which permeated their consciousness for centuries, is an important part of Walker's thesis because it attempts to reinforce the notion that the toll of casualties would be great in a U.S. invasion of Japan. Miscamble suggests a similar theme, explaining that the "the twisted neo-*samurai* … geared up with true *banzai* spirit to engage the whole population in a kind of national *kamikaze* campaign." [58]Maddox is slightly less crude, suggesting that that the "very idea of surrender was alien to the Japanese samurai tradition."[59]

Thus, within the traditionalist camp one finds a remarkable degree of unanimity. While some authors, such as Miscamble and Newman, focus on the moral argument, others, such as Maddox, implore the military aspect. Others still emphasize the "savage" culture of the "Oriental enemy" a la Paul Walker. Yet, all of the traditionalists tend to converge in their main analysis. There is little disagreement among them on any vital issues. In one way this greatly distinguishes them from the revisionist camp, which presents a quite heterogeneous and diverse array of analyses.

The Revisionist Camp

The traditionalists and revisionists part ways on the fundamental divide of atomic diplomacy. Within the traditionalist camp arguments are largely convergent, whereas within the revisionists camp the nuances are far more pronounced. All tend to agree that some level of atomic diplomacy was in play. Most, however, disagree on a variety of other issues. Gar Alperovitz and Martin Sherwin heavily emphasize the role of atomic diplomacy. In contrast, Takaki suggests race and racism as primary variables. Hasegawa maintains that an "international" perspective is vital, and criticizes past revisionists for heavily focusing on leaders in Washington. As Gar Alperovitz is the first and quintessential revisionist, much of the internal discussion amongst revisionists is characterized by correcting, expanding, or challenging certain assumptions Alperovitz has made.

The first distinction of analysis can be seen in the characterization of the Roosevelt and the Truman administration. Alperovitz imbues individual political actors, particularly Harry Truman and his adviser James Byrnes, with immense agency over the use of the bomb. He warns against "analyses which assert that a combination of factors-political, military, racial, and financial-produced the decision."[60]He also makes the case against "momentum theories," which may have "an odd feeling of seeming plausibility about them," but which go against the evidence that top U.S. military officials were against the bombing.[61] Throughout his work it is stressed that individual political actors were absolutely fundamental in the decision, and that no sort of "momentum theory" is capable of capturing the dynamics of the top-level discussions that led to the final decision. Alperovitz emphasizes the importance of the Truman-Byrnes relationship, implicitly suggesting that the outcome may have been different with Roosevelt in office.

Martin Sherwin articulates a somewhat distinct argument that draws a strong line of continuity between the Roosevelt and Truman administrations. For Sherwin, an "analysis of the policies [Roosevelt] chose...suggests that the diplomatic value of the bomb began to shape his atomic energy policies as early as 1943."[62] Although Sherwin cites Roosevelt's elusive decision making process and sudden death as inhibitors to fully understanding his policy, he posits that Roosevelt "consistently opposed international control and acted in accordance with Churchill's monopolistic, anti-Soviet views."[63] He concludes that Roosevelt's commitment to amicable postwar relations with the Soviets has "often been exaggerated," and that "his prescriptions for the diplomatic role of the atomic bomb... reveal a carefully guarded skepticism regarding the Grand Alliance's prospects for surviving the war intact."[64] Thus, Sherwin argues that Truman did not "inherit the question" of whether to employ the bomb as a means of atomic diplomacy, but he "inherited the answer" since by 1943 the diplomatic value of the bomb had already begun to shape atomic energy policies. The decision to use the bomb, and its diplomatic implications, were prescribed by Roosevelt. Truman's decisions were more or less technical, revolving around how specifically to use the bomb. Where Alperovitz has attempted to present a break or disconnect between what he perceives as Roosevelt's uncertain and wavering atomic policies, Sherwin presents a forceful analysis suggesting strong continuity between the two administrations.

A second point of contention amongst revisionists is the role of race and racism in the decision to use the bomb. Here Alperovitz argues that while "it is certainly possible" that racism amongst U.S. officials played a role in the decision to drop the bomb, "it is all but impossible to find specific evidence that racism was an important factor."[65] In contrast, while Takaki adopts Alperovitz's notion of atomic diplomacy, he drastically parts with him on the issue of race. Takaki's primary focus is understanding the decision within the trajectory of US racism. [66] In this regard, it seems his argument is best encapsulated when he declares, borrowing from John Dower, that "in this 'war without mercy,' Truman made the deadly mushroom cloud of 'Manhattan' appear over Japan in order to destroy an enemy he regarded as 'a beast'."[67] Takaki explicates upon the "racialization of the Pacific War," positioning it within the historic context of racism and US expansionism. After briefly addressing Japanese notions of racial superiority, Takaki attempts to place Truman's decision to use the atomic bombs within the "sociological imagination" of anti-Japanese racism in US society. In doing so, he links the war in the Pacific to earlier periods of conquest. His analysis focuses on the complex processes by which the US idea of democracy was intricately bound up with westward expansion and slavery, all institutions saturated with racialized notions of superiority. Citing the Chinese Exclusion Act, "Yellow Peril" hysteria, the American Federation of Labor anti-Japanese agitation, and the Asiatic Exclusion League, Takaki draws a long line of continuity culminating in the internment of Japanese Americans and the atomic bombing of Hiroshima and Nagasaki. For Takaki, notions of racial superiority and anti-Asian racism were key variables in the "sociological imagination" which facilitated the bombing of hundreds of thousands of civilians. It is in this context of a society deeply permeated with both institutional and individual racism that Truman's actions must be analyzed. Takaki analyzes Truman's biography, emphasizing the implicit notions of racial superiority deeply embedded in him and his family of ex-slave owners. Takaki outlines Truman's broadly anti-Asian sentiments, such as in 1911 when he explained that he "does hate Chinese and Japs" and that the "yellow men [ought to be] in Asia." [68] By 1945, Truman referred to the "Japs" as "savages, ruthless, merciless and fanatic." Thus, the "sociological imagination" was a highly racialized one that helped rationalize the slaughter of innocent Japanese civilians in the minds of men like Truman.

Tsuyoshi Hasegawa also takes Alperovitz to task on more than one occasion. Throughout *Racing the Enemy* he points out that he views his work as a corrective to the mistakes of revisionist historians. As he explains, the "sharp division between revisionist and orthodox historians in the Unites States" has failed to address the crucial international dimension because "the main point of contention is over American perceptions of Soviet intentions" that "depict Soviet actions as a sideshow and assign to Moscow a secondary role at best."[69] Furthermore, although Hasegawa is certainly not an orthodox historian, he is mildly critical of the revisionists who have preceded him: "Although much of what revisionist historians argue is faulty and based on tendentious use of sources, they nonetheless deserve credit for raising an important moral issue that challenges the standard American narrative of Hiroshima and Nagasaki."[70] Thus, Hasegawa strengthens the revisionist narrative by correcting some of the errors and increasing the attention to the international dynamic at work.

Alperovitz in large part bases his argument on the conclusions of the 1946 United States Strategic Bombing Survey which argued that Japan "would likely have surrender in 1945 without atomic bombing, without a Soviet declaration of war, and without an American invasion." [71] In contrast with Alperovitz and most other revisionist historians who uncritically accept the United States Strategic Bombing Survey's conclusion, Hasegawa maintains that "defeat and surrender are not synonymous," and Paul Nitze's "conclusion was repeatedly contradicted by the evidence in the Survey itself."[72] He largely accepts the critique of the USSBS findings put forward by Barton Bernstein. Instead, he argues that "even without the atomic bombs, the war most likely would have ended shortly after Soviet entry into the war-before November 1."[73] Strangely, Hasegawa tends to overemphasize his departure from Alperovitz on this point, or he must have simply overlooked Alperovitz contention that, even had the atomic bomb not been used, it is "almost a certainty that the Japanese would have capitulated upon the entry of Russia into the war."[74]

On a number of other points Hasegawa and Alperovitz certainly do disagree, however. Whereas Alperovitz characterizes the Sino-Soviet negotiations between Stalin and the Nationalists as a U.S. ploy to prolong Russian entry in the war, Hasegawa responds that in the Sino-Soviet negotiations, the "interests of Truman, Stalin, and Chiang Kai-shek all converged: the successful conclusion of a Sino-Soviet treaty could make everyone happy." [75] Hasegawa does not view the difficult negotiating by the Chinese as a concocted plot by the U.S. to keep the Soviets out of the war. "Revisionist historians are wrong," Hasegawa explains, "in asserting that Harriman's actions were meant to pressure Soong to resist Stalin's demand in order to prevent Soviet entry into the war against Japan."[76] Likewise, throughout his work Hasegawa repeatedly attempts to re-characterize Byrnes are someone not nearly as bent on geopolitical conflict with the Soviet Union as other revisionist historians have made him out to be. For instance, in response to the Soviet Kurils Operation as part of August Storm, Hasegawa argues that Byrnes, "though often regarded by revisionist historians as an ardent advocate for a tough stance against the Soviet Union... favored a conciliatory position on this issue."[77] Thus, the internecine differences amongst the revisionists exist. They are not nearly as pronounced or as heated as the differences between the traditionalists and the revisionists, but significantly more obvious than any real disagreement amongst traditionalist scholars.

Consensus Historians vs. the Traditionalists and the Revisionists

Between the traditionalist and revisionist historians lay a murky "middle ground" that encompasses a group of scholars who posit quite different arguments regarding the atomic bomb but tend to share in common a notion that alternatives existed. These "consensus" historians, as J. Samuel Walker refers to them, [78] in some way suggest that Truman and his advisers were aware of alternatives that seemed likely to end the war. The "consensus" historians reject the traditionalist argument that the atomic bombs were a military necessity and at the same time greatly distance themselves from the atomic diplomacy thesis. Samuel Walker's*Prompt and Utter Destruction: Truman and the Use of the Atomic Bombs Against Japan* (1997), Dennis Wainstock's*The Decision to Drop the Atomic Bomb: Hiroshima and Nagasaki* (1996), and Sean L. Malloy's *Atomic Tragedy: Henry L. Stimson and the Decision to Use the Bomb Against Japan* (2008) form the core of this "consensus" or middle ground camp.

Dennis Wainstock argues that the policy of unconditional surrender was a "policy of revenge, and it hurt America's national self-interest." [79] He continues, suggesting that had the United States given Japan conditional surrender terms, including retention of the emperor, Japan would have surrendered significantly earlier than it did. This means that neither the atomic bombs nor Soviet intervention would have been required. By prolonging the war in Europe and East Asia the policy of unconditional surrender expanded Soviet power in both areas, thereby harming U.S. interests. The dropping of the atomic bomb only "hastened the surrender of an already defeated enemy." [80] Wainstock does not neatly align with either the traditionalist or revisionist camp. First, he aligns his critique of unconditional surrender within "U.S. national interests." His emphasis is that unconditional surrender unnecessarily prolonged the war, and Truman's commitment to it subsequently harmed U.S. interests since the prolonged war eventually allowed the Soviet Union to enter the arena and exercise increased influence in East Asia. This "policy of revenge [unconditional surrender]… hurt America's national self-interest" because it "prolonged the war… and helped to expand Soviet power."[81]

It is in this way that Wainstock differs sharply from all of the traditionalists who, in one way or another defend the policy of unconditional surrender. Whereas Paul Walker, Richard Frank, and Wilson Miscamble tend to be generally supportive of the unconditional surrender policy, James Maddox, in a rather reserved way, argues that "there is no way of telling whether the doctrine prolonged the war in any way." [82] Robert Newman is Wainstock's primary adversary in this regard, however. Newman argues two main points: first, Truman "had no good reason" to believe that permitting retention of the emperor would have led to early capitulation and, second, the "Potsdam Declaration defined surrender in a fashion acceptable to the Japanese

175

peace forces."[83] To "those who insist that unconditional surrender was a purely punitive stance," he proclaims that the "leaders of the Japanese peace party... saw in the Potsdam terms an acceptable alternative to the destruction Japan would otherwise sustain."[84] The reason that Truman eventually accepted the condition that the emperor be retained was, according to Newman, because "peace was too tantalizing to resist." [85] In the end, however, Newman is sure that retaining the emperor, "what Hiroshima cultists insist was a viable alternative for Truman to end the war early... was really no alternative at all."[86] Furthermore, the conditions outlined at Potsdam were not unconditional surrender, and the Japanese knew it. Thus, for Newman the entire thesis constructed by Wainstock rests on dubious grounds.

Regarding his differences with the revisionists, Wainstock concedes that "perhaps Truman's decision to drop the bombs was an attempt to both impress the Soviets... and to end the war before the Soviets entered and seize the Far Eastern territories."[87] Even if this were true, however, it was totally counterproductive since in the end it prolonged the war and allowed Soviet entry, something that could have been prevented by altering the policy. This brief commentary is all the space that Wainstock provides for the atomic diplomacy thesis. In other words, despite accepting that atomic diplomacy may have played some minor role, Wainstock contends that a blind policy of unconditional surrender was of prime importance in the decision. This is where his greatest disagreement comes to the fore with the revisionists, and in particular Hasegawa. Hasegawa contends that even if Truman had "accepted a provision in the Potsdam declaration allowing the Japanese to retain a constitutional monarchy," it would "not have immediately led to Japan's surrender."[88] It is doubtful, Hasegawa maintains, "that Japan would have capitulated before the atomic bomb was dropped on Hiroshima and the Soviet Union entered the war."[89] Thus, whereas the policy of unconditional surrender is the fundamental variable for Wainstock, it is significantly less so for Hasegawa. Wainstock significantly minimizes the significance of atomic diplomacy and inflates the importance of the unconditional surrender policy.

Sean Malloy, like Takaki, attempts to analyze the decision to use the atomic bomb through the "lens of biography." [90] Malloy attempts to approach "the use of the bomb through a conceptual framework he calls the "context of use," positioning the use of the bomb as a "compound product of a series of choices" rather than "the result of single decision." [91] Malloy makes the argument that Stimson, as secretary of war, unintentionally "presided over a set of policies that accelerated the budding nuclear arms race with the Soviet Union,"[92] despite his "deep concern with limiting the effects of war on civilians and fostering trust between nations as the foundation of the peace that followed." [93] In essence, *realpolitik* dominated Stimson's approach to the atomic bomb and undermined his moral commitments.

One example of this is Stimson's oversight of the 1945 Stassfurt operation intended to secure Anglo-American hegemony over uranium supplies. By the time of Strassfurt, when the U.S. moved in to seize the largest known stock of uranium in Europe, they "did as so as part of a one-sided nuclear arms race" in which, "by 1945, the Soviet Union was already America's primary nuclear rival."[94] Thus, while Stimson is the tragic hero with a fatal flaw, James Byrnes is his foil, presented as the bad apple in the administration who desires conflict with the Soviet Union. Malloy's key argument, then, is that "by his own actions during World War II, the secretary of war had helped to set in motion exactly the kind of destructive international competition in armaments that he had spent much of his long public career attempting to avoid." [95] The almost capricious nature of his rapidly changing positions, and the tenuous justifications which frequently accompanied them, indicates that Stimson's moral convictions were more often than not drown out for the sake of political expediency. Malloy's conception of the atomic bomb as a "tragedy" is the principle departure from the traditionalists who tend to glorify the use of the bomb and celebrate it for ending the war and saving lives.

Malloy's differences with the revisionist camp are rather nuanced, but significant. Once again, his conception of the bombs as a "tragedy," rather than a calculated diplomatic initiative, separates him from the revisionists. Second, he makes the argument that the secretary of war "was in a unique position to shape many of the decisions about the use of the bomb."[96] This is in direct contradistinction to other historians, such as Alperovitz, who emphasize the agency of actors such as James Byrnes at Stimson's expense. Second, Malloy attempts to put forward a sort of "momentum theory" that Alperovitz considers "seemingly plausible" but in reality historically bankrupt. During the various decisions that led to the atomic bombing, the morals and convictions of officials were often sublimated for political expediency. For Malloy, this was particularly true of Stimson. In this way, a sort of "momentum theory" is employed by Malloy to mitigate the pernicious intent of certain actors and explain away the "failures" of their decisions. Thus, the atomic bombs were not intentionally used as diplomatic tools by most of the Truman administration, but policy "failures" as individuals were swept up in events. Further modifying the arguments of Alperovitz and Hasegawa, Malloy argues that "American domestic politics" were a primary reason that Truman "failed at Potsdam" to use the "two potentially useful, if imperfect, diplomatic levers... in an effort to end the war." [97] Furthermore, whereas Hasegawa presents Soviet entry as vital, Mallow suggests that "neither the public threat of Soviet entry nor the lure of allowing the Japanese to retain the emperor after the war were diplomatic panaceas." [98] Thus, Malloy's differences with the revisionists are perceptible.

A slightly different approach is apparent in J. Samuel Walker's book. He sets out to answer two interrelated questions: was the bomb "necessary at all" and, "if so, what exactly did it accomplish?"[99]By the conclusion of the book, Walker asserts that the answer to the first question "seems to be yes and no. Yes, it was necessary to end the war as quickly as possible. No, it was not necessary to prevent an invasion of Japan."[100] Addressing the second question, he maintains that the bomb "shortened the war and saved the lives of a relatively small but far from inconsequential number of Americans."[101] By situating his thesis within these parameters, S. Walker avoids having to take a position regarding the morality of the atomic bombings and instead focuses on rather narrow notions of "military necessity." He presents a variegated list of reasons Truman dropped the bomb: "(1) the commitment to ending the war successfully at the earliest possible moment; (2) the need to justify the effort and expense of building the atomic bombs; (3) the hope of achieving diplomatic gains in the growing rivalry with the Soviet Union; (4) the lack of incentives not to use atomic weapons; and (5) hatred of the Japanese and a desire for vengeance."[102]

Walker's differences with the traditionalists are quite clear: Walker suggests three rectifications to the popular narrative, a narrative the traditionalists largely accept: first, "there were other options available for ending the war... without the bomb and without an invasion"; second, due to Japan's enervated capacity for war, Truman and his advisers did not regard invasion as inevitable; last, even if invasion was necessary to end the war, military planners "projected the number of American lives lost at far fewer than the hundreds of thousands that Truman and his advisers claimed after the war."[103]Furthermore, Walker relies on the USSBS, a point of divergence between himself and both the traditionalists and Hasegawa, to conclude "the war would probably have ended before an American invasion of Kyushu became necessary." [104] Walker essentially dismisses the entire traditionalist approach, with the caveat that Truman was indeed concerned with saving as many American lives as possible.

It is important to note that he is rather critical of the revisionist approach as well. First and foremost, Walker specifically outlines what Alperovitz disparages as an analysis asserting "that a combination of factors-political, military, racial, financial-produced the decision." Alperovitz's criticism of such an approach is that it "is easy to assemble fragments of evidence" that suggest such an analysis, but jumping from these "fragments to an explanatory conclusion about decision-making at the very top of the U.S. government is suspect."[105] Thus, Walker's "five fundamental considerations" are a significant departure from Alperovitz. More significantly, Walker actually considers the entire atomic diplomacy thesis as a sideshow. For instance, he maintains that "Truman did not drop the bomb primarily to intimidate the Soviets." It was at best an ancillary consideration, a "bonus."[106]

Thus, the "consensus" historians, largely agree that potential alternatives existed, that invasion may not have been necessary, and that the atomic bombs were probably not responsible for saving hundreds of thousands of lives. In other words, they were not a military necessity. At the same time, the atomic bombs were not deployed primarily as diplomatic mechanisms. Even if they eventually came to fulfill this role, it was either the unintentional result of "momentum" or a tertiary variable barely perceptible vis-à-vis other considerations.

Conclusion: The Myth, the Cult, Nuclearism, and Nuclear Consciousness

In the post-war era, the debate and discussion over the bomb has been of tremendous importance. Both the traditionalist and revisionist camps have plotted the trajectory of the discourse surrounding Hiroshima and Nagasaki in different ways. Gar Alperovitz has suggested that officials promulgated propaganda in a top-down manner in order to manufacture an "American myth" surrounding the use of the atomic bombs. Robert J. Lifton's preface to Martin Sherwin's *A World Destroyed* laments the emergence of "nuclearism," the ideology that the atomic bomb is a "deity" capable of both "destroying the world" and "capable of ruling and protecting the world, even of keeping the world going."[107] In contrast, Robert Newman denounces Alperovitz and other revisionists as "Hiroshima cultists," "Truman bashers," and a host of other pejoratives for creating a "cult" that worships at the altar of Hiroshima.   Lastly, Paul Boyer, in his book *By the Bomb's Early Light: American Thought and Culture at the Dawn of the Atomic Age* (1994), suggests that a sort of "nuclear consciousness" has infused itself in the perceptions and ideology of Americans in the post-war era.[108] In fact, "nuclear reality" so deeply pervades our "consciousness that it is hard to imagine what existence would have been like without it."[109] In these various ways authors have interpreted the post-war world after the atomic bomb.

In the second part of his book, Alperovitz explores the creation of the mythology surrounding the ostensibly "inevitable" use of the bomb. He maintains that three decisions, including the rejection to provide enough time for Japan to surrender, the choice to not offer the Japanese emperor assurances, and the explicit decision not to test a Russian entry into the war, "set the terms of reference for the bomb's subsequent seemingly 'inevitable' use... [and] so tightly framed the remaining issues as to make it all but impossible thereafter to oppose the bombings." [110] This "framing of the bomb," alongside the top-down campaign of disinformation immediately after the war, were key factors that facilitated the permeation of American consciousness with the "inevitability" narrative.

Stimson, Truman, Byrnes, and Groves were key figures in this top-down propaganda campaign. Despite what Alperovitz argues was an ancillary role in the actual decision to drop the bomb, Stimson did play a vital role in propagating the official discourse, citing Stimson's 1947 *Harper's* article which was presented as "a mere recital of the facts." Stimson posited a rigid dichotomy later picked up by traditionalist historians: either a costly invasion or use of the bomb was required to end the war. As Alperovitz explains, the article was an "extraordinary success," with the *New York Times*, the *Washington Post*, *Reader's Digest*, the *Bulletin of Atomic Scientists*, and an indeterminate number of other media outlets "decidedly uncritical and, indeed, often effusive in praise."[111] Truman's argument that "the dropping of the bombs stopped the war" and "saved millions of lives" was the main line of thought he propagated continuously after the war. He maintains that the "over a million" figure "became the essential source for a myth which has been repeated with only occasional challenge for much of the last half century" despite modern scholarship demonstrating "the estimate to be without any serious foundation in the documents of that period." [112] Byrnes systematically distorted and revised the past by shrouding himself in secrecy and meticulously managing his personal writings. Groves' role as "an expert public relations artist and news 'spin' master" also comes to light when he devised a strategy whereby U.S. officials would "saturate" the "huge market hungry for information with officially approved material from the only authoritative source available."[113] In Japan itself a Civil Censorship Division of the Occupation had some 8,700 staffers engaged in examining thousands of newspapers, magazines, textbooks, motion pictures, and even private mail to ensure they did not stray too far from the official discourse.[114] The most pernicious form of censorship was also the most ubiquitous; namely, government classification. Thus, as Alperovitz argues, "the 'normal' functioning of government... is even more effective than the occasional excesses which make the headlines."[115] In these ways the historical narrative from beginning to end was "managed" by U.S. officials.

Part of Martin Sherwin's work is intended to combat the legacy of nuclearism. In a world where humans have "infused [the atomic bomb] with a constellation of awe and mystery. That constellation has included tendencies to embrace the bomb, to become fiercely dependent upon it, indeed, to render it something close to a deity."[116] The "willful embrace of the cruelest weapon ever created is the essence" of nuclearism.[117] Suggesting a line of continuity with Paul Boyer, *A World Destroyed* suggests that an "idealistic aura of peacemaking was inseparable from the bomb's lure of ultimate technology and ultimate power-all of which became part of the transcendent technology of nuclearism."[118] Hence, "the bizarre emphasis on the bomb's ostensible function of 'saving lives' rather than destroying them, of rendering the world peaceful rather than bringing to it a specter of annihilation."[119] This "bizarre emphasis" has been the plaything of traditionalist scholars for decades.

In sharp contrast with Alperovitz and Sherwin, Robert P. Newman's thesis in *Truman and the Hiroshima Cult* is the paradigmatic post-revisionist account of the atomic bomb and its aftermath. In it he argues that a "cult," with attendant cultists, has arisen around Truman and the Hiroshima decision. These "Hiroshima cultists" argue, in a variety of forms, that Japan was on the verge of surrender, that the "unconditional surrender" formula unnecessarily prolonged the war, and that Truman's decision to drop the bomb was driven either by racism towards the Japanese or diplomatic concerns vis-à-vis the Soviets, or some combination thereof. Newman vehemently rejects what he refers to as the "Japanese-as-victim cult," suggesting that any and all of the above suggestions are fundamentally incorrect. Newman proclaims that neither "Hiroshima cultists nor professional moralists had even considered the possibility that Hiroshima and Nagasaki were legitimate retribution for the millions of deaths caused by Japan's fourteen-year rampage through China and the Pacific."[120]

Newman traces the development and growth of what he maliciously and interchangeably refers to as the "Japan-as-Victim myth" or "Hiroshima cult." He begins by explaining how in the immediate aftermath of the war "the whole world viewed Japan as villainous." [121] After 1948, however, things began to change, in both Japan and the United States. In 1949 John Hersey's *Hiroshima* was published, which Newman credits with having the opposite but equally powerful impact that Anne Frank's diary had on Germany. Where Anne Frank's diary forced Germany to come to terms with its atrocities, *Hiroshima* shielded Japan from having to do so, and helped begin the "Japan-as-Victim" myth. Furthermore, in 1951 P. M. S. Blackett published *Fear, War, and the Bomb*, which argued that the bomb was not the last act of the Second World War but the first act of the Cold War. Finally, in 1954 when the U.S. tested the new H-bomb and the crew of a tuna trawler were affected by radioactive fallout, the "five most important Japanese newspapers took a common position: this was the third atomic bombing." [122]

Despite all this, however, in 1964 a public opinion poll suggested that 49 percent of the Japanese public viewed the United States as their "favorite foreign country." By 1973, after the U.S. atrocities in Vietnam and use of Japan to accomplish them, this "popularity" had dropped to 18 percent. [123] By the late sixties people were questioning earlier U.S. military endeavors, notably the dropping of the atomic bombs, as a reflection of the changing political tide and anti-Vietnam war sentiment. By 1989, the "majority opinion even among Japanese scholars" was accepting of both the Blackett thesis and racism as primary factors in the dropping of the atomic bomb. In the United States, the gradual buildup of anti-nuclear activism, starting with *The Bulletin of the Atomic Scientists* in the late 1940s to the "Scientists' Declaration on Nuclear Power" in 1975, had a major impact on retroactive views of the bombings. Thus, "accurate charges" of postwar "overkill... seemed to legitimate chargers of overkill levied at the Hiroshima and Nagasaki bombs."[124] Furthermore, many "who became disillusioned with the American terror bombing in Vietnam became converts to the Hiroshima guilt trip."[125] Newman also cites Ian Buruma's *The Wages of Guilt*, which explores the myriad of factors for why a "Japan-as-Victim" cult developed but no comparably "cult" developed around Germany. The key factor as Newman sees it, however, was Vietnam. Without it, "the Japanese-as-victims cult in the United States would still be puny."[126] Newman's work is a vicious attack on the legacy of revisionists like Gar Alperovitz and Martin Sherwin.

Paul Boyer's study, *By the Bomb's Early Light: American Thought and Culture at the Dawn of the Atomic Age*, addresses the "unsettling new cultural factor" of the atomic bomb that had been introduced in immediate post-war period from 1945 to 1950. [127] His contention is that the bomb "had transformed not only military strategy and international relations, but the fundamental ground of culture and consciousness" in the United States.[128] These five formative years shaped how Americans first "confronted the bomb, struggled against it, and absorbed it into the fabric of the culture." [129] In short, Boyer maintains that the 1945 to 1946 period was a time of "obsessive post-Hiroshima awareness of the horror of the atomic bomb," while in the period from 1947 to 1950 and after there was a "diminished cultural attention and uneasy acquiescence" as the "dread destroyer of 1945 had become the shield of the Republic by 1950."[130] In essence, Sherwin's "transcendent technology of nuclearism" permeated what Boyer calls America's "nuclear consciousness." This "nuclear consciousness" was infused into the very core of American ideology in the post-war era and so deeply pervades American "consciousness that it is hard to imagine what existence would have been like without it."[131]Hiroshima and Nagasaki, Boyer argues, "stand as signposts marking both a gash in the living flesh of our historical consciousness and a turning point in our ethical history." [132]

From 1945 to 1946 an "intense discourse" had surrounded the atomic bomb, where after 1947 this "diminished to scattered murmurs and faint echoes" and by 1950 "America's nuclear culture... would appear as a gray and largely deserted landscape."[133] Around this time the Atomic Energy Commission began a full throttle propaganda campaign to associate atomic energy with health, happiness, and prosperity. This campaign drew in scientists, educators, radio personalities, health workers, and others, directly reaching some four million Americans and indirectly affecting many more. A "policy of deep secrecy about atomic-bomb research and stockpiling," alongside the "pervasive official practice... of playing down the bomb's dangers" continued to condition the American public.[134] In this context, and with the ensuing Cold War schism that dominated international relations, the "civil defense" paradigm displaced the "international control" slogan dominant during 1945-6. This multifaceted propaganda campaign was so successful that by 1950 Americans had overwhelmingly, if not unanimously, embraced the atomic bomb. The mid-1950s saw a resurgence of debate over the atomic bomb and then a re-decline after 1963. He argues that the illusion of diminished risk, the loss of immediacy, the promise of a world transformed by atomic energy, the complexity and comfort of deterrence theory, and the importance of the Vietnam War led to the decline of atomic prominence. Interestingly, whereas Newman positions the Vietnam as the central feature in establishing the "Hiroshima cult," Boyer contends that the Vietnam War actually lessened discussion and debate over the atomic bomb.

Although Boyer aligns neatly with revisionist historians, he does refocus the chronological lens. Where other historians have drawn a line of continuity between the development of the bomb and its use, or between the Roosevelt and Truman administrations, Boyer furthers that line of continuity by exploring the state's role in managing post-Hiroshima public discourse. In this way Boyer's work partially overlaps and agrees with but significantly transcends Alperovitz "architecture of an American myth." By focusing on the state's institution of a broad, far-reaching propaganda campaign that helped shape popular opinion, Boyer repositions the role of the state not just as user of the atomic bomb, but also as manager of the dominant discourse after its use. In this way, Boyer provides a unique historiographical contribution by arguing that atomic policies "transformed not only military strategy and international relations, but the fundamental ground of culture and consciousness" in the United States.

Thus, not only is the discourse surrounding the actual use of the atomic bomb split into competing camps, the post-war discourse itself is a topic of debate. In this regard, Paul Boyer's work is the most thorough, sophisticated, and systematic cultural analysis of the post-war discourse. For those of us interested in challenging not only the excesses of war, but the inter-imperial rivalries that ultimately lead to the use of the bomb, understanding the nuances of the historiographical debate is vital. More importantly, in the wake of the

1995 Smithsonian controversy and the ever-expanding list of countries with access to nuclear armaments, those of us on the left must continue to wage war on the post-war discourse justifying and rationalizing the atomic bomb.

Bibliography

Alperovitz, Gar. *The Decision to Use the Atomic Bomb and the Architecture of an American Myth*. New York: Alfred A. Knopf, 1995.

Boyer, Paul. *By the Bomb's Early Light: American Thought and Culture at the Dawn of the Atomic Age*. Chapel Hill: The University of North Carolina Press, 1994.

Frank, Richard B. *Downfall: The End of the Imperial Japanese Empire.* New York: Penguin Books, 1999.

Hasegawa, Tsuyoshi. *Racing the Enemy: Stalin, Truman, and the Surrender of Japan.* Cambridge, MA: The Belknap Press of Harvard University Press, 2005.

Maddox, Robert James. *Weapons for Victory: The Hiroshima Decision*. Columbia: University of Missouri Press, 2004.

Malloy, Sean L. *Atomic Tragedy: Henry L. Stimson and the Decision to Use the Bomb Against Japan*. Ithaca: Cornell University Press, 2008.

Miscamble, Wilson D. *The Most Controversial Decision: Truman, the Atomic Bombs, and the Defeat of Japan*. Cambridge: Cambridge University Press, 2011.

Newman, Robert P. *Truman and the Hiroshima Cult.* East Lansing: Michigan State University Press, 1995.

Walker, J. Samuel. *Prompt and Utter Destruction: Truman and the Use of the Atomic Bombs Against Japan*. Chapel Hill: The University of North Carolina Press, 2004.

Walker, Paul D. *Truman's Dilemma: Invasion or the Bomb*. Gretna: Pelican Publishing Company, 2003.

Stimson, Henry L. "The Decisions to Use the Atomic Bomb." *Harper's Magazine* (1947).

Sherwin, Martin J. *A World Destroyed: Hiroshima and Its Legacies*. Stanford: Stanford University Press, 2003.

Takaki, Ronald. *Hiroshima: Why America Dropped the Atomic Bomb*. Boston: Little, Brown and Company, 1995.

Wainstock, Dennis. *The Decision to Drop the Atomic Bomb.* New York: Enigma Books, 2011.

Citations

[1] I borrow the term "consensus" from J. Samuel Walker.

[2] Tsuyoshi Hasegawa utilizes "orthodox" to describe this position.

[3] Henry L. Stimson, "The Decisions to Use the Atomic Bomb," *Harper's Magazine* (1947). See full article: http://classrooms.tacoma.k12.wa.us/stadium/mberggren-2/us-history/download/Stimson%2B-%2BHarper%2BFeb%2B1947%2B-%2BDecision%2Bto%2BUse%2Bthe%2BAtomic%2BBomb.pdf?id=230795

[4] J. Samuel Walker, *Prompt and Utter Destruction: Truman and the Use of the Atomic Bombs Against Japan* (Chapel Hill: The University of North Carolina Press, 2004), 105.

[5] Originally published in 1995.

[6] A reiteration and strengthening of his 1965 work *Atomic Diplomacy*.

[7] Originally published in 1973.

[8] Truman, Stimson, Byrnes, Stalin, Hirohito, and the Big Six in Japan are examples where disagreement is most pronounced.

[9] Gar Alperovitz, *The Decision to Use the Atomic Bomb and the Architecture of an American Myth*(New York: Alfred A. Knopf, 1995), 19.

[10] Alperovitz, *The Decision to Use the Atomic Bomb,* 225.

[11] Martin J. Sherwin, *A World Destroyed: Hiroshima and Its Legacies* (Stanford: Stanford University Press, 2003), 6.

[12] Sherwin, *A World Destroyed*, 7.

[13] This argument maintained that the US should share atomic technology with the Soviet Union in exchange for political cooperation.

[14] This position stated that the US should maintain a monopoly over atomic technology as long as possible and advance its diplomatic aims through harsh bargaining from its position of atomic power.

[15] Tsuyoshi Hasegawa, *Racing the Enemy: Stalin, Truman, and the Surrender of Japan* (Cambridge, MA: The Belknap Press of Harvard University Press, 2005), 140.

[16] Hasegawa, *Racing the Enemy*, 154.

[17] Ibid., 135.

[18] Ibid., 139.

[19] Alperovitz, 19.

[20] Robert James Maddox, *Weapons for Victory: The Hiroshima*

Decision (Columbia: University of Missouri Press, 2004), xv.

[21] Maddox, *Weapons for Victory*, 146.

[22] Ibid., 113.

[23] Richard B. Frank, *Downfall: The End of the Imperial Japanese Empire* (New York: Penguin Books, 1999), 104.

[24] This is Newman's term for revisionist historians.

[25] The USSBS maintained that in all likelihood Japan would surrender prior to November 1, 1945 without the atomic bombing or the entrance of the Soviet Union into the war. It further states that had Japan not surrendered by November 1, it would definitely have surrendered prior to the end of 1945.

[26] Robert P. Newman, *Truman and the Hiroshima Cult* (East Lansing: Michigan State University Press, 1995), 36.

[27] Newman, *Truman and the Hiroshima Cult*, 47.

[28] This is one of Newman's other terms for revisionists.

[29] Ibid., 49.

[30] Wilson D Miscamble, *The Most Controversial Decision: Truman, the Atomic Bombs, and the Defeat of Japan* (Cambridge: Cambridge University Press, 2011), 91.

[31] Frank, 95.

[32] Ibid., 96.

[33] Ibid., 197.

[34] Paul D. Walker, *Truman's Dilemma: Invasion or the Bomb* (Gretna: Pelican Publishing Company, 2003), 171.

[35] Miscamble, 115. Original emphasis.

[36] Maddox, 153.

[37] Hasegawa, 5.

[38] Maddox, 131.

[39] Frank, 348.

[40] Miscamble, 89.

[41] Ibid., 91.

[42] Sakomizu was chief secretary to the cabinet of Japan during World War II.

[43] Hasegawa, 250.

[44] Miscamble, 3.

[45] Ibid., 44.

[46] Ibid., 113.

[47] Ibid., 119.

[48] Ibid., 124.

[49] Newman, xiii. Emphasis added.

[50] Ibid., 120.
[51] Ibid., 130.
[52] Ibid., 138. Emphasis original.
[53] Paul Walker, 15.
[54] Ibid., 17.
[55] Ibid., 18-19.
[56] Ibid., 27.
[57] Ibid., 43-44.
[58] Miscamble, 120-1.
[59] Maddox, xv.
[60] Alperovitz, 656.
[61] Ibid., 657.
[62] Sherwin, 6.
[63] Ibid., 7.
[64] Ibid., 8.
[65] Alperovitz, 655.
[66] Ronald Takaki, *Hiroshima: Why America Dropped the Atomic Bomb* (Boston: Little, Brown and Company, 1995), 8.
[67] Takaki, *Hiroshima*, 100.
[68] Ibid., 94.
[69] Hasegawa, 2.
[70] Hasegawa, 300.
[71] Alperovitz, 4
[72] Hasegawa, 295.
[73] Ibid., 296.
[74] Alperovitz, 85.
[75] Hasegawa., 129.
[76] Ibid., 188
[77] Ibid., 275
[78] Samuel Walker cites Barton Bernstein as one of the pioneering "consensus" historians of Hiroshima.
[79] Dennis Wainstock, *The Decision to Drop the Atomic Bomb* (New York: Enigma Books, 2011), 178.
[80] Wainstock, *The Decision to Drop the Atomic Bomb*, 178.
[81] Ibid., 178.
[82] Maddox, 8.
[83] Newman, 57.
[84] Ibid., 71.
[85] Ibid., 73.
[86] Ibid., 77.

[87] Wainstock, 171

[88] Hasegawa, 290

[89] Ibid., 291

[90] Sean L. Malloy, *Atomic Tragedy: Henry L. Stimson and the Decision to Use the Bomb Against Japan* (Ithaca: Cornell University Press, 2008), 7.

[91] Malloy, *Atomic Tragedy*, 8.

[92] Ibid., 81.

[93] Ibid., 11.

[94] Ibid., 67.

[95] Ibid., 70.

[96] Ibid., 9.

[97] Ibid., 129. Here he is referring to retention of the emperor (modifying unconditional surrender) and the public threat of Soviet entry into the war.

[98] Malloy, 129

[99] Samuel Walker, 6.

[100] Ibid., 109.

[101] Ibid., 109.

[102] Ibid., 92.

[103] Ibid., 5-6.

[104] Ibid., 89.

[105] Alperovitz, 656.

[106] Walker, 95.

[107] Sherwin, xi.

[108] Paul Boyer, *By the Bomb's Early Light: American Thought and Culture at the Dawn of the Atomic Age* (Chapel Hill: The University of North Carolina Press, 1994), xix.

[109] Boyer, *By the Bomb's Early Light*, xx.

[110] Alperovitz, 631.

[111] Ibid., 455.

[112] Ibid., 466.

[113] Ibid., 598.

[114] Ibid., 610.

[115] Ibid., 613.

[116] Sherwin, xi.

[117] Ibid., xi.

[118] Ibid., xii.

[119] Ibid., xi.

[120] Newman, xiii.

[121] Ibid., 153.
[122] Ibid., 161.
[123] Ibid., 164.
[124] Ibid., 177.
[125] Ibid., 183.
[126] Ibid., 184.
[127] Boyer, xxi.
[128] Ibid., xxi.
[129] Ibid., xx.
[130] Ibid., 352 and 349.
[131] Boyer, xx
[132] Ibid., 182.
[133] Ibid., 291.
[134] Ibid., 303.

Organized Terror and Ethnic Cleansing in Palestine

Andrew Gavin Marshall

The official Israeli government explanation for the 'disappearance' of 750,000 Palestinian Arabs from the land (roughly half the Arab population in Palestine in 1948) was that they left "voluntarily." The "new history" of Israel emerged within the past couple decades due to declassified documents relating to the 1948 war and its origins, and with a number of Israeli historians recreating the history of Israel and challenging the official story. David Ben-Gurion, who would become Israel's first Prime Minister, was a leading Zionist at the time. He and other Zionists "accepted" the UN partition plan, wrote Jerome Slater, "only as a necessary tactical step that would later be reversed." In a 1937 letter to his son, Ben-Gurion wrote:

A partial Jewish state is not the end, but only the beginning. The establishment of such a Jewish state will serve as a means in our historical efforts to redeem the country in its entirety... We shall organize a modern defense force... and then I am certain that we will not be prevented from settling in other parts of the country, either by mutual agreement with our Arab neighbors or by some other means... We will expel the Arabs and take their places... with the forces at our disposal.[1]

In the same year, Ben-Gurion also wrote that, "The Arabs will have to go, but one needs an opportune moment for making it happen, such as a war."[2] A year later, in 1938, Ben-Gurion told a Zionist meeting that, "I favor partition of the country because when we become a strong power after the establishment of the state, we will abolish partition and spread throughout all of Palestine." Palestine, as defined by the Zionists, had included the West Bank, Golan Heights in Syria, Jerusalem, southern Lebanon, and a significant degree of Egypt's Sinai Peninsula.[3]

For any settler colonies, as the Zionists were, there are roughly four conditions which have to met if they are to survive. Graham Usher, an Israeli journalist, wrote that:

They must obtain a measure of political, military, and economic independence from their metropolitan sponsors. They must achieve military hegemony over, or at least normal relations with, their neighboring states. They must acquire international legitimacy. And they must solve their "native problem."[4]

The Jewish state, as defined by leading Zionists such as David Ben-Gurion, was not to simply be Jewish in its sociopolitical structure, explained Ilan Pappé, "but also in its ethnic composition." Further, this would be made possible "only by force." To accomplish this task, an efficient military organization was built over several years, with extensive financial resources. The main Jewish paramilitary organization in Palestine was founded in 1920 in order to protect the Jewish colonies, assisted by "sympathetic" British officers. Orde Wingate, a British officer, was central to convincing Zionist leaders of the need for such a military organization, associating the idea of   a Jewish state with militarism and an army. Wingate was assigned to Palestine in 1936, and had established close connections between the Jewish paramilitary organization Haganah and the British forces during the 1936-39 Arab Revolt.[5]

In 1940, Ben-Zion Luria, a historian at Hebrew University who was also employed by the Jewish Agency in Palestine suggested that the Jewish National Fund (JNF) should conduct a registry of all the Arab villages in Palestine, numbering some 1,200 in all, which had spread across the countryside for hundreds of years. Luria stated that, "This would greatly help the redemption of the land" into Jewish hands. The Jewish National Fund (JNF) was founded in 1901 as one of the principal colonization organizations focused on buying Palestinian land to settle

Jewish colonies. By the end of the Mandate in 1948, the Zionists had control over 5.8% of the land in Palestine.[6]

When news about the "village files" reached Yossef Weitz, the chief of the JNF settlement department (a major Zionist colonialist), he suggested that it be transformed into a "national project." Other top Zionists became very enthusiastic about the project, of which the main emphasis was on mapping the villages. In several cases, these maps in the Israeli State Archives are all that remains of the entire villages. The British, aware of these projects, were unable to find the headquarters for the secret intelligence network that was established to construct the maps. By the later 1940s, the "village files" included much more than mere locations of villages, but rather had details about road access, the quality of the land, water resources, common sources of income for the local population, religious and sociopolitical affiliations, and even the age of individual men within the village. One important category, explained Israeli historian Ilan Pappé, was the index of "hostility," referring to those individuals and communities which were 'hostile' to the Zionist project of colonization, which was largely determined according to examining the participation of certain villages and people in the Arab Revolt of 1936-39, which "included lists of everyone involved in the revolt and the families of those who had lost someone in the fight against the British. Particular attention was given to people alleged to have killed Jews."[7]

The British, who had the Mandate over Palestine from 1923, when it was given to the British by the League of Nations, always saw Palestine as a highly strategic and vital imperial possession, largely due to its proximity to the Suez Canal, and thus, the route to Britain's colonial "Jewel", India. Palestine was considered a 'buffer' in the Middle East, in a land of potentially hostile peoples infused with the ideas of Arab nationalism. Just prior to World War II, the Arab population in Palestine revolted against the British rule in reaction to the dramatically increased rate of Jewish immigration and colonization of the land. The Arab Revolt (1936-39) presented the British with a civil war situation, which was suppressed by force of arms. Where the Arabs were a major problem for the British in the 1930s, the Zionists became a problem for the British in the 1940s, for they too turned to terrorist tactics to make British rule over Palestine impossible. Following World War II, the British Security Service (MI5), according to declassified documents from the agency, focused on the threat to Britain posed by Zionist terrorism, both within the Mandate and within Britain itself. The two main organizations identified by MI5 as terrorist groups were the Irgun Zvai Leumi and the Stern Gang, who had planned on taking the war against Britain to its home, hoping to send several terrorist "cells" to London to "beat the dog in his own kennel." As the secret documents reveal, "MI5 was actually more concerned about the threat of Zionist terrorism than about the looming threat of the Soviet Union."[8]

MI5's wartime Director-General, Sir David Petrie, stated in 1946 in regards to the threat of Zionist terrorism that, "the red light is definitely showing." From a network of informers within Zionist organizations, Britain uncovered plots to assassinate British politicians associated with Palestine policy, including the Prime Minister himself. The Stern Gang had, in 1944, assassinated the British Minister of State in the Middle East, Lord Moyne, and had also tried (on several occasions) to assassinate the British High Commissioner for Palestine, Sir Harold MacMichael. On July 22, 1946, the Irgun bombed the King David Hotel in Jerusalem, which was home to British government officials and personnel, and resulted in the deaths of 91 individuals, some of them Jews. Both MI5 and MI6 had offices in the Hotel at the time. As Britain responded with force against Zionist terrorist groups and other organizations, the extremist nature of the groups naturally increased. In October of 1946, the Irgun bombed the British Embassy in Rome, and conducted several sabotage operations against British military transportation routes in occupied Germany. In April of 1947, the British Colonial Office in London discovered an Irgun bomb consisting of 24 sticks of explosives, but the timer had broken, so the bomb did not detonate. In June of 1947, the Stern Gang launched a letter bomb campaign in Britain, "targeting every prominent member of the Cabinet," totaling 21 in all, but none of them ultimately got through to their targets. Another letter bomb assault was undertaken by the Stern Gang in 1948.[9]

In June of 1946, the British Army in Palestine undertook a search for the Jewish Agency, Haganah, and Palmach to retrieve their arms and arrest specific members and leaders. The Zionist organizations, however, had infiltrated the British just as the British had infiltrated the Zionist organizations; thus, the Zionists had advanced warning of the raid and some top officials were able to avoid arrest. The chief of the Haganah, Moshe Sneh, which was the military branch of the Jewish Agency, was in liaison with the terrorist organizations Irgun and Lehi. David Ben-Gurion, the president of the Jewish Agency, was also wanted by the British for his complicity in terrorist attacks. All in all, during the raid, roughly 2,700 people were arrested, including a significant portion of the political leadership within the Palestinian Jewish community, and some arms caches were retrieved. The result, predictably, was to multiply the violence committed against the British in retribution for the raids and arrests. Thus, the British High Commissioner in Palestine, Sir Alan Cunningham, concluded that, "immediate partition is the only solution which gives a chance of stability."[10]

This was largely the result of the Jewish Resistance Movement (JRM) which had emerged and developed between 1945 and 1946, consisting of the Haganah, Palmach, Irgun and Lehi, "directed and coordinated by the Jewish Agency for Palestine, despite the objections of some of its left-wing members." The aims of the JRM were to "weaken or destroy British rule in Palestine." The Haganah was founded as a territorial militia to defend Zionist settlements in Palestine, and in 1938, several Haganah units worked with the British to help crush the Arab Revolt. The British created the Palmach during World War II as an "elite offensive unit" in order "to assist [the British] in the event of a German invasion of Palestine." In 1945, the Haganah engaged in a secret agreement with the terrorist groups Irgun and Lehi against the British Mandate government. The Irgun was formed in 1931 when several officers separated from the Haganah over socialist sympathies within the defense forces, and became a right-wing paramilitary army, standing in opposition to the original conception of socialist and labour Zionism. The Stern Gang (also known as Lehi) separated from the Irgun during World War II when the Irgun agreed to cooperate with the British. The Stern Gang was a radical far-right group which held many fascist sympathies, and even "pursued agreements with Mussolini and the Nazis in 1940," though unsurprisingly, Hitler did not respond to the requests.[11]

It was within these various terrorist and paramilitary organizations that Plan D was formed among several Zionist leaders, most notably, David Ben-Gurion, to plan for the ethnic cleansing of Palestine. Throughout the 1940s, the planning stages of the village files went through many revisions, and encapsulated Plans A through D. In the planning stages during 1940, as one member of the data collection team, Moshe Pasternak, later recalled:

We had to study the structure of the Arab village. This means the structure and how best to attack it. In the military schools, I had been taught how to attack a modern European city, not a primitive village in

*the Near East. We could not compare it [an Arab village] to a Polish, or
an Austrian one. The Arab village, unlike the European ones, was built
topographically on hills. That meant we had to find out how best to
approach the village from above or enter it from below. We had to train
our "Arabists" [the Orientalists who operated a network of
collaborators] how best to work with informants.[12]*

A large network of informants had been established to gain
intelligence on the Palestinian villages throughout the Mandate. The
intelligence which was provided allowed for even more details into the
village files, especially after 1943, as the expanded information
included: "detailed descriptions of the husbandry, cultivation, the
number of trees in plantations, the quality of each fruit grove (even of
individual trees!), the average land holding per family, the number of
cars, the names of shop owners, members of work shops, and the
names of the artisans and their skills." As time passed, and the village
files collected more information, political affiliations were added in
regards to individuals within the villages, and in 1945, information
regarding village mosques, the names of the imams and even accounts
of the inside of particular homes. As the end of the Mandate grew close,
the village files increasingly provided information of a more militaristic
nature: "the number of guards in each village (most had none) and the
quantity and quality of arms at the villagers' disposal (generally
antiquated or even nonexistent)." In 1944, a small village was home to
the training of informants and spies and from which they would conduct
reconnaissance missions. The final report for the village files was in
1947, focusing on forming lists of "wanted" individuals. As Ilan Pappé
explained:

*In 1948, Jewish troops used these lists for the search-and-arrest
operations they carried out as soon as they had occupied a village. That
is, the men in the village would be lined up and those whose names
appeared on the lists would be identified, often by the same person who
had informed on them in the first place, but now wearing a cloth sack
over his head with two holes cut out for his eyes so as not to be
recognized. The men who were picked out were often shot on the spot...
Among the criteria for inclusion in these lists, besides having
participated in actions against the British and the Zionists, were
involvement in the Palestinian national movement (which could apply to
entire villages) and having close ties to the leader of the movement, the*

Mufti Haj Amin al-Husayni, or being affiliated with his political party. Given the Mufti's dominance of Palestinian politics since the establishment of the Mandate in 1923, and the prominent positions held by members of his party in the Arab Higher Committee that became the embryo government of the Palestinians, this offense too was very common.[13]

Villages of roughly 1,500 people had about 20-30 individual "suspects" within them. In November of 1947, the Zionist military command concluded that, "the Palestine Arabs had nobody to organize them properly," and that, "If not for the British, we could have quelled the Arab riot [the opposition to the UN Partition Resolution in 1947] in one month." The Arabs, while constituting a demographic challenge to the Zionist aspirations for Palestine, were not a military threat. Their military structures and leadership were largely destroyed by the British during the Arab Revolt and the Zionists were also aware that the Arab states were disorganized and hesitant to move forward on the Palestine issue. Thus, it was the British that primarily stood in the way of the Zionist plans for Palestine, and with 100,000 troops stationed in the an area with roughly 2 million people, it was no small force to contend with. Thus, the Zionist leadership, and specifically David Ben-Gurion, began advocating to support the Partition in the hopes of establishing a small Jewish state in order to have a base from which to expand. In 1946, Ben-Gurion told a gathering of the Zionist leadership that they could accept a smaller state, but that, "We will demand a large chunk of Palestine." Within a few months, the Jewish Agency created a map of a partitioned Palestine. The UN produced a partition map with less land allotted for the Jewish state. After the 1948-49 war, however, the new Jewish state had - through ethnic cleansing - established itself along the lines set out for it in the Jewish Agency map: all of Palestine, save the West Bank and Gaza.[14]

It was in this context that Plan C was evolved from Plans A and B. The British could not repress the eventual Jewish uprising in Palestine after World War II as they had the Arab Revolt prior to the war, and it was clear to the Zionist leadership that the British were on the way out, in no small part due to pressure from Zionist terrorism. In 1946, Plan C was finalized to prepare the Jewish military structures for their offense against the Palestinian population, including striking against political leadership, anti-Zionist Arabs, senior Arab officials, transportation routes, economic infrastructure, etc. Plan C added upon the village files information regarding leaders and activists within the Arab population and other "potential human targets." Within a few months, the addition of "operational specifics" became the basis for Plan D, which envisioned a Jewish State composed of 78% of the land of Palestine, as set out in the Jewish Agency map. As for the one million Palestinians within those lands, Plan D was very specific:

These operations can be carried out in the following manner: either by destroying villages (by setting fire to them, by blowing them up, and by planting mines in their rubble), and especially those population centers that are difficult to control permanently; or by mounting combing and control operations according to the following guidelines: encirclement of the villages, conducting a search inside them. In case of resistance, the armed forces must be wiped out and the population expelled outside the borders of the state.[15]

As Ghazi Falah wrote in the journal, *Annals of the Association of American Geographers*, Plan D's "underlying objective was the nationwide conquest and control of territories." Among the tactical objectives of Zionist forces were to occupy "all police fortresses/stations evacuated by British forces, and of Arab villages close to Jewish settlements; creating continuity between Jewish cities and neighbouring Jewish settlements; gaining control of lines of communications; besieging enemy cities; capturing forward bases of the enemy; counter attacks both inside and outside the borders of the State."[16]

In November of 1947 the UN proposed the partition plan into two states, with Jerusalem and Bethlehem as an international zone. The UN partition plan vastly increased the amount of land for the Zionists, as Jewish land amounted to less than 7% of the total of Palestine in 1947, which was increased to 56% in the UN partition plan, leaving 42% for the Palestinians, who prior to partition had over 90% of the land. The Zionists immediately began the ethnic cleansing in December of 1947 prior to the British leaving, and the first Arab army did not invade until May of 1948, when the British left. Thus, under British rule, wrote Falah, "Jewish forces initiated a war of demographic and territorial expansion which took on the dimension of space purification - expulsion and prevention on the return of the expellees." All able-bodies Jews within Palestine were mobilized by the Zionist forces to partake in the operation, with civilian Jews settling in the depopulated Palestinian villages in order to prevent any possible return of refugees. Civilians also imposed economic sanctions, disseminating propaganda, and preventing Palestinians from harvesting their crops. Destruction of Arab crops was a general policy, or to have Jewish settlers move in and harvest existing Arab fields in cleansed towns.[17]

Certain towns were then selected for massacres, usually carried out in small villages which had previously good relations with their Jewish neighbours. These towns were selected with the specific purpose of providing "lessons in toughness" for other Palestinians villages to incite them to leave and not return. Between May 1947 and March 1948, there were 92 cases of Zionist terrorism and massacres against Palestinians, organized by the Haganah in cooperation with the Irgun and Stern Gang. The small villages were chosen to be "victims," to be an example - a terror campaign - to incite fear in the Palestinian population. One such massacre in April of 1948 killed 254 Arab civilians in one village. On top of the massacres, the rape of Arab Palestinian women, whether Christian or Muslim, was also a prominent feature of the more brutal cleansings. When the British left Palestine and the Arab states invaded, they prevented the Zionist forces from occupying the West Bank and the Gaza Strip.[18]

All in all, some 400 Palestinian villages were cleansed, forcing roughly 750,000 Palestinians to flee, leaving roughly 100,000 Palestinians within the newly conquered Jewish territories, who remained under a virtual state of martial law and concentrated in small pales within Israel, the state which was declared by the Zionists in May of 1948. Massive Jewish immigration commenced for survivors of the Holocaust as well as Jews from Arab nations and the Soviet Union.[19]

The men who carried out the ethnic cleansing of Palestine became the mythical heroes of the founding of the state of Israel, most notably David Ben-Gurion, and the future leaders of the Israeli army, Yigael Yadin and Moshe Dayan, along with prominent Arabist academics, who, much like the intellectuals of the Nazi state, were among the most systematically malevolent, responsible for the final decisions regarding which villages were to be eradicated and which villagers were to be executed. The operations of the Arabists - Orientalist intellectuals - "were supervised by Issar Harel, who later became the first head of Mossad and the Shin bet, Israel's secret services."[20] The ruthless murders, assassinations, and massacres - even of women and children - were not a mere 'result' of the war, as many historians have claimed, but were a matter of policy. As Ezra Dannin, the Israeli government adviser on Arab affairs stated that, "If the High Command believes that by destruction, killing, and human suffering its aims will be achieved faster, then I would not stand in its way. If we don't hurry up, our enemies will do the same things to us."[21]

Notes

[1] Jerome Slater, "What Went Wrong? The Collapse of the Israeli-Palestinian Peace Process,"*Political Science Quarterly* (Vol. 116, No. 2, 2001), pages 173-174.

[2] Ilan Pappé, "The 1948 Ethnic Cleansing of Palestine," *Journal of Palestine Studies* (Vol. 36, No. 1, Autumn 2006), page 9.

[3] Jerome Slater, "What Went Wrong? The Collapse of the Israeli-Palestinian Peace Process,"*Political Science Quarterly* (Vol. 116, No. 2, 2001), page 174.

[4] Graham Usher, "Unmaking Palestine: On Israel, the Palestinians, and the Wall," *Journal of Palestine Studies* (Vol. 35, No. 1, Autumn 2005), page 26.

[5] Ilan Pappé, "The 1948 Ethnic Cleansing of Palestine," *Journal of Palestine Studies* (Vol. 36, No. 1, Autumn 2006), pages 9-10.

[6] Ibid, pages 10-11.

[7] Ibid, page 11.

[8] Calder Walton, "British Intelligence and the Mandate of Palestine: Threats to British National Security Immediately After the Second World War," *Intelligence and National Security* (Vol. 23, No. 4, 2008), pages 435-436.

[9] Ibid, pages 439-440.

[10] Steven Wagner, "British Intelligence and the Jewish Resistance Movement in the Palestine Mandate," *Intelligence and National Security* (Vol. 23, No. 5, 2008), pages 629-630.

[11] Ibid, pages 630-631.

[12] Ilan Pappé, "The 1948 Ethnic Cleansing of Palestine," *Journal of Palestine Studies* (Vol. 36, No. 1, Autumn 2006), pages 11-12.

[13] Ibid, pages 12-13.

[14] Ibid, pages 13-15.

[15] Ibid, pages 15-16.

[16] Ghazi Falah, "The 1948 Israeli-Palestinian War and its Aftermath: The Transformation and Se-Signification of Palestine's Cultural Landscape," *Annals of the American Association of American Geographers* (Vol. 86, No. 2, 1996), page 259.

[17] Ibid, page 261.

[18] Ibid, page 262.

[19] Graham Usher, "Unmaking Palestine: On Israel, the Palestinians, and the Wall," *Journal of Palestine Studies* (Vol. 35, No. 1, Autumn 2005), page 27.

[20] Ilan Pappé, "The 1948 Ethnic Cleansing of Palestine," *Journal of Palestine Studies* (Vol. 36, No. 1, Autumn 2006), pages 18-19.

[21] Jerome Slater, "What Went Wrong? The Collapse of the Israeli-Palestinian Peace Process,"*Political Science Quarterly* (Vol. 116, No. 2, 2001), page 175.

Indigenous Rights
DEPARTMENT

An Anarchistic Understanding of the Social Order

Environmental Degradation, Indigenous Resistance, and a Place for the Sciences

Andrew Gavin Marshall

This article was originally written for the Spanda Foundation's Journal, Vol. IV, 1, 2013, entitled, "Anarchy and Non-Profit: An Emerging Affair." It may be accessed for free at http://www.spanda.org/publications.html. A full bibliography may also be viewed there.

For roughly five hundred years, indigenous peoples have been struggling against the dominant institutions of society, against imperialism, colonialism, exploitation, impoverishment, segregation, racism, and genocide. The struggle continues today under the present world social order and against the dominant institutions of 'neoliberalism' and globalization: the state, corporations, financial institutions and international organizations. Indigenous communities continue to struggle to preserve their cultural identities, languages, histories, and the continuing theft and exploitation of their land. Indigenous resistance against environmental degradation and resource extraction represents the most direct source of resistance against a global environmental crisis which threatens to lead the species to extinction. It is here that many in the scientific community have also taken up the cause of resistance against the destruction of the global environment. While Indigenous and scientific activism share similar objectives in relation to environmental issues, there is a serious lack of convergence between the two groups in terms of sharing knowledge, organization, and activism.

Indigenous groups are often on the front lines of the global environmental crisis - at the point of interaction (or extraction) - they resist against the immediate process of resource extraction and the environmental devastation it causes to their communities and society as a whole. The continued repression, exploitation and discrimination against Indigenous peoples have made the struggle - and the potential consequences of failure - significantly more problematic. This struggle has been ongoing for centuries, and as the species heads toward extinction - as it is along our current trajectory - Indigenous peoples will be on the front lines of that process. Many in the scientific community have been struggling for decades to address major environmental issues. Here, the focus is largely on the issue of climate change, and the approach has largely been to work through institutions in order to create enough pressure to reform. Yet, after decades of organizing through academic and environmental organizations, lobbying governments, corporations and international organizations, progress has been slow and often ineffectual, with major international conferences being hyped up but with little concrete results. Indigenous peoples continue to struggle against the dominant institutions while many in the scientific community continue to struggle within the dominant institutions, though their objectives remain similar.

A major problem and disparity becomes clear: Indigenous peoples - among the most repressed and exploited in the world - are left to struggle directly against the most powerful institutions in the world (states and transnational corporations), while many in the sciences - an area of knowledge which has and continues to hold enormous potential to advance the species - attempt to convince those powerful institutions to profit less at exactly the point in history when they have never profited more. Indigenous communities remain largely impoverished, and the scientific community remains largely dependent for funding upon the very institutions which are destroying the environment: states, corporations and international organizations. Major barriers to scientific inquiry and research can thus be established if the institutions feel threatened, if they choose to steer the sciences into areas exclusively designed to produce 'profitable' forms of knowledge and technology. As humanity enters a critical stage - perhaps the most critical we have ever faced as a species - it is important to begin to acknowledge, question, and change the institutional contradictions and constraints of our society.

It seems only logical that a convergence between Indigenous and scientific activism, organization, and the sharing of knowledge should be encouraged and facilitated. Indeed, the future of the species may depend upon it. This paper aims to encourage such a convergence by applying an anarchistic analysis of the social order as it relates to environmental degradation, specifically at the point of interaction with the environment (the source of extraction). In classifying this as an anarchistic analysis, I simply mean that it employs a highly critical perspective of hierarchically organized institutions. This paper does not intend to discuss in any detail the issue of climate change, since that issue is largely a symptom of the problem, which at its source is how the human social order interacts directly with the environment: extraction, pollution, degradation, exploitation and destruction at the point of interaction.

This analysis will seek to critically assess the actions and functions of states, corporations, international organizations, financial institutions, trade agreements and markets in how they affect the environment, primarily at the point of interaction. It is also at this point where Indigenous peoples are taking up the struggle against environmental degradation and human extinction. Through an anarchistic analysis of Indigenous repression and resistance at the point of interaction between the modern social order and the environment (focusing primarily on examples from Canada), this paper hopes to provide encouragement to those in the scientific community seeking to address environmental issues to increase their efforts in working with and for the direct benefit of Indigenous peoples. There exists a historical injustice which can and must be rectified: the most oppressed and exploited peoples over the past five hundred years of a Western-dominated world are on the front lines of struggling for the survival of the species as a whole. Modern science - which has done so much to advance Western 'civilization' - can and should make Indigenous issues a priority, not only for their sake, but for the species as a whole. Indeed, it is a matter of survival for the sciences themselves, for they will perish with the species. An anarchistic analysis of the social order hopes to encourage a convergence between Indigenous and scientific knowledge and activism as it relates to resolving the global environmental crisis we now face.

Global Corporate Power

Corporations are among the most powerful institutions in the world. Of the top 150 economies in 2010, 58% were corporations, with companies like Wal-Mart, Royal Dutch Shell, ExxonMobil, and BP topping the charts[1]. According to Fortune's Global 500 list published in 2012, the top ten corporations in the world were: Royal Dutch Shell, ExxonMobil, Wal-Mart, BP, Sinopec Group, China National Petroleum, State Grid, Chevron, ConocoPhillips, and Toyota Motor[2]. The Global 500 corporations posted record revenues for 2011 at USD 29.5 trillion, up 13.2% from the previous year. Eight of the top ten conglomerates were in the energy sector, with the oil industry alone generating USD 5 trillion in sales, approximately 17% of the total sales of the Global 500. The second largest sector represented in the Global 500 was commercial banks, followed by the auto industry[3].

A scientific study conducted by the Swiss Federal Institute of Technology in Zurich analyzed the 'network of control' wielded through 43,000 transnational corporations (TNCs), identifying "a relatively small group of companies, mainly banks, with disproportionate power over the global economy." The researchers identified a 'core' of 1,318 companies which owned roughly 80% of the global revenues for the entire network of 43,000 TNCs. Above the core, the researchers identified a 'super-entity' of 147 tightly-knit corporations - primarily banks and financial institutions - collectively owning each other's shares and 40% of the wealth in the total network. One researcher commented, "In effect, less than 1 per cent of the companies were able to control 40 percent of the entire network[4]."

Writing in the Financial Times, a former US Treasury Department official, Robert Altman, referred to financial markets as "a global supra-government," explaining:

They oust entrenched regimes where normal political processes could not do so. They force austerity, banking bail-outs and other major policy changes. Their influence dwarfs multilateral institutions such as the International Monetary Fund. Indeed, leaving aside unusable nuclear weapons, they have become the most powerful force on earth[5].

The "global supra-government" of financial markets push countries around the world into imposing austerity measures and structural reforms, which have the result of benefiting the "super-entity" of global corporate power. The power and wealth of these institutions have rapidly accelerated in the past three decades of neoliberal 'reforms' promoting austerity, liberalization, deregulation, privatization and financialization. Neoliberal ideology was politically championed by Ronald Reagan in the United States and Margaret Thatcher in Great Britain, but was largely imposed upon the so-called 'Third World' (Latin America, Asia, and Africa) through major international organizations like the World Bank and the IMF. The results of this massive transfer of wealth and power to an increasingly connected and small fraction of the world's population have been devastating for humanity and the world as a whole. This process guided by neoliberal dogma has been most often referred to as 'globalization.'

As the 1980s debt crisis gripped the 'Third World,' the IMF and World Bank came to the 'rescue' with newly designed loan agreements called 'Structural Adjustment Programs' (SAPs). In return for a loan from these institutions, countries would have to adhere to a set of rigid conditions and reforms, including austerity measures (cutting public spending), the liberalization of trade, privatization, deregulation, and currency devaluation[6]. The United States controls the majority shares of both the World Bank and IMF, while the US Treasury Department and Federal Reserve work very closely with the IMF and its staff[7]. If countries did not adhere to IMF and World Bank 'conditions,' they would be cut off from international markets, since this process was facilitated by "unprecedented co-operation between banks from various countries under the aegis of the IMF[8]." The conditions essentially opened up the borrowing countries to economic imperialism by the IMF, World Bank, and transnational corporations and financial institutions, which were able to gain access and control over the resources and labour markets of poor countries. Thus, the 1980s has been known as the "lost decade of development," as many 'Third World' countries became poorer between 1980 and 1990[9]. Joseph Stiglitz, a former chief economist at the World Bank, wrote that, "such conditions were seen as the intrusion by the new colonial power on the country's own sovereignty[10]."

The structural adjustment programs imposed upon the Third World devastated the poor and middle classes of the borrowing countries, often resulting in mass protests against austerity[11]. In fact, between 1976 and 1992, there were 146 protests against IMF- sponsored austerity measures in 39 different countries, including demonstrations, strikes and riots. The governments, in response, would often violently repress protests[12]. The government elites were often more integrated with and allied to the powerful institutions of the global economy, and would often act as domestic enforcers for the demands of international banks and corporations. For many countries imposing structural adjustment programs around the world, authoritarian governments were common[13]. The IMF and World Bank structural adjustment programs also led to the massive growth of slums around the world, to the point where there are now over a billion people living in urban slums (approximately one out of every seven people on earth)[14]. Further, the nations of the Third World became increasingly indebted to the powerful financial institutions and states of the industrial world with the more loans they took. The wealthy elites within the Third World plunder the domestic wealth of their countries in cooperation with global elites, and send their money into Western banking institutions (as 'capital flight') as their domestic populations suffer in poverty. The IMF and World Bank programs helped facilitate capital flight through the deregulation and 'liberalization' of markets, as well as through the opening up of the economies to unhindered exploitation. Some researchers recently compared the amount of money in the form of aid and loans going into Africa compared to that coming leaving Africa in the form of capital flight, and found that "sub-Saharan Africa is a net creditor to the rest of the world by a substantial margin." The external debt owed by 33 sub-Saharan African countries to the rest of the world in 2008 stood at USD 177 billion. Between 1970 and 2008, capital flight from those same 33 African countries amounted to USD 944 billion. Thus, "the rest of the world owes more to these African countries than they owe to the rest of the world[15]."

The neoliberal ideology of 'profit before people' - enforced by the dominant states, corporations, banks and international organizations - has led to a world of extreme inequality, previously established by centuries of empire and colonialism, and rapidly accelerated in the past three decades. As of 2004, one in every three human deaths was due to poverty-related causes. In the twenty years following the end of the Cold War, there were approximately 360 million preventable deaths caused by poverty-related issues. Billions of people go hungry, lack access to safe drinking water, adequate shelter, medicine, and electricity. Nearly half of humanity - approximately 3.1 billion people as of 2010 - live below the USD 2.50/day poverty line. It would take roughly USD 500 billion - approximately 1.13% of world income (or two-thirds of the US military budget) - to lift these 3.1 billion people out of extreme poverty. The top 1% own 40% of the world's wealth, while the bottom 60% hold less than 2% of the world's wealth. As Thomas Pogge wrote, "we are now at the point where the world is easily rich enough in aggregate to abolish all poverty," but we are "choosing to prioritize other ends instead." Roughly 18 million people die from poverty-related causes every year, half of whom are children under the age of five. Pogge places significant blame for these circumstances upon the "global institutional arrangements that foreseeably and avoidably increase the socioeconomic inequalities that cause poverty to persist [...] [policies which] are designed by the more powerful governments for the benefit of their most powerful industries, corporations, and citizens[16]."

In 2013, Oxfam reported that the fortunes made by the richest 100 people in the world over the course of 2012 (USD 240 billion) would have been enough to lift the world's poorest people out of poverty four times over. An Oxfam executive, Barbara Stocking, noted that this type of extreme wealth - which saw the world's richest 1% increase their income by 60% in the previous twenty years - is "economically inefficient, politically corrosive, socially divisive and environmentally destructive [...] We can no longer pretend that the creation of wealth for few will inevitably benefit the many - too often the reverse is true[17]." A study by the Tax Justice Network in 2012 found that the world's superrich had hidden between USD 21 and 32 trillion in offshore tax havens, meaning that inequality was "much, much worse than official statistic show," and that "for three decades extraordinary wealth has been cascading into the offshore accounts of a tiny number of superrich," with the top 92,000 of the world's superrich holding at least USD 10 trillion in offshore accounts[18].

The Environmental Impact of Inequality

The human social order - dominated by states, corporations, banks and international organizations - has facilitated and maintained enormous inequality and poverty around the world, allowing so few to control so much, while the many are left with little. This global social and economic crisis is exacerbated by the global environmental crisis, in which the same institutions that dominate the global social order are simultaneously devastating the global environment to the point where the future of the species hangs in the balance.

Just as the dominant institutions put 'profit before people,' so too do they put profit before the environment, predicating human social interaction with the environment on the ideology of 'markets': that what is good for corporations will ultimately be good for the environment. Thus, the pursuit of 'economic growth' can continue unhindered - and in fact, should be accelerated - even though it results in massive environmental degradation through the processes of resource extraction, transportation, production and consumption[19]. Trading arrangements between the powerful rich nations and the 'periphery' poor nations allow for the dominant institutions to exploit their economic and political influence over weaker states, taking much more than they give[20]. These trading relationships effectively allow the rich countries to offshore (or export) their environmental degradation to poor countries, treating them as exploitable resource extraction sources. As the resources of poor nations are extracted and exported to the rich nations, the countries are kept in poverty (with the exception of their elites who collude with the powerful countries and corporations), and the environmental costs associated with the high consumption societies of the industrial world are ultimately off-shored to the poor countries, at the point of interaction[21]. Thus, international trade separates the societies of consumption from the effects of extraction and production, while the poor nations are dependent upon exports and exploiting their cheap labour forces[22]. This process has been termed ecological unequal exchange[23].

Between the mid-1970s and mid-1990s, the majority of the world's non-renewable resources were transferred from poor to rich nations, accelerating in volume over time (due to technological advancements), while decreasing in costs (to the powerful nations). Thus, between 1980 and 2002, the costs of resource extraction declined by 25% while the volume of resource extraction increased by more than 30%. Environmentally destructive processes of resource extraction in mining and energy sectors have rapidly accelerated over the past few decades, resulting in increased contamination of soils, watersheds and the atmosphere. Negative health effects for local populations accelerate, primarily affecting Indigenous, poor and/or migrant populations, who are subjected to excessive pollutants and industrial waste at nearly every part of the process of extraction, production and transportation of resources and goods[24].

In an examination of 65 countries between 1960 and 2003, researchers found that the rich countries "externalized" the environmentally destructive consequences of resource over-use to poor, periphery nations and populations, thus "assimilating" the environments of the less-developed nations into the economies of the powerful states, disempowering local populations from having a say in how their resources and environments are treated[25]. Rich societies consume more than can be sustained from their own internal resource wealth, and thus, they must "appropriate" resource wealth from abroad by 'withdrawing' the resources in environmentally destructive (and thus, more economically 'efficient') ways. Apart from ecologically destructive 'withdrawals,' the rich nations also facilitate ecologically destructive 'additions,' in the form of pollution and waste which cause environmental and health hazards for the poor societies. This is facilitated through various trading arrangements (such as the development of Export Processing Zones), consisting of minimal to no environmental regulations, cheap labour and minimal restrictions on corporate activities[26].

While Japan and Western Europe were able to reduce the amount of pollutants and 'environmental additions' they made within their own societies between 1976 and 1994, they accelerated their 'additions' in waste and pollutants to the poor countries with which they traded, "suggesting a progressive off-shoring over the period onto those peripheral countries" not only of labour exploitation, but of environmental degradation[27]. Foreign Direct Investment (FDI) by transnational corporations has been linked to extensive environmental hazards within the countries in which they are 'investing,' including growth in water pollution, infant mortality, pesticide use, and the use of chemicals which are often banned in the rich nations due to high toxicity levels and dangers to health and the environment, and greater levels of carbon dioxide emissions. Indeed, between 1980 and 2000, the total anthropogenic CO_2 emissions from the rich countries increased by 21%, while over the same period of time in the poor countries it more than doubled. While forested areas in the rich nations increased by less than 1% between 1990 and 2005, they declined by 6% over the same period of time in poor countries, contributing to soil erosion, desertification, climate change and the destruction of local and regional ecosystems[28].

According to an analysis of 268 case studies of tropical forest change between 1970 and 2000, researchers found that deforestation had shifted from being directed by states to being directed and implemented by corporations and 'economic' interests across much of Latin America, Africa, and Asia. This was largely facilitated by the IMF and World Bank agreements which forced countries to reduce their public spending, and allowed for private economic interests to obtain unprecedented access to resources and markets. The rate of deforestation continued, it simply shifted from being state-led to "enterprise driven[29]."

Using a sample of some sixty nations, researchers found that IMF and World Bank Structural Adjustment Programs (SAPs) were associated with higher levels of deforestation than in countries which did not sign the SAP agreements, as they allowed rich nations and corporations to "externalize their forest loss" to poor nations. Further, "economic growth" as defined by the World Bank and IMF was related to increased levels of deforestation, leading the researchers to acknowledge that, "economic growth adversely impacts the natural environment[30]." World Bank development loans to countries (as separate from structural adjustment loans) have also been linked to increased rates of deforestation in poor nations, notably higher rates than those which exist in countries not receiving World Bank loans[31].

Military institutions and armed warfare also have significant environmental impacts, not simply by engaging in wars, but simply by the energy and resources required for the maintenance of large military structures. As one US military official stated in the early 1990s, "We are in the business of protecting the nation, not the environment[32]." While the United States is the largest consumer of energy among nations in the world, the Pentagon is "the world's largest [institutional] consumer of energy[33]." The combination of US tanks, planes and ships consume roughly 340,000 barrels of oil per day (as of 2007)[34]. Most of the oil is consumed by the Air Force, as jet fuel accounted for roughly 71% of the entire military's oil consumption[35].

Nations with large militaries also use their violent capabilities "to gain disproportionate access to natural resources[36]." Thus, while the US military may be the largest single purchaser and consumer of energy in the world, one of its primary functions is to secure access to and control over energy resources. In an interview with two McKinsey & Company consultants, the Pentagon's first-ever assistant secretary of defense for operational energy and programs, Sharon E. Burke, stated bluntly that, "My role is to promote the energy security of our military operations," including by increasing the "security of supply[37]."

In a study of natural resource extraction and armed violence, researchers found that, "armed violence is associated with the extraction of many critical and noncritical natural resources, suggesting quite strongly that the natural resource base upon which industrial societies stand is constructed in large part through the use and threatened use of armed violence." Further, when such armed violence is used in relation to gaining access to and control over natural resources, "it is often employed in response to popular protest or rebellion against these activities." Most of this violence is carried out by the governments of poor nations, or by mercenaries or rebels, which allows for distancing between the rich nations and corporations which profit from the plundering of resources from the violent means of gaining access to them. After all, the researcher noted, "other key drivers of natural resource exploitation, such as the IMF, World Bank, WTO, and global marketplace, cannot, on their own, guarantee core nation access to and control over vital natural resources[38]." Perhaps unsurprisingly, then, the United States - and other powerful nations - and the major arms companies within them are the largest arms dealers in the world[39].

It is clear that for scientists - and anyone else - interested in addressing major environmental issues, the source of the problem lies in the very structure and function of our dominant modern institutions, at the point of interaction. In short: through states, armed violence, banks and corporations, international organizations, trade agreements and global 'markets,' the environment has become a primary target of exploitation and destruction. Resources fuel the wealth and power of the very institutions that dominate the world, and to maintain that power, they engage in incredibly destructive activities with negative consequences for the environment and the human species as a whole. The global environmental crisis is intimately related to the global social and economic crises of wealth inequality and poverty, labour exploitation, and 'economic growth.' To address the environmental crisis in a meaningful way, this reality must first be acknowledged. This is how an anarchistic understanding of the environmental crisis facing the world and humanity can contribute to advancing how we deal with these profound issues. For the sciences, the implications are grave: their sources of funding and direction for research are dependent upon the very institutions which are destroying the environment and leading humanity to inevitable extinction (if we do not change course). Advancing an anarchistic approach to understanding issues related to Indigenous repression and resistance to environmental degradation can help provide a framework through which those in the scientific community - and elsewhere - can find new avenues for achieving similar goals: the preservation of the environment and the species.

Indigenous Repression and Resistance

Indigenous peoples in the Americas have been struggling against colonialism, exploitation, segregation, repression and even genocide for over 500 years. While the age of formal colonial empires has passed, the struggle has not. Today, Indigenous peoples struggle against far more powerful states than ever before existed, transnational corporations and financial institutions, international organizations, so-called "free trade" agreements and the global 'marketplace.' In an increasingly interconnected and globalized world, the struggle for Indigenous peoples to maintain their identity and indeed, even their existence itself, has been increasingly globalizing, but has also been driven by localized actions and movements.

Focusing upon Indigenous peoples in Canada, I hope to briefly analyze how Indigenous groups are repressed, segregated and exploited by the dominant institutions of an incredibly wealthy, developed, resource-rich and 'democratic' nation with a comparably 'good' international reputation. Further, by examining Indigenous resistance within Canada to the destruction of the natural environment, I hope to encourage scientists and other activists and segments of society who are interested in environmental protection to reach out to Indigenous communities, to share knowledge, organizing, activism, and objectives.

A Legacy of Colonialism

Historically, the Canadian government pursued a policy of 'assimilation' of Indigenous peoples for over a century through 'Indian residential schools,' in what ultimately amounted to an effective policy of "cultural genocide." In 1920, Canada's Deputy Minister of Indian Affairs Duncan Campbell Scott bluntly explained: "I want to get rid of the Indian problem [...] Our object is to continue until there is not a single Indian in Canada that has not been absorbed into the body politics and there is no Indian question, and no Indian Department[40]." The segregation, repression and exploitation of Indigenous communities within Canada is not a mere historical reality, it continues to present day. Part of the institutional repression of Indigenous peoples is the prevalence of what could be described as 'Third World' conditions within a 'First World' nation. Indigenous communities within Canada lack access to safe drinking water at a much higher rate than the general population[41]. Indigenous people and communities in Canada also face much higher levels of food insecurity, poverty, unemployment, poor housing and infant mortality than the rest of the population[42]. Accounting for roughly 4% of the population of Canada (approximately 1.2 million people as of 2006), Indigenous peoples also face higher rates of substance abuse, addiction, and suicide[43].

Indigenous people - and especially women - make up a disproportionate percentage of the prison population[44]. Further, as Amnesty International noted, "Indigenous women [in Canada] are five to seven times more likely than other women to die as a result of violence[45]." The Native Women's Association of Canada has documented roughly 600 cases of missing or murdered indigenous women in Canada, more than half of which have occurred since 2000, while Human Rights Watch reported that the Royal Canadian Mounted Police (RCMP) in northern British Columbia had "failed to properly investigate the disappearance and apparent murders of [indigenous] women and girls in their jurisdiction[46]."

Resource Extraction, Environmental Degradation, and Indigenous Peoples

Industries seeking to develop land and extract resources are increasingly turning to Indigenous territories to develop and seek profits on the land and environment upon which such communities are so often dependent for survival. At the point of interaction with the environment, Indigenous peoples are left to struggle with the damaging environmental and health consequences caused by state and corporate interests extracting resources and wealth from the land and environment.

The Alberta tar sands (or oil sands) is a primary example of this process. Many environmental, indigenous and human rights organizations consider the tar sands development as perhaps "the most destructive industrial project on earth." The United Nations Environmental Programme identified the project as "one of the world's top 100 hotspots of environmental degradation." The dense oil in the tar sands (diluted bitumen) has to be extracted through strip mining, and requires enormous amounts of resources and energy simply to extract the reserves. It has been documented that for every one barrel of oil processed, three barrels of water are used, resulting in the creation of small lakes (called 'tailing ponds'), where "over 480 million gallons of contaminated toxic waste water are dumped daily." These lakes collectively "cover more than 50 square kilometres (12,000 acres) and are so extensive that they can be seen from space." The processing of the oil sands creates 37% more greenhouse gas emissions than the extraction and processing of conventional oil[47].

While the United States consumes more oil than anywhere else on earth, Canada is the main supplier of foreign oil to the United States, exporting roughly 1.5 million barrels per day to the US (in 2005), approximately 7% of the daily consumption of oil in the US. The crude bitumen contained in the tar sands has been estimated at 1.7 trillion barrels, lying underneath an area within Alberta which is larger than the entire state of Florida and contains over 140,000 square km of boreal forest. In 2003, the United States Department of Energy officially acknowledged the reserves of crude bitumen in the Alberta tar sands, and elevated Canada's standing in world oil markets from the 21st most oil-rich nation on earth to the 2nd, with only Saudi Arabia surpassing[48].

Alberta's tar sands have attracted the largest oil companies on earth, including Royal Dutch Shell, ExxonMobil, BP, and Total S.A. Local indigenous communities thus not only have to struggle against the devastating environmental, health and social consequences caused by the tar sands development, but they also have to struggle against the federal and provincial governments, and the largest corporations on earth. The Athabasca River (located near the tar sands development) has been depleted and polluted to significant degrees, transforming the region "from a pristine environment rich in cultural and biological diversity to a landscape resembling a war zone marked with 200-foot-deep pits and thousands of acres of destroyed boreal forests." Indigenous peoples have been raising concerns over this project for years[49].

Disproportionate levels of cancers and other deadly diseases have been discovered among a local Indigenous band, the Fort Chipewyan in Athabasca. These high levels of cancers and diseases are largely the result of the enormous amounts of land, air, and water pollution caused by the tar sands mining[50]. One Indigenous leader in Fort Chipewyan has referred to the tar sands development as a "slow industrial genocide[51]." As pipelines are planned to be expanded across Canada and the United States to carry tar sands oil, this will have devastating impacts for "indigenous communities not only in Canada, but across the continent[52]."

Between 2002 and 2010, the pipeline network through Alberta experienced a rate of oil spills roughly sixteen times higher than in the United States, likely the result of transporting diluted bitumen (DilBit), which has not been commonly transported through the pipelines until recent years. In spite of the greater risks associated with transporting DilBit, the US agency responsible for overseeing the country's pipelines decided - in October of 2009 - to relax safety regulations regarding the strength of pipelines. In July of 2010, a ruptured Enbridge pipeline in Michigan spilled 800,000 gallons of DilBit, devastating the local communities in what the government referred to as the "worst oil spill in Midwestern history." In July of 2011, an Exxon pipeline spilled 42,000 gallons of DilBit into the Yellowstone River in Montana[53].

Idle No More: The Rise of Indigenous Resistance

In 2009, the Canadian Ministry of Indian Affairs and Northern Development announced the Federal Framework for Aboriginal Economic Development which sought to "improve the participation" of Indigenous people "in the Canadian economy," primarily by seeking "to unlock the full economic potential of Aboriginal Canadians, their communities, and their businesses[54]." An updated report on the *Framework* in 2012 reaffirmed the intent "to modernize the lands and resource management regimes on reserve land in order to increase and unlock the value of Aboriginal assets[55]." As John Ibbitson wrote in the *Globe and Mail*, "businesses that want to unlock the potential of reserves, from real estate development to forestry and mining, need the legal certainty that a property regime makes possible[56]." In late 2012, Canadian Prime Minister Stephen Harper's Conservative Party introduced an omnibus Budget Bill (C-45) which amended several aspects of the Indian Act (without proper consultations with Indigenous groups). Bill C-45 also moved forward to "unlock" barriers to resource extraction, environmental degradation, and corporate profits with an amendment to the Navigable Waters Act, which dramatically reduced the number of protected lakes and rivers in Canada from 40,000 to 97 lakes, and from 2.5 million to 63 rivers[57].

Following the introduction of Bill C-45 to the Canadian Parliament, a group of four Indigenous women in the province of Saskatchewan held a "teach-in" to help increase awareness about the Bill, quickly followed by a series of rallies, protests and flash mobs where Indigenous activists and supporters engaged in 'round dances' in shopping malls, organized through social media networks like Twitter and Facebook. This sparked what became known as the 'Idle No More' movement, and on December 10, 2012, a National Day of Action took place, holding multiple rallies across the country. The immediate objectives of the Idle No More movement were to have the government "repeal all legislation that violates treaties [with Indigenous peoples], including those that affect environmental regulations," such as Bill C-45 and the previous omnibus Bill C-38. The longer-term objectives of the movement were to "educate and revitalize aboriginal peoples, empower them and regain sovereignty and independence[58]."

Pamela Palmater, a spokesperson for Idle No More and a Ryerson University professor noted that Indigenous people in Canada were opposing Bill C-45 "not just because it impacts their rights, but also because we know that it impacts the future generations of both treaty partners," referring to both Indigenous and non-Indigenous Canadians. "The question," she added, "really should be whether Canadians will rise to protect their children's futures alongside First Nations[59]." Theresa Spence, an Indigenous chief from a northern Ontario community (Attawapiskat) went on a hunger strike for 44 days to support Idle No More and raise awareness about a serious housing crisis in her community. Spence only ended her hunger strike upon being hospitalized and placed on an IV drip[60]. Her community of Attawapiskat had been experiencing a major housing crisis for a number of years, and in 2011, a state of emergency was declared in response to the fact that for over two years, many of the community's 1,800 residents were "living in makeshift tents and shacks without heat, electricity or indoor plumbing." James Anaya, a United Nations human rights expert expressed his "deep concern about the dire social and economic condition" of the Attawapiskat community to the Canadian government, which reflected a situation "akin to third world conditions[61]." The Conservative government of Stephen Harper (which came to power in 2006) blamed the crisis on the internal handling of funds within Attawapiskat, claiming that the government provided CAD 90 million in funding for the community since 2006. However, analysis of the funds revealed that only CAD 5.8 million in funding had gone toward housing over the course of five years. Meanwhile, estimates put the necessary funds to resolve the housing crisis alone at CAD 84 million[62]. The former Minister for Aboriginal Affairs acknowledged that the government had known about the housing crisis for years, saying that it "has been a slow-moving train wreck for a long time[63]."

In 2005, the community of Attawapiskat had signed a contract with the international mining conglomerate De Beers to develop a diamond mine 90 km near their community. The mine officially opened in 2008, projecting a 12-year contribution to the Ontario economy of CAD 6.7 billion[64]. In 2005, De Beers dumped its sewage sludge into the Attawapiskat community's lift station, causing a sewage backup which flooded many homes and exacerbated an already-developing housing crisis, followed by another sewage backup potentially caused by De Beers in 2008[65]. Afterward, the company donated trailers to the community to serve as "short-term emergency shelters," yet they remained in place even four years later[66].

As the Idle No More movement took off in late 2012 and early 2013, members of the Attawapiskat community undertook road blockades leading to the De Beers mine. The company sought a legal injunction against the protesters, and the blockade was ended just as a large number of police were headed to the community to "remove the barricades." After successfully blocking the mine from properly functioning for nearly twenty days, the company announced that it was considering taking legal action against the protesters[67].

The Idle No More mission statement called "on all people to join in a revolution which honors and fulfills Indigenous sovereignty which protects the land and water [...] Colonization continues through attacks to Indigenous rights and damage to the land and water. We must repair these violations, live the spirit and intent of the treaty relationship, work towards justice in action, and protect Mother Earth." The movement's manifesto further declared that, "the state of Canada has become one of the wealthiest countries in the world by using the land and resources. Canadian mining, logging, oil and fishing companies are the most powerful in the world due to land and resources. Some of the poorest First Nations communities (such as Attawapiskat) have mines or other developments on their land but do not get a share of the profit[68]." As Pamela Palmater noted, Idle No More was unique, "because it is purposefully distances from political and corporate influence. There is no elected leader, no paid Executive Director, and no bureaucracy or hierarchy which determines what any person or First Nation can and can't do [...] This movement is inclusive of all our peoples[69]."

The Athabasca Chipewyan Indigenous band which had been struggling for years against the tar sands development were further mobilized with the eruption of Idle No More onto the national scene, including by establishing a blockade on Highway 63 leading to the tar sands development[70]. As Chipewyan chief Allan Adam noted, "The way I look at it, the First Nations people are going to cripple this country if things don't turn out [...] Industry is going to be the target." He also added: "We know for a fact that industry was the one that lobbied government to make this regulatory reform[71]." Indeed, this was no hyperbole.

The State in Service to Corporations

Greenpeace obtained - through access to information laws - a letter sent to the Canadian government's Environment minister and Natural Resources minister dated December of 2011, written by a group called the Energy Framework Initiative (EFI), representing the Canadian Association of Petroleum Producers, the Canadian Energy Pipeline Association, the Canadian Fuels Association, and the Canadian Gas Association. The letter sought "to address regulatory reform for major energy industries in Canada" in order to advance "both economic growth and environmental performance." It specifically referenced six laws that it wanted amended, including the National Energy Board Act, the Canadian Environmental Assessment Act, the Fisheries Act, the Species at Risk Act, Migratory Birds Convention Act, and the Navigable Waters Protection Act. Referring to many of these laws as "outdated," the letter criticized environmental legislation as "almost entirely focused on preventing bad things from happening rather than enabling responsible outcomes[72]."

Less than a month after receiving the letter, the Canadian Natural Resources Minister Joe Oliver lashed out at activists opposing the construction of Enbridge's Northern Gateway pipeline shipping oil from Alberta's tar sands to the B.C. coast for shipment to Asia, stating, "Unfortunately, there are environmental and other radical groups that would seek to block this opportunity to diversify our trade... Their goal is to stop any major project no matter what the cost to Canadian families in lost jobs and economic growth. No forestry. No mining. No oil. No gas. No more hydro-electric dams." Oliver went on, saying that such "radical groups" were threatening "to hijack our regulatory system to achieve their radical ideological agenda," and accused them of using funding from "foreign special interest groups[73]."

Documents from the energy industry revealed that big corporations advised the Harper government not to amend the many environmentally related acts separately, but to employ "a more strategic omnibus legislative approach," which resulted in the two omnibus bills over 2012, Bills C-38 and C-45, which included "hundreds of pages of changes to environmental protection laws [...] weakening rules that protect water and species at risk, introducing new tools to authorize water pollution, as well as restricting public participation in environmental hearings and eliminating thousands of reviews to examine and mitigate environmental impacts of industrial projects[74]." The energy industry got virtually everything it asked for in the two omnibus bills, including - as their letter to the Harper government suggested - reforming "issues associated with Aboriginal consultation[75]."

Documents from Environment Canada showed how the minister informed a group of energy industry representatives that the development of pipelines were "top-of-mind" as the government pursued "the modernization of our regulatory system." When the new legislation passed, the Canadian Environmental Assessment Agency announced that it has cancelled roughly 3,000 environmental assessments, including 250 reviews related to pipeline projects[76]. Other documents showed that at the same time the minister was informing energy corporations that he was serving their interests, he was to inform Indigenous leaders that any "changes to the government's environmental assessment or project approvals regime" were "speculative at this point" and that they would "respect our duties toward Aboriginal peoples[77]."

As the Harper government became the primary lobbyist for the Alberta tar sands, documents showed how the government compiled a list of "allies" and "adversaries" in its public relations campaign, referring to energy companies, Environment Canada and the National Energy Board as "allies," and the media, environmental and Indigenous groups as "adversaries[78]." The Canadian government even ran an "outreach program" where diplomats would attempt to secure support among American journalists for the Keystone XL pipeline project - taking oil from the Alberta tar sands to the Gulf Coast in the United States[79]. As the Canadian government revised its anti-terrorism strategy in early 2012, it listed "eco-extremists" alongside white supremacists as a threat to national security[80]. A review of Canadian security documents from the national police force (RCMP) and the Canadian intelligence agency (CSIS) revealed that the government saw environmental activism such as blockades of roads or buildings as "forms of attack" and "national security threats." Greenpeace was identified as "potentially violent," as it had become "the new normal now for Canada's security agencies to watch the activities of environmental organizations," noted one analyst[81].

Idle No More and Oil Pipelines

The government of Canada acknowledged in early 2013 that it expected - over the following decade - that there would be "a huge boom in Canadian natural resource projects," potentially worth CAD 600 billion, which is foreseen to be taking place "on or near" Indigenous lands. One Indigenous chief in Manitoba warned that the Idle No More movement "can stop Prime Minister Harper's resource development plan and his billion-dollar plan to develop resources on our ancestral territory. We have the warriors that are standing up now, that are willing to go that far[82]."

In an official meeting between the Harper government and the Assembly of First Nations in January of 2013, Indigenous 'leaders' presented a list of demands which included ensuring there was a school in every indigenous community, a public inquiry into the missing and murdered Indigenous women, as well as several other very 'moderate' reforms. For the government, the objectives were much more specific, as internal documents revealed, written in preparation for Harper's meeting with Indigenous leaders. As one briefing memo stated, the government was working towards "removing obstacles to major economic development opportunities[83]."

For the Idle No More movement, which does not consider itself to be 'represented' by the Assembly of First Nations leaders, the objective is largely "to put more obstacles up," as Martin Lukacs wrote in the Guardian. Indigenous peoples, he noted, "are the best and last defense against this fossil fuel scramble," specifically in mobilizing opposition to "the three-fold expansion of one of the world's most carbon-intensive projects, the Alberta tar sands[84]."

In March of 2013, an alliance of Indigenous leaders from across Canada and the United States announced that they were "preparing to fight proposed new pipelines in the courts and through unspecified direct action," specifically referring to the Northern Gateway, Keystone XL and Kinder Morgan pipeline projects. One Indigenous leader at the formation of the alliance warned, "We're going to stop these pipelines one way or another." Another Indigenous leader commented: "We, as a nation, have to wake up [...] We have to wake up to the crazy decision that this government's making to change the world in a negative way[85]."

The territories of the ten allied Indigenous groups "are either in the crude-rich tar sands or on the proposed pipeline routes." One Indigenous leader from northern British Columbia referred to the Canadian government, stating, "They've been stealing from us for the last 200 years [...] now they're going to destroy our land? We're not going to let that happen [...] If we have to go to court, if we have to stand in front of any of their machines that are going to take the oil through, we are going to do that. We're up against a wall here. We have nowhere else to go[86]."

Roughly one week after the Indigenous alliance was formed, an ExxonMobil pipeline carrying Alberta tar sands oil through the United States ruptured in the town of Mayflower, Arkansas, spilling thousands of barrels of oil into residential neighbourhoods and the surrounding environment. Exxon quickly moved in with roughly 600 workers to manage the cleanup and sign checks "to try to win over the townsfolk and seek to limit the fallout[87]." The United States Federal Aviation Administration (FAA) put in place a "no fly zone" over Mayflower, Arkansas, within days following the oil spill. The 'no fly zone' was being overseen by ExxonMobil itself, thus, as Steven Horn commented, "any media or independent observers who want to witness the tar sands spill disaster have to ask Exxon's permission[88]."

Between March 11 and April 9 of 2013 (in a span of roughly thirty days), there were 13 reported oil spills on three separate continents, with more than a million gallons of oil and other toxic chemicals spilled in North and South America alone. The oil spills included an Enbridge pipeline leak in the Northwest Territories in Canada (March 19), a tar sands 'tailing pond' belonging to Suncor leaking into the Athabasca River in Alberta (March 25), a Canadian Pacific Railway train derailment spilling tar sands oil in Minnesota (March 27), the Exxon spill in Mayflower (March 29), oil-based hydraulic fluid spilling into the Grand River from a power plant in Michigan (March 31), a CN Rail train derailment in Ontario (April 3), a drilling leak in Newfoundland (April 3), the Shell pipeline leak in Texas (April 3), a condensate spill at an Exxon refinery in Louisiana (April 4), and a pump station 'error' in Alaska (April 9)[89]. Another spill took place in June on Kinder Morgan's Trans Mountain pipeline in British Columbia, one of the pipeline extensions being opposed by Indigenous groups[90].

Meanwhile, Stephen Harper was in New York in May, speaking to the highly influential US think tank, the Council on Foreign Relations, where he explained that the proposed Keystone XL pipeline "absolutely needs to go ahead," adding that it was "an enormous benefit to the US in terms of long-term energy security[91]." TransCanada, the company aiming to build the Keystone XL pipeline, along with the government of Alberta, hired a team of lobbyists with connections to the Obama administration and Secretary of State John Kerry in particular to pressure the US government to approve the pipeline[92]. In late April, the president of the American Petroleum Institute confidently declared, "When it's all said and done, the president will approve the pipeline[93]." In late May, the CEO of TransCanada said, "I remain extremely confident that we'll get the green light to build this pipeline[94]."

Leaders from 11 different Indigenous bands in the United States "stormed out" of a meeting in May being held with federal government officials in South Dakota in protest against the Keystone XL pipeline. The leaders criticized both the project and the Obama administration, with one leader commenting, "We find ourselves victims of another form of genocide, and it's environmental genocide, and it's caused by extractive industries." Another Indigenous leader who walked out of the meeting warned, "What the State Department, what President Obama needs to hear from us, is that we are going to be taking direct action[95]." TransCanada has even been supplying US police agencies with information about environmental activists and recommendations to pursue charges of "terrorism" against them, noting that the company feared such "potential security concerns" as protests, blockades, court challenges, and even "public meetings[96]."

While Indigenous communities in Canada and elsewhere are among the most repressed and exploited within our society, they are also on the front lines of resistance against environmentally destructive practices undertaken by the most powerful institutions in the world. As such, Indigenous groups are not only standing up for environmental issues, but for the future of the species as a whole. With the rapidly accelerating 'development' of the tar sands, and the increasing environmental danger of huge new pipelines projects, resistance to how our modern society treats the environment is reaching new heights. Indigenous organizing - much of which is done along anarchistic ideas (such as with the Idle No More movement) - is presenting an unprecedented challenge to institutional power structures. Thus, there is an increased need for environmentalists, scientists, and others who are interested in joining forces with Indigenous groups in the struggle against environmental degradation and the potential extinction of the species. In Canada, there is an even greater impetus for scientists to join forces with Indigenous communities, for there is a state-sponsored assault upon environmental sciences that threaten to devastate the scientific community in the very near term.

The Canadian Government's Attack on Environmental Science

Since Stephen Harper's Conservative government came to power in 2006, there has been a steady attack upon the sciences, particularly those related to environmental issues, as the government cut funding for major programs and implemented layoffs. One major facet of this attack has been the 'muzzling' of Canadian scientists at international conferences, discussions with the media, and the publication of research. At one conference hosted in Canada, scientists working for Environment Canada were forced to direct all media inquiries through the public relations department in an effort "to intimidate government scientists[97]." Under new government guidelines, scientists working for the Department of Fisheries and Oceans (DFO) cannot publish material until it is reviewed by the department "for any concerns/impacts to DFO policy." The Canadian Association of University Teachers (CAUT) expressed in a letter to Stephen Harper their "deep dismay and anger at your government's attack on the independence, integrity and academic freedom of scientific researchers[98]." Hundreds of Canadian scientists marched on Parliament Hill in July of 2012 in what they called a "funeral procession" against the government's "systematic attack on science[99]."

One of the world's leading science journals, Nature, published an editorial in March of 2012 calling on the Canadian government to stop muzzling and "set its scientists free[100]." Journalists requesting interviews with Canadian government scientists on issues related to the Arctic or climate change have had to go through public relations officials, provide questions in advance, adhere to "boundaries for what subjects the interview could touch upon," and have a PR staffer "listen in on the interviews[101]."

Dozens of government agencies and programs related to environmental sciences have had their budgets slashed, scientists fired, or were discontinued altogether[102]. The Environmental Law Centre at the University of Victoria lodged a formal complaint with Canada's Federal Information Commissioner about the muzzling of scientists, outlining multiple examples "of taxpayer-funded science being suppressed or limited to prepackaged media lines across six different government departments and agencies." Natural Resources Canada now requires "pre-approval" from the government before any scientists give interviews on topics such as "climate change" or the "oilsands[103]."

The attack upon the sciences is part of the Harper government's 2007 strategy, Mobilizing Science and Technology to Canada's Advantage, which directed "a major shift away from scientific goals to economic and labour-market priorities," aiming to focus on science and research which would be directly useful to industry and for commercial purposes. The Natural Sciences and Engineering Research Council of Canada (NSERC) has been steered by the government "toward industry-related research and away from environmental science." The government's minister of state for science and technology noted that the focus for research was to be on "getting those ideas out to our factory floors, if you will, making the product or process or somehow putting that into the marketplace and creating jobs[104]." Further, the National Research Council (NRC) was "to focus more on practical, commercial science and less on fundamental science" which wouldn't be as beneficial to corporate interests. The minister of state for science and technology, Gary Goodyear, announced it as "an exciting, new journey - a re-direction that will strengthen Canada's research and innovation ecosystem for many years to come." The president of the NRC noted that, "We have shifted the primary focus of our work at NRC from the traditional emphasis of basic research and discovery science in favour of a more targeted approach to research and development[105]."

As Stephen Harper said, "Science powers commerce," but apparently to Harper, that is all it should do, even though many scientists and academics disagree[106]. The implications should be obvious: just as society's interaction with the environment is unsustainable, so too is the dependency of the sciences upon those institutions which are destroying the environment.

Moving Forward

Regardless of one's position in society - as a member of an Indigenous group, an activist group, or within the scientific community - all of human society is facing the threat of extinction, accelerated by our destruction of the environment sourced at the point of interaction (the location of extraction) between the dominant institutions of our world and the natural world itself. Roughly half the world's population lives in extreme poverty, with billions living in hunger, with poor access to safe drinking water, medicine and shelter, monumental disparities in wealth and inequality, the production and maintenance of unprecedented weapons of death and destruction, we are witnessing an exponentially accelerating plundering of resources and destruction of the environment upon which all life on Earth depends. If there has ever been a time in human history to begin asking big questions about the nature of our society and the legitimacy of the institutions and ideologies which dominate it, *this is it.*

An anarchistic understanding of the institutions and ideologies which control the world order reveals a society blinded by apathy as it nears extinction. The institutions which dictate the political, economic and social direction of our world are the very same ones destroying the environment to such an extent that the fate of the species is put at extreme risk. To not only continue - but to accelerate - down this path is no longer an acceptable course of action for humanity. It is time that socially segregated populations begin reaching out and working

227

together, to share knowledge, organizational capacity, and engage in mutual action for shared objectives. With that in mind, it would appear to be beneficial not only for those involved - but for humanity as a whole - if Indigenous peoples and segments of the scientific community pursued the objective of protecting the environment together. Acknowledging this is easy enough, the hard part is figuring out the means and methods of turning that acknowledgement into action. This is again where anarchist principles can become useful, emphasizing the creative capacity of many to contribute new ideas and undertake new initiatives working together as free individuals in collective organizations to achieve shared objectives. This is not an easy task, but it is a necessary one. The very future of humanity may depend upon it.

Confronting Columbus

Revisionism Versus Reality

Colin Jenkins

Regarding the painstaking process of historiography, someone of relative importance once remarked, "History is written by the victors." A statement which echoes Plato's dictum that, "those who tell the stories also hold the power," its modern source is unclear. Still, many do not hesitate to attach these words to Winston Churchill, Britain's renowned Prime Minister during the Second World War. Considering Churchill's own history - born into an aristocratic family; his grandfather the 7th Duke of Marlborough; his father, Lord Randolph Churchill, a wealthy British statesman; his mother, Jennie Jerome, an "American socialite," herself the daughter of a financier, speculator, and mass landowner - and the fact that he made an early living overseeing the mass killing of indigenous Africans and Indians located everywhere from Bombay to Sudan to South Africa, such a statement would hardly come as a surprise. If "victory" is defined in terms of deploying one's immense privilege - whether socioeconomic, "racial," or national - to enslave, oppress, and murder others who lack such privilege in order to maintain that very system for oneself and generations to come, then Winston Churchill was certainly one of history's "victors."

The act of whitewashing history - whether literally through the domination of Eurocentric perspectives, or figuratively through blatant omission and revisionism - is certainly common practice. It is the "victors" main tool in shaping history. Historical revisionism has been defined as "a consciously falsified or distorted interpretation of the past to serve partisan or ideological purposes in the present;" "a collective task in a nation's cultural development, the full significance of which is emerging only now: to redefine a nation's status in a changing world;" or the act "of 'truth-seekers' finding different truths to fit the needed political, social, or ideological context." In the United States of America, such revisionism becomes immediately apparent when one steps into a public school classroom - where histories of indigenous genocide and human enslavement are, at best, minimized; and, at worst, utilized to stroke a false sense of superiority and exceptionalism; and where the perpetrators of these crimes against humanity are magically transformed from conquerors to "explorers," from murderers to "adventurers," and from slave masters to "patriots" and "founding fathers," all in the stroke of a pen or the voice of a lecture.
The act of historical revisionism has deep-seated cultural effects.

Essentially, it creates two worlds:

- The first based in quasi-fiction, informed on selective data and historical accounts from either the actual "victors" or the direct beneficiaries of the perceived "victory;" and one that enjoys unquestioned dominance through manipulation and a process of layered assimilation where commonly accepted "knowledge" is constantly reproduced through academia and seamlessly delivered to its intended audience.

- The second based in reality, informed on factual data and historical accounts from not only the "victors," but also from the supposed "losers;" and one that faces almost certain or near-extinction through numerous acts of manipulation and/or omission which are carried out over a number of years, decades, or even centuries.
Historiography is the proving ground for this ongoing struggle between revisionism and reality. The ruling classes deploy their army of "traditional intellectuals," born and bred of privilege and churned through the most prestigious schools and universities, to protect the dominant ideology through a sophisticated presentation of *revisionism*.

The working classes, struggling to maintain actualities, look upon their own ranks to create a semblance of *reality* as the torchbearers of truth. Hanging in the balance is the direction of society: towards continued polarization, inequities, and dehumanization; or towards a sense of being - something that cannot be realized without truth:

Revisionism gives us *Columbus Day*; a federal holiday "in commemoration of Christopher Columbus's historic 1492 voyage," for which, in 1934, the U.S. Congress "duly requested the President proclaim the second Monday of October of each year as such"

Reality gives us *Indigenous People's Day*; "a holiday celebrated in various localities in the United States, begun as a counter-celebration to Columbus Day, with the "purpose of promoting Native American culture and commemorating the history of Native American peoples."

Revisionism gives us the following announcement from the White House: "When the explorers laid anchor in the Bahamas, they met indigenous peoples who had inhabited the Western hemisphere for millennia. As we reflect on the tragic burdens tribal communities bore in the years that followed, let us commemorate the many contributions they have made to the American experience, and let us continue to strengthen the ties that bind us today."

Reality gives us the words of Columbus himself: "(The natives) are so naive and so free with their possessions that no one who has not witnessed them would believe it. When you ask for something they have, they never say no. To the contrary, they offer to share with anyone."

Revisionism gives us the words of Michael Berliner of the Ayn Rand Institute: (Western civilization) brought "reason, science,self-reliance,individualism, ambition, and productive achievement" to a people who were based in "primitivism, mysticism, and collectivism," and to a land that was "sparsely inhabited, unused, and underdeveloped."

Reality gives us yet another dispatch from Columbus: "I promise this, that if I am supported by our most invincible sovereigns with a little of their help, as much gold can be supplied as they will need, indeed as much of spices, of cotton, of mastic gum, also as much of aloes wood, and as many slaves for the navy as their Majesties will wish to demand."

Revisionism gives us this official statement from the U.S. government: "In the centuries since that fateful October day in 1492, countless pioneering Americans have summoned the same spirit of discovery that drove Christopher Columbus when he cast off from Palos, Spain, to pursue the unknown. Engineers and entrepreneurs, sailors and scientists, explorers of the physical world and chroniclers of the human spirit -- all have worked to broaden our understanding of the time and space we live in and who we are as a people."

Reality gives us Columbus' words: "They (the Arawak Indians) brought us parrots and balls of cotton and spears and many other things, which they exchanged for the glass beads and hawks' bells. They willingly traded everything they owned.... They were well-built, with good bodies and handsome features.... They do not bear arms, and do not know them, for I showed them a sword, they took it by the edge and cut themselves out of ignorance. They have no iron. Their spears are made of cane.... They would make fine servants.... With fifty men we could subjugate them all and make them do whatever we want."

The "whitewashing" of history has an intended purpose -to control information and knowledge, to keep the "huddled masses" ignorant, and to maintain the status quo. The Churchills of the world and their keepers would have it no other way. For if history were reality-based, the immense wealth and power they have enjoyed and continue to enjoy - of which has been accumulated through the stolen resources of indigenous peoples, and multiplied on the backs of the enslaved, the imprisoned, the working classes and the peasantry - would cease to exist. If history were reality-based, the hierarchical systems that keep this illegitimate wealth and power intact, and the government watchdogs that protect these systems, would cease to exist.

On this day, reality begins with recognizing the real consequences of Christopher Columbus' "expeditions," which continued far beyond the hallowed year of 1492. "In 1493, Columbus returned with an invasion force of seventeen ships, appointed at his own request by the Spanish Crown to install himself as 'viceroy and governor of [the Caribbean islands] and the mainland' of America, a position he held until 1500," explains Ward Churchill. "Setting up shop on the large island he called Espa-ola (today Haiti and the Dominican Republic), he promptly instituted policies of slavery (encomiendo) and systematic extermination against the native Taino population." In all, "Columbus' programs reduced Taino numbers from as many as eight million at the outset of his regime to about three million in 1496. Perhaps 100,000 were left by the time of his departure" some seven years later.

As working class women and men, we have an intimate connection with indigenous peoples who were "so free with their possessions" that "they would offer to share with anyone," just as we do with our neighbors. We have a bond with those whose only wish was to be left alone, to live and carry on as they please, to progress their livelihoods, and to care for their families, loved ones and neighbors, just as we do. The conditioned need to possess "worldly goods" at the expense of enslaving and murdering other human beings does not exist for our benefit, and should not be celebrated. Reality *does* and *should*mean something.

Reject revisionism. Embrace reality. We have nothing to lose but our chains.

Notes

James McPherson, Revisionist Historians. Perspectives, 2003. American Historical Association.
Harold D. Lasswell, Propaganda Technique in World War I (1927), MIT Press, pp. xxii-xxvii.
Matthew d'Ancona, History men battle over Britain's future. The Times, May 9, 1994.
Presidential Proclamation, Columbus Day 2012. http://www.whitehouse.gov/the-press-office/2012/10/05/presidential-proclamation-columbus-day-2012 . Accessed on 10/13/13.
"Winston Churchill" . Historylearningsite.co.uk. 30 March 2007. Accessed 10/13/13.
Zinn, Howard. *A People's History of the United States: 1492-present.* New York: HarperCollins, 2003.
http://www.amstudy.hku.hk/columbusletter.html . Accessed 10/13/13.

F. David Peat, Blackfoot Physics: A Journey into the Native American Universe (2005), Weiser, pg. 310.

Medieval Sourcebook: Christopher Columbus: Extracts from Journal, Fordham University archives.http://www.fordham.edu/halsall/source/columbus1.asp. Accessed 10/13/13.
History Not Taught is History Forgot: Columbus' Legacy of Genocide. An excerpt from Ward Churchill's book, Indians Are Us (Common Courage Press, 1994)http://www.mit.edu/~thistle/v9/9.11/1columbus.html. Accessed on 10/13/13.

Labor Issues
DEPARTMENT

On My Free Time, Too?

The Pervasiveness of Corporate Culture

Lige English

Capitalism and democracy are more than strange bedfellows. They are actively antagonistic forms of social organization. The expansion of one necessarily comes at the diminution of the other. This fact is poorly understood in America, where there is a default assumption that the two forms are corequisite. This essay seeks to outline the argument as to how and why this is the case. In consideration of space, this essay will come in multiple installments. The first installment, this post, will discuss briefly the fact and the consequences of capitalism's growing role in every aspect of our personal lives. The second will discuss the same for capitalism's encroachment into our political life. Third, I will briefly discuss why these tendencies are endemic to the system in which we find ourselves.

The commercialization of baking soda provides an interesting example of the expansion of capital into our personal lives. It may seem like a small thing that such products, once purchased in bulk from the local grocer, have become a branded commodity. But this advent is a useful allegory for the trajectory of capital in our lives. And with only a little bit of abstract reasoning, it can be seen that this reality has a far greater impact than a modest yellow and red box would suggest.

The local grocer has become the exception and not the rule. There are many reasons for this, and the phenomenon would make for an interesting study in its own right. Accepted as fact for now, it is a small leap to say the decline of the local grocer is a powerful symbol for the decline of local control of the economy. Groceries are one of those rare things which cut across class, race, gender identity, etc. without exception. We all need to eat, and whether we acquire our food from regional or national corporations, there is one effect that I'd like to highlight with many concomitant results.

Shopping at national brands has the effect of stripping profits away from local communities and sending them to executives and shareholders. This discussion can go on broadly but I will limit it to two points. This sets the stage for local underinvestment. Where profit is stripped from its source, there is little incentive for the profiteers to reinvest in the community. This is especially true with necessary goods like food. Where the local grocer has loyalty to their constituency, the corporation doesn't even have loyalty to its executives' country of origin. Second, the resulting upward trickle of wealth creates the circumstances, namely excess of capital, for the institution to spread its hold by establishing new outposts in new regions. This begins the cycle of profit bilking and underinvestment anew.

A final point on the commercialization of baking soda: it once was that we would scoop our baking soda from an unlabeled barrel and take whatever poundage we required for our homes. Now we arise to our Sony alarm clocks, put Folgers into our Cuisinart coffee makers before jumping into the shower where we use Suave hair products and Irish Spring soap. Before we've even rubbed the sleepiness from our eyes, we have interacted with and contributed to the trend a dozen times over.

Another way that money power has expanded into our personal lives to the detriment of democracy is the expansion of the scope and scale of the workday. Personally, I do not awake to a Sony alarm clock; my HTC smartphone's alarm function does that. One of the very first things I do before hitting the Cuisinart is to check both of my email accounts to make sure that there are no work-related updates which demand my immediate attention. All of this in spite of the fact that I work for a rather progressive institution. Indeed, surveys have consistently found this to be the new "normal." According to Bob

Collins' report on Minnesota Public Radio, "One in five employees has checked work email by 7 in the morning, and the average employee has spent 46 minutes working before ever getting to the office."

And this reality is not limited to professional and salaried workers. As we begin our work earlier and end it later, there is a demand for services stretching through ever greater hours of the day. Various forms of transit, from rail to cab service, must operate throughout increasing hours; gas stations maintain increasing hours; and assorted food services expand the scope of their hours of operation. This happens both in response to the effective demand created by longer working hours in general and also as the capitalists are forced into competition with one another.

There are numerous anti-democratic consequences of these trends as well. The most obvious is that we are spending more hours of the day operating within the context of an authoritarian institution. It is telling, on the face of it, that we spend these extra hours following the rules and etiquette of our workplaces and responding to the imperatives created by the same. It also demonstrates the degree to which we have internalized our own oppression. While, on average, we leave work at 5:48pm, we are working in one form or another until about 7:19pm. So, we are willingly providing nearly twelve hours of labor each day - half again the eight-hour standard fought for by the labor movement (Murphy).

Another side effect of these increased hours is the diminution of personal time which could otherwise be spent enriching our families and our communities. It also reduces the amount of time available to us for civic engagement. Lack of time is a commonly cited excuse for people's failure to be active members of their social and political communities. Voting patterns are an insufficient proxy for general civic engagement but it can be a useful stand-in when discussing liberal, bourgeois democracy. According to the U.S. Census Bureau, 34.9% of non-voters cite being too busy as their reason for not voting. However, I would be quick to point out that a huge volume of those are probably bullshit; in my research, I came across articles that cited things like sports and manicures as being part of people's business.

Capitalism has injected itself evermore deeply into every realm of our lives, including the personal. This expansion has necessarily come at the expense of democracy in the social and political spheres, and it results in a diminishing space for local control of resources and wealth. We not only allow these intrusions in seemingly small ways, like our individual consumption choices, but we become active participants in the process as we spend ever-increasing amounts of our personal time interfacing directly with the system through work. The expansion of capital requires the diminution of democracy, and when we become active participants in the process, we begin to internalize the authoritarian tendencies of the system.

Notes

Collins, Bob. "The expanding workday." Minnesota Public Radio, June 25, 2012:
(http://minnesota.publicradio.org/collections/special/columns/news_cu t/archive/2012/06/the_expanding_workday.shtml) May 11, 2013.

Murphy, Samantha. "Why Bosses No Longer Care If You're Late for Work [STUDY]." Mashable.com, June
25, 2012: (http://mashable.com/2012/06/25/coming-in-late-study/). May 11, 2013.

"Table 12. Reasons for Not Voting, by Sex, Age, Race, and Hispanic Origin, and Educational Attainment:
November 1998." United States Census Bureau, July 19, 2000: (http://www.census.gov/population/socdemo/voting/cps1998/tab12.tx t). May 11, 2013.

On the Front Lines of Class War

Why the Fight for a Livable Wage is Everyone's Fight

Colin Jenkins

"There's class warfare, all right, but it's my class - the rich class - that's making war, and we're winning."
- Warren Buffett (2006)

In the spring of 2004, amid the thaw of a frigid New York City winter, a brave group of Starbucks baristas began organizing. Like most service-sector employees in the United States, they were faced with the daunting task of trying to live on less-than-livable wages. Inconsistent hours, inadequate or non-existent health insurance, and less-than-dignified working conditions paled in comparison to their inability to obtain the most basic necessities. Apartment meetings, backroom discussions, and after-hours pep talks - all fueled by a collective angst - culminated into a sense of solidarity, the natural bond that occurs when workers take the time to realize their commonalities and shared struggle. On May 17, 2004, they officially announced their affiliation with the Industrial Workers of the World, an all-encompassing union with an impressive history of labor activity in the US. A petition for unionization followed suit. Their demands were simple: Guaranteed hours with the option for fulltime status, an end to understaffing, a healthier and safer workplace, and increased pay and raises.

"Solidarity Unionism," Grassroots Organizing, and the Formation of a New Front

It is only fitting that such a daring endeavor would fall under the banner of the IWW. Proudly asserting itself as "One Big Union" and "A Union for All Workers," the "Wobblies" shun hierarchical and highly-bureaucratic union models that have dominated the American labor scene for much of the past half-century, instead promoting and utilizing direct action that is member-run and member-driven. Deploying what they refer to as "solidarity unionism," as opposed to "business unionism," the preamble to the IWW's constitution echoes an old-school, militant, trade-union tone, boldly (and correctly) proclaiming, "The working class and the employing class have nothing in common. There can be no peace so long as hunger and want are found among millions of the working people" - a far cry from the timid and capitulating modus operandi of the modern adaptation.

However, it is not just a much-needed infusion of labor militancy that makes the IWW attractive, it is its grassroots approach to labor organizing. In a post-industrial landscape that is overrun with underemployment, the IWW's model represents accessibility and a sense of empowerment for disconnected workers who find themselves on virtual islands - outside the potentially radical confines of a traditional shop floor. And when considering that wages have either dropped or remained stagnant in the midst of ever-growing costs of living over the past 30 years, it is no surprise that American workers are reaching their collective breaking point and seeking refuge in the form of a shared struggle.

After decades of a disastrous neoliberal agenda that has placed the American working class in an all-out sprint to the bottom, the growing needs of low-wage workers coupled with the "wobbly way" to create a perfect storm. As such, the Starbucks Union captured a vibe and sparked a movement. 2007 saw the arrival of Brandworkers, "a non-profit organization bringing local food production workers together for good jobs and a sustainable food system." Following a similar grassroots blueprint, the NYC-based organization was founded "by retail and food employees who identified a need for an organization dedicated to protecting and advancing their rights," and stands on "a simple principle: **that working people themselves, equipped with powerful social change tools, were uniquely positioned to make positive change on the job and in society.**" Their direct-action, "Focus on the Food Chain (FOFC)" initiative specifically targets "the rapid proliferation of sweatshops among the food processing factories and distribution warehouses that supply the City's (NYC) grocery stores and restaurants" and that of which "increasingly relies on the exploitation of recent immigrants of color, mostly from Latin America and China." In an unprecedented effort, FOFC "creates space for the immigrant workers of NYC's industrial food sector to build unity with each other, gain proficiency in the use of powerful social change tools, and carry out member-led workplace justice campaigns to transform the industry." Ultimately, "Focus members and their allies are using organizing, grassroots advocacy, and legal actions to build a food system that provides high-quality local food and good local jobs."

Groups like the Starbucks Workers Union and Brandworkers created momentum. In 2010, six years after baristas came together in Manhattan, a band of sandwich makers gathered 1,200 miles westward, in Minneapolis, Minnesota. Thus, the next wave of grassroots, low-wage labor activity - this time stemming from the fast-food industry and, more specifically, the corporate brand of Jimmy John's sandwiches - took hold. Sporting T-shirts that read, "Wages So Low You'll Freak" - a mockery of JJ's corporate slogan, "Subs So Fast You'll Freak" - JJ workers, also under the direction of the IWW, embarked on the first ever unionization drive for fast-food workers. Emily Przybylski, a bike delivery worker at the restaurant chain, captured the spirit of the moment. "A union in fast food is an idea whose time has come," she told reporters. "There are millions of workers in this industry living in poverty, with no consistent scheduling, no job security and no respect. It's time for change." As Labor Day 2010 approached, JJ workers at one Minneapolis store filed for a union election, and actions such as leafleting and picketing were coordinated at stores in 32 states, "from Clovis, California to Miami, Florida."

The embryo created by baristas in NYC, and nurtured over the better part of a decade by the likes of the Brandworkers and Jimmy John's workers in Minneapolis, came to a head in 2012. On Thursday, October 4th, 2012, the spread of low-wage discontent struck the epicenter of corporate exploitation, as "more than 70 Los Angeles Wal-Mart workers from nine stores walked off the job." These walkouts accompanied over "20 charges of unfair labor practices" filed with the

National Labor Relation Board. A week later, Wal-Mart workers across 28 stores in 12 states, staged labor protests in the form of strikes and walk-outs. The first workers' strike in the company's 50-year history spread to stores in Los Angeles, San Francisco, Seattle, Chicago, Dallas, Miami, Washington, D.C., and Orlando.

This movement, much like its predecessors, was largely formed out of grassroots organizing efforts that were over a year in the making. In June 2011, "OUR Walmart," a workers advocacy organization supported by and coordinated with store associates from across the country, dispatched "nearly 100 Associates representing thousands of OUR Walmart members from across the United States to the Walmart Home Office in Bentonville, Ark., and presented a Declaration of Respect to Walmart executive management." The Declaration included a list of requests: Listen to us, the Associates; Have respect for the individual; Recognize freedom of association and freedom of speech; Fix the Open Door policy; Pay a minimum of $13/hour and make full-time jobs available for Associates who want them; Create dependable, predictable work schedules; Provide affordable healthcare; Provide every Associate with a policy manual, ensure equal enforcement of policy and no discrimination, and give every Associate equal opportunity to succeed and advance in his or her career; and provide wages and benefits that ensure that no Associate has to rely on government assistance.

In November of 2012, merely weeks after Wal-Mart workers took a courageous stand, fast-food workers from McDonald's, Wendy's, Burger King, Taco Bell and KFC staged protests in various locations around New York City, "demanding $15 an hour in pay and the right to form a union." A few months later, in the spring of 2013, fast food strikes gained momentum with numerous walk-outs across the country. In April, NYC workers - backed by labor, community and religious groups - staged protests at more than five dozen restaurants. Over the course of the next month, similar actions were carried out in Pennsylvania and Chicago. In Chicago, the actions spread from the fast-food industry to retail, with low-wage workers from Macy's, Sears, and Victoria's Secret also participating. On Friday, May 10th, "400 workers at more than 60 fast-food restaurants in the Detroit metro area walked off the job" in what may have been "the largest fast food strike in American history."

The Detroit event was significantly effective as it "shut down multiple restaurants entirely, including multiple McDonald's outlets, a Long John Silver's, a Burger King, two Popeye's restaurants, and a KFC."

"One McDonald's worker, Jay Robinson, told reporters that when he started at McDonald's over two years ago, he was paid $7.40 an hour," writes Aaron Petkov for Socialistworker.org. "Robinson has gotten raises since then - and now makes $7.48 an hour." In his efforts to care for himself and a 2-year-old daughter, "It's a day-to-day struggle," he told reporters. "And the owners make millions." At another McDonald's restaurant, "management attempted to avert a shutdown by bringing in replacement workers, but those replacement workers (in a moment of incredible solidarity) then promptly joined the strike."

This wave of low-wage labor militancy continued through the summer. On Thursday, August 29th, workers at numerous fast-food chains participated in coordinated strikes in nearly 60 cities nationwide. Citing poverty wages and the need for more rights in the workplace, "a dozen workers didn't show up for their shift at a McDonald's on 8 Mile Road (in Detroit), forcing the closure of the dining room." In Raleigh, N.C., about 30 workers picketed outside a Little Caesars location. One employee, Julio Wilson, expressed the discontent of his peers, saying the $9-an-hour he was paid was not nearly enough to support himself and his 5-year-old daughter. "I know I'm risking my job, but it's my right to fight for what I deserve," Wilson said. "Nine dollars an hour is not enough to make ends meet nowadays."

In Indianapolis, "several employees walked off the job from a McDonald's outlet at 16th and Meridian streets." "Most people here have a family to support, and most people here barely make enough to make ends meet,'" employee Dwight Murray said. "We're here today because we feel like McDonald's is a $6 billion entity and it's not unfeasible for them to pay $15 an hour.

Corporate Greed, Propaganda, and Union-Busting

Despite the obvious needs for livable wages, there is much opposition. Union-busting has become a staple of employee orientations throughout the corporate landscape, with retail giants like Target and Wal-Mart regularly unleashing "aggressive anti-union push (es), and distributing pamphlets and other propaganda to employees." Corporations like Target have become notorious for making employees watch dramatized "training videos" on the so-called "dangers" of unionization in an attempt to convince workers that higher wages, more benefits, and an overall sense of dignity at the workplace would somehow **not** be good for them.

This concerted effort to maintain a grip on poverty wages has led to the formation of intricate networks of union-busting firms that employ corporate lawyers and "anti-union strategists" to offer "continuing education" for business owners and executives. "At these seminars," writes Kim Phillips-Fein, "lawyers and labor relations consultants from the nation's top union-busting law firms come to speak to rapt, intimate groups of executives, advising them on how to beat union election drives, do end runs around the National Labor Relations Board (NLRB), and decertify unions, all the while hawking their own firms' services." Of course, "union members are expressly banned."

To complement this behind-the-scenes movement, corporate mouthpieces like Fox News have taken up the propaganda charge against unions by referring to them as "monopolies" that prevent non-union workers from securing jobs, coining terms like "union thugs" as a fear tactic, displaying video snippets of supposed "union violence," utilizing doublespeak like "right to work" to suggest that accepting low wages is somehow a *right* that should be fought for, and airing modern-day snake oil salesmen to convince its working class viewers that unions are given extra benefits at *their* expense. In addition to ideological propaganda, special interest groups, wealthy donors, and Super PACs fueled by the Supreme Court's infamous Citizens United decision - such as Koch Industries PAC - have placed virtual ATMs in Governor's mansions and Congressional offices to ensure political opposition to workers' needs while remaining corporate (and thus profit)-friendly.

Starbucks' corporate response to the organizing efforts made by those fateful NYC workers in 2004 was fierce. "Faced with the first serious effort in decades to unionize one of its stores, Starbucks launched what a former worker called 'a scorched-earth campaign' against pro-union employees," reported Josh Harkinson. "The union busting has just been absolutely relentless," says the worker, Daniel Gross, who was fired in 2006 due to his involvement in the initial organizing efforts at the Manhattan store where he worked.

The Minneapolis Jimmy John's workers were met with similar tactics, which included bizarre personal attacks from store owners and management through social media. On March 22, 2011, after lobbying for sick days from the restaurant chain, six workers - all of whom were "key figures" in the union organizing efforts - were fired for "defaming the brand and disloyalty to the company." Shortly thereafter, another "pro-union" employee was berated and humiliated on social media by owners and managers, some of whom went as far as posting the employee's personal telephone number on a public Facebook page and asking people to text the employee to "let him know how they feel." An Assistant Manager then posted disparaging personal comments about the pro-union employee, making fun of his appearance and including a picture of the employee for all to see.

In addition to these reactive measures deployed by some companies, corporate behemoths like Wal-Mart have relied on proactive union-busting programs for years. In 2007, Washington-based Human Rights Watch released an extensive report accusing the retail giant of "routinely flouting its workers' human rights through a sophisticated strategy of harassing union organizers, discriminating against long-term staff, and indoctrinating employees with misleading propaganda." The report includes examples of "workers forced into unpaid overtime and an alleged strategy of squeezing out long-serving staff who are more costly than low-wage, temporary, younger workers," highlights "elaborate tactics to stop staff from coming together to fight for better conditions," and even describes detailed measures such as "focusing security cameras on areas where staff congregate and shifting around loyal workers in 'unit packing' tactics to ensure votes for union recognition are defeated."

The report also found that each store manager, as a part of their training, receives a "manager's toolbox" manual which instructs them on "how to remain free in the event union organizers choose your facility as their next target," and that managers are also given access to and instructed to call a 'union hotline' if they suspect staff are discussing unionization - an action that would deploy corporate specialists from the company's headquarters to "address the situation."

The reasons for such opposition are clear. Corporate profits remain at an all-time high because companies are able to pay poverty wages to their employees and rely on government welfare programs to cover the rest (ironically, while also enjoying historically low corporate tax rates). Additionally, the economic storm that has lingered over the heads of the American working class for the past five years has equaled a virtual paradise for corporate America. Three simple facts highlight this current economic landscape:

- **Corporate profit margins just hit another all-time high** as companies are making more per dollar of sales than they ever have before.
- **Wages as a percent of the economy just hit another all-time low** as companies are paying employees less than they ever have as a share of GDP.
- **Fewer Americans are working than at any time in the past three decades** as companies don't employ as many workers as they used to. As a result, the employment-to-population ratio has collapsed.

Maintaining this environment has become a top priority for wealthy investors, the corporations themselves, and the politicians who are funded by both. By gutting the middle class through the destruction of unions (as of 2011, only 11.9% of the American workforce was unionized - a 70-year low) over the past three decades, corporations have enjoyed a relatively clear path towards establishing these beneficial conditions of today - where 20% of the population owns 89% of all "privately held wealth;" and where the top 1% of the population owns 42.1% of all "financial wealth (total net worth minus the value of one's home)."

In addition to corporate-friendly policies that became commonplace starting with the Reagan years and continuing through both Bush', Clinton, and now Obama, the emergence of globalization has allowed for the replacement of American workers through the process of offshoring and the subsequent exploitation of extremely impoverished populations of workers abroad. Therefore, this latest surfacing of labor militancy from within the ranks of the domestic, low-wage, service-sector workforce represents the biggest threat - not only in its tangible fight for economic justice in the form of a livable wage, but also in its potentially revolutionary orientation which identifies with the modern working class and, most notably, the working poor - that corporate hegemony has faced within the geographic confines of the U.S. in decades.

"If these guys are seen to succeed, it could really light a fire, because the dissatisfaction is unquestionable," labor historian Peter Rachleff explains. "The corporation knows that, and they have a lot of resources [and] plenty of lawyers" to combat these working class movements.

Workers' Victories and Building Momentum

Despite a well-funded and highly-coordinated opposition, there have been many victories and positive developments along the way. The mere emergence of a new labor resistance - let alone the fact that it has developed from within the low-wage service-sector and from one of the most disenfranchised demographics of the working class - is very encouraging. While some have questioned the roots of the movement and the extent of the involvement of more traditional, hierarchical unions like SEIU (Service Employees International), there is no denying the politicization and sense of empowerment that is being internalized by the involved workers themselves.

Considering the near-death of working class consciousness in the U.S., this development simply cannot and should not be underestimated. The infusion of a direct-action model that insists on a worker-controlled approach to labor battles (i.e. the IWW) is certainly a leap forward. And this method has proven effective in more ways than one. On Tuesday, December 28, 2008, NYC Starbucks baristas were vindicated by National Labor Relations Board judge, Mindy E. Landow, when she ruled that Starbucks had "illegally fired three workers and otherwise violated federal labor laws in seeking to beat back unionization efforts at several of its Manhattan cafes" and ordered Starbucks "to pledge to end what she said was discriminatory treatment toward workers who supported the union at four of its Manhattan shops: 200 Madison Avenue at 36th Street, 145 Second Avenue at 9th Street, 15 Union Square East and 116 East 57th Street."

Two years later, the IWW Starbucks Workers Union, following a "determined campaign of grassroots actions in Starbucks stores and communities all over the country," secured another victory when the company's corporate office gave in to demands for workers to receive time-and-one-half pay for working on Martin Luther King, Jr. Day. "We're deeply moved to have been able in our modest way to increase respect for Dr. King's legacy while ensuring that Starbucks employees who work on his holiday are fairly compensated," said Anja Witek, a Starbucks barista and SWU member in Minnesota. "This is a great example of what baristas and all low-wage workers can achieve by getting organized and taking direct action in support of workplace justice issues." In February of 2012, after a long and drawn-out battle with Jimmy John's, a federal judge ruled the company illegally fired the six employees who had campaigned for sick time, and ordered the company to "reinstate the workers with back pay within 14 days." In a spirited testimony, Erik Forman, one of the fired employees, remarked:

"It has already been over a year since we were illegally fired for telling the truth. For all the hard work and dedication of the NLRB's civil servants, employers like Jimmy John's prefer to break the law and drag cases through the courts for years rather than let workers exercise their right to win fair pay, sick days, and respect through union organization. The dysfunctional U.S. labor law system gives Mike and Rob Mulligan (JJ franchise owners) and their cronies in the 1% carte blanche to trample on workers' rights. Jimmy John's workers, and the rest of the 99%, will only be able to win a better life by taking our fight from the courtroom back to the shop floors and the streets."

The latest low-wage workers strike, which took place on December 5th across "100 cities through the day," signified, according to the Guardian's U.S. affiliate, "a growing clamour for more action on income inequality." In front of a Walgreen's in downtown Chicago, nearly 200 protestors chanted, "We can't survive on eight-twenty-five...Walgreen's, Walgreen's, you can't hide. We can see your greedy side!" In Washington, D.C., dozens of workers carrying signs singing loudly, "Jingle bells, jingle bells, jingle all the way, it's no fun, to survive, on low low low low pay." "In New York City, about 100 protesters blew whistles and beat drums as they marched into a McDonald's chanting "We can't survive on $7.25."

This collective outrage has empowered workers while also placing the problem of income inequality back on the public agenda. Major media sources that had barely uttered a word about such inequality in recent decades have now begun to showcase it. The Catholic Church's latest Pope, Francis, has made waves during a near-month-long tirade exposing the flaws of capitalism, recently asking, "How can it be that it is not a news item when an elderly homeless person dies of exposure, but it is news when the stock market drops 2 points?" and referring to the "widening gap between those who have more and those who must be content with the crumbs." And calls for a federal minimum wage increase have gained steam with U.S. Labor Secretary, Thomas Perez, writing on his blog, "To reward work, to grow the middle class and strengthen the economy, to give millions of Americans the respect they deserve - it's time to raise the minimum wage." Though, of course, the Democratic Party's proposal to raise the current rate from $7.25 to $9.00, or even $10.10 in other proposed legislation, would hardly equal a significant change for tens of millions of working poor. Still, despite reformist-based rhetoric from politicians, the agenda is being shaped by the brave workers who have risked all to take a stand.

The battle cry "Fight for $15" has stuck. Numerous small and localized labor organization like Detroit 15- a group of fast-food and retail workers from the Detroit area fighting "for fair wages and the right to form a union without interference" - and Fast Food Forward - a movement of NYC fast-food workers coming together to "build community engagement, hold corporations and their CEOs accountable, and to raise wages so that all Americans can prosper" - have sprung up amidst the movement-at-large, helping to form collaborative efforts with community and religious organizations which possess built-up social capital to be used, and to make the collective decision-making process more accessible to the workers themselves.

Socialist candidate, Kshama Sawant, who made the "Fight for $15" cause a key part of her election campaign, made history by winning a seat on the Seattle City Council in November. Sawant's victory was significant not only for working class interests that have been in dire need of a true "left wing" for decades, but also for the fact that her platform was able to pull local Democrats toward a more authentic (though still reformist), left-wing, working-class agenda. As Seattle Times columnist, Danny Westneat, reported:

"You can't look at the stagnant pay, declining benefits and third-world levels of income disparity in recent years and conclude this system is working. For Millennials as a group, it has been a disaster. Out of the wreckage, left-wing or socialist economic ideas, such as the 'livable wage' movement in which government would seek to mandate a form of economic security, are flowering."

The Future of the American Working Class

If you're reading this, chances are you are a member of the working class - not because the article specifically pertains to your interests but because, by definition, a large majority of us are compelled to work for a wage or salary to survive. The Occupy slogan which may seem a bit hyperbolic on the surface - breaking society into two camps: the 99% and the 1% - is actually not far off. The 99% essentially refers to the working class - those of us who are underemployed, unemployed, making minimum wage, making an hourly wage, working multiple jobs, earning a salary, working as "salaried professionals," working "under-the-table," etc.. In other words, if you weren't born with enough privilege and generational wealth to carry you through life, you are likely working for a wage in some form or another, or would be compelled to do so if left to your own means.

Jay Robinson, Julio Wilson, Dwight Murray, and their fellow employees are correct in their estimation: Multi-billion dollar corporations *can* and *should* pay their workers a livable wage. Considering how far removed we are from the age-old concept of workers "enjoying the fruits of their labor," a seemingly minimal expectation of earning a livable wage for fulltime work has become a revolutionary notion. But it shouldn't be. This issue is not just a low-wage problem - it's a working class problem. It's a middle class problem. It's a societal problem that destroys living standards for everyone outside of elite circles. And, while it is nowhere near the end-all, be-all of solutions to a toxic system, the premise of "a chain being only as strong as its weakest link" is certainly an improvement over the neoliberal, "greed is good" mantra which has dominated monetary and governmental policy over the past thirty years.

For low-wage workers themselves, besides allowing the dignity of "earning a living," a livable wage infuses more expendable income into the economy while allowing for the opportunity to live without a chronic reliance on public assistance. "If you earn your money through wages (unlike many of the 1 percent, who earn through things like investments and a tax system biased in favor of capital gains over income) then a higher wage, minimum or otherwise, would mean that you'd spend the additional dollars, creating jobs for other workers," explains market analyst Marshall Auerback. "You'd pay down your mortgages and car loans, getting yourself out of debt. You'd pay more taxes - on sales and property, mostly - thereby relieving the fiscal crises of states and localities. More teachers, police and firefighters would keep their jobs. America would get a virtuous cycle toward higher employment and, more importantly, the cycle would be based on a policy which creates higher incomes, not higher debt via credit expansion."

251

Furthermore, the establishment of livable wages eases the burden placed on the rest of the working class, which has contributed approximately $7 billion per year to fund public assistance programs that serve as a form of subsidization for Fortune 500s. That figure, from an October 2013 report by UC Berkeley's Labor Center, includes four major social benefits programs that low-wage workers are forced to use in order to provide basic necessities for themselves and their families. Specifically, the amount is broken down to Medicaid and the Children's Health Insurance Program ($3.9 billion), the Earned Income Tax Credit ($1.9 billion), food stamps ($1 billion), and Temporary Aid for Needy Families ($200,000), and doesn't include other publicly funded programs like child care assistance, WIC, or section 8 housing, among others.

For those who see low-wage workers protesting for higher pay and think, "why don't they just get a better job" or "why don't they go to college, like I did, and earn a degree?" - think again. In 2012, nearly 300,000 Americans with college degrees were working minimum wage jobs. Furthermore, nearly one-half of all recent college graduates with jobs are underemployed. "Of 41.7 million working college graduates in 2010, about 48 percent of the class of 2010 work jobs that require less than a bachelor's degree, and 38 percent of those polled didn't even need high school diplomas." Even worse yet, 40% of recent college graduates are unemployed. In other words, the idea that earning a degree guarantees a livable wage is exactly that - an idea, no longer based in reality.

For those who see low-wage workers striking for a livable wage and think, "what do they expect, they're working at McDonald's" or "these aren't careers we're talking about" - think again. Fact is, since the arrival of globalization, American manufacturing companies - the traditional suppliers of a livable wage - have jumped ship, moving their operations overseas to exploit impoverished workforces that are compelled to labor for next-to-nothing. Since this shift, America's working class has become largely reliant on the service industry. In other words, low-wage, service sector jobs are now careers - not by choice, but by necessity. The 2008 economic crisis and subsequent "recovery" only intensified this shift as "mid-wage occupations ($13.84 to $21.13 per hour) constituted 60 percent" of job losses during the 2008 recession, but only 22 percent of the job gains during the recovery. In contrast, "low-wage occupations ($7.69 to $13.83 per hour) constituted 21 percent" of job losses during the recession, while representing 58 percent of new jobs created during the aftermath. This is a staggering displacement that has seen once-livable employment virtually replaced by now-unlivable wages. As a result, the "characteristics of minimum wage workers" are changing, as 75 percent of them are now adults, many of whom have dependents to care for, and 70 percent of who have at least a high school degree.

The American working class has found itself in a breakneck "race to the bottom" during the corporatist era. However, recent developments stemming from "solidarity unionism," low-wage worker revolts, and a backlash against neoliberal policies and the extreme income inequality which they have bred have shown that American workers are, in fact, beginning to "rise like lions after slumber." If the thundering wave of low-wage labor militancy that has swept the country is any indication, the slumber is officially over. And if the "dramatic actions by and on behalf of workers" in places likes Seattle the past few months - including a "defeat of concessions at major grocery chains, Boeing workers' big 'no' vote on concessions, a $15 minimum wage voted in for airport workers, and election of a socialist (a candidate who made a city-wide $15 minimum wage the centerpiece of her campaign) to city council" - represent a microcosm of things to come, the proverbial race to the bottom - whether it has struck bedrock or not - is over.

Because of their emergence as a viable sector of embedded labor, courageous, low-wage workers in the service industry now represent the front lines of an ongoing class war. They represent, as Dave Frieboth notes, "a general uprising of young, displaced workers trapped in low-wage jobs;" people who "looked at the wage disparities and saw that, as a simple matter of fact, the system isn't working." The further they can be kept down in terms of wages, benefits, and overall standards of living, the more effectively their lowly presence may be used as leverage to drive all working Americans' standards down. Thus, their status affects the status of the working class as a whole. They are not only fighting for themselves - they are fighting for all of us. In this sense, "an injury to one" truly is "an injury to all." Their fight is everyone's fight.

References

Sylvia Allegretto, Marc Doussard, Dave Graham-Squire, Ken Jacobs, Dan Thompson and Jeremy Thompson. "FAST FOOD, POVERTY WAGES: THE PUBLIC COST OF LOW-WAGE JOBS IN THE FAST-FOOD INDUSTRY." A report by UC Berkely's Labor Center. October 15, 2013.http://laborcenter.berkeley.edu/publiccosts/fastfoodpovertywage s.shtml

Arnade, Chris. "Pope Francis is a whistleblower for the poor. Thank you Time for recognising it." The Guardian, December 11, 2013. http://www.theguardian.com/commentisfree/2013/dec/11/time-pope-francis-whistleblower-poor-right-choice

Auerback, Marshall. "Why Low Minimum Wages Kill Jobs and Crush Living Standards for Everyone." AlterNet, April 24, 2012.http://www.alternet.org/story/155132/why_low_minimum_wage s_kill_jobs_and_crush_living_standards_for_everyone?page=0%2C1

Bacon, John. "Fast-food workers strike, protest for higher pay." USA Today, December 5, 2013.http://www.usatoday.com/story/money/business/2013/12/05/fas t-food-strike-wages/3877023/

Bigman, Paul. "How'd Seattle Do It?" Labor Notes, December 16, 2016.http://labornotes.org/2013/12/howd-seattle-do-it

Blodget, Henry. "Profits Just Hit Another All-Time High, Wages Just Hit Another All-Time Low." Business Insider, April 11, 2013. http://www.businessinsider.com/profits-at-high-wages-at-low-2013-4

Brandworkers: Good Jobs, Local Food. http://www.brandworkers.org/our-mission

Brandworkers campaigns: Focus on the Food Chain. http://www.brandworkers.org/campaigns

Callahan, David . "The Global Context of Wal-Mart's Illegal Union Busting Tactics." Demos, September 6, 2013. www.demos.org/.../global-context-walmarts-illegal- **union-busting**-tactics

Casselman, Ben. "College Grads May Be Stuck in Low-Skill Jobs." The Wall Street Journal, March 26, 2013. http://online.wsj.com/news/articles/SB10001424127887323466 204578382753004333838

Characteristics of Minimum Wage Workers: 2011. US Department of Labor Bureau of Labor Statistics report. March 2, 2012. http://www.bls.gov/cps/minwage2011.htm

Noam Chomsky interviewed by Tom Morello. "On Democracy." Summer 1996.http://www.chomsky.info/interviews/1996summer.htm

Clark, Andrew. "Security cameras and HQ squads: Wal-Mart's union-busting tactics." The Guardian, April 30, 2007. http://www.theguardian.com/business/2007/may/01/usnews.supermarkets

Cooper, Michael. "Lost in Recession, Toll on Underemployed and Underpaid." The New York Times, June 18, 2012. http://www.nytimes.com/2012/06/19/us/many-american-workers-are-underemployed-and-underpaid.html

Dimaggio, Dan. "Union-Busting: Six Fired After Demanding Sick Days for Fast-Food Workers." AlterNet, March 25, 2011. http://www.alternet.org/story/150375/union-busting%3A_six_fired_after_demanding_sick_days_for_fast-food_workers

Discounting Rights: Wal-Mart's Violation of US Workers' Right to Freedom of Association. Human Rights Watch, May 2007. http://www.hrw.org/sites/default/files/reports/us0507webwcover.pdf

Dolan, Ed. "US Corporate Profits at All-Time High as GDP Growth Holds at 2.5 Percent." EconoMonitor, September 26, 2013. http://www.economonitor.com/dolanecon/2013/09/26/us-corporate-profits-at-all-time-high-as-gdp-growth-holds-at-2-5-percent/ Domhoff, G. William. "Wealth, Income, and Power." Who Rules America? UC Santa Cruz Sociology Department. http://www2.ucsc.edu/whorulesamerica/power/wealth.html

Eidelson, Josh. "Fast Food Strike Wave Spreads to Detroit." The Nation, May 10, 2013.http://www.thenation.com/blog/174270/fast-food-strike-wave-spreads-detroit#

Eidelson, Josh. "McDonald's Guest Workers Stage a Surprise Strike." The Nation, March 6, 2013.http://www.thenation.com/blog/173217/mcdonalds-guest-workers-stage-surprise-strike#

Fast Food Forward: Higher Pay for a Stronger New York. http://fastfoodforward.org/

Fast Food, Poverty Wages: The Public Cost of Low-Wage Jobs in the Fast-Food Industry. Report by the UC Berkely Labor Center. http://laborcenter.berkeley.edu/publiccosts/fast_food_poverty_wages.pdf

Gabbatt, Adam. "US fast-food workers strike over low wages in nationwide protests." The Guardian, December 5, 2013. http://www.theguardian.com/world/2013/dec/05/fast-food-workers-strike-minimum-wage

Greenhouse, Steven. "Starbucks Loses Round in Battle over Union." The New York Times, December 23, 2008. http://www.nytimes.com/2008/12/24/nyregion/24starbucks.html?_r=0

Greenhouse, Steven. "Union Membership in U.S. Fell to a 70-Year Low Last Year." The New York Times, January 21, 2011. http://www.nytimes.com/2011/01/22/business/22union.html?_r=0

IWW Starbucks Workers Union homepage. http://www.iww.org/unions/dept600/iu660/starbucks

IWW Campaigns: Current and Historic. http://www.iww.org/history/campaigns

Jenkins, Colin. "Corporatism 2.0: Wal-Mart and the Modern Corporate Business Structure." The Hampton Institute, May 24, 2013. http://www.hamptoninstitute.org/corporatism2.0.html

Jimmy John's Workers Union homepage. http://www.jimmyjohnsworkers.org/

Kroll, Andy. "Wisconsin Governor Scott Walker: Funded by the Koch Bros." Mother Jones, February 18, 2011. http://www.motherjones.com/mojo/2011/02/wisconsin-scott-walker-koch-brothers

Lott, John. "Why Unions are Harmful to Workers." Fox News, March 17, 2011.http://www.foxnews.com/opinion/2011/03/17/unions-harmful-workers/

Lydersen, Kari. "Jimmy John's Workers Hope Management 'Freaks Out' Over Union Drive." In These Times, September 10, 2010.http://inthesetimes.com/working/entry/6422/jimmy_johns_workers_hope_management_freak_out_over_union_drive/

McGuinness, William. "Half Of Recent College Grads Work Jobs That Don't Require A Degree: Report." Huffington Post, January 29, 2013. http://www.huffingtonpost.com/2013/01/29/underemployed-overeducated_n_2568203.html

Miles, Kathleen. "Walmart Strike: Dozens Of LA Workers Walk Off The Job In First-Ever Strike Against Retailer." Huffington Post, October 4, 2012. http://www.huffingtonpost.com/2012/10/04/walmart-strike-la-workers-walk-off-first-ever_n_1940710.html

Mobley, Chris. "Election breakthrough for a Seattle socialist." Socialistworker.org, November 14, 2013.http://socialistworker.org/2013/11/14/election-breakthrough-in-seattle

OUR Wal-Mart: Organization United for Respect at Wal-Mart. http://forrespect.org/

Petkov, Aaron. "We'd Like a Living Wage with that Order." Socialistworker.org, May 20, 2013.http://socialistworker.org/print/2013/05/20/wed-like-a-living-wage

Phillips-Fein, Kim. "A More Perfect Union Buster." Mother Jones, September/October

2008.http://www.motherjones.com/politics/1998/09/more-perfect-union-buster

Powell, Michael Orion. "The Hunt for Red November: Third-Party, Working-Class Politics Get a Boost with Socialist Victory." The Hampton Institute, November 20, 2013.http://www.hamptoninstitution.org/rednovember.html

Pullella, Philip. "Pope Francis in Peace Message Attacks Mega-Salaries With 'Crumbs' For Poor." Huffington Post, December 12, 2013. http://www.huffingtonpost.com/2013/12/12/pope-attacks-mega-salarie_n_4431701.html

Resnikoff, Ned. "Hundreds of Service Workers Strike in Chicago." MSNBC, April 24, 2013.http://www.msnbc.com/all-in/hundreds-service-workers-strike-in-chicago

Resnikoff, Ned. "Largest fast food strike yet as workers walk out in Michigan." MSNBC, May 10, 2013.http://www.msnbc.com/all-in/largest-fast-food-strike-yet-workers-walk

Sands, David. "Detroit Fast Food Strike Employees Gather At Protest to Demand Unions And A $15 Per Hour Wage." Huffington Post, May 10, 2013. http://www.huffingtonpost.com/2013/05/10/detroit-fast-food-strike-15-hour_n_3254861.html

Sands, David. "Fast Food Strike: Detroit Walkouts, Protests Continue National Movement For Higher Wages, Union." Huffington Post, May 10, 2013. http://www.huffingtonpost.com/2013/05/10/fast-food-strike-detroit-protests-living-wage_n_3252944.html?utm_hp_ref=detroit

Semuels, Alana. "Fast-food workers walk out in N.Y. amid rising U.S. labor unrest." Los Angeles Times, November 29, 2012. http://articles.latimes.com/2012/nov/29/business/la-fi-mo-fast-food-strike-20121129

Shapiro, Lila. "American Labor's Next Target." Huffington Post, June 16, 2011.http://www.huffingtonpost.com/2011/06/16/target-union-labor-movement_n_877741.html

Strauss, Gary. "Fast Food Workers Strike for Higher Pay." USA Today, August 30, 2013.http://www.usatoday.com/story/news/nation/2013/08/29/fast-food-workers-strike-for-higher-pay-in-nearly-60-cities/2726815/

Thompson, Derek. If Corporate Profits Are at an All-Time High, Why Are Corporate Taxes Near a 60-Year Low?" The Atlantic, May 23, 2013. http://www.theatlantic.com/business/archive/2013/05/if-corporate-profits-are-at-an-all-time-high-why-are-corporate-taxes-near-a-60-year-low/276164/

Townsend, Allie. "First Fast-Food Workers Union Planned." TIME Newsfeed, October 5, 2010.http://newsfeed.time.com/2010/10/05/first-fast-food-workers-union-planned/

Tracking the Recovery after the Great Recession. A report by the National Employment Law Project.http://www.nelp.org/index.php/content/content_about_us/tracking_the_recovery_after_the_great_recession

Zweifel, Dave. "There is a Class War, and Rich are Winning." The Capital Times (Wisconsin), October 6, 2010. https://www.commondreams.org/headline/2010/10/06-5

"284,000 College Graduates Had Minimum-Wage Jobs Last Year." Huffington Post, March 13, 2013.http://www.huffingtonpost.com/2013/03/31/college-graduates-minimum-wage-jobs_n_2989540.html

"The $7-billion dollar problem of low-wage, fast-food jobs." NASDAQ "Minyanville" blog.http://www.nasdaq.com/article/the-7-billion-problem-of-lowwage-fastfood-jobs-cm288226

"Historic First in Nation's Fast Food Industry, 200 Jimmy John's Workers to Vote in NLRB Union Election on October 22." Jimmy John's Workers Union homepage, September 28, 2010.http://www.jimmyjohnsworkers.org/news/201009/labor-day-jimmy-johns-faces-coast-coast-actions-support-nations-first-ever-fast-

food-
uni%20http://www.workdayminnesota.org/index.php?news_6_4609

"NYC's fast-food workers expected to strike in bid for higher wages."
NBC News - Reuters, April 4,
2013. http://www.nbcnews.com/business/nycs-fast-food-workers-
expected-strike-bid-higher-wages-1C9212578

"Wal-Mart Workers in 12 States Stage Historic Strikes, Protests Against
Workplace Retaliation." Democracy Now online, October 10,
2012.http://www.democracynow.org/2012/10/10/walmart_workers_in
_12_states_stage

"Hourly wages of entry-level workers by education, 1973-2011." Report
by the Economic Policy Institute. http://www.epi.org/chart/ib-327-
table-1-hourly-wages-entry-level-2/

Labor Study Groups
How, Can, or Do They Work?

Daniel J. Kelly

I have one really big problem to overcome as I sit here writing this article: I can't tell you where I work. That would be a problem except that I'm going to provide just enough detail that the reader will still have a reasonable understanding of the subject. Additionally, the problems faced by employees at my workplace are not significantly different than those faced by working people anywhere in the United States.

I work in a factory but it's a factory that makes absolutely nothing in the way of a tangible commodity. The employees sit in the same place all day, tethered to two machines, and performing essentially the same tasks over and over again. The employees have practically no say over the conditions under which they work and are subject to ongoing surveillance. If you guessed that the "factory" in question is a 'call center' you'd be one hundred percent correct - and it is a factory. The two machines to which workers are tethered are a computer and a telephone. Of course the only "products" manufactured are little abstract packets of information. And those "packets" are worth a lot of money to a lot of powerful people. This call center/factory is a function of a public agency and its workers are, of course, public employees. A generation ago, the employees of this call center would have worked at actual factories that made things like electrical equipment, rototillers, hair brushes, and sausages. Those were the products that used to be made in the urban community where my call center is located. That was before capitalists figured out they could make a lot more money by moving operations to the Global South (or in some cases the American South). That gray, smoggy paradise of good-paying, union jobs in manufacturing is now just a memory to most Americans. On the other hand, most so-called "white-collar" jobs were long ago "proletarianized" and, nowadays, most good-paying, union jobs are found in the public sector.

The reason I can't name my exact workplace has a lot to do with the recent political attacks on public employees in general. If I were to publically disclose my employer's name in a written opinion piece, that might imply I'm speaking for this public agency rather than just for myself and, now that the neoliberal ideology has entered every workplace, it's better to be careful.

In early 2011, one of my fellow shop stewards, an old activist, approached me with the idea of starting a labor study group at our workplace. So, we gathered a small group of fellow employees to meet during lunch in order to read and discuss chapter one of Michael Yates' 2009 book, "Why Unions Matter." The reason we chose this book had more to do with the fact that my friend and I each owned a copy than anything to do with its content. That being said, Yates' book happens to be very good.

My friend, the fellow steward, became the initial coordinator of the group that consisted of four men and one woman. We scheduled our meetings for alternate Wednesdays from 12:30 PM to 1:00, which conveniently overlaps with our scheduled lunch time. The "coordinator" set up a program by which we'd each read the entire chapter and present an oral report. His instructions were that the oral reporters should stand in turn at the end of the meeting room table and deliver the report. No doubt he was trying to instill leadership qualities in each of us. Unfortunately, our initial attempt at a study group ended after only a few meetings.

We probably wouldn't have attempted to revive the study group several months later were it not for two events. At the final meeting of our first study group, I gave my personal report-back on the Yates book. I barely finished speaking when the lone woman in our group remarked, "this country needs a goddamn revolution!" Since most of my coworkers have always impressed me as a bit conservative, often voting against their own best interests, this was a response I had not counted on - especially since this woman was hardly what one would call a firebrand. Maybe there is still some revolutionary potential in the American working class, I thought.

Nonetheless, the labor study group languished for several months until the second event. This event was the rapid, spontaneous spread of the Occupy movement in late 2011. I had not counted on the second event either.

I had become actively involved in Occupy since the first planning meeting in my own city following the initial encampment in New York City. Early in October 2011, Occupy meetings in my community attracted hundreds of attendees. The accepted wisdom that the Occupy movement was made up mostly of upper middle-class white kids simply does not agree with my own experience. I encountered numerous working-class people at Occupy events throughout that initial month. What surprised me more was the keen interest shown in this movement by my co-workers. My fellow steward and I decided this would be an ideal time to try to resurrect the labor study group. This time, I took on the role of coordinator and, for our next book, I chose several sections of "Solidarity Divided" by Bill Fletcher Jr. and Fernando Gapasin, published by University of California Press in 2008. "Solidarity Divided" is, by most standards, a dense, academic text. I had found it a bit difficult to get through when I'd first read it myself. Thus, a few other union members suggested this was way too difficult a piece for my co-workers to handle, to which I always answered, "I just don't happen to think people are stupid; besides, I understood it and I'm really no smarter than anyone else who works here."

Our study group had, in the wake of Occupy, grown from six to about fifteen members. Yes, people complained that the text was difficult but, nevertheless, most of them read it and gave interesting reports (seated this time). We spent months on the book and responses ranged from denunciations of capitalism by a number of participants to one man who said he was a libertarian and nothing in that book had changed his mind.

In the months since then, our study group has leveled off to around six regular members. We've revisited "Why Unions Matter" (chapter three this time), and even started watching documentaries. One of the films we watched and discussed is "Class Dismissed," narrated by Ed Asner, which explores the mostly negative ways television portrays the American working class. Despite showing films in multiple 30-minute

263

segments on a computer monitor in our union's office, people always return to see the conclusion. This is most encouraging.

I was also encouraged when I loaned a copy of "State of The Unions," a book by labor journalist Philip Dine. I had hoped the interested party would skim a few chapters and find a couple of ideas we could discuss in our meetings. He, instead, returned a couple of weeks later and said he'd been so fascinated with the book that he'd stayed up all night on a couple of occasions to finish reading it. He then delivered an incisive 30-minute report on its content.

In conclusion, I have to say that workers are hungry to learn more about the things that affect their status as a class, even if they don't put it in those words. While many of the people in my worksite have more formal education than many other working class people, I don't believe that alone is a deciding factor as to why they show an interest in studying labor. It's not the quantity of the education, but the content that makes the difference. If the U. S. working class is ever to become the transformative force it once was, workers will need to take the initiative to educate themselves. Specifically, they will have to understand their role, as a class, in the Neoliberal economy. The primary impediment to this understanding is the social and pol itical apathy born of a learned helplessness that undermines the aspirations of working-class people. One thing I learned from the Occupy movement is that when people's voices are heard they become aware of their immense potential for power. Do labor study groups work? My only answer is that anything which gives workers the chance to be honestly heard works.

LGBTQ Rights

DEPARTMENT

Cut From the Same Rigid Cloth

Hate Crimes and Militarism

Jonathan Mathias Lassiter

Recent shifts in the tides of American life have lead to the defeat of the Defense of Marriage Act, defeat of California's Proposition 8, and repeal of Don't Ask Don't Tell, the policy of discrimination against same gender loving (SGL) members of the military. Alongside these shifts, hate crimes against SGL and trans people have seen an uptick. News reports from across the country have recounted stories of violence against SGL and trans people in cities including New York and Los Angeles (Lloyd, 2013; Prokupecz, 2013; Yakas, 2013). One of the most heinous crimes occurred in New York City this Spring wherein an SGL man was shot in the face and killed in Greenwich Village (Yakas, 2013). At the beginning of the summer, the "leaking" of classified information about the United States' government's Orwellian actions upon its citizens and those of other countries have placed American militarism in the spotlight (democracynow.com, 2013). It is interesting that these two phenomena-hate crimes against SGL and trans people on one hand, and militarism on the other-seem to be moving center stage around the same time. There is significance in these occurrences. Hate crimes and militarism are not unrelated and neither is new. Both are extreme, chronic, and global. Both are born of ideological systems that aim to define and structure the world. And in both cases, violence is the method of choice to sustain hegemonic ideologies and values.

Hate crimes against SGL and trans people typically seek to intimidate and punish nonheterosexual or gender nonconforming people in order to sustain the ideologies of heteronormativity and heterosexism. Heteronormativity assumes the heterosexuality of all people and their conformity to the binary roles of male and female. Heterosexism places heterosexuality in a privileged position at the top of a social hierarchy and casts other expressions of sexual and romantic engagement as deviant and inferior. Both of these ideologies pack people who fall along the spectrum of diversity into overly simplified, restrictive and dichotomous categories: heterosexual man and heterosexual woman. These categories serve two purposes: first, to preclude self-definition, and second, to provide comfort and reinforcement to those who hold heterosexist/heteronormative ideologies.

Militarism functions in a similar way. The use of armies, invasions, coercion, and other manners of militaristic violence are the means by which imperial gains are achieved and maintained. The American empire provides a salient case study of militarism in action. America uses its military forces to secure economic and cultural investments in places all over the world. These military forces render targeted countries at best-subjective to the whims of the United States-and at worst-thoroughly controlled by it. Within this militaristic framework, violence is the accepted method used to sustain the narrow interests, comforts and way of life of the United States and its citizens, but gives no guarantee of regard for the lives of those upon whom the empire imposes itself. Furthermore, societal acceptance of militarism fosters a culture of rigidity and control within the borders of the United States.

The Shared Motivations and Consequences of Hate Crimes Against SGL and Trans People and Militarism

Like American militarism, hate crimes against SGL and trans people are often said to have been committed in self-defense against unwanted advances from threatening SGL and trans people (similar to the national security argument-in that the United States purports militarism is appropriate to protect itself from foreign threats and terrorism that might harm American lives). People who commit hate crimes against SGL and trans people often feel justified in their offenses and are convinced that they are doing what is right by punishing or sending a message of intolerance to sexual and gender deviants who transgress the predominate heteronormative ideological system. Similarly, the United States often view the use of its military power over others as moral and just. A recent speech made by President Barack Obama at the National Defense University on May 23, 2013 illustrates this. During the speech in which the President discusses the United States current militaristic actions, he stated, "America's actions are legal. We were attacked on 9/11. Within a week, Congress overwhelmingly authorized the use of force. Under domestic law, and international law, the United States is at war with al Qaeda, the Taliban, and their associated forces. We are at war with an organization that right now would kill as many Americans as they could if we did not stop them first. So this is a just war-a war waged proportionally, in last resort, and in self-defense" (whitehouse.gov, 2013).

Homoantagonistic hate also crimes strike terror and promote anxiety among other SGL and trans people even if they are not directly targeted. Being SGL or trans or being perceived as SGL or trans is enough for one to be assaulted. Akin to this is the American insistence on prosecuting whistleblowers that expose the illegal actions of the empire. This type of retaliation on behalf of the United States, sends a message to other would-be fighters for democracy that their actions will be punishable.

Hate crimes represent the eroding of relatedness across differences and the outright rejection of SGL and trans people as human beings. Hate crimes also serve to maintain the heteronormative tenor of society and perpetuate negative stereotypes about SGL and trans people. In a parallel process, American militarism is creating more dissenters than allies. Pure, honest discussion across ideological lines without economic or exploitative strings is almost nonexistent in any of America's international relationships. For example, America provides economic and diplomatic backing to Israel and in return Israel shares intelligence information with America about possible security threats as well as its technological innovations that contribute to the United States economic gain (Eisenstadt & Pollock, 2012). Even the United States "friendly" relationships are splattered by the muck and mire of militaristic symbiosis. While the United States benefits from feelings of more security, economic advantages, and cultural influence, it is narrowing its image in the world from that of a fiercely democratic nation struggling for justice for all but to that of a nation obsessed with dominance and superiority.

American Militarism

Militarism has been defined as "1) a strong military spirit or policy; 2) the principle or policy of maintaining a large military establishment; 3) and the tendency to regard military efficiency as the supreme ideal of the state and to subordinate all other interests to those of the military" (dictionary.com). Scholars have conceptualized militarism as the spread of militaristic attitudes (Vagts, 1937) and social practices (Mann, 2003) into civilian life. The injection of militarism into contemporary American civilian life is evident when one examines both historical and current modes of interaction among citizens and the ways in which society-as a whole-treats those they deem as "other." Throughout history, those of us who are defined as the deviant other have often been subjected to aggressive treatment, surveillance, and social control. Examples include Jim Crow laws that greatly restricted the mobility and civil rights of ex-slaves in America, the internment of Japanese people during World War II, and hate crimes committed against Muslim Americans in the aftermath of the September 11, 2001 attacks. Societal level militarism is seen in official and de facto policies such as the war on drugs, the school-to-prison pipeline, the prison industrial complex, and the Stop and Frisk policy in New York City-all of which disproportionately police and confine low-income citizens and people of color.

The origins of America's long militaristic history can logically be traced to the Manifest Destiny doctrine-a religiously tinted belief purporting that America was "predestined" to occupy the entire North American continent (ushistory.org, 2013a). Action upon this doctrine resulted in the Mexican American War and the Treaty of Guadalupe Hidalgo in 1848, which secured ownership of what are now Texas, California, Nevada, Utah, and parts of Arizona, New Mexico, Oklahoma, Colorado and Wyoming (pbs.org, n.d.). American militarism began to get its footing in other parts of the globe in 1898 when the United States took possession of the Philippines, gained oversight of Cuba via the Platt Amendment, and annexed the Hawaii islands as part of its dealings in the Spanish-American War (Trask, n.d.; ushistory.org, 2013b). Both of these acquisitions contributed, and was attributable to the ideology of righteous possession and superiority. And as such, the United States could and did allow itself to regard the acquired as inferior, to ignore their concerns or dismiss them as pawns for goal achievement. The displacement of indigenous and Mexican people living in the western part of North America prior to American possession, as well as deaths of Pilipino people at the hands of the United States war machine all exemplify the fallout of an imperialist self view that relegates others to lesser status, and defines them as dispensable through violence. Several militaristic conquests have succeeded these early ones; and all have contributed to what is now-virtually-American rule of the globe. As of September 30th, 2011, the United States had a physical presence through military bases and personnel in 760 territories and foreign countries across the globe (Department of Defense, 2012) and a cultural or economic presence in many more. Furthermore, since September 11th, 2001, American military exploits, owing to perceived threats to the American way of life, have proliferated. To achieve sustainability and social order, the United States has enacted a series of counterterrorism policies that are promoted as security measures while insidiously stripping away American civil liberties. Policies such as the Patriot Act, the Homeland Security Act, and the Foreign Intelligence Surveillance Act all increased the federal government's power to invade other countries and to conduct surveillance of foreigners and American citizens through programs such as the PRISM project (democracynow.org, 2013). Militarism is entrenched in American policies both historically and currently and affects not only other countries but the domestic environment as well.

Hate Crimes Against SGL and Trans People

Those who commit hate crimes find inspiration and justification in a militaristic society that preferences violence and control over democracy and relatedness. Hate crimes are "words or actions intended to harm or intimidate an individual because of her or his membership in a minority group; they include violent assaults, murder, rape, and property crimes motivated by prejudice, as well as threats of violence or other acts of intimidation" (Finn & McNeil, 1987 as cited by Herek, 1989, p. 1) Herek (1989) suggests that hate crimes are an outgrowth from intolerance. This is not hard to understand. When we think about specific hate crimes that target SGL and trans people, the perpetrators often openly profess the bigotry that motivate their actions. For example, in a hate crime committed in October of 2006 against two gay male residents of Atlanta, GA, James Carter and R'heem Turner, heard their assailants exclaim, "Get yo faggot ass down" (McCullom, 2006). The use of derogatory sexual epithets makes it clear that the men's assumed sexual orientations were the motivation for the assault. Unfortunately, hate crimes are not isolated events. There have been a multitude of homoantagonistic hate crimes in recent decades including Sakia Gunn, Michael Sandy, Terrance Aeriel, Iofemi Hightower, Dashon Harvey, Lateisha Green, and Matthew Shepard. In fact, the Federal Bureau of Investigation has been collecting hate crime statistics since 1996 and in 2011, 20.8% of all single-bias incidents of hate crimes resulted from sexual orientation bias (Federal Bureau of Investigations, 2011). Also, in a sample of 402 trans people, researchers found that almost sixty percent of the participants in their study reported some form of trans bias harassment or violence in their lifetime (Lombardi, Wilchins, Priesing, & Malouf, 2001). These statistics make it clear that hate crimes against SGL and trans people are prevalent in the United States.

Further analysis of hate crimes paint a picture of when and how hate crimes against SGL and trans people occur. Many SGL and trans people become the victims of hate crimes before they become adults. Herek, Gillis, Cogan, & Glunt (1997) found that 41% of nonheterosexual people reported being victims of hate crimes since the age of 16. Furthermore, women are more likely to report being sexually assaulted because of their sexual orientation than men. These findings make sense in a society where some believe that people can be forced into heterosexuality, via methods ranging from exorcism to rape (Herek, Cogan, & Gillis, 2002; McCullom, 2009). While hate crime victims typically report being assaulted by strangers, many suffer harassment at the hands of family members and friends. SGL and trans people report most often that their antagonizers are male, white, and between the ages of 19 and 25 (Herek et al., 2002; Herek et al., 1997). Again this makes sense in a society where heterosexual men report higher levels of negative attitudes toward SGL and trans people than heterosexual women (Herek & Capitanio, 1999; Kite & Whitley, 1998). Heterosexual white men represent the hegemon in the white supremacist society of the United States. It is not hard to understand why they might be the most invested in maintaining the status quo-as it benefits them the most-and the use of violence is not seen as an inappropriate tool for ensuring the status quo is maintained. With that said, people across sociodemographic characteristics whom tend to hold more rigid worldviews, and whom are invested in heteronormativity and heterosexism have been known to use violence to maintain these ideologies of oppression and to punish those who challenge them.

Hate crimes have negative physical and psychological consequences for SGL and trans people. Victims of violent hate crimes can suffer bruises, broken bones, and sometimes death, in addition to stolen or vandalized property. Hate related homicides against SGL and trans people made up 16.7% of all hate crime deaths (National Coalition of Anti-Violence Programs People [NCAVP], 2013). People of color were the most affected and made up 73.1% of all hate crimes committed against SGL and trans people. In addition, with the exception of death, physical consequences of hate crimes often go unreported by SGL and trans people (Herek et al., 2002; Herek, Gillis, & Cogan, 1999). Many SGL and trans people choose not to report hate crimes to police for fear of being victimized a second time by law enforcement officers thought-and in some cases known-to engage in homoantagonistic discrimination and mistreatment. The NCAVP (2013) found that among SGL and trans people who did report hate crime incidents to police, 48% reported police misconduct and 26.8% reported that the police had hostile attitudes. Indeed, police are sometimes the violent offenders of SGL and trans people. In 2012, police comprised 23.9% of the homoantagonistic violent perpetrators whom victims did not know personally (National Coalition of Anti-Violence Programs People [NCAVP], 2013). Violence against SGL and trans people is often committed by those closest to the victim as well as members of institutions who are suppose to protect the vulnerable.

Hate crime victimization is also related to poor mental health among SGL and trans people. Researchers have found that depression, anxiety, and PTSD symptoms are higher in victims of hate crimes than those who have not experienced such victimization (Herek et al., 1997; Herek et al., 1999). They have also found that SGL and trans victims of hate crimes are more afraid of being victimized again, perceive themselves as more vulnerable, have lower sense of mastery, and view others as less benevolent (Herek et al., 1997; Herek et al., 1999). Hate crimes against SGL and trans people create an atmosphere of dread among nonheterosexual and gender nonconforming people.

The Rigid Need for Control: A Link Between Militarism and Hate Crimes

The need for control is a very human one. We all have it. In and of itself, it is not an unhealthy need. Rigidity of worldview, and the obsessive quest to impose, enact and enforce it, is what is dangerous-both physically and psychologically, at micro and macro levels. Instead of being able to grapple with the need to predict and manipulate one's environment in a flexible manner, rigidity causes one to adopt restrictive, one-size fits all tactics to achieve a sense of control. Rigidity is conceptualized in this paper as the inability to approach and engage with people, places, things, and ideas in a manner that is exploratory and unhindered by bias. People and societies who have high levels of rigidity tend to lack appreciation of others' viewpoints and emotions. Rigid people and societies tend to lack empathy and have negative attitudes toward difference. From a psychodynamic framework, rigidity can be seen as a defense against anxiety (Eriksen & Eisenstein, 1953). The highly rigid person may have a heightened sense of internal conflict, and deny an aspect of her/himself, because gratification of that aspect may clash ideologically with her/his rigid self-definition (Cattell & Ghosetiner, 1949). For example, a bicurious person who chooses to rigidly define her/himself as heterosexual is less likely to explore her/his same-sex attraction because gratification of that desire might conflict with her/his sense of self as a moral woman or man.

Rigidity hampers one's cognitive abilities. Very rigid people and societies have low tolerance for ambiguity and often display an inability to break from old perceptual habits and ways of thinking, or ideational inertia (Cattell & Ghosetiner, 1949). For example, a highly rigid society would find it difficult to think of itself in objective terms and instead cast its role in the world in idealistic terms. This is evident in the words of former President George W. Bush when he stated, nine days after September 11, 2001, that "[terrorists] hate what they see right here in this chamber: a democratically elected government. Their leaders are self-appointed. They hate our freedoms: our freedom of religion, our freedom of speech, our freedom to vote and assemble and disagree with each other" (cnn.com, 2001). While for some terrorists these statements may apply, ideational inertia prevents people who share the former president's beliefs to consider how American militarism and

273

foreign policies could fuel anti-American sentiment. The non-rigid, objective observer may on the other hand conclude that these policies contribute to poverty and exploitation of other countries and people around the world. And that while there is no justification for murder as carried out on September 11, these effects may explain the profound frustration that lead to the attacks. Rigidity can render a nation blind to its role in conflict and prevent it from taking peaceful, responsible steps toward resolution and instead resort to familiar retaliatory violence.

Researchers have found that a variety of personality traits are associated with rigidity. In one study, people who scored high on a measure of rigidity also scored significantly higher on measures of social introversion and submissiveness and scored significantly lower on measures of social presence and leadership ability (Rehfisch, 1958). This suggests that people who have high levels of rigidity may find more comfort in their inner world than in interactions with others. They may also be more likely to follow rules, acquiesce to the status quo and accept the ideas and actions of others in power without challenging them. Rehfisch (1958) also found that people who scored high on a measure of rigidity also scored significantly higher (compared to those who had low scores on the rigidity measure) on measures of anxiety, depression and self-dissatisfaction. They were also found to express themselves in more forcible manners. These findings suggest that highly rigid people may experience more negative emotion, and may be more confrontational and direct in their expressions than less rigid people.

High levels of rigidity tend to predominate in men. Indeed, men have been found to be more rigid than women (Vollhardt, 1990). Researchers have found that those with high levels of rigidity and need for control are more prone to violence and more likely to view role violation negatively than people who have lower levels of rigidity. In a study of 595 men who were the victims of childhood sexual and physical abuse, men who also later became abusers reported more gender rigidity than those who did not perpetuate the cycle of violence (Lisak, Hopper, & Song, 1996). This finding suggests that rigidity concerning one's gender and what it means to be a man is related to passing along abuse to others. If a child with high mental rigidity is abused he may come to accept abuse as being part of the default landscape of the male child and, as an adult, may therefore think of abusing children, and possibly others, as normal and more masculine. It should be noted that this formulation of the interactions and temporal relation of gender rigidity and violence perpetration assumes a very high level of mental rigidity around concepts of "right and wrong". However, this is not an entirely unrealistic formulation in a society where often masculinity is tied to notions of violence and dominance. Similarly in a study that included a random sample of 17 different cultures-cultures as defined by the Human Relations Area Files, a cultural anthropology organization-researchers found that at the societal level, sex-role rigidity was correlated with acts of violence (McConahay & McConahay, 1977). These findings may explain why men overwhelmingly are the perpetrators of homoantagonistic hate crimes and the orchestrators of militaristic actions.

Rigidity has restrictive effects on a rigid person or society's ability to think reflexively, pursue new methods of engagement, and deal with conflict in nonstereotyped ways. Eriksen and Eisenstein (1953, p. 386-387) stated that "in an attempt to control and reduce anxiety the [rigid] individual restricts his[/her] psychological field to the point where he[/she] feels he can master and control it. Through repression of threatening ideas and activities the field of alternatives is reduced and associations lose their freedom and flexibility....There is a strong need for certainties and for black-and-white solutions which are reflected not only in emotional relationships, but in perceptual and cognitive functions as well." Given these implications of rigidity and its association with violence, it is not hard to understand the link between rigidity, hate crimes, and militarism.

Moving Forward

Our world is rapidly changing. The granting of civil rights for SGL people publically acknowledges the existence of same-sex attracted people and lend legal and cultural legitimacy-on a national scale-to sexual matters outside of heteronormative confines. The increasing worldwide uprisings and protests against inequality in places like Turkey, Bulgaria, Spain, Egypt, and domestically represent the freedom call in a world dominated by oppressive systems. People like Bradley Manning, Julian Assange, and Edward Snowden upset the mystique of American militaristic operations and threaten the cloak that enables governmental avoidance of accountability. All of these things agitate the presumed principles of society. For some-especially those high in rigidity, these accumulating shifts threaten their very foundation and the cognitive schemas that organize their world. This type of core threat can cause people to respond in drastic ways to protect the stability and functions that provide comfort for them.

In order to combat the mental rigidity of worldview that fosters hate crimes and militarism we must be reflexive in our thoughts and actions. We must challenge ourselves to move beyond our comfort zones and we must be willing to take chances. Take chances to listen with unbiased ears, share without need to persuade, and give without receiving. To overcome our rigidity we must be willing to venture into unknown territory and give up notions of predictability, stability, control, and manipulation. We must be willing to be anxious and uneasy and accept foremost that as people, in the global and American community, we are not evil or just, not gay or straight, but human. Until we can do these things, until we can let go of our rigid worldviews and the need to enforce them, hate crimes and militarism will flourish, and we will continue to perish.

Works Cited

Cattell, R., & Ghosetiner, L. (1949). The varieties of structural rigidity. *Journal of Personality, 17*, 321-341. doi: 10.1111/j.1467-6494.1949.tb01217.x

cnn.com. (2001, September 21). *Transcript of President Bush's address.* Retrieved from http://archives.cnn.com/2001/US/09/20/gen.bush.transcript/

democracynow.com. (2013, June 7). *"A massive surveillance state": Glenn Greenwald exposes covert NSA program collecting calls, emails.* Retrieved from http://www.democracynow.org/2013/6/7/a_massive_surveillance_stat e_glenn_greenwald

Department of Defense. (2012). *Base structure report: FY 2012 baseline.* Retrieved from www.acq.osd.mil/ie/download/bsr/BSR2012Baseline.pdf

Eisenstadt, M., & Pollock, D. (2012). *Asset test: How the United States*

benefits from its alliance with Israel. Retrieved from
http://www.washingtoninstitute.org/policy-analysis/view/asset-test-
how-the-united-states-benefits-from-its-alliance-with-israel

Eriksen C., & Eisenstein, D. (1953). Personality rigidity and the
Rorschach. *Journal of **Personality**, 21*, 386-391. doi: 10.1111/1467-
6494.ep8930322

Federal Bureau of Investigations. (2011). *Hate crime statistics 2011:
Incidents and offenses*. Retrieved from http://www.fbi.gov/about-
us/cjis/ucr/hate-crime/2011/narratives/incidents-and-offenses

Herek, G. (1989). Hate crimes against lesbians and gay men: Issues for
research and policy. *American Psychologist, 44*(6), 948-955.

Herek, G., & Capitanio, J. (1999). Sex differences in how heterosexuals
think about lesbians and gay men: Evidence from survey context effects.
Journal of Sex Research, 36(4), 348-360.

Herek, G., Cogan, J., & Gillis, J. (2002). Victim experiences in hate crimes
based on sexual orientation.*Journal of Social Issues, 58*(2), 319-339.

Herek, G., Gillis, J., & Cogan, J. (1999). Psychological sequelae of hate-
crime victimization among lesbian, gay, and bisexual adults. *Journal of
Consulting and Clinical Psychology, 67*(6), 945-951.

Herek, G., Gillis, J., Cogan, J., & Glunt, E. (1997). Hate crime victimization
among lesbian, gay, and bisexual adults: Prevalence, psychological
correlates, and methodological issues. *Journal of Interpersonal Violence,
12*, 195-215. doi: 10.1177/088626097012002003

Kite, M., & Whitley, B. (1998). Do heterosexual women and men differ
in their attitudes toward homosexuality? A conceptual and
methodological analysis. In G. Herek (Ed.), *Stigma and sexual
orientation: Understanding prejudice against lesbians, gay men, and
bisexuals. Psychological perspectives on lesbian and gay issues , Vol.
4.* (pp. 39-61). Thousand Oaks, CA: Sage Publications, Inc.

Lisak, D., Hopper, J. & Song, P. (1996). Factors in the cycle of violence:
Gender rigidity and emotional constriction. *Journal of Traumatic Stress,*

9(4), 721-743.

Lloyd, L. (2013, June 17). Anti-gay hate crime leaves man's car undrivable. *Laist*. Retrieved from http://laist.com/2013/06/17/anti-gay_hate_crime_leaves_mans_car.php

Lombardi, E., Wilchins, R., Priesing, D., & Malouf, D. (2001). Gender violence. *Journal of Homosexuality, 42*, 89-101. doi: 10.1300/J082v42n01_05

Mann, M. (2003). *Incoherent empire*. London: Verso.

McConahay, S. & McConahay, J. (1977). Sexual permissiveness, sex-role rigidity, and violence across cultures. *Journal of Social Issues, 33*, 134-143. doi: 10.1111/j.1540-4560.1977.tb02009.x

McCullom, R. (2006, October 27). Atlanta gay bash victims speak out: "I didn't want to die". Retrieved from http://rodonline.typepad.com/rodonline/2006/10/atlanta_gay_bas.htm

McCullom, R. (2009, June 25). Black Connecticut church focus of gay teen "exorcism" video. Retrieved http://rodonline.typepad.com/rodonline/2009/06/antigay-black-connecticut-church-focus-of-teen-exorcism-video.html

Militarism. (n.d.). In dictionary.com free online English dictionary. Retrieved from http://dictionary.reference.com/browse/militarism?s=t

National Coalition of Anti-Violence Programs People. (2013). A report from the national coalition of anti-violence programs (NCAVP): Lesbian, gay, bisexual, transgender, queer and HIV-affected hate violence in 2012. Retrieved from http://www.avp.org/about-avp/coalitions-a-collaborations/82-national-coalition-of-anti-violence-programs

pbs.org. (n.d.). *The Mexican American war*. Retrieved from http://www.pbs.org/wgbh/americanexperience/features/general-article/grant-mexican-american-war/

Prokupecz, S. (2013, May 22). Gay couple, man assaulted in 2 separate attacks hours after rally against hate crimes. *NBC New York*. Retrieved from http://www.nbcnewyork.com/news/local/Anti-Gay-Hate-Crime-SoHo-Broadway-Attack-208337881.html

Rehfisch, J. (1958). Some scale and test correlates of a personality rigidity scale. *Journal of Consulting Psychology, 22*(5), 372-374.

Trask, D. (n.d.). *The Spanish-American war.* Retrieved from http://www.loc.gov/rr/hispanic/1898/trask.html

ushistory.org. (2013a). *Manifest destiny*, Retrieved from http://www.ushistory.org/us/29.asp

ushistory.org. (2013b). *Hawaiian annexation*. Retrieved from http://www.ushistory.org/us/44b.asp

Vagts, A. (1937) *A history of militarism: Romance and reality of a profession*. New York: W. W. Norton & Co.

Vollhardt, L. (1990). Rigidity: A comparison by age and gender. Social Behavior and Personality, 18(1), 17-26.

whitehouse.gov. (2013, May 23). *Remarks by the President at the National Defense University*. Retrieved from http://www.whitehouse.gov/the-press-office/2013/05/23/remarks-president-national-defense-university

Yakas, B. (2013, May 19). Greenwich Village hate crime murder victim was "proud hay man" from Brooklyn. *Gothamist*. Retrieved from http://gothamist.com/2013/05/19/greenwich_village_hate_crime_murder.php

Homonegativity In Black

A Culturally Sensitive Historical Perspective

Jonathan Mathias Lassiter

It is a popular belief that African American people are more homonegative than people of other races. This belief is more delusion than fact. Homonegativity is a problem within African American communities. I am not too idealistic to know that some African Americans express homonegativity in subtle and extreme ways toward same gender loving people (SGL). However, African Americans do not have a monopoly on homonegativity. They are people just like individuals of other races and are not the exception to the rule. They have their prejudices and areas for growth just like their other human brothers and sisters. The purpose of this essay is not to excuse homonegativity among African Americans but to provide an examination of the historical context of homonegativity in African American communities and provide strategies to mitigate it.

The myth of hyper-homonegativity within African American communities is just another example of the portrayal of African Americans (and people of color in general) as hyper aggressive, intolerant, and ideologically stagnant. To my dismay, people of African descent often perpetuate this fallacy. Recently Lee Daniels, an African American filmmaker, commented in an interview that "black men can't come out" (Hernandez, 2013). His reasoning was that because African American SGL men receive messages from religious, familial, and community sources touting the deviance of homosexuality that there is no way that they could possibly disclose their sexual identities to others and live an authentic life. He spewed, "the black culture and the Hispanic culture have a thing about [homosexuality]" (Hernandez, 2013).

This type of myth dissemination paints a picture of SGL people as victims of African American homonegativity who must deny their sexual selves or be punished through rejection and possibly violence. It also paints a picture of African Americans and other people of color as draconian sexual and gender role police. Homonegative sexual and gender role policing do take place in African American communities but it is not a given. It is not the case for many and it does not happen exclusively in African American communities. Heterosexual African American people have nuanced relationships with SGL people in and outside of their communities. All SGL people are not stuck in closets fearing for their lives. In fact, a recent survey found that SGL people from communities of color (including African Americans, Latino(a)s, and Asian Americans) identify as SGL more openly than Non-Latino(a) European Americans (Gates & Newport, 2012). Furthermore, research has consistently shown that religion (most often Abrahamic religions-i.e. Christianity, Islam, and Judaism) not race is the most significant predictor of homonegative bias (Schulte & Battle, 2004). Indeed, religion and the deviant sexualization of bodies of color can be understood as the biggest contributors to the homonegativity that is seen in communities of color today. This essay will provide a brief exploration these major factors related to homonegativity in African American communities, specifically, and discuss methods for moving away from homonegativity and towards tolerance and affirming relatedness for African Americans and SGL people of all colors.

The Influence of Racism and the Deviant Sexualization of the Body on Black Americans' Expression of Homonegativity

Audre Lorde (1984) provides powerful insight in her book *Sister Outsider* when she discusses the actions often taken by people in response to difference. The following passage provides a synopsis of the engagement patterns people and government historically has had-and in many ways, currently have-with each other.

Institutionalized rejection of difference is an absolute necessity in a profit economy, which needs outsiders as surplus people. As members of such economy, we have all been programmed to respond to the human differences between us with fear and loathing and to handle that difference in one of three ways: ignore it, and if that is not possible, copy it if we think it is dominant, or destroy it if we think it is subordinate. But we have no patterns for relating across our human difference as equals. As a result, those differences have been misnamed and misused in the service of separation and confusion. (p.115).

While I do not propose that pre-colonial African peoples were free of bias toward SGL people, or any peoples deemed different for that matter, colonialism had a potent programming effect on Africans subsequent engagement with SGL people. The subsequent treatment of SGL people by Africans and African Americans mirror the model set forth by European colonists in their treatment of African peoples and their differences. Since the early introduction of the two races, it has been a constant struggle for African people and their descendents to resist blight (Douglas, 1999). Almost immediately, European people began a process of defining and redefining African people. The definitions conjured by them and their offspring-European Americans-often cast them not only as other, but as deviant other (Murray & Roscoe, 1998).

European explorers first defined African people as primitive (Murray & Roscoe, 1998). The primitive was viewed in predominately two ways: as the noble savage or the sylvan wild man (Murray & Roscoe, 1998). Murray and Roscoe (1998) reported that the noble savage was perceived as "healthier, better adjusted, and the bearer of wisdom" (p. xi) and the sylvan wild man was considered monstrous and someone to be feared. Roscoe and Murray (1998) noted that the primitive African person served to highlight the differences between western and non-Western culture. Whatever the African person was, the European person was not and vice versa. In contrast to the sophistication of European culture, African peoples were judged to be "close to nature, ruled by instinct, culturally unsophisticated...heterosexual, [their] sexual energies and outlets devoted exclusively to their 'natural' purpose: biological reproduction"

(Murray & Roscoe, 1998, p. xi). Early European anthropologists bolstered this heterosexist claim with reports of the absence of same-sex relationships and practices among African peoples (Murray & Roscoe, 1998). When they did acknowledge it, they either explained it as a necessity due to lack of women available for men or a temporary phase among adolescents (Murray & Roscoe, 1998). The European perception of African peoples and their African American descendents as primitive and impulsive-and thus, inferior-came to define all aspects of them, including their intelligence and sexuality (Guthrie, 2004; Murray & Roscoe, 1998). (See Guthrie, 2004, for a detailed account of European American people's misuse of science to define African people and their African American descendents as unintelligent.)

The European notions of African sexuality were codified among American slave owners and dictated the beliefs and behaviors of European Americans regarding African Americans (both past and present). American slave owners conceptualized the enslaved Africans as "oversexed, to have animalistic large genitals and to be characterized by predatory sexual behavior" (Griffin, 2004, p. 133). African male slaves were perceived as violent bucks. The use of the word buck conjures the image of a beast. This term had the effect of stripping African male slaves of their humanity and linking them with the animal kingdom, the primitive. As violent bucks, they were seen as powerful sources of production in the plantation fields and as virile inseminators of female slaves in the slave quarters (Donoghue, 2008; Douglas, 1999). Both of these roles had positive implications for slave owners' profits. However, they also constituted a threat to white society (Douglas, 1999). If African male slaves became too powerful, they might overtake slave owners. If their sexual lust became too strong, they might rape white women or worst, seduce them into voluntary erotic liaisons. In a Freudian manner, slave owners projected their ills and insecurities onto their slaves. While they accused the African male slave of conspiracies of domination and sexual subjugation of white women, they were the real perpetrators of these crimes against African slave women and white women (Donoghue, 2006; Douglas, 1999; Hernton, 1992). Slave owners viewed African women as sexually deviant as well. They formulated African women as either asexual domestics or hypersexual seductresses. These formulations allowed slave owners to cast African women in the roles cooks, maids, and nurses as well as justify the rape and sexual torture inflicted upon these women.

The detrimental effects of these definitions stamped upon African bodies persist in the present. African men have gone from the violent, overly sexual buck to the violent, sex crazed African American thug that still have all of the attributes of the former incarnation. The incessant rendering of African American men in this manner has made them the target of systematic castration, lynching, and incarceration (Douglas, 1999). It has also caused them to be objectified as body parts for sexual gratification by both men and women (West, 1994). These stereotypes negatively affect both SGL and heterosexual African American men (McBride, 2005). In the eyes of many, African American women are also stamped with the stamp of abnormality in regards to their sexuality and sexual roles. Overall, they are still conceptualized in the imaginations of many as either overbearing caretakers who are asexual and who emasculate their sons and male partners through their caretaking. Many African American women are also seen as sexually undesirable and interpersonally unappealing by many men (of all colors) due to their body shapes, skin color, or nontraditional gender role qualities such as being opinionated and forthright in their interactions. On the other hand, some African American women are oversexualized and fetishized as "video vixens" and "big booty hoes" with large sexual appetites and uninhibited sexual practices. Such deviant conceptualizations of black sexuality have caused African Americans to be not only homonegative but also sex negative in general (West, 1994). Given these factors, it is not surprising that the policing of sexuality is a problem in too many African American communities.

In an effort to prove their morality and humanity, many African Americans have cast SGL people as the deviant other (Douglas, 1999). They have done this in the same manner that it was done to them by European explorers and American colonists. In order to be above someone in a hierarchy of oppression, someone must be below. In an effort to gain approval within a white supremacist society, some African Americans use homonegativity as a way to separate themselves from "depraved" SGL people. Many African Americans have internalized the notion of SGL as morally corrupt, unnatural, and perverted (Griffin, 2006). Just as early Europeans defined themselves by distinguishing between what was Western and what was not, African Americans have engaged in the same differentiating. It is as if with their homonegativity, many African Americans are saying to their oppressors (i.e. white supremacists and white supremacist institutions): "we are not as bad as them (i.e. SGL people), accept us." In some ways, the homonegativity of

African Americans unifies them with their homonegative Caucasian counterparts. The supposed depravity of SGL people is a rallying call for all purported "pure, good moral people." In accordance with this reasoning, some African Americans' objection to same-sex practices and relationships can be viewed as a testament to their purity and humanity as heterosexual African Americans.

Religion as Justification of Homonegativity in Black Communities

Religion is often used to justify the oppression of the *other* in many communities (Farajaje-Jones, 1993). (*Other* is defined by this author to mean anything or anyone that does not fit within the notions of the mainstream or the status quo in a society or community). Just as European colonists used Christianity to justify the enslavement of Africans in the American colonies, it was and is used by many African American Christians to condemn SGL people. This horizontal oppression is particularly unfortunate and has negative effects on the well being of many African American SGL people (Boykin, 1996; Griffin, 2006). As a Pew study (2008) indicated, 55% of African Americans believe that religious scriptures should be interpreted literally. This might explain why Biblical text is often cited as the authoritative source providing support for Christians' disdain for SGL people and their behaviors. In the Old Testament of the Bible, scriptures from the book of Genesis (particularly, the story of Sodom in Chapter 19) and Leviticus (Chapter 18) are used to admonish same-sex sexual behaviors and attractions. Paul's words are used to condemn them in the New Testament.

Chapter 19 of the book of Genesis describes the arrival of two male angels in the city of Sodom. These two angels were staying at Lot's house when some men from the city came to Lot's house and requested to "know" the angels carnally. When Lot would not allow the city's men access to the angels, the city's men tried to forcefully gain entry into Lot's house. As a result, the angels blinded the men and then destroyed the cities of Sodom and Gomorrah with brimstone and fire. Many Christians interpret the destruction of Sodom and Gomorrah as evidence that the Christian God condemns same-sex sexual behaviors and attraction. Same-sex attraction and intent of same-sex sexual behaviors are interpreted in the passages by the request of the city's men to know- *know* in the Old Testament has traditionally been interpreted to mean sexual intercourse-the angels, who were also male.

However, many scholars debate the true sin of Sodom (Long, 2004). Many dispute whether the men's sin was homosexuality or the violation of hospitality (Long, 2004). Given that it was custom for strangers to be treated hospitably when they entered into a new town. Some argue that it could have been both, that they were inhospitable and desired to rape the angels (Long, 2004). Yet, nowhere else in the Hebrew scriptures is the story of Sodom used to condemn same-sex sexual behaviors and attraction and the sin of Sodom is never explicitly identified (Long, 2004).

Leviticus 18:22 forbid men from lying with other men as if with women. Scholars have pointed out that this scripture is a part of what is known as the Holiness Code, which is comprised of chapters 18-20 of the book of Leviticus (Long, 2004). It is hypothesized that the Holiness Code is the work of a priestly writer or school that through contemplation of the Sodom story wrote a set of laws to distinguish the Israelites from their foreign neighbors (Long, 2004). Indeed, these chapters not only forbid same-sex sexual behaviors but the mixing of fabrics and imposed rigid diet restrictions. Whatever the rationale of the Holiness Code, it is clear that it was written for a particular people in a particular moment in history and is now outdated.

Just as the author of the Holiness Code wrote his list of laws to make sure the Israelites were distinct from their neighbors, so did Paul prohibit early Christians from engaging in several behaviors in an attempt to differentiate them from non-Christians (Long, 2004). One such behavior was sexual intercourse between partners of the same sex. In Romans 1:24-27, 1 Corinthians 6:9-10 and 1 Timothy 1:8-10, he warns against the evils of same-sex intercourse. These scriptures cast homosexuality as the result of ungodliness and people that engage in same-sex intercourse as unrighteous people that will not go to heaven in the afterlife.

Such judgments in the scriptures and literal interpretation of these scriptures about same-sex sexual behaviors and attractions have caused many people in African American churches to hold homonegative beliefs. The literal interpretation of these scriptures is shocking and contradictory given the historical use of Biblical scriptures by African Americans. African Americans have a history of using Biblical scriptures to foster liberation and not oppression (Douglas, 1999). For example, when slave owners attempted to use Paul's words to justify slavery, enslaved people rejected that interpretation and instead focused on the story of the Exodus, which emphasized deliverance from oppression. It is unfortunate that some African American clergy and congregants would then cite an author whose words were once utilized to facilitate their oppression-as slaves-to contribute to the persecution of SGL people. It is a classic example of the oppressed becoming the oppressor.

The "Unnatural" Argument against Same-Sex Attractions and Behaviors

Some homonegative African Americans not only cite religious scripture for the basis of their homonegativity but also rely on ideologies that purport the sexual behaviors and attractions of SGL people are the result of unnatural aberrations and contaminations (Douglas, 1999). The fact that two same sex people cannot procreate through their sexual activity with each other is perceived as proof for many homonegative people that it is unnatural. These people claim to believe that sexual intercourse was designed exclusively for procreation. It is not uncommon to hear homonegative Christians say, "Adam and Eve not Adam and Steve." This mantra expresses their belief that the natural order is for men and women to be sexually and romantically paired with the opposite sex and not in same sex dyads.

Anal intercourse among men is often viewed in a particularly negative way. Some clergy and homonegative people cast anal intercourse as the manifestation of a double deformity that separates the natural from the unnatural (Long, 2004). Even though anal intercourse is practiced among heterosexual and SGL people alike, SGL men are often the only ones considered to be deformed for engaging in this practice. They are seen as deviating from the "good form" of men having sexual relations with women. Furthermore, because at least one partner in anal intercourse is penetrated, receptiveness is also conceptualized as a deviation from nature because, stereotypically, a man is only a penetrator in the act of intercourse. Thus, not only are African American men seen as abandoning their sexual relationships with women but some are also accused of assuming a feminine role, further deviating from gender norms-or what is natural.

Some homonegative people in the African American communities have constructed the mythology of same-sex sexual behaviors and attraction as a disease transmitted to African American people by European colonists during slavery, and European American men, in modernity, in an attempt to sabotage the survival of the Black community (Fullilove & Fullilove, 1999; Griffin, 2004). Interestingly, as described above, Europeans first propagated this myth (Murray & Roscoe, 1998). However, historians and anthropologists have found evidence that clearly prove that the assertion is indeed fictional (Murray & Roscoe, 1998). Several African tribes all throughout the African continent engaged in same-sex sexual practices and had same-sex romantic relationships (Murray & Roscoe, 1998). In Africa, however, egalitarian same-sex relationships-in which both partners have relatively equal social status-were not as widespread as they were among Europeans (Murray & Roscoe, 1998). Murray and Roscoe (1998) reported that the two most common and widespread types of same-sex relationships among males were age-based and gender-based. Age-based patterns of same-sex relationships were those in which one partner was older than the other. The older partner usually was the penetrator and the younger partner was receptive. Often the older partner would also serve as a mentor to the younger one. In gender-based same-sex relationships, the penetrating partner is not deemed SGL. However, the penetrated partner was expected to perform the gendered role of a woman. That meant dressing and behaving like a woman. Also, in some African societies, same-sex sexual activity was a rite of passage (Murray & Roscoe, 1998). For example, among tribes in Cameroon and in parts of West Africa, it was common among children and adolescents in the years that preceded their marriages to engage in sexual activity with members of the same sex. Some even continued their same-sex sexual activities into adulthood (Murray & Roscoe, 1998). It was more common for African women to enter into same-sex relationships as adults than it were for their male counterparts. There were even tribes composed entirely of women who worked together and had romantic liaisons. It was not unheard of for widows to take the money left by their husbands and start romantic symbiotic relationships with other women-often younger-for whom they provided financially. The evidence presented by Murray and Roscoe (1998)-and the other authors-in their anthology provide substantial proof that homosexuality is not a foreign transmission to African people and their descendents-African Americans. As Audre Lorde (1984) wrote, many African Americans have given "false power to difference" (p.15). This false power is often destructive in nature. However, this deleterious use of difference was greatly influenced by European colonists. Europeans did not introduce same-sex sexual behaviors and attraction to Africans but encouraged them and their descendents to distrust and thus antagonize

SGL people (Griffin, 2004; Murray & Roscoe, 1998). African American people's homonegative attitudes and behaviors may be influenced by endemic and outside factors but it is their sole responsibility to move away from homonegativity. Such negative ideologies separate African American people from their loved ones and others struggling for justice.

Moving Away From Homonegativity

Heterosexual African Americans have and continue to become more tolerant and affirming of SGL people within and outside of their communities. Scholars have found that African Americans are in favor of policies that benefit SGL people such as nondiscrimination employment measures and civil liberties at rates higher than their Caucasian counterparts (Lewis, 2003; Rivas, 2012). Heterosexual African Americans have made great strides and still have some growing to do in regards to making their communities more inclusive of their SGL brothers and sisters.

SGL people, their allies, and heterosexual African Americans have the responsibility of furthering this inclusion. Some strategies (adapted from Gibbs & Jones, 2013) toward this aim include educating African American people about SGL people, both past and present; engaging in individual contact with heterosexuals in an open and mutual manner that is not condemnatory or entitled; group contact between heterosexual African American organizations and SGL organizations with members of all colors; and realistic public health and public education initiatives that display SGL people as diverse-not cookie cutter clones aping heterosexual norms-in their identities, races, socioeconomic statuses and other ways while providing accurate, nonstigmatizing information.

Most people do better when they know better. It should not be assumed that African American heterosexual people automatically understand same-sex attraction and behaviors or the wants and needs that are unique to SGL people. Educational efforts should be made in schools, churches, and community organizations. These efforts should incorporate SGL history and civil liberty issues into curriculums and discussions within African American institutions in a way that is relevant to African Americans. One of the best ways to do this is by featuring the narratives of African American and other people of color who are also SGL. SGL people should not be painted with the brushstrokes of whiteness that centers on European American gays and lesbians. It is imperative that these curriculums and discussions do not intentionally or inadvertently position the struggles of SGL people as greater than or identical to those of African Americans. This diminishes the very real and current injustices that African Americans continue to experience and will hinder relatedness.

Individual and group contact might be the most important method of fostering community among seemingly different groups. Members of SGL communities and African American communities (which are not mutually exclusive) must be willingly to reach beyond their comfort zones to commune with each other in a way that is not antagonistic and is without motivations to persuade. Relationships formed must be genuine with the sole purpose of getting to know the other person. Relationships should not be a means to an end but the end itself. These types of relationships involve real, whole people who do not lead with their difference. SGL people should not enter heterosexual spaces as SGL people but as human people. African American people should not consider their blackness as their most important attribute in their engagements with others. While differences should be respected and affirmed in relationships, it is not necessary for them to be primary. Humanness, complicated and complex, should always be at the center.

Public health and public education initiatives have the potential to foster attitude change and shift interpersonal relations at the macrolevel. Public health and public education initiatives such as marketing campaigns and research agendas that focus on accurate, diverse, and nonstigmatizing subject matter can help positively progress attitudes about SGL people. Too often the images and information disseminated about SGL people is narrowly focused and color-coded. For example, while there is a range of issues important to SGL people, marriage equality-most often with a white face-has been the most highlighted one in the current millennium. Also, while there are a number of ills that affect African American SGL people, government agencies overwhelming fund research projects that focus on pathology such as HIV-risk behaviors and drug use. More attention should be given to the resilience and normal development of SGL people and not just their shortcomings. The relationships of SGL people-and not just the sexual ones-should be examined and highlighted. This treatment of SGL people shows their diversity while accentuating their humanness. For example, racial and ethnic minority lesbian couples in the Southern United States are more likely to be raising children than their male and

European American counterparts (Gates, 2013), however; these narratives are hardly ever heard in mainstream discourses. These strategies when implemented in an inclusive and reflexive manner have the potential to mitigate homonegativity among African Americans and the SGL people in and outside of African Americans communities.

Homonegativity is still an issue in African American communities. However, it is not a problem unique to African Americans and it is not more of a problem for African American communities than for other communities. Homonegativity has a long and complex history in the African American community stemming from human ineptness at engaging with difference, colonization and religious indoctrination, and "natural" order ideologies. The history of homonegativity and its current presence in African American communities do not mean that SGL people have no place there. It does not mean that African American SGL people "can't come out" and live authentic lives. Indeed, many currently do lead fulfilling, honest lives. Homonegativity in African American communities means the same thing that its presence means in any other place: there is more work to do.

References

Boykin, K. (1996). *One more river to cross: Black and gay in America.* New York: Doubleday.

Donoghue, E. (2008). *Black breeding machines: The breeding of Negro slaves in the diaspora* . Bloomington, IN: AuthorHouse.

Douglas, K. (1999). *Sexuality and the Black church: A womanist perspective.* Maryknoll, NY: Orbis Books.

Farajaje-Jones, E. (1993). Breaking silence: Toward and in-the-life theology. In J. Cone & G. Wilmore (Eds.), *Black Theology: A Documentary History, Vol. 2: 1980-1992* (pp. 139-159). Maryknoll, NY: Orbis Books.

Fullilove, M., & Fullilove, R. (1999). Stigma as an obstacle to AIDS action: The case of the Black community. *American Behavioral Scientist, 42,* 1117-1129. doi: 10.1177/00027649921954796

Gates, G. (2013). *LGBT Parenting in the United States*. Retrieved from the Williams Institute: http://williamsinstitute.law.ucla.edu/wp-content/uploads/LGBT-Parenting.pdf

Gates, G., & Newport, F. (2012). *Special Report: 3.4% of U.S. adults tdentify as LGBT: Inaugural Gallup findings based on more than 120,000 interviews*. Retrieved from http://www.gallup.com/poll/158066/special-report-adults-identify-lgbt.aspx

Gibbs, J. M., & Jones, B. E. (2013). The Black community and its LGBT members: The role of the behavioral scientist. *Journal of Gay & Lesbian Mental Health, 17*, 196-207. doi: 10.1080/19359705.2013.766563

Griffin, H. (2004). *Toward a true Black liberation theology: Affirming homoeroticism, Black gay Christians, and their love relationships.* In A. Pinn & D. Hopkins (Eds.), *Loving the body: Black religious studies and the erotic* (pp. 133-153). New York: Palgrave Macmillian.

Griffin, H. (2006). *Their own receive them not: Black lesbians and gays in Black churches.* Cleveland, OH: The Pilgrim Press.

Guthrie, R. (2004). *Even the rat was white: A historical view of psychology.* Boston: Allyn and Bacon.

Hernandez, G. (2013, August 19). Gay filmmaker Lee Daniels says 'black men can't come out'. Retrieved from http://www.gaystarnews.com/article/gay-filmmaker-lee-daniels-says-black-men-cant-come-out190813

Hernton, C. (1992). *Sex and racism in America.* New York: Anchor.

Lewis, B. (2003). Black-white differences in attitudes towards homosexuality and gay rights. *Public Opinion Quarterly, 67*, 59-78. doi: 10.1086/346009

Long, R. (2004). *Men, homosexuality, and the gods.* Binghamton, NY: Harrington Park Press.

Lorde, A. (1984). *Sister Outsider: Essays and speeches.* New York: Ten Speed Press.

McBride, D. (2005). *Why I hate Abercrombie and Fitch: Essays on race and sexuality.* New York: New York University Press.

Murray, S. & Roscoe, W. (Eds.), (1998). *Boy-wives and female husbands: Studies of African homosexualities.* New York: Palgrave Macmillian.

Pew Forum on Religion & Public Life (2008). A religious portrait of African-Americans. Retrieved from http://pewforum.org/A-Religious-Portrait-of-African-Americans.aspx

Rivas, J. (2012, May 23). Poll: People of color more likely to support gay marriage than whites. Retrieved from http://colorlines.com/archives/2012/05/people_of_color_more_likely_to_support_gay_marriage_than_whites_abc_poll_finds.html

Schulte, L. J., & Battle, J. (2004). The relative importance of ethnicity and religion in predicting attitudes towards gays and lesbians. *Journal of Homosexuality*, *47*(2), 127-142. doi: 10.1300/J082v47n02_08

West, C. (1994). *Race matters.* New York: Vintage.

Housing Works

A Trans Analysis

Jonathan Mathias Lassiter

One of my favorite poets, JP Gordon, wrote: "in the grey i've looked for you..." (Gordon, 2010). He's a lot more daring than most. The human mind, in general, does not like grey. It looks for the black and white; grey is too much of a hassle. As human beings, but especially as Americans, we love our categories that put things in place. We categorize small and large things, the concrete and the abstract. These categories give us comfort. Unfortunately, these categories and their accompanying comforts are illusions. These illusions allow us to convince ourselves that we have control over the uncontrollable, that things exist that do not, or that we can understand the unknowable. They give us power. Indeed, many categories empower the things placed within them and disempower the things that do not fit inside of them. One such thing is gender. Gender has traditionally been categorized as male and female. Male is positioned in a space of power over female, and people that do not identify or conform to either of those are disempowered through their erasure. In a very real way, people along the continuum of male and female, in the space between those two poles—"in the grey"—are marginalized and erased in many areas of American life. These people are often referred to as trans.

Trans people upset and unsettle our categories of male and female. They call into question the validity of the power transcribed to those categories and indicts the very concept of male and female. They expose these categories to interrogation and remove their cloak of authority. While trans people—their very existence and interrogation—unhouses the categories of gender, many are unhoused—quite literally—in various ways by society. (I use the word *unhouse*, both conventionally, meaning "to drive from a house or habitation; deprive of shelter" (dictionary.com, 2014) and unconventionally, as Cornel West (2000) does, meaning to incite a "kind of existential vertigo" that throws one off balance and fosters the questioning of the foundation of one's worldview.) For many trans people housing discrimination is a major barrier to physical security and social enfranchisement (Grant, Mottet, Tanis, Harrison, Herman, & Keisling, 2011). They are disproportionately pushed from their homes of origin, denied housing, and evicted because of their gender identity/expression. Trans people are too often unhoused, unsheltered, and left exposed to all sorts of physical and social dangers.

This essay attempts to examine the parallel process of trans people's unhousing of gender categories and the literal unhousing of trans people due to housing discrimination. To facilitate mutual understanding, the essay begins with an explanation of gender terms used throughout. A review of the literature on housing discrimination and homelessness experienced by trans people is then presented. The essay moves to an examination of queer theory and its application to gender. Next, an exploration of the unhousing of gender and its connection to the unhousing of trans people is undertaken. The essay culminates in a presentation of a theory aimed at unhousing gender as a process to facilitate the housing and liberation of trans and non-trans people, both literally and figuratively.

Gender Terms

Gender is a socially constructed concept and there are many terms that can be used to describe it and its categories. (All terms presented here are taken from *Teaching Transgender: A Resource from the National Center for Transgender Equality* ([NCTE]; 2009), unless otherwise noted.) Commonly gender is related to one's sex or sex organs. Sex is defined in this essay as the designation of biological reproductive organs that are usually different for people at the opposite ends of the gender spectrum. Most often a female is considered a person born with female sex organs and who behaves in a way that is feminine, and has a female gender identity. A male is considered a person who is born with male sex organs, who behaves in a way that is considered masculine, and has a male gender identity. These people would be considered cisgender because their sex organs, behavior, and identity align in a way that is customary and at the same end of the gender spectrum. For many societies, currently including America, these are the only two genders. Even when a person is born intersex (i.e. with both male and female sex organs or chromosomal expressions), the person is expected to choose a gender category with which to identify and forsake all other options.

Trans people are a heterogeneous group. Trans does not necessarily denote an endpoint where one tries to or desires to become identified or presented as 100% male or 100% female (Roen, 2002). Instead, trans can be the notion of fluidity where one has "ongoing oscillation between more feminine and more masculine aspects of internal gender identity and outward physical presentation" (Diamond & Butterworth, 2008, p. 369). Trans people may be transsexual, crossdressers, genderqueer, or gender nonconforming (Goodrum, 2002). Transsexual people are often considered to be individuals who have a desire to or who physically transition from their birth sex to the opposite sex with the use of hormones or through sexual reassignment surgeries. Transwomen are people born with male genitalia who have transitioned into a female gender identity/expression and transmen are people who were born with female genitalia who transitioned into male female gender identity/expression. Crossdressers are people who dress in the clothing of the opposite sex but do not desire to transition into the opposite sex. Genderqueer people are people who are usually androgynous and have gender identities/expressions that are between the poles of male and female. People who are gender nonconforming have gender expressions that do not align with traditional male and female gender roles. Trans people may possess SGL or heterosexual sexual orientations. Though often confused, their sexual orientation is distinct from their gender identity. Regardless of their identification along the gender and sexual orientation spectrums, homelessness remains a threat and problem for many trans people.

Homelessness among Trans People

Research identifies housing discrimination and homelessness as a major concern for trans people (Grant et al., 2011; Minter & Daley, 2003). In Washington, D.C. 19% of trans people reported not having their own living space (Xavier, 2000) and in San Francisco researchers found that 32% of trans people endorsed being the victim of housing discrimination (Minter & Daley, 2003). Housing discrimination often takes place in the form of unfair rent prices (i.e. landlords forcing trans tenants to pay more in rent for the same accommodation that other non trans tenants receive); being harassed by landlords and fellow tenants; and being denied housing all together. It is unfortunate, because this housing discrimination often leads to homelessness for many trans people. As many as 19% of trans people reported being homeless at some point in their lives and, in 2009, 2% of trans people were currently homeless at the time they were surveyed—which is twice the percentage of the general population (Grant et al., 2011). In addition to housing discrimination, trans people become homeless because of mental health issues, substance abuse problems, physical abuse from family members, violence at the hands of intimate partners, and estrangement from their families (Mottet & Ohle, 2003; Ray, 2006; Xavier, 2000). Once rendered homeless, trans people often have difficulty accessing shelter services and finding adequate long-term housing due to discrimination in the shelter system and among social service workers as well as having fewer legal protections than other sexual minorities (Mottet, 2004). Many trans people face myriad obstacles to gaining and maintaining adequate, fair housing and thus struggle with homelessness.

The majority of research studies that examined homelessness among trans people focused on trans youth (Hunter, 2008; Quintana, Rosenthal, & Krehely, 2010; Ray, 2006; Reck, 2009; Wilson et al., 2009). These studies provide a wealth of information about the forces and events that make homelessness so prevalent among trans people. Some researchers estimate that 320,000 to 400,000 gay and trans youth are homeless at some point each year (Quintana et al., 2010). These youth, which are classified as unaccompanied youth between the ages of 12 and 24, usually disclose or come out about their gender identity in their mid adolescence and frequently find themselves homeless shortly thereafter due to abuse, neglect, and family conflict (Quintana et al., 2010).

After these youth are rendered homeless, they are often the victims of violent crimes. Homeless trans youth are seven times as likely than heterosexual homeless youth to be victims of physical violence while living on the street (The National Switchboard as cited in Ray, 2006). Most of the time, they experience violence on the street after experiencing it in their homes of origin (Wilber, Ryan, & Marksamer, 2006). Trans people do not only experience physical assault as youth but throughout their tenure on the street. In one study, 60% of the homeless trans people surveyed reported that they were the victims of harassment or violence (Lombardi, 2001). Many homeless trans people also suffer from mental health issues and substance abuse (Mottet & Ohle, 2003; Clements, Katz, & Marx, 1999). Researchers have found that trans youth experience disproportionate rates of depression, suicide, loneliness, and psychosomatic illness (Cochran, Stewart, Ginzler, & Cauce, 2002; McWhirter, 1990). It is not unreasonable to conclude that many homeless trans adults experience the same mental maladies.

Homelessness results in a severe lack of resources. Some homeless trans people engage in exchanging sex for their basic needs such as money, food, or a place to sleep for the night (Mottet & Ohle, 2003). This survival sex can increase the likelihood that they become infected with sexually transmitted diseases and HIV (Vanwesenbeeck, 2001). In one study, 35% of the transwomen were infected with HIV (Clements, Katz, & Marx, 1999). Another study conducted in California found that transwomen's rates of HIV infection surpassed those of both homosexual and bisexual men (Lombardi, 2001). Some homeless trans people also share needles to inject hormones (Mottet & Ohle, 2003). This practice can also lead to HIV infection as well as Hepatitis C. This information is alarming and even more serious given that many trans people have inadequate healthcare, health insurance, and are often treated unfairly by healthcare workers (Mottet & Ohle, 2003; Ray, 2006). Beyond sexually transmitted diseases, trans people are denied appropriate medical tests and treatment due to their gender identity/expression. For example, many transmen still need gynecological and breast cancer screenings even though they may have transitioned because they are still susceptible to illnesses associated with people of their birth sex such as ovarian or breast cancer (Mottet & Ohle, 2003). Yet, insensitive and unknowledgeable medical staff often deny many of these procedures to their trans patients.

When homeless trans people do access the shelter system, they often encounter hostility and prejudice. Sometimes they are denied shelter services; forced to live with people of their same birth sex; and are harassed and/or assaulted by shelter staff and residents (Grant et al., 2011; Mottet & Ohle, 2003). Furthermore, many shelters do not provide adequate privacy and safety for trans clients. The available research concerning trans people presents a harrowing picture of the difficulties and obstacles related to housing discrimination and homelessness, which include lack of resources, lack of physical and mental healthcare access and ethical treatment, and unsafe and demeaning shelter accommodations.

Queer Theory and Unhousing Gender

One of the reasons trans people are assaulted with oppressive discrimination at such high rates is because, for many, trans people assault the foundations (one of them being gender) of the world (mostly the western and contemporary parts of it). Gender is traditionally and most popularly thought of as a binary: male and female. This binary approach to gender has been termed bigenderism by Gilbert (2009). Gender is one of the most ingrained, and often unspoken, concepts. It comes with its own rules and assumptions that strictly order the world with virtually no effort. Bigenderism sets up a system that polices gender identity and expression. This policing is evident in the rules and laws that govern, both implicitly and explicitly, day-to-day life. These rules dictate people's interactions in governments, religious institutions, schools, hospitals, professional and artistic settings, and virtually all other settings through the classification of people into male and female and prescribing the parameters of appropriate gender-based behavior in those spaces. This type of policing places people in boxes. At times these boxes can be comfortable and sometimes they may be confining, but they are always barriers to ways of being not defined by gender. Bigenderism is a cornerstone of heteronormativity. Heteronormativity assumes and prescribes that people are either male or female and that these two genders will only romantically and sexually partner with the opposite gender. Giblert (2009, pp. 97-98), writes:

> "...bigenderism and heteronormativity are symbiotic: heterosexuality relies on the assumption that an

*individual's genitals are in accordance with their
gender appearance, and bigenderism ensures that the
categories are demonstrative. Bigenderism and
heteronormativity ensure that the world is divided into
woman and man, and sexism sees to it that woman is
undervalued and man overvalued. Eliminating the
categories themselves is one way of eliminating the
[systems of oppression including sexism, heterosexism,
homonegativity, and transphobia] that depend on
them."*

Bigenderism and its sibling, heteronormativity, underpin a system that
reinforces the status quo and a hegemonic point-of-view that defines
the rules in a system that only serves those who sufficiently adhere to
the notions of masculine male and feminine female. Those who do not
are designated as abnormal and marginalized in a hegemonic society of
binaries. This binary-ordered society with rules related to gender (in
conjunction with hierarchies related to race, sex, class, ability status,
etcetera) demands assimilation and similarity (Rodriguez, 2003) and
shuns—"the grey"—the dissented and dissident. Queer theory attempts
to interrogate and deconstruct the systems of bigenderism and
heteronormativity. Smith (2003, p. 346) outlines the core tenets of
queer theory:

*"(1) all categories are falsifications, especially if they are binary
and descriptive of sexuality; (2) all assertions about reality are
socially constructed; (3) all human behavior can be read as
textual signification; (4) texts form discourses that are exercises
in power/knowledge and which, properly analyzed, reveal
relations of dominance within historically-situated systems of
regulation; (5) deconstruction of all categories of normality and
deviance can best be accomplished by queer readings of
performative texts ranging from literature (fictional,
professional, popular) to other cultural expressions (geographic
distribution, body piercing, sit-coms, sadomasochistic
paraphernalia)."*

While queer theory has mostly been concerned with academic
notions—with a focus on literature and performance arts—of sexuality,
I attempt to focus on the real world implications of "unhousing" gender.

Thus, I will focus on core tenets one and two. All categories are socially constructed illusions machinated in the human mind for the purpose of providing structure to the world. In this way, categorization and bigenderism is a natural outgrowth of human nature. This, in and of itself, is not pathological. However, when this categorization is then used to dehumanize, oppress, and confine those within and outside of those categories, systems of oppression are created. The interrogation and the critical analyses of gender categories can unhouse them and rob them of their oppressive power. Oppressive power is prescriptive and superimposes its vision—or lack thereof—onto the lived experiences of those it subjects. Human beings are more diverse and fluid than bigenderism proposes. Bigenderism squashes originality, creativity, spontaneity, and liberation. It tells people who and how a male should feel, how a female should behave (and what they are not allowed to feel or do), and that there are no legitimate alternatives. Within this society of binaries, power produces the illusion it purports to represent (Butler, 1990). In actuality, gender—and all identities—is fluid; it is perpetually changing (Fuss, 1991). As human beings, we are constantly making decisions about how we want to present ourselves at a given moment. We are constantly discovering ourselves. These constant discoveries are "reflections of an inner state of consciousness" (Phillips & Stewart, 2008, p. 396) and queer theory seeks to manifest that inner process externally whereby "gender is an expression of a cosmic duality principle that extends far beyond male and female bodies" (Phillips & Stewart, 2008, p. 396).

There is historical evidence that bigenderism is not universal nor "natural." Gender expressions along the continuum has been documented in many—but not all—precolonial locations such as Africa (Murray & Roscoe, 1998; Wekker, 1993), Southeast Asia (Williams, 1986), East Asia and the Pacific Islands (Murray, 2002), Central and South America (Murray, 1987, 1995) and among Islamic societies (Murray, 1995) and indigenous peoples of the Americas (Phillips & Stewart, 2008). In many cases, these diversely gendered people—who would probably be considered trans in contemporary society—were considered to be spiritual and often had elevated positions within their societies. Bigenderism is in fact "unnatural." It has created gender categories that can rob human beings of the full human experience. It is "a fiction and a postmodern mixing and matching of body parts...related to other fictional forms like clothing or fantasy" (Halberstam, 1994, p.

226). Queer theory, through interrogation and critical analyses, seeks to unhouse and eliminate restrictive bigenderism of male and female that assigns people to boxes and orders them within a heteronormative system. This unhousing allows for fluidity along a continuum of being. This notion may seem absurd, unrealistic, delusional, or frightening for some. However, it may be the ultimate liberation. This unhousing does not necessarily destroy the concept of gender but unconfines it and gives it room to move. In such an unhoused space, everyone could be considered trans, moving along a continuum of gender identity and expression that feels most natural for them in each moment.

Unhousing Gender to Erase Margins, Housing Discrimination to Marginalize

I do not think it is a coincidence that a group (i.e. trans people) that raises the biggest questions about gender categories (i.e. questions their validity and power) is also one of the most marginalized groups. Trans people unhouse gender and are—by many—considered freaks. Baldwin (1985, p. 689), in his essay *Here Be Dragons*, wrote "freaks are called freaks and treated as they are treated—in the main, abominably—because they are human beings who cause to echo, deep within us, our most profound terrors and desires." I propose that it is the terror of being unconfined by bigenderism and the possible desire to transgress gender categories that one suppresses in one's self that fuels much of the social hatred and marginalization aimed at trans people. Trans people embody and make physically manifest the reality that bigenderism is indeed an illusion. And, if it is an illusion, its power is tenuous. Thus, the power of bigenderism must be protected at all cost even if it means using that power to erase (and if that is not entirely possibly, neutralize) the threat through marginalization. People will often go to extreme lengths to maintain the foundation of their psychological and physical structures and environments.

In general, people of all genders and sexual orientations are tied to their understandings of gender categories. As explained before, bigenderism serves cisgender and heterosexual people by organizing societal hierarchies based on gender. These hierarchies endow males with power over females and outlines "appropriate" behavior between the two. Therefore, the investment of cisgender and heterosexual people in bigenderism is understandable—even if it is unfortunate, oppressive, and restrictive. The policing of gender by SGL people seems more tragic. Some SGL people, and it would seem the "mainstream" (read white, cisgender, and male) SGL community as a whole, have a large investment in bigenderism. This investment is closely tied to profit and politics of respectability. Some SGL people are granted assess to resources in the oppressive heteronormative system as long as the cultural flavorings of SGL people can be commodified and sold (Ferry, 2012). The value of SGL people is dependent upon how palatable and digestible they are to heterosexual consumers. The more SGL people fit into a box or boxes (or a model queer identity)—which usually means presenting as cisgender, white, not poor, able-bodied, sexually nonthreatening, comical, neat, fashionable, sassy, and male—the more predictable they are in the heteronormative marketplace. Predictability translates into comfort and comfort translates into access. The farther outside the box and boxes people live, the less access they are likely to have. Trans people are often shamed and marginalized by cisgender SGL people for their lack of adherence to the model queer identity (Ferry, 2012). In an attempt to safeguard their own access within the heteronormative system, some cisgender SGL people shame and marginalize trans people for their lack of adherence to the predictable model (Ferry, 2012). What better way to shame and marginalize trans people than by denying them their basic needs?

I have already discussed the detrimental implications of housing discrimination for trans people's physical, psychological, and social well being. If trans people are stuck fighting to meet their basic needs, it is almost impossible for them to fully actualize the successful unhousing of gender categories and all the oppressive systems (based on race, sex, class, ability status, religion, etcetera) that intersect with them. The unhousing of bigenderism and its related systems of oppression requires the housing of trans people. However, the housing of trans people may only be achievable after the successful unhousing of bigenderism. The point of intervention is hard to determine.

Looking and Struggling In the Grey

One thing that I do know is that while trans people represent the physical evidence of bigenderism's fictitious nature, the unhousing of bigenderism requires the efforts of both cisgender and trans people,

SGL and heterosexual people, and all those people along the spectrum and intersections of identities and expressions. I am a cisgender, SGL, African American man writing about these issues and do not attempt to be or present as an expert on the lived experiences of trans people's lives. I do write this essay in attempt to call attention to the discrimination—specifically, housing discrimination—faced by trans people at grossly disproportionate rates. I write this essay in an attempt to call attention to how my struggle as a cisgender man is tied to the struggle of trans people—and all oppressed people—against bigenderism. Bigenderism hinders us all. I want to be clear that I am not opposed to gender, in and of itself, I am opposed to bigenderism and its limiting and oppressive consequences. This essay is an attempt at unhousing bigenderism in myself and society, one reader at a time. I have attempted to unhouse bigenderism through an application of queer theory that does not seek to define but disturb the commonly held notions of it (Edelman, 2004). Gender categories are socially constructed illusions. While these illusions give our world shape, and make it easily definable, they can be barriers to authentic and fluid ways of being. Unhousing gender categories mixes the black and white and throws the world into grey. A grey that is realistic and probably—at least initially—uncomfortable, but ultimately liberating.

References

Baldwin, J. (1985). Here be dragons. In James Baldwin (Ed.), *The price of the ticket: Collected nonfiction 1948-1985* (pp. 677-690). New York: St. Martin's.

Butler, J. (1990). *Gender trouble: Feminism and the subversion of identity*. New York: Routledge.

Clements, K., Katz, M., & Marx, R. (1999). *The Transgender Community Health Project.* Retrieved from http://hivinsite.ucsf.edu/InSite?

Cochran, B., Stewart, A., Ginzler, J., & Cauce, A. (2002). Challenges faced by homeless sexual minorities: Comparison of gay, lesbian, bisexual, and transgender homeless adolescents with their heterosexual counterparts. *American Journal of Public Health, 92*, 773-777.

Diamond, L., & Butterworth, M. (2008). Questioning gender and sexual identity: Dynamic links over time. *Sex Roles, 59*, 365-376. doi: 10.1007/s11199-008-9425-3

dictionary.com (2014) *unhouse*. Retrieved from http://dictionary.reference.com/browse/unhouse

Edelman, L. (2004). *No future: Queer theory and the death drive*. Durham, NC: Duke University Press Books.

Ferry, 2012

Fuss, D. (1991). Inside/out. In D. Fuss (Ed.), *Inside/out: Lesbian theories, gay theories* (pp. 1–10). New York: Routledge.

Gilbert, M. (2009). Defeating bigenderism: Changing gender assumptions in the twenty-first century. *Hypatia*, 24 (3), 93-112.

Goodrum, A. J. (2002). *Gender identity 101: A transgender primer*. Retrieved from http://www.sagatucson.org/tgnetaz/gender_101.htm

Gordon, JP. (2010). To a man yet to be met. Retrieved from https://www.facebook.com/pages/JP-Gordon/217350108440771

Grant, J., Mottet, L., Tanis, J., Harrison, J., Herman, J., & Keisling, M. (2011). Injustice at every turn: A report of the national transgender discrimination survey, executive summary. Retrieved from http://transequality.org/PDFs/Executive_Summary.pdf

Halberstam, J. (1994) F2M: the making of female masculinity. In L. DOAN (Ed.) *The Lesbian Postmodern* (pp. 210-228). New York: Columbia University Press.

Hunter, E. (2008). What's good for the gays is good for the gander: Making homeless youth housing safer for lesbian, gay, bisexual, and transgender youth. *Family Court Review, 46,* 543-557. doi: 10.1111 /j.1744-1617.2008.00220.x

Lombardi, E. (2001). Enhancing transgender health care. *American Journal of Public Health, 91,* 869-872. Retrieved from *ajph.aphapublications.org/cgi/reprint/91/6/869.pdf*

McWhirter, B. (1990). Loneliness: A review of current literature with implications for counseling and research. *Journal of Counseling and Development, 68,* 417-423.

Minter, S., & Daley, C. (2003). *Trans realities: A legal needs assessment of San Francisco's transgender communities.* Retrieved from Transgender Law Center website: http://www.transgenderlawcenter.org /publications.html

Mottet, L. (2004). The education and policy needs of transgender individuals. *SIECUS Report, 32,* 35-38. Retrieved from http://www.highbeam.com/doc/1G1-127059598.html

Mottet, L., & Ohle, J. (2003). *Transitioning our shelters: A guide to making homeless shelters safe for transgender people.* Retrieved from Homeless Resource Center website: http://www.thetaskforce.org/downloads/reports/reports/Transitioning OurShelters.pdf

Murray, S. (1987). *Male homosexuality in Central and South America.* San Francisco: Instituto Obregon.

Murray, S. (1995). *Latin American male homosexualities.* Albuquerque: University of New Mexico Press.

Murray, S. (2002). *Pacific homosexualities.* Unknown Location: iUniverse.

Murray, S., & Roscoe, W. (1998). *Boy-wives and female husbands: Studies of African homosexualities.* New York: St. Martin's.

National Center for Transgender Equality [NCTE], (2009). *Teaching transgender: A resource from the National Center for Transgender Equality*. Retrieved from http://transequality.org/ ResourcesNCTE_Teaching_Transgender.pdf

Phillips, L., & Stewart, M. (2008). "I am just so glad you are alive": New perspectives on non-traditional, non-conforming, and transgressive expressions of gender, sexuality, and race among African Americans. *Journal of African American Studies, 12,* 378-400. doi: 10.1007/s12111-008-9053-6

Quintana, N., Rosenthal, J., & Krehely, J. (2010). *On the streets: The federal response to gay and transgender homeless youth.* Retrieved from Center for American Progress website: www.americanprogress.org/issues/2010/06/pdf/lgbtyouthhomelessnes s.pdf

Ray, N. (2006). *Lesbian, gay, bisexual and transgender youth: An epidemic of homelessness*. Retrieved from www.thetaskforce.org/downloads/HomelessYouth.pdf

Reck, J. (2009). Homeless gay and transgender youth of color in San Francisco: "No one likes street kids"—even in the Castro. *Journal of LGBT Youth, 6*, 223-242, doi: 10.1080/19361650903013519Rodriguez, J. (2003). *Queer Latinidad: Identity practices, discursive Spaces*. New York: New York University Press.

Roen, K. (2002). 'Either/or' and 'both/neither': Discursive tensions in transgender politics. *Signs, 27*(2), 501–522.

Smith, R. (2003). Queer theory, gay movements, and political communication. *Journal of Homosexuality, 45*, 345-348. doi: 10.1300/J082v45n02_18

Xavier, J. (2000). *The Washington, DC transgender needs assessment survey.* Retrieved from http://www.glaa.org/archive/2000/tgneedsassessment1112.shtml

Vanwesenbeeck, I. (2001). Another decade of social scientific work on sex work: A review of research 1990–2000. Annual Review of Sex

Research, 12, 242–289. Retrieved from http://scholar.google.com/scholar?cluster=1169220840182422934&hl=en&as_sdt=2000

Wekker, G. (1993). Mati-ism and Black lesbianism: Two ideal typical constructions of female homosexuality in Black communities of the diaspora. *Journal of Homosexuality, 24*, 145–158. doi: 10.1300/J082v24n03_11

West, C. (2000). *Cornel West's opening remarks.* Retrieved from http://old.essentialschools.org/pub/ces_docs/fforum/2000/speeches/west_00.html

Wilber, S., Ryan, C., & Marksamer, J. (2006). *Best practice guidelines: Serving LGBT youth in out-of-home care.* Retrieved from National Center for Lesbian Right website: www.nclrights.org/site/DocServer/BPG_execsummary.pdf?docID=2801 Best practice guidelines: Serving LGBT youth in out-of-home care

Williams, W. (1986). *The spirit and the flesh: Sexual diversity in American Indian culture.* Boston: Beacon.

Wilson, E., Garofalo, R., Harris, R., Herrick, A., Martinez, M., Martinez, J Adolescent Medicine Trials Network for HIV/AIDS Interventions. (2009). Transgender female youth and sex work: HIV risk and a comparison of life factors related to engagement in sex work. *AIDS Behavior, 13,* 902-913. doi: 10.1007/s10461-008-9508-8

Politics & Government
DEPARTMENT

The Breakdown of The Rule of Law
America's Descent Into Authoritarianism

Devon Douglas-Bowers

From early in one's life, an American is taught the law and American institutions of justice are great equalizers within our society, ensuring that everyone is treated the same, no matter one's class, race, or ethnicity. Yet, what has been happening quite recently, especially within the past decade or so, is that we have been seeing an increasing breakdown in the rule of law and the use of the justice system to enforce injustices.

President Obama rode in on a high horse in the 2008 presidential elections, specifically on his slogan of hope and change. He rightly criticized the Bush administration on a number of issues, from the economy to the wars abroad, as well as the use of drones.[1] Yet, Obama subsequently went and not only increased the use of drones, but used them to kill Anwar Al-Awlaki, a member of Al Qaeda who was still legally an American citizen at the time of his death.[2] However, the story gets even more shocking as not only does such as act create a legal precedent where the President can kill any US citizen that he deems a terrorist[3], but the Obama administration's attorney general argued that such assassinations of American citizens on US soil "would be legal and justified in an extraordinary circumstance.'"[4] Some would argue that Attorney General Eric Holder cleared the entire domestic drone debacle when he sent a letter to Senator Rand Paul which read: It has come to my attention that you have now asked an additional question: "Does the President have the authority to use a weaponized drone to kill an American not engaged in combat on American soil?" The answer to that question is no.[5]

However, the problem with that answer is the vagueness of the phrase "engaged in combat." While it may seem obvious to someone what that phrase means, it becomes murky when one sees that the Defense Department has labeled protests as a form of low-level terrorism[6] and that environmental activists are being prosecuted as terrorists.[7] Does this means that protesters and environmental activists are "engaged in combat on American soil" and thus it is OK to attack them with armed drones?

This is deeply problematic as it essentially nullifies the due process clause of the Fifth Amendment and paves the way for future Presidents to potentially label their political opponents as terrorists or an enemy combatant (both have vague definitions), assassinate them with a drone, and hide the evidence under the guise of national security. The breakdown of the rule of law has been furthered in the economic sphere as the wealthy elites are able to crash the economy and receive no jail time whatsoever, even though crimes were committed.[8] These economic elites are so powerful that even "the Department of Justice fears bringing criminal charges against them because of the possible repercussions such proceedings would have on the greater economy."[9] The fact that these corporate fatcats can crash the economy without fear of prosecution is only a testament to their political and economic clout. They have established institutions that are so firmly entrenched within the American economy that even the Department of Justice fears the effects of bringing them to court. These corporations have cheated the government out of what they owe by using tax havens or shell companies, as was the case with Apple.[10] This corporate tax evasion does not only send money overseas, but these corporations can tap that money at will by "simply by taking out loans and using foreign cash as collateral."[11] Activity such as this reveals our two-tiered justice system where individuals get prison time for tax evasion, while bankers run free.[12]

A final- and perhaps the most disturbing of all of these examples- in the breakdown of the rule of law in America is that those who reveal injustices are harshly punished. Bradley Manning revealed information of US war crimes and was demonized as a traitor even though he had a legal duty to tell of these war crimes as "in the US Army Subject Schedule No. 27-1 is 'the obligation to report all violations of the law of war.'"[13] Manning was treated with such harshness that the UN Torture Chief classified Manning's treatment as being in "violation of his right to physical and psychological integrity as well as of his presumption of innocence."[14] More recently, Edward Snowden released information that the US has been spying on its citizens and he has been deemed a traitor even though

Treason is the only crime specified in the Constitution, and here is what our founding document says about it, from Article Three, Section Three:

Treason against the United States, shall consist only in levying War against them, or in adhering to their Enemies, giving them Aid and Comfort.

The Supreme Court has interpreted this to mean that no one can commit treason unless it's with a country against whom our Congress has declared war. This means that neither the Vietnam War nor the Korean War nor the War on Terror can yield treasonous Americans, as none of these wars were declared by Congress. [15] The actual law is being ignored in order to demonize and prosecute those who go against the state.

Yet, what does this the breakdown of the rule of law mean for the United States? For one it means that the US is a nation where "There are two sets of laws: one set for the government and the corporations, and another set for you and me,"[16] yet on a deeper level it signals that the US is becoming more and more of an authoritarian state. There are many characteristics of authoritarianism that the US is currently engaged in or has shown since the dawn of the 21st century. They include:

· Constraints on political institutions (Think the political constraints on third parties[17])

· Constraints on the mass public

· Ill-defined executive power[18]

The descent of the US to an authoritarian nation signals the destruction of the rule of law. Yet, there is hope. We the people can reverse this situation, but we will have to work outside the system. We are our only hope.

Notes

1. Tom Curry, "Obama Continues, Expands Some Bush Terrorism Policies," *NBC News*, June 6, 2013 (http://nbcpolitics.nbcnews.com/_news/2013/06/06/18804146-obama-continues-extends-some-bush-terrorism-policies?lite)

2. Joshua Keating, "Was Anwar Al-Awlaki Still A US Citizen?" *Foreign Policy*, September 30, 2011 (http://blog.foreignpolicy.com/posts/2011/09/30/was_anwar_al_awlaki_still_a_us_citizen)f

3. Adam Serwer, "Obama's Dangerous Awlaki Precedent," *Mother Jones*, September 30, 2011 (http://www.motherjones.com/mojo/2011/09/al-awlakis-innocence-beside-point#13725235717251&action=collapse_widget&id=3279092)

4. Jon Swaine, "Barack Obama 'has authority to use drone strikes to kill Americans on US soil," *The Telegraph*, March 6, 2013 (http://www.telegraph.co.uk/news/worldnews/barackobama/9913615/Barack-Obama-has-authority-to-use-drone-strikes-to-kill-Americans-on-US-soil.html)

5. Amy Davidson, "Rand Paul Gets A Letter From Eric Holder," *The New Yorker*, March 7, 2013 (http://www.newyorker.com/online/blogs/closeread/2013/03/rand-paul-gets-a-letter-from-eric-holder.html)

6. American Civil Liberties Union, *ACLU Challenges Defense Department Personnel Policy To Regard Lawful Protests as "Low-Level Terrorism*," http://www.aclu.org/national-security/aclu-challenges-defense-department-personnel-policy-regard-lawful-protests-%E2%80%9Clow-le, June 10, 2009

7. Kevin Gosztola, *Environmental Activist, Prosecuted as If He Was Terrorist, Was Held in Isolation for Political Speech*, Firedoglake, http://dissenter.firedoglake.com/2013/04/01/environmental-activist-prosecuted-as-if-he-was-terrorist-was-held-in-isolation-for-political-speech/ (April 1, 2013)

8. All Gov, *Why No Prison for Banksters Who Caused Financial Crisis...Yet?*, http://www.allgov.com/news/top-stories/why-no-prison-for-banksters-who-caused-financial-crisisyet?news=842515, April 15, 2011

9. Halah Touryalai, "The Real Reason Wall Street Always Escapes Criminal Charges? The Justice Dept Fears The Aftermath," *Forbes*, June 3, 2013 (http://www.forbes.com/sites/halahtouryalai/2013/03/06/the-real-reason-wall-street-always-escapes-criminal-charges-the-justice-dept-fears-the-aftermath/)

10. Brendan Sasso, "Senate report: Apple using shell companies to dodge taxes," *The Hill*, May 20, 2013 (http://thehill.com/blogs/hillicon-valley/technology/300791-senate-report-accuses-apple-of-using-shell-companies-to-dodge-taxes)

11. Christopher Matthews, "The Next Big Thing In Corporate-Tax Avoidance," *Time*, April 3, 2013 (http://business.time.com/2013/04/03/the-next-big-thing-in-corporate-tax-avoidance/)

12. Jamie Satterfield, Ex-lawyer Sentenced to Prison For Tax Evasion," *Knoxnews*, June 24, 2013 (http://www.knoxnews.com/news/2013/jun/24/ex-lawyer-sentenced-to-prison-for-tax-evasion/)

13. Marjorie Cohn, "Bradley Manning's Legal Duty to Expose War Crimes," *Truthout*, June 3, 2013 (http://www.truth-out.org/news/item/16731-bradley-mannings-legal-duty-to-expose-war-crimes)

14. Kim Zetter, "UN Torture Chief: Bradley Manning Treatment Was Cruel, Inhuman," *Wired*, March 12, 2012

(http://www.wired.com/threatlevel/2012/03/manning-treatment-inhuman/)

15. Evan Puschak, "Lawrence O'Donnell: Why Edward Snowden Cannot Be A Traitor,"*MSNBC*, June 25, 2013 (http://tv.msnbc.com/2013/06/25/why-edward-snowden-cannot-be-a-traitor/)

16. John W. Whitehead, *The Age of Neo-Feudalism: A Government of the Rich, by the Rich, and for the Corporations*, The Rutherford Institute, https://www.rutherford.org/publications_resources/john_whiteheads_commentary/the_age_of_neo_feudalism_a_government_of_the_rich_by_the_rich_and_for_the_c, January 28, 2013

17. Roy L. Behr, Edward H. Lazarus, Steven J. Rosenstone, *Third Parties in America* 2nd edition (Princeton, NJ: Princeton University Press, 1984), Chapter Two "Constraints on Third Parties"

18. Gretchen Casper, *Fragile Democracies: The Legacies of Authoritarian Rule* (Pittsburgh, PA: University of Pittsburgh Press, 1995), pg 40

The Socialist Party of America

A Historiographical View

P. Josh Hatala

For more than a century historians, political theorists, and social commentators have attempted to explain the absence of a robust, socialist party in the United States, capable of winning elections or framing political discourse.[1] Over the last half century the United States has stood nearly alone in its lack of a viable socialist or social democratic party capable of meaningfully influencing national politics. There was, however, a brief period of limited success for American socialists at the beginning of the twentieth century. In 1912 Eugene V. Debs, Socialist Party presidential candidate, received six percent of the national vote. In the same year socialists held 1200 public offices, sent one member of their party to congress, and had an impressive roster of 118,000 dues paying members.[2] Then, suddenly, the Socialist Party ceased its expansion and receded even further into the backdrop of American political life. What happened? This challenging and persistent question has garnered a wide array of responses from historians who, from the 1950s to the present, have made it the subject of book length monographs, essays, and journal articles. These authors, while sharing a common focal point, have approached this question employing historical frameworks reflective of the age in which they were interpreting and writing history. An analysis written in the 1950s on the decline of the Socialist Party, for example, will not be the same as one written in the 1980s by virtue of the fact that the historical profession itself has expanded its repertoire and developed new theoretical "lenses" through which to interpret the past- a reality that becomes evident through the primarily chronological format I have used in this non-exhaustive historiographical essay. In spite of this diversity of lenses, the question of why socialism has failed, as well as what this failure says in broad terms about American life, were central concerns of these historians who blamed the Socialist Party's decline on party factionalism, external pressures brought by World War One and the Russian Revolution, the appeal of mainstream reformism, lack of Leninist style organizing, and more. As socialists in the 21st century begin to reassess electoral and movement strategy, exposure to this work might serve to allow socialists, even in some small measure, to better analyze and contextualize the current and future state of the socialist movement in the United States

In 1952 Iris Kipnis presented the first book length monograph on the socialist movement in the United States, *The American Socialist Movement, 1897-1912*. Kipnis dealt with the origins and rise of socialist movements from 1897-1912, but focused primarily on the decline of the Socialist Party of America. Before Kipnis's work, only a handful of journal articles on the socialist movement had been published. This paucity of research on the socialist movement, Kipnis believed, was attributable to the notion adopted by historians that the socialist movement was something of an historical aberration in US history, making it unworthy of extensive research and study. Kipnis rejected this point of view, positing that an understanding of the Socialist Party of America was an essential component in understanding other developments connected to the Progressive Movement of the early 20th century. Kipnis's seminal study was to be referenced, supported, altered, or rejected by subsequent historians of the American Left.

Kipnis examined the Socialist Party as both a political party and a social movement, focusing on the internal developments and discord within the Socialist Party itself. Conceptually, he relied heavily on the "Rankian model" of history with its focus on politics, diplomacy, and political parties as the prime agents of historical change.[3] His primary pool of sources was official- coming directly from the Socialist Party: Socialist Party newsletters and newspapers, proceedings from Socialist Party conventions, and official party statements made up the bulk of his research material. Kipnis focused on leaders of different factions within the party, as well as the factions as entities within themselves, and how they respond to external political forces, and to each other. In discussing his view of agency in history Kipnis wrote, "Surely the activities of the Socialists themselves had something to do with the nature of the results they achieved. If not, history must be merely the record of the movements of human puppets pulled by invisible strings."[4] However, the workers and dues paying members of the party are conspicuously absent from his account. Kipnis built a case for a growing factionalism within the Socialist Party that led to its demise following the height of its success- the presidential election of 1912 when Socialist Party candidate Eugene V. Debs earned roughly six percent of the national vote. In choosing 1912 as an end date in his study, Kipnis made it clear that to him this date marked the end of the Socialist Party as a viable force against the two party system- an assertion that will be challenged fifteen years later (1967) by James Weinstein, whose work will be discussed below.

Kipnis argued that leading up to the elections of 1912 two factions had emerged within the party- both a left and right wing. The party's left wing was concerned with revolutionary change and strategy, focusing its energies on developing strong bonds with industrial unions in hopes of revolutionary upheaval. In 1901, the year of the party's founding, most leaders and members belonged to the left and center factions. "They held that socialism would be ushered in only after the working class had gained state power through Socialist control of a majority of national and local offices." [5] To do this, socialists would educate workers in "scientific socialism" and aid unions in struggles. Kipnis argued that the left's orientation, however, which relied heavily upon the concept of class solidarity, was faulty because American workers had little developed sense of class consciousness. Although the left and center factions did concern themselves with electoral success, for them the purpose of elections was primarily educational because true change could only be won through a workers' revolution, not elections.

The bulk of the blame for the Socialist Party's decline, according to Kipnis, lay with the party's right-leaning members and eventual orientation. Kipnis argued that the right saw socialism evolving gradually in America by influencing American political and economic structures. As elections *were* won across the nation, the center elements within the party began to move to the right, seeing electoral success as a more expedient path to change. As the Socialist Party veered right, the left faction became increasingly disillusioned and left the party, leaving the Socialist Party to represent a kind of extreme form of American reformism, but not a revolutionary party. Emblematic of this shift in the party's orientation was the expulsion of Bill Haywood, a prominent leader of the left faction. After Haywood's dismissal, the party fell too much in line with the progressivism of the era, Kipnis believed, leaving it irrelevant in an era in which the banner of reform was carried by larger and more influential parties.

Also published in 1952, Daniel Bell's *Marxian Socialism in the United States* did not deal exclusively with the Socialist Party, yet remains a frequently cited work in the historiography of the Socialist Party, socialist movements, and the failure of the American left broadly speaking. In a 1967 paperback edition of his work, Bell found fault with Kipnis's thesis that the Socialist Party would have succeeded if it had only increased its militancy, calling it simply, "wishful thinking about history".[6] Additionally, Bell criticized Kipnis's seemingly static labeling of "left" and "right" factions within the Socialist Party as arbitrary, arguing that the composition and principles of these tendencies within the party meant different things at different stages in the party's history.

Trained as a sociologist, Bell took a self-described Weberian approach to interpreting history and contended that the decline of the American left, of which the Socialist Party was an integral part, could be attributed to its being "in the world but not of the world". [7] Working from Weber's premise that modern politics cannot be guided by ethical absolutes but must be grounded in pragmatism, Bell posited that the socialists failed because they refused to accept the basic rules for political discourse, of which compromise is a component, while attempting to be a part of American political life. "The socialist movement", he wrote, "by its very statement of goal and in its rejection of the capitalist order as a whole, could not relate itself to the specific problems of social action in the here-and-now, give-and-take, political world... so it could only act, and then inadequately, as the moral, but not political, man in immoral society". [8] Bell's use of Weber was indicative of the post-war years during which some historians came under the influence of sociology, employing it as a tool for historical inquiry.[9]

Bell went on to argue that the Socialist Party, like much of the radical left, was infected with chiliastic sensibilities which caused it to be too ideologically driven to adapt to real world circumstances. Living in "another world" made the party irrelevant to most people. While employing Weber for his theoretical framework, Bell's sources were similar to those of Kipnis and Shannon- socialist periodicals, proceedings from conventions, and the writings of major party leaders like Eugene V. Debs. In addition to Weber, Bell stood apart in citing the theoretical considerations of Socialist Party leader and historian Morris Hillquit whose occasional Marxist orthodoxy, Bell argued, led the party to accept ideological principles divorced from pragmatic politics.

In addition to his theoretical considerations, Bell examined more tangible, tactical errors of the Socialist Party as well as external constraints. At the forefront of his argument, Bell contended that the Socialist Party's opposition to World War One placed the party firmly outside of mainstream politics and the labor movement, thereby causing it to lose the trust of the American people. While Kipnis saw a "left" and "right" vying for control of the party up until 1912, Bell saw between 1917 and 1921 "a complete shift of the *entire* socialist movement to a frame of reference completely outside the structure of American life"[10] which led to the death of the Socialist Party. This "frame of reference" was connected to an ethical rigidity that served to further remove the party from mainstream discourse. Additionally, Bell cited as reasons for decline the expulsion of the left-wing of the party from 1912-1913, the expulsion of the growing Bolshevik contingent following the Russian Revolution, as well as the attractiveness of Wilson's reforms for the intellectuals of the Socialist Party who left *en masse* in favor of "The New Freedom", forming the Woodrow Wilson Independent League.

David Shannon's, *The Socialist Party of America*, published in 1955, relied on sources similar and sometimes identical to Kipnis's, yet branched out to include a more diverse range of evidence. Along with official Socialist Party convention minutes, essays in socialist journals, and official party pronouncements, Shannon made more frequent use of personal correspondence between party leaders as well as materials from the Columbia University Oral History Project. Shannon also made use of the official records of the Socialist Party housed at Duke University and criticized Kipnis for overlooking such a valuable pool of source materials. Along with this criticism of Kipnis's work, Shannon faulted Kipnis for being, "too uncritical of Haywood and his wing of the party and overly critical of the more conservative groups among the Socialists"[11]. Furthermore, Shannon remaiend completely unconvinced of Kipnis's thesis that "the failure of the Socialist Party is to be understood in terms of the party's factionalism..."[12] Shannon's alternative thesis will be discussed below.

Like Kipnis, Shannon examined disagreements within the party as resulting from conflict between factions, but also focused on conflict between the personalities of leaders within the party as well as their decisions and motives. Instead of seeing the Socialist Party from the "ground up" as later historians would, Shannon interpreted the party in terms of the moves of its great leaders as well as within the context of an American culture that held to traditions that socialists could do nothing to change. America's two-party system that is difficult for third parties to break into played a role in this but, more importantly, it was America's lack of class-consciousness that prevented the Socialist Party from gaining more ground. The historical absence of a feudal system or aristocracy, the fact that capitalism, despite its problems, gave people a better life, as well as a high degree of class mobility, all made the Socialist Party's appeal to the "working class" irrelevant. Though this argument is not presented in Marxist terms, Shannon did take class into account to a larger degree than Kipnis in his interpretation of socialism's failure. In the discussion of class, however, he focused on the movement's leaders and their interactions with a "national character". For example, Shannon wrote, "When Debs during his war trial said, 'While there is a lower class I am in it; while there is a criminal element, I am of it; while there is a soul in prison, I am not free,' he expressed a noble sentiment, but relatively few Americans recognized the statement as an expression of solidarity with themselves."[13]

Shannon also moved beyond 1912 as an ending point for the Socialist Party as a viable political force, arguing that after the Russian Revolution of 1917, the Socialist Party saw world revolution as imminent and became *more* radical. It was not, as Kipnis argued, the post-1912 election fallout and move to more mainstream politics that destroyed the Socialist Party, but the radicalization of the party that took place in the latter half of the 1910s and into the 1920s.

In almost direct contrast to Kipnis, Shannon argued that the Socialist Party failed because it aimed its propaganda at a non-existent American proletariat. America, he believed, was not nearly class conscious enough to accept socialism as presented by the Socialist Party. "The Left", he wrote, "thought the Right was hopelessly bourgeois, and the Right thought the Left's radicalism was more glandular than philosophical". [14] To Shannon, the party became too dependent on doctrine and a working-class ideology, leaving it irrelevant. He also cited the rise of incompetent leaders in the party as a major reason for the party's decline. It was these leaders of the party and the party's factions who, by becoming too ideologically driven, failed to control the party as a *true* American political party willing to make compromises. As a result, the party lost its appeal. Other historians, of course, would disagree.

James Weinstein was the first to argue that the socialist movement did not decline before and during World War One, but in fact "grew in size and prestige during the war"[15], despite government repression during this period. The height of American socialism, he argued in *The Decline of Socialism in America, 1912-1925*, was not the election of 1912 when Eugene V. Debs won the largest number of votes a socialist candidate would ever receive. Instead, Weinstein showed growth in the party and electoral success in the years during and immediately following World War One, with the Socialist Party finally falling away as a real force around 1919. In opposition to Kipnis who argued that the Socialist Party met its end with the expulsion of Bill Haywood from the National Committee of the Socialist Party and the decline of the left faction in 1912-1913, Weinstein claimed that this reorganization led to no major shift in the party's orientation, nor to its decline.

In his refutation of Kipnis, Weinstein focused on the continued inclusiveness of the party from 1912-1919. He showed a broad membership base and a party that served as a kind of umbrella organization for members of the Industrial Workers of the World (IWW), Christian Socialists, atheists, those involved in mainstream politics, as well as those apathetic to electoral success. The party did not, as Kipnis suggested, become too right-leaning in its orientation and thereby irrelevant in an age of more viable progressive political parties. Weinstein argued that though the Socialist Party *did* lose support from those who sided with Wilson's reforms, as well as those socialists who left the party to support the war, the party managed to grow. As the only political party in America that did not support the war, some of this new membership came from fellow war resisters. Even more significant were those immigrants who joined the party following the Russian Revolution- many of whom were of Slavic descent and supported the Russian Revolution. The percentage of foreign-born party members jumped from 20 percent before the war to 52 percent following it.[16] By 1920 the party had 109,000 members- just a few thousand below its 1912 levels.[17] These demographic changes were mirrored in geographic changes with much of the party's membership being concentrated in eastern cities. With the supporters of Wilson and the war gone from the Socialist Party, a more revolutionary element had entered through this new membership.

Weinstein's thesis was built upon an alternative reading of the sources used by Kipnis and Shannon and, perhaps more importantly, the use of local labor newspapers. It is in examining the local, as opposed to the national character of the Socialist Party, that Weinstein was able to arrive at his conclusions. Despite a poor showing in the 1916 presidential election (as compared to 1912), the Socialist Party grew in 1917 and 1918 at the *local* level through election to local, less prominent offices. Weinstein's focus on changes in the local character of the Socialist Party placed his work in opposition to Kipnis and Shannon who focud primarily on major party leaders, factional disputes, and America's "national character". Likewise, the oversight of Kipnis and Shannon regarding the obvious importance of the foreign-born membership in revitalizing the party during and immediately after the war is mysterious. Being aware of the increase in party membership from foreign-born rank and file members while still declaring the party dead in 1912 makes one wonder if their theses were not informed by an element of xenophobia. Weinstein, on the other hand, saw growth as growth, even if the Socialist Party ceased to be primarily a party of native-born Americans. In fact, it was the foreign-born who had the greatest impact on the party in the post-war years. Still, despite the growth, Weinstein too recognized the Socialist Party's decline. So what *did* destroy the Socialist Party?

Weinstein argued that the party's downfall as a viable force was purely the result of internal factionalism spurred by Bolshevism. Following the Russian Revolution the Bolsheviks preached the necessity and inevitability of world revolution. The foreign-born members of the Socialist Party, many of whom were of Slavic origin, accepted the Bolshevik call and began a struggle for control of the party. By 1919 the "old guard" of the party, recognizing the impossibility of immediate revolution in America, fought for unity and re-organization while the new left of the party pushed for insurrection. Battles for supremacy of vision ensued and in little time those calling for revolution, primarily the foreign-born, left the party for one of the new Communist organizations. This split marked the death of the Socialist Party.

Accepting Weinstein's thesis that World War One and its consequences effectively ended the viability of the Socialist Party, Sally Miller examined the role of Victor Berger and his faction within the party in her 1971 work, *Victor Berger and the Promise of Constructive Socialism, 1910-1920.* Miller worked from sources nearly identical to the ones used by the authors discussed above, yet naturally focused more narrowly on those documents relating to Victor Berger, the first socialist to obtain a seat in the United States Congress (1910) and leader of the party's center-right, reformist bloc. As the fifth work in a historiography concerned with the inability of the Socialist Party to survive in the American political landscape, Miller also worked from and refutes the findings of the authors above.

Through her focus on Berger, Miller set out to challenge Bell's belief that the Socialist Party was "in the world but not of the world". Instead, Miller highlighted the ability of Berger and the center-right faction of the party to retain socialist belief in the midst of American political realities. Whereas Bell saw the maintenance of socialist ethics as an impossibility in the American political arena, Miller saw the real application of these ethics through the person of Berger and his followers. Miller believed that in Berger's "willingness to act as a moral man in immoral society" and "in his attempt solve the ethical paradox inherent in political action, he was striving to become Max Weber's 'genuine man' with a 'calling for politics'". [18] It is this attempt by Berger to embody Weber's theory that was the main focus of Miller's study. In choosing this focus, Miller was therefore greatly concerned with the agency of individuals in the workings of history. Even though Berger had achieved a measure of success in integrating socialist idealism with politics, internal and external obstacles, as well as personal failings, prevented the growth of the Socialist Party.

Miller accepted a number of the findings of her predecessors in her discussion of the party's failure. She agreed with Shannon that the Bolshevik Revolution galvanized the leftist elements in the party, spurring them to preach an imminent socialism divorced from American realities that relied on appeals to a non-existent class-consciousness. Miller also accepted Weinstein's view that the foreign-born members who came to dominate the party were central to this leftist orientation, adding that they sought to graft European realities onto an America where the same opportunities for revolution did not exist. Miller, however, did not place all of the blame on the left. She agreed with Bell that the intellectuals who left the party in support of Wilson's reformism, as well as those who left in support of the war, were also responsible for the party's disintegration.

Miller's central thesis was that because of the loss of many stable, center-right leaders, by the end of World War One the Socialist Party was not equipped to combat the rise of the left faction. "Old leaders who were responsible for the consistent tenor of party policy", she wrote, "were unable to guide the Socialist Party in its moment of agony. At a time when the old left merged into a new one, cemented by stimuli that produced its greatest momentum, the right wing found itself fatally crippled and incapable of meeting vigorously the severest internal challenge." [19] Berger was among those leaders criticizing the left while calling the party back to a reformist position. However, in opposing the war, Berger and the Socialist Party had become too far removed from the sentiments of most Americans. Miller also suggested that Berger's egotistical and aggressive character played a role in the deterioration of the center-right. Berger *could* have united the center-right, Miller argued, were it not for his unsavory personality. The party found itself without a strong reformist component while the left was about to leave the party in favor of a more revolutionary position. This combination of "external events and internal errors combined to destroy the dream". [20]

Another biography, Nick Salvatore's 1982 *Eugene V. Debs: Citizen and Socialist,* examined the life of Eugene V. Debs, perennial presidential candidate for the Socialist Party in the early part of the twentieth century. Salvatore set out to correct what he perceived to be misrepresentations of Debs promulgated by preceding histories of the man and the period. Salvatore wrote that, "Too often Debs became a larger-than-life hero, a born radical eternally at odds with the culture that nurtured him."[21]

Salvatore extended his focus beyond the political life of the leader to try and capture the actions and values of Debs as springing from specific historical contexts. Salvatore wrote that, "the book is... a piece of social history that assumes individuals do not stand outside the culture and society they grew in and from."[22] In this sense, Salvatore's work stood in the tradition of the "new labor history", with its lack of emphasis on "great men" or labor organizations as the primary agents in history. Instead, it is the culture of the masses of rank and file workers[23], as well as pre-industrial American cultural*values*, channeled through Debs within a socialist context that most interested Salvatore. His work was also something of a psychohistory, in that it ascribes psychological characteristics to Debs that were acquired through his childhood and upbringing. Debs's psychological makeup, in effect, motivated his actions and responses to the changing world around him. Additionally, manhood and dignity, within the context of the family, were central values to the working class climate from which Debs came. The value of manhood, "demanded that [a man] secure a living wage; establish through industry and proper habits his own self-respect; and in this manner secure the respect of other men- goals defined primarily from the work experience." [24] The values which informed Debs' and other Americans' worldview were challenged by the growth and abuses of the advent of large-scale American industry and capitalism, leading to a point where, "The meaning of manhood no longer seemed a given birthright, and this still earnest native son began his search for another beacon light upon a hill."[25] This "beacon light" would be based upon a vision of justice and equality derived from the nineteenth century American political and social experience.

Debs was successful, Salvatore argued, not because of who he was, but because of what he represented. In this vein, Debs was not the kind of historical anomaly that preceding biographies or textbooks have interpreted him to be, and the socialism Debs represented was not a foreign import of a strictly theoretical Marxist bent. Instead, Debs's socialist political thought stemmed from his immersion in America's democratic traditions and values. In his discussion of these values, America's character, and Debs' place within this world, Salvatore addressed the question of socialism's failure in the United States. Salvatore rebutted those historians and leftist critics who, "have suggested that [Debs's] particular adaptation of Karl Marx and American political thought was reformist and have argued that this lack of orthodox Marxism in large part accounts for the failure of Socialism in America." [26] Here Salvatore had in mind those like Iris Kipnis who argued that the Socialist Party pandered too much to the middle-class, or the right-wing, and that a more leftist orientation would have led to greater growth and success. And, although writing fifteen years before Brian Lloyd (discussed below), refuted his thesis that the party was not Marxist-Leninist enough in orientation and failed because of its refusal to accept doctrinaire Marxism. Instead, Salvatore argued something quite different.

Salvatore appears to accept an element of the "American Exceptionalism" thesis when he writes of the working class that, "the task of affirming a collective identity in a culture that boasted of its individualistic mores was difficult indeed."[27] The author suggested that America's unique character, in contrast with Europe's, for example, prevented greater class-consciousness from taking root among workers.

In this context, Salvatore said that preceding historians formed a badly posed question in asking why the Socialist Party failed. He wrote that, "Failure assumes the possibility for success, but that was never a serious prospect for the Debsian movement." [28] Because of America's character, nothing the Socialist Party could have done would have led to revolution. It was a doomed project from the start. However, Salvatore remained somewhat optimistic about the *meaning* of the Socialist Party for American society, seeing the principles and program of the Socialist Party as an example to those in the future committed to issues of social and economic justice.

Moving into newer history, Richard Judd's 1989 urban history, *Socialist Cities: Municipal Politics and the Grass Roots of American Socialism,* focused on grassroots efforts to make socialism a reality in the United States. Instead of focusing on the party's leadership as other works did, Judd looked at the Socialist Party from below in a kind of microhistory concerned with the Socialist Party in urban areas. This microhistory, influenced by anthropology, (an influence seen in Judd's concern with parades and picnics, for example) "place[s] small communities, single events, or even one individual under minute scrutiny."[29] Judd was concerned with the, "grass roots level [which]offers a picture of boundless energy and enthusiasm- Socialist lectures, rallies, parades, picnics, and street-corner speeches held weekly, tons of Socialist literature, hand-carried throughout the cities, and Socialist papers circulated to hundreds of thousands of readers." [30] From these phenomena, Judd draws broad conclusions about the party's failures.

In the first chapter of his book, "The Debate on American Socialism", Judd provided a thorough review of the literature which preceded him, separating most previous interpretations of the Socialist Party's failure into two camps- one which has dealt with the party in terms of internal factions, and the other which suggested external factors, namely "American Exceptionalism", prevented the party's success. In the first camp, Judd placed Kipnis, Shannon, and Miller, while he placed Bell in the latter. Suggesting that each point of view possessed shortcomings, he wrote, "taken singularly, each explanation appears too comprehensive; the overarching presumptions of each analysis ignore the complexity of the whole. In light of the plausible alternatives, none of the explanations-external or internal-seems to yield definitive answers."[31] Judd went on to criticize much of the preceding historiography, with the exception of Salvatore's work, as lacking, "a view of the worker as an active historical agent." [32] His critique extended to these historians' focus on the "great men" of the socialist past, namely Debs and DeLeon, as indicators of trends within American socialism and the relationship of the rank and file to the party. Because of his emphasis on the rank and file, local elections, and the social character of the party, Judd's work was an amalgam of social and urban history, as well as a microhistory. Along with Salvatore, Judd was a product of the 1960s theory explosion within the field, naturally responding to and utilizing the diversity of theoretical and historical frameworks that emerged in those and subsequent years.

Judd's sources reflected his local focus. He relied on material not employed by the previous historians such as contemporary scholarly articles on local socialist activity in the Midwest, an unpublished dissertation on socialist municipal administration of the same era, and newspaper and journal articles focusing on local socialist administration written in the early twentieth century. Judd also utilized local Socialist Party newspapers from the period, convention minutes, and socialist pamphlets written and distributed in Midwestern cities. With these sources he weaved together the meaning of socialist politics in five Midwestern cities where socialist candidates experienced various levels of success. These types of cities, he argued, were where socialists saw their greatest chances of establishing solid bases of support which would in turn influence national politics.

Judd saw the Socialist Party in the cities as having a changing base of support. At first, members of the middle-class who were displeased with corruption in the political parties, along with industrial workers, united to put socialists into office. Once in office, socialists faced opposition from businesses and middle-class reformers, stifling the possibility for real change. The working classes continued to support the Socialist Party but the middle-class gravitated towards other, more powerful progressive movements. Bound up with this explanation was a more complicated view of the decline of the Socialist Party than previously expressed. Judd cited nearly all of the previously mentioned internal and external crises mentioned by previous historians-factionalism, external pressures brought by World War One and the Russian Revolution, the appeal of Wilson's reforms, and others, as multiple factors precipitating the decline of the party. However, other than this "synthesis", he did not put forth any kind of original thesis, opting instead to suggest that the history of the Socialist Party's decline, whether it be from a kind of "American Exceptionalism" or not, be a lesson to future radicals. What the lesson is that they should take away is ambiguous at best.

Pittenger's 1993 intellectual history of the American socialist movements, *American Socialists and Evolutionary Thought, 1870-1920,* considered the impact nineteenth century evolutionism had on socialist thought. Interpreting American socialism and the Socialist Party through the field of the "history of ideas", Pittenger returned to a framework initiated by historian and philosopher Arthur Lovejoy in the early decades of the twentieth century that assumed ideas have the ability to shape outcomes.[33] In examining the "inner world" of late nineteenth and early twentieth century socialist thinkers, Pittenger concluded that evolutionist principles supplanted theoretical Marxism, leading American socialists to accept the gradual, seemingly inevitable evolution of society. Evolutionary thought also explained why American socialists were not as critical of racism, sexism, and nativism, as they could have been. And, perhaps more importantly, why American socialists were not as radical as many of their European counterparts. Even though a more theoretical, Marxist approach came to characterize the tenor of the Socialist Party in the early part of the twentieth century, the party's thinkers still remained infused with a spirit of optimism and positivism, while maintaining a reliance on progress in "scientific" terms.

Pettinger made his case using writings of well known, and lesser known, authors of the late nineteenth and early twentieth century-many of whom have become associated with "Utopian Socialism". He looked to prominent authors like Jack London, Charlotte Perkins Gilman, and Edward Bellamy to tease out evolutionary thinking. This approach was aided by late nineteenth and early twentieth century journals like the International Socialist Review, as Pettinger sometimes read "against the grain" to see the ebb and flow of evolutionary thinking on socialism. Socialist authors from the period, especially Morris Hilquit and Laurence Gronlund, were also cited to support his thesis.

For American socialists in the early twentieth century, "attaining scientific literacy often seemed a first step toward socialist commitment." [34] Pittenger cited the fact that even Bill Haywood, leader of the left faction expelled from the Socialist Party in 1913 for his radical positions and call for direct action, was known to read Darwin and Spencer in his formative years and considered their thought an influence in his own political awakening.[35] Pittenger cited the prevalence of this phenomenon- American socialists moving from evolutionary thought, or a belief in the natural progression of society toward a better end, to more scientific socialism, while they retained the residual influence of evolutionary thinkers on their Marxism. This worldview, to Pittenger, influenced both the right and left wings of the party. Pittenger wrote that evolutionary theory came to be, "...seen as a part of the Marxist intellectual tradition," [36] and that, "Socialist Party members, like their predecessors, ...found in Darwin and Spencer ways to unite ardent desire with scientific certainty."[37]

For American socialists, Marxism was influenced by the hopeful positivism and scientific determinism of the nineteenth century. These philosophical underpinnings provided a space for racism, sexism, and nativism to exist within a "socialist" framework in a time when, "One could consistently be a socialist and, by modern standards, a reactionary on a wide array of issues that were understood in evolutionary terms." [38] In other words, exclusion based on race, sex, and ethnicity were "scientifically" justified in the minds of many early twentieth century socialists. This pervasive pseudo-science which colored American Marxism also allowed for a kind of political passivity which, Pittenger suggests, aided in the decline of the Socialist Party. While socialists *did* fight for change, they relied too heavily on the notion that progress would inevitably come for the worker in the course of humanity's evolution, leaving socialists less effective than if they had operated without this principle. This evolutionary approach was weak and ineffectual according to theorist Brian Lloyd who thought that the Socialist Party could have been more successful if built and organized along Leninist lines.

Situating his work within the context of Marxist-Leninist historical and political theory, while supported by intellectual history, Lloyd set out to attack the "American Exceptionalism" thesis. Through his Marxist paradigm, which interprets events and movement in history through a lens of class conflict, Lloyd argued that it was a lack of understanding of true Marxist theory by American radicals that defeated socialism's chances for success. Although his work dealt with the American left in broad terms, Lloyd did address the Socialist Party using his theoretical framework. Lloyd's thesis stood in direct conflict with Bell's, which argued that the left's failure can be attributed to its acceptance of doctrinaire Marxism, as well as Shannon's, which saw factional disputes over the meaning of Marxism as the prime culprit.

In place of theory, Lloyd's 1997 *Left Out: Pragmatism, Exceptionalism, and the Poverty of American Marxism, 1890-1922* argued, radicals before the rise of Eugene V. Debs accepted a version of Marxism infused with positivism and Darwinism. Lloyd's thesis fell in line with Pittenger's discussion while delving more deeply into the reasons for socialism's decline and offering an alternative historical outcome if only the application of theory had trumped pragmatism. During and after Debs, socialists relied too heavily on experience and pragmatism- a natural outgrowth of positivist thinking. This version of American socialism, infused with excessive pragmatism, essentially watered down Marxist principles to the point where it was easy for adherents to accept similar brands of a more powerful progressivism. By this process Marx, writes Lloyd, was "whittled down to the size of a social historian."[39] This absence of theory and ideology, which stood in sharp contrast to the theory driven Bolsheviks, for example, explains the failure of the Socialist Party. Lloyd believed that this brand of doctrinally sapped "Marxism" was an ideological trap that continues to ensnare the American left to this day.

To make his case, Lloyd closely examined socialist theorists of the late nineteenth and early twentieth century, and drew conclusions similar to those of Pittenger. He probed the works of economist and sociologist Throrstein Veblen, particularly his work, *Socialist Economics*, as an intellectual pathway from Marx to an outright acceptance of pragmatism by socialists sometime between 1905 (the date of the book's publication in English) and 1912. Lloyd also explored the pragmatism of William James and John Dewey as influences on American socialist thought in addition to a number of the sources used by Pittenger (Hillquit, for example), and early twentieth century socialist periodicals. Lloyd contrasted the character of these influences and sources with what he interpreted as genuine Marxism- a Marxism that, "reflects a sympathetic engagement with the works of Marx and Engels, Lenin, Georgy Lukacs, and Mao Tse-tung."[40]

With such a departure from "pure Marxism" on the part of American socialists, historical debates over the role of factionalism in the party as a prime culprit in the Socialist Party's failure was trivial in Lloyd's analysis. The main problem, which ran much deeper than infighting, was an ideological one. Toward the end of his work, Lloyd implied a Marxist-Leninist solution to the "poverty" of American socialists and what he perceived to be their belief that electoral success, or working within a capitalist framework, can create revolution. He wrote, "No matter how patiently it was awaited or urgently it was summoned, no natural agent of revolution emerged from the cauldron of modern industry. Trade unionism has never, of its own volition, transmuted into anti-capitalism; no electoral socialist, on either side of the Atlantic, has used a bourgeois state to dismantle capitalism." [41]

Investigating why something *did not* happen, rather than why it *did,* presents a unique set of problems for historians, as well as socialists today. To present an argument for the absence of a strong, viable socialist movement in the United States, or its decline in the early part of the twentieth century, is to argue something about the forces that prevented the growth of this movement. While some historians have argued that internal disputes or party orientation are primarily to blame, others have pointed to external factors, positing that there is something unique about America's character that secured the triumph of capitalism and the death of a strong left. This "internal vs. external" debate has been colored by shifts within the discipline of history. These changes have allowed historians to reassess the socialist movement with fresh theoretical frameworks and provide new analysis that further elucidates the period while laying the groundwork for future historians to continue to solve this perennial question. We know that, "Men make their own history, but they do not make it as they please; they do not make it under self-selected circumstances, but under circumstances existing already, given and transmitted from the past." With these future historians, a future socialist movement can and should learn from the successes and failures of our own American past and be fully cognizant and realistic about the circumstances given and transmitted from that past that continues to weigh heavily on the present.

Notes

[1] This question was first posed by the German Werner Sombart's 1906 publication, *Why is there no Socialism in the United States?*, (New York: Sharpe, 1976).
[2] Christopher Lasch, *The Agony of the American Left*, (New York: Knopf, 1969), 35.
[3] Anna Green and Kathleen Troup, *The Houses of History*, (New York: New York University Press), 2-3.
[4] Iris Kipnis, *The American Socialist Movement, 1897-1912,* (New York: Columbia University Press, 1952), 5.

[5] Ibid., 425.

[6] Daniel Bell, *Marxian Socialism in the United States*, (Princeton: Princeton University Press, 1952), 195.

[7] Ibid., 5.

[8] Ibid.

[9] Green and Troup, 110-114.

[10] Bell, 116.

[11] David Shannon, *The Socialist Party of America*, (New York: The Macmillan Company, 1955), 270.

[12] Ibid.

[13] Ibid., 264.

[14] Ibid., 129.

[15] James Weinstein, *The Decline of Socialism in America, 1912-1925*, (New Brunswick: Rutgers University Press, 1967), 327.

[16] Ibid., 328.

[17] Ibid., 327.

[18] Sally Miller, Victor Berger and the Promise of Constructive Socialism, 1910-1920, (West Port: Greenwood Press, Inc., 1973), 14-15.

[19] Ibid., 231.

[20] Ibid., 244.

[21] Nick Salvatore, Eugene V. Debs: Citizen and Socialist, (Chicago: University of Illinois Press, 1982), xi.

[22] Ibid., xi.

[23] Green and Troup, 38.

[24] Salvatore, 23.

[25] Ibid., 55.

[26] Ibid., 271.

[27] Ibid.

[28] Ibid.

[29] Green and Troup, 174.

[30] Richard W. Judd, Socialist Cities: *Municipal Politics and the Grass Roots of American Socialism,*(Albany: State University of New York, 1989),183.

[31] Ibid., 9.

[32] Ibid., 10.

[33] Arthur Lovejoy, The Great Chain of Being, (Cambridge: Harvard University Press, 1976).

[34] Mark Pittenger, *American Socialists and Evolutionary Thought, 1870-1920, (*Madison: The University of Wisconsin Press, 1993), 121.

[35] Ibid., 122.

[36] Ibid., 123.
[37] Ibid., 124.
[38] Ibid., 198.
[39] Brian Lloyd, *Left Out: Pragmatism, Exceptionalism, and the Poverty of American Marxism, 1890-1922,* (Baltimore: The Johns Hopkins University Press, 1997), 91.
[40] Ibid., 457.
[41] Ibid., 414.

Challenging Liberty

The Danger of DNA Databases

Devon Douglas-Bowers

In 2013, the Supreme Court passed down a ruling stating that it is legal to take DNA swabs from arrestees without a warrant on the grounds that "a DNA cheek swab [was similar] to other common jailhouse procedures like fingerprinting;"[1] and yesterday, it was reported that the New Jersey state senate passed a bill that "would require the collection of DNA samples from people convicted of some low-level crimes, including shoplifting and drug possession."[2] While many are praising the passing of such legislation, it ignores the inherent dangers of allowing the government to collect DNA.

While DNA databases may seem new, this is only because they are recently coming back into the news. They have been around for quite some time as, since 1988, "every US state has established a database of criminal offenders' DNA profiles" with the goal of "quickly and accurately [matching] known offenders with crime scene evidence."[3] Politicians are arguing that taking DNA samples of criminals will actually lower crime, as the DNA works as a deterrent by increasing the likelihood that a criminal will be convicted if they are

335

caught. However, this may not be the case, as a working paper from the University of Virginia found last year that, " **The probability of reoffending and being convicted for any offense is 3.7 percentage points (23.4%) higher for those with a profile in the DNA database than those without** ," (emphasis added) and, that DNA profiling mainly affects younger criminals with multiple convictions, as they are "85.6% more likely to be convicted of a crime within three years of release than their unprofiled counterparts."[4] Thus, on a practical level, we should be skeptical as to whether or not DNA databases will actually lower crime in the long-term.

A separate but equally important issue in regards to these DNA databases is the assault on our privacy. Barry Steinhardt, then-Associate Director of the ACLU, stated back in 2000 that:

"While DNA databases may be useful to identify criminals, I am skeptical that we will ward off the temptation to expand their use," said Barry Steinhardt, Associate Director of the ACLU. "In the last ten years alone, we have gone from collecting DNA only from convicted sex offenders to now including people who have been arrested but never convicted of a crime."[5]

Indeed, Steinhardt is quite correct in that law enforcement has a history of expanding the use of their tools. One example is tasers, which, when first introduced, were seen as a way to apprehend criminals without resorting to lethal force, have now gone so far astray from that original purpose that they have been used on children.[6] Thus, it would not be a stretch to assume that, over time, this DNA database could be used improperly, such as in the case of Earl Whittley Davis, where his DNA was uploaded and he subsequently became a subject of a 2004 cold case murder:

*Earl Whittley Davis was a shooting victim whose DNA profile was subsequently uploaded into CODIS even though he had done nothing wrong. This victim then became the subject of a cold case hit for a murder that occurred in 2004. **Although the Maryland District Court found that crime control was a generalized interest that did not outweigh Davis' privacy when placement of his DNA profile in CODIS was not in response to a warrant or to an applicable statute, the Court held that the DNA evidence was nonetheless admissible.** The Court reasoned that placement of Davis' profile in CODIS was not reckless, flagrant or systematic, that exclusion would result in only marginal deterrence, if any, and that any deterrent effect would be* *greatly outweighed by the cost of suppressing "powerfully inculpatory and reliable DNA evidence."*

This case should lead people to fear that utilizing such practices to expand the DNA database would open a backdoor to population-wide data banking. *By denying certiorari, the U.S. Supreme Court is implicitly affirming the rulings of the Second and Eleventh Circuits. This will make it more challenging for those opposing DNA database statutes on Fourth Amendment grounds.[7] (emphasis added)*

In the dissenting opinion of the Supreme Court case, *Maryland v. King*, many of the Justices echoed this worry of law enforcement using the DNA databases to attempt to solve old crimes, with Justice Scalia stating, "Solving unsolved crimes is a noble objective, but it occupies a lower place in the American pantheon of noble objectives than the protection of our people from suspicionless law-enforcement searches. The Fourth Amendment must prevail." [8]

DNA databasing is dangerous as it provides a future diary of sorts, which "has the potential to reveal to third parties a person's predisposition to illnesses or behaviors without the person's knowledge; and it is permanent information, deeply personal, with predictive powers" and thus "[calls] into question the very meaning and possibility of human liberty"[9] as it can lead into the slippery slope of pre-crime, especially with regard to a person's behaviors.

In addition to this, DNA databasing could negatively impact minorities and the poor, and even allow people's family members to be arrested, as *Wired* reported back in 2011:

Civil rights advocates have warned that demographically unbalanced forensic DNA data banks could "create a feedback loop." **Because samples are stored and compared against DNA collected at future crime scenes, police will be more likely to pursue crimes committed by members of overrepresented groups, while underrepresented groups can more easily evade detection.**

The potential for problems expands when states permit so-called familial DNA searches, in which police who can't find a database match to crime scene DNA can search the database for partial matches, ostensibly from the suspect's family and relatives, who can then be targeted. *It's even possible to imagine situations in which some* *races or groups become universally covered, while others remain only partially surveyed. [10] (emphasis added)*

Yet, what is most worrying is the expansion of DNA databasing from major criminal offenders such as murderers and rapists to now including "some low-level crimes, including shoplifting and drug possession."[11] This expansion of DNA databasing to include even victimless crimes is quite worrisome as it shows that we are moving to a state of law where virtually any crime will allow the police to draw and database one's DNA.

With the passing of this ruling and the steadily increasing implementation of DNA databasing on the state level, an ember in the light of freedom is quietly extinguished.

References

[1] Jesse Holland, "Supreme Court Rules Police Can Take DNA Swabs From Arrestees," *Time Magazine*, June 3, 2013 (http://swampland.time.com/2013/06/03/supreme-court-rules-police-can-take-dna-swabs-from-arrestees/)

[2] Ryan Hutchins, "Bill to require DNA collection for some low-level crimes passes N.J. Senate," *The Star Ledger*, June 24, 2013 (http://www.nj.com/politics/index.ssf/2013/06/bill_to_require_dna_collection_for_some_low-level_crimes_passes_nj_senate.html#incart_river)

[3] L. Doleac, Jennifer, "The Effects of DNA Databases On Crime," University of Virginia, Frank Batten School of Leadership and Public Policy, Working Paper 01, 2012.http://www.batten.virginia.edu/content/2013-001-effects-dna-databases-crime-jennifer-doleac-860

[4] Ibid

[5] American Civil Liberties Union, DNA Databases Hold More Dangers Than Meet the Eye, ACLU Says, http://www.aclu.org/technology-and-liberty/dna-databases-hold-more-dangers-meet-eye-aclu-says, March 23, 2000

[6] Pam Spaulding, Police use Taser on unarmed, nude child with autism wandering on highway ,

Firedoglake, http://pamshouseblend.firedoglake.com/2013/06/21/polic e-use-taser-on-unarmed-nude-child-wandering-on-highway/ (June 21, 2013)

[7] Candice Roman-Santos, "Concerns Associated with Expanding DNA Databases," *Hastings Science & Technology Law Journal* 2:267 (2010), pg 20

[8] Liz Goodwin, "In dissent, Scalia joins with court's liberals to blast police DNA testing without warrant," *Yahoo! News*, June 3, 2013 (http://news.yahoo.com/blogs/lookout/dissent-scalia-joins-court-liberals-blast-police-dna-184252969.html)

[9] Christine Rosen, "Liberty, Privacy, and DNA Databases," *The New Atlantic*, 1:1 Spring 2003, pg 39

[10] Brandon Keim, "Forensic DNA Could Make Criminal Justice Less Fair," *Wired*, October 7, 2011 (http://www.wired.com/wiredscience/2011/10/forensic-dna/)

[11] *The Star Ledger* , June 24, 2013

The New Politics of the Twenty-First Century

Global Resistance and Rising Anarchism

Devon Douglas-Bowers

A number of occurrences have taken place in the past 13 years since the rise of the new millennium; we have seen and are seeing the rise of popular movements all over the world and a resistance to the forces of imperialism, capitalism and subjugation, from the most recent Arab Spring to the world's largest coordinated anti-war gathering in history with the global protests against the Iraq War[1], to the rise of the Occupy Movement and the surfacing of indigenous resistance as in the Idle No More campaign of Canada's First Nations population. While not all movements are pushing for the elimination of the state, or are even anarchistic in nature, they are rebelling against the current societal structures and creating an opportunity for radical change. What we are seeing around the world is a global resistance that, in some cases, has anarchist undercurrents. We are witnessing the new politics of the 21st century.

While many movements such as the Occupy Movement and the Arab Spring included anarchist influences within them, anarchism as a political philosophy is still quite misunderstood, and some time should be taken to understand it.

340

Anarchism is defined by the *American Heritage Dictionary* as "The theory that all forms of government are oppressive and should be abolished." [2] While it does advocate the abolition of the state, anarchism also includes "a heightened and radical critique and questioning of power and authority: if a source of authority cannot legitimize its existence, it should not exist." [3] This has led to anarchism being critiqued by a number of individuals and an increase in anarchist thought to the point where there are a large number of anarchist ideas being championed today, from anarcho-feminism to queer anarchism to black anarchism.

Anarchism and the Labor Movement

In the United States, anarchism has had a rather interesting history with regards to not only Occupy, but also the 19th century labor movement. Anti-statism isn't anything new in the US as there have been a large number of crusaders who "condemned [the government] as an oppressive tyranny" when slavery wasn't abolished in the newly founded country. This abhorrence of slavery and hypocrisy caused "men like William Lloyd Garrison and Wendell Phillips [to renounce] their allegiance to it, John Brown openly declared war upon it, and thousands of others regarded it as unfit to command their respect and loyalty."[4] Anti-statism only increased in the 19th century with the inclusion of anarchists in the labor movement.

The International Working Men's Association (IWMA) advocated for the 8-hour workday in its 1866 Congress. The IWMA "had influence amongst the German-speaking immigrant anarchist and socialist workers of Chicago,"[5] and after it was disbanded, the International Working People's Association, being founded in 1881 by anarchists, took up the struggle.

This struggle for better working conditions culminated in what became known as the 1886 Haymarket Square Riot in which 40,000 workers went on strike to fight for an 8-hour day. The strikes beget protests which beget police confrontation. "On May 3, police fired on strikers who were menacing the strikebreakers at McCormick Harvester, and several strikers were injured. Labor leaders then convened a mass meeting for the following evening at the city's Haymarket Square."[6] As the police demanded the rally be shut down, someone threw a dynamite bomb towards a group of officers, to which the police responded with gunfire. The result: seven dead police officers and several workingmen injured. A total of eight anarchists were charged, which resulted in seven people being sentenced to death in addition to one life sentence in prison. Two death sentences were commuted to life imprisonment by Illinois governor Richard J. Oglesby, one committed suicide and four were hung.

Occupy Wall Street

While anarchism continued until World War 1 with massive anti-war protests, it was eventually forced underground. However, the Occupy movement breathed new life into anarchist ideas. OWS's focus on "direct action and leaderless, consensus-based decision-making,"[7] embodied into the General Assembly, was an anarchistic aspect of Occupy. It also was anarchistic in its refusal to " recognize the legitimacy of existing political institutions," "accept the legitimacy of the existing legal order," and its "embrace of prefigurative politics." [8] This refusal to recognize the political institutions is anarchistic in nature as it refuses to appeal to political powers to alleviate societal ills. By rejecting the two-party system, and rather than fighting for a third-party, OWS rejected the state and worked to create a community based on horizontal (as opposed to hierarchical) organization. By rejecting the legal order in the form of ignoring " local ordinances that insisted that any gathering of more than 12 people in a public park is illegal without police permission," [9] OWS refused to subjugate itself to the very forces that worked to establish and uphold the current status quo. Occupy embraced political ideas and experimented with them, which resulted in the creation of new institutions, from kitchens to clinics to media centers; all of which were consistently built around the ideas of working together, horizontal organization, and voluntary cooperation - elements that are central to anarchist thought. While the encampments may no longer exist, the Occupy movement is still alive in the form of offshoots; and the activists that made up Occupy didn't disappear, rather they have moved on into other forms of resistance[10], though just not under the Occupy banner. They have even been involved in organizations that have provided large amounts of aid to damaged communities, such as Occupy Sandy, which stepped in when the federal government could not.[11]

Global Uprisings

This resistance to the status quo has not just been taking place in America, but also all over the world. In 2008, Zbigniew Brzezinski warned of a global political awakening. In a *New York Times* op-ed, he stated "For the first time in history, almost all of humanity is politically activated, politically conscious and politically interactive. Global activism is generating a surge in the quest for cultural respect and economic opportunity in a world scarred by memories of colonial or imperial domination."[12] This "global activism" is quite real and very well may upend the entirety of the current political, social, and economic systems.

In Brazil, protests have been occurring over issues ranging from inflation to education reform and forced evictions. Among all of this, teachers went to the streets to "demand better wages and school conditions when police decided to disperse the demonstration." [13] There had already been violent clashes between teachers and police, highlighted by several striking teachers that were occupying a city council building in Rio de Janiero being beaten and dragged out by the police. During the demonstration in late October 2013, the police decided to repress the teachers by using heavy-handed tactics such as shooting tear gas canisters. Brazilian anarchists came to the aid of the teachers by protecting them from the state-sponsored violence. As one teacher, Andrea Coelho, said, "It was the Black Bloc that protected me in that protest."[14] This protection of teachers has caused the teachers union to declare unconditional support for the black bloc protesters.[15]

These protests in Brazil come amidst a time when there was "less than 1% growth last year and less than 3% forecast this year compared to 7.5% in 2010," and where its political leaders convinced the world that it "was developed enough to host the soccer World Cup this year and the Summer Olympics in Rio de Janeiro in 2016, yet seemed so unwilling to show their own people they could improve the country's pathetically underfunded schools, staffed by just as woefully underpaid and undertrained teachers."[16] Just last year, a UN study indicated that wealth inequality was increasing with "the richest 20% of the population on average earn 20 times more than the poorest 20%." [17] It is among this massive increase in wealth inequality on a regional level, along with a corrupt government and lack of educational investment, that the people have finally decided enough is enough and are demanding there be massive changes to the current system.

In Europe, where in places like Greece, children are starving in order to repay banks, revolt is taking place. Last year in Bulgaria, around 4,000 people demonstrated "calling for an end to the 'reign of the oligarchy' and demanding that the nation's government step down to make way for early elections." [18]They argue that the country is still unstable, unprosperous, and not well governed 24 years after Communist rule was ended. The protest was part of a five-month old anti-government movement that alleges the government has mafia ties. Such accusations were confirmed to be, in part, true after a 2008 investigation by the European Union's anti-fraud office exposed the Nikolov-Stoykov group, a conglomerate with businesses from meat processing and storage to a Black Sea Resort, had connections to the government and has been accused of being a front for a criminal company network comprised of over 50 Bulgarian companies as well as other European and offshore companies. [19]More recently, the European Commission issued a report discussing the government-mafia ties in Bulgaria, with puts the blame on "both the executive and the judiciary in Bulgaria, which have been engulfed by power struggles, with each accusing the other of serving the mafia."[20]

In Italy, there have been anti-austerity protests going on for quite some time. The violence escalated at a 2013 demonstration as police fired tear gas at anti-austerity protesters and at least 16 people, including four officers, were injured and eight protesters were arrested. The protesters were "calling for more affordable housing, better wages and improved conditions for immigrants and refugees, tens of thousands of whom live in a twilight zone of semi-legality in Italy, with many forced to squat in disused buildings or sleep rough."[21] More protests are continuing in Italy where there have been cuts in education spending, and are spreading to all of Europe as the EU proposed spending cuts in its 2014 budget.[22]

Amidst the talk and fervor of the Arab Spring, anarchist activists were heavily involved in organizing after Mubarak's ousting. Egyptian anarchist Mohammed Hassan Aazab noted that after Mubarak was gone, they "started gathering, talking to people, printing up writing about our ideas, and organizing meetings in downtown cafes in front of whoever was there."[23] The organizing continues and the fight against the oppressive Egyptian regime goes on, even as the Egyptian government bans protests of more than ten people without a police permit; effectively an attempt to end all protests.

In Bahrain, the protests against the Sunni monarchy continue as Shiites protest "repression against the opposition amid an ongoing crackdown on the largely peaceful demonstrations."[24] These protests occur despite the Bahraini government's history of using violence against peaceful demonstrators, even going so far as killing children.[25] The majority Shiite nation has been repressed for years; they face employment and educational discrimination, have little political representation, and are barred from most government and military positions.[26]

Protests have even hit nations in sub-Saharan Africa, such as Sudan. In 2012, protesters took to the street initially to protest a cut in fuel subsidies, but since then the demonstrations have evolved "to wider dissent against the country's leadership after security forces killed at least 50 people [in late September], according to the African Center for Justice and Peace Studies and human rights watchdog Amnesty International." [27] The Sudanese government admitted "that 87 people were killed, while activists and human rights groups say the number was at least 200."[28] The main catalyst to the protests was the decrease of fuel subsidies following the separation between Sudan and South Sudan, which was home to about 75% of Sudan's oil production. All of this is occurring when "the Sudanese pound hit an all-time low on the key black market on [September 21, 2013] as people sought to shift their savings into hard currency in anticipation of higher inflation."[29] This increase in inflation, coupled with the cut in fuel subsidies, has led to a massive increase in costs of living, and especially to food prices as Sudan is a major food importer.

While quite sparse in certain areas of the region, protests have spread to Asia as well. In China, "Strikes have become increasingly frequent at privately owned factories in recent years, often involving workers demanding higher wages or better conditions," and technology has helped grow this protest movement as "the explosive growth in the use of home-grown versions of Twitter has made it easy for protesters to convey instant reports and images to huge audiences."[30] These protests are in response to the continuation of low wages and unsafe working conditions amidst a landscape where the number of millionaires and billionaires continues to increase while China has become the world's second largest economy. As if growing discontent among the workforce wasn't enough, the government's surprisingly

345

slow response to alleviate the disastrous effects of the July 2013 floods has caused flood victims to protest. The Chinese government has responded to these protests by sending out riot police whom may have used violence to quell the protesters as "Photographs showed several residents [of Yuyao city] bleeding from the head" [31] following a confrontation.

There are also protests in Thailand, as Thais seek to oust current Prime Minister Yingluck Shinawatra, the sister of former premier Thaksin Shinawatra, who protesters say control her. Shinawatra's older brother was wildly unpopular in 1998 after using his American connections to boost his political image, committing Thai troops to aiding the US invasion of Iraq amid protest from both the military and the public,[32] and allowing the CIA to use Thailand for its extraordinary rendition program. [33] In addition to the suspicion of corruption, Yingluck Shinawatra has also been criticized for "her alleged ignorance, lack of political experience, and tendency to stay adrift of key issues."[34]

On literally every continent, there is resistance to the current political power structures. And while many may not be pushing for the end of the state, they are pushing for radical change toward a society where 'the many' will benefit rather than 'the few'.

Indigenous Resistance

For all of these protests and uprisings, this analysis would not be complete without a group that has been exploited, ignored, stereotyped, and victimized by acts of genocide across the world: the indigenous population.

In Canada, Elsipogtog First Nation members located in New Brunswick province have been fighting against fracking plans as neither the government nor industries discussed the issue with them, despite the fact that "Rulings by the Supreme Court of Canada and lower courts have established a duty to consult and accommodate aboriginal people when development is considered on their land, even non-reserve traditional lands." [35] The First Nations argue that they have never ceded their lands and that the treaties signed in the 1700s were only to acknowledge peace and friendship between the immigrants and the indigenous population. This revolt has culminated in the Idle No More movement which is aimed to protect not only indigenous lands, but also the larger environment in Canada from corporations which aim to use the land for the sole purpose of extracting its resources through harmful techniques such as fracking.

Indigenous resistance is also occurring in Israel. In November 2013, the Israeli parliament moved to begin debating and possibly approving the Prawer Plan. The Prawer Plan, if passed, would have resulted in "the destruction of 35 'unrecognized' Arab Bedouin villages, the forced displacement of up to 70,000 Arab Bedouin citizens of Israel, and the dispossession of their historical lands in the Naqab."[36] On November 30th, it was reported that "In the Negev village of Houra, clashes broke out at the main demonstration where about 1,200 protesters had gathered," with protesters eventually throwing stones at Israeli security forces and the police responding with "tear gas, stun grenades and water cannon."[37] While the Prawer Plan was not approved, the Israeli government still "[failed] to recognize the Bedouin communities and villages, thus still rendering them vulnerable to displacement." [38] It is rather interesting that even though they are citizens of Israel, the Bedouins were still pushed to be subjugated at the interest of the Jewish majority.

Canada and Israel are not the only places where the indigenous population is fighting back. In addition to being wracked with protests regarding education, corruption and a generally inefficient government, Brazil is also witnessing protests from indigenous people. In October 2013, 500 people set up camp in front of Congress to "oppose a constitutional change that would let lawmakers participate in the demarcation of territories. Indigenous people and their supporters say the proposal would allow agricultural interests to encroach on their lands."[39] The fight of Brazil's indigenous population to protect their lands has been going on for over a year now, with many of the conflicts resulting in deaths. According to a 2012 report done by the Indigenist Missionary Council, "54 Indians were murdered in 2012, most of them as a result of land conflicts," [40] and the problem only continues into 2013, with a total of three murders occurring during the first half of the year.

Conclusion

Yet, what does this all mean? Why does it even matter? This global resistance is extremely important as it reveals to global elites that their façade of democracy and consumerism is rapidly falling apart in the face of lagging economies, high unemployment rates, and a political class that is more concerned with its own personal needs rather than that of the people who they have charge over. It serves as a message to people worldwide that they can and must fight back against the current political, social, and economic systems if they are to survive; that they can create new communities and new institutions that don't rely on the current systems of power, and that are organized horizontally rather than hierarchically.

These protests show that the people will not sit idly by and let the government serve them on a platter to corporations, or, even worse, neglect to uphold the promises they took to protect the population. These movements represent a mass awakening of humanity which has the potential to radically change the entire landscape of society on a global scale.

We must be willing to fight for as long as it takes to alter societies that currently serve small sectors of industry or financial elites at the expense of the many to societies that foster a climate of peace - peace with each other and peace with the environment - and encourage education and cooperativeness for the good of all while respecting the autonomy of the individual. Most importantly though, we must foster peace within ourselves and not be afraid to engage with those in our immediate area on these issues; for if not, we will risk the continuation of this broken system and lose what may have been a great chance to change the current situation for the better.

Notes

[1] Phyllis Bennis, "February 15, 2003. The Day the World Said No to War," *Institute For Policy Studies*, February 15, 2013 (http://www.ips-dc.org/blog/february_15_2003_the_day_the_world_said_no_to_war)

[2] *American Heritage Dictionary* , 5th edition, s.v. "anarchism"

[3] Devon Douglas-Bowers, *On Anarchism: An Interview with Andrew Gavin Marshall*, Hampton Institute, http://www.hamptoninstitution.org/onanarchism.html#.UpatMVQ9La8 (October 2, 2013)

[4] Charles A. Madison, "Anarchism in the United States," *Journal of the History of Ideas* 6:1 (1945), pg 50

[5] International Workers Association, *The 8 Hour Day, the Anarchists and the IWPA: Haymarket and the Radicalization of Labour Demands in the 1880s*, http://www.iwa-ait.org/content/8-hour-day-anarchists-and-iwpa-haymarket-and-radicalization-labour-demands-1880s (May 6, 2013)

[6] David Greenberg, "Anarchy in the US: A Century of Fighting The Man," *Slate*, April 28, 2000 (http://www.slate.com/articles/news_and_politics/history_lesson/2000/04/anarchy_in_the_us.html)

[7] Dan Berrett, "Intellectual Roots of Wall St. Protest Lie in Academe," *The Chronicle of Higher Education*, October 16, 2011 (http://chronicle.com/article/Intellectual-Roots-of-Wall/129428/)

[8] David Graeber, "Occupy Wall Street's Anarchist Roots," *Al Jazeera*, November 30, 2011 (http://www.aljazeera.com/indepth/opinion/2011/11/2011112872835904508.html)

[9] Ibid

[10] Democracy Now, *Two Years After Occupy Wall Street, a Network of Offshoots Continue Activism for the 99%,* http://www.democracynow.org/2013/9/19/two_years_after_occupy_wall_street (September 19, 2013)

[11] Alan Feuer, "Occupy Sandy: A Movement Moves to Relief," *New York Times*, November 9, 2012 (http://www.nytimes.com/2012/11/11/nyregion/where-fema-fell-short-occupy-sandy-was-there.html?_r=0)

[12] Zbigniew Brzezinski, "The Global Political Awakening," *New York Times*, December 16, 2008 (http://www.nytimes.com/2008/12/16/opinion/16iht-YEbrzezinski.1.18730411.html?pagewanted=all)

[13] Bradley Brooks, "Anarchist Tactics Grow Among Brazil's Protests," *Associated Press*, October, 22, 2013 (http://news.yahoo.com/anarchist-tactics-grow-amid-brazils-protests-040814619.html)

[14] Ibid

[15] Revolution News, Brazil: Teachers Union Officially Declares Unconditional Support for Black Bloc,http://revolution-news.com/brazils-teachers-union-officially-declares-unconditional-support-for-black-bloc/ (October 9, 2013)

[16] Tim Padgett, "What Brazil's Protests Say About Latin America's Fumbling Elites," *Time*, June 19, 2013 (http://world.time.com/2013/06/19/what-brazils-protests-say-about-latin-americas-fumbling-elites/)

[17] BBC News, *UN Study Says Wealth Gap in Latin America Increases*,http://www.bbc.co.uk/news/world-latin-america-19339636 (August 21, 2012)

[18] Al Jazeera, *Bulgarians Protest Against Government Policy*,http://www.aljazeera.com/news/europe/2013/11/bulgarians-protest-against-government-policy-2013111015288976392.html (November 10, 2013)

[19] Doreen Carvajal, Stephen Castle, "Mob Muscles Its Way Into Politics in Bulgaria," *New York Times*, October 15, 2008 (http://www.nytimes.com/2008/10/16/world/europe/16bulgaria.html?pagewanted=all&_r=0)

[20] Turkish Weekly, *EC Draft Report Slams Bulgaria over Govt-Mafia Ties*,http://www.turkishweekly.net/news/138606/ec-draft-report-slams-bulgaria-over-govt-mafia-ties.html (July 17, 2012)

[21] Nick Squires, "Anti-austerity Protesters Clash With Police in Rome," *Telegraph*, October 31, 2013 (http://www.telegraph.co.uk/news/worldnews/europe/italy/10418497/Anti-austerity-protesters-clash-with-police-in-Rome.html)

[22] BBC, *Students Protest Over Austerity Cuts in Italy*, http://www.bbc.co.uk/news/world-europe-24956693 (November 15, 2013)

[23] Joshua Stephens, "Anarchism in Egypt: An Interview From Tahrir Square," *Waging Nonviolence*, July 2, 2013 (http://wagingnonviolence.org/2013/07/anarchy-in-egypt-an-interview-from-tahrir-square/)

[24] Russia Today, *Thousands Protest in Bahrain Capital, Demand 'torturers be brought to justice,'*http://rt.com/news/bahrain-protests-opposition-repression-194/ (November 23, 2013)

[25] Huffington Post, *Bahrain: Hundreds Mourn After Boy Is Killed In Demonstration*,http://www.huffingtonpost.com/2011/11/19/bahrain-hundreds-mourn_n_1102730.html (Novemer 19, 2011)

[26] Rannie Amiri, "Bahrain: Days of Rage, Decades of Oppression," *Antiwar*, February 21, 2011 (http://original.antiwar.com/rannie-amiri/2011/02/20/bahrain-days-of-rage/)

[27] Henry Austin, "Is The Arab Spring Moving South? Violent Anti-government Protests Hit Sudan,"*NBC News*, October 1, 2013 (http://worldnews.nbcnews.com/_news/2013/10/01/20769020-is-the-arab-spring-moving-south-violent-anti-government-protests-hit-sudan)

[28] BBC, *Sudan Feels The Heat From Fuel Protests*, http://www.bbc.co.uk/news/world-africa-24938224 (November 14, 2013)

[29] Khalid Abdelaziz, Ulf Laessing, "Sudan to Lift Fuel Subsidies Posing 'Great Risk' For Economy-Bashir," *Reuters*, September 22, 2013 (http://www.reuters.com/article/2013/09/22/sudan-economy-idUSL5N0HI0OG20130922)

[30] The Economist, *Unrest In China: A Dangerous Year*, http://www.economist.com/node/21543477(January 28, 2012)

[31] Sui-Lee Wee, "China Sends Riot Police to Block New Protests by Flood Victims," *Reuters*, October 16, 2013 (http://www.reuters.com/article/2013/10/16/us-china-protest-idUSBRE99F0BN20131016)

[32] Fox News, *Thailand Vows to Keep Troops in Iraq*,http://www.foxnews.com/story/2003/12/28/thailand-vows-to-keep-troops-in-iraq/ (December 28, 2003)

[33] Max Fisher, "A Staggering Map of the 54 Countries That Reportedly Participated in the CIA's Rendition Program," *Washington Post*, February 5, 2013 (http://www.washingtonpost.com/blogs/worldviews/wp/2013/02/05/a-staggering-map-of-the-54-countries-that-reportedly-participated-in-the-cias-rendition-program/)

[34] Samudcha Hoonsara, Somroutai Sapsomboon, Kittipong Thavevong, "Yingluck Enters 2013 A Survivor," *The Nation*, January 1, 2013 (http://www.nationmultimedia.com/politics/Yingluck-enters-2013-a-survivor-30197064.html)

[35] Mark Gollom, Daniel Schwartz, "N.B. Fracking Protests and the Fight for Aboriginal Rights," *CBC News*, October 19, 2013 (http://www.cbc.ca/news/n-b-fracking-protests-and-the-fight-for-aboriginal-rights-1.2126515)

[36] Adalah: The Legal Center for Minority Rights in Israel,*Demolition and Eviction of Bedouin Citizens of Israel in the Naqab (Negev) - The Prawer Plan*, http://adalah.org/eng/?mod=articles&ID=1589

[37] Russia Today, *'Day of rage': Police, protesters clash in Israel at plans to evict 40,000 Bedouins*,http://rt.com/news/britain-protest-prawer-plan-511/ (November 30, 2013)

[38] NSBNC International, *Israel drops Prawer Plan but fails to recognize Bedouin Villages*,http://nsnbc.me/2013/12/13/israel-drops-prawer-plan-fails-recognize-bedouin-villages/ (December 13, 2013)

[39] Fox News, *Indigenous Groups Stage Protests Across Brazil to Press*

For Demarcation of Their Lands, http://www.foxnews.com/world/2013/10/01/indigenous-groups-stage-protests-across-brazil-to-press-for-demarcation-their/ (October 1, 2013)

[40] David Dudenhoefer, "Brazil's Natives Protest Threats to Their Rights From Congress," *Indian Country*, October 8, 2013 (http://indiancountrytodaymedianetwork.com/2013/10/08/brazils-natives-protest-threats-their-rights-congress-151644)

Bearing Witness

A Discussion on Paying Attention and Creating Awareness

Devon Douglas-Bowers

Seeing the bombings, killings, and general injustices committed in the US and around the world is extremely disheartening and discouraging. Hopelessness and a general feeling that nothing can be done can easily over-wash a person. It is even more frustrating if you are in a situation where you are unable to attend protests, rallies, or marches. However, there is something that we can all do: bear witness. By that I mean we keep abreast of what is going on in the world and make a point to discuss important issues and topics with people in our everyday lives, especially those who may not be too interested in politics. To discuss this in more detail, I recently had an email interview with Melissa R. and Geoff W. about "bearing witness."

Melissa R. is a queer woman living in the southern United States. She works full time in healthcare and encourages self-education.

Geoffrey W. is an activist and economics student at Washington State. He is the president of his campus' Queer-Straight Alliance, and enjoys spending his time attempting to overthrow the colonialist, patriarchal, discriminatory powers that be. When asked for comments, one person said Geoff was, "...born in the cesspool of multiculturalist liberal propaganda."

1. How do you define this idea of 'bearing witness?'

Melissa: I think of this in a broader sense so that it includes practices of mine as well as what I imagine would be a more common interpretation. By a more common interpretation I mean those interactions with other people that involve sharing experiences, knowledge, and ideas without the religious missionary aspect. In my broader explanation it's really about developing a wide ranging base of knowledge and ideas without being locked into any so that others are off limits. There is self study and education at the core. I suppose that bearing witness would come in again to personal practices of mine would in conversation, observation, conflict resolution, and then again sharing information and ideas. For me it isn't about changing someone's core ideas or bringing them over to a team but more about giving them an impetus to consideration on their own.

I also take bearing witness to mean putting thoughtful attention to what is going on around me or in the world. One could on a level know that there is a drone program and maybe even know details of it to the extent they are available. Many people do and yet choose to turn off at the junction of seeing the testimony of the families who were fortunate enough to have survived, such as Rafiq ur Rehman and his two children. They came to D.C. to testify about the drone attack on Waziristan in which Rafiq's mother was killed and children injured. Only five "lawmakers" and very few journalists showed. Hearing and spreading these truths be it pretty or harsh is a form of bearing witness that is essential, in my opinion.

Geoff: Christians have the best definition, "to share the good news." Unfortunately, not everything lefties bear witness to can be considered remotely close to "good," so we must adopt our own definition. Let the truth be said, then. At the least, let your truth be said.

2. Why do you think that bearing witness is important?

Melissa: So many are in debt to extend their education, didn't complete their high school education, or are engaging in self education because they don't want to add to debt in order to go to college. In addition to these means of education bearing witness can be educational moments as well. Even if this is watching documentaries, listening to programs, talking to people of varying opinions, a new takeaway can be gained. I think there is also something gained for both parties when a compassionate or attentive audience is present for particularly important moments. It doesn't have to lead to a change of mind or an urge to move. It could just give someone perspective or give one person a sense of dignity for being recognized.

Geoff: Bearing witness startles people. I can't speak for humans globally, but in America we tend to segregate ourselves based on personal beliefs. When an individual has the opportunity to say something contrary to their peers' opinions, there is a small moment where people have to decide either to dismiss the new opinion out of hand, or think critically about both options presented. It's that latter action we as activists should hope to prompt.

3. How do you go about doing this in your own lives?

Melissa: I feel in addition to having a wide base of knowledge we also need to take in a wide variety of experiences and kinds of life, not necessarily through having them ourselves. We can do this by earnestly communicating them with other people. It's never been easier for this to take place than in this time of instant mass information. One problem that I see is what I call "teaming" which is really just tribalism. The corporate media is only distributing limited information and even within those there are sides to be chosen. Even with so much information available many people still choose to wall themselves off in these reinforcement chambers. What I think we can do in our own lives is just engage with people, read a wider variety of information with a critical eye, but not with the intent of moving from one side to another. This whole notion of "sides" is problematic and exactly what enhances power structures. Be with people and give them compassion. Smile at people who flick you off in traffic.

Geoff: I'm a student and an activist, so an overwhelming number of opportunities to discuss controversial issues are made available to me. They run the gamut, from voicing an opinion in a classroom to directing weekly workshops. My university is in a fairly conservative region, so many people are unfamiliar with concepts of neocolonialism, of queer theory, feminist thought, racism, and most all of the anti-prejudice work radicals in left-leaning areas take for granted. As a queer transgender individual, I find myself most often bearing witness to my own experience, through questions asked by professors and students alike. It's not something I can keep on all the time, eventually any person becomes weary of defending their own existence. This leads into the next question.

4. Would you consider bearing witness a form of activism?

Melissa: The label of activism has been contested over the past few years in such a manner that it is constantly changing but that happens with language so I do and I don't. In certain situations, I can see where it could be applicable but I don't seek that label out. There is a real problem with language policing even among more conscientious people so I don't really think too much about if I am being an activist today or not. I do think that the spreading of knowledge and information is an act that is so important that it is activism even if you aren't outside with a microphone, especially when you don't have the means or opportunity to do other things. Arthur Ashe said "Start where you are. Use what you have. Do what you can." It's simple but it says it all.

Geoff: Is bearing witness a form of activism? Yes. Unabashedly, whole-heartedly yes. The first time I realized how important bearing witness is as a form of activism, I was fresh into college. A professor had decided we'd spend the quarter having a variety of conversations around controversial issues, and would let the students work things out between ourselves. For one day of class, affirmative action was the topic at hand. Unsurprisingly, no one in the class supported (or had bother reading up about) affirmative action, except for myself and one woman. The conversation quickly devolved from any constructive discussion of the policy, or even of systemic prejudices, into one peppered with seriously racist commentary.

357

As a white person, this would have been an opportunity to cash in my privilege card and step back. Instead, I decided it'd be better to "bear witness." The woman and I spent the entire 50 minute class period arguing against 33 other students. It wasn't fun, nor did it feel terribly productive. It was after the class, however, that the significance of what seems to be a small action was explained to me. The woman, whose name I have since forgotten, pulled me aside and thanked me. It turns out, this wasn't the first time she'd had to discuss racism in class, but as a woman of color in a predominantly white campus, she was always forced to be the sole defender of anti-racist, anti-discriminatory policy. She'd gone into the discussion expecting to play the role again, but having a second person there to back her up, and to call out bullshit as I saw fit, meant that the burden of proof was shared.

In a similar vein, every time an issue in classes or conversation comes up that relates to me specifically, I wish desperately that I'll not be the only person defending the politics I align with. Because it's isolating, exhausting, and downright demoralizing to be the only person in a class of 60 who speaks up in defense of transgender people. It puts minority groups on the defense, and perpetuates a campus environment that effectively excludes us. This can be applied to the workplace, social spaces, activist groups, and more.

5. How would you contrast it with more traditional ideas of protesting such as marches and rallies?

Melissa: Marches and rallies seek to bring masses together. What I'm talking about is examining everything and not taking a single issue focus, which is one of the things that has bothered me. It should be noted that I do not live in a large city that is noted for even good turnout at protests. The few that I have been to were very disheartening. I do see that among protests taking place when they do happen they are single issue focuses and it appears that nationwide there is a problem with this. Another thing that keeps me from participating with causes I would mostly agree with is their tactics. I'm not going to go and join a PETA protest outside of Barnum and Bailey's Circus even though it is a tortuous affair because I don't see how dousing a naked person in fake blood on a busy street for children to walk by conveys that message. That is just the tip of the disaster that is PETA.

I'm not trying to downplay the work of activists; I am speaking from my perspective as someone who thinks that there should be a broader focus. The handful of Gay Groups receiving millions in funding pushing marriage initiatives are a prime example of single issue focus. They completely leave out the trans community, issues of elder rights, job protections, and have written off Chelsea Manning as if she isn't still serving a prison sentence for telling the truth. This is just my perspective as one queer person.

Geoff: Rallies and marches are effective tools for changing top down policies. Campus administration, corporations, and especially governments are more responsive to a rally and other forms of direct action. I don't know how effective they are at changing the hearts and minds of people. In many instances, just making your opinion known is a radical action. Ideally, traditional forms of activism and bearing witness should go hand in hand.

6. Some would criticize this as doing nothing and not having any major impact. What would be your response to such an argument?

Melissa: Doing nothing will have no impact. Like I mentioned before, use what you have and do what you can. I didn't know about Leonard Peltier until a teacher of mine in high school told me his story. I learned about Leonard Peltier, AIM, John Trudell, read Malcolm X's autobiography, and began relearning history. You never know the thing that will be a catalyst for change whether for yourself or someone else. It could be a book, a documentary, being with a person through an experience, living through intense trauma or bullying just to name a few.

Geoff: I would say the people arguing against it need to step back and think critically about their position. There are many people who cannot safely do more than voice their opinions. There are even more people whose opinions are unsafe to voice. In some areas of the country, probably more areas than people in urban areas might believe, bearing witness can and does result in a job loss, isolation, and violence.

Race & Ethnicity
DEPARTMENT

Education and Architecture In Black

Two Sides of the Same Coin

Mike Perry

Education is regarded as one of the most essential components of any society. It is generally accepted that schools are one of the most vital parts of an education that act as vessels, facilitating learning environments to help cultivate knowledge and other various experiences. However, it is important to understand that 'education' and 'learning' are broad terms that can define all forms of attaining, understanding and expressing knowledge, irrespective of sociocultural context and place. It should be noted that within the broader definition of 'learning' exists a schism that bifurcates the word into two separate understandings: the ideological (school) and the theoretical (education). As the ideological, it is widely accepted that schools are the single most important component and facilitator of education within the United States. These facilities are built and established to promote and make available knowledge and information for those who partake in its educational system. Schools, as institutions, are typically thought of as a standard way of attaining a 'proper' education; however, 'schools' are not synonymous with learning as is made evidenced on the most basic of levels: its definition.

A school is defined by Merriam-Webster as:

an organization that provides instruction: as
a: an institution for the teaching of children
b: college , university
c (1) : a group of scholars and teachers pursuing knowledge together
that with similar groups constituted a medieval university (2) : one of the
four faculties of a medieval university (3) : an institution for specialized
higher education often associated with a university <the school of
engineering>
d: an establishment offering specialized instruction .

The keywords/phrases here are "organization," "institution,' 'college, university," "a group of scholars and teachers," and "an establishment offering specialized instruction." All of these definitions seem to reject the fact that learning can be, and is, in fact, fluid and administered/administrable outside the walls of an organized (physical) institution. As a matter of fact, education, as the theoretical, is quite frankly, the exact opposite. Its definition paints a picture very different than what is typically thought of as learning, since, generally, in the United States, education *is* synonymous with school. It goes unquestioned; however, one can see that this is a fallacy, as Merriam Webster defines education as:

a : the action or process of educating or of being educated ; also : a
stage of such a process
b : the knowledge and development resulting from
an educational process <a person of littleeducation >
2: the field of study that deals mainly with methods of teaching and
learning in schools

With the understanding of 'school' and 'education' as two separate entities and philosophies, it becomes easier to analyze the machinations and operations of each. Schools are clearly defined as a (sometimes specific) system (of many possible types of systems) employed to facilitate learning and cultivate knowledge. However, schools are not particularly necessary for either of these phenomena to take place. When a definition is applied with such rigidity to the act of learning, one must begin to question why and how. In questioning the role and purpose of 'school,' as defined by Merriam Webster, it should be understood that the idea of 'school' is within a certain sociocultural context, even if it permeates different societies and cultures. That is to say, a particular philosophy of 'teaching' might have been constructed by one group of people/culture and then, for any number of reasons (trade, imperialism, racial segregation, etc), have been applied to (actively/forcibly) or assimilated (passively) to the new society/culture. And while most people would argue that schools, as a physical and philosophical representation of education and learning, are in and of themselves beneficial to societies and the individuals for whom they are established and maintained, it could also be argued to the contrary. Take, for instance, *diagram 1:1*, which shows the separation of school and education.

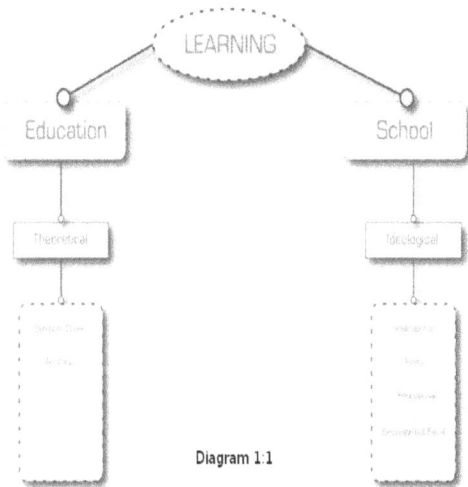

Diagram 1:1

Education is the theoretical manifestation of learning. On the other hand, school is the ideological manifestation. Within the theoretical are the subcategories of 'aesthetic' and symbolic order that represent the actual and/or potential process of learning irrespective of sociocultural context. Under the ideological are the subcategories: institutional, policy, education and 'separate but equal.' These subcategories represent the machinations of 'learning' or the ways in which schools can be detrimental to the educating of its constituents.

Given the fact that schools and education do *not* operate in the same fashion, it is safe to assume that schools *can* operate in the exact *opposite* manor as education/learning. As a matter of fact, schools can, in certain instances, stifle one's own attainment of knowledge and education. One such instance is the racist educational system of 1960s/70s United States. Let's, for a minute, consider some of the most horrific and insidious acts done in the name of education: Desegregation busing, segregated schools, etc. As W.E.B. DuBois once cogently stated, "For the business of the public schools, always recognized from the beginning, has been to break down social lines, to do away with silly distinctions not based on individual work, to be the melting pot out of which comes the great and dreamed of democracy. Of course the South opposes it because it opposes democracy." [1] In this statement, DuBois recognized the separation of school and education, and believed that schools could be used a means to break down social lines. He is referring to education, as opposed to the generally accepted idea of the school.

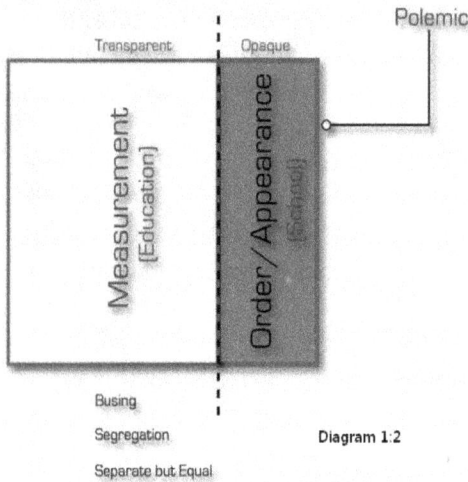

Polemic

Transparent | Opaque

Measurement (Education)

Order/Appearance (School)

Busing
Segregation
Separate but Equal

Diagram 1:2

Given these historical examples, it is clear to see that schools have had, and continue to have, a particular predilection for the explicit and deliberate omission of race, gender, class and sexual orientation in regards to the learning experience. As can be seen in *diagram 1:2*provided below, 'schools,' as an order/appearance, allege to/are promoted as all-inclusive, non-discriminatory institutions where the path to one's success can only be found within their walls and ideology. Unfortunately, that is hardly the case. If one looks beyond the polemic - that is, the order/appearance - one can and will, indeed, find the measurement (education), which more thoroughly defines schools and their true purpose, irrespective of social/racial/economic/etc context. Ideally, or theoretically, the main intent is to educate equally - regardless of one's socioeconomic status. Schools, as demonstrated by segregation and desegregation busing, to name a few, have not always been - and arguably, still, are not - all-inclusive.

Doctoral Candidate, Paul T. Miller, discusses DuBois' ideas in his essay entitled, '*W.E.B. Du Bois: Education, Race and Economics from 1903-1961*," in which he states:

Education as the chief means of ameliorating problems of race and class held sway with Du Bois his entire life. As a sort of response to "The Negro Question", Du Bois advocated planned education that would cultivate the intellect as well as direct the actions of students for the purpose of improving the life chances of African Americans in specific and the condition of all people in general. In chapter six of The Souls of Black Folk, he writes... to stimulate wildly weak and untrained minds is to play with mighty fires; to flout their striving idly is to welcome a harvest of brutish crime and shameless lethargy in our very laps. The guiding of thought and the deft coordination of deed is at once the path of honor and humanity (1969:123). Du Bois (1969) notes that effective education will develop training that will best use the labor of all men without enslaving or brutalizing, and that such training will, ...encourage the prejudices that bulwark society, and stamp out those that in sheer barbarity deafen us to the wail of prisoned souls within the Veil (123-4).[2]

What is being suggested here is the conscious effort to develop *learning* that addresses education in a formal and programmatic way. This should also be done through policy as well, which can have a direct impact on its constituents.

Architecture operates in a similar fashion to schools in which there is a divide between architecture and "architecture." Architecture as discipline and object, has a particular predilection for omission; particularly the expurgation of race, gender, class and sexual orientation from the aesthetic. As architect Diana Agrest once pointed out, "this system is defined not only by what it includes, but also by what it excludes, inclusion and exclusion being parts of the same construct. Yet that which is excluded, left out, is not really excluded but rather repressed; repression neither excludes nor repels an exterior force for it contains within itself an interior of representation, a space of repression." [3] To clarify, architecture demands aesthetics be absolved of any scrutiny, and worse yet, actively refuses to *acknowledge* its, sometimes negative, influences on - or repressions of - one or more of the aforementioned social groups. Architecture's refusal of acknowledgement is a machination of repression that is fueled by a culture and ideology of independence/exclusion from other disciplines; however, it should be made clear that this ideology is problematic at best and insidious at worst. With that being said, explorations will be made in regards to 'modern' architecture as a Western born discipline that operates within a system of repression and omission.

To begin, it is of utmost importance to understand the discipline of architecture as a binary discipline/system. On the one hand, there exists the theoretical side of architecture, which encompasses the symbolic order and the aesthetic. And on the other hand, there exists the ideological, which encompasses the institution, profession and education within architecture (**Diagram 1:3**).

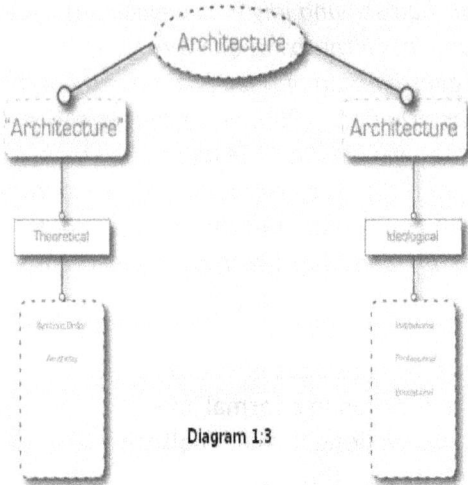

Diagram 1:3

Diana Agrest often talks about the machinations of the theoretical, namely the symbolic order, in regards to women and the identity of women within architecture. And while Agrest talks about gender in her analysis of architecture, race can easily be inputted in lieu of gender to explain the same phenomena. In Agrest's essay, "*Architecture from Without: Body, Logic and Sex*," she explains, "the system of architecture from within is characterized by an idealistic logic that can assume neither contradiction nor negation and, therefore, is based upon the suppression of either one of two opposite terms. This is best represented by the consistent repression and exclusion of woman. Woman does not fit the symbolic order. She is offside, in the cracks of symbolic systems, an outsider." [4] To clarify, Agrest's argument infers that, within the theoretical side of architecture, one can begin to recognize, understand and critique the omission of certain elements which is made manifest by the ever-so-apparent 'idealistic logic that can assume neither contradiction nor negation.' Because of this, one can also assume that the same applies to other disenfranchised persons, not only women.

Agrest continues with the iconoclastic deconstruction of the theoretical versus the ideological in her other essay entitled, " *Semiotics and Architecture: Ideological Consumption or Theoretical Work*," in which she cogently and accurately argues that, "the function of these 'theories,' now as always, has been to adapt architecture to the needs of Western social formations, serving as the connection between the overall structure of a society and its architecture." [5] It is within this statement that we find ourselves at a crossroad. If architecture is a discipline that alleges to be all-inclusive, why is it that one often finds race and gender, as made apparent by Agrest, absent from the discipline? As stated before, architecture has a particular predilection with omitting and repressing. If the absence of something represents the repression of another then one must question why and try to recognize, understand, critique, and eventually make a change.

The ideological side of architecture is the 'opaque' side of architecture - the side that presents itself as all-inclusive and the theoretical allows the analysis of its opposite: the repression of those who are disenfranchised and women in particular, at least, in regards to Agrest's essay (**Diagram 1:4**).

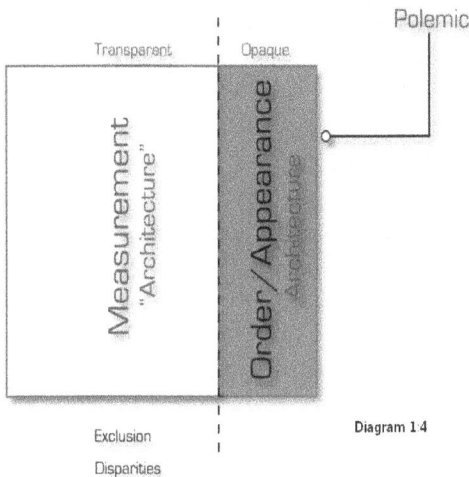

Diagram 1:4

The most obvious problem with this (opaque) demand/claim is that it eschews engaging in a dialogue about the potential problems within the discipline; namely the previously mentioned 'refusal of acknowledgement.' Another problem, directly related to the first, is that architecture becomes unable to address real problems because of its lack of acknowledgement of its role in the problems. The third and most damaging problem is the negative impact that architecture, as discipline and object, may have on those groups of people for whom it ignores and expurgates. The purpose of the built environment is to, in some way, shape or form, influence and/or change society, or, at the very least, the group of people that will occupy and experience the aforementioned environment. And because Architecture has this ability it can be used, if it is will to address itself and engage in a dialogue between the world and itself, for the socioeconomic benefit of disenfranchised persons. But first architecture needs to be willing to engage with that with which it pretends to have no association. Architecture has had a negative impact on the black American community through this repression and omission. The socioeconomic/opportunistic implication of architecture on disenfranchised persons is vast. However, architecture is a discipline that often addresses the aesthetic without addressing anything else. Things other than the aesthetic are also a significant part of architecture and its relationship to class and race. The 19th century Germany architectural theorist, Heinrich Hübsch, pointed out this very fact; the fact that architecture is not aesthetic alone and the assumption that it is has ultimately been damaging to persons for which it is supposed to, or, at the very least, can, help. Hübsch states:

Whoever looks at architecture primarily from its decorative aspect and perhaps asks himself why he likes one form of leafwork on a capital better than another will easily despair on the possibility of establishing reliable principles. Yet, however starts his investigation form the point of view of practical necessary will find a secure base… It is obvious that two criteria of functionality - namely, fitness for purpose (commodity) part of every building. These formative factors derives from function, are surely as objective and as clear as they possible could be.

A clear distinction should be made between the style, or aesthetic, and the programmatic or its commodity. Often times, it can be argued, architecture and architects - those in practice and theorists - forget this basic and imperative fact.

Considering architecture often plays a significant role within society and on its inhabitants and black Americans who might partake in the discipline on an academic or professional level, it is peculiar that that connection is so rarely talked about. Its impact is implicit and explicit; voluntary and involuntary. Its negation and preclusion of the involvement of black Americans by way of an architectural strategy/language is, quite frankly, terrifying. In order to address and engage, and, hopefully, advance, the nature and dynamic(s) of these, often ignored, relationships, one must consider several theories to come to a sound conclusion. To begin, it should be noted, while self evident, that architecture does not exist within a vacuum. It is not perceived and felt by the designer alone but its occupants and users as well. Architecture is directly (and indirectly) related to the politics of the society within which it is erected, how can it be separated from other things.

It should also be made clear that architecture and public policy go hand in hand - as architecture's survival and development is completely dependent on and limited by government policy. Because of this, architecture also has a legal/political contract and obligation as well as social obligation to benefit those for whom it is designed and erected. To answer this it might help to take a look at WEB DuBois' theories on education, race and economics to further develop the ideas and connections between the aforementioned topics and an architectural strategy to develop and promote said ideas.

In conclusion, schools and architecture operate in much the same fashion. They both exist as a binary between the opaque (order/appearance) and the transparent (measurement). It is through the understanding of the operations of the opaque that one can move beyond and into the transparent to understand thoroughly the machinations and operations of the theoretical of schools and architecture.

Notes

[1] DuBois, W.E.B. *Mixed Schools. Resources on the life and legacy of W.E.B. DuBois*. UMass Amherst, 13 Feb. 2013. Web. 28 April 2013. ‹http://www.library.umass.edu/spcoll/digital/dubois/EdMixedSchools.pdf›

[2] Miller, Paul T. *W.E.B. Du Bois: Education, Race and Economics from 1903-1961. Department of African American Studies*Temple University, 02 June. 2010. Web. 16 March 2013, pp. 123-124. ‹http://www.jpanafrican.com/docs/WEBDuBoisEducationRaceEconomics.pdf›

[3] Agrest, Diana, and Mario Gandelsonas. "Semiotics and Architecture: Ideological Consumption or Theoretical Work."

[4] Agrest, Diana, and Mario Gandelsonas, p. 28.

[5] Agrest, Diana. Simiotics, p. 21.

DuBois, W.E.B. *The Crisis*. Trans. S. H. Butcher. *Resources on the life and legacy of W.E.B. DuBois*. UMass Amherst, 13 Feb. 2013. Web. 28 April 2013. ‹http://www.library.umass.edu/spcoll/digital/dubois/EdEducation.pdf›

"school." *Merriam-Webster.com*. 2011. http://www.merriam-webster.com (05 April 2013).

"education." *Merriam-Webster.com*. 2011. http://www.merriam-webster.com (05 April 2013).

Slavery By Another Name

The Convict Lease System

Devon Douglas-Bowers

After the Civil War, the 13th, 14th, and 15th Constitutional amendments were passed with the intention of establishing equality under the law for newly freed slaves, or so the story goes. The fact of the matter is that slavery was - and still is - completely legal in the United States, only in a much different form. The institution of slavery, as we've come to understand it, actually underwent an evolution of sorts. Instead of having the direct enslavement of blacks with an entire apparatus used to keep slaves in their condition, certain elements of the state apparatus were piecemealed over time to enslave blacks, namely the legal and prison systems. Hence, the act of enslavement itself changed as black convicts were no longer slaves to individual masters, but rather they were enslaved to the companies which they were leased out to. To create this system, there not only had to be the involvement of the Southern judicial system and individual Northern and Southern elites, but also the involvement and reinstitution of slavery within a corporate context.

The 13ᵗʰ Amendment

To attain a full understanding of the convict lease system, there must first be a reexamination of the 13ᵗʰ amendment. It has been stated in history books and in classrooms across America that this amendment ended slavery, yet this is quite false. The 13ᵗʰ Amendment states "neither slavery nor involuntary servitude, **except as a punishment for crime whereof the party shall have been duly convicted**, shall exist within the United States, or any place subject to their jurisdiction." [1] (emphasis added) Thus, slavery is completely and totally legal if it is part (or the whole) of a punishment for someone who was and is convicted of a crime.

When debating the 13ᵗʰ amendment, many in Congress were not thinking of slaves, but rather white labor, as Senator Henry Wilson said, "The same influences that go to keep down and crush down the rights of the poor black man bear down and oppress the poor white laboring man." [2] Senator Richard Yates of Illinois was much blunter, stating that he had "never had the negro on the brain" [3] when discussing the amendment. Such notions are in the absurd! Wilson is correct to an extent when he argues that both slave and white labor are oppressed by the same system; both are oppressed in that they are being manipulated and played off one another by the elite of both the North and South. Still, Wilson ignores the fact that white labor was *very* much less oppressed than black slave labor - as white laborers were seen as human beings, deserving of at least a minimal degree of dignity and respect, rather than viewed and treated worse than animals. White laborers were free to do as they pleased, without having to worry about having papers on their person as to prove their freedom.

Therefore, the passing of the 13ᵗʰ amendment should be examined within the context of an economic competition between black slave labor and free white labor. The South's economy was built around slave labor and the ability to have the slaves produce more than they were 'worth,' seeing as how slaves were viewed as not just general property but a long-term economic investment which helped the Southern plantation elite. Yet, due to the existence of slavery, white labor indirectly suffered, as not only did they lose out on the income they were making when slavery was first introduced - in addition to any potential future income - but, also, white labor was unable to make advances within the South, as slavery provided a source of labor that was less expensive in the long-term.

Senator Henry Williams illustrates these points and other problems that white labor had with slavery. He stated:

Slavery was evil because it destroyed much of the richest land in the South; it degraded labor and the meaning of labor for poor white working men in the South; it robbed the South of culture by degrading the efforts of laborers; and it allowed southern aristocrats to further insult northern white workers by demeaning their laboring efforts as crabbed and mean. *It was the association between labor and slavery in the minds of southern aristocrats that demeaned the efforts of industrious northern laborers.* Thus, slavery pulled white workers down in two ways: one, by direct competition with slave labor in the South, and two, by associating all the industrious efforts of workers with those of the degraded slaves. *[4]*

Thus, the only way for white labor to triumph in their struggle for rights such as a fair wage and regular working hours was for the abolition of slavery. White labor had a direct interest in the nullification of slavery. Yet, there was a difference of opinion in the minds of Southern elites who wanted to continue slavery, but on different terms.

Southern Elites

Before discussing the Southern elites, one must first examine them within the context of the Southern economy after the Civil War. It was utterly in shambles; in fact, one could make an argument that it had been decimated and demolished in virtually every conceivable way. The entire economy of the South was built upon the institution of slavery and agriculture. With the end of the Civil War, not only was the Southern economy damaged by the freeing of black slaves, but the land was deeply scarred and hurt as well, thus creating an immediate economic problem. However, among all of this, there was an opportunity reorient and reconstruct the economy around a new labor source, as cheap labor would surely be needed to rebuild the region.

The social order must be examined as well. While the slaves were now free and able to do as they pleased, there was still a deeply embedded racism within the minds of Southern whites. The fact that blacks had fought in the Civil War did not suddenly mean that the perception of blacks had changed; rather, to the Southern elites, they still viewed blacks as inferior and only good for labor, longing to perpetuate the slave system within a new industrial framework that would transcend the agricultural framework which been destroyed. This new system was to be found in convict leasing.

The leasing out of state convicts to private hands has its basis in the minds of such people as John T. Milner of Alabama. Milner was no ordinary man, rather he was a Southern elite who "was in the vanguard of that new theory of industrial forced labor," writing in 1859 that "black labor marshaled into the regimented productivity of factory settings would be the key to the economic development of Alabama and the South." [5] Milner's idea of using regimented black labor can be seen in his involvement of a project for the Blue River railroad company in Alabama. In 1859, he issued a plan for the laying of rail in Montgomery, "presenting statistical evidence to demonstrate the potential economic benefit to Montgomery of securing connections with Decatur," a city north of Montgomery. He argued that the Blue River could build its own track in nearby Jones Valley with the use of slave labor. Yet, in Milner's mind, this slave labor had to be managed by whites. He stated "A negro who can set a saw, or run a grist mill, or work in a blacksmith shop, can do work as cheaply in a rolling mill, even now, as white men do at the North, provided he has an overseer, a southern man, who knows how to manage negroes." [6] After the end of the Civil War, Milner's plan changed, but he was convinced that "the future of blacks in America rested on how whites *chose* to manage them." [7] To this end, in the 1870s, he moved with purpose to acquire the black convict labor that Alabama's prisons were offering up. He took these convicts and put them to work in coal mines, treating them barbarically.

Records of Milner's various mines and slave farms in southern Alabama, some of which were owned by one of his business partners - a cousin to an investor in the Bibb Steam Mill - tell the stories of black women stripped naked and whipped, of hundreds of men starved, changed, and beaten, of workers perpetually lice-ridden and barely clothed. [8]

Black Americans, many of them former slaves, were essentially re-enslaved - but within the context of a corporate structure characterized by an alliance between the state and the corporation. Additionally, the judicial system was greatly involved in allowing this to occur, from the laws passed to sheriffs selling off convicts to companies.

The Judicial System

In order to allow for the convict lease system to exist, and for blacks to be reduced to their former state as a labor source, it required purposeful laws aimed at limiting the rights of "newly freed" blacks. The object was to criminalize black life to the point where blacks could be imprisoned on the most frivolous of offenses. Such laws took the form of "Black Codes."

To understand the creation of Black Codes, it is necessary to understand the social order that motivated elites to push for such legislation. North Carolina is a prime example. After the war, the elite would have preferred a return to the status quo that existed under the slave system, yet this was not possible due to the liberation of blacks created by the destruction of the slave system. This problem was greatly exacerbated by the fact that, "in suppressing the war to dissolve the Union, the whites were deprived of arms while many Negroes had easily obtained them;" thus, "A general feeling of insecurity on the part of the whites" resulted. [9] Armed blacks were viewed as an immediate threat to elite interests as they now possessed the ability to defend and protect themselves - in other words, blacks were able to ensure they would not be re-enslaved. Furthermore, it presented a problem to the overall white power structure, as having weapons would empower blacks to stand up for themselves and assert their rights not only as Americans but also as human beings; and such a situation brought the memories and worries of a slave revolt back to the forefront of the minds of elites.

To put blacks back 'in their place,' the elite pushed several laws that were passed in the state legislature, such as defining "a Negro as any person of African descent, although one ancestor to the fourth generation might be white." [10] The fact that racial identity was dependent on the mother rather than the father made the situation all the worse for blacks who had white fathers - whether by marriage or by rape - as they were now considered to be black and thus would be subject to the worst aspects of living within a white supremacist society, and with little recourse.

Another example of the law being used to target and punish blacks was those laws concerning vagrancy. In North Carolina, there was a problem concerning labor as, after the Civil War, blacks and whites were working on their own fields, yet:

Many others less energetic, white and black, were flooding the towns and refusing work of any sort, for in the days of bondage, master and slave had been taught that to labor with the hands was undignified: consequently, freedom to many Negroes meant a deliverance from hard labor. [11]

These workers proved a problem to North Carolinian industrialists and agriculturalists as few could afford to pay workers a wage until the crop had been grown, not to mention that neither employee nor employer were familiar with a wage system. A solution was found in the creation of vagrancy laws. Regarding the workers who refused to do any labor, vagrancy laws ensured that "a person who had no means of survival or refused to work would be regarded a vagrant and sent to court;" however, a payment could be offered which would be conditional upon the "good behavior of the vagrant for one year." Yet, if the person was unable to make such a payment, they would be deemed a vagrant, duly convicted, and consequently fined, imprisoned, or both. When concerning newly-freed slaves, the laws were much harsher as many of them, once convicted, were "apprenticed to their former owners under a contract" or were "leased" to a corporation. In the contract, the owner was to feed, clothe, and instruct the freed slave in reading, writing, and arithmetic; and, upon the end of the apprenticeship, they were to be given money, a new set of clothes, and a new Bible as payment for the work done. However, such repayment rarely occurred or was enforced by the state government.

Overall, in the South, vagrancy laws were so ill-defined that any free black who was not under the protection of a white person could be arrested. Such laws allowed for police to "round up idle blacks in times of labor scarcity, and also gave employers a coercive tool that might be used to keep workers on the job." [12]

With the judicial system having established a means to ensure a continuous supply of cheap labor, the leasing could now begin.

Convict Leasing

The act of leasing out convicts is nothing new in states such as Alabama, where the government had no interest in caring for convicts, and thus prisoners were leased out to companies. While this may have helped prisons get convicts off their hands, they made no extra revenue from it. After the Civil War, such leasing began to pick up steam as corporations had access to an abundance of near-free labor.

Labor scarcity between states was a major problem; therefore, concerted efforts were made by each state to keep black prison labor within their borders. This was accomplished by waging war on emigrant agents - people who specialized in moving labor from where it was abundant to where it was scarce. They had done this when slavery was still existent, and it continued under the newly-freed slaves. Such agents were viewed as a threat to white farmers who disliked the idea of transient black labor threatening the establishment of a stable labor source. Many states established anti-emigrant agent laws due to their need to keep black labor accessible. One example took place in 1876, when Georgia, "Hard hit by black movement to the West," passed legislation that "levied an annual tax of $100 for each county in which a recruiter sought labor. A year later, the amount was raised to $500." [13]

Convict leasing, interestingly enough, resulted in power being taken from the state level and given to those on the local level. As a result, sheriffs became quite powerful soon after the Civil War ended as "County sheriffs and judges had dabbled with leasing black convicts out to local famers, or to contractors under hire to repair roads and bridges, beginning almost immediately after the Civil War." [14] The economic empowerment awarded to sheriffs created an incentive for them to convict and lock up as many freedmen as possible in order to keep a steady supply of labor. Entire economies eventually formed around the convict lease system, including the development of a speculative trade system in convict contracts.

The witnesses and public officials who were owed portions of the lease payments earned by convicts received paper receipts - usually called scripts - from the county that could be redeemed only after the convict had generated enough money to pay them off. Rather than wait for the full amount, holders of scripts would sell their notes for cash to speculators at lower-than-face-value. In return, the buyers were to receive the full lease payments - profiting handsomely from those convicts who survived, and losing money on the short-lived. [15] While there was much profit to be made in the convict lease system, not everyone was happy with it - namely, white labor.

Labor's Reaction to Convict Leasing

Just as how white labor was against slavery due to it undermining their struggle for better working conditions, they were also against the convict lease system for the very same reasons. Never did they stop to consider the fact that both worker and freedman were being manipulated by the very same systems that governed them. Labor's anti-convict leasing sentiments were felt long before the Civil War began. In 1823, in New York City, journeymen cabinet makers conducted a mass meeting to discuss prison-made goods being introduced to the market and how it threatened their trade. In that same year, also in New York City, mechanics petitioned the state legislature to end the use of prison labor. [16]

During the Civil War, labor unions were opposed to the use of convict labor, arguing that it "tended to lower the wages of thousands of laborers, and in some instances has virtually driven certain kinds of labor out of the field," and that" the contractor is seeking cheap labor and cares nothing for the welfare of the prisoner." [17] However, it should be noted that unions were not opposed to all convict labor, as they were fine with prisoners being relied upon to build state prisons. Thus, opposition from labor unions in general certainly wasn't rooted in morality and presented as a protest to the brutal, inhumane treatment of convicts, but rather whether or not the convicts were encroaching on their area of employment.

Still, this should not be examined as a separate battle between free labor and convict labor, but rather a continuation of the struggle between the two groups. Once again, the only way white labor's goals could be achieved was through the destruction of most of the convict lease system. While the convict leasing may have been profitable for a select few, it was a thorn in the side to many - a fact that signified its eventual demise.

The End of Convict Leasing

Due to a mixture of changes in the economic and social landscapes, convict leasing would eventually die out. However, it is important to note that economic and social justifications for such a system reinforced each other as not only was it "an expedient by which Southern states with depleted treasuries could avoid costly expenditures; it was also one of the greatest single sources of personal wealth to some of the South's leading businessmen and politicians." [18] The Southern elites benefited greatly from the system and thus put all of their efforts into perpetuating the system for as long as possible.

If one only looks on the surface at the abolition of convict leasing, they may assume its demise was due to the public indignation which arose against the system; yet this is not the case - far from it. Rather, it involved a combination of factors stemming from race, politics, and economics - depending on the state. For example, in Louisiana, convict leasing was abolished due to it being "part of a reform package which had as its purpose the complete triumph of white supremacy in political affairs;" whereas in Tennessee, its leaders:

..decided that the demands of fiscal responsibility dictated abolition when the expense of maintaining the militia at convict stockades-a cost incurred by an armed rebellion on the part of free miners who were displaced by convict gangs-proved greater than the income from the leasing contract. [19]

This system was embedded with racism, politics, and economics, as well as violence and brutality. Men and women were beaten, bloodied, bruised, and valued only so long as they were able to perform labor. They were reduced to nothing more than human resources, human tools used to enrich white industrialists and agriculturalists from the North and the South. From the Civil War to World War Two, Black Americans were re-enslaved under a new system that was no better than the first.

Notes

1: Legal Information Institute, *13ᵗʰ Amendment of the US Constitution*,http://www.law.cornell.edu/constitution/amendmentxiii
2: Lea S. VanderVelde, "The Labor Vision of the Thirteenth Amendment," *University of Pennsylvania Law Review* 138:2 (1989), pg 440
3: VanderVelde, pg 446
4: VanderVelde, pg 466
5: Douglas A. Blackmon, *Slavery by Another Name: The Re-enslavement of Black Americans from the Civil War to World War 2* (New York, New York: Anchor Books, 2008) pg 51
6: W. David Lewis, "The Emergence of Birmingham as a Case Study of Continuity between the Antebellum Planter Class and Industrialization in the 'New South'," *Agricultural History* 68:2 (1994), pg 67
7: Blackmon, pg 51
8: Blackmon, pg 52
9: James B. Browning, "The North Carolina Black Code," *The Journal of Negro History* 15:4 (1930) pg 462
10: Browning, pg 464
11: Browning, pg 466
12: William Cohen, "Negro Involuntary Servitude in the South, 1865-1940: A Preliminary Analysis," *The Journal of Southern History* 42:1 (1976) pg 34
13: Cohen, pg 39
14: Blackmon, pg 64
15: Blackmon, pg 65
16: Henry Theodore Jackson, "Prison Labor," *Journal of the American Institute of Criminal Law and Criminology* 18:2 (1927) pgs 244, 245
17: Theodore Jackson, pg 246
18: Matthew J. Mancini, "Race, Economics, and The Abandonment of Convict Leasing," *The Journal of Negro History* 63:4 (1978) pg 339
19: Mancini, pg 340

An Empire of Poverty

Race, Punishment, and Social Control

Andrew Gavin Marshall

Between 1619 and 1860, the American legal system, from that imposed by the British Empire to that constructed following the American Revolution, "expanded and protected the liberties of white Americans - while at the same time the legal process became increasingly harsher as to the masses of blacks, with a steady contraction of their liberties." This process marked the 'social construction' of race and with it, racial superiority and inferiority, delegated to whites and blacks, respectively.[1] Interesting to note was that between 1619 and the 1660s, the American colonial legal system was "far more supportive for blacks; or, phrased differently, the early legal process was less harsh." Georgia's original charter, in fact, had three prohibitions: no alcohol, no free land titles, "and no Negro slaves." In Virginia, as late as 1672 and 1673, there were legal records of some slaves "serving limited terms as indentured servants rather than being sentenced to the eternity of slavery."[2]

The colonies in the Americas required a massive labour force, "Between 1607 and 1783, more than 350,000 'white' bond-labourers arrived in the British colonies."[3] The Americas had both un-free blacks and whites, with blacks being a minority, yet they "exercised basic rights in law."[4] Problems arrived in the form of elites trying to control the labour class. Slaves were made up of Indian, black and white labourers; yet, problems arose with this "mixed" population of un-free labour. The problem with Indian labourers was that they knew the land and could escape to "undiscovered" territory, and enslavement would often instigate rebellions and war:

The social costs of trying to discipline un-free native labour had proved too high. Natives would eventually be genocidally eliminated, once population settlement and military power made victory more or less certain; for the time being, however, different sources of bond labour had to be found.[5]

Between 1607 and 1682, more than 90,000 European immigrants, "three-quarters of them chattel bond-labourers, were brought to Virginia and Maryland." Following the "establishment of the Royal African Company in 1672, a steady supply of African slaves was secured." Problems became paramount, however, as the lower classes tended to be very rebellious, which consisted of "an amalgam of indentured servants and slaves, of poor whites and blacks, of landless freemen and debtors." The lower classes were united in opposition to the elites oppressing them, regardless of background.[6]
Bacon's Rebellion of 1676 was of particular note, as bond-labourers, black and white, rebelled against the local elites and "demanded freedom from chattel servitude." For the colonialists, "[s]uch images of a joint uprising of black and white, slave and bondsman, proved traumatic. In the face of a united rebellion of the lower orders, the planter bourgeoisie understood that their entire system of colonial exploitation and privilege was at risk."[7]
In response to this threat, the landed elite "relaxed the servitude of white labourers, intensified the bonds of black slavery, and introduced a new regime of racial oppression. In doing so, they effectively created the white race - and with it white supremacy."[8] Thus, "the conditions of white and black servants began to diverge considerably after 1660."
Following this, legislation would separate white and black slavery, prevent "mixed" marriages, and seek to prevent the procreation of "mixed-race" children. Whereas before 1660, many black slaves were not indentured for life, this changed as colonial law increasingly "imposed lifetime bondage for black servants - and, especially significant, the curse of lifetime servitude for their offspring."[9]

A central feature of the social construction of this racial divide was "the denial of the right to vote," as most Anglo-American colonies previously allowed free blacks to vote, but this slowly changed throughout the colonies. The ruling class of America was essentially "inventing race." Thus, "[f]reedom was increasingly identified with race, not class."[10]

The 'Reconstruction' of Slavery in Post-Civil War America

Important to note has been the ways in which slaves were used as the main labour force, and thus blacks were identified and being sustained as a lower-class labour force. Following the Civil War, abolition of slavery and the Reconstruction Period, there were coordinated moves - a 'compact' - between the North and South in the United States, to devise a way of keeping blacks as a submissive labour force, and one which was confined to a new form of slavery: penal slavery. Thus, we see emerging in the 1870s and into the 20th century, a rapid expansion of prisons, and with that, of southern penal systems using prisoners as forced labour. This new legal system, which was "far less rigid than slavery," had been referred to as "involuntary servitude," and, wrote one scholar, "was a fluid, flexible affair which alternated between free and forced labor in time to the rhythm of the southern labor market."[11]

A famous American botanist and agricultural editor of the *Weekly News and Courier* wrote in 1865 that, "There must... be stringent laws to control the negroes, & require them to fulfill their contracts of labour on the farms." Southern legislatures, then, began to enact what were referred to as Black Codes, "designed to preserve white hegemony."[12] The 12-year period following the end of the Civil War, known as the 'Reconstruction,' saw the continued struggle of newly-freed blacks to attempt to break free from being "forced back under the political and economic domination of the large landowners," and to do so, they were demanding land ownership rights to the tune of "40 acres and a mule." This was, of course, unacceptable to vested interests. While the Republic Party had freed the slaves, the main core of the Party had become dominated by Northern wealthy interests, and "were unwilling to press for thoroughgoing reform, and by 1877 had become convinced that their interests were better served by an alliance with Southern white conservatives than the largely illiterate and destitute ex-slave population." In the North at this time, the captains of industry and kings of capital (the bankers and industrialists) were waging a continued war against organized and increasingly radicalized labour. Thus, there was very little interest in seeking to enfranchise black labour in the South. As the *New York Times*suggested, the demands for "40 acres and a mule" hit at "the fundamental relation of industry to capital," and "strikes at the root of all property rights in both sections. It concerns Massachusetts quite as much as Mississippi."[13]

The legal system was used to essentially criminalize black life, without making specific references to race, laws that were passed specifically targeted blacks in attempting to limit their mobility, the price of their labour, and to make several aspects of typical black southern life to be deemed "criminal." This process was paralleled in South Africa in the construction of the apartheid system. As one historian wrote:

Prior to the 1860s, neither the South nor South Africa had an extensive history of large-scale imprisonment or of hiring out prison labour to private contractors. Before the Civil War, slave-owners had punished their own slaves. African Americans accounted for less than 1 per cent of Alabama's pre-war prison population; the bulk of the 200-300 inmates of the first penitentiary built in 1841 comprised, as in northern prisons, mostly of newly-arrived European immigrants.[14]

Many of the South's prisons were destroyed during the Civil War, and thus, as the Black Codes were subsequently enacted, legislation was increasingly passed which aimed to facilitate the leasing of convicts to private contractors, and as a result, there was little need to rebuild the prison infrastructure; instead, have prisoners build the new infrastructure of an industrializing South, with the convict population from the 1870s onward largely being leased to farmers and railroad contractors, which saved state revenues from building new prisons as well as procuring revenue. In 1874, the governor of Alabama had complained about spending $100,000 on convicts, and within two years of leasing out Alabama's inmates to private contractors, he boasted of a $15,000 profit. Thus, prisons would never "be anything but a source of immense revenue to the state." Largely the same process was undertaken in South Africa to secure labour for the diamond mines run by the De Beers Company.[15] As William Worger wrote of the dual development of the American South and South African convict labour systems:

[C]apitalists in both areas establishing new industries and constrained by expensive capital, high fixed costs for plant and operations, and competitive struggles for market share, viewed convict labour as essential to the introduction of machine production, the defeat of organized labour, and the overall cheapening of the costs of production... [I]n both cases the state, when viewed in its local and regional rather than national and metropolitan manifestations, enthusiastically supported the leasing of convicts to private employers... because of the enormous financial benefits to their administrations of selling prison labour... and because imprisonment with hard labour in industrial enterprises offered a means to 'discipline' (in the discourse of the South) and to 'civilise' (in that of British colonialism) African Americans and Africans convicted on the basis of their race for acts - such as petty theft and burglary... that would not have resulted in lengthy terms of incarceration for whites... [In both cases] convict labour was used to divide and defeat organized labour and to enable employers to segregate the workplace on the basis of race.[16]

Migration, Housing, and Organizing Ghettos

It was no coincidence that each of these convict labour systems emerged in the context and circumstances of the development of Jim Crow segregation laws in the South and official apartheid in South Africa. At the same time as this was taking place in the South, massive migration of blacks from the South to the North began, concurrently with a period of radical labour militancy and class crisis. As such, this era saw the development of the ghettoes in major Northern cities "as a space of containment in urban areas." The harsh legal racism, segregation, and cultural hatred of blacks in the South also spurred the migration to Northern cities. Between 1882 and 1968, there were 4,723 reported lynchings of African Americans, 90% of which took place in the Deep South. Between 1910 and 1960, roughly 5 million African Americans migrated to the North, Midwest, and Northeast. As Eduardo Mendieta wrote:

It is significant that the process of northern urbanization takes place in tandem with the process of racial gentrification. This racial gentrification is overseen by the state itself through its housing policies. These policies ensure that the poor and colored are concentrated in the dilapidated and poorly serviced urban centers while wealthy whites... are granted the license and funding to flee to the suburbs. In other words, the development of the ghetto has to be seen in tandem with the suburbanization of the US... An overview of the different agencies and acts used by Congress to regulate housing policies and availability reveals that the government conspired to segregate through its loaning practices, and actually participated in the very act of destroying housing that was and could have been available to African Americans and poor people in the inner cities.[17]

In fact, amazingly, "the government [had] destroyed more low-incoming housing than it actually built." This process had extended right into the post-World War II period. Between 1960 and 1977, "as the number of whites living in suburbs increased by 22 million... the inner-city African-American population grew by 6 million." Kenneth T. Jackson wrote, "American housing policy was not only devoid of social objectives, but instead helped establish the basis for social inequities. Uncle Sam was not impartial, but instead contributed to the general disbenefit of the cities and to the general prosperity of the suburbs."[18]

Most American ghettos first came into existence just as economic inequalities were reaching "new heights" in the 1920s in the midst of the long-worn battle between industrialists and organized labour. At this time, racial segregation was increasingly a global phenomenon, when imperial and national states were implementing social and geographical forms of segregation "by equating urban problems such as 'vice', crime, disease and social unrest with blacks and other people of color and suggesting urban division as a means to solve these problems." As Carl H. Nightingale wrote in the *Journal of Urban History*:

In the United States, this global "racial urbanism" informed the actions of the white homeowners, realtors, and banks that transformed an urban landscape marked by scattered minority-black enclaves into one of the large-scale segregated majority-black communities we know as ghettos. These first ghettos were also marked by the founding of separate black-run institutions that served their residents.[19]

The second phase of ghettoization in the United States occurred with the Great Depression, New Deal, and World War II-era, a time in which there was a continued growth of northward migration of black

Americans to the industrial cities. In this context, the New Deal's Home Owner's Loan Corporation and the Federal Housing Administration "instituted highly discriminatory housing policies... [which] were aggravated by similarly racially biased urban renewal, public housing, and transportation policies, which not only solidified the boundaries of ghettos but also pushed them outward from downtown."[20]

The third major phase of ghetto reform came about as a result of the Civil Rights Movement. Working with a major Civil Rights organization, the Congress of Racial Equality (CORE), the Ford Foundation sought to "organize the ghetto" through a program aimed at "making working-class blacks a decipherable and controllable constituency," and thus:

[The Ford] foundation sought black leaders who could be brought into the establishment fold and could engineer orderly change in the ghetto. Having found a model to control the black community by containing it... the Ford Foundation would use its experience with CORE in Cleveland as a base to complete its vision for African Americans in a post-civil rights America.[21]

A national housing program, organized around new public-private partnerships which would benefit the elite class, was developed to create housing for the poor. The development of this plan - the Rockefeller Program - was the most controversial of the initiatives under the 1968 housing legislation, which placed "little emphasis on expanding homeownership opportunities," and instead, stressed "the importance of involving private enterprises in the rebuilding of cities and make use of tax incentives to encourage such involvement." The interesting features of the Rockefeller Program, implemented under New York Governor Nelson Rockefeller, were that it contemplated "that government will sponsor, develop, construct, and possibly manage the housing project," and while the "actual construction work will be done by private firms as contractors... it is government which is to rebuild the slums." Thus, the "incentives to enlist the active involvement of the private sector are not directly related to the task of rebuilding the slums, except insofar as they enable private enterprise to participate in the profits which will accrue."[22]

The Rockefeller Foundation itself had a significant impact upon the changing focus of urban design. As Peter L. Laurence wrote, "between 1955 and 1965, the Rockefeller Foundation research programme for Urban Design Studies contributed significantly to post-war urban theory and to the emergence of the new discipline of urban design out of the overlapping interests of the fields of architecture, city planning and landscape design."[23] Rockefeller influence on city planning was thereafter established and institutionalized through the formation of the fields of urban studies and city planning.

Educating Africans to be "Junior Partners in the Firm"

In the first half of the 20th century, the Rockefeller Foundation and Carnegie Corporation undertook joint projects aimed at constructing an education system for black Americans in the South as well as for black Africans in several British colonies. In 1911, the Phelps-Stokes Fund was chartered with the purpose of managing "the education of Negroes both in Africa and the United States." This restrictive educational system for black Americans had already been institutionalized, beginning with the 'philanthropic' endeavours of Wall Street bankers and northern industrialists and capitalists at several conferences in 1898. The education was constructed on the basis that, as one conference participant stated, "the white people are to be the leaders, to take the initiative, to have direct control in all matters pertaining to civilization and the highest interest of our beloved land. History demonstrates that the Caucasian will rule, and he ought to rule." As one conference organizer stated:

Time has proven that [the 'negro'] is best fitted to perform the heavy labor in the Southern states... He will willingly fill the more menial positions, and do the heavy work, at less wages, than the American white man or any foreign race... This will permit the Southern white laborer to perform the more expert labor, and to leave the fields, the mines, and the simple trades for the negro.[24]

The conferences resulted in what became known as the 'Tuskegee educational philosophy,' which was decided upon by 1901. Three major decisions were taken at the conferences. The first major decision was that "it was necessary that provision be made to train a Negro leadership cadre":

For this purpose, then, it was concluded that certain Negro colleges would be strengthened to educate a strong professional class - doctors, lawyers, ministers - which would be responsible for raising the general physical and moral level of the race in the segregated black communities... [Second], it was decided that the Negro had been educated away from his natural environment and that his education should concern only those fields available to him. This key decision marked the formulation of the concept of a special Negro education. Third, it was decided that this special education - vocational and agricultural in focus - of the Negro had to be directed toward increasing the labor value of his race, a labor value which, not surprisingly, would see the white capitalist as chief beneficiary.[25]

Thus, in 1901 the fourth conference on the issue established the Southern Education Board. The following year, John D. Rockefeller established the General Education Board (a precursor to the Rockefeller Foundation), which "alleviated any financial concerns which the planners of southern Negro education might have experienced."[26] The Rockefeller philanthropy had extensive influence on implementing the 'Tuskegee educational philosophy,' particularly through the Southern Education Board, of which it not only helped finance, but had a shared leadership. Eleven members of the Southern Education Board were also members of Rockefeller's General Education Board. With time, other funds and philanthropies became involved, such as the Jeanes Fund, the Slater Fund, and eventually the Phelps-Stokes Fund. Again, there was significant overlap between these organizations. The first president of the Jeanes Fund was James H. Dillard, a member of the Southern Education Board, an agent of the Slater Fund, and a member of Rockefeller's General Education Board. In 1923, Dillard became a trustee of the Phelps-Stokes Fund. The Jeanes Fund, headed by Dillard, instituted the concept of the 'Jeanes teacher':

a local Negro who could make contact in the rural communities as no one else could and who could adapt the school curriculum to the conditions of these communities. Hygiene, home economics, and industrial and agricultural training were to form the backbone of the curriculum for Jeanes rural schools. In 1925, the Jeanes school concept was transferred to Kenya, largely owing to the vigorous advocacy for such a transplantation by representatives of the Phelps-Stokes Fund.[27]

The Tuskegee/Phelps-Stokes educational philosophy quickly garnered the attention of British missionary educators in Africa. Two influential

British missionary educators visited the Tuskegee Institute in 1912, with the idea in mind that they could adapt this educational philosophy to Britain's colonies in Africa. One of these missionaries was J.H. Oldham, former secretary of the World Missionary Conference, and editor of the *International Review of Missions*, "the quasi-official journal of the Protestant missionary societies in Great Britain from its inception in 1912." Having become well-acquainted with the American philanthropists involved in organization black education, Oldham introduced Thomas Jesse Jones to British colonial officials in charge of educational policy in Africa, and in 1924, "Oldham became the Phelps-Stokes Fund's representative in the United Kingdom and intensified his vigorous lobbying efforts to have Phelps-Stokes Fund/Tuskegee concept incorporated into official mission and colonial educational policy."[28] As Kenya's colonial secretary stated, the educational philosophy would ensure "an intelligent, cheerful, self-respecting, and generally docile and willing-to-learn African native." In 1925, Jones successfully negotiated for financial aid from the Carnegie Corporation to finance the establishment of a Jeanes training school in Kenya. The funding from Carnegie included direct funding for the school, as well as facilitating white educators from Africa to come to the U.S. to "investigate" the Southern educational system, as well as implementing intelligence tests for Africans (just as the major philanthropies had been propagating around the United States as part of their support for eugenics programs). Jones also turned to other major foundations for support, such as Rockefeller's International Education Board (which had Anson Phelps-Stokes as a trustee), as well as the Laura Spellman Rockefeller Memorial, which all subsequently provided major grants to establish several schools across Africa.[29]

Jones and the major foundations further supported the development of black education in South Africa, helping cement the apartheid system that was being developed. As Jones himself stated, the education of black South Africans in the Tuskegee philosophy can maintain their subordination to the white ruling class, and keep them as "junior partners in the firm."[30]

Managing the Poor through Social Welfare

Another major area of concern in these chapters is on the 'moral construction' of the poor, going beyond (but not ignoring) the ways in which the poor are 'created' and 'maintained' as a social group (i.e., noting the political, economic, and social policies and institutions that create and sustain poverty as a powerful social force), but also in looking at how the poor are, as a group, "regulated" and how society "morally constructs" views and perceptions of the poor, so that they are vilified, demonized, and politicized as "deviants."

The origins of 'welfare policies' and other forms of 'social welfare' emerged several hundred years ago as a response to the inability of the economic system to benefit the masses of society, and thus, to prevent - often in the midst of an economic crisis - mass social unrest, rebellion, or potentially, revolution, social welfare policies were implemented as a means of social control: to alleviate some of the tensions from the gross systemic inequalities, and secondly, and often overlooked, as a means of regulating the behaviour, "work ethic" and prospects of the poor; to maintain them as a cheap labour force. This is done through the methods in which social welfare is provided: the process of applying for social services and welfare, the conditions required to be applicable, the demands which must be met by the applicant as determined by the state, the state intervention in the family and personal life of recipients (often through social workers), and other means of both expanding and detracting the amount of people on welfare as a means to sustain the labour force according to the demands of industry. As such, it is important to analyze the origins of "social work" as a means of "social control" and "managing the poor."

Originating in the 16th century, relief giving to the poor began to be transferred from the private realm to the state. In Britain, the poor had to be registered and begging had to be authorized, and the Elizabethan Poor Laws, passed in 1572, "established a 'poor rate' tax and provided for secular control of the poor by justices of the peace, so-called overseers of the poor." The poor were separated into three categories: "a) the poor by impotency, b) the poor by casualty, and c) the thriftless poor." The third category, "thriftless poor," were viewed as being responsible for their own condition, and thus had to "work for relief." In the 18th century, workhouses began to emerge as a "policy innovation" to establish "worth" among the poor, to make them productive to the industrial class through contracting cheap labour in return for minor poverty relief. In the 19th century, the poorhouse "had become the official last resort for the poor."[31]

The poorhouse and workhouse were often examined in the works of Charles Dickens. One is often reminded of the character Ebenezer

Scrooge in *A Christmas Carol*, when approached by collectors seeking donations for poor relief, with the collector stating, "At this festive time of year, Mr. Scrooge, it is more than usually desirable that we should make some slight provision for the poor and destitute." To which Scrooge replied, "Are there no prisons?"

"Plenty of prisons."

"And the union workhouses - are they still in operation?"

"They are. I wish I could say they were not."

"The Treadmill and the Poor Law are in full vigour, then?"

"Both very busy, sir."

"Oh, from what you said at first I was afraid that something had happened to stop them in their useful course. I'm very glad to hear it."

Refusing to donate, Scrooge stated, "I help to support the establishments I have mentioned - they cost enough; and those who are badly off must go there."

"Many can't go there; and many would rather die."

Scrooge replied, "If they would rather die... they had better do it, and decrease the surplus population."

   This scene reflected the ideology and philosophy of elites in that era, and indeed, up until present day. The poorhouses of that era were terrible, where "conditions were so awful, the act of relief itself became the test of necessity." Much like the stigma of welfare in today's context, "[t]hose who presented themselves to the poorhouse were casting themselves outside of moral society," as entrance into that situation "symbolized and made painfully concrete a loss of social status, citizenship, and even the right to one's own labor and physical freedom." The New Deal following the Great Depression in the 1930s reaffirmed, with its expanded welfare and social services, the stipulation that relief must only be in exchange for work and labour. This represents a "moral construction" of poverty and "the poor," because they are deemed as being required to work for relief, as in, they are undeserving of relief without conditions, regardless of their circumstances. The "stigma" of poverty and welfare are such that the poor are viewed as generally undeserving of anything, of being the cause of their own poverty, and thus, if they want/need relief, they had better work for it. It was through working and labour that the poor, then, were able to provide a "social worth" in return for "poor relief." It is thus no coincidence that social security and unemployment insurance were "restricted to individuals classified by policy as workers, that is, individuals with a relatively prolonged and steady formal work history." As a result, this led to the exclusion of "agricultural and domestic workers as well as those in marginal jobs who moved in and out of work," which, not coincidentally, included a significant portion of the black population in the United States.[32]

With the New Deal, the state in America moved into the realm of activity previously the focus of the philanthropic foundation. In fact, these private foundations were pivotal in the formation of the New Deal. As Barry Karl and Stanley Katz noted, "Franklin Roosevelt preferred to conceal the fact that so many of his major advisers on policy and some of his major programmes in social reform were the result of support by one of more of the private foundations," particularly through the Rockefeller Foundation and the Social Science Research Council, funded by the Rockefeller and Carnegie foundations.[33] The support from such foundations, which represent the most elite interests within society and the capitalist class itself, founded and run by the wealthiest and most powerful bankers and industrialists of the era, represented an elite fear generated by the mass social unrest of the era brought on by the Great Depression, which was created by that very same class. Thus, social security and the New Deal were a means of securing social control.[34] The New Deal, however, also had a profoundly negative impact upon the "race question" in the United States, which broadly affected the black community. As Christopher G. Wye wrote in the *Journal of American History*:

[T]he New Deal public housing and emergency work programs played an important part in alleviating the problems generated by the Depression, [but] they also contributed to the preservation of perhaps the two salient components which combine to produce a caste-like Negro social structure - residential segregation and a distinctly racial occupational pattern.[35]

Civil Rights: From "Black Power" to "Black Capitalism"

The major foundations - Ford, Carnegie, and Rockefeller - were also heavily involved in the Civil Rights movement, but with specific aims of social control. In the 1950s, the Ford Foundation began taking an interest in the Civil Rights movement, and after convening a study on how to "improve race relations," the Ford Foundation began giving grants to black colleges "to improve the quality of their educational offerings."[36] By 1966, the Civil Rights movement was one of the major areas of Ford Foundation funding. Against the backdrop of the summer of 1966 in which there were 43 "urban disorders" (riots in ghettos), which had been "precipitated by confrontations between blacks and the police," the Ford Foundation announced that it would "direct significant resources to the social justice area." Among the aims of the Foundation were: "to improve leadership and programming within minority organizations; to explore approaches to better race relations; to support policy-oriented research on race and poverty; to promote housing integration; and to increase the availability of legal resources through support of litigating organizations and minority law students."[37] The Ford Foundation also sponsored the Grey Areas program in the early 1960s, which evolved into President Johnson's "War on Poverty," as a program for "urban renewal," but was, in fact, concerned with issues arising out of poor people's (and particularly poor people of colour's) resistance to major urban growth projects undertaken by a coalition of corporations and corporatist labour unions following World War II. As Roger Friedland wrote:

Political challenge by the poor, and especially the nonwhite poor, threatened the dominance of the corporations and labor unions and the growth policies they pursued. It was the poorest neighborhoods which were displaced by urban renewal and highway construction, whose housing stock was depleted by clearance, whose employment opportunities were often reduced both by the expansion of office employment stimulated by central business district growth and by restrictive unionization on large construction projects and municipal jobs, and whose services were constrained by the enormous fiscal costs of the growth programs.[38]

It was in this context that the Ford Foundation established programs aimed at ameliorating the antagonisms within the impoverished communities, not through structural or systemic change of the causes of poverty, but through organization, institutionalization, and legalistic reform programs, thus leading to the government's "War on Poverty." The same approach was taken in regards to the Civil Rights movement.

There was a transformation between 1966 and 1967 of the notion of 'black power', which was increasingly viewed by elites and 'authorities', such as J. Edgar Hoover of the FBI, as "the beginning of a true black revolution." Many advocates of 'black power' saw it as the beginnings of a revolt against "white western imperialist" America.[39] The Civil Rights movement was originally "launched by indigenous leadership and primarily mobilized the southern black community." Thus, it was essential for large foundation funding of the movement, to effectively control its direction and impetus. This "elite involvement would seem to occur only as a response to the threat posed by the generation of a mass-based social movement." The major foundations "supported the moderate civil rights organizations in response to the 'radical flank' threat of the militants, while non-elites (churches, unions and small individual donors) spread their support evenly."[40]

Elite patronage of the Civil Rights movement "diverted leaders from indigenous organizing and exacerbated inter-organizational rivalries, thereby promoting movement decay."[41] Foundation funding for civil rights did not become significant until 1961-62, five years after the Birmingham bus boycott, and the peak of foundation support for civil rights was in 1972-73, four to five years after the assassination of King.[42] This indicated that foundation grants to civil rights were 'reactive', in that they were designed in response to changes in the movement itself, implying that foundation patronage was aimed at social control. Further, most grants went to professionalized social movement organizations (SMOs) and in particular, the NAACP. While the professional SMOs initiated only 14% of movement actions, they accounted for 57% of foundation grants, while the classical SMOs, having carried out roughly 36% of movement actions, received roughly 32% of foundation grants. This disparity grew with time, so that by the 1970s, the classical SMOs garnered 25% of grants and the professional SMOs received nearly 70% of grants. Principally, the NAACP and the NAACP Legal Defense Fund were the most endowed with foundation support.[43] Many of the foundations subsequently became "centrally involved in the formulation of national social policy and responded to elite concerns about the riots."[44]

It became clear that the older, established and moderate organizations received the most outside funding, such as the National Urban League, the NAACP and the Legal Defense and Educational Fund.[45] As the black struggles of the 1960s increasingly grew militant and activist-oriented in the latter half of the 1960s, "foundation contributions became major sources of income for the National Urban League, the Southern Regional Council, and the Legal Defense and Educational Fund."[46] The attempt was to promote reform instead of losing their vested powers and interests in the face of a growing revolution.

The NAACP and the National Urban League represent the more moderate civil rights organizations, as they were also the oldest, with membership primarily made up of middle class African Americans, leading to many, including King himself, to suggest they were disconnected from the reality or in representing poor blacks in America.[47] The radicalization of the black protest movement led to the emergence of challenges to the NAACP and Urban League in being the 'leaders' in civil rights, as new organizations emerged which represented a broader array of the black population. Among them were the Congress of Racial Equality (CORE), the Student Non-violent Coordinating Committee (SNCC), and the Southern Christian Leadership Conference (SCLC), which Martin Luther King led. Foundations increased funding for all of these organizations, but as activism and militancy accelerated in the latter half of the 1960s, the funding declined for the more radical, militant and activist organizations and increased dramatically for the established and moderate organizations. This trend continued going into the 1970s.

In 1967, Martin Luther King's SCLC received $230,000 from the Ford Foundation, yet after his assassination, the organization received no more funding and virtually fell to pieces. That same year, the Ford Foundation gave the NAACP $300,000, and gave the Urban League $585,000. The Rockefeller Foundation granted the League $650,000, with the Carnegie Corporation coming in with $200,000. The Ford Foundation also gave the Congress of Racial Equality (CORE) $175,000 in 1967.[48]

In 1968, with the SCLC out of the picture, Ford increased funding for CORE to $300,000, increased grants to the NAACP to $378,000, and gave the Urban League a monumental grant of $1,480,000. The same year, the Rockefeller Foundation and the Carnegie Corporation gave the NAACP $500,000 and $200,000 respectively. Clearly, the foundations were supporting the older established and moderate organizations over the new, young and activist/radical organizations. For the following year, 1969, CORE received no more grants from foundations, while the Ford, Rockefeller and Carnegie foundations increased their grants to the NAACP and the Urban League. In 1974, the NAACP received grants of $950,000 from the Ford Foundation, $250,000 from the Rockefeller Foundation, and $200,000 from the Carnegie Corporation. The Urban League received grants of $2,350,000 from the Ford Foundation and

$350,000 from the Rockefeller Foundation.[49] The strategic use of foundation funding helped undermine and outmaneuver the radical and militant civil rights organizations, while strengthening and institutionalizing the reform-oriented organizations.

This co-optation of the civil rights movement was so vital to these elite interests for the principle reason of the movement taking its natural course, out of an ethnic or race-based focus and into a class and global social focus. A. Philip Randolph, a civil rights leader, spoke in 1963 at an ALF-CIO convention at which he stated, "The Negro's protest today is but the first rumbling of the 'under-class.' As the Negro has taken to the streets, so will the unemployed of all races take to the streets."[50] The aim of foundation funding for the Civil Rights movement was to direct it from a potentially revolutionary position - that of 'Black Power' - and transform it into a reformist and legalistic movement, ostensibly to establish "Black Capitalism." Thus, instead of changing the systemic and institutional structures of society which had created racism, segregation, and exploitation, the "success" of the Civil Rights movement (apart from the very real achievements of securing basic civil rights for black citizens) was seen by elites as the ability of blacks to rise within the institutional and hierarchical system which dominated society, not to challenge or change it fundamentally.

The "Excess of Democracy"

In the 1970s, elite intellectual discussion was dominated by what was referred to as "democratic overload," or what the Trilateral Commission referred to in a report of the same title as, "The Crisis of Democracy." One of the principal authors of this 1975 report was Samuel Huntington, who wrote that the 1960s saw a surge in democracy in America, with an upswing in citizen participation, often "in the form of marches, demonstrations, protest movements, and 'cause' organizations."[51] Further, "the 1960s also saw a reassertion of the primacy of equality as a goal in social, economic, and political life."[52] Of course, for Huntington and the Trilateral Commission, which was founded by Huntington's friend, Zbigniew Brzezinski, and banker David Rockefeller, the idea of "equality as a goal in social, economic, and political life" is a terrible and frightening prospect. Huntington analyzed how as part of this "democratic surge," statistics showed that throughout the 1960s and into the early 1970s, there was a dramatic increase in the percentage of people who felt the United States was spending too much on defense (from 18% in 1960 to 52% in 1969, largely due to the Vietnam War).[53]

Huntington wrote that the "essence of the democratic surge of the 1960s was a general challenge to existing systems of authority, public and private," and that, "People no longer felt the same compulsion to obey those whom they had previously considered superior to themselves in age, rank, status, expertise, character, or talents." He explained that in the 1960s, "hierarchy, expertise, and wealth" had come "under heavy attack."[54] He stated that the three key issues which were central to the increased political participation in the 1960s were:

social issues, such as use of drugs, civil liberties, and the role of women; racial issues, involving integration, busing, government aid to minority groups, and urban riots; military issues, involving primarily, of course, the war in Vietnam but also the draft, military spending, military aid programs, and the role of the military-industrial complex more generally.[55]

Huntington presented these issues, essentially, as the "crisis of democracy," in that they increased distrust with the government and authority, that they led to social and ideological polarization, and ultimately, to a "decline in the authority, status, influence, and effectiveness of the presidency."[56] Huntington concluded that many problems of governance in the United States stem from an "excess of democracy," and that, "the effective operation of a democratic political system usually requires some measure of apathy and noninvolvement on the part of some individuals and groups." Huntington explained that society has always had "marginal groups" which do not participate in politics, and while acknowledging that the existence of "marginality on the part of some groups is inherently undemocratic," it has also "enabled democracy to function effectively." Huntington identifies "the blacks" as one such group that had become politically active, posing a "danger of overloading the political system with demands."[57] Huntington, in his conclusion, stated that the vulnerability of democracy, essentially the 'crisis of democracy,' comes "from the internal dynamics of democracy itself in a highly educated, mobilized, and participant society," and that what is needed is "a more balanced existence" in which there are "desirable limits to the indefinite extension of political democracy."[58] Summed up, the Trilateral Commission Task Force Report essentially explained that the "Crisis of Democracy" is that there is too much of it, and so the 'solution' to the crisis, is to have less democracy and more 'authority'.

To have "less democracy," however, required careful and strategic moves and considerations. Primarily, the means through which this objective would be reached was through the disciplinary measures of the "free market" and "regulation of the poor." This led to the neoliberal era, where this program of "reducing democracy" took place not only in the United States, but on a global scale. The disciplinary means undertaken in the 'Third World' nations were brought on by the 1980s debt crisis, and the World Bank and IMF "structural adjustment programs" which invariably expanded poverty, debt, and supported ruthless dictatorships which suppressed their own populations. This era also saw the "globalization of the ghetto" with the rapid development of urban slums around the world, to the point where over one billion people today live in slums. In the United States, the middle classes began to be mired in debt, particular the expansion of student debt, which served as a disciplinary feature, so that students were no longer activists or mobilized, but simply had to graduate and get jobs to pay off their debts.

A 1971 memo written by a representative of the U.S. Chamber of Commerce reflected the fear inherent in the Trilateral Commission report of a few years later at the problems posed to elite interests by the "excess of democracy." It referred to these "excesses" as a "broad attack" on the American economic system. The memo noted that, "the assault on the enterprise system is broadly based and consistently pursued. It is gaining momentum and converts." While noting that sources of the attack include leftists and revolutionaries, it also acknowledged that the "attack" was being joined "from perfectly respectable elements of society: from the college campus, the pulpit, the media, the intellectual and literary journals, the arts and sciences, and from politicians." The author of the memo stated that, "If our system is to survive, top [corporate] management must be equally concerned with protecting and preserving the system itself." It went on:

But independent and uncoordinated activity by individual corporations, as important as this is, will not be sufficient. Strength lies in organization, in careful long-range planning and implementation, in consistency of action over an indefinite period of years, in the scale of financing available only through joint effort, and in the political power available only through united action and national organizations.[59]

The memo then went on to articulate a major program of "counter attack" with an emphasis on changing the educational system, the media, and bringing the state and courts more directly into the business community's orbit. This era saw the emergence of the major right-wing think tanks, and the expanded influence of business leaders in the media, government, and universities, crowned with the Reagan-Thatcher era of neoliberalism: privatization, deregulation, debt-expansion, impoverishment, and punishment.

Punishing the Poor

In regards to the black population, who created quite a stir among the American elites in the 1960s and into the 1970s, the response from the elite sector was similar as to what it was during the Reconstruction period following the Civil War: mass incarceration. Reagan's "war on drugs" led to a rapid expansion of legislation purportedly aimed to reduce the problems of the illicit drug trade in the United States (while the Reagan administration secretly supported the drug trade in covert operations abroad, such as in Nicaragua, the Iran-Contra Scandal, etc.). The growth of the prison population in the United States from 1975 onward was marked simultaneously by a decline in welfare recipients. In fact, the largest prison systems were established in states with the weaker welfare systems. Between 1980 and 2000, "the number of people incarcerated in the United States increased by 300 percent, from 500,000 to nearly 2 million." The parole and probation population, by 2000, included 3.8 million people, and by 1998, "nearly 6 million people - almost 3 percent of the adult population - were under some form of correctional supervision." As reported in the journal,*Punishment & Society*:

The impact of these developments has fallen disproportionately on young African-Americans and Latinos. By 1994, one of every third black males between the ages of 18-34 was under some form of correctional supervision, and the number of Hispanic prisoners has more than quintupled since 1980. These developments are not primarily the consequence of rising crime rates, but rather the 'get-tough' policies of the wars on crime and drugs.[60]

As sociologists Katherine Beckett and Bruce Western wrote, "in the wake of the Reagan revolution, penal and welfare institutions have come to form a single policy regime aimed at the governance of social marginality," or, in other words, the management of the poor and non-white populations. Thus, reduced welfare spending as a method of social control was replaced with increased incarceration and imprisonment.[61]

The prison system itself, which had its origins in the application of social control, functioned through segregation and discrimination, has not evolved from these institutional ideologies that saw its development over several hundred years. The prison and incarceration, according to philosopher and historian Michel Foucault, was "a new form of repression, designed to consolidate the political and economic power of capitalism under the modern state," in what he termed, "the disciplinary society."[62]

Just as took place during the criminalization of black life following the Civil War, the criminalization of black life following the Civil Rights Movement saw not only the growth of incarceration rates for the black community, but also saw the growth of the use of the prison population as a source of cheap labour. In today's context, with privatization of prisons, outsourcing of prison labour, and other forms of exploitation of the "punished" population, this has given rise to what is often referred to as the "prison-industrial complex."[63]

This article was but a brief sampling of some of the information, issues, ideas, events, and processes that will be thoroughly researched and written about in two chapters for The People's Book Project. If you found the information enlightening, interesting, or important, please contribute to the People's Grant goal of raising $1,600 to finance the completion of two chapters on this subject, which will include a great deal more than was sampled above, deeper analysis, more detailed and documented understandings, and a much wider, global contextualization. This was but a minor fraction of what can be completed with the support of readers. Help get this important information into the public sphere. As the global economic crisis rapidly expands the global rates of impoverishment, as the middle class vanishes into debt and poverty, and as our societies are reorganized to "manage" these social, political, and economic changes, this history is vital to understanding not only the objectives, ideas and actions of elites, but also the ways in which the people may challenge them.

Notes

[1] A. Leon Higginbotham, Jr., "Racism and the Early American Legal Process, 1619-1896," *Annals of the American Academy of Political and Social Science* (Vol. 407, No. 1, May 1973), page 1.
[2] Ibid, page 6.
[3] David McNally, *Another World is Possible: Globalization and Anti-Capitalism* (Arbeiter Ring Publishing, 2006), page 149.
[4] Ibid, page 150.
[5] Ibid, pages 151-152.
[6] Ibid, pages 152-153.
[7] Ibid, page 153.
[8] Ibid, pages 153-154.
[9] Ibid, pages 154-155.
[10] Ibid, page 155.
[11] William Cohen, "Negro Involuntary Servitude in the South, 1865-1940," *The Journal of Southern History* (Vol. 42, No. 1, February 1976), page 33.
[12] Ibid, page 34.
[13] Brian Kelly, "Labor, Race, and the Search for a Central Theme in the History of the Jim Crow South," *Irish Journal of American Studies* (Vol. 10, 2001), page 58.
[14] William H. Worger, "Convict Labour, Industrialists and the State in the US South and South Africa, 1870-1930," *Journal of Southern African Studies* (Vol. 30, No. 1, March 2004), page 68.
[15] Ibid, pages 68-69.
[16] Ibid, page 85.
[17] Eduardo Mendieta, "Plantations, Ghettos, Prisons: US Racial Geographies," *Philosophy and Geography* (Vol. 7, No. 1, February 2004), page 52.
[18] Ibid, pages 52-53.
[19] Carl H. Nightingale, "A Tale of Three Global Ghettos: How Arnold Hirsch Helps Us Internationalize U.S. Urban History," *Journal of Urban History* (Vol. 29, No. 3, March 2003), page 262.
[20] Ibid, page 265.

[21] Karen Ferguson, "Organizing the Ghetto: The Ford Foundation, CORE, and White Power in the Black Power Era, 1967-1969," *Journal of Urban History* (Vol. 34, No. 1, November 2007), pages 69, 96.

[22] William J. Quirk and Leon E. Wein, "Homeownership for the Poor: Tenant Condominiums, the Housing and Urban Development Act of 1968, and the Rockefeller Program," *Cornell Law Review* (Vol. 54, No. 6, July 1969), pages 849, 855.

[23] Peter L. Laurence, "The Death and Life of Urban Design: Jane Jacobs, The Rockefeller Foundation and the New Research in Urbanism, 1955-1965," *Journal of Urban Design* (Vol. 11, No. 2, June 2006), page 145.

[24] Robert F. Arnove, ed., *Philanthropy and Cultural Imperialism: The Foundations at Home and Abroad* (Indiana University Press, 1980), pages 180-181.

[25] Ibid, page 181.

[26] Ibid.

[27] Ibid, page 182.

[28] Ibid, pages 185-186.

[29] Ibid, pages 188-190.

[30] Ibid, page 194.

[31] Evelyn Z. Brodkin, "The Making of an Enemy: How Welfare Policies Construct the Poor," *Law & Social Inquiry* (Vol. 18, No. 4, Autumn 1993), pages 655-656.

[32] Ibid, pages 656-658.

[33] Barry D. Karl and Stanley N. Katz, "The American Private Philanthropic Foundation and the Public Sphere 1890-1930," *Minerva* (Vol. 19, No. 2, Summer 1981), page 268.

[34] J. Craig Jenkins and Barbara Brents, "Capitalists and Social Security: What Did They Really Want?" *American Sociological Review* (Vol. 56, No. 1, February 1991), page 129.

[35] Christopher G. Wye, "The New Deal and the Negro Community: Toward a Broader Conceptualization," *The Journal of American History* (Vol. 59, No. 3, December 1972), page 639.

[36] Lynn Walker, "The Role of Foundations in Helping to Reach the Civil Rights Goals of the 1980s,"*Rutgers Law Review*, (1984-1985), page 1059.

[37] Ibid, page 1060.

[38] Roger Friedland, "Class Power and Social Control: The War on Poverty," *Politics & Society* (Vol. 6, No. 4, December 1976), pages 459-461.

[39] Robert C. Smith, "Black Power and the Transformation from Protest to Policies," *Political Science Quarterly*, Vol. 96, No. 3, (Autumn, 1981), page 438

[40] J. Craig Jenkins and Craig M. Eckert, "Channeling Black Insurgency: Elite Patronage and Professional Social Movement Organizations in the Development of the Black Movement," *American Sociological Review*, Vol. 51, No. 6, (Dec., 1986), page 814.

[41] Ibid, page 815.

[42] Ibid, pages 819-820.

[43] Ibid, page 821.

[44] Ibid, page 826.

[45] Herbert H. Haines, "Black Radicalization and the Funding of Civil Rights: 1957-1970," *Social Problems*, Vol. 32, No. 1, Thematic Issue on Minorities and Social Movements, (Oct., 1984), page 38.

[46] Ibid, page 40.

[47] Martin N. Marger, "Social Movement Organizations and Response to Environmental Change: The NAACP, 1960- 1973," *Social Problems*, Vol. 32, No. 1, Thematic Issue on Minorities and Social Movements, (Oct., 1984), page 22.

[48] Ibid, page 25.

[49] Ibid.

[50] Howard Zinn, *A People's History of the United States* (Harper: New York, 2003), page 464.

[51] Michel J. Crozier, Samuel P. Huntington and Joji Watanuki, The Crisis of Democracy. (Report on the Governability of Democracies to the Trilateral Commission, New York University Press, 1975), page 61.

[52] Ibid, page 62.

[53] Ibid, page 71.

[54] Ibid, pages 74-75.

[55] Ibid, page 77.

[56] Ibid, page 93.

[57] Ibid, pages 113-114.

[58] Ibid, page 115.

[59] Lewis F. Powell, Jr., "Confidential Memorandum: Attack of American Free Enterprise System," U.S. Chamber of Commerce, 23 August 1971:http://www.pbs.org/wnet/supremecourt/personality/sources_do cument13.html

[60] Katherine Beckett and Bruce Western, "Governing Social Marginality: Welfare, Incarceration, and the Transformation of State Policy," *Punishment & Society* (Vol. 3, No. 1, January 2001), pages 43-44.
[61] Ibid, page 55.
[62] Robert P. Weiss, "Humanitarianism, Labour Exploitation, or Social Control? A Critical Survey of Theory and Research on the Origin and Development of Prisons," *Social History* (Vol. 12, No. 3, October 1987), page 333.
[63] Rose M. Brewer and Nancy A. Heitzeg, "The Racialization of Crime and Punishment: Criminal Justice, Color-Blind Racism, and the Political Economy of the Prison Industrial Complex," *American Behavioral Scientist* (Vol. 51, No. 5, January 2008).

Social Economics

DEPARTMENT

Invisible Chains

Consumerism, Debt, and Consciousness

Colin Jenkins

Critical analyses regarding the effects of "consumerism" have been a staple of Leftist theory for the past century. The Situationist International, appearing in the 1950s as an extension of Lukacs' unique brand of social analysis from the 20s, famously ridiculed the "western lifestyle" as a "fake reality which masks the capitalist degradation of human life."[1] The Situationists viewed the "spectacle" as the process for which people's desires are shaped and molded towards consumerist tendencies through mass media, marketing and advertising, and advanced techniques like "recuperation." This counter-cultural examination quickly became synonymous with a Left that had already come to terms with the "economic injustice" which characterized "the predatory phase of human development."[2] In opposition to this "rigged game," a determined and conscious working class countered with radical unionism and activism, direct action, stacks of polemics, studies on socio-economics, and avant-garde artistic techniques that fell under the banner of "culture jamming." "Detournement" turned the act of recuperation upside down by attempting to radicalize and politicize the corporate slogans and logos that flooded the "spectacle," leading to modern alternative media outlets such as Adbusters, the unsung catalysts of Occupy Wall Street and Rolling Jubilee, and street artists like

Banksy, who combines detournement techniques with urban graffiti to send powerful counter-cultural messages via concrete canvass.

Naturally, any opposition to consumerism, especially from within those societies historically classified as "western" or "industrialized," is counter-hegemonic and proto-revolutionary. After all, the cultures derived from them have come to be dominated by ideals rooted in capitalism and market economies, naturally leading to intense daily routines that consist of celebrity worship at the altar of reality television and a multi-billion dollar "gossip industry." And when considering the dominant culture is one of superficiality, where our identities are based on what we own, wear and drive - in other words, consumerism - any stance in opposition to this is naturally "against the grain." The current counter-culture is one that not only recognizes the inherent dangers of a society where meaningful human concerns like impoverishment, homelessness, ever-increasing militarism, racism and misogyny take a backseat to Reality Housewives, American Idol and Jersey Shore; but also one that dares to make conscious lifestyle decisions which run contrary to this domination, while also working to break the collective trance that derives from such. Despite the obvious legitimacies found in this stance, and assuming we haven't conceded to nothingness, it's important to consider (1) how this opposition affects the Left's ability to function as a real alternative to the embedded socio-political hegemony, and (2) how it affects the Left's relationship with a working class that has embraced much of this culture as its own. The inherent risks of elitist-like diatribes against what have essentially become "cultural norms" beg for a re-evaluation which must recognize the need to accommodate both scathing cultural critiques *and*working-class political means. And while this seemingly half-assed approach to addressing such reactionary psychology may be debatable, the dangerous effects and continued escalation of consumerism clearly represent a powerful barrier to reaching any semblance of a collective working class consciousness. Its roots are not always as clear.

In 1901, following the conquest of Madagascar, French General Joseph Simon Gallieni immediately introduced a franc-based currency in order to impose an "educational tax" on the native population. This move had three implied purposes: "To teach the natives the value of work;" to create an immediate and effective monetary form of debt; and to instill consumerist tendencies within the population. While the first "function" followed the typical blueprint of colonialism by creating cheap forms of "human resources" to exploit, the latter two incorporated tangible debts to "legitimize" servitude (a tactic that would soon take hold in the "modern international financial system") and a culture of consumerism as the psychological means to establish and maintain what Antonio Gramsci once referred to as "cultural hegemony." As David Graeber explains, "The colonial (French) government was quite explicit about the need to make sure that (indigenous) peasants had at least some money of their own left over, and to ensure that they became accustomed to the minor luxuries - parasols, lipstick, cookies - available at the shops."[3] Understanding the connection between alienation, debt and consumerism - and how each may be used as a form of control - goes beyond the "inferiority complex" that Fanon once attributed to colonized populations which are "physically and symbolically destroyed, and in their place the colonizer produces a people who deserve only to be ruled."[4] Essentially, these are tools that transcend international and inherently racist relations between the "core" and "periphery" - making class analyses absolutely vital in regards to the "forced dependency" created by the architects of the dominant culture, not only from the perspective of an indigenous population, but also from that of the domestic working classes. "It was crucial that they (the colonized) develop new tastes, habits and expectations; that they lay the foundation of a consumer demand that would endure long after the conquerors had left, and keep Madagascar forever tied to France."[5]

Establishing a "cultural hegemony" runs analogous to principles that drive the market business model, which relies solely on individual "desires" to sell products. Since most of these desires do not constitute basic needs in the Maslovian sense, advertising and marketing must convince consumers that they need big screen televisions, new clothes, technological gadgets, and so forth. With such a task at hand, the business community had to look no further than the colonizers' experience in establishing control over its subject population. In a 1955 edition of *The Journal of Retailing*, Economist and Marketing Consultant, Victor Lebow, urged business "leaders" and marketers to cultivate and exploit this consumerist mentality with full force:

(Our economy) demands that we make consumption our way of life, that we convert the buying and use of goods into rituals, that we seek our spiritual satisfactions, our ego satisfactions, in consumption. The measure of social status, of social acceptance, of prestige, is now to be found in our consumptive patterns. The very meaning and significance of

our lives today expressed in consumptive terms. The greater the pressures upon the individual to conform to safe and accepted social standards, the more does he tend to express his aspirations and his individuality in terms of what he wears, drives, eats- his home, his car, his pattern of food serving, his hobbies.... We require not only "forced draft" consumption, but "expensive" consumption as well. We need things consumed, burned up, worn out, replaced, and discarded at an ever increasing pace. We need to have people eat, drink, dress, ride, live, with ever more complicated and, therefore, constantly more expensive consumption.[6]

To them, the ultimate challenge was not merely establishing a monetary system which allows for widespread consumer spending (fiat-based, supply-side economics) - a task that is handled in conjunction by the "financial wizards" of the hegemonic class - but rather creating the psychological desire to drive such spending. Essentially, as Lebow implied, this may only be accomplished by deflating the "meaning" out of life and replacing it with artificial "spiritual and ego satisfactions" that are achieved through false consciousness and "forced draft consumption." In a scene from the movie *Fight Club*, Tyler Durden famously rails against the effects of this conditioned psychology on the working classes:

I see all this potential, and I see squandering. God damn it, an entire generation pumping gas, waiting tables - slaves with white collars. Advertising has us chasing cars and clothes, working jobs we hate so we can buy shit that we don't need. We're the middle children of history, man. No purpose of place. We have no Great War. No Great Depression. Our Great War's a spiritual war; our Great Depression is our lives.

While Durden's underground sermon accurately characterized the nihilistic decadence of America's Generation X - a generation born at the pinnacle of this consumerist assault - he was merely echoing the theoretical basis of "commodity fetishism" espoused by Marx nearly a century and a half prior:

(With the spread of markets) there will come a time when everything that people consider as inalienable will become an object of exchange, of traffic, and can be alienated. This is the time when the very things which till then had been communicated, but never exchanged, given, but

never sold, acquired but never bought - virtue, love, conviction, knowledge, conscience - when everything, in short, passed into commerce. It is the time of general corruption, of universal venality. It has left remaining no other nexus between man and man other than naked self-interest and callous cash payment. [7]

As predicted, this commodity-consumer paradigm has dominated life for much of the past century. Just as workers are commodified and alienated by their role within the labor-capital relationship, they are doubly commodified and exploited in the consumer-capital relationship. Marx recognized this; western imperialists recognized this; and the corporate business community recognizes this. Hence, the appearance of an extensive "propaganda model" that is carried out in the form of a multi-billion-dollar marketing and advertising industry - which is controlled to a large extent by "a relatively concentrated network of major corporations, conglomerates and investment firms."[8] And while there are certainly examples of acute organization within this corporate community (i.e. The Business Roundtable, Chamber of Commerce, etc...), the maintenance of its hegemony ultimately falls on a loosely connected arrangement of entities that share one powerful commonality: the search for profit. It is this very dynamism that makes it such a formidable foe for the Left in its attempt to deploy class-conscious politics.

Long before the onset of industrialization, capitalism, and even market economies, there were many examples of cultures partaking in the act of accumulation for reasons other than need. Therefore, it seems such "gathering" is likely inherent in our DNA. So what's the problem? Well, first of all, it's important to differentiate between a superficial condemnation that borders on envy, and an analytical assessment that attempts to identify and deconstruct mindless, narcissistic and reactionary societal tendencies. By doing so, it brings much needed legitimacy to the latter purpose, while avoiding further alienation from folks who find natural enjoyment in the acquisition of things. In other words, it's not the act of "wanting" that's inherently bad, it's the totality of a "consumerist" society that intensifies the process of degradation and dehumanization which has already been established within the realms of capital, labor and property relations. And while the battle against exploitation via labor and property is complex, multi-layered and formidable, especially when considering its collective nature and the multitude of external factors involved, the battle against anti-consciousness perpetuated by consumerism can be won on an individual basis, from within. Ultimately, it is this compounding "superstructure" which houses many aspects of superfluous want, where the transition from a civil society to a "surface society" has been made complete; and ironically, where the reversal of such may begin. Therefore, juxtaposing "superficial condemnation" and "analytical analysis" is absolutely vital when breaking down this inherently destructive process. Secondly, it is important to identify such characteristics of a "surface society," with the most dangerous of those coming in the form of personal identity, whether internally through the self or externally through the perception of others. Historically, this process of "self-worth through accumulation" and its reciprocal effect on public perception has blurred the lines between consummation for personal enjoyment and "conspicuous consumerism" as a means of establishing human value. Thorstein Veblen's observations of more than a century ago, though somewhat obvious, still ring true:

Since the consumption of these more excellent goods is an evidence of wealth, it becomes honorific; and conversely, the failure to consume in due quantity and quality becomes a mark of inferiority and demerit."[9]

As if the illegitimacy and consequences of personal fortune and unequal distribution are not enough, the cultural norms that are created through consumption and public display serve to compound and further entrench such inequity on a social scale. As such, the "cultural hegemony" becomes a self-sustaining phenomenon that persists without the need for direct manipulation. "This principle has had the force of a conventional law," explains Veblen. "It has served as the norm to which consumption has tended to conform, and any appreciable departure from it is to be regarded as an aberrant form, sure to be eliminated sooner or later in the further course of development."

A civil society is one that recognizes the collective nature which exists within a community *and* realizes the inherent connection between a common good and the individual "pursuit of happiness." The essence of civility was captured by Peter Kropotkin in his historical work, *Mutual Aid: A Factor of Evolution*:

The mutual-aid tendency in man has so remote an origin, and is so deeply interwoven with all the past evolution of the human race, that it

411

has been maintained by mankind up to the present time, notwithstanding all vicissitudes of history. It was chiefly evolved during periods of peace and prosperity; but when even the greatest calamities befell men --when whole countries were laid waste by wars, and whole populations were decimated by misery, or groaned under the yoke of tyranny --the same tendency continued to live in the villages and among the poorer classes in the towns; it still kept them together, and in the long run it reacted even upon those ruling, fighting, and devastating minorities which dismissed it as sentimental nonsense. And whenever mankind had to work out a new social organization, adapted to a new phase of development, its constructive genius always drew the elements and the inspiration for the new departure from that same ever-living tendency.[10]

A "surface society" is one that ignores this commonality and replaces it with narcissistic tendencies that are centered within a false sense of identity - one that constantly pursues wealth or, at the very least, the appearance of such. In *Prosperity without Growth*, Tim Jackson writes, "The profit motive stimulates a continual search for newer, better or cheaper products and services. Our own relentless search for novelty and social status locks us into an iron cage of consumerism. Affluence itself has betrayed us."[11] This society, in sharp contrast to its civil counterpart, has been intensified by the maturation and successive mutations of capitalism, a system that has far outlived the spotty improvements it once offered to its ancestral systems of feudalism and mercantalism.

The development of a "surface society" is as much intentional as it is incidental. On one hand, it represents a regression to what Kant once referred to as "man's self-imposed infancy." On the other hand, it represents a product of invention - the intended result of a social and economic system that is manipulated and shaped through intensely concentrated power structures and profit-seeking motives. The latter brings us back to the French subjugation of Madagascar, where a noted "strategy" used to gain control of the indigenous population was to mold them into consumers who become "accustomed to the minor luxuries available at the shops." Thus, by doing so, they are not only assimilated into the "western mindset," but also dependent on the perceived need for otherwise worthless commodities. Post-industrialized societies are marked by similar dynamics, some of which are natural byproducts of the corporatized market system, and others which are products of design through hierarchical decision-making and political and monetary policy. Ultimately, if the interests of the "ruling-class" (the super minority) not only differs from that of the "working-class" (the super majority), but actually runs adversarial to such, then the need to "manipulate a culturally diverse society so that the ruling-class worldview becomes the worldview that is imposed and accepted as the cultural norm," like Gramsci once suggested, is logical on face value.

As we embark well into the 21st century, debt has officially replaced "labor surplus value" as the fundamental tool used by "the rich to extract wealth from the rest of us."[12] However, below its tangible use for "extracting" and funneling wealth to the top lies a crucial weapon in the battle for consciousness and working-class servitude. One of the most notable instances of "assimilation through policy" is reflected within America's love affair with home ownership, which has been intensely subsidized by the federal government for the past century. Interestingly enough, the push for home ownership was rooted in two essential motives: to quell the radical working-class uprisings of the early 1900s, and to serve as a subtle avenue for transferring public funds to private finance. Federal support of home ownership "began as an extension of anti-communist efforts in the wake of the Bolshevik Revolution in Russia; as on organization of realtors put it at the time, "socialism and communism do not take root in the ranks of those who have their feet firmly embedded in the soil of America through homeownership."[13] The working-class angst that had begun to surface, both internationally with the events in Tsarist Russia and nationally with the groundswell of union activity and workers' strikes, presented the need to ramp up capitalist intervention in domestic policy. What followed were the federally-backed "Own Your Own Home" campaign, the Home Owners' Loan Corporation (HOLC), the Federal Housing Administration (FHA) and the Federal National Mortgage Association (better known as "Fannie Mae."). The consensus among the "owning-class" was that indebted homeowners do not go on strike. The subsidization of private home ownership through tax incentives (where the federal government actually pays homeowners a portion of their expenses at the end of the year) allowed for the manipulation of working-class interests, and were eventually fortified by modern advents of the same, such as consumer debt (rampant through the 1980s and 90s) and student loan debt (dominant from the 1990s to present). It is no surprise that this "control by debt" mantra has intensified during an historical macroeconomic transition from tangible production economies to highly abstract "financial" economies. In contrast to the potentially negative perception of debt, the introduction of seemingly positive forms of class connections have been deployed in the form of "privatized" retirement plans, company "profit sharing," 401Ks and "deferred compensation" plans - all of which urge workers to give portions of their earnings to Wall St. in the promise of long-term returns. Yet another artificial creation of vested (in the form of a direct monetary medium), though contradictory, interest in the owning-class' well-being. The result: A working-class that cheers on the Dow, Nasdaq and S & P 500 under the false impression of inclusion and mutual interest, all the while being fleeced.

Naturally, as "financialization" has sprung up as the dominant paradigm, so has the near-complete fusion of what C. Wright Mills once referred to as "The Power Elite." Graeber writes:

Financialization is not just the manipulation of money. Ultimately, it's the ability to manipulate state power to extract a portion of other people's incomes. Wall Street and Washington, in other words, have become one. Financialization, securitization and militarization are all different aspects of the same process. And the endless multiplication, in cities across America, of gleaming bank offices-   spotless stores selling nothing while armed security guards stand by-is just the most immediate and visceral symbol for what we, as a nation, have become.[14]

So, where does consumerism fit into this bleak reality? It's rather simple. Without a constant effort to ensure people remain "accustomed to the minor luxuries - parasols, lipstick, cookies- available at the shops," the potential reach of debt is limited. Of course, basic necessities like housing, health care, food, clothing, and even water can and have been commodified in this fashion - but this isn't enough. Without creating and maintaining an insatiable "need" for luxuries, immense avenues of profit (on one side) and debt (on the other side) are essentially shut down. Furthermore, beyond the basic pursuit of monetary gain (profit) and wealth extraction (debt) lies the foundation of the status quo: the struggle for consciousness. A working class that remains ignorant to its role in this struggle; that remains indignant towards members of its own class through artificial divisions (race, gender, nationality) or false consciousness (by foolishly blaming the poor, homeless, welfare recipients, etc..); that buys into the *Weltanschauung* established by the "owning-class," is one that stands idle in the face of its own collective disenfranchisement. It allows "the norms of gender, class, and culturally circumscribed behavior, the requirements of work, the pressures of seeking status through consumption, and, in the absence of viable social alternatives, the need to find almost all enjoyment from private commodities" to dictate human life.[15] In this sense, consumerism is the enemy of solidarity; and solidarity is the catalyst of social awareness. Because if and when genuine class consciousness takes flight, society runs the risk of offering a *meaningful* human existence - an inevitable death to the status quo and the collective realization that "you're not your fuckin khakis."

Notes

[1] Guy Debord. The Society of the Spectacle.
[2] Albert Einstein. Why Socialism? Monthly Review: May 1949. (Paraphrasing Thorstein Veblen)
[3] David Graeber. *Debt: The First 5,000 Years* (New York: Melville House, 2011)
[4] Franz Fanon. *Black Skin, White Masks* (New York: Grove Press, 1967)
[5] Graeber, Debt.
[6] Karl Marx. The Poverty of Philosophy, 1847.
[7] Victor Lebow. Journal of Retailing, Spring of 1955.
[8] Edward Herman and Noam Chomsky. Manufacturing Consent: The Political Economy of the Mass Media (New York: Pantheon, 1988)
[9] Thorstein Veblen. The Theory of the Leisure Class: An Economic Study of Institutions (New York: Macmillan, 1902), pp. 68-101
[10] Kropotkin, Peter. Mutual Aid: A Factor of Evolution. 1902
[11] Is rampant consumerism ruining our lives? The Guardian, March 17, 2011.
[12] "Can Debt Spark a Revolution?" David Graeber. The Nation, September 5, 2012.
[13] Vincent Cannato, A Home of One's Own, National Affairs, Spring 2010.
[14] The Nation.
[15] Michael Albert. *Parecon: Life After Capitalism* (New York: Verso, 2003), p. 205.

In a System of Coercion and Predetermined Choices, 'Freedom' Is Just A Word

Kali Ma

Freedom is a word and idea that has become synonymous with America. President George Bush told Americans in the wake of 911 that the reason terrorists attacked the country was because "they hate our freedoms." The national anthem proudly proclaims that America is "the land of the free." Every July 4, Americans celebrate Independence Day and the *freedoms* that America represents. But what does *freedom* actually mean? What do politicians, those in power, and everyday individuals mean when they use *freedom* to describe the essence of America? In the sense that we have been conditioned to think of freedom and America as synonymous, there is actually no true meaning or definition of *freedom*. It is what George Orwell termed a "meaningless word" because it conveys nothing specific.[1] In reality, freedom means different things to different people: the right to free speech; the right to vote and participate in the political process; the right to privacy; the ability to accumulate great wealth and consume various products; or the right to live unmolested and to move about freely without constraints. [2] Essentially, the meaning of freedom is a personal one that has no official consensus.

According to the Merriam-Webster Dictionary, freedom means: a)*the absence of necessity, coercion, or constraint in choice or action*; b) *liberation from slavery or restraint or from the power of another.* Freedom, then, is about autonomy and independence - to be in control of oneself and to *choose* one's destiny. If we apply *this* definition as the standard, do we truly have freedom?

"Work Until We Keel Over and Die"

The reality for most people in the world today is one in which we serve the needs of the economic system, and in turn, those at the top who benefit from the status quo. For a human being to do anything in the world, his or her most basic needs - such as food, shelter, and clothing - must first be met. Since all individuals need money to survive, the economic system within a country is one of the primary - if not *the* primary - determinant of an individual's course and quality of life. Since money is directly tied to survival, it serves as a major factor that guides our decisions.

Frontline's recently released documentary *Two American Families* vividly depicts the extent to which money and the economic system affect our everyday reality. The film follows the lives of two working-class families (the Neumanns and the Stanleys) over the course of twenty years as they struggle to live the "American Dream." Their troubles begin when both Tony Neumann and Claude Stanley lose their well-paying, unionized manufacturing jobs to overseas outsourcing. What follows in the next two decades for both families is a painful struggle to keep up with their bills, feed their children, and cope with the constant stress of being unemployed, underemployed, and on the brink of poverty and homelessness. Throughout the years, the Neumanns and Stanleys work various demanding jobs (sometimes two at a time) and eventually hope to live a life of "purpose and a lot more self-respect." The Neumann kids worry about the family's finances and, at one point, even offer to sell their baseball cards. The Stanley boys start their own lawn care business and have no time for fun during the summer because, as the oldest son Keith says, "You have to go out there and help your mom and dad." Only one Stanley child makes it through college while the rest are unable to attend due to medical bills that put the family $30,000 in debt. Even with all their hard work, resilience, and refusal to give up, both families express their disappointments and blame themselves for the struggles they have endured over the years.

One of the most disturbing examples of the injustice and ruthlessness of our system is the foreclosure of Terry Neumann's home. After 24 years, Terry loses her house in 2011 because her part-time job wages are not enough to cover the mortgage. If we assume that the monthly mortgage payments stayed the same for 24 years, the Neumann family paid JP Morgan close to *$236,160* for a house the bank sold for $38,000 in foreclosure and for which they demanded an *additional* $120,000 from Terry as a buy-out.[3] After years of barely "making it," Terry has little faith in the future and believes that most of us will simply "work until we collapse, keel over and die."

Poverty - As American as Apple Pie

Unfortunately, the Stanleys and the Neumanns are not unique. Their stories are typical and happen to millions of Americans every day. According to recent surveys, 76% of Americans live paycheck to paycheck and 80% of Americans struggle with unemployment and near-poverty at some point in their lives. Since the 2008 economic crash, millions of Americans have slipped into poverty, lost their homes, gone bankrupt, become unemployed, and are now working part-time jobs in an economy where not even full-time wages are enough to make a decent living. But these conditions have always been present, as evidenced by families like the Stanleys and Neumanns; it's just that now an increasing number of Americans are living this reality that had previously gone mostly unacknowledged. Currently, there are more than 47 million Americans on food stamps (most of the employed), and almost a third of working class families earn wages below the official poverty threshold. In the more updated poverty measures, which include additional living costs such as medical expenses, almost 50% of Americans - 146. 4 million people - are considered poor or low-income.[4] On top of all this, 69% of Americans today hold some form of debt with the median household owing $70,000. Unfortunately, the odds of overcoming these dire economic circumstances are slim: the U.S. ranks consistently at the bottom when it comes to income equality and offers much less economic mobility than other developed countries. So, who is benefitting from this system?

The top 1% richest households in America received 121% of all income gains from 2009 to 2011, and median CEO pay increased to $15.1 million last year. Today, the richest 1% of Americans take in 24%of all new income, while in 1976 they took home 9%. The 400 wealthiest individuals - the *real* owners of America - have more wealth than the bottom 150 million Americans. Corporations have also raked in record profits, yet somehow none of this prosperity has "trickled down" to the rest of us.

Freedom to *Live*, Not Merely Exist

When we look at the Stanleys, Neumanns, and millions of other families struggling to (literally) survive, one has to ask: are they *free* human beings? What *freedoms* do they enjoy? For the overwhelming majority of us, our whole lives revolve around meeting our basic needs and keeping our families from starvation and homelessness. Most individuals are at the mercy of the economic system and have little time for anything else - survival is their main concern. What kind of a life is that? Is this a life lived in *absence of necessity, coercion, or constraint in choice or action*? People spend most of their lives working for a ruthless system and benefit very little from the incredible work and labor they put into it. And despite their best efforts, they are barely making it.

But being a human is about more than just earning a living, working 40 plus hours a week for someone else's benefit, and wasting countless more hours commuting to and from work. We get a few hours to ourselves for lunch or at home after work, and (if we are lucky) two weeks of vacation per year. This is not freedom - it's more like temporary release. *Living* means more than merely *existing*; *living* is about experiencing life by expressing one's passions, connecting with one another, and contributing creatively to our communities. For the most part of our existence, our bodies and our time belong to our employers, the "owners." The only reason the current system "works" is because it threatens us with starvation and homelessness - this is coercion. It is not *freedom* by any definition.

According to studies, most workers today have completely checked out from their jobs and are practically sleepwalking through their workdays. This even includes high-income workers, which suggests that money has little effect on whether we actually enjoy our jobs. These statistics fly in the face of those who argue that our current system is necessary because it creates an incentive for people to be productive. Studies have repeatedly shown that money is actually a bad motivator, and what people really care about is to have *autonomy* at their jobs and the opportunity to apply their talents and be recognized for their work. Turns out, self-expression and the ability to make one's own decisions are more important than money. This may be surprising to many of us because we have been indoctrinated into an economic ideology that sees profit as the ultimate value without any consideration for human beings and the natural world. Today, our global economy is mostly geared toward consuming and producing products we don't need at the expense of exploited workers and the degradation of our environment. In other words, we are lending our labor to forces of death and destruction while ignoring the consequences of our work. No wonder most people cannot relate to their jobs.

Unfortunately, many individuals cannot afford to quit their jobs even if they find their work morally repugnant because they have to worry about paying their bills and taking care of their families. Moreover, in an economy based on consumption and exploitation, there are few meaningful jobs that provide us with a deep sense of purpose and that create a positive impact on society. If they do exist, these jobs are mostly reserved for privileged individuals who get to choose between careers of profit or lives of purpose. It is these kinds of choices that working class people do not have in our system today.

No one is suggesting that people should not be "productive" or contribute to society; on the contrary, people *want* to have a purpose in life and we should be able to utilize our talents and passions for the benefit of society while still working in harmony with each other and the environment. A coercive economy only creates widespread discontent and fails to meet even the basic physical and psychological needs of the majority of people.

Unfortunately, there are still those who blame others for being poor, unemployed, or struggling in this economy. While those in power often blame people for their misfortunate in order to evade responsibility for creating and perpetuating a system of oppression, there are also those within the working class who echo their sentiments. Clearly these individuals have internalized the authoritarian and coercive mindset that keeps them obedient to the needs of those in power. Their anger, criticism and disgust are misplaced and should be directed at the ruling class who benefits from this system of oppression and degradation. They have sharp words of "personal responsibility" for working people, yet no calls for accountability of Wall Street criminality and general belligerence of the ruling class. The victim-blamers never stop to ask themselves why there is no space in our economy for people to express their passions and talents; or why every person must adapt to the needs of the system - isn't the system supposed to work for us, the people? But, of course, it is much easier to blame the victims than to confront our own powerlessness.

Limited, Predetermined Choices

Our every decision depends on the system's approval, and we forego many of our wishes, desires, hopes, and dreams because we have to labor to survive. This is simply a sophisticated and updated version of slavery that has most people serving the interests of the powerful with minimal benefits to themselves. And make no mistake about it - the ruling class - if they could get away with it - would make all of us work for free. They are certainly not above slavery, as the history of African Americans and today's corporate exploitation of farmworkers, temp workers, prisoners, and millions of sweatshop laborers around the world clearly shows. We are only putting up with this system because we have no other choice; we are blackmailed and rendered passive because our survival depends on our servitude to the interests of a ruthless authoritarian structure. No one in their right mind would willingly choose this type of existence because it goes against every natural human instinct that pushes against oppression and yearns for self-expression and creativity.

We cannot even choose our own education because we have to look to the system to determine which majors will land us a job or make us a lot of money. Knowledge and education have been commodified, stripped of their inherent value, and turned into assembly-line products to be bought and sold on the market. We have lost the most basic and personal freedoms to determine how we wish to cultivate our lives - it is all about the system and how we can be used to serve its needs. This type of thinking is so deeply ingrained into our psyche that most people do not even realize that this is how they approach life. Living our passions and having autonomy should not be a privilege - we all deserve the opportunity to express our talents, not just the lucky (mostly privileged) few. Anything less than that is psychological and spiritual suicide.

The issue of freedom boils down to autonomy - the dignity of self-determination which recognizes that we as human beings are more than just commodities to be used and exploited for the benefit of the few; to exercise our inherent rights as living beings to make decisions about our own lives without facing catastrophic consequences from a system created by those in power who benefit from our oppression. So the next time you hear the word "freedom," ask yourself: do I have the autonomy to direct my life as I wish, to pursue my passions, interests, and desires without facing the consequences of starvation, homelessness or alienation? Am I free to do as I wish (without harming anyone) or am I dependent and beholden to a greater force and power than myself - one that makes those fundamental decisions for me? Do I have *real* choices in my life or only the superficial "choice" of Pepsi or Coke, Democrat or Republican, CNN or Fox News? In other words, do our choices have *substance* or is it just the same shit in a different package?

Notes

[1] Because the word "freedom" conveys nothing, individuals (and governments) can conceal the true nature of their ideas and actions behind such ambiguous words, while allowing their audience to fill in the missing definition. For instance, when politicians speak of a *free* economy (or economic *freedom*), what they really mean is an economy free to exploit workers and the environment without any regulation, rules, or oversight of corporations; however, many individuals interpret economic *freedom* to mean the right to work, decent wages, or better opportunities to start small businesses. Clearly, there is a disconnect between the politician's meaning of the word and its interpretation by the audience.

[2] Even the rights we think we have are vanishing before our eyes: as a result of mass surveillance, the right to privacy no longer exists; our votes have become meaningless because regardless of who we vote for, Wall Street and the military industrial complex always win; many of us

cannot even walk around freely without being harassed in the age of codified racial profiling under "Stop and Frisk"; and of course the "chilling" effect on free speech resulting from unprecedented persecutions of journalists and whistleblowers by an establishment so afraid of the truth that it jails those who expose corruption and war crimes.

[3] $820 (monthly mortgage) x 12 months x 24 years = $236,160. This sum does not include fees and penalties the Neumanns paid over the years when they fell behind on their mortgage.

[4] Some critics argue that even these figures are too low because the standards for calculating the poverty line have not been updated since the 1960s. If the measures had kept pace with living standards over the years, today the poverty threshold would be $34,000 for a family of four instead of the $25,222 in the more "updated" version under the Poverty Supplemental Measure.http://www.cepr.net/index.php/blogs/cepr-blog/raising-minimum-wage-to-9-not-enough-to-ensure-that-families-with-fulltime-workers-live-above-poverty-line

More on the Sociology of Development

Towards a Re-articulation of Dependency Theory

David Fields

The sociology of development as a field of study, a structure of knowledge, providing an interpretive grid through which to render impoverished regions of the world intelligible has its roots after the completion of Second World War with the crystallization of 'Modernization theory', which constituted an ideation that societies are understood to move from social positions of tradition to modernity polar ends of an evolutionary continuum. At some point, incremental changes give way to a qualitative jump into modernity, marked by the essence of industrialism. In this sense, the Third world is perceived to be below the threshold of modernity, with a preponderance of traditional-like features such as an extended kinship social structure and, due to the lack of progress towards political differentiations, similar to that of Western forms of democratization, strict hierarchical sources of authority, altogether negating the possibilities to move beyond disintegrated autarkic primary economic activities (Parsons, 1964).

The development of a high extent of differentiation: the development of free resources which are not committed to any fixed, ascriptive groups; the development of wide non-traditional, "national," or even super-national group identifications; and the concomitant development, in all major institutional spheres, of specialized roles and of special wider regulative or allocative mechanisms and organization, such as market mechanisms in economic life, voting and party activities in politics, and diverse bureaucratic organizations and mechanisms in most institutional spheres (Eisenstadt (1973: 23).

According to Rostow (1960), all societies can be placed along a linear continuum from undeveloped to developed along a 'stages of economic growth' path, derived from an extensive study of Western economic development. In 'traditional society', the first stage, it is deemed that economic output is limited because of inaccessibility to innovative technology. At the second stage, 'the preconditions for take-off, modern science, attributed to "Western Europe of the late seventeenth and early eighteenth centuries" (Rostow, 1960, p. 6) ensues new innovations in production in agriculture and industry, fostering widespread education, entrepreneurship, and institutions capable of mobilizing industrial capital; capitalistic investments increase, especially in transport, communication and raw materials. Nevertheless, despite the development of some modern manufacturing, traditional social structures and production techniques remain:

In many cases, for example, the traditional society persisted side by side with modern economic activities, conducted for limited economic purposes by a colonial or quasi-colonial power (Rostow, 1960, p.7)

Rostow's third stage is 'the Take-off', in which traditional barriers to economic growth, like the effect of a dual economy, are overcome. At this point, capital investment increases rapidly and new industries expand exponentially, as does an 'entrepreneurial class'-economic growth becomes a normal condition" (Rostow, 1960, p. 36). At the fourth stage, 'the Drive to Maturity', technology becomes more complex and what produced is now less a matter of economic necessity, and more a question of consumer choice. This leads to the final fifth stage of high consumption, in which economic sectors specialize in the manufacturing of highly sought after consumer durables and basic life needs are mutually satisfied. In a play on Marx, Rostow's analysis suggests that the West, which "is more developed industrially only shows, to the less developed, the image of its own future' (Marx, 1954,

p. 19). The assumption is that capitalism is a historically progressive system, which is transmitted from the privileged economically advanced countries to the rest of the world by a continual process of destruction and replacement of pre-capitalist social structures (Palma, 1978).

The problem with modernization theory is that it is quite ahistorical, with respect to the global capitalist exploitation. 'Modernization' theory can, and has been, be interpreted as a 'blame the victim' approach to problems affecting the 'Third World'. Rostow ignores the external influences like colonialism that contributed to social in the Third World. Rostow's, and for most of 'modernization' theory, the unit of analysis is the nation-state of the 'Third World', emphasizing internal dynamics, sectors and sub-sectors, combined with the causal role of technology. As such, conclusions drawn from this approach are that all nations, regardless of the history of imperialism, colonialism, etc., should be able to modernize with emulation of more developed economies and their diffusing of highly advanced technology.

Paul Baran and Paul Sweezy, in Monopoly Capital (1960), building on the path-breaking work of Michel Kalecki and Joseph Steindl, assess the degree to which monopoly, as measured by the market concentration ratio of large capitalist firms (corporations) in economically advanced countries, ensues an inverse of Marx's famous hypothesis that the 'laws of motion' of capitalist development in produces a 'tendency for the surplus to fall. Rather, the economic surplus, defined as the gap, at any given level of economic activity-effective demand in Keynesian terminology-, between what is produced and the socially necessary costs of producing it, under monopoly capitalism has a tendency to rise (Baran & Sweezy,1966, pp. 9, 52-57).

Since aggregate levels of effective demand for total output determine the level of economic activity, crises of capital accumulation are inevitable if the monopoly sector cannot sustain its power via sufficient investment opportunities to absorb its accumulating share of the total surplus produced. Rather than let this insufficiency put downward pressures on potential profits as a whole, various stabilizing factors are set in motion, which include classical Keynesian government deficit spending, research & development (although risky without reliable forecasts potential spillover effects), waste (as evidenced by a sales effort, i.e. consumerism), or imperialism-the last of which provides the foundations for the dependency theoretical approach to economic development.

In this sense, for an understanding of the fundamental division between economically advanced countries and impoverished ones, it is requisite to place attention to the extent to which foreign investment acts as an outlet for investment-seeking surplus generation. Unlike Lenin's theory of imperialism, foreign investment is a method of extracting wealth, not a channel through which surplus is directed, ensuing underdevelopment (Baran & Sweezy, pp. 104-105). Underdevelopment is, thus, a process by which monopoly capital in economically advanced nations exploit economically weaker countries by exporting capital to the extent that profits produced (from the production of cheaper consumer goods or raw materials via lower wages in these countries, for example) are repatriated. It is the process by which the expropriation of "foreign sources of supply and foreign markets, ena[ble] [the agents of] monopoly capital to buy and sell on specially privileged terms" (Baran & Sweezy 1966, p. 201), ensuring, caeteris paribus, their positions of power in the world are sustained. The result is that economically weaker countries suffer the retardation of the requisite forces to spawn autonomous and dynamic process of self-governance of the conditions that constitute independent social/political/economic coordination, planning and control.

The argument is that (Baran & Sweezy, pp. 9,178-179) monopoly capitalism is tantamount to the degree to which large capitalist firms in economically advanced countries have as their counterpart the "exploitation of much of the rest of the world" and, as a result, constitute international relations as a "hierarchical system with one or more leading metropolises, completely dependent colonies [even if not name, certainly in practice] at the bottom, and many degrees of superordinate and subordination in between [...] [t]hese features are of crucial importance to the functioning of both the system as a whole and its individual components [...] (Baran & Sweezy, 1966, pp. 178-179). As such, "we cannot hope to formulate adequate development theory and policy for the majority of the world's population who suffer from [impoverishment] without first learning how their past economic and social history gave rise to their present underdevelopment" (Frank, [1966] 1969). Underdevelopment is neither an original nor traditional social position. Hence, it cannot be assumed that the contemporary position of the Third World can be understood as solely a reflection of its internal historically specific social, political, economic, and organizational characteristics. The process by which monopoly capital in economic advanced countries extract surplus from less-developed countries through capital exports limits the latter's ability to achieve the status of the former. Thus, 'modernization theory' is utterly unsatisfactory, for such an approach

[...] in all its variations, ignores the historical and structural reality of the underdeveloped countries. This reality is the product of the very same historical process and systemic structure as is the development of the now developed countries' (Frank 1969, p. 47).

To suggest that social, political, and economic advancement of the underdeveloped world can be generated by the diffusion of what is deemed modernizing institutions, values, etc. is fundamentally erroneous. If development fails to occur, it is not because within the Third World there are mere obstacles to diffusion because of innate poverty arising from some form Gerschenkronian 'backwardness', but due to the net outflow of vital resources, whether natural, monetary, human, technological etc. The implication is that underdevelopment is not because of the "the survival of archaic institutions", or some inability to contract some 'modern man' (Inkles, 1969) syndrome; on the contrary, it is generated by the same capitalist development that led to the domination by economic advanced countries, that is, "the development of capitalism itself" (Frank, [1966] 1969). Capitalism, hence, is an operation that cements a peripheral latifundium system, via the constant forces of 'primitive-accumulation', what Myrdal (1957) defined as international 'backwash' effects, that reproduces a cleavage between 'town and country', centre and periphery, on a tremendously enlarged basis (cf. Bukharin & Lenin, 1929).

Viewed from this standpoint, dependency theory is a manifestation of what David Harvey (1978, 2007) defines as 'accumulation by dispossession' by virtue of which dialectical forces of motion and contradiction generate vast disparities of wealth and power on a worldwide scale. The world economy is reproduced as a world-system (Wallerstein, 1979) of 'unequal exchange' (Emmanuel, 1972; Amin 1974, 1976), in which 'underdevelopment' ensues peripheral internal long-run stagnation (Bornschier & Chase-Dunn, 1985, pp. 39-40). The terms of trade for the periphery fall precipitously - this is the Prebisch-Singer hypothesis (Prebisch 1950). As Samir Amin (1976, p. 292) notes, "whereas at the center growth means development, making the economy more integral, in the periphery growth does not mean more development, for it dis-articulates the economy. Since the imbalance of international trade defines the mechanisms by which capital is drained from former colonized countries, there is no way for peripheral

428

countries in the world economy to 'catch up' in Rostowian fashion (p. 383).

Nevertheless, the social facts that constitute the particular social conditions for the constant negation of a 'just price' in international trade 'admits of varying interpretation' (Frank, 1977). Case in point is the extent to which the periphery is in fact 'peripheralized'. To suggest that the capitalist world economy simply, by definition, produces a centre-periphery polarity (Frank, 1967; Wallerstein, 1974), is to pay insufficient attention to understanding the extent to which economic development in the periphery is a convoluted association of varying social processes, rather than the mere result of a state's homogenized world-systemic position (Gellert, 2010).

According to Cardoso and Faletto ([1967] 1970), for instance, development in the periphery, while controlling for socioeconomic income differentials, is likely if foreign capital penetration creates spillover effects. That is, partial economic growth is viable through what Peter Evans (1995) describes as the practice of an 'embedded autonomy'-an apparent solidified social network between the state and civil society (which consists of economic elites from the centre) that creates the capacity for the state, as such, to engage in domestic Keynesian aggregate demand management. Whether this is manifested is the extent to which a peripheral country does not suffer the inability to borrow in its own currency, in which a country, most likely a developing one, supplements its domestic unit account of fiduciary reserve assets with a foreign currency. This is the exemplification of a country foregoing its national 'monetary sovereignty' (Mundell, 1961).

The essence of national 'monetary sovereignty' is the cartelist (or chartelist) (Goodhart, 1998) conception that emphasizes state power to establish a particular unit of account, a national currency, which allows economic calculations to take place (Ingham, 2004). In this sense, money is a means for accounting for and settling of financial debts, the most important of which are tax debts, which, in turn, regulate the level of aggregate demand, and thus determination of national income through the use of fiscal policy; it represents a [store of financial value] [...] [of which] general purchasing power is held [...] (Keynes, 1930, p. 3).

In the United States, for example, and in contrast to James O'Connor ([1973] 2002) and Erik Olin Wright's (1979) fiscal sociological model for analyzing the intricacies of public finance, which narrowly centers on a hypothetical natural limit to fiscal policy (Wright 1979, p.157), the federal government, through open-market operations, sells government bonds, Treasury securities, which are either bought or foregone by the Federal Reserve (Fed). If the Fed commits to a policy of purchasing Treasury securities, the interest rate by which the Federal government is liable on Treasury securities held by the Fed is lowered. Symmetrically, if the Fed sells Treasury securities, the Federal Government's interest burden, which is paid through taxes denominated in dollars, is raised. By providing a guarantee for State debt, the Fed delivers the capability for the federal government to use fiscal policy to regulate aggregate demand. Thus, the extent to which fiscal policy is an option is determined by the burden of the federal government's interest payments on Treasury securities to the Fed (cf. Lerner, 1943; Domar, 1944).

From this perspective, 'underdevelopment', or 'dependency', is the powerlessness a peripheral country to establish its own unit of account and thus is forced to variably peg its national currency to a foreign reference currency. What ensues is the inability to use monetary policy-central bank purchasing and selling of government bonds denominated in the domestic currency for purposes of controlling the money supply, and thus the cost of credit-, and fiscal policy, via deficit spending, for domestic economic needs. Since the central bank is forced to maintain a certain level reserves of the foreign reference currency such that the price of the domestic currency, in terms of the reference currency, does not change, this produces a negative money-multiplier that sets in motion an inherent deflationary bias, which, if not counteracted by capital inflows to spur aggregate demand, can lead to abrupt contraction of the monetary base, stinting any supposed progress towards economic sustainability (cf. Fields & Vernengo, 2012, 2013).

Thus, if any form of government spending is to be engaged, an 'underdeveloped' country has to issue bonds that are not denominated in its own currency. This amounts to the attraction of external commercial loans with the faith of the country's financial markets by foreign investors used as collateral. As such, country risk is most likely going to exist. If confidence is lost in the strength of the country's financial markets, leading to a spread over bonds like US treasury securities, if the foreign reference currency is the dollar, for example, interest rates on domestic foreign currency denominated bonds are likely to rise, making government spending very costly, which removes any form of domestic capacity to spur public investment as an effective countercyclical policy in the face of economic downturns. This has been essentially the case of Argentina before the 2001-2002 crisis, and of the

European periphery since the intensification of the Greek crisis in 2011.

Balance of payments constraints can be quite unsupportable, spawning self-fulfilling financial collapses. Moreover, they altogether constitute an ideological mask that normalizes the advance of global cosmopolitan money-capitalist power to dictate the terms of domestic democratic politics (Ingham, 2008). As such, the extent to which a country is 'peripheralized', is the degree to which its creditworthiness is essentially evaluated in terms of the degree to which the state takes steps toward lowering the social wage for the benefit of multinational corporations from the centre (or core).

Works Cited

Amin, Samir. 1972. "Underdevelopment and dependence in black Africa: Historical origin." Journal of Peace Research 9(2): 105-119.

Amin, Samir. 1974. "Accumulation and development: a theoretical model." Review of African Political Economy 1(1): 9-26.

Amin, Samir. 1976. Unequal Exchange. Brighton, UK: Harvester.

Baran, Paul and Paul Sweezy. 1966. Monopoly Capital: An Essay on the American Economic and Social Order. New York: Monthly Review Press

Block, Fred. 1981. "The Fiscal Crisis of the Capitalist State." Annual Review of Sociology 7:1-27

Bomschier, Volker, and Christopher K. Chase-Dunn. 1985. Transnational Corporations and Underdevelopment. New York: Praeger

Bukharin, Nikolaï, and Vladimir Il'itx Lenin. 1929. Imperialism and world economy. Vol. 4. New York: International Publishers

Cameron, Angus. 2008. "Crisis? What Crisis? Displacing the Spatial Imaginary of the Fiscal State." Geoforum 39: 1145-1154

Campbell, John L. 1993. "The State and Fiscal Sociology." Annual Review of Sociology 19: 163-185

Cardoso, Fernando H., and Enzo Faletto. 1967[1970]. Dependência e desenvolvimento na América Latina. Rio de Janeiro: Zahar.

Cox, Kevin R. 2004. "Globalization and the Politics of Local and Regional Development: The Question of Convergence." Transactions of the Institute of British Geographers 29: 170-194

Devine, Joel A. 1983. "Fiscal Policy and Class Income Inequality: The Distributional Consequences of Governmental Revenues and

Expenditures in the United States, 1949-1976." American Sociological Review 48(5): 606-622

Domar, Evsey D. 1944. "The burden of the debt and the national income." The American Economic Review 34(4): 798-827.

Dymski, Garry A. 1990. "Money and Credit in Radical Political Economy: A Survey of Contemporary Perspectives." Review of Radical Political Economics 22(2-3):38-65

Dymski, Gary A. 2005. "Poverty and Social Discrimination: A Spatial Keynesian Approach." Pp. 230-250 in Reimagining Growth: Towards a Renewal of Development Theory, edited by Silvana De Paula and Gary A. Dymski. New York: Zed Books.

Ebner, Alexander. 2006. "Institutions, Entrepreneurship, and the Rational of Government: An Outline of the Schumpeterian Theory of the State." Journal of Economic Behavior & Organization 59: 497-515.

Eisenstadt, Shmuel N. 1973. Traditional Patrimonialism and Modern Neopatrimonialism. Beverly Hills: Sage Publications

Fields, David, and Matías Vernengo. 2012. "Hegemonic Currencies during the Crisis: The Dollar versus the Euro in a Cartelist Perspective." Review of International Political Economy

Fields, David, and Matías Vernengo. 2013. "Dollarization." Wiley-Blackwell Online Encyclopedia of Globalization.

Emmanuel, Arghiri. 1972. Unequal Exchange: An Essay on the Imperialism of Trade. New York: Monthly Review Press

Evans, Peter. 1995. Embedded Autonomy: States and Industrial Transformation. Princeton: Princeton University Press.

Flacks, Richard and Gerald Turkel. 1978. "Radical Sociology: The Emergence of Neo-Marxian Perspectives in US Sociology." Annual Review of Sociology 4: 193-238

Frank, Andre Gunder. 1966. The development of underdevelopment. Boston: New England Free Press

Frank, Andre Gunder. 1969 "The Development of Underdevelopment." Monthly Review

Frank, André Gunder. 1977. "Long Live trans-ideological enterprise! The Socialist Economies in The Capitalist International Division of Labor." Review (Fernand Braudel Center): 91-140.

Gellert, Paul K. 2010. "Extractive regimes: toward a better understanding of Indonesian development." Rural Sociology 75(1): 28-57.

Goodhart, Charles. 1998. "The Two Concepts of Money." European Journal of Political Economy, 14(3): 407-432

Harvey, David. 1978. "The Urban Process under Capitalism: A Framework for Analysis." International Journal of Urban and Regional Research 2(1-4): 101-131

Harvey, David. 2007. "Neoliberalism as creative destruction." The Annals of The American Academy of Political and Social Science 610(1): 21-44

Ingham, Geoffrey. 1984. Capitalism Divided? London: Macmillan.

Ingham, Geoffrey. 1996a. "Money is a Social Relation." Review of Social Economy 54(4): 507-529

Ingham, Geoffrey. 1996b. "Some Recent Changes in the Relationship Between Economics and Sociology." Cambridge Journal of Economics 20: 243-275

Ingham, Geoffrey. 1998. "On the Underdevelopment of the 'Sociology of Money'." Acta Sociologica 41(10): 3-18

Ingham, Geoffrey. 1999. "Capitalism, Money, and Banking: A Critique of Recent Historical Sociology." British Journal of Sociology 50(1): 76-96

Ingham, Geoffrey. 2000. "Class Inequality and The Social Production of Money." in Renewing Class Analysis, edited by Rosemary Crompton, Fiona Devine, Mike Savage, and John Scott. Oxford: Blackwell Publishers.

Ingham, Geoffrey. 2003. "Schumpeter and Weber on the Institutions of Capitalism: Solving Swedberg's 'Puzzle'." Journal of Classical Sociology 3: 297-311

Ingham, Geoffrey. 2004. The Nature of Money. Cambridge UK: Polity Press

Inkles, Alex. 1969. "Making Men Modern: On the Causes and Consequences of Individual Change in Six Dveloping Countries." American Journal of Sociology 75(1): 208-224

Keynes, John Maynard. 1930. A Treatise on Money: Vol. 1. London: Macmillan

Lerner, Abba P. 1943. "Functional Finance and the Federal Debt." Social Research 10(1): 38-51

Marx, Karl. 1954. Capital, Vol. 1. Moscow: Progress Publishers

Mundell, Robert A. 1961. "A Theory of Optimum Currency Areas." American Economic Review 51(4): 657-665

Myrdal, Gunnar. 1957. Economic theory and underdeveloped countries. London: Duckworth

O'Connor, James. 2002. The Fiscal Crisis of the State. New Brunswick, NJ: Transaction Publishers.

Palma, Gabriel. 1978. "Dependency: a formal theory of

underdevelopment or a methodology for the analysis of concrete situations of underdevelopment?" World Development 6(7): 881-924.

Parsons, Talcott. 1964. "Evolutionary Universals in Society." American Sociological Review 29(1)3: 339-357

Prebisch, Raul. 1950. "El Desarrollo Económico de la América Latina y sus principales problemas." Revista de Economía Argentina 48(379-380): 17-24.

Rostow, Walt Whitman. 1960. The stages of economic growth: A non-communist manifesto. London: Cambridge University Press.

Smart, Barry. 2012. "Fiscal Crisis and Creative Destruction: Critical Reflections on Schumpeter's Contemporary Relevance." Journal of Classical Sociology 12(3-4): 526-543

Wallerstein, Immanuel. 1979. The capitalist world-economy. Vol. 2. London: Cambridge University Press,

Wright, Erik Olin. 1979. Class, crisis and the state. London: Verso

Vernengo, Matias. 2006."Technology, finance, and dependency: Latin American radical political economy in retrospect." Review of Radical Political Economics 38(4): 551-568.

Calibrating the Capitalist State in the Neoliberal Era

Equilibrium, Superstructure, and the Pull Towards a Corporate-Fascistic Model

Colin Jenkins

Since the capitalist formation of relations between what is perceived as the 'public sector' and the 'private sector,' traditional nation-states and their governing bodies have played a major role as facilitators of the economic system at-large. This became a necessary supplemental component as localized economies, which were dominated by agrarian/plantation life, gave way to industrialization and subsequent mass migration into urban centers, thus introducing new industrial economies based in the manufacturing/production process. With the advent of wage labor came predictable outcomes of "capital accumulation" and a perpetually increasing polarization between the "owning class" and "working class." And with this growing inequality came the notions of worker collectivization and unionism which, absent any equalizing measures taken by the State, were the only sources of hope for workers who quickly found themselves, their livelihood, and their family's well-being at the mercy of a rapidly fluctuating and exploitative labor market. Work was often hard to come by and,when it was available, the wages "earned" were barely enough to cover basic necessities like food, clothing and shelter - provisions which had long been commodified to create expanding avenues of profit for the "owning class."

The inherent instabilities created by this economic system - a system that exists for the sole purpose of creating or maintaining individual/personal wealth (as opposed to preserving collective/societal wealth) - require components that act solely as stabilizers. Despite its shunning, the existence of*society* - or "the aggregate of people living together in a more or less ordered community" - not only remains, but actually serves as the casing for which this system must rely on, or more aptly, *capitalize*from within. And because of this reliance, the instabilities and contradictions that simultaneously represent natural byproducts and threats become common growths as the result of a counterintuitive and inhumane arrangement, and must be kept in check through a delicate (though not necessarily intricate) balancing act.

In order to "balance" competing interests - in this case the "dominant" and "dominated" classes - the political sphere, a major element of the State apparatus, assumes a vital role. As such, Nicos Poulantzas, building upon earlier theoretical contributions from the likes of Antonio Gramsci, details the dynamic process whereas the state serves as a facilitator to the *unstable equilibrium* that is produced by the internally antagonistic capitalist system. Ultimately, through this act of facilitating, the state (by deploying its political power) negotiates a perpetual series of "compromises" in the form of economic "sacrifices" which are accepted as a necessity by the dominant classes; and which are precisely aimed at creating a *limited* equilibrium that ensures a minimal degree of social stability (maintained by the political superstructure) atop the inherently asymmetrical economic base.

Poulantzas explains:

"...political power is thus apparently founded on an unstable equilibrium of compromise. These terms should be understood as follows:
1) Compromise: in the sense that this power corresponds to a hegemonic class domination and can take into account the economic interests of certain dominated classes even where those could be contrary to the short-term economic interests of the dominant classes, without this affecting the configuration of political interests;
2) Equilibrium: in the sense that while these economic 'sacrifices' are real and so provide the ground for an equilibrium, they do not as such

*challenge the political power which sets precise limits to this equilibrium; and 3) **Unstable**: in the sense that these limits of the equilibrium are set by the political conjuncture."* [1]

Gramsci tells us, "The life of the state is conceived of as a continuous process of formation and superseding of unstable equilibria… between the interests of the fundamental group and those of the subordinate groups - equilibria in which the interests of the dominant group prevail, but only up to a certain point, i.e. stopping short of narrowly corporate interest."[2] In other words, as the capitalist system naturally bends toward a corporate-fascistic state of being through the simultaneous developments of capital accumulation and mass alienation - thus forming structures of domination that extend from the economic base and into the political, social, and cultural realms - there develops a need to stabilize the fragile nature (in the sense that such imbalance is a constant threat to the societal structure at-large) of this system.

The need to maintain this equilibrium exists as long as a wholly functioning society is requisite for capitalist expansion - or, as long as worker-consumers represent viable targets of exploitation. In *Political Powers and Social Classes*, Poulantzas identifies certain measures that represent embedded concessions on the part of the owning class, carried out by the state apparatus through a systematic process that is relatively fluid and effortless (though, as Poulantzas points out, competing interests exist even within this elite bureaucracy). In recognizing the function of the state and its role atop the capitalist formation of relations, Poulantzas explains, "The notion of the general interest of the 'people', an ideological notion covering an institutional operation of the capitalist state, expresses a *real fact*: namely that this state, by its very structure, gives to the economic interests of certain dominated classes guarantees which may even be contrary to the short-term economic interests of the dominant classes, but which are compatible with their political interests and their hegemonic domination."[3]

Political systems based on grand "democratic" narratives like "representative democracy" and "republicanism," as well as Rousseau's "social contract," are ideal enablers for this societal arrangement. This is the very reason why liberalism and the modern adaptation of the "liberal politician" play such a crucial role in their opposition to the proto-fascist nature of "conservatism." Their superficially adversarial relationship represents the ultimate stabilizer as its reach is limited to the confines of the political superstructure. And, because it deals primarily with "social issues" (including passive measures of economic redistribution), it is ultimately relegated to directing the aforementioned "compromises" of the dominant class. It does not and can not transform the economic base (the capitalist hierarchy) as these compromises, while representing "real economic sacrifices" that are necessary to provide the ground for equilibrium, "do not as such challenge the political power which sets precise limits to this equilibrium."

"Democratic" systems which involve periodic elections of "representatives" to "public" office accomplish two important tasks in this regard. First, they create a façade of civil empowerment - a form of political compromise which gives the dominated classes the appearance of choice vis-a-vis universal suffrage. Second, they create a political sphere that, while completely fused with the long-term interests of the dominant classes (through its sole purpose as a facilitator), operates as a separate entity existing outside the economic base - a separation that is, as Poulantzas explains, both an exclusive and necessary element to the capitalist system. It reminds us of John Dewey's claim that, "As long as politics is the shadow cast on society by big business, the attenuation of the shadow will not change the substance." In the US, the two-party political system has proven extremely effective in this regard. Aside from differences on social issues like abortion and gay marriage, as well as socioeconomic issues like unemployment insurance and public assistance, both parties ultimately embrace capitalist/corporatist interests in that they both serve as facilitators for the dominant classes: The Republican Party in its role as *forerunner*, pushing the limits of the capitalist model to the brink of fascism; and the Democratic Party in its role as *governor*, providing intermittent degrees of slack and pull against this inevitable move towards a "corporate-fascistic state of being."

The distinction made between 'the political' and 'the economic' is important to consider, though these boundaries have seemingly blurred in the age of neoliberalism and the intensification of the merger between "public" and "private." And while Poulantzas insists this separation is inherent and theoretically unbreakable, he (along with Gramsci) may have underestimated the extent to which compromises may be reined in without destabilizing the equilibrium beyond repair. During the neoliberal era, there have been many developments which have pushed this long-standing balance to the verge of "narrow corporatism" and beyond, including factors related to technology and government surveillance, growth in the banking industry, the development of corporate media and intricate propaganda, financialization's role in supplementing monopoly capitalism, and the maturation of the international economic system and all of its mediating components, to name a few; but that discussion is for another place and time.

For the purpose of this analysis, we are focused on national electoral politics and political parties, and the specific role they play in maintaining the status quo - in this case, not only the capitalist hierarchy, but also the stage of monopoly capitalism which has come to fruition over the past few decades. The distinction between base and superstructure allows us to see how the political apparatus, through the actions of political parties, exists solely as a tool for the "power bloc." Furthermore, it allows us to divert from reductionist theories which attempt to highlight a singular cause, and move towards a more nuanced critique of the capitalist state, especially in the "pluralist" form that we see in the US and other "western democracies."

"As far as the terrain of political domination is concerned, this is also occupied not by one single class or class fraction, but by several dominant classes and fractions," explains Poulantzas. "These classes and fractions form a specific alliance on this terrain, the power bloc, generally functioning under the leadership of one of the dominant classes or fractions, the hegemonic class or fraction."[4] In this instance, even with a government that includes separate branches - legislative, executive, and judicial - and represents several interests, as in Robert A. Dahl's "polyarchy," the state still exists and operates on the foundation of a capitalist system that creates its own hierarchy. The members of this "political terrain" are not necessarily synchronized with one another when it comes to geography, special interests, localized interests, and priorities when maintaining the equilibrium, and they don't have to be. Despite these various pieces which make up the power bloc, in its own formation the base forces the political "superstructure" to adjust accordingly. This is why modern practices like "blanket financing" of political campaigns, which consists of corporations or private interests providing monetary support to opposing candidates and political parties in a particular election, have become so prevelant. Politicians, despite what their personal beliefs or aspirations may be, are put into power by the very hierarchy that depends on the economic base. Their positions of power cater to and are reliant on not only the power bloc which put them there, but the maintenance of the very system that allows them to stay there. Therefore, while they may possess some leeway in terms of pushing superficial agendas, their ability to do so is granted by the hierarchy extending from the economic base. Ultimately, in order to maintain its own existence, the political apparatus must protect the base - and is essentially designed (or is ever-evolving) to do so despite its "relative autonomy" which is "inscribed in the very structure of the capitalist state."

According to Poulantzas, by recognizing both the autonomy of the "state machine" as well as the existence of a "power bloc" which mimics society's pluralist form, it will "enable us to establish theoretically, and to examine concretely, the way in which the relative autonomy of the capitalist state develops and functions with respect to the particular economic-corporate interests of this or that fraction of the power bloc, in such a way that the state always guards the general political interests of this bloc - which certainly does not occur merely as a result of the state's and the bureaucracy's own *rationalizing will*."[5] This understanding includes "firmly grasping the fact than an institution (the state) that is destined to reproduce class divisions cannot really be a monolithic, fissureless bloc, but is itself, by virtue of its very structure (the state is a relation), divided."[6] Poulantzas continues:

The various organs and branches of the state (ministries and government offices, executive and parliament, central administration and local and regional authorities, army, judiciary, etc.) reveal major contradictions among themselves, each of them frequently constituting the seat and the representative - in short, the crystallization - of this or that fraction of the power bloc, this or that specific and competing interest. In this context, the process by whereby the general political interest of the power bloc is established, and whereby the state intervenes to ensure the reproduction of the overall system, may well, at a certain level, appear chaotic and contradictory, as a 'resultant' of these inter-organ and inter-branch contradictions.[7]

This "division," and these "contradictions," were never more evident than with President Dwight Eisenhower's 1961 farewell address and sobering warning against the rising "military industrial complex," which publicly displayed a major fission within the power bloc. According to Poulantzas, this splitting is irrelevant in the capitalist scheme of things because it remains, by design, autonomous from the base; and, therefore, will naturally work itself out to accommodate that base, whether through conscious coordination or through inherent process. In the age of neoliberalism and monopoly capitalism, the state has become highly concentrated out of necessity. In this sense, C. Wright Mills' assessment rings true:

As each of these domains becomes enlarged and centralized, the consequences of its activities become greater, and its traffic with the others increases. The decisions of a handful of corporations bear upon military and political as well as upon economic developments around the world. The decisions of the military establishment rest upon and grievously affect political life as well as the very level of economic activity. The decisions made within the political domain determine economic activities and military programs. There is no longer, on the one hand, an economy, and, on the other hand, a political order containing a military establishment unimportant to politics and to money-making. There is a political economy linked, in a thousand ways, with military institutions and decisions. [8]

This intertwined political economy exists within the superstructure. It's increased centralization, coordination, and synchronization over the past half-century has undoubtedly pushed the US government to the brink of a "corporate-fascistic state of being." In this development, the equilibrium has never been more delicate and fragile. The two-party system, thriving from the pluralist nature of both the electorate and power bloc, has proven efficient in carrying out trivial "concessions" that give "the economic interests of certain dominated classes guarantees which may even be contrary to the short-term economic interests of the dominant classes, but which are compatible with their political interests and their hegemonic domination."[9] The expansion of domestic militarization and the intensification of "austerity measures" have introduced a degree of "corporate-fascistic" torque unseen before from within a mature capitalist state. How far these embedded "compromises may be reined in without destabilizing the equilibrium beyond repair" remains to be seen.

References

[1] Poulantzas, Nicos (Timothy O'Hagan translating). Political Power and Social Classes. Verso, 1975, p. 192.

[2] Gramsci, Antonio. Prison Notebooks, p. 182.

[3] Poulantzas, Political Power and Social Classes, p. 191.

[4] Poulantzas, Nicos. Classes in Contemporary Capitalism (Translated from French version by David Fernbach). Verso, 1978, p. 93.

[5] The Poulantzas Reader: Marxism, Law and the State. Verso Books: London/New York, 2008, p. 284.

[6] Ibid, p. 285.

[7] Ibid, p. 285.

[8] C. Wright Mills. The Power Elite, New Edition. Oxford University Press: 2000, p. 76.

[9] Poulantzas, Political Power and Social Classes, p. 191

From Class to Privilege

A Post-Industrial Marxist Analysis

Colin Jenkins

Marx's analysis of developing 19th-century industrial economies represented a broad focus on society's division into two distinct camps: those who owned the means of production (Capital) and those whose livelihoods relied solely upon their wages earned (Labor). The inevitable confrontation between the owning class and the working class was the ultimate conclusion to Marx's revolutionary theory, and was predicated upon excessive capital accumulation for the capitalists as a result of the perpetual exploitation and alienation of the proletariat. The work of Marx and Engels has been validated not only by its widespread acceptance as a major ideological influence, but also by its seemingly never-ending relevance. However, as valuable as Marx's original work remains, and as important as it is to understand the painstakingly scientific approach that much of it was rooted in, it is also crucial to expand upon this school of thought. In other words, as times have changed, so shall the ways in which we apply this incredibly complex ideology onto real-world problems.

Since Marx's time, the capitalist system has experienced significant change through both its natural evolution (i.e. globalization) and a series of artificial interventions (i.e. the construction of a modern international financial system). In terms of Marxist philosophy, perhaps the most potentially damaging aspect of this change has come in the form of increased ambiguity regarding the structure of class. In other words, while class antagonisms have seemingly intensified, they have also expanded and morphed into a structure that presents complexities which can no longer be simplified through a mere "dual class war" analysis. The bottom line is this: The evolution of capitalism, the development of the "modern international financial system," and the subsequent arrival of post-industrialization and financialization have prompted a restructuring of the class hierarchy, especially within the international hotbed of the capitalist system – the former "western industrialized nations."

From a strict economic perspective, Marx's analysis focused on newly emerging economies which developed out of the protectionist nature of mercantilism, and that existed within a global "national" system which was predominately shaped by industrial manufacturing and agriculture. Today, the agro-industrial system which once characterized the "western" landscape has given way to a complex arrangement of technological and service-based economies, all of which are controlled by a global "international" system that has made traditional nationalist trade tactics such as protectionism nearly obsolete.

This capitalist evolution has directly affected the demographics of the working class in the former western industrialized bloc, once consisting mainly of farmers and industrial wage laborers, and now consisting of a wide range of low-wage service workers and salaried "professionals." It has also led to increased volatility within the class hierarchy, which has been caused by the creation of a substantial and multi-generational impoverished class along with the arrival of a newly formed "petite bourgeoisie" that has been heavily penetrated by parts of the former industrialized proletariat (at least temperamentally, if not economically). In addition to this identity crisis for the working class, the modern system has also spawned an uber-bourgeois class that can no longer be simply thrown into the pool of traditional "owners of the means of production," especially when considering both their roles as international economic players and their incredible influence over the political spectrum.

A major development within the United States during its WW2-era boom was the bourgeoization of the middle classes. Its formation, which was markedly homogenous (white, male, suburban) and largely due to imperialist endeavors abroad (including the Marshall Plan, which turned post-WW2 European reconstruction into US-based profit), led to a distinct break in the working class. This newly emerged American middle class differed from Marx's petite bourgeoisie in that, in terms of the fundamental capital-labor relationship, it existed solely on the spectrum of labor. As opposed to the strata described by Marx, the industrialized middle class does not (typically) possess the ability to "purchase the labor of others" and does not (typically) work for itself, like the "semi-autonomous peasantry and small-scale merchants" of the past.

Since its arrival in the 1940s, the American middle class, despite owing much of its birth to the battles fought by radical and progressive labor unions, has become controlled by an internal schism that has frequently led to widespread support of self-destructive economic agendas. This unconscious "self-loathing" has been made possible through an intensification of the pro-capitalist cultural hegemony, which often exploits deeper psychological insecurities such as racism, classism, jingoism and xenophobia. Simply stated, this bourgeoization is characterized by a middle class that has become "temperamentally conservative" at the expense of its own working-class interests, choosing the near-sighted nature of consumerism over the far-sighted nature of citizenship.

Common knowledge suggests that traditional political thought pits the left against the right. In Marx's time, the right would likely represent those who owned the means of production while the left would represent those within the working class; however, today, with the onset of an increasingly influential cultural hegemony as well as the development of a broad synthesis between the proletariat and petit bourgeoisie, this is no longer the case.

Because post-industrialization has led to increasingly blurred class divisions, it has become beneficial to examine modern societies and their respective economies in terms of privilege. When shifting Marxist perspective from its traditional focus on class antagonisms to a modern adaptation rooted in privilege, we may reasonably assume that, in the modern United States, the agenda of the left is to fight privilege and the agenda of the right is to protect privilege. Now, the question becomes, "How do we gauge an abstract concept like privilege?"

Within the context of historical materialism, the economic structure ultimately determines and shapes society. And, naturally, with capitalism, the economic structure develops in an asymmetrical manner that eventually becomes top-heavy; with the effects of such development creating massively unequal amounts of privilege, which ultimately exist as both a natural byproduct of this system (accumulation) and as a means to preserve the capitalist structure (maintaining through power and coercion). In Marx's time, privilege could more easily be recognized as existing solely within the bourgeoisie (with perhaps some minor exceptions), however, in modern times, with the restructuring of class, privilege presents itself in varying degrees throughout the top of the class hierarchy.

Therefore, from a post-industrial Marxist perspective that shifts traditional focus from class to privilege, we must first attempt to define and identify pockets of privilege. Next, we must ponder fundamental questions regarding privilege: Is privilege merely represented by generational wealth or are there other external factors that must be considered? What interest does society hold in protecting and/or redistributing privilege? How shall privilege be regulated and/or redistributed? Does the government's role consist of a perpetual intervention in "the affairs of the people" or is it simply enough to extract the existing hierarchy and lay a new foundation? This analysis does not pretend to cover every aspect of such a complex inquiry, and therefore, factors including generational wealth, white supremacy, estates rights and so forth will not be examined. Rather, this analysis intends solely to present a broad neo-Marxist alternative to traditional Marxist philosophies regarding class structure, class consciousness, cultural hegemony and proletariat activism – nothing more and nothing less. It is but a small section on the ideological bridge connecting 19th-century Marxism to 21st-century reality.

Post-Industrialization and the Emergence of a New Class Structure

Perhaps the most crucial step within any post-industrial Marxist analysis is to attempt to redefine Marx's two-class societal configuration, which no longer seems applicable. Since the emergence of a post-WW2 international economic system, the society's that boast the greatest degree of capitalist attributes (the former western industrialized bloc) have experienced a vast restructuring of their respective class hierarchies. In the example of the United States, we can see three major developments regarding this class structure: 1) the arrival of a distinct uber-bourgeoisie class; 2) a widespread bourgeoization of the middle classes; and 3) a separation between the working classes and the impoverished.

Developments that occurred within the political arena during the last quarter of the 20th century, most notably represented by a so-called "Conservative Revolution" and characterized by government deregulation as well as an oxymoronic public financial backing of the private sector, led to the development of an uber-bourgeoisie class in the United States. From 1978 until 2007, this exceptional class experienced economic growth that rivaled, and eventually surpassed, that of the Gilded Age. In real terms, the top 1 percent of the financial hierarchy, which accounted for roughly 9 percent of the U.S. Income Share (market income including capital gains) in 1978, now represents nearly 25 percent of the total income share; and the top .01 percent of the population (approximately 14,000 families), which accounted for 1 percent of the U.S. Income Share in 1978, now represents nearly 7 percent of the total income share. This highly concentrated growth, which outpaced traditional bourgeois growth (the top 10 percent) by nearly 800 percent, as well as "working class" growth by a rate of 45:1, allowed for the greatest degree of capital accumulation that has occurred since Adam Smith threw down his gauntlet in the path of mercantilism. The realization and inclusion of not only the arrival of the uber-bourgeoisie, but also the contrasts they present to the traditional bourgeoisie, is crucial for the continuation of Marxist philosophy.

The development of the uber-bourgeoisie paralleled an equally important enlargement within the petit bourgeoisie, which was intensely penetrated by the upper strata of the proletariat through the bourgeoization of the middle class. Peculiarly, this expansion of the petit bourgeoisie was not fueled by widespread economic growth within the middle class (which was actually stagnant throughout this period), but rather by a psychological transformation that redirected middle class angst towards the lower rungs of the socioeconomic hierarchy. This redirection of angst, along with an increasingly influential cultural hegemony rooted in consumerism and an overall political ideological shift to the right, has allowed for the creation of a class buffer. This buffer has been maintained through the widespread exploitation of ignorance that lies embedded in the shallow mentalities of racism, classism, xenophobia and nationalism – and has even spawned "successful" corporate news outlets like Fox News ("Rich people paying rich people to tell middle class people to blame poor people").

Through the artificial construction of "evil elements" that include ethnic minorities, foreigners, immigrants, "welfare queens," terrorists and criminals, the ruling classes have been able to redirect middle class angst that would otherwise target their own greedy, oligarchic interests. This misdirected anger that is embraced by many within the proletariat meshes with the mere presence of the petit bourgeoisie middle classes to allow for a distinct separation from the ever-distant bourgeoisie and virtually invisible uber-bourgeoisie. As long as the middle classes hold on to the false hopes of penetrating the bourgeoisie, they will ultimately be left admiring the bourgeoisie lifestyle from afar; and, most importantly, will continue to see (1) working-class (majority) agendas as detrimental to their self-interests, and (2) bourgeois and uber-bourgeois (elite minority) agendas as beneficial to their existence – a perception that is completely reversed from reality.

A third development that has paralleled the arrival of the uber-bourgeosie and the coordinated redirection of middle-class angst is the creation of multi-generational, First World impoverishment and a gradual separation between the working class and the impoverished. Much like the formation of the uber-bourgeoisie and its separation from the traditional bourgeoisie at the top of the economic hierarchy, the formation of the perpetually impoverished has created a similar partition at the bottom of the socioeconomic ladder – one that can no longer be ignored within any neo-Marxist analysis. This chronic disconnect between the traditional working class and the post-industrialized underemployed and unemployed has been manufactured in a similar fashion to that of the bourgeoization of the middle class in that it promotes the destruction of class-consciousness through the exploitation of shallow mentalities, therefore constructing a misdirection of working-class angst from the top (where it belongs) to the bottom.

Industrialized Class Divisions

Bourgeoisie (including Petit Bourgeoisie)

Proletariat

Post-Industrialized Class Divisions
Uber-Bourgeoisie
Bourgeoisie
Petit Bourgeoisie/Middle Class
Proletariat
Impoverished

From Class to Privilege

Considering the dynamics of post-industrialization, it has become just as important to consider privilege as it is to consider class, especially within the former industrialized bloc. Regardless of which Marxist sect is followed, the premise behind all such theory has always been rooted in class consciousness and collective action on the part of the oppressed – that action being the widespread transfer of the means of production from the hands of the ruling class minority to the working class majority. In contrast to the traditional focus on the "means of production," which was certainly relevant throughout the period of industrialization, a refocus onto "privilege" allows flexibility within the practical application of Marxist philosophy within the post-industrialized society, which, as stated before, poses unique challenges related to increased ambiguity of class divisions and an overall identity crisis within the working class. It also begins to address and fill the void of revolutionary, working-class environments - like shop floors, production lines, and factories - where workers were traditionally huddled together like cattle.

Because Marxism is based on the goal of redistributing illegitimate control (theoretically, all wealth and power is illegitimate within a capitalist structure), traditionally represented by the transfer of economic control and therefore social and political power from the bourgeoisie minority to the proletariat masses, this newfound flexibility allows for an avenue of revolutionary change that is rooted in the process of privilege enhancement. While the abstract nature of privilege presents a challenging task for Neo-Marxists, it is this very nature that provides an ironic opportunity to transcend the traditional dual-class societal structure in order to address the multi-layered, post-industrial class structure. Rather than target the broad transfer of power, which would theoretically amount to a mutual transaction consisting of the massive loss of bourgeoisie control and the equally massive gain of proletariat control, this Neo-Marxist approach allows for a gradual accumulation of privilege for the proletariat classes that is not dependant on a reciprocal relinquishment of privilege from the bourgeoisie classes. Although, at the same time, it allows for the simultaneous occurrence of privilege enhancement and reduction from opposing ends of the spectrum, if and when this opportunity presents itself. Granted, this approach borders on reformism, but seems to be the best way to approach current conditions given the lack of class-consciousness, especially in the US. It reminds us of Huey P. Newton's notion of "surviving until we can transform society."

Now, when considering this emphasis on privilege, the task of identifying specific pockets of privilege within a post-industrialized society like the United States becomes imperative. With self-determination being the ultimate privilege anyone could hope for in life, it becomes sensible to focus on particular advantages found within the context of a post-industrialized market society that allow for greater degrees of self-determinism. In an attempt to identify significant privileges, we can locate five that remain highly relevant and may be applied throughout the socioeconomic class structure: home and property ownership, credit, education, employment, and a livable wage. In keeping with the premise of a materialist concept of history, we may identify these privileges as key factors regarding personal growth within a modern market economy.

When applying privilege rates to the class hierarchy, it is reasonable to assume that the higher we ascend on this structure, the more abundant privileges become, and the lower we descend, the scarcer they become. In other words, it is safe to assume that all of those existing within the uber-bourgeoisie have copious access to each and every privilege listed above while, in contrast, those existing within the impoverished sector often fail to realize any of these privileges. In keeping with Marxist philosophy, any examination based in privilege capacity first recognizes that privilege is both a cause and effect within the socioeconomic hierarchy; rather, those who find themselves in a relatively impoverished predicament do so because they have not been presented with reasonable opportunities resulting from an overall deficit of privilege (cause); and in addition to this, fail to realize legitimate means to escape poverty for the same reasons (effect). The same can be said regarding the opposite end of the spectrum, only in completely reversed terms.

The identification of privilege, and an overall shift from class consideration, allows for a differentiation between traditional Marxist analysis, which addressed the agro-industrial society, and modern Neo-Marxist analysis, which addresses the post-industrialized society. The key to this demarcation process is found in the Neo-Marxists ability to locate elements of the bourgeois agenda within areas of the socioeconomic structure that were rarely considered within traditional Marxist analysis, mainly because they did not exist. In other words, while the landscapes of the bourgeoisie and newfound uber-bourgeoisie still represent the final frontiers to be overcome in the ongoing struggle, there exists the potential for significant peripheral battles throughout the multi-tier class spectrum spawned by post-industrialization; including, in some cases, those of the proletariat and impoverished. Ultimately, rather than engaging in a singular, ideological war that pits the increasingly untouchable bourgeoisie upper classes against the ever-ambiguous and thoroughly divided working classes, this philosophical shift allows for intermittent political battles to exist simultaneously within the post-industrial landscape.

The creation of this new Marxist blueprint addresses two crucial obstructions that have stymied the proletariat movement throughout the former industrialized bloc of nations for several decades. First, it circumvents the "all-or-nothing" revolutionist fervor that is often embraced (sometimes to a fault) by those who subscribe to Marxist philosophy by allowing for the creation of simultaneous, peripheral battles that focus on privilege enhancement, yet do not lose their "revolutionary" nature. Second, it streamlines Marxist politics to make it compatible for use within the "modern pluralist democracies" that have virtually lost all of their democratic elements at the expense of market ideology. In other words, this Neo-Marxist approach escapes the confines of the required singular, mass proletariat movement and instead allows for a pluralist proletariat movement that focuses on privilege enhancement throughout the multi-layered class structure, as opposed to the immediate, overall transfer of the means of production (which, in a world of financialization and globalization, themselves have lost influence). Ultimately, within the context of the ongoing "Reform vs. Revolution" debate, this approach may aptly be described as a "prolonged, multi-layered Revolutionary" method in that it seeks the overthrow of the ruling classes through a systematic attack on the peripherals of the superstructure.

Restoring Class Consciousness and Addressing the Cultural Hegemony

Despite the changing dynamics within this Neo-Marxist approach, it is impossible to escape the importance of reviving class-consciousness and engaging the cultural hegemony that permeates within the post-industrialized society much in the same ways that it endured, and intensified, throughout the industrialized period. In fact, many of the changes that have taken place within the class hierarchy have represented direct byproducts of not only the broad capitalist base, but more specifically that of the far-reaching and increasingly influential superstructure, which ultimately shapes and determines the cultural orthodoxy. In terms of the former western industrialized bloc of nations, this cultural hegemony has fully synthesized with that of ruling-class interests, hence the temperamental bourgeoization of the middle class and proletariat that has persisted despite and through widespread economic stagnation and depression.

Within the context of classical Marxist doctrine, the "coming of the revolution" has been deemed both inevitable (through various interpretations of Marx's early work, which suggested the capitalists would eventually become their own "gravediggers") and, in contrast, completely reliant upon class-consciousness and the subsequent actions stemming from some sort of catalyst: In Leninist circles, this consists of a "vanguard party" made up of professionally-trained cadre; and in Gramsci circles, this consists of enough "organic intellectuals" to equal critical mass. In light of many developments that have occurred throughout the 20th century, most notably those of globalization and the formation of an international financial system that offers public protection to private business, it has become increasingly clear that any hopes of a natural evolution consisting of "capitalism to class-consciousness to revolution to communism" has become futile.

As long as the capitalist system (which, in itself, is becoming increasingly ambiguous) continues to be propped up by trillion-dollar government interventions, the system will remain on perpetual life support; and furthermore, as long as capitalism represents the main thread that is interwoven throughout the international community, nearly every nation's ruling class will find it in their best interest to keep this system alive through government and military action/coercion. Therefore, the main objective of Neo-Marxism must be to address the formidable cultural hegemony that continues to obstruct the widespread realization of class-consciousness. The working classes, despite the increased ambiguity of class divisions that have paralleled the arrival of post-industrialization, still remain as the standard bearers of societal change; however, an overall deficit and ongoing erosion of class consciousness amongst the working classes in the "former western, industrialized bloc of nations" has led to a de-facto reliance on "vanguard" philosophies that call on socialist leadership to attack the cultural orthodoxy head-on. The problem with this reliance is two-fold: (1) it creates a hierarchical structure within the working-class movement that often times ignores the most disenfranchised, and (2) it has a tendency to reject any efforts that may be considered reformist; therefore, failing to reach a swath of the working class by ignoring their immediate needs (again, Newton's call for survival preceding revolution).

In this newly found, post-industrial landscape that lacks traditional, radical, working-class space, there are two crucial avenues for change. The first is in peripheral battles that reflect the immediate needs of the working class, even if considered "reformist" in nature. These battles may include, but are certainly not limited to, affecting the legislative process. Examples of these causes include the fast-food workers' movement in the US (Fight for 15, etc), despite the involvement of hierarchical and even pro-capitalist unions; and grassroots actions against police brutality, an epidemic that has life-and-death consequences for the most disenfranchised of the American working class and is a large part of capitalism's inevitable slide towards fascism.

The second avenue, and most important, is in creating class consciousness. With the temperamental bourgeoization of the "middle class" and large parts of the working class, such consciousness has become almost non-existent in the post-industrial landscape. This is largely due to the slow death of labor unions that began with the neoliberal assault in the 1980s, as well as a gradual transformation from radical unions based in internationalism and a foundational understanding of political economy (i.e. the Industrial Workers of the World) to hierarchical and capitalist-friendly unions which lack a broad-based philosophical grounding. The creation of class consciousness may be realized on multiple fronts, many of which will inevitably be found on the latter avenue of direct action and activism, even if reformist in nature. For example, the fast-food workers' movement which calls for a $15-dollar minimum wage does not seek a revolutionary overhaul of the capitalist system and has been influenced and coordinated in many aspects by reformist and even reactionary union structures. However, it is a crucial step towards promoting and developing class consciousness amongst a population (low-wage service sector workers) that has had very little or no exposure to a class analysis. At the very least, such movements allow for the formation of organic solidarity between the workers, who find themselves taking a stand together, walking the picket lines together, holding hands and realizing a common struggle, together – all keys to realizing class consciousness.

Social Movement Studies
DEPARTMENT

The Pre-War Japanese Left

A Survey and Critique

Derek A. Ide

The 2009 upheaval in Japanese politics, manifested in the ouster of the Liberal Democratic Party and their decades-long rule, signaled a significant shift to the left on the part of Japanese masses. Despite the caricature of Japanese society as one dominated by traditionally conservative and reactionary currents, Japanese leftists from the nineteenth century onward have articulated and maintained a diverse line of political thought that has played a vital role in challenging, both theoretically and materially, the dominant ideology and the capitalist economic structure which maintains it. Early leftist thought was originally rooted in Christian Humanism, only later developing an emphasis on socialist currents represented by reformism, anarchism, and Marxism. Popular forms of organization that struggled against the oppressive economic, political, and social institutions which constitute Japanese society have historically aligned themselves with a variety of leftist political thought.

Ultimately, however, two primary variables have existed in a dynamic interrelationship which has assured the dominance of the Japanese ruling class and excluded popular leftists elements from restructuring Japanese society along lines of social justice, equality, and democratic control over the economic sphere: intense state repression and the failures of the Japanese left to articulate a consistent praxis to achieve fundamental change. These two variables, important to varying degrees in different periods of recent Japanese history, provide a framework in which the weaknesses of the Japanese left can be critically assessed and allow for the synthesis of a new revolutionary praxis to emerge.

Modern leftist political thought has only been a material possibility within the last century and a half in Japan. Japanese society, from the mid-seventh to the mid-nineteenth century, was dominated by a conservative feudal system of extreme hierarchy. This top-down administration consisted of a ruling Shogun who presided over nearly 250 regional Daimyo Lords and maintained a semblance of ideological legitimacy through a mandate from the relatively powerless monarch, referred to as the Heavenly Sovereign, and a unique borrowing of Chinese Confucianism which strictly defined social roles and was utilized to legitimate strict political, social, and economic stratification.

Changing Social Relations in the Tokugawa Period (1603-1868)

An urban revolution under the rule of the House of Tokugawa was facilitated by the development of new agricultural techniques which, from 1550 to 1650, nearly doubled the amount of land under cultivation. This allowed for the rapid influx of ex-farmers into urban areas that were clustered primarily around castles used in the past by the Daimyo as military centers. This demographic shift from an agrarian to urban society fostered the growth of new markets, especially around luxury items associated with the nobility such as silk, which augmented the size of the urban proletariat.

The transformation under the Tokugawa period from a largely agricultural, semi-feudal society to an early industrial society brought with it the burgeoning of new social classes. Namely, the bourgeoisie, both large and small, which bought up labor to extract surplus from the relatively nascent modern working class, a class which sold its labor and produced valuable commodities for the market. The development of these new social classes, demarcated by their relation to the means of production, were a result of a complex array of factors including centralization of political power, agricultural improvements driven by military competition, technological advancements spurred by the fact that fewer farmers were needed, and the rapid urbanization resulting from these processes. Yet, despite all this economic development Japan remained within the ossified class structure of a feudal society.

The rigid social hierarchy of Neo-Confucian ideology was maintained as official dogma and a multitude of social, political, and economic benefits were assigned to the nobility. Merchants and artisans often lived precariously, some enjoying exponential success and others failing miserably under the heel of the emerging capitalist machine. For laborers and the poor, dangerous, onerous work earned them paltry wages, forced consumption restrictions, hereditary occupational status, and atrocious housing. It was, however, these economic conditions which foresaw the emergence in Japan of an entirely new economic order, one dominated not so much by military generals but by capitalists and bureaucrats in a rapidly urbanizing economy.

Combined with these new social forces emerging on the economic scene, peasant uprisings threatened the stability of the Tokugawa regime which lived off their exploitation. These uprisings, regardless of what particular historians [1] may presume, were not entirely apolitical, even if demands were largely relegated to economic issues. Within the midst of this complex transition in Japanese society came the controversial gunboat diplomacy of Western powers, manifested in the arrival of the Americans under the leadership of Matthew Perry in 1853, which triggered a national debate over the role of foreigners and how Japan should interact with them. A political formation of conservative Japanese nationalists and monarchists, forerunners of the ultranationalist tendencies in Japan, rallied around the banner of "revering the emperor and repelling the barbarians (Westerners)."[2] This group, the *sonnō jōi*, utilized the social force of the peasantry to overturn the dominance of the Shogun, who they saw as capitulating to foreigners. It was during this tumultuous period that a complex series of events led to the eventual downfall of the feudal power of the Shogun and the transfer of power to the emperor in what was called the Meiji Restoration.

Early Socialist Thought and Christian Humanism (1870-1911)

Until the late nineteenth century modern strains of leftist political thought were not only an impracticality, they were nearly impossible to articulate given the feudal social relations. On conjunction with these feudal restraints, traditional Buddhist, Shinto, and Confucian thought, which dominated the ideology of the masses, did not provide a framework in which working class oppositional politics could be easily developed.[3] Therefore, as Japanese philosophical historians Piovesana and Yamawaki point out, it is "difficult to associate materialism with Socialism during the period 1870-1911, primarily because early socialist thought in Japan was connected with a humanistic and Christian view of social problems."[4] The bond between early socialism and Christian humanism was strengthened during the Russo-Japanese war, which brought together members of both groups to participate in anti-war meetings.[5] It was not until the Russian Revolution of 1917 that Japanese socialists en masse would orientate themselves towards a scientific, rather than purely moralistic, critique of the existing social relations.

Elites in Japan during the late nineteenth century were driven primarily by two goals: national independence and "civilization and enlightenment." The first was to be achieved by cultivating a national identity and articulating strong economic goals while the second required industrialization, the removal of past pre-capitalist traditions, and the fostering of beneficial relationships with technologically advanced Western states. Both policies were intended to galvanize the rapid industrialization that would augment Japan's economic power. Subsequently, a brutal process of primitive accumulation occurred that brought with it a stripping of the power from the old nobility, a fundamentally new and more efficient tax structure, and the establishment of a primitive parliamentary system. The new constitution developed in 1889 was largely anti-democratic in its nature and highly exclusionary; it served primarily to enhance the political power of the "sacred and inviolable" emperor.

The pursuance of these goals lead to a rapid modernization process and the growth of nascent social forces. The number of factory workers grew from "a few thousand in the 1870s...to somewhat more than 400,000 in the late 1890s."[6] The number of female textile workers jumped from 26,800 in 1886 to 184,000 in 1909.[7] During this time, Japanese urban centers grew enormously and, for the first time in Japanese history, currents of modern leftist political thought based upon a technologically advanced industrial society could be cultivated. The very foundations of these ideas, such as democratically controlling the means of production and equal distribution of society's material wealth, were the result of the new economic forces that were developing a reality of class conflict.

The intense industrialization process that Japan underwent during the last part of the nineteenth century was spearheaded by the new Japanese government. Communications, transportation, and heavy industry were put forth as key components for economic development. The vast majority of the Japanese people were poor and those who already maintained the resources to invest in new industries quickly gained the upper-hand. Capital accumulation by certain economic titans only accelerated the concentration of economic power away from ordinary people and into the hands of a new capitalist class, the *zaibatsu*. Four giant conglomerates, Mitsui, Mitsubishi, Sumitomo, and Yasuda, grew to rival the robber barons of the West. Japan's trading capabilities with the West were prodigiously increased as industrial output skyrocketed.

This economic development did not ameliorate the miserable conditions of the new laboring class or the peasantry. Women in particular faced the brunt of the newly emerging industrial madness; they were often forced to work in conditions akin to slave labor at a fraction of the price of men who were often involved in more skilled trades.[8] The vast majority of Japanese people were excluded from the democratic process, subjected to a centralized government authority of which they did not choose, and forced to sell their labor to powerful economic titans who dominated vital Japanese industries as agriculture became increasingly mechanized and less reliant upon labor-intensive practices. Thus, the seeds of class strife were sewn.

The product of these developments did not materialize into practical organization just yet, however. Prior to the establishment of the Japan Socialist Party in 1906, early socialist groups were primarily theoretical in nature and acted more as intellectual study groups than practical organizational structures. One of the earliest of these was the Society for the Study of Socialism (*Shakaishugi Kenkyukai*) established in 1898 by a circle of Christian intellectuals in Tokyo.[9] The Social Democratic Party was formed in 1901, established on the tenants of Christian humanism, social democracy, and pacifism, things they believed achievable through electoral means. The state saw such a development towards leftist politics, even of such a mild variety, as a threat and forced the group to disband. [10] As long as the movement remained theoretical, academic, and abstract, the state tolerated it. The breaking point was when the party desired, even through reformist and parliamentary means, to alter the structures of society that worried government officials.

One example of this is the Socialist Society which held around 180 meetings from 1902 to 1903. Once the group decided to shift from a purely academic pursuit to become, even if only slightly, an activist-oriented organization by attempting to inculcate the idea of socialism in the popular consciousness, it was no longer permissible. Almost immediately government harassment became routine as police disrupted distribution of socialist newspapers, confiscated printing materials, and fined or imprisoned members. Subsequently, the Socialist Society was forced to disband in 1904. The long history of government repression of Japanese leftists had begun.

A range of debate concerning strategy, tactics, and the role of the state resulted from the intense government repression. This debate split socialists into two overarching camps: reformists and revolutionaries. Although not every leftist theoretician can be pigeonholed into each group perfectly, the two categories best reflect the two primary currents of leftist thought during this period. Reformists such as Abe Isoo, Kinoshita Naoe, and Katayama Sen were the equivalents, more or less, of European social democrats who advocated change through parliamentary means and promulgated their ideas through a monthly periodical called New Era (*Shin Kigen*). The revolutionaries, whose ranks included Kōtoku Shūsui, Sakai Toshihiko, and Yamaguchi Koken among others, were inspired primarily by German and French materialists and anarcho-syndicalists. Subsequently, they viewed a mix of class struggle and direct action as the primary tactics to be utilized in the transformation of society. They organized around two primary publications called The Light (*Hikari*) and the more theoretical Studies in Socialism (*Shakaishugi Kenkyu*). [11] The range of ideas and debate within the left at this time were enormous.

Kōtoku began as a liberal involved in the Popular Rights movement and quickly developed a blend of anti-war pacifism and social democratic sympathies. He did not become, in his own words, a "radical anarchist" until his experience anti-war organizing forced him to clash with the state apparatus where he met severe repression and imprisonment. After this period he adopted a sort of ultra-leftism and argued that fighting for universal suffrage was a waste and the Diet, or Japanese parliament, was only a tool of propertied class. His focus rested upon utilizing the general strike as the primary weapon of the working class, a position reinforced after the apparently spontaneous labor agitation that occurred in 1906 and 1907. [12] One position, articulated by a reformist named Yamakawa, upheld that political action for reforms, such as struggling for universal suffrage, were essential to bolster the class consciousness of the proletariat. A third position, closest perhaps to reality, was advocated by socialists such as Sakai who argued a synthesis of both political and direct action was essential. Even some, such as Katayama from the reformist camp, advocated a similar position when he stated that:

Although I advocate Universal Suffrage as the best means of educating the working classes and as a peaceful method for the development of the socialist movement in Japan, I have also belief in the direct action of workers and in general strikes as the best means of strengthening the position of the workers against the capitalist classes.[13]

At this point in time it was apparent that socialists found Marxism useful for analyzing and critiquing the structures of class society but could not articulate where or how it was useful in developing socialist strategy or tactics in how to transcend class society. A crucial weakness that enervated the left during this period was the inability to adopt a comprehensive strategy that utilized tactics both legal and illegal, political and direct, to develop a framework under which effective socialist organization could be established and allowed to grow. Given the restrictive external conditions it is unclear that even if a majority of the left had adopted this position, articulated best by socialists like Sakai, that they would have been able to overturn the state. Regardless, the potential for developing the socialist organization necessary for mobilizing the masses and capitalize on the struggles to come in the future would have been much greater.

The epitome of this failure is shown in the brief history of the Japan Socialist Party (*Nihon Shakaito*) formed in 1906. Around 200 activists from both camps came together in an attempt to unify around common principles. The schism between reform and revolution, however, did not allow this union to remain intact long. Factionalism was rife and although a strong plurality of members held predilections towards Kōtoku's anarcho-syndicalism and direct action, he did not have enough to form a solid majority. Despite the internal power struggles inherent in groups attempting to reconcile two contradictory forms of praxis for social change, the JSP was ultimately crushed by external forces. [14] General Katsura, a rabid conservative, took power for a second time in 1908 and was bent on crushing any forms of socialist organization. The government quickly forced the party to disband because, according to them, it agitated labor unrest. The party was forced to cease print of their paper, the*Commoners' News*. Many prominent socialist voices were arrested. Twelve, including Kōtoku, were arrested on grounds they were attempting to assassinate the emperor and were swiftly executed three days after sentencing without any form of appeal. It is not clear to this day whether or not Kōtoku was involved at all. [15] Regardless, the trial and conviction was a government attempt to discredit the socialist movement and create a climate of fear that would incriminate leftist thought.

Taishō Period (1910-30)

Not until the Taishō period, lasting roughly from 1910 to 1930, was the zenith of democratic participation by masses reached in the prewar era. Social movements that had burgeoned during the Meiji era blossomed into life during the early part of the twentieth century. Class conflict and participatory, democratic movements on behalf of the masses reached their apex during this period and were, at least partly, reflected in the evolving political institutions in Japan. Ironically, all of this internal development occurred within the context of the imperial ambitions of Japan's leaders. The Japanese empire consolidated its power after World War I and increased its control over China, Manchuria, Karafuto, Korea, Taiwan, and other areas of the South Pacific. By 1922, Japan had secured its hegemony in the region.

It was within this imperial advancement that the internal division sown during the early Meiji years of industrialization began to sprout. Class conflict became more concrete, a serious reflection of the material conditions in Japanese society. Factory workers grew in numbers while wages and workplace rights remained stagnant or declined. In 1914, only fifty strikes occurred in Japan while in 1919, only five years later, nearly 500 instances of labor disputes were recorded and tens of thousands of workers took action against unfair conditions. By 1930, this number has risen above 900 recorded disputes with over 80,000 participants. [16] The number of unions rose significantly from 187 in 1919 to 818 by 1931. Likewise, union membership increased dramatically from around 100,000 members in 1921 to over 350,000 in 1931. [17] A hailstorm of calls for the implementation of universal suffrage, democratization of the educational system, and abolition of draconian anti-labor laws were put forth. By 1921, a landmark labor battle occurred at shipyards in Kobe where the army was called in to break a massive strike, a crucial turning point. Afterwards, moderates advocating gradualism and labor-capital harmony were marginalized and more radical elements became active in the movement.

Subsequently, an avenue was opened for radical activists to win support for their ideas. The foundations for a revolutionary socialist alternative had already been laid by four principle socialists during this period: Sakae Ōsugi, Toshihiko Sakai, Kanson Arahata, and Hitoshi Yamakawa. Each had felt the wrath of the state and, after serving prison terms for their political activism, advanced their own theoretical positions in which posited methods of organization that would best serve radicals within the context of Japanese society. All four became heavily involved in labor organizing during World War I and all but Ōsugi converted to Marxism-Leninism after the Russian Revolution. [18] Ōsugi maintained his commitment to anarcho-syndicalism until being murdered by police in 1923. [19] The other three were founding members of the Japanese Communist Party (*Nihon Kyōsan-tō*) in 1922. The Russian Revolution had marked the end of anarcho-syndicalism being the primary force in socialist theory. However, the contributions that Lenin had put forth were not clearly understood immediately within Japanese arena of struggle. The first article on Leninism did not appear until 1918 and vital critiques of capitalism such as Marx's Capital were not fully available in Japan until 1924.

Labor was not the only area where social change and democratic organization was occurring. Many who participated in the Popular Rights movement, a reform movement for political democracy, turned towards more radical, left-wing thought as it became apparent that political demands, let alone social and economic concerns, could not be addressed through the extremely exclusionary democratic forms available in Japan. A multitude of examples symbolize this transformation. The editors of *Democracy*, a journal from the New Men Society, articulated the theoretical shifts of those previously involved in the Popular Rights movement. As one participant, Akamatsu Katsumaro, describes, "Our groups fell away from democratic theory and we lost our calmness. We now focused our attention on discussion of how to lead the class struggle in Japan... Socialism and anarchism became topics of interest." [20] Similarly, the Friendly Society (*Yuaikai*), a welfare labor organization that promoted harmony between classes, started off very moderate but quickly developed kernels of radicalism within it. Radicals had pushed through demands within the *Yuaikai,* arming with a left critique that denounced the evils of capitalism, called for an end to wage slavery, and demanded workers' control over their work, culture, and society at large. There were not simply vague abstractions, however, as the organization called for material demands to be met: eight hour work day, a 48 hour work week, a minimum wage, equal pay for equal work, social insurance, accident compensation, and arbitration of labor disputes among other things. Politically, they demanded universal suffrage, a repeal of oppressive laws against labor organizations and the democratization of Japan's political system. [21] These lucid examples lead one to believe that it was through struggle for democratic, parliamentary reforms that people were opened up to more radical, leftist critiques of society. Essentially, this points to the idea that peoples' consciousness change through struggle, even if that struggle is one for reform. This concept is a fundamental tenant in the theory of "socialism-from-below" that rejects elitist methods of revolutionary organization.

Agrarian reform was also a major issue during this period. Tenant farmers began to organize themselves to fight for rent reduction and better wages. From 1920 to 1929 over 18,000 tenant disputes were recorded; some ended in outright victory for the tenants while the majority ended in some form of compromise. [22] Regardless of outcome, such a dramatic rise in tenants articulating their own demands against landlords signaled that peasants were increasingly prepared to challenge fundamentally undemocratic social relations. Similarly, minority groups such as the *burakumin* began to affiliate themselves with radical social movements, especially Marxists who advocated revolutionary change and control over society by working people. Even more significant was the advance of Women's rights and early feminists who articulated demands for equality, both politically and economically. Some organizations were headed primarily by bourgeois, middle-class sectors while the more militant, radical women's rights activists agitated along socialist lines.

All of this activity, in conjunction with the changing social conditions, opened up the possibility for a large sector of the population to break away from the ideological stranglehold of traditional Japanese culture and the class collaborationism of the bourgeois academics and labor reformists. Many saw this opportunity to augment the strength of radical ideas and disseminate radical critiques of the capitalist system. Kawakami Hajime, professor of economics at Kyoto University, was one of the most famous Marxist academics who popularized socialist ideas on university campuses among students. [23]

Ideas were not just for academics, however. After a successful May Day rally in 1920 where protestors violently clashed with police forces, an attempt was made to unite a variety of different tendencies under an umbrella group called the Labor Union League. Despite being an important step in bridging the gap between leftists and forming a unified force, this effort was marred by ideological clashes that did not permit the organization to last long. [24] In the same year the Socialist League was formed and the group postulated a rigorous denunciation of capitalism:

We will destroy the present capitalist system. We will destroy systems, organizations, customs, thoughts, arts, and other bourgeois culture that go with the capitalist system. In order to create a truly human life, we are resolved to realize a society without wealth and poverty, a society in which all people work and all people receive security of food, clothing, and housing... We believe that our main power in this class conflict lies in...the worker class, and we will struggle for their awakening, unifications, and training. [25]

They also made calls for the "salaried class, the small entrepreneurs" who were "basically workers" to come join in their movement. By October of 1920 the SL boasted one-thousand members, a significant advance for radical politics. However, police continually harassed the group by breaking up meetings and conventions, as well as arresting leaders and activists. They were forced to disband in May of 1921. Regardless of the SL's short-lived existence, it was vitally important for the role it played in popularizing radical thought. It did this in three ways: first, even after the forced dispersion of the group members continued work in small groups and clarified theoretical differences in various schools of thought. Second, the SL bridged the gap between older Bolshevists and a new generation of radicals from the universities. Lastly, they greatly increased contact and strengthened the bond between left-wing intellectuals and labor organizers, opening more avenues for working people to take up radical left wing thought. [26]

It was, however, the reccurring weakness of the Japanese Left that ultimately ended in the demise of the SL. According to Beckmann and

Ōkubo, authors of *The Japanese Communist Party*, the Japanese left suffered primarily from their lack of unity:

Even if the attitude of the authorities had been different, the league was probably doomed to failure because of the disparity of the ideological and personality groupings within it. None of these groups could properly be called an organization, and except for the anarcho-syndicalists, none had worked out action programs. [27]

The social democrats advocated legal reform but lacked the political capital to make any serious inroads, even in terms of piecemeal reformism. Marxists spoke abstractly of socialist revolution but their theory was severed from action as they had no strategic methods to accomplish this goal; they lacked a concrete praxis that could synthesize reflection and action or fuse theory and practice. No lucid, comprehensive conception of Leninism, something that could have potentially given Japanese radicals a blueprint for how to operate under extremely oppressive conditions, had been articulated in Japan at this point. The anarcho-syndicalists, of course, suffered from their ultra-leftist orientation that isolated them from any form of reformist struggle and, subsequently, from those who were not already radicalized. While their romanticism attracted some followers, their strategy of relying purely upon direct action and rejecting political demands was extremely detrimental.

The Japanese Communist Party (1922)

It was at this juncture, after the repressive apparatus of the state had enervated and debilitated any autonomous forms of radical organization, that the need for an underground party of revolutionaries became apparent. Thus, in 1922 a few radicals, including Sakai, Arahata, and Yamakawa, formed the Japanese Communist Party. By this time, Lenin had already warned that unless the "young working class of Japan rapidly becomes sufficiently strong to seize the Japanese bourgeoisie by the throat" than "as sure as morning follows night, so will the first imperialist war, which ended in 1918, be followed by a second war that will center around the Far East and the problem of the Pacific." [28]
Despite this, Lenin's advice to the Japanese Communists remained

abstract and primarily rhetorical. It was Georgy Safaro, the Comintern's leading expert on East Asia, who first developed a coherent plan for revolution in Japan. He argued that the working class could not create a workers' revolution immediately but must first strategically align themselves with the peasantry and call for a "democratic republic, land nationalization, and the nationalization of large industry" which would be placed under workers' control. [29] When Katayama Sen was sent as a representative of the JCP to the Comintern he eagerly expressed his optimism about the prospects for revolution as he laid out the changing social conditions:

I think that the Japanese worker has made as much progress in the last half century as the worker of Europe has made during the last two or three centuries...the Japanese proletariat will soon learn how to fight against the capitalist oppressors more successfully than the workers of America or Europe, where the capitalist system is fully developed and established. [30]

Despite this enthusiasm, it was not Katayama's projection that rang true for Japan but Lenin's warning of impending imperialist war. Due to serious restrictions and a lack of resources, Japanese Communists did not maintain steady contact with leaders in the Soviet Union. This was, perhaps, a veiled gift given the soon-to-come Stalinist reaction that would grip the post-1924 Soviet sphere.

Eventually, most of the JCP came to accept that universal suffrage was a real goal with material and subjective consequences that ought to be struggled for. They did not, however, concede in the early years of the party that political democracy, even if it could be achieved, could light the pathway to true democracy where working people maintained control over the organization and distribution of the wealth of society. Furthermore, Yamakawa argued that Japan would not reach any sort of political democratic state for three primary reasons: first, the Japanese bourgeoisie had established its power by combining with the remnants of medieval autocracy and had lost its revolutionary spirit of a new class, second, Japan had no basis for the development of political liberalism and democracy since it had already reached the stage of imperialism, and third, the Japanese bourgeoisie had no loyal supporters and was threatened by an ever-advancing class-conscious proletariat. [31] The position commonly accepted at this time in the party was as follows:

A certain degree of political liberalism and democracy is necessary for the maturity of the proletariat as a class. To that extent-to that extent only-the proletariat has a common interest with the petty bourgeoisie and can make use of a petty bourgeois party. But the proletarian movement must act as an independent political force. [32]

The leaders of the JCP struggled over the question of how to utilize universal suffrage. For instance, the development of a broad electoral party was potentially a double-edged sword. Any sort of parliamentary party that hoped to achieve electoral results could not, especially given Japanese conditions, articulate the need for a socialist revolution. Similarly, the more the party became inclusive of all workers and all people, regardless of what sort of reactionary ideas they brought with them, the more the party would become bogged down in petty reformism that channeled struggle purely into the Diet. Without such a broad platform, however, the party would remain isolated and separated from the working class and would struggle to reach the broad audiences they hoped for.

The party was not challenged with this conundrum long. Under intense pressure from the state and forced to operate under the watchful guise of highly repressive government institutions, the JCP decided to dissolve itself in 1924. Instead, they would attempt to create a broad parliamentary party that would no longer be "alienated from the masses" and "reduced to factionalism." [33] It is apparent that:

The state destroyed its organization...But the party itself suffered from certain basic weaknesses. It was not a unified body with a concrete platform, but was instead an amalgam of personal factions whose members could not agree on the strategy and tactics of revolution...the party had not developed to the point where it was based on mass organizations of workers and peasants. [34]

Yamakawa argued that these fatal weaknesses were the result of maintaining a small, elite, illegal party. [35] Instead, the hope was that universal suffrage would allow the communist movement to grow by organizing a broad workers party which would allow communists to work inside of, or "burrow from within," and by doing so reach a wider layer of people. His ideas arose from a rigid conception of Marxism that maintained Japan was still in the feudal stage of economic development and, therefore, the stage of capitalism had not been reached where the proletariat would be able to take power.

In 1925, Fukumoto Kazuo emerged as the foremost Japanese Marxist theorist attacking Yamakawa's interpretation, arguing instead that Japan should be considered an economically developed capitalist state. He criticized Yamakawa's reliance upon universal suffrage and the dissolution of the vanguard party. Disliked by Moscow, Fukumoto was greatly influenced by the Hungarian Marxist George Lukács and, subsequently, was concerned with postulating a workable praxis. He "developed the dialectical aspects of historical materialism, as well as the practical aspects in the line of Lenin's *What Is To Be Done*?" [36] His position signified a definite break with the directives from Moscow and his ideas became quite popular on the left with something of a personality cult evolving around him. By 1926 the need for the reestablishment of the JCP became apparent as the small bureau that was maintained after the dissolution of the party could do very little by itself. The plan for the JCP was to function within the framework of the broader Labor-Farmer Party and form strong blocs with other groups that would attempt to gain hegemony. A new draft for the party was established that asserted the need for rejecting the "100 per cent" conception of membership in order to be more inclusive. Abstract discussions were to be replaced with more concrete issues. [37] The Party was rejecting both its former sectarianism and its desperate self-destruction. Unfortunately, these developments came too late to beat back the reactionary forces that were too be unleashed upon the left by the Japanese state.

The Dismantling of the Left in the Pre-War Era (1928-1935)

Despite the developments within the JCP, the party had very little time to effectively implement any of them. In 1928 and 1929 thousands of left-wing activists, accused of being communists, were arrested up in a national offensive led by General Tanaka Giichi to root out leftists. On one day alone, March 15, 1928, over 1,600 people were arrested. [38] By the early 1930's the majority of the JCP leadership and membership had been arrested, killed, tortured, or forced into renouncing their radicalism. In a one year span from 1931 to 1932 over 300 members of the party were sentenced. The trials were intended to show that the JCP had violated the Peace Preservation Law, passed in 1923, which "made it illegal to advocate either change in the national polity or the abolition of private property." [39] Any defendant who refused to publicly recant communism with written statements were punished harshly. This sort of intimidation and coercion literally decimated the party. After the forced coercion of two leaders in 1933 over 500 over members followed suit and renounced the JCP under state coercion. [40]

By 1931 conditions had become so unbearable that the JCP, now forced to operate underground, articulated the call for an immediate socialist revolution. They received no help from Russia which, by this time, lacked any vestige of the workers' revolution of 1917 and had already felt the degeneration from socialist revolution to state-capitalism manifested in Stalin's ascension. The Comintern was in the midst of an ideological struggle against Trotsky and other "Left Opposition" members who attempted to uphold an opposition to Stalin. Accordingly, the JCP was suspected of harboring Trotskyist currents and ostracized. This was not without its truth, as members such as famed Kyoto University professor and Labor-Farmer candidate Kawakami Hajime had insinuated their affiliation with Trotsky by translating articles which Stalin had labeled Trotskyist. [41] Kawakami himself was sent to prison in 1933 as the "red hunt" hit the university campuses. The last ditch effort of openly calling for immediate revolution without a mass base to follow through on such demands led to the isolation and defeat of the JCP as the government augmented their repressive activities. By 1935 the JCP and all its all organizational structures ceased to operate; the Japanese communist movement had been crushed by the state apparatus.

Conclusion (1928-1935)

The history of the pre-war Japanese left, then, is a history of vibrant resistance but ultimate defeat. All of this vital democratic activity and popular participation coalesced under, and was enormously influenced by, the emergence of left-wing political thought. While pre-war Japanese leftist thought offered an impressive display of diversity and the possibility for united action, the potential for revolutionary transformation was viciously stamped out. National minorities, women, and others began to organize themselves into groups and parties that struggled for fundamental change in Japanese society, articulating another important critique of Japan's material base and ideological components. Economic equality, workplace democracy, agrarian reform, minority recognition, and women's rights were all issues debated and discussed within leftist currents and struggled for during the pre-war era. Working people began to harbor subversive thoughts and radical ideas became more popular as class struggle and liberation movements became a reality. Subsequently, a prodigious wave of repression hit Japanese society as officials attempted to stamp out radical thought in Japan. New laws were passed that facilitated the imprisonment and murder of left-wing activists and it became illegal to challenge the supremacy of private property or to advocate change in the structure of government.

Undoubtedly the legitimacy of the Japanese ruling class was challenged by democratic forces during the prewar era. Despite significant repression, radical thought became popular in Japan as leftists attempted, but ultimately failed, in applying a revolutionary theory to pragmatic, material goals. Socialists and leftists became vital proponents of the various radical causes in Japan, including the abolition of wage labor, the implementation of workplace democracy, and the liberation of oppressed minorities. Political and economic elites recognized the precarious situation that would occur for their power if such an excess of democratic force was unleashed by the masses. Therefore, harsh repression had to be woven into superficial political reform and small concessions granted to popular movements. Simultaneously, this mix of conciliation and dismantling of radical thought facilitated the imperial project by limiting dissent and critique of Japan's militarist ventures. Subsequently, the most reactionary and nationalistic currents would take power and set Japan's political, economic, and social trajectory on a militaristic course that would succeed in stamping out leftist dissent and any challenges to the system.

Ultimately, the demise of the prewar left in Japan was the result of two irrevocably interconnected phenomena. State repression and the internal weaknesses of the left enervated the only potential force capable of stemming the tide towards xenophobic ultra-nationalism and quasi-fascist militarism. It is possible that a united front, one in which the revolutionary left could unify with progressive elements of Japanese society to combat the rise of the reactionary sectors that took state power in Japan, could have shifted the course of history and averted the country's disastrous entrance into World War II. Such a policy that could work strategically outside the system by maintaining autonomy and revolutionary independence, but tactically inside the system through whatever legal means accessible, could have provided the left the potential to avoid severe isolation. It is apparent that, given the nature of the Japanese state and the state apparatus in general, government repression would have resulted against radical elements regardless of their strategy. Still, a coalescing, unified strategy, incorporating a wide array of flexible and diverse tactics, could have reduced the efficiency of state persecution. Instead, rampant factionalism ate away from the left within and devoured its potential for transformative action while the ever-strengthening forms of semi-fascist state repression dealt the deathblow. Had the left been able to combat the augmentation of militaristic and ultra-nationalist sentiments in Japan, an objective requiring a much deeper understanding of not only theoretical Marxism but practical, applicable praxis, it is possible to conceive that a culture of resistance may have been cultivated that would have changed the course of history, averted Japanese entrance into World War II, and saved the lives of the hundreds of thousands of Japanese who became victims of brutal American firebombing and atomic devastation.

Notes

[1] Mikiso Hane, *Modern Japan: A Historical Survey*, *Third Edition* (Colorado: Westview Press, 2001), 87. For instance, Hane maintains that the "end of more than 260 years of Tokugawa rule...was primarily a political event, although it has been interpreted by many Japanese historians as the product of the new social and economic forces..."
[2] Hane, Modern Japan, 76.
[3] Gino Piovesana, Naoshi Yamawaki, *Recent Japanese Philosophical Thought, 1862-1996* (Great Britain: Japan Library, 1997), 55.
[4] Piovesana, Recent Japanese Philosophical Thought, 52.
[5] Ibid.
[6] James McClain, *A Modern History: Japan*, (New York: W.W. Norton & Company, 2002), 248.
[7] McClain, *A Modern History: Japan*, 249.
[8] Ibid.

[9] George M. Beckmann, Genji Ōkubo, *The Japanese Communist Party 1922-1945* (Stanford: Stanford University Press, 1969), 1.
[10] Beckmann, *The Japanese Communist Party*, 2.
[11] Ibid.
[12] Ibid.
[13] Katayama Sen, *The Labor Movement in Japan*, "Chapter 5: The Socialist Party and Its Activities," accessed 7 December 2009; available from
http://www.marxists.org/archive/katayama/1918/labor_movement/ch05.htm; Internet.
[14] Beckmann, *The Japanese Communist Party*, 6.
[15] Ibid.
[16] McClain, 372.
[17] Ibid.
[18] Beckmann, 7-8.
[19] Ibid.
[20] Ibid.
[21] Ibid.
[22] McClain, 368.
[23] Piovesana, *Recent Japanese Philosophical Thought*, 170.
[24] Beckmann, 23.
[25] Ibid.
[26] Ibid.
[27] Ibid.
[28] Ibid.
[29] Ibid.
[30] Ibid.
[31] Ibid.
[32] Ibid.
[33] Ibid.
[34] Ibid.
[35] Ibid.
[36] Piovesana, 175.
[37] Beckmann, 106.
[38] Hane, 232.
[39] Ibid.
[40] Ibid.
[41] Piovesana, 173.

How Capitalism Underdeveloped Hip Hop (Part 1)

A People's History of Political Rap

Derek A. Ide

Disclaimer: The language expressed in this article is an uncensored reflection of the views of the artists as they so chose to speak and express themselves. Censoring their words would do injustice to the freedom of expression and political content this article intends to explore. Therefore, some of the language appearing below may be offensive to personal, cultural, or political sensibilities.

Introduction: Historical Phenomena, Hip-Hop Culture, and Rap Music

Historical phenomena never develop in a vacuum, isolated from reality; nor are they mechanistically manifested from the historical material conditions lacking the direction of human agency. Rather, historical phenomena are products of a specific environment at a particular time period that have been molded, processed, and transformed by human beings who attempt to define and control their own destiny. The culture fostered in the grimy streets of the South Bronx during the 1970s is no different. Heavily influenced by the economically and socially oppressed ghettoes, along with the echoes of the last generation's movements for liberation and the street gangs that filled in the void they left, the South Bronx provided the perfect matrix in which marginalized youth could find a way to articulate the story of their own lives and the world around them. In this historically unique context, a culture would be created through an organic explosion of the pent-up, creative energies of America's forgotten youth. It was a culture that would reach every corner of the world in only a couple decades; this is hip-hop.

Many people mistakenly narrowly define hip-hop as a particular style of music. The reality, however, is that Hip-hop is an extremely multifaceted cultural phenomenon. As hip-hop pioneer DJ Kool Herc explains, "People talk about the four hip-hop elements: DJing, B-Boying, MCing, and Graffiti. I think that there are far more than those: the way you walk, the way you talk, the way you look, the way you communicate." [1] Indeed, each component presents its own unique history, heroes, and tales of resistance; each acts as a distinct piece of a larger puzzle. Viewed in its totality, hip-hop is undoubtedly a global phenomenon, reaching across the borders of nation-states and touching entire generations. One integral aspect of this culture, familiarly labeled rap, is the musical element which combines MCing and DJing; it is "is the act of speaking poetically and rhythmically over the beat." As Black intellectual Michael Eric Dyson eloquently explains, "Rap artists explore grammatical creativity, verbal wizardry, and linguistic innovation in refining the art of oral communication." [2] The characteristic east coast sounds of New York City, the intricate Hip-hop scene in France, the nascent grime subgenre in London, and the politically charged rap developing in Cuba demonstrate just how global the influence of rap music truly is.

Hip-hop was born from the ashes of a community devastated by a capitalist economic system and racist government officials. At first independent and autonomous, it would not be long before corporate capitalism impinged upon the culture's sovereignty and began the historically familiar process of exploitation. Within a few years the schism between the dominant, mainstream rap spewed across the synchronized, consolidated radio waves and the dissident, political, and revolutionary lyrics expressed throughout the underground network would develop, separating hip-hop into two worlds. Rapper Immortal Technique frames this dichotomy in a political context emphasizing the opposition between the major label "super powers of the industry" and the "underground third world of the street." [3]Indeed, the stark difference between the commodified songs and albums pumped out by the mainstream rap industry and the creativity and resistance exemplified in the underground movement cannot be overemphasized.

Hip-hop's glamorized, commercialized image, made familiar through every aspect of pop culture and privately centralized radio stations, is viewed by some as a justification for the prevailing "boot strap" ideology derived from thirty years of neoliberal economic policies and the dominant ideological formulations supporting them. Time argues capitalism allowed for "rap music's market strength [to give] its artists permission to say what they pleased." [4] Indeed, some argue that one's ability to market a product in a capitalist society is what has allowed rap music to flourish and become as large of an industry as it is today.[5] This simplistic view, however, ignores one crucial aspect; the culture has been manipulated by a handful of industry executives for capital gain. Meanwhile, hip-hop activists who advocate for social change, formulate political dissent, and fight for economic redistribution have been systematically marginalized and excluded from the mainstream discourse. Corporate capitalism, aided by neoliberal deregulation and privatization, have stolen the culture, sterilized its content, and reformatted its image to reflect the dominant ideology. Independent, political rap containing valuable social commentary has been replaced with shallow, corporate images of thugs, drugs, and racial and gender prejudices filled with both implicitly and explicitly hegemonic undertones and socially constructed stereotypes. Hip-hop has been underdeveloped by the mainstream industry in the same sense that third world countries were underdeveloped by traditionally oppressive first world nations: it has been robbed of its content like a nation is robbed of its resources, its artists exploited like a country's labor is exploited, and its very survival hinged upon complete subservience to an established political, economic, and social institution. The following is an outline of a culture's musical resistance to subjugation by the economic, political, and social authority of American capitalism and its ruling elites.

The South Bronx in the 1970's and Material Conditions in Hip-Hop's Birthplace

Until 1979 with the release of Sugarhill Gang's six minute track titled "Rapper's Delight," hip-hop's musical component, rap, had not spread far beyond the South Bronx where it originated. To highlight 1979 as the year rap music began, however, would be a disservice to not only historical accuracy, but to any serious understanding of the roots through which hip-hop music blossomed. Comprehending the rise of a culture inevitably entails a holistic approach where the political, economic, and social institutions and conditions are analyzed to derive an understanding of their effects on the thoughts, ideas, and actions of the generation who created the culture. Therefore, the rise of hip-hop is inevitably linked with a host of changes during the 1970s to the political economy and the dominant ideology supporting it. These changes include the fading of the nonviolent civil rights movement and the subsequent black power movement, a massive restructuring from the failed Keynesian economic policies of state-interventionism to neoliberal, trickle down economics, the prodigious deindustrialization and the resulting unemployment, and the abandonment of urban spaces by government divestment and white flight. The Bronx of the early 1970s provides a paragon for such conditions and how they impacted the residents of these urban spaces; these conditions, however, were not limited to one area but were widely represented in many urban areas during this decade. Hip-hop culture, springing from such a particular set of conditions, would spread like wildfire into other areas where a similar combination of political and economic changes was rapidly advancing.

As Akilah Folami explains, "Historically, Hip-hop arose out of the ruins of a post-industrial and ravaged South Bronx, as a form of expression of urban Black and Latino youth, who politicians and the dominant public and political discourse had written off, and, for all intent and purposes, abandoned." [6]These youth were alienated from decent employment opportunities and confined to under-funded schools with little community resources; New York would suffer immense job losses coupled with decreased local and federal funding for social services. [7] The South Bronx alone would lose:

600,000 manufacturing jobs; 40 percent of the sector disappeared. By the mid-seventies, average per capita income dropped to $2,430, just half of the New York City average and 40 percent of the nationwide average. The official youth unemployment rate hit 60 percent. Youth advocates said that in some neighborhoods the true number was closer to 80 percent.[8]

Such conditions would leave "30 percent of New York's Hispanic households...and 25 percent of black households...at or below the poverty line. [9] This massive loss of employment was not the only contributing factor, however. Urban renewal programs, such as the one directed by elite urban planner Robert Moses, helped fuel white flight and suburban sprawl along with subsequent capital divestment from the city. Moses would go on to plan and build the Cross Bronx Expressway, which would "cut directly through the center of the most heavily populated working class areas in the Bronx," tearing apart the homes of some 60,000 Bronx residents. [10] Utilizing "urban renewal rights of clearance," Moses and local legislators would effectively enforce economic and legal segregation of poor and working-class Blacks and Latinos whom were pushed into "tower-in-a-park" model public housing units where they "got nine or more monotonous slabs of housing rising out of isolating, desolate, soon-to-be crime-ridden 'parks'."[11] Thus, it was deep within these hellholes of poverty, unemployment, segregation, and desperation that hip-hop's first birth pangs would be felt. As hip-hop historian Jeff Chang poignantly explains, it's "not to say that all hip-hop is political, but hip-hop comes out of that particular political context." [12]

The enormous influence of material conditions on hip-hop are lucidly illuminated with the 1982 release of a song titled "The Message" by pioneering rap group Grandmaster Flash and the Furious Five. Hesitant at first to record such a "preachy" rap song by a self-titled "party group," eventually Melle Mel, the lead rapper of the group, decided to give it a try.[13] Thus, the group helped to pioneer "the social awakening of rap into a form combining social protest, musical creation, and cultural expression."[14]Although not the first to provide social commentary on institutional racism and abject living conditions, as evidenced by earlier rappers such as Kurtis Blow, Brother D and the Collective Effort, and Tanya "Sweet Tee Winley,[15] "The Message" would provide the first mainstream, commercial success to speak seriously on these issues. The immense frustration and alienation of being confined to run-down ghettoes presents itself repeatedly throughout the song. Wrapped in each and every line is piercing social commentary on the condition of America's rotting inner city slums. The song opens by describing the horrendous conditions found specifically in the South Bronx during this period but could also be applied most the nation's abandoned urban centers:

Broken glass, everywhere / People pissing on the stairs, you know they just don't care / I can't take the smell, I can't take the noise / Got no money to move out, I guess I got no choice / Rats in the front room, roaches in the back / Junkies in the alley with a baseball bat / I tried to get away, but I couldn't get far / Cause the man with the tow-truck repossessed my car [16]

The sentiment expressed in the last two lines of being unable to escape the projects is one that runs consistently throughout the history of Hip-hop. Tupac, nearly a decade later, would articulate this despair further in his song "Trapped" where he speaks to the agonizing feeling of hopelessness and anger at being segregated into ghettoes and harassed by police.[17]

Dyson notes that as rap evolved it "began to describe and analyze the social, economic, and political factors that led to its emergence and development: drug addiction, police brutality, teen pregnancy, and various forms of material deprivation."[18] The Message takes up many of these issues and more, commenting repeatedly on the terrible state of education children in the projects are confined to. One line provides an explanation of how in the ghetto one rarely gets more than "a bum education" alongside "double-digit inflation." Another verse tells the story of a young boy who exclaims to his father that he feels alienated and dumb at school, due at least in part to his teachers' attitudes towards him; as the child explains, "all the kids smoke reefer, I think it'd be cheaper, if I just got a job, learned to be a street sweeper." In this succinct rhyme, the postulation put forth by educational theorist Jean Anyon that working-class and poor students are pushed into occupations which perpetuate the existing class structure is brilliantly summarized.[19] The despair and bleakness of abject ghetto life is articulated in a rather percussive manner in the last verse, "You grow in the ghetto, living second rate, and your eyes will sing a song of deep hate, the places you play and where you stay, looks like one great big alley way."[20]

Although "The Message" was not the first social commentary on ghetto life to be produced, it was the first mainstream success to reach a broader layer of listeners and proved that socially conscious rap had an audience. By the early 1980's hip-hop had already exploded onto the scene through particular mediums in certain areas. Graffiti had already provided a way in which alienated and seemingly invisible youths could make themselves visible outside the Bronx through creative, counter-hegemonic acts that signaled to the ruling authorities they were claiming their own space. Break dancing, or B-Boying, provided an outlet for youths to engage each other in peaceful competition and while it "did not dissolve the frustrations of being poor, unemployed, and a forgotten youth, it certainly served... as a catalyst to increasing the youth led community based peace effort." [21] However, it was rap music that, arguably, would have the largest impact in the future:

At a time when budget cuts lead to a reduction in school art and music programs, and when vocational training in high schools lead to jobs that had significantly decreased or no longer existed, "inner city youth transformed obsolete vocational skills from marginal occupations into the raw materials for creativity and resistance," with "turntables [becoming] instruments and lyrical acrobatics [becoming] a cultural outlet." [22]

This cultural outlet would not remain isolated in the South Bronx for long. Neither would it be confined to simply describing the harsh reality of living in the projects.

Afrocentricity, Black Power, and Hip-Hop's New School

Hip Hop was originally honed in house parties, parks, community centers, and local clubs by pioneers such as DJ Kool Herc, Afrika Bambaataa, and Grandmaster Flash. Independent record labels were quick to pick up on the enormous buzz generated by this new street sound. Small record executives, with their ears to the street, realized that "there were potentially many more millions of fans out there for the music," but they needed a way to push it from the traditional arenas where spontaneity reigned into the lab where Hip-hop could be researched, developed, and put into radio rotation. [23] Rap had to "fit the standards of the music industry" and labels had to pursue methods which in which they could "rationalize and exploit the new product" to "find, capture, package, and sell its essence...Six-man crews would drop to two. Fifteen-minute party-rocking raps would become three-minute ready-for-radio singles. Hip-hop was refined like sugar."[24] The laws of capitalism dictated that the art form had to be commodified, manufactured, and sold to a market. After the initial commercial success of "Rapper's Delight" and "The Message," corporate encroachment would quickly invade Hip-hop sovereignty. This seminal musical format would act as a medium through which two distinct worlds would mesh; young, black youth who aspired to spit rhymes and find a way out of their seemingly despondent condition would be introduced to nascent white record executives, opening what ostensibly appeared as new, untested feasibilities to previously marginalized artists. As early Hip-hop head and B-boy Richie "Crazy Legs" Colon would comment, "it was getting us into places that we never thought we could get into. So there was an exchange there... [but] that was also the beginning of us getting jerked...that's a reality."[25]

The struggle over control of the culture would be a reminiscent theme for the next decade. Dissident rap presenting a critique of the political economy would briefly touch mainstream society in the early and mid 1980's before being stifled and ostracized. In the next few years, the crossover of rap acts like Run-D.M.C. and the rise of overtly political rap groups such as Public Enemy, along with lesser known but highly controversial artists such as Paris, would trigger intense debate over the nature of Hip-hop and the direction it was headed. Passing from the pioneering old-school, a new era of Hip-hop would develop consisting of a fresh blend of Afrocentricity, cultural nationalism, calls for a neo-Black power, and a focus on the African diaspora. It would delve into the questions of race and racism and the legacy of slavery, along with a critique of institutionalized forms of oppression and ideas of what methods could adequately challenge them. It also presented artists with the first taste of corporate control over creative expression, a tension that would remain a prominent theme throughout the history of rap music. Any definite time frame would only succeed in confining the progression of Hip-hop into arbitrary, categorical stages that lack accurate representation of the often overlapping and dynamic evolutionary process of the art. However, in the mid 1980s it became apparent that rap was burgeoning into uncharted territory.

Afrocentric rap, advocating a unique mix of cultural nationalism and Pan-Africanism, can trace its roots to Afrika Bambaataa and the Zulu Nation, an organization of reformed gang members who attempted to take back their streets through the creation of innovative cultural outlets, many of which would develop into early Hip-hop culture. Bambaataa "started to believe that the energy, loyalty, and passion that defined gang life could be guided toward more socially productive activities...he saw an opportunity to combine his love of music and B-boying with his desire to enhance community life." [26] After some initial musical success, however, tensions began to mount between Bambaataa and the man who signed him, Tom Silverman, founder of the independent label Tommy Boy Records. Bambaataa recounts, "The record companies would try to tell us what we should make, what we should do...We said, 'Listen, we're the renegades, we sing what we want to sing, dress how we want to dress, and say what we want to say."[27] This sort of outright resistance to artist manipulation worked for a time, when artists dealt primarily with small, independent stations during the nascent stages of Hip-hop's development. Later, however, when the corporate structures completely enveloped the art, it would be nearly impossible to individually challenge such enormous institutions.

Queens rap trio Run-D.M.C. "is widely recognized as the progenitor of modern rap's creative integration of social commentary, diverse musical elements, and uncompromising cultural identification"[28] into what would become known as the New School of Hip-hop. [29] Fueled by Jam Master Jay' complex, percussive beats and brilliant lyrical deliverance, Run-D.M.C. would burst into the mainstream by signing a distributing deal with Colombia records.[30] Bridging the gap between rap and rock, Run-D.M.C. appealed to a wide range of audiences from rugged, street hustlers to well-to-do white kids in a desperate search to branch out from the cultural confinement of suburbia. As their album *Raising Hell* rushed to platinum status, they catapulted rap music into mainstream discourse and charted a new path for commercial success. The group presented an interesting dynamic where, challenging corporate-driven consumerism with lines such as "Calvin Klein's no friend of mine, don't want nobody's name on my behind," [31] they simultaneously promoted a specific style of apparel with tracks such as "My Adidas" that would break with previous, flashily clad rap artists and forever tie Hip-hop's look to the styles of the street. *Raising Hell* would end with "Proud to Be Black," a track emphasizing African history and the struggle against slavery while documenting the historical progress of black people. Involving themselves in specific struggles or causes, such as doing benefit performances for the anti-Apartheid struggle, [32] they did not shy away from political issues.

On "Wake Up," the trio echoed calls for democratic participation of the masses, full employment, fair wages, and an end to racial prejudice that would be familiar to any socialist activist. They provided a glimpse of the shape a truly humanizing society could take:

There were no guns, no tanks, no atomic bombs / and to be frank homeboy, there were no arms... / Between all countries there were good relations / there finally was a meaning to United Nations / and everybody had an occupation / 'cause we all worked together to fight starvation... / Everyone was treated on an equal basis / No matter what color, religion or races / We weren't afraid to show our faces / It was cool to chill in foreign places... / All cities of the world were renovated / And the people all chilled and celebrated / They were all so happy and elated / To live in the world that they created... / And every single person had a place to be / A job, a home, and the perfect pay...[33]

The song is haunted by the chorus proclaiming that all the hopes and desires for the fanciful world articulated are "just a dream." The group switches gears on "It's Like That," citing unemployment, atrocious wages, ever-increasing bills, and the struggle to survive within the confines of a capitalist political economy. At the end of each verse they communicate their prodigious frustration manifested from the despair and helplessness prevalent in oppressed communities, leaving the listener with little hope for change: "Don't ask me, because I don't know why, but it's like that, and that's the way it is!"[34] Grand ideals aside, Run-D.M.C. ultimately did not pursue a confrontational approach to the dominant institutions in society and, thus, their commercial success in part reflects their desire to integrate into the established system rather than attempt to dismantle the established structures.

Ideas of collective social change would be articulated more thoroughly by artists such as Public Enemy. Coming from a relatively well-to-do, although still highly segregated, post-white flight neighborhood, Public Enemy's ambitions were to "be heard as the expression of a new generation's definition of blackness."[35] As opposed to artists who may record a political song or sneak a witty, politically charged punch line into a mainstream hit, Public Enemy would focus entire albums around counter-hegemonic themes reflecting their constantly evolving political philosophy. Their Black Nationalist ideology did not go unnoticed in their first album, but it would augment over time as the group developed their own conception of a new Black Power. On *It Takes a Nation of Millions to Hold Us Back* and *Fear of a Black Planet* they delved deeply into race relations, the oppression of the black community at home and abroad, and brought into question entire institutions of society they viewed as perpetuating racism. The group also spoke openly of their support for

Palestinian liberation and against U.S. imperialism. On "Bring the Noise," they challenged black radio to play their music and on "Party for Your Right to Fight" they evoked images of Martin Luther King Jr., Malcolm X, and the Black Panther Party in a "pro-Black radical mix"[36] while aiming verbal invectives at J. Edgar Hoover and the FBI for their historically repressive roles against the black community.

Public Enemy undoubtedly pushed political hip-hop to a new level. Their intense, in-your-face rhymes promoted a historical revival amongst black youth previously separated from prior cultural developments and struggles of the past. However, as Dyson points out, this can lead to rappers hoping to emulate the methods of the past without a critical analysis of its strengths and weaknesses or, worse yet, to promoting vacuous calls to past movements' cultural icons intended to draw reverence without attempting to augment the organizational infrastructure required to proactively challenge oppressive institutions. Still, given the tyrannical nature of the society in which they lived, the group labeled themselves "the Black Panthers of rap" [37] as a symbolic expression of their hostility towards the system. However, the framework within which they operated, borrowing large portions of their theoretical interpretation of society to the Nation of Islam and Louis Farrakhan, did not allow them to adopt the Panthers' revolutionary, socialist critique of the political economy. It was replaced instead with a form of black militancy aligned primarily with a narrow conception of Black Nationalism. Public Enemy would drastically differ from the Panthers who had come to reject Black Nationalism as a racist philosophy, aiming their crosshairs more broadly on capitalism [38] and arguing racism was a byproduct of that particular economic mode of production.[39] Regardless, Public Enemy's prodigious contributions to political hip-hop cannot be ignored. They fostered political discussion and pushed hip-hop to embrace black liberation. Yet, they would fail to propose a cohesive, theoretical alternative or method through which this could be achieved.

Other times, political hip-hop took the form of cathartic, impulsive depictions of violence stemming from the wrath manifested within oppressed black communities. One example, Oakland rapper Paris, who adhered early in his career to a form of Black Nationalism similar to Public Enemy's, would seek a sort of lyrical revenge against individuals and institutions he found oppressive and exploitative. Through songs like "Bush Killa," where he fantasized about assassinating then President George H. Bush, he would decisively embrace a black militancy that challenged the past legacy of King's non-violence: "So don't be tellin' me to get the non-violent spirit, 'cause when I'm violent is the only time you devils hear it!" Later in the song he goes on to poignantly express his disgust with the predatory nature of military recruitment while uniquely mimicking the famous line from Muhammad Ali, [40] "Yeah, tolerance is gettin' thinner, 'cause *Iraq never called me nigger*, so what I wanna go off and fight a war for?" [41]Presumably due to the radical nature of his music, Paris was dropped from his record label, Tommy Boy, after parent company Time Warner reviewed the content of his album.[42] He distanced himself from the Nation of Islam, and thought that they were "more concerned with what was wrong with society than with how to change it." [43] Nearly two decades later, and still rapping under his own label, Paris would go on to develop a political stance that, while still bonded to certain aspects of his previous Black Nationalist thought, would become decidedly more working-class in its orientation, emphasizing class struggle and interracial solidarity rather than a simple black-white dichotomy.

The 1980s were, undoubtedly, a time of creativity, diversity, and cultural exploration within the musical realm of Hip-hop. Artists even tested the waters with politically significant album covers. Paris placed a potent photo of riot police choking a black protestor in his 1989 release*Break the Grip of Shame*.[44]Rapper KRS-One, paraphrasing Malcolm X on his album title *By All Means Neccesary* (1988), poses on the front cover in a fashion reminiscent of Malcolm's famous photograph; Malcolm, standing with AK-47 in his right arm and peering out of the drapes with his left, symbolized the vision of armed self-defense and intellectual self-determination. KRS-One, adorned in a fashionable outfit and carrying a more contemporary Uzi, personified these principles Malcolm so vehemently defended throughout his life. [45] Chuck D of Public Enemy explains, given the group's extensive list of politically charged album covers, that sometimes "the covers were thought out more than the songs."[46] Corporate control was illuminated in this artistic arena as well when hip-hop trio KMD attempted to release an album titled *Black Bastards* which featured a "Little Sambo"[47] character being hung; Elektra, their label, quietly rejected the album and its politically charged album artwork.[48]

Some rappers, such as Rakim, toyed with abstract ideas of personal and spiritual development, meshed with political Islam and the elitist vision of the Five Percenters, a group who believed that a gifted five percent of the world's population was destined to fight against the exploitative ten percent on behalf of the ignorant, backwards eighty-five percent.[49] Others, like rap group Naughty by Nature, found unique ways to tie in urban culture and style to the historic legacies of the past. On one of the group's most political tracks, "Chain Remains," rapper Treach vividly explicates on the cultural significance of the chain commonly worn by black, urban youth, tying it into the past history of slavery and the prison-industrial complex:

Bars and cement instead of help for our people / Jails ain't nothin' but the slave day sequel / Tryin' to flee the trap of this nation / Seein' penitentiary's the plan to plant the new plantation... / Free? Please, nigga, ain't no freedom! / Who's locked up? Who's shot up? Who's strung out? Who's bleeding? Keep reading / I'm here to explain the chain remain the same / Maintain for the brothers and sisters locked / The chain remains...[50]

The last verse ends with an incendiary call to revolution, although the terms for which are not specifically outlined: "the only solutions revolution, know we told ya', the chain remains 'til we uprise, stuck in a land where we ain't meant to survive." Despite calls for racial solidarity and social empowerment, the violence found in poverty-stricken urban areas often followed artists into the realm of entertainment.

When violence broke out at various rap venues in 1987, the hip-hop community was quick to respond with a Stop the Violence Movement. A group of artists organized a project "that would include a benefit record, video, book, and a rally around the theme."[51] On the record "Self Destruction," a wide assortment of rappers came together to urge black youth to "crush the stereotype" and "unite and fight for what's right,"[52] by stopping the senseless violence that plagued the black community. Unfortunately, it was not a sustained political campaign and, as Jeff Chang argues, Stop the Violence "was always less a movement than a media event." [53] KRS-One, re-launching the Stop the Violence 2008 campaign in a similar fashion, disagrees, claiming Chang's interpretation is "inaccurate history and fake scholarship."[54] Regardless, media event or movement, Stop the Violence provided another example of rappers attempting to take control of their communities and control their own destinies.

New School Hip Hop was defined by its seminal, independent spirit of artists' attempts to maneuver within the confines of an ever-increasing hierarchal, corporate, top-down structure. Indeed, as Chang notes, "Rap proved to be the ideal form to commodify the hip-hop culture. It was endlessly novel, reproducible, malleable, and perfectible. Records got shorter, raps more concise, and tailored to pop-song structures." [55] The infrastructure needed to solidify corporate power over the culture was being rapidly built but originality and autonomy would not yet be completely shattered. The day would soon come, however, when creativity and free political expression would be stomped out and replaced with denigrating images of black men, as self-destructive gangsters and intellectually bankrupt drug-pushers, and black women, whose sole contribution is their sexual appeal, vigorously promoted by the dominant ideology. Generally, during this period artists would attempt to hold on "to the Black Panther ethic of remaining true to Blackness... to the people in the lower classes" while, on the other hand, rejecting the Party's anti-capitalist stance; "Rappers wanted a piece of the American pie while staying grounded to the urban culture, and wanted to speak in their own voice and on their own terms."[56]Given the political, social, and economic conditions of the mid-1980s, this was no surprise.

The sort of individualistic response exemplified by New School artists was developed within the context of a detrimental political vacuum left by the simultaneous failure and systematic repression of revolutionary left groups of the 1960s and early 1970s. Instead of political organizers, rappers would view themselves as reporters whose primary vocation was to give the voiceless a form of expression and relay the conditions of ghetto life to the rest of the world. Public Enemy articulated this concept when he explained that rap was "Black America's CNN, an alternative, youth-controlled media network."[57] Tupac would echo this concept, "I just try to speak about things that affect me and our community. Sometimes I'm the watcher, and sometimes the participant," he commented, and likening himself to reporters during the Vietnam War, he explicated on his role, "That's what I'll do as an artist, as a rapper. I'm gonna show the graphic details of what I see in my community and hopefully they'll stop it." [58] Rather than broad-reaching, collective social change achieved through organized resistance, rap music would act as a means to express counter-hegemonic, yet radically individualized forms of resistance that captured the very essence of the urban youth existence. This concept would be carried further into the realm of musical performance:

Rap...found an arena in which to concentrate its subversive cultural didacticism aimed at addressing racism, classism, social neglect, and urban pain: the rap concert, where rappers are allowed to engage in ritualistic refusals of censored speech. The rap concert also creates space for cultural resistance and personal agency, losing the strictures of the tyrannizing surveillance and demoralizing condemnation of mainstream society and encouraging relatively autonomous, often enabling, forms of self-expression and cultural creativity. [59]

It was this anti-authoritarian impulse, fostered in the hard streets of Los Angeles where police brutality was rampant and socioeconomic conditions were dire, that galvanized the next phase of Hip-hop which would take the nation by storm.

Notes

[1] DJ Kool Herc quoted in Jeff Chang, *Can't Stop Won't Stop*, (New York City: St. Martin's Press, 2005), xi.
[2] Michael Eric Dyson, *The Michael Eric Dyson Reader*, (New York City: Basic Civitas Books, 2004), 408.
[3] Immortal Technique, "Death March" *The 3rd World*, 2008, Viper Records. DJ Green Lantern makes the opening remarks.
[4] Ta-Nehisi Coates, "Hip-hop's Down Beat," *Time*, accessed 5 April 2009; available from http://www.time.com/time/magazine/article/0,9171,1653639,00.html; Internet.
[5] David Drake, "The 'Death' of Hip-Hop," *Pop Playground*, accessed 5 April 2009; available from http://www.stylusmagazine.com/feature.php?ID=1525; Internet. Implicit in Stylus's 2005 article about the "death" of hip-hop is the idea that capitalism allowed for hip-hops growth. They argue the history of hip-hop cannot be separated and "well-behaved politicos with either leftist or moralist agendas" only "imagine a fictional past" since "capitalism was involved from the second it spread, from the moment a rhyme was laid to wax capitalism was there." While this is partly correct, as hip-hop developed within the confines of a capitalist society, and was thus influenced by the dominant ideological forces that perpetuate such a society, the early independence and autonomy from corporate

capitalism and the art form that developed without the profit incentive, but instead for reasons of pure enjoyment (Kool Herc house parties) or political and social transformation (Zulus) shows that hip-hop and capitalism can not only be separated, but at it's earliest stages were separate entities.

[6] Akilah N. Folami, "From Habermas to 'Get Rich or Die Trying': Hip Hop, The Telecommunications Act of 1996, and the Black Public Sphere," *Michigan Journal of Race and Law, Vol. 12(June 2007)*(Queens, NY: St. John's University School of Law, 2007), 240.

[7] Folami, *Habermas to "Get Rich or Die Trying,"* 254.

[8] Chang, *Can't Stop Won't Stop*, 13.

[9] Tricia Rose, *Black Noise: Rap Music and Black Culture in Contemporary America 27* (Middletown, CT: Wesleyan University Press, 1994), 28.

[10] Rose, *Black Noise*, 31.

[11] Chang, 11-12.

[12] Jeff Chang interviewed by Brian Jones, "Interview with Jeff Chang, Hip Hop Politics," *International Socialist Review*, Issue 48, (July-August 2006), accessed 5 April 2009; available fromhttp://www.isreview.org/issues/48/changinterview.shtml; Internet.

[13] Craig Watkins, *Hip Hop Matters: Politics, Pop Culture, and the Struggle for the Soul of a Movement* (Boston: Beacon Press, 2005), 21.

[14] Dyson, *Michael Eric Dyson Reader*, 402.

[15] Chang, 179.

[16] Grandmaster Flash and the Furious Five, "The Message," *The Message*, 1982, Sugar Hill.

[17] Tupac Shakur, "Trapped," *2Pacalypse Now*, 1991, Jive. Tupac, who, originally just repeating stories from his peers, would have a violent run in with police not long after he released the song. Accused of jaywalking, Tupac would be knocked to the ground and have his face slammed into the concrete, leaving life-long scars across his right cheek bone. After a long court battle, he finally settled with the police department for a small sum. "You know they got me trapped in this prison of seclusion / Happiness, living on tha streets is a delusion... / Tired of being trapped in this vicious cycle / If one more cop harrasses me I just might go psycho / And when I get 'em / I'll hit 'em with the bum rush / Only a lunatic would like to see his skull crushed / Yo, if your smart you'll really let me go 'G' / But keep me cooped up in this ghetto and catch the uzi... / They got me trapped / Can barely walk the city

streets / Without a cop harassing me, searching me / Then asking my identity... / Trapped in my own community / One day I'm gonna bust / Blow up on this society / Why did ya' lie to me? / I couldn't find a trace of equality...

[18] Dyson, 402.

[19] Jean Anyon, *"Social Class and the Hidden Cirriculum."* Journal of Education, 162(1), Fall, 1980. Online version available here http://cuip.uchicago.edu/~cac/nlu/fnd504/anyon.htm; Internet.

[20] Flash, "The Message."

[21] Folami, 258.

[22] Ibid., 257.

[23] Chang, 133.

[24] Ibid., 134

[25] Ibid., 177

[26] Watkins, *Hip Hop Matters*, 23.

[27] Chang, 190.

[28] Dyson, 402.

[29] Chang, 255.

[30] Ibid., 204.

[31] Run-D.M.C., "Rock Box," *Run-D.M.C.*, 1983, Profile/Arista Records.

[32] Chang, 218.

[33] Run-D.M.C., "Wake Up," *Run-D.M.C.*, 1983, Profile/Arista Records.

[34] Run-D.M.C., "It's Like That," *Run-D.M.C.*, 1983, Profile/Arista Records.

[35] Chang, 249.

[36] Public Enemy, "Party For your Right to Fight," *It Takes a Nation of Millions to Hold Us Back*, 1988, Def Jam/Columbia/CBS Records.

[37] Chang, 248.

[38] *Bobby Seale, Seize the Time (Baltimore: Black Classic Press, 1997), 23, 256, 383.*

[39] Fred Hampton, "Murder of Fred Hampton, Reel 1," accessed 5 April 2009; available from http://mediaburn.org/Video-Priview.128.0.html?uid=4192; Internet. In this clip, Hampton is talking to a church crowd about how Blacks and the Black Panther Party should interact with Whites and White radicals.

[40] In 1966 Muhammad Ali, in his denunciation of the Vietnam War and U.S. attempts to draft him, explained "I ain't got no quarrel with the Vietcong... No Vietcong ever called me nigger." For more information, see here: http://www.aavw.org/protest/homepage_ali.html; Internet.

[41] Paris, "Bush Killa," *Sleeping With the Enemy*, 1992, Scarface.

[42] Peter Byrne, "Capital Rap" *San Francisco News*, accessed 5 April 2009; available from http://www.sfweekly.com/2003-12-03/news/capital-rap/2; Internet.

[43] Byrne, "Capital Rap," 2.

[44] Andrew Emery, *The Book of Hip Hop Cover Art*, (Mitchell Beazly, 2004), 95.

[45] Emery, *Hip Hop Cover Art*, 133.

[46] Ibid., 81.

[47] "Sambo" is a racial slur for African-Americans in the United States but the image of the Little Black Sambo became famous after a children's book by Helen Bannerman was published in London in 1899. The original story can be found here: http://www.sterlingtimes.co.uk/sambo.htm

[48] Emery, 112.

[49] Chang, 258-9.

[50] Naughty by Nature, "Chain Remains," *Poverty's Paradise*, 1995, Warner.

[51] Chang, 274.

[52] Lyrics for the song can be found here: http://www.lyricsmania.com/lyrics/krs-one_lyrics_3454/other_lyrics_10824/self_destruction_lyrics_125592.html

[53] Chang, 274.

[54] KRS-One interviewed by Brolin Winning, "KRS-One: You Must Learn," *MP3.com*, accessed 5 April 2008; available from http://www.mp3.com/news/stories/9464.html; Internet.

[55] Chang, 228.

[56] Folami, 263.

[57] Chang, 251.

[58] Tupac Shakur, "Tupac Resurrection Script - The Dialogue," *Drew's Script-O-Rama*, accessed 5 April 2008; available from http://www.script-o-rama.com/movie_scripts/t/tupac-resurrection-script-2pac-Shakur.html ; Internet.

[59] Dyson, 403.

How Capitalism Underdeveloped Hip Hop (Part 2)

A People's History of Political Rap

Derek A. Ide

West Coast Projects, the Rise of Gangsta Rap, and Congress's War on the Youth

Gangsta Rap burst forth in its nascent form in the late 1980's in the heart of Los Angeles. To comprehend how this subgenre of rap developed, however, the ruthless conditions which originally produced the gang epidemic must be recognized. Institutionalized racial segregation, economic deprivation, and social degradation, enforced by hegemonic government and business structures, had historically plagued communities of color in the area and produced a distinct history which would give rise in the 1980's to a prodigious spike in gang activity and violence. Historically marginalized groups would be pitted against one another in despondent economic conditions and forced to compete amongst themselves for the paltry scraps that fell from society's table. Government departments, banking agencies, and the real estate industry would play into the game of get-rich-quick racial segregation. Redlining, the practice of denying or increasing costs of housing and insurance to economically segregate communities along racial lines, played a fundamental role in the homogenous racial composition of west coast urban areas. In 1938, the Federal Housing Administration released an underwriting manual which all lenders were forced to read, explaining that areas should be investigated in order to determine "the probability of the location being invaded" by "incompatible racial and social groups" and, more importantly, that for a "neighborhood is to retain stability" it must "be occupied by the same social and racial classes" because a change in these would lead to "instability and a decline in values." [1] Some entrepreneurs "figured out how to hustle racial fear" [2] by buying at low prices from whites fleeing their homes and selling to blacks at prices significantly higher than market level. This effectively kept blacks and whites segregated into different neighborhoods.

After World War II, public housing projects were constructed, giving Watts the highest concentration of public housing on the West Coast. [3] Combined with this historic segregation, the 1980s brought with it "deindustrialization, devolution, Cold War adventurism, the drug trade, gang structures and rivalries, arms profiteering, and police brutality" which would combine to "destabilize poor communities and alienate massive numbers of youth." [4] In the same decade 131 manufacturing plants closed their doors, Los Angeles's official unemployment was at 11 percent in 1983 and in South Central youth unemployment was over 50 percent, one quarter of Blacks and Latinos lived below the poverty line, and living conditions had drastically declined. [5] Even when gangs attempted to make peace and establish long-standing treaties with one another, no infrastructure was in place to maintain stable communities with jobs and social services. In fact, when the leaders from seven rival gangs called a truce and marched to City Hall to request funding for social services, they were told they could apply for a paltry $500 grant. [6] This denial was on top of the conservative economic agenda dominating the political domain at the time which had already cut spending on subsidized housing by 82 percent, job training and employment by 63 percent, and community service and development programs by 40 percent from post-World War II era progressive spending policies. [7]

It was within these conditions that by the 1980s, after the dismantling of political organizations such as the Black Panthers and Young Lords, 155 gangs would claim over 30,000 members across the city. [8]Gangsta rap, as it was labeled, would attempt to articulate, and in some instances glorify, the street life so common in Los Angeles. Immortal Technique points out that a "factoid of information probably purposely forgotten through the years is that before it was labeled 'Gangsta Rap' by the industry itself it was called 'Reality Rap' by those individuals that created it." [9] Political prisoner and former Black Panther Mumia Abu-Jamal explains that the music was spawned by young people whom felt "that they are at best tolerated in schools, feared on the streets, and almost inevitably destined for the hell holes of prison. They grew up hungry, hated and unloved. And this is the psychic fuel that seems to generate the anger that seems endemic in much of the music and poetry." [10] This anger would shine through on tracks such as "Straight Outta Compton" by N.W.A., where rapper Ice Cube explains that he's "From the gang called Niggaz With Attitudes" and "When I'm called off, I got a sawed off, squeeze the trigger, and bodies are hauled off!" [11]

Their rhymes signified a shift from the revolutionary programs set forth by previous political rappers and instead focused on a complete self-indulgence in instant gratification; drugs, women, the murder of enemies and assassination of police, everything was fair game. It was N.W.A.'s track entitled "Fuck tha Police," released in 1988, which garnered national media attention. The rather prophetic song would become a universal slogan in ghetto communities just four years later with the police beating of Rodney King and subsequent urban uprisings. Disgusted with the police brutality they witnessed regularly, N.W.A. would take up the issue, not politically, but with an individual vengeance and wrath previously unmatched. Beginning with fictitious court hearing in which "Judge Dre" would preside "in the case of NWA versus the police department," the "prosecuting attorneys" MC Ren, Ice Cube, and Eazy E would each lay out their case against the Los Angeles Police Department. Ice Cube's opening lines, brimming with unparalleled virulence, would set the tone: "Fuck the police comin' straight from the underground, young nigga got it bad cuz I'm brown, and not the other color so police think, they have the authority to kill a minority." Reminiscent of Paris's earlier fantastical verbal assassination of President Bush, MC Ren would warn police "not to step in my path" because "Ren's gonna blast," and, turning the tables, he confidently proclaims his hatred towards the police "with authority, because the niggas on the street is a majority." Eazy E finishes the last verse, emphasizing that fact that cops should not be perceived as immune to violent resistance: "Without a gun and a badge, what do ya got? A sucka in a uniform waitin' to get shot." [12] The controversy revolving around this song would push the album it was featured on, *Straight Outta Compton*, to double platinum status. By June of 1989, the right-wing backlash against N.W.A. would be front page news, an entertainment manifestation of the "War on Gangs" which L.A. Police Chief Darryl Gates had already brought to South Central.

The atmosphere of late 1980's was dictated by punitive measures explicitly directed at youth and relentless attacks on youth culture. The Street Terrorism Enforcement and Prevention Act was passed in 1988 and enhanced punishments for "gang-related offenses," created "new categories of gang crimes," and gave up to three years in state prison for even claiming gang membership. [13] This piece of legislation had profoundly harmful repercussions for youth who identified with, or even may have displayed certain characteristics of, being involved with a gang; police considered any combination of two of the following examples to constitute gang membership: "slang, clothing of a particular color, pagers, hairstyles, or jewelry." [14] Within a decade most major cities and at least nineteen states had similar laws. [15] The crossover into what became a congressional attack on Gangsta rap was facilitated by opportunistic politicians who pounced excitedly on the chance:

Tipper Gore, the wife of former vice president Al Gore, and Susan Baker, the wife of Bush's former campaign manager, James Baker, formed Parents Music Resource Center (PMRC) which called for, and received, a congressional hearing on record labeling. Every song listed by the PMRC and presented at the congressional hearing as being too explicit and obscene and in need of censorship labeling was done by a Black artist. [16]

While politicians and networks of Christian fundamentalist groups had already begun anti-hip-hop campaigns under a guise of protecting morality, what Thompson labeled the "cultural civil war," [17] it was failed liberal politician and head of the National Political Congress of Black Women, C. Delores Tucker, who spearheaded the congressional war on Gangsta rap. Teaming up with cultural conservatives, Tucker, through a façade of feminism and racial pride, organized a concerted campaign against rap in order to push through legislation that strengthened juvenile-crime laws and crackdowns on youth. Inverting cause and effect, she argued that the hip-hop generation would become internalized "with the violence glorified in gangster rap" and that rap music created a "social time bomb" which would "trigger a crime wave of epidemic proportions," only to be stopped by smothering the cultural and musical developments of ghetto youth. [18]

Among some of her chief targets was Tupac Shakur (2Pac), who was not quiet in his opposition to Tucker and her political opportunism. Tupac, staying true to his roots on "Nothin' But Love," outlines the composition of his family tree as one of "Panthers, pimps, pushers, and thugs;" [19] this unique mixture helped him to articulate a conception of the rebellious ghetto lifestyle blended with the legacy of black struggle into what he termed "Thug Life." An acronym, which stood for "The Hate U Gave Little Infants Fucks Everybody," [20] his idea of "Thug Life" was a "new kind of Black Power" [21] that young black males were forced to live through:

These white folks see us as thugs, I don't care if you a lawyer, a man, an 'African-American,' if you whatever...you think you are, we thugs and niggas [to them]...and until we own some shit, I'ma call it like it is. How you gonna be a man when we starving?... How we gonna be African-Americans if we all need a gun? [22]

Tupac, whose mother Afeni Shakur was a prominent Black Panther and political activist, would utilize his connections with the streets and balance his music with historical connections to political organizers such as Huey Newton and chilling urban tales of despondent situations such as the fictitious tale of the teenage mother Brenda and the ever-present black-on-black violence. Through this unification of social commentator and street participant, Tupac would authenticate his image to millions of youth, black and white alike. Tupac's response to Tucker's critique of the lyrical content of his music was redolent of Chuck D's interpretation of rappers as journalists who help to show the world the gruesome reality of urban street life; as he argued, "I have not brought violence to you. I have not brought Thug Life to America. I didn't create Thug Life. I diagnosed it." [23]

Furthermore, according to Dyson, the attempt to suppress "gangsta rap's troubling expressions" is manipulated for "narrow political ends" that fail to "critically engage...artists and the provocative issues they address." [24] While dialogue concerning rampant homophobia, sexism, and other dehumanizing aspects of certain rap artists should be challenged, it should be done so in a way that does not alienate and isolate, but engages and allows for the artist to transcend both actions that reflect the dominant ideology and the use of oppressive language. Rapper and activist Son of Nun summarizes his position:

Some real rappers spit truth every night, but say stupid shit when it comes to gay rights. They talk about the Panthers, but they never knew that Huey woulda' called their asses out for what they do...So, in my music, I try not to call out specific emcees...[because] I realize that I have more in common with them, then I'll ever have in common with the label head or the corporate people putting that music out... [Despite sexist or homophobic remarks] when you read the interview and listen to some lyrics, you'll see that there's a revolutionary consciousness that's there at the same time...and I'd rather see those brothers as my comrades whom I can build with, as opposed to people I need to chop down and diss... [25]

   This extension of the right-wing economic attack on working class and poor youth into the cultural realm, as exemplified by politicians like Tucker, should not be viewed in isolation from the larger historical trends occurring at the same time; it operated within a certain political economy and aided the perpetuation the dominant ideology required in order to push through neoliberal economic policies.
The mental framework in which Gangsta rap functions is articulated by Immortal Technique, drawing on the theoretical contributions to education outlined in Paulo Freire's *Pedagogy of the Oppressed*, he explains, "Our youth and young adults see these gangstas and other ruthless men [famous gangsters, drug kingpins, etc.] as powerful beyond the scope of a government that holds them prisoner. People*emulate their oppressor* and worship those that defy him openly." [26] This does not, however, mean that Gangsta rap is devoid of a political foundation or that it should be ostracized by the Hip-hop community. As Dyson argues, "While rappers like N.W.A. perform an invaluable service by rapping in poignant and realistic terms about urban underclass existence, they must be challenged...[to understand] that description alone is insufficient to address the crises of black urban life." [27] Thus, this fusion of gangster and rebel, a sort of misguided revolutionary, groping in the darkness of urban decay and abandonment for a way to challenge oppressive, hegemonic institutions, finds its musical expression in the West Coast rap scene. Today, gangsta rap has spread far beyond the streets of L.A. and into every neighborhood, ghetto, suburb, country, to every corner of the

world. The rebellious, gangster appeal, devoid of social content and reality, continues to be marketed on every street corner; a sort of "manufactured, corporate bought thug image" is pushed to the youth while "the Revolutionary element is for the most part completely sanitized by the corporate structure."[28]

Corporate Consolidation and the Telecommunications Act

This rejection of the revolutionary and embrace of the thug caricature so common in contemporary hip-hop is, in large part, a result of corporate monopolization of radio airwaves and dismantling of independent record labels. For years, questions concerning rap's viability as a musical genre and it's viability as a pop music sensation surrounded the relatively young art. Industry executives looked upon rap with disdain, viewing it as a niche market unsuitable for broad consumption. This allowed the genre to slip under corporate radar and maintain a sense of independence from major pop labels for a significant period of time. After the innovative development in 1991 of SoundScan that utilized bar-code recording to garner hard data on music sales and replaced the previous "archaic method" which had relied on the retail personnel who compiled weekly, subjective reports of sales trends "open to interpretation," [29] rap was found to have a much broader appeal than originally thought. With this new, more objective methodology of measuring music consumption, rap jumped from the relative obscurity of being a subcultural phenomenon to a major competitor with rock and pop music on the *Billboard* charts. [30] The "underreporting of rap was a result of long-standing cultural sensibilities and racial assumptions" [31] on the part of retail personnel. Subsequently, industry executives who still may have "harbored ill feelings toward the genre" could no longer "ignore the sales data SoundScan provided...[or] the huge financial payoff it offered." [32] As hip hop observer and critic Craig Watkins explains, "In an industry that had long ago sold its soul to the guardians of capitalism, the commercial compulsions that operate among culture industry executives are a powerful force." [33] The music, however, would have to be tamed considerably.

These commercial compulsions galvanized industry executives to tighten their stranglehold on rap music. In order to protect their status within the capitalist framework and pop music industry, executives were forced to marginalize and reject progressive, dissident, revolutionary, socialist, or any other form of independent and autonomous rap that may present a systemic critique of the established relations of power in society. Corporate hip-hop, as exemplified with the rise of rappers like 50 Cent in 2003, "rested almost entirely on its ability to sell black death" where "guns, gangsterism, and ghetto authenticity brought an aura of celebrity and glamour to the grim yet fabulously hyped portraits of ghetto life." [34] Statistics are not conclusive, but Mediamark Research Inc. estimates that whites constitute around sixty percent of the consumer market for rap in the United States. [35] Other sources, such as Def Jam CEO Russell Simmons, place the number somewhere closer to eighty percent. [36] Regardless, it is obvious that hip-hop is not an exclusively black culture; the composition of the consumer market facilitates a sort of "cultural tourism" where a "staged authenticity" [37] filled with racial stereotypes of black culture can be marketed to white youth.

Corporate consolidation of media outlets has galvanized this process of promoting a certain image of ghetto youth while downplaying the revolutionary or counter-hegemonic sentiments expressed in the music. Major labels and corporate conglomerates have very little interest in promoting artists who question capitalism or the free market fundamentalism. After all, it was that very system which originally granted them the ability to garner the enormous capital required to build their constantly expanding media empire. Immortal Technique articulates this concept:

The hood is not stupid, we know the mathematics / I make double what I would going gold on Atlantic / 'Cause EMI, Sony, BMG, Interscope / Would never sign a rapper with the white house in his scope / They push pop music like a religion / Anorexic celebrity driven / Financial fantasy fiction. [38]

Without an understanding of the significant role that major media outlets play in promoting a specific paradigm, especially in the case of a popular musical juggernaut such as rap, the rise of the glorified, gangster image cannot be concretely analyzed. Chang comments that "a lot of times people will talk about 50 Cent, but they won't talk about the structures that have made a 50 Cent possible." [39] The structures Chang refers to are multifaceted, and include broad neoliberal market deregulations that, since the 1970s, allowed for massive corporate takeovers of independent record labels and a consolidation of radio and other media outlets. For instance, by 2000, five companies - Vivendi Universal, Sony, AOL Time Warner, Bertelsmann, and EMI - dominated eighty percent of the music industry. [40] One act in particular, however, the Telecommunications Act passed by Congress in 1996, presented "a landmark of deregulation," a "legal codification of the pro-media monopoly stance" that allowed the free market to shift power "decisively in the direction of the media monopolies." [41]The passage of this act had a percussive impact on the artists' creative control over their music.

The Telecommunications Act relaxed ownership limits over radio and television for corporate entities, essentially creating fewer corporate conglomerates with concentrated control over various media outlets. Congress ostensibly passed the act under the tenuous postulation that "a deregulated marketplace would best serve the public interest." [42] As to be expected, its passage spurred a rapid absorption of smaller, local radio stations into the hands of large, already established companies such as Clear Channel,[43] Cumulus, Citadel, and Viacom. [44] The result was that hundreds of jobs were decimated, community programming was abandoned, and radio playlists became standardized across the country. [45] For a stations like KMEL-FM in the Bay Area, whom prided themselves on being a "people's station" by engaging in social issues affecting the San Francisco community, this meant being bought out and merged with competing stations; playlists became nearly identical, specialty shows were cut, local personalities were fired, and local or underground artists "unable to compete with six-figure major label marketing budgets" were left without a venue. [46] Artists like Binary Star, who challenged the gangster caricature, would become, even more than before, systematically excluded by these corporate structures. Rhymes, such as those displayed on one of Binary Star's most well-known tracks "Honest Expression," [47] would be consistently ostracized from airplay.

Conglomerates like Clear Channel, unlike locally controlled radio, had no community affairs department to foster dialogue or promote local artists with fresh sounds or unique lyrics. [48] Companies downsized to maximize profits and regional programmers overtook local ones, signifying a further shift from local interests of listeners. [49] The ever-present need to increase profitability also galvanized some stations to replace live disc jockeys with prerecorded announcers who would create localized sound bites and patch together entire shows based upon a master copy that was filtered down through regional and local distributors; [50] radio truly became top-down. Subsequently, the public sphere in which artists could contest the image of the apolitical gangster or socially devoid party-goer shrunk rapidly. Corporate rap became a medium through which content was filtered and sterilized while dissident voices were marginalized or shut out completely. Even political rap was reworked into a specific consumer niche; "defanged as 'conscious rap,' and retooled as an alternative hip-hop lifestyle," the prefix became "industry shorthand for reaching a certain kind of market" instead of an authentic, organic title. [51]

Thus, as is the trend in a capitalist society where the "market...does not assure that all relevant views will be heard, but only those that are advocated by the rich [and can market a product of mass appeal that will attract advertisers, which dominate the programming message]," the Telecommunications Act has had profoundly negative implications upon hip-hop's autonomy and ensured that the media landscape was "dominated by those who are economically powerful."[52] Likewise, the prodigious increase in corporate consolidation facilitated the process by which consumption could be artificially managed and manipulated by the "mass media's capacity to convey imagery and information across vast areas to ensure a production of demand." [53] Therefore, the exclusion of particular forms of musical expression, especially those deemed political or controversial, are replaced with corporate-driven, marketed images of young black males adhering to a socially constructed thug stereotype. Fokami explains:

Corporations which dominate the media, have heavily marketed (to influence consumer demand), produced and perpetuated, the gangsta image by, among other things, playing gangsta rap lyrics, almost to the exclusion of other alternative voices that would contest such lyrics or image... The Act has made it virtually impossible for alternative voices in rap (either by the gangsta rappers themselves through their alternative "positive" tracks or by other "positive" rap artists) to be heard on the radio, since corporate conglomerates are less concerned with diversity in ideas but in meeting market created consumer demand for such lyrics. [54]

Thus, while congressional attacks were pummeling rap music for degrading lyrical content and demeaning music videos, the same politicians were simultaneously passing laws which facilitated the crystallization of apolitical, socially devoid gangsta rap into mainstream pop culture. This apparently blatant contradiction is, when viewed in the context of the capitalist state, much more consistent than at first glance; the political establishment sought to promote corporate consolidation and media monopolization, thus limiting public space for dialogue and debate in the hip-hop community, which, in turn, allowed them to pursue a the preferable path of blaming the victims for society's woes. Avoiding an uncomfortable and possibly incriminating dialectical analysis which would address the root cause, namely the dominant political and economic system, that perpetuates many of the social blights expressed in rap music, politicians attack the youth, and especially Black and Latino youth, for problems that plagued urban communities long before rap music hit the scene.

Bursting Onto the Mainstream Scene and Contemporary Political Rap

Hip-hop stepped forward into the mainstream political establishment in 2004 when it had a brief, rather superficial media campaign targeting youth voters. Rap mogul Sean "Diddy" Combs used hip-hop as a platform to organize a campaign under the sensationalist title "Vote or Die" as an attempt to register younger voters, garner youth participation, and generate excitement about the elections. While registering voters was only a marginal success, [55] it was clear the goals were decidedly apolitical with little actual political motivation for urban youth who, for years, had felt alienated from mainstream political discourse. The two candidates put forward by America's ruling elites, George Bush and John Kerry, had platforms so similar it was challenging to generate enough interest for young people to mobilize within the context of the two-party duopoly. Four years later, however, hip-hop would emerge as an unimaginably powerful advertisement for Barack Obama. His 2008 campaign sparked immense interest within the hip-hop community and debate flourished over whether or not hip-hop should stand behind Obama. It was little more than a decade prior that Tupac hopelessly exclaimed "although it seems heaven sent, we ain't ready, to see a Black president" on the song "Changes." [56] Now, energized by a candidate whom, for the first time, they felt would reach out to the hip-hop generation, many artists, such as Jay-Z, took center stage in fundraising concerts and spoke proudly of their involvement in his campaign. Nas, one of hip-hops "most brilliant orators" [57] whose own political trajectory involved going from conscious gangster with his first album *Illmatic* (1994) to passionate revolutionary with his latest release *Untitled* (2008), "captures the gambit of fears, hopes and doubts that swirl together in the consciousness" [58] of the black community on the track "Black President:"

KKK is like "what the fuck," loadin' they guns up / Loadin' mine too, ready to ride / Cause I'm ridin' with my crew / He dies--we die too / But on a positive side / I think Obama provides hope and challenges minds / Of all races and colors to erase the hate / And try and love one another, so many political snakes / We in need of a break / I'm thinkin' I can trust this brotha / But will he keep it way real? / Every innocent nigga in jail gets out on appeal / When he wins--will he really care still? [59]

Nas is not alone in his critical support for Obama; Mary J. Blige and rapper Big Boi from Outkast compose a song of solidarity for the working class and poor in "Something's Gotta Give," which challenges Obama to truly listen to the concerns and pressures of urban communities while earnestly calling for desperately needed social change. Big Boi articulates his working class consciousness when he rhymes, "You know the common folk, blue collar, day-to-day workers that squeeze a dollar / so maybe they can swallow a little, not a lot, just enough to fill that bottle / But it's a million dollars a gallon for gas to get to work tomorrow." [60] Unapologetically political, well-known artists creatively maneuvered political dialogue and discussion into the mainstream discourse.

Still, these odes to Obama were able to push through corporate outlets partly because their content and message remained safely within the established political borders. Obama, after all, garnered large support from many of the capitalist classes ruling elites, whom viewed the Republicans eight-year run as disastrous for the United State's economic power and image abroad. Despite this brief stint within mainstream circles, political hip-hop did not begin, and it will not end, with Obama. Radical hip-hop and revolutionary artists like Immortal Technique, Dead Prez, Paris, Lupe Fiasco, Son of Nun, and an innumerable amount of other artists remain marginalized and embroiled in the struggle to spread their message in the face of a competitive, cut-throat jungle of corporate conglomerates and consolidated, top-down radio. Often, hip-hop artists formulate unique narratives or relay stunningly academic critiques of society that tie together seemingly separate issues and help the listener foster a more critical, holistic analysis of larger societal forces.

On his latest single, "3rd World," Immortal Technique utilizes a percussive, hard-hitting instrumental produced by DJ Green Lantern to expose U.S. imperialism and militarism across the globe, brilliantly explicating on the concept of contemporary war as a natural outgrowth of capitalism. Born in Peru and representing his "Third World" roots, Technique explains that he is:

From where the only place democracy's acceptable, is if America's candidate is electable... from where they overthrow Democratic leaders, not for the people but for the Wall Street journal readers... So I'ma start a global riot, that not even your fake anti-Communist dictators can keep quiet!

On "Ghetto Manifesto," The Coup humorously outline ghetto conditions, sardonically utilizing hip-hop lingo to emphasize their point, "Got a house arrest anklet but it don't bling bling, got a homie with a cell but that shit don't ring!" Later, they put out a call for organization and mobilization, explaining "even renowned historians have found that, the people only bounce back when they pound back." They simultaneously challenge nationalist ideology, "the trees we got lifted by made our feet dangle, so when I say burn one I mean the Star-Spangled." A plethora of underground and independent rap artists express similar themes which address the need for autonomous political organization and present alternative, more humane visions for society.

Hip-Hop at a Crossroads: Conditions Today and Where Do We Go From Here?

Hip-hop was cultivated in the streets as an innovative response of urban minorities, traditionally marginalized by dominant political and economic structures, seeking a voice of their own. Alienated by harsh conditions imposed upon them by an advanced capitalist society, these urban youth sought an outlet where they could foster their own conceptions of identity and challenge institutional oppression, whether individually or collectively. Poverty, unemployment, a decrepit educational system, cuts in social services, and capitalism's inherent need to maintain a permanent underclass blended together to create a matrix in which a new, counter-hegemonic culture would emerge with the dialectically opposed characteristics of both the oppressor and the liberationist. Today, the devastating conditions which birthed hip-hop remain a reality and, in some instances, have intensified. The recent crisis capitalism has found itself in continues the downward spiral and the world economy appears close to collapse. The conditions for the working-class and the poor, however, have only worsened over the thirty years since hip-hop established itself as a cultural entity.

Unemployment is skyrocketing nationally across color lines but in many cities, such as Milwaukee, Detroit, and Chicago, black unemployment is at or near 50 percent. [61] Already claiming the highest rates of poverty in the industrial world, U.S. poverty statistics have risen drastically since the onset of the world banking crash, placing both Blacks and Latinos at or above 20 percent; youth minority statistics are often much higher. [62] The loss of jobs, combined with the collapse of the housing market and sub-prime predatory lending, has pushed an immense amount of working-class residents out of their homes[63] and left nearly fifty million people without healthcare. [64] Schools, after a brief glimmer of hope with post-civil rights integration, have become more segregated now than they were thirty years ago with public school systems in Chicago, St. Louis, Los Angeles, Detroit, Philadelphia, Cleveland, and many other urban areas 80-95 percent Black and Hispanic. [65]

Thus, the conditions in which hip-hop originally arose have not improved. Social commentator and activist Keeanga-Yamahtta Taylor postulates these are rational outcomes of the dominant political economy:

The material impact on the lives of Black workers should be clear enough, but ideologically, the systematic and institutional impoverishment of African American communities perpetuates the impression that Blacks are inferior and defective. These perceptions are perpetuated and magnified by the mass media, Hollywood and the general means of ideological and cultural production in bourgeois society. The recurrence and persistence of racism in this economic system is not accidental or arbitrary. American capitalism is intrinsically racist. [66]

Like Taylor, independent hip-hop has, throughout its existence, maintained a critical approach to the capitalist mode of production and the material conditions resulting from it. On "Window to My Soul," Stic.man of Dead Prez painfully professes the emotional trauma he experienced as he watched his older brother develop a serious drug addiction. Rather than blame the individual, an old rhetorical tactic utilized to conceal social inequality and displace blame, even more prevalent now that a Black man occupies the Whitehouse, [67] Stic.man addresses the larger socioeconomic forces which often dictate and limit choices for the urban poor:

The same conditions that first created the drug problems still exist... / And on days off, we blow off them crumbs like nothing / Getting high cause a nigga gotta get into something / But we get trapped in a cycle of pain and addiction / And lose the motivation to change the condition... / How did Black life, my life, end up so hard? [68]

He questions the entire wage system and bourgeois morality with piercing lines such as "got to go to the job or starve, without a gun every day employees get robbed." Questioning whose interests are served in the perpetuation of the current system, he concludes that it's "the police, lawyers, and judges, the private owned prison industry with federal budgets." He ends with an unapologetic proclamation that the oppression of blacks is systemic, but oppressed communities cannot turn to individualized forms of escapism and instead must discuss the organization of society as it currently exists, "I blame it on the system but the problem is ours, it's not a question of religion; it's a question of power." [69] The call to a revolutionary alternative, although not always explicitly detailed, has been a persistent theme in the language of political rap. This, undoubtably, is due to the fact that many within the oppressed communities share Taylor's conviction that the dynamic interrelationship between wealth, power, poverty, and the institutional forms in which oppression is manifested.

The landscape of independent, political hip-hop is constantly changing, progressing, and evolving. In the last few years, the augmentation of revolutionary hip-hop which aims to combat traditionally oppressive societal institutions and entrenched corporate structures provides a glimpse of the potential for the art's future. Hip-hop's place in politics extends far beyond a presidential election or congressional debates on explicit content; hip-hop, in the words of Dead Prez's M-1, "means sayin' what I want, never bitin' my tongue / hip-hop means teachin' the young." [70] Immortal Technique tells it like this, "I live and breathe Revolution, Rebellion is in my blood and Hip Hop is the heart that pumps it." [71] Two decades into the rap game, Paris provides a way forward with the newest single, "Don't Stop the Movement," from his independently owned label Guerrilla Funk:

Givin' power to the people to take back America / Panic in the head of the state, pass the Derringer / Aim and shoot, Beruit to Bay Area... / Panther power, acid showers/ This land is ours, stand and shout it... / Hard truth revolutionary black militant / Death to the Minutemen, checks to the immigrants / Streets still feelin' it, we still killin' it / We still slaughterin' hawks, feed the innocent / Read the imprint / Guerrilla Funk was birthed outta' necessity, collectively / Respectively, to behead the beast / On behalf of the left wing scared to speak, NOW GET UP! [72]

Expressing the need for solidarity between the struggles against militarism in the Middle East, black oppression in the U.S. and dehumanizing anti-immigration policies, the chorus warns activists to not stop the movement for social justice and liberation. It ends with a recording of the common protest chant which proclaims that "the people, united, will never be defeated." KRS-One comments that hip-hop is the only place Dr. Martin Luther King's dream is visible, "black, white, Asian, Latino, Chicano, everybody. Hip-hop has formed a platform for all people...that, to me, is beyond music." [73] As underground rap artist Macklemore urges his listeners, "to my real hip-hop heads, please stand up, because the only ones who can preserve this art is us." [74]

The battle continues to rage over hip-hop's soul. Two contradictory forces clash to gain dominance: one representing the great wealth and power of the established order, the other struggling for independence, autonomy, and social change. Black intellectual Manning Marable makes the argument that "cultural workers," such as hip-hop artists, "must be able to do more than rhyme about problems: they have got to be able to build organizations as well as harness the necessary monetary resources and political power to do something about them." [75] To answer the question of what role hip-hop will play in the formation of such revolutionary organizations and movements depends on which side wins, the power of profit or the power of the people. For hip-hop activists to rescue the art form from capitalism's corporate clutches it will take dedication, organization, and education; time will tell if the hip-hop generation is up to this onerous task. The very essence of the culture is at stake.

Notes

[1] Keeanga-Yamahtta Taylor, "Origins of Housing Discrimination," *International Socialist Review*, Issue 59, (May-June 2008), accessed 5 April 2009; available from http://www.isreview.org/issues/59/letters.shtml; Internet.
[2] Chang, 307.
[3] Ibid., 308.
[4] Ibid., 315.
[5] Ibid., 314-5.
[6] Ibid., 367-8.
[7] Ibid., 279.
[8] Ibid., 314.
[9] Immortal Technique, "Gangsta Rap is Hip Hop," *HipHopDX.com*, accessed 5 April 2008; available from http://www.hiphopdx.com/index/columns-editorials/id.692/title.is-gangsta-rap-hip-hop-by-immortal-technique ; Internet.
[10] Mumia Abu-Jamal recording on Immortal Technique, "Homeland and Hip Hop," *Revolutionary Vol. 2*, 2003, Viper Records.
[11] N.W.A., "Straight Outta Compton," *Straight Outta Compton*, 1988, Ruthless/Priority.
[12] N.W.A., "Fuck tha Police," *Straight Outta Compton*, 1988, Ruthless/Priority.
[13] Chang, 388.
[14] Ibid., 388.
[15] Ibid., 388.
[16] Folami, 263.
[17] Chang, 292.
[18] Ibid., 453.
[19] Tupac Shakur, "Nothin' But Love," *R U Still Down? (Remember Me)*, 1997, Jive.
[20] Urban Dictionary, accessed 5 April 2009; available fromhttp://www.urbandictionary.com/define.php?term=thug+life; Internet.

[21] Shakur, "Tupac Resurrection Script."

[22] Ibid.

[23] Ibid.,

[24] Dyson, 414.

[25] Son of Nun, "Son of Nun - Hip Hop Artist and Activist," SleptOn Magazine, accessed 5 April 2009; available from http://www.slepton.com/slepton/viewcontent.pl?id=1955; Internet.

[26] Immortal Technique, "Gangsta Rap is Hip Hop."

[27] Dyson, 407.

[28] Immortal Technique, "Gangsta Rap is Hip Hop."

[29] Watkins, 36-7.

[30] Ibid., 39.

[31] Ibid., 39.

[32] Watkins, 41-2.

[33] Ibid., 42.

[34] Ibid., 2-3

[35] Manning Marable, "The Politics of Hip Hop," World History Archives, accessed 5 April 2009; available from - http://www.hartford-hwp.com/archives/45a/594.html; Internet.

[36] Carl Bialik, "Is the Conventional Wisdom Correct in Measuring Hip Hop Audience?" The Wall Street Journal, accessed 5 April 2009; available fromhttp://online.wsj.com/public/article/SB111521814339424546.html; Internet.

[37] Dean MacCannell, In The Tourist: A New Theory of the Leisure Class (Schocken Book 1976), 153.

[38] Immortal Technique, "Watch Out," The 3rd World, 2008, Viper Records.

[39] Chang quoted in Jones, "Politics of Hip-Hop."

[40] Chang, 443.

[41] Ibid., 440-1.

[42] Anastasia Bednarski, From Diversity To Duplication Mega-Mergers And The Failure of the Marketplace Model Under The Telecommunications Act of 1996 , (2003), 273, 275.

[43] Adam J. Van Alystyne, Clear Control: An Antitrust Analysis Of Clear Channel's Radio And Concert Empire, (2004), 627, 640.

[44] Folami, 291-2.

[45] Chang, 441-2.

[46] Folami, 300.

[47] Binary Star, "Honest Expression," *Masters of the Universe*, 2000, Infinite Rhythm/Subterraneous/L.A. Underground. Lyrics such as these present a challenge to the corporate gangster image: "I ain't hardcore, I don't pack a 9 millimeter / Most of y'all gangster rappers ain't hardcore neither... So what you pack gats and you sell fiend's crack / You ain't big time, my man / You ain't no different from the next cat in my neigberhood who did time."

[48] Chang, 442.

[49] Eric Boehlert, "Radio's Big Bully," *Salon.com Arts & Entertainment*, accessed April 5 2009; available from http://archive.salon.com/ent/feature/2001/04/30/clear_channel/print.html; Internet.

[50] Van Alystyne, *Clear Control*, 660.

[51] Chang, 447-8.

[52] Owen Fiss, *Free Speech and Social Structure*, 71 Iowa L. Rev. 1405 (1986), 340.

[53] Rosemary J. Coombe, *Objects Of Property And Subjects Of Politics: Intellectual Property Laws And Democratic Dialogue*, 69 Tex. L. Rev. 1853 (1991), 1862-3.

[54] Folami, 301.

[55] Mark Boyer, "What Happened to 'Vote or Die'?" *Fresh Cut Media*, accessed 5 April 2009; available from http://getfreshcut.com/2008/02/04/what-happened-to-vote-or-die/; Internet.

[56] Tupac Shakur, "Changes," *2Pac's Greatest Hits*, 1998, Interscope Records.

[57] Zach Mason, "Hip Hop Speaks Out for Obama," Socialist Worker, accessed 5 April 2009, available from http://socialistworker.org/2008/10/28/hip-hop-speaks-for-obama; Internet.

[58] Mason, "Hip Hop Speaks Out for Obama."

[59] Nas, "Black President," *Untitled*, 2008, Def Jam.

[60] Lyrics quoted in Mason, "Hip Hop Speaks Out for Obama."

[61] Keeanga-Yamahtta Taylor, "Race in the Obama Era," accessed 5 April 2009; available from http://socialistworker.org/2009/04/03/race-in-the-obama-era; Internet. Taylor cites a study by social scientist Marc Levine from the University of Wisconsin-Milwaukee.

[62] Sylvia A. Allegretto, "U.S. Government Does Relatively Little to Lessen Child Poverty Rates," *Economic Policy Institute*, accessed 5 April 2009; available

from http://www.epi.org/economic_snapshots/entry/webfeatures_snap shots_20060719/ ; Internet. *Research by Rob Gray. After taxes, child poverty rates in the U.S. are 26.6 percent. Black and Latino minor poverty rates are higher.

[63] Taylor, "Race in the Obama Era." Taylor notes that "Black homeownership has dropped from 49 percent to 46 percent... By 2007, 30 percent of Black households had zero net worth, compared to 18 percent of white households... Households of color lost between $164 billion and $213 billion over the past eight years... Combined, this could lead to a one-third reduction in the Black middle class."

[64] "Facts on Health Insurance Coverage," National Coalition on Healthcare, accessed 6 Dec 2008; available from http://www.nchc.org/facts/coverage.shtml; Internet.

[65] Jonathan Kozol, "Still Separate, Still Unequal: America's Educational Apartheid," Harper's Magazine, Vol. 311, September 2005, accessed 5 April 2009; available from http://www.mindfully.org/Reform/2005/American-Apartheid-Education1sep05.htm; Internet.

[66] Taylor, "Race in the Obama Era."

[67] Dinesh D'Souza, "Obama and Post-Racist America," To The Source, accessed 5 April 2009; available from http://www.tothesource.org/1_21_2009/1_21_2009.htm; Internet. Pundits have already used Obama's election as an example that institutional racism does not exist in America. For instance, author Dinesh D'Souza wrote after his victory: "As I watched Obama take the oath of office...I also felt a sense of vindication. In 1995, I published a controversial book The End of Racism. The meaning of the title was not that there was no more racism in America...My argument was that racism, which once used to be systematic, had now become episodic...racism existed, but it no longer controlled the lives of blacks and other minorities. Indeed, racial discrimination could not explain why some groups succeeded in America and why other groups did not...for African Americans, their position near the bottom rung of the ladder could be better explained by cultural factors than by racial victimization."

[68] Dead Prez, "Window to my Soul," Turn off the Radio: The Mixtape, Vol. 2: Get Free or Die Tryin', 2003, Landscape Germany.

[69] Dead Prez, "Window to my Soul."

[70] Dead Prez, "It's Bigger Than Hip Hop," Let's Get Free, 2000, Relativity.

512

[71] Immortal Technique, "About Immortal Technique," *Myspace*, accessed 5 April 2009; available from http://www.myspace.com/immortaltechnique; Internet.

[72] Paris, "Don't Stop the Movement," *Acid Reflux*, 2008, Guerrilla Funk.

[73] Manning Marable, "The Politics of Hip Hop."

[74] Macklemore, "B-Boy," *The Language of My World*, 2008, Integral Music Group.

[75] Marable, "The Politics of Hip Hop."

Society & Culture
DEPARTMENT

Human Potential

A Testament to Drive and Fortitude

Syard Evans

Every trip to a children's hospital is an inspiring, and often, life-changing event, regardless of the reason for the visit. Whether you are a child going for treatment, touring the facilities on a school trip, a parent accompanying your sick child for treatment, or, as in my case, a professional making a referral visit to meet a young person in need of a foster home placement, it is impossible to leave this type of environment without an enhanced perspective of the world and your place in it.

I have made more of these visits than I can count. In my work, I get called upon frequently to assist in finding placement for kids who are in state custody and difficult to place. Beyond the stark supply-and-demand issues of overloaded social service systems with more kids needing homes than families willing and/or able to provide appropriate homes, the kids I get called about generally possess one of two significant characteristics that pose additional barriers to placement. They are either medically fragile, requiring a significant level of care and support to address medical or health-related issues, or they have substantial behavioral challenges and have promptly worn out their welcomes at a variety of placement types, including foster homes, residential facilities, psychiatric hospitals, and sometimes even juvenile correctional facilities.

I have learned more from these kids than I have ever read in any book or absorbed in any lecture, about them, about me, about life, and about humanity. One of the most important lessons I have learned is that all human beings are capable, worthy, positive creatures. Every last one. Regardless of the intensity and quantity of the challenges and difficulties a person experiences, every person has value and contributes to the collective fabric of us all. The young man I met on my most recent trip to the local children's hospital illustrates this well. For the sake of anonymity, let's call him Henry.

Henry was a two-year-old little boy who had encountered a mountain of obstacles since his first day in this world. He was born at 24-weeks premature, a feat that, according to the Quint Boenker Preemie Survival Foundation, gave him just a 39% chance of survival. His lungs were underdeveloped, he experienced significant heart problems, and he endured a life-threatening brain bleed. Henry spent almost the entire first year of his life at the children's hospital fighting for his life but eventually stabilized enough to be discharged to his mother's care. Unfortunately, that was not the victory you and I might have hoped it would be for him.

I can only speculate that the overwhelming needs of Henry's care, a drastic lack of support, information, and resources, combined with the debilitating consequences of drug addiction influenced his mother's decision to take him home, place him in his bed, and do little-to-nothing with Henry for the next year of his life. Henry relied on a ventilator to compensate for his ineffective, still developing lungs and a continuous feeding pump to ensure he received proper nutrition to continue to strengthen and develop. Unfortunately, Henry's feeding pump was not filled regularly while in the care of his mother, and he did not receive enough nutrients to sustain the hard-won progress he made in the first year of life, much less continue growth and development.

It is unclear how state officials were finally alerted to the neglect that Henry was experiencing or, more importantly, why it took almost a year for anyone to notice. By the time I met him, he had been readmitted to the children's hospital weighing the same amount he had weighted at his discharge almost a year before and been taken into state custody. Henry was no stronger in any of the areas expected and had lost a significant amount of muscle tone in his malnourished little body. He is actually a pretty overwhelming sight to see. His tiny little body looks as if it belongs to an infant, not a two-year-old, but his head is robust and oddly shaped.

Henry's head is substantially oversized. The nurse introducing me to him explained that his body was so invested in self-preservation that the sparse calories he obtained during his year of neglect were utilized for brain development while the rest of his body was unnourished and left to remain stagnate, even deteriorate in some ways. Additionally, the back of Henry's oversized head was completely flat due to the excessive amount of time he spent lying on his back during such a crucial period in his physical development.

As I stood looking at Henry for the first time, two things struck me. The first, and least significant for our purposes here, was that, with his fair skin, freckles, and orange-red curls, Henry brought to my mind the idea of Tim Wise as a baby. I'm sure there is a significant opportunity to explore the irony of Wise's powerful message of the debilitating influences of privilege on our society and Henry's circumstances despite the privileges he possessed or because of the ones he lacked. However, that is analysis for another time.

The remarkable occurrence for me as I stood there watching this child connected to a multitude of life-sustaining machines, playing with the nursing aid working with him, was the undeniable life and vigor that radiated from him. He chased after brightly colored toys that the aid held over his head and smiled with a wide, sparsely toothed smile that made me smile right along with him. There was an undeniable drive present in Henry that made it unnecessary to ask the most reasonable question, "How in the world has he endured all of this?" Standing next to his hospital crib, it was clear that it was never a consideration for him to not endure. Henry met each obstacle with an admirable determination. He did not know any other way.

I listened as the nurse explained that Henry quickly learned that the machines connected to him to keep him alive were equipped with alarms that gave audible alerts when they were not functioning properly. So, when he was alone in his room and wanted some company, he would pop the hose off of his ventilator and patiently wait for a frantic nurse to come respond to the alarming system.

I watched as Henry's respiratory therapist attempted to conduct his scheduled treatment. He would allow the therapist to position him in a certain position and then jerk and flail his little body around causing her to have to reposition him again. As the therapist fussed about this, he laughed a deep and hardy chuckle, very entertained by the interaction.

Her affection for him was evident. His teasing and enjoyment of the teasing gave her significant joy as well.

While interacting with Henry, I noticed that he would often grab at his face, and I inquired with the nurse about this behavior. She explained that in addition to all the other aspects of Henry's body that did not function properly, he was born with a condition that precluded his eyelids from operating as designed. As a result, his eyes closed when he moved around, and he was unable to open them on his own. To compensate, Henry figured out that he could grab the skin on his cheek and pull down to manually open his eyes and allow himself to see. As he gets older, the nurse informed, there is a corrective procedure that can be done to remedy this condition, but until he is old enough, Henry has reserved himself to enthusiastically improvising.

What a compact, larger-than-life testament to human drive, fortitude, and potential.

Henry's story is one that can illuminate the difficulties of life that, to some degree, we all must face, but his story is also one that provides ample support for the idea that each person is valuable and has the potential for valuable contributions to our greater society. And he is not alone. Every day stories of children paint a picture of our possibilities. Each story provides an example of children who have either learned and implemented the best lessons from those around them or, maybe more likely the case, have relied on their innate abilities and instincts to be able to overcome the poor instructions and care provided by society to simply figure out the "right" way on their own.

No one taught Henry how to operate his eyes or to make the hospital staff smile. Similarly, there weren't specific instructions provided to Jeremiah Anthony, an Iowa City West High student who set up and operates an anti-bullying Twitter account that provides compliments to students and promotes positivity at his school. The adults in Zach Sobiech's life were likely ill equipped to instill in him in his short 18 years the wisdom and courage it took him to face a losing battle with cancer and create an uplifting musical YouTube contribution that will undoubtedly inspire and encourage every person who takes the time to watch it for the rest of time. And the members of the Phi Alpha Tau fraternity at Emerson College in Boston, Massachusetts who raised over $16,500 to cover the cost of top surgery for their transgendered fraternity brother were almost certainly not armed with ideas and information from society that lead to their valiant decision and action.

These kids and many others like them provide significant evidence that innate human potential is strong and good. Of course there are ample illustrations of the harm and destruction human beings are capable of, but, for the following two reasons, those are not the focus here: 1) we all have access to the nightly news for review of those examples, and 2) in each situation where people do harm, unlike the examples listed above, we can almost always trace back to influencing factors in the person's environment including, but not limited to, abuse, neglect, trauma, indoctrination, and more.

Our focus, rather, needs to be on recognizing the raw potential that exists in each of us, most importantly, our children and in figuring out how to provide space to nurture, sustain, and develop this potential. Unfortunately, there is not a definitive answer to this, but there are important factors that experience in the social service system yields.

Individuals must be given the ability to develop who they are and not be forced to become who they are expected to be. Societal expectations regarding gender identity, race, religion, socioeconomic status, educational attainment, age, sexual orientation, ability, etc. all serve to stunt and often kill human potential. Additionally, educational and service systems must be structured to focus on person-centered services. Statistical analysis of thousands of data points from a standardized test question or a social services survey will not provide us with the insight we need to nurture and develop the true potential of the individuals we encounter. Only nurturing relationships will provide the knowledge and insight necessary to support people to the greatest magnitude of who they can potentially become. Our quantitative systems must figure out how to provide qualitative supports. We must ensure that basic needs are met and understand that basic needs are different for different individuals.

Henry and so many others like him force us to consider that the answers we need to the problems we've created are already here among us. We just have to figure out how to grow, develop, and avoid harming our most valuable resource: human potential.

Identity

The Mental and Social Barrier to Solidarity

Kali Ma

What keeps the working class from coming together in a united front against the current system of oppression and exploitation? It is a question that, perhaps, has many answers, yet one that must be addressed if we are to understand what it will take to bring about the change that benefits us all. Division within the working class is a major problem that comes in many forms. In addition to living in an economic system that keeps us estranged through competition and an emphasis on self-interest, we are also separated from one another based on our identities and social conditioning. It is a more subtle division that on the surface might seem benign, but one that is extremely insidious because of its perceived insignificance. Even if a revolution occurred tomorrow and the power shifted to the people - how would we deal with each other after centuries of pain, persecution, division, and discrimination, created and antagonized by our identities? Would we slip back into the same roles and slowly recreate the same society we revolted against in the first place? Obviously, there is more to a revolution than simply changing of the guards. If it is to become real and lasting, it has to first and foremost revolutionize the human mind and, in turn, how we relate to one another.

The Shaping of Identity Through Conditioning

Conditioning is "the act or process of training a person or animal to do something or to behave in a certain way in a particular situation." Social conditioning molds our behavior by directly and indirectly promoting certain beliefs, ideas, and values through various institutions within society, most notably, the family and the education system. The belief system created by conditioning expresses itself through a personality or set of identities. [1] Identity within a social context is "[t]he set of behavioral or personal characteristics by which an individual is recognizable as a member of a group."[2] Each identity is, thus, shaped by conditioning and associated with certain behaviors and values recognized by the rest of society. We simply slip into a particular role or identity (black, white, mother, father, professor, boss, employee, athlete, artist, etc.) with its predetermined expectations and play out the script of what society agrees defines that role or a member of that particular group.

Identity gives us stability, direction, and a sense of belonging within society. It is natural for human beings to want to find this type of security in a world that is often unstable and uncertain. There is safety in identity because it ties us to others 'like us' and may even offer us social, economic, and political benefits.

While we are free to express our unique individuality through various identities, this expression occurs within the confines of a particular persona, which serves as a subtle mechanism that controls our actions. After all, we cannot stray too far from our chosen persona; if we do, we would be acting 'out of character' or contrary to the expectations of that particular identity. In essence, once an individual identifies with a role or identity, he or she begins to default to the set of expectations tied to that role and often (consciously or unconsciously) ignores his or her true desires and inclinations. [3] As a result, most of us never reach our true potential because we let our identities (personas) tell us what to do, how to act, and how to be in the world. As psychiatrist C.G. Jung observed, "[The persona] is, as its name implies, only a mask of the collective psyche, a mask that *feigns individuality*, making others and oneself believe that one is an individual, whereas one is simply acting a role through which the collective psyche speaks."[4]

Essentially, most of us never live as full, whole, actualized, unique individuals; rather, each of us consists of fragments of identities, roles, and personas stitched together into a personality, which we mistake for our true individuality. We interact with one another through these artificial personas and images, which serve as invisible armor that prevent us from relating to each other on a deeper, more genuine level. Meanwhile, the real individuality rarely comes out, and if it does, it is often in fleeting moments only to go back to one of its established personas through which it interacts with the world.

Identity Conflicts

Because there are many different identities, they often conflict with one another and create division among the people. [5] There are countless examples of social roles and designations with their corresponding identities and set of expectations, many of which directly clash with one another: religion (Christian/Muslim), nationality (Russian/American), gender (man/woman), age (young/old) sexual orientation (gay/straight/bi), social status (poor/middle class/rich), political beliefs (Democrat/Republican/Communist/Anarchist), occupation (doctor/lawyer/janitor), relationship roles (wife/husband/friend), race (black/white/Latino) and so on. While there can be conflict between individuals of different identities, division can also occur within the individual.

Internal identity clashes manifest when conflicting (or incompatible) identities reside within one person. For instance, an African-American police officer who participates in racial profiling through "Stop and Frisk," and similar official and unofficial police programs that disproportionately target minorities, is actively perpetuating the racist culture historically present within law enforcement. We can assume that this individual identifies as a police officer *first* (and African-American second), and as such, has internalized the police culture to such an extent that even though he himself would be a victim of these policies, he has become the aggressor acting out the conditioned set of beliefs associated with the identity of a police officer.[6] Thus, the set of values tied to the primary persona we identify with provides the lens through which we view ourselves and, in turn, others.[7]

Which identity we embrace as the dominant one seems to be in large part dependent on the privileges and advantages it bestows on us in various situations. In the above example of the African-American cop, his status and identity as a law enforcement officer puts him in a position of power and privilege over most other citizens, thus, his dominant identity is tied to his occupation. In certain situations it might be advantageous for this same police officer to emphasize his race in order to relate to other African-Americans, while in other instances his identity as, say, a former college athlete might bring him social prestige and the admiration of others. Thus, persona identifications change based on the environment and circumstances in order to confer to the individual the greatest amount of security, sense of belonging, privilege, and often, power.

At the same time, many of us suppress certain identities for the same reasons, whether it is our sexual orientation, ethnicity, social status, educational background, and so on. This suppression, in turn, might prevent us from expressing ourselves more fully because we are clinging to a perception of ourselves from the perspective of the dominant identity that finds parts of us to be inferior or undesirable. What all identities and social conditioning have in common, however, is that they are internal hierarchical authorities that we strive to obey. As a result, our consciousness becomes enslaved to internalized standards that prevent our unique individuality from expressing itself fully without distortion from limiting identities and beliefs.

We Are Not Our Identities

Identities are like costumes - they are not who we are, but merely reflections of parts of us which we express through the many different outfits (roles) we wear throughout our lives. If we cling to one identity, we essentially become its slave. If that identity clashes with another person's identity, it often creates a deep barrier to coming together and recognizing our commonalities as human beings. On the other hand, if we suppress parts of ourselves, we deny a huge element of who we are and diminish our power through shame, guilt, and denial. Only when we embrace all aspects of ourselves and realize that identities are too limiting to define us as human beings, will we begin the process of liberation from our conditioned mindset and all definitions of who we 'should' be.

Essentially, our task is to break through our limiting personas that mask our true individuality and perpetuate division between others and ourselves. This is by no means an easy task - the process of dissolving social conditioning tied to our identities is often experienced as a kind of death because it extinguishes our 'old' self-identification and a perspective that provides us with stability, security, and a sense of belonging. This is precisely why people will defend certain ideas and beliefs even in the face of irrefutable facts and evidence - because an acknowledgment of their beliefs' non-existence or fallacy would threaten the person's worldview and, in turn, their core identity that gives them significance, meaning and a point of reference from which they interact with the world. In other words, the individual experiences the attack on their beliefs as a direct attack on them.

The process of shedding the layers of identity and conditioning is uncomfortable and results in a state of uncertainty and tension because it removes our set of instructions, our map of how to be in the world. We are then forced to live from an internal point of reference, which in our current identity obsessed society, will often lead to a sort of estrangement from the world. The gift of this process, however, is that (with courage and strength) a person is much more likely to live from their core self and express their true potential as a unique being. Consequently, this person gains the ability to relate to others on a more profound, honest level and is more likely to be open to other people's life experiences without the distorted, judgmental lens of conditioned identities and personas.

As so often, the solution resides in a paradox: the more we become our unique selves, the more likely we are to unite with others. From this perspective, we find common ground in the fact that we are all different, unique individual beings and any standards of who we are *supposed* to be simply fade away. Unity through individuality creates true solidarity and paves the way to a revolution actually worth having.

Notes

[1] In this essay, identity, persona and role are used interchangeable. However, there are slight differences in how these concepts express themselves: *identity* denotes the person's primary way of identifying, or how they view themselves in relation to the outside world; *persona* is the image the person presents to others, which can be an identity or a

role; and a *role* is the 'part' the person plays in a certain situation, which can be an identity or a persona.

[2] *See also* the Merriam-Webster Dictionary definition of identity: "the qualities, beliefs, etc., that make a particular person or group different from other"

[3] Take for example an individual who identifies as a Democrat and who, during the Bush presidency, was strongly anti-war, anti-corporate welfare and vehemently pro civil liberties, pro social welfare programs for the people. Now, however, that the Democrats' superstar President Obama is in the White House, suddenly this same individual finds excuses and justifications for all the wars, civil liberties violations, corporate welfare and bailouts, the cutting of social safety nets, and even chuckles gleefully when President Obama jokes about drones. What has happened to this individual? He or she is so identified with being a Democrat that all rational, critical, independent thinking has been outsourced to the identity of a Democrat, no matter how hypocritical and inconsistent this now seems. It was the identity this person clung to all along; it was never about the issues.

[4] C.G. Jung, Two Essays on Analytical Psychology, Second Edition, Bollingen Series XX, (Princeton University Press 1972) p. 157

[5] One key proposition of the social identity theory is that membership in a particular group provides individuals with self-esteem and that groups oftentimes seek to increase their self-image by discriminating against members of outside groups, thus creating an "us vs. them" mentality.

[6] *See* Janaye Ingram, "(Intra)Racial Profiling: When Blacks Profile Each Other," February 5, 2014,http://www.empowermagazine.com/editorial-board-intraracial-profiling-blacks-profile/ .

[7] Internalized homophobia, sexism, and racism as well as general self-hate based on our perceived inferiority to a 'superior' ideal are some other common manifestations of this internal identity conflict. To illustrate one of many examples this internalized phobia and identity conflict might manifest, think of a gay, female, Christian who identifies as a Republican. What is the expected or 'proper' way of identifying for this woman in our society? If she primarily identifies as gay, then most likely her Christian and Republican identities will conflict with her homosexuality; if her dominant identity is that of a Christian, then her homosexuality might be suppressed or infused with feelings of guilt and shame.

Coming Home to Roost

American Militarism, War Culture, and Police Brutality

Colin Jenkins

"President Kennedy never foresaw that the chickens would come home to roost so soon..."
- Malcolm X, December 1, 1963

"Americans love to fight, traditionally. All real Americans love the sting and clash of battle... you are here because you are real men and all real men like to fight!" The thundering voice rang out from the large box speakers situated across the damp, cement floor. *" Americans love a winner! Americans will not tolerate a loser! Americans despise cowards! Americans play to win all of the time. I wouldn't give a hoot in hell for a man who lost and laughed. That's why Americans have never lost nor will ever lose a war; for the very idea of losing is hateful to an American! "* The words surged violently from the mesh screens, ostensibly louder by the second. A quick glance across the concrete quad produced a herd of silhouettes, all frantically running to their predetermined spots in the haze of a 4:00 AM-fog. *"We don't want yellow cowards in this Army. They should be killed off like rats! If not, they will go home after this war and breed more cowards! The brave men will breed more brave men. Kill off the God-damned cowards and we will have a nation of brave men!"*

It was the summer of 1994. I was 19 years old. The words screaming from those speakers - a daily sound that I would become accustomed to over the course of a few weeks - were those of U.S. Army General George Patton (through the voice of George C. Scott). The location was Columbia, South Carolina, though it might as well have been halfway across the world because the only things I would see for the next two months were marching drills, firing ranges, fields of mud and grass, and miles upon miles of indistinguishable running terrain. This was US Army Basic Training and I was one of thousands of recruits eager to soak up the glory of "defending our country."

Everything that is done in basic military training is done with intent. The primary goal is to develop and condition killing machines - human beings who are capable of exterminating other human beings on command. The corollary effects of this development are vast. The transforming of one's self to a component of a "well-oiled machine." The suppressing of human emotion, and even human reason. The extraction of, as Patton suggested, cowardice - in other words, compassion, understanding, empathy, or simply anything that would cause a soldier to stop and question what they are doing at any given time. The ultimate goal of this training is to make one robotic - the finished product of a process of dehumanization, whereas one is forced to shed elements of humanity out of necessity; and, in doing so, runs the risk of viewing others in less than humane ways. It is difficult to deny that, in the event a person finds themselves in the midst of war, this training becomes invaluable. The chaotic, unpredictable, and nerve-rattling environment that is inherent with any battlefield does not allow for time to think. It does not allow for time to reflect. It only allows for conditioned reaction - proactive and reactive measures that are designed to create efficient "soldiering" and optimum survival.

Soldiers, themselves, lose a great deal of autonomy in this process. On a hot and hazy July afternoon, just a few days before my introduction to the words of Patton, as I joined hundreds of others in a frantic scramble off a convoy of refurbished school buses, I lost myself. I became a blank slate. I became a shell of a young man, readily available for shaping, sculpting and conditioning as my new makers saw fit. Life suddenly took on a whole new meaning. I was now accountable to others, as they were accountable to me; and our accountability was on parade for all to see. If anyone stepped out of line, questioned anything, considered alternatives, or attempted to think for themselves, their "irresponsible defiance" was immediately transferred to public humiliation. However, our forced accountability to one another - something we as a society could certainly use more of - was not an issue. It was the underlying purpose of this accountability that becomes questionable in retrospect. Ultimately, it rested on the acceptance of our roles as tools of war, something that would develop steadily in our subconscious. Already armed with abstract notions of patriotism, American exceptionalism and moral superiority, our self-inscribed 'greater good' was now supplemented with an inescapable obligation to fulfill orders. This is the inherent psychology of 'soldiering' - a role that requires a prolonged and nuanced conditioning that begins at a very early age.

Objectification, Empathy Erosion, and an Internalized Culture of War and Oppression

In the United States, the process of objectification begins at a young age. Americans are conditioned by everything from television, music, and marketing to sports, pornography, and even their parents, to objectify others. Gender roles play a major part in this process. Males are taught to objectify the female body; and females are taught to embrace this objectification by basing their self-worth on outward appearance. Correspondingly, females are taught to objectify males as dominant protectors; and males are taught to embrace this objectification by basing their worth on machismo, aggression, and physical prowess.

According to philosopher Martha Nussbaum, objectification occurs in various ways. A person may be objectified if they are treated:

- as a tool for another's purposes (instrumentality);

- as if lacking in agency or self-determination (denial of autonomy, inertness);

- as if owned by another (ownership);

- as if interchangeable (fungibility);

- as if permissible to damage or destroy (violability);

- as if there is no need for concern for their feelings and experiences (denial of subjectivity).[1]

Our collective conditioning runs the gamut of Nussbaum's list. First and foremost, objectification (or reification) is a prerequisite to our dominant economic system of capitalism. By objectifying others, people become more suitable participants in this scheme that thrives off exploitation and alienation. With this conditioning, the CEO is more apt at seeing employees as numbers on a spreadsheet, the banker is able to view clients as nothing more than borrowers, the landlord is able to view a family simply as renters, and the boss sees nothing but workers who need to be prodded like cattle. People, essentially, become sources of income and profit to those who are willing to use them as such. And, perhaps more importantly, these "sources" are gradually shaped into willing participants along the way, apathetically giving in to systems of power and control.

This coercive nature naturally extends into the socio-political realm, where wealthy politicians are more than willing to use working class children as pawns of war, allowing their lives to be extinguished and bodies to be mangled for stock portfolios. This dehumanizing process also creates a world where these same politicians see citizens as nothing but fickle subjects, the government seeks to control "the mob," the soldier sees only enemies, and the police officer only criminals in desperate need of order and discipline. It is, as Vasily Grossman once warned, a society where man has ceased to exist, unavoidably being replaced with "man-like creatures that have undergone an internal transformation."[2]

"When people are solely focused on the pursuit of their own interests, they have all the potential to be unempathic," explains Simon Baron-Cohen, a professor at Cambridge University. What has occurred in this process, according to Baron-Cohen, is a societal phenomenon of "empathy erosion." Quite simply, "When our empathy is switched off, we are solely in the 'I' mode. In such a state, we relate only to things or to people as if they were just things."[3] While this naturally occurs within everyone from time to time, its expansion in American culture has become the pervasive product of a "me, first" mentality created by the marketization and commodification of everything from sex and violence to human services and education.

The significance of this development is profound. Essentially, the more we dehumanize interactions, or the more we make human contact impersonal, the more willing we are to engage in forceful, aggressive, and unempathic interactions with others - behaviors that are (it's worth noting) viewed as positive attributes within the sports world many of us grow up in, and the business world many of us enter as adults. In this sense, it is not competition - in and of itself - that represents a problem; but rather, it is the objectifying nature of coercive relations that pose as competition within any hierarchical society.

The act of objectifying others, whether treating them as "interchangeable tools" to be used at your disposal or simply stunting their self-determination in some manner, is a reciprocal process that is internalized by both parties. The objectifier, through the process of dehumanizing the objectified, becomes less human themselves. This internalization is what allows for a culture of war and oppression to persist. America's "war culture" is shaped by a myriad of factors. First and foremost, we are an imperialist country. The US has been at war, involved in a foreign conflict, or militarily occupied foreign territory (or all three) for 216 years of its 237-year existence. [4]

War is our business, and we do it well. And yes, common, everyday Americans have benefitted in some form or another from war (i.e. the formation of an "industrialized middle class"); however, these "benefits" haven't come without sacrifice - the most prominent of which is a collective misery that has been brought to much of the world's population through colonialism, geopolitical land grabs, and the theft of natural resources. War is, essentially, nourishment for a parasitical corporate hierarchy that takes what it wants and discards of the scraps, allowing them to "trickle down" to the rest of the world, including the working class in the US.

With a vast majority of Americans coming from this working class, widespread victimization - and a stubborn acceptance of it - represents a "rite of passage" in our culture. Whether through impoverished circumstances, socioeconomic limitations, substandard education, a general sense of exploitation that is realized as we grow older, or the grueling, existential crisis we all seem to face at one point or another, we are all victims of repression and exploitation on some level. This has never been more evident than during the past four decades. And the notion that we are to avoid "the victim card" at all costs - as it is supposedly a sign of "weakness" - is laughable when considering the immense amount of injustice we face as a whole: drowned out by corporate power, strangled by government suppression, working more and more while making less and less, forced into consumer debt, dealing with skyrocketing costs of living, chained by student debt, etc.

The class-based oppression and victimization which stem from our embedded hierarchy present peculiar dynamics in terms of carrying out the violent projection of war culture. The fact that soldiers and police officers - the hired guns of the ruling classes - almost always come from working-class backgrounds is especially interesting when considering their roles as enforcers of the very ideology that attacks their class peers. However, when combined with this process of objectification that has become commonplace, an immersion into a deep-seated "war culture" and militarism, and the robotic programming of military or police training, it comes as little surprise that a demographic consisting predominantly of white males is able to complete this transition from working-class oppressed to working-class oppressor with relative ease. Educator and philosopher, Paulo Freire, eloquently describes this process of transformation through internalization:

The very structure of their thought has been conditioned by the contradictions of the concrete, existential situation by which they were shaped. Their ideal is to be men; but for them, to be men is to be oppressors. This is their model of humanity. This phenomenon derives from the fact that the oppressed, at a certain moment of their existential experience, adopt an attitude of "adhesion" to the oppressor. Under these circumstances they cannot "consider" themselves. This does not necessarily mean that the oppressed are unaware that they are downtrodden. But their perception of themselves as oppressed is impaired by their submersion in the reality of oppression. At this level, their perception of themselves as opposites of the oppressor does not yet signify engagement in a struggle to overcome the contradiction; the one pole aspires not to liberation, but to identification with its opposite pole.[5]

This widespread process of internalization is crucial to those wishing to maintain an inherently unjust and oppressive status quo. For, in order to keep such a system intact, the very few who benefit from this arrangement must rely on some members of the working class to ignore or shed themselves of class-consciousness on their way to breaking class ranks and carrying out the violent acts needed to sustain. Professor Abdul JanMohamed tells us, "according to (Antonio) Gramsci, any hegemony is subtended, in the final analysis, by the deployment of violence; and for hegemony to function as such, the masters' rules, including the deployment of violence, must be adequately internalized."[6] Without this internalization, human beings - and especially those coming from the working classes - would be left to act on their own interests, something that would not serve the ruling classes well.

American Militarism and White Supremacy

Any discussion involving American militarism must include the underpinnings of white supremacy, an all-encompassing ideology which has ravaged the lives and communities of non-white peoples for centuries. White supremacy is fueled by objectification and, more specifically, the collective dehumanization of peoples of color. Its power lies in the fact that it not only transcends the fundamental societal arrangement of class, but that it is embraced largely by working class whites who have shown a willingness to internalize and project their own oppression onto others - in this case, the non-white working classes.

Not surprisingly, this foundation extends far beyond the geographic confines of the US, representing the basis for which the "White Man's Burden" and age-old foreign policies like the Roosevelt Corollaryof the Monroe Doctrine operate. The ties that bind what Martin Luther King, Jr. once referred to as "the giant triplets of racism, materialism, and militarism" cannot be underestimated, as they provide the self-righteous, societal "justification" necessary to carry out indiscriminate acts of aggression both here and abroad. Social theorist bell hooks' assessment of George Zimmerman, the self-appointed neighborhood watchman turned murderer of Trayvon Martin, captures this mindset: "White supremacy has taught him that all people of color are threats irrespective of their behavior. Capitalism has taught him that, at all costs, his property can and must be protected. Patriarchy has taught him that his masculinity has to be proved by the willingness to conquer fear through aggression; that it would be unmanly to ask questions before taking action."[7]

When Muhammad Ali refused to fight in Vietnam, famously stating, "I ain't got no quarrel with them Viet Cong; No Viet Cong ever called me nigger," he was referring to the dominant power structure of white supremacy that had not only subjugated him in his own country, but also had global implications regarding imperialism, colonialism, and ever-increasing militarism. Ali, along with other conscious Black Americans, recognized life in the U.S. as a microcosm of the war in Vietnam. Whether in Birmingham, Alabama or the Ben Tre Province in South Vietnam, black and brown people were being murdered indiscriminately. African Americans had their share of enemies at home - Bull Connor, George Wallace, the Ku Klux Klan, the FBI, Jim Crow - and, for good reason, had no vested interest in wars abroad. Their priorities were defense and self-preservation in their homeland; not offense and destruction in Vietnam.

Racism is a cousin to militarism, and its influence on shaping American culture over the years is undeniable. Despite misconceptions, reconstruction in the post-slavery US was no more kind to Black Americans than during colonial years, especially in the southern states. "In the last decades of the nineteenth century, the lynching of Black people in the Southern and border states became an institutionalized method used by whites to terrorize Blacks and maintain white supremacy," explains Robert A. Gibson. "In the South, during the period 1880 to 1940, there was deep-seated and all-pervading hatred and fear of the Negro which led white mobs to turn to 'lynch law' as a means of social control."[8] These lynchings were almost always spontaneous, rooted in white supremacist and racist emotion, and void any semblance of due process. They were also mostly supported - whether through direct supervision or "turning a blind eye" - by local politicians, judges, and police forces.

According to Tuskegee Institute figures, between the years 1882 and 1951, 3,437 African Americans were lynched in the United States - a tally that amounts to roughly 50 per year, or a little over 4 per month through the lifespan of an entire generation.[9] Essentially, for nearly a century, "freed" slaves were still very much at the mercy of, as WEB DuBois once noted, "men who hated and despised Negroes and regarded it as loyalty to blood, patriotism to country, and filial tribute to the fathers to lie, steal or kill in order to discredit these black folk." [10] This general hatred was not only projected by white citizens throughout the country, but remained institutionalized by laws of racial segregation - also known as "Jim Crow" - in much of the US until the 1960s.

While the courageous and awe-inspiring Civil Rights movement of the '60s was successful in curbing some government-backed segregation, the ugly stain of white supremacy has endured well into the 21st century through a convoluted lens of extreme poverty, poor education, lack of opportunity, and disproportionate imprisonment. It has become blatantly evident within the world of 'criminal justice,' and more specifically through the ways in which law enforcement engages and interacts with Black communities across America.

Modern forms of lynching have gained a foothold with laws such as New York City's "Stop and Frisk" and Florida's infamous "Stand Your Ground" - with both providing legal outlets to harass and kill Black Americans at an alarming rate. However, even before such laws, police officers terrorized inner-cities for decades. The most glaring example occurred in 1991 with the beating of Rodney King - an incident that uncovered a deliberate and widespread brand of racist policing as well as "an organizational culture that alienates itself from the public it is designed to serve" while teaching "to command and confront, not to communicate."[11]

The 2012 murder of Trayvon Martin by George Zimmerman served as a sobering reminder of the tragically subhuman value that has been placed on Black life in America. Martin's death rightfully brought on cries of an "open season on young black men," while another 2012 murder, this time of 17-year-old Jordan Davis, who was shot and killed by Michael Dunn in broad daylight while sitting in a car with three friends, reiterated this fact. Like Martin, Davis was unarmed and posed no threat - and certainly not enough of a threat to justify lethal force. In Davis' case, the murderer, Dunn, indiscriminately fired 8 bullets into the vehicle where Davis and his friends were sitting. The public reaction to the two murders (adults killing unarmed children, mind you), especially from those who somehow felt compelled to defend the killers, as well as the subsequent trials, the posthumous (and false) 'criminalizing' of the victims with decontextualized images and information, and the total absence of justice on both accounts - all products of a long-standing culture of white supremacy - exposed the lie that is "post-racial" America.

However, these reactions were and are nothing new. It has been "open season" on young black males for many years in the US, and very few outside African American or activist communities couldn't care less. One study estimates that "one Black person is killed every 24 hours by police, security guards, or vigilantes."[12] Furthermore, "43% of the(se) shootings occurred after an incident of racial profiling," Adam Hudson tells us. "This means police saw a person who looked or behaved "suspiciously" largely because of their skin color and attempted to detain the suspect before killing them. [13]

Many of the victims of these "extrajudicial" killings posed no threat at the time of their murders, as was the case with Amadou Diallo, Sean Bell, Oscar Grant, Aaron Campbell, Orlando Barlow, Steven Eugene Washington, Ervin Jefferson, Kendrec Mcdade, Kimani Gray, Wendell Allen, Ronald Madison, James Brisette, Tavares McGill, and Victor Steen, to name a few. [14] Some, like Brisette (17), Gray (16), McGill (16), and Steen (17), were children. Others, like Madison and Steven Eugene Washington, were mentally ill or autistic. All were unarmed.

If the Rodney King trial taught us (and police) anything, it was that officers in the US can inexplicably beat an unarmed and non-threatening Black man to near-death and face no consequences for doing so. Twenty years later, this unaccountability on the part of law enforcement has evolved into an overly-aggressive and often fatal approach to interacting with innocent, young black men. This has never been more evident than during a rash of indiscriminate and blatant acts of police brutality in recent years. All peoples of color have become viable targets, and some of the most alarming examples have been directed at children and people with special needs and disabilities.

In 2009, a 16-year-old autistic boy, Oscar Guzman, was chased into his family's restaurant by two Chicago police officers after they questioned him for "watching pigeons." Guzman, who was posing no threat and breaking no laws, was "struck in the head with a retractable baton, causing a four-centimeter laceration that had to be closed with staples at a nearby hospital."[15]

In 2011, two Miami-Dade officers stopped 22-year-old Gilberto Powell, who has Down syndrome, due to a "suspicious bulge" coming from his waistband. When the officers confronted Powell and began patting him down, Powell became frightened and ran. The officers caught up and beat him. The "bulge" turned out to be a colostomy bag. Powell was unarmed and breaking no laws.[16]

In November of 2013, a 14-year-old child was "roughed up" and tasered by police in Tullytown, Pennsylvania after being caught shoplifting at a local Wal-Mart. The child suffered a broken nose, multiple abrasions, and two swollen and black eyes as a result. He was unarmed and posed no threat to the officers.

On January 3, 2014, 64-year-old Pearl Pearson was pulled over by police on suspicion of leaving the scene of an accident. After Pearson failed to show his hands when instructed by officers, a "7-minute altercation ensued" and Pearson was severely beaten. He was unarmed and posed no threat. The reason he did not show his hands as ordered: he's deaf - a fact that is displayed on a sign attached to his car.[17]

Other examples include the unnecessary brutalization of incapacitated individuals, as well as the emergence of a universal, reckless "shoot-first" mentality. The most recognizable incident was the 2009 street execution of Oscar Grant by Bay Area Rapid Transit (BART) Policeman, Johannes Mehserle. Following a brush-up with other passengers, Grant and a friend were apprehended by officers who had them lay prone on the ground. Grant was "restrained, unarmed," and had "his hands behind his back," when the officer shot him in the back, killing him. The entire incident was caught on video.

Shockingly, occurrences like this have become common with relatively little fanfare. In May of 2013, 33-year-old David Sal Silva was beaten to death by California officers after he was stopped and questioned for suspected public intoxication. "When I got outside I saw two officers beating a man with batons, and they were hitting his head so every time they would swing, I could hear the blows to his head," said witness Ruben Ceballos, who told the Californian the noise was so loud it woke him up. Sal Silva, unarmed, "begged for his life" before being bludgeoned to death for no apparent reason.[18]

In September of 2013, following a car accident, 24-year-old Jonathan Ferrell was shot 10 times by Charlotte police officer, Randall Kerrick. After knocking on the door of a nearby home, Ferrell spotted the officer and began running towards him for help when Kerrick opened fire. Ferrell was unarmed, posed no threat, and was merely seeking assistance after accidentally crashing his car into a tree line off the road. He died instantly.[19] That same month, Long Beach police officers were captured on a video posted to YouTube repeatedly Tasering and striking Porfirio Lopez with a baton as he lay in the street. Lopez was unarmed and posed no threat to the officers.[20]

In October of 2013, Sheriff's deputies in Santa Rosa, California shot and killed a 13-year-old boy who was carrying a pellet gun. The boy, Andy Lopez, was walking down the sidewalk on his way to return the "low-powered, air pellet gun" to a friend who he had borrowed it from. Before realizing the gun was a toy, and despite having no reason to believe the child was a threat, an officer shot him dead.[21]

In 1968, Huey P. Newton noted that "the country cannot implement its racist program without the guns. And the guns are the military and the police."[22] 45 years later, this comment rings true. Institutions and lawmakers alone cannot carry out racial and class-based oppression on their own - they need willing participants. Domestically, police officers must become these willing participants; and their psychological makeup, which is shaped by a process of objectification and a prolonged internalization of "war culture," is crucial. On a global scale, this task is left to our soldiers - working-class women and men who are routinely placed in harm's way for the wrong reasons, and many of whom suffer a compounded and severe mental toll in the process.

The Mental Toll and Savagery of War

America's "war culture" goes far beyond psychological preparation and conditioning. Ultimately, and most significantly, it includes the physical projection of this collective mentality. It includes, as social commentator Joe Rogan simply put it, "sending these big metal machines that kill people" halfway across the world.[23] The young, working-class women and men (like myself) who become the willing participants of this projection are the very products of this conditioned mentality. As children, our inherent submission to objectification and subsequent immersion into "war culture" makes this possible.

Unfortunately, the effects of war are real. They are shocking. And they are horrifying. The mental health effects on the participants of these wars are vast, especially with regards to the modern battlefield. Soldiers are returning to the US with a variety of such conditions - most notably Post Traumatic Stress Disorder (PTSD), Traumatic Brain Injury (TBI), Depression, and Anxiety.

Dr. Deborah Warden, of the Defense and Veterans Brain Injury Center at Walter Reed Army Medical Center, noted in a report for the *Journal of Head Trauma Rehabilitation* that elements specifically related to modern warfare have resulted in a significant increase in head trauma-related injuries.[24]Two major factors in this development are technological advances in protective equipment and a relative increase in "blast attacks." "In the current conflict, mortality has declined, and it is believed that this is because of the advances in body armor worn by the military personnel," explains Dr. Warden. "With the high-quality body armor, individuals who may have died in previous wars may survive with possible injuries to extremities and head and neck." In addition to this, "more TBI may be occurring in the current war because of the frequency of explosive, or blast attacks. Military sources report that approximately two thirds of army war zone evacuations are due to blast," and "88% of injuries seen at second echelon treatment sites were due to blast."

In a study conducted nearly six years after the beginning of the US occupations of Iraq and Afghanistan, it was determined that, out of 1.64 million military service members who were deployed into these arenas, "approximately 300,000 individuals currently suffer from PTSD or major depression, and that 320,000 individuals experienced a probable TBI during deployment." [25] Additionally, "about one-third of those previously deployed have at least one of these three conditions, and about 5 percent report symptoms of all three." A separate study found that "21 percent of active duty soldiers and 43 percent of reserve soldiers developed symptoms significantly related to mental health disorders."[26]

According to another study:

"15,204 soldiers who had completed their first deployment participated in two questionnaires about their mental health and sleep patterns from 2001 to 2008. During baseline questionnaires before deployment, most soldiers did not have any psychiatric disorders or a history of one. However, during follow-up questionnaires, 522 soldiers had post-traumatic stress disorder (PTSD), 151 have anxiety, and 303 were depressed. Fifty percent of the soldiers studied reported combat-related trauma and 17 percent reported having insomnia prior to their deployment." [27]

The increase in mental illness among soldiers has been identified as the main cause of increasing suicide rates. In 2012, the Army reported that 325 suicides occurred within its ranks - "Our highest on record," according to Lt. Gen. Howard Bromberg, deputy chief of staff, manpower and personnel for the Army.[28]

Naturally, within any arena of combat where young, impressionable adults are moved around like pawns on a chessboard, human emotion runs wild. Despite the robotic conditioning that occurs during basic training, this chaotic environment has a tendency to penetrate the human psyche, bringing about an extreme range of feelings, vexations, actions, and reactions. Human beings are simply not equipped to handle the terrors that accompany war - the sight of human corpses, charred and mangled bodies, some of them children - in their totality. And coping skills, whether inherent or forced, vary in effectiveness from person to person. Unfortunately, some cope by internalizing the terror. In these cases, we see the worst in humanity.

The infamous Wikileaks video that leaked in 2010, showing "thirty-eight grisly minutes of US airmen casually slaughtering a dozen Iraqis in 2007" - including two Reuters newsmen - puts this savagery into focus "not because it shows us something we didn't know, but because we can watch it unfold in real time. Real people, flesh and blood, gunned down from above in a hellish rain of fire."[29] The video footage, which immediately went viral, came on the heels of the haunting images taken at Abu Ghraib, where Iraqi prisoners were physically and sexually abused, tortured, raped, sodomized, and killed by American and Iraqi soldiers.[30] Other such incidents were inevitable.

2010 was an especially gruesome year in Afghanistan. A February 12th nighttime raid by U.S. Special Operations forces near Gardez killed five people, including two pregnant women.[31] Another airstrikeby U.S. Special Operations forces helicopters on February 23 killed more than 20 civilians and injured numerous others. Among the injured was a 4-year-old boy who lost both of his legs. A few months later, during a visit with the child at a hospital in Kabul, Afghan President Hamid Karzai "scooped him up from his mattress and walked out to the hospital courtyard," and asked, "Who injured you?" as helicopters passed overhead. "The boy, crying alongside his relatives, pointed at the sky."[32] A few months later, in April, American troops "raked a large passenger bus with gunfire" near Kandahar, Afghanistan, killing 5 civilians and wounding 18.[33]

In January of 2014, numerous photos showing US Marines burning and looting the dead bodies of Iraqi soldiers were obtained by the media. "Two of the photos show a Marine apparently pouring a flammable liquid on two bodies. Other shots show the remains on fire and, after the flames went out, charred. A Marine in another photo is shown apparently rifling through clothing amid one corpse's skeletal remains. Another Marine is shown posing in a crouch with his rifle pointing toward a human skull." [34] Overall, more than a dozen bodies were shown in the photos, some of which were covered with flies and one being eaten by a dog.

Considering the savagery that accompanies such an environment, it is not difficult to see how undervalued human life becomes. The soldiers who carry out, witness, or even hear of this brutality are almost certain to suffer long-standing mental health effects. According to the Department of Veterans Affairs website, symptoms of PTSD include "bad memories or nightmares" and "flashbacks"; triggered and impulsive emotions; intense feelings of fear, guilt, or shame; and "hyperarousal" - feeling jittery, paranoid, and "always on the lookout for danger."[35] The effects of TBI include numerous sensory problems, depression and anxiety, and severe mood swings and/or aggressive behaviors, among many other things. [36]

When all is said and done, and the politicians decide to bring them home, the soldiers who are lucky enough to return in one physical piece are often shattered into bits and fragments of mental and emotional distress. Often times, these soldiers face limited options - one of the most common of which is transitioning to a career in law enforcement.

From Fallujah to Philadelphia: Bringing the Wars Home

Police training mimics military training, both physically and mentally. Transition programs that funnel soldiers to police forces have become common at all levels of government. The changing face of law enforcement is indicative of this process as forces that are traditionally advertised to "protect and serve" have become noticeably militaristic. Perhaps even more concerning is the fact that soldiers, many of whom carry the mental baggage of war, are being streamlined from the streets of Fallujah to the city blocks of the US.

In a recent article for "Police: The Law Enforcement Magazine," Mark Clark tells us that military veterans seeking employment in police ranks "is happening right now in numbers unseen since the closing days of the Vietnam War." To assist with job placement and transitioning, organizations like "Hire Heroes USA" works with "about 100 veterans each week" - at least 20% of whom are seeking law enforcement jobs.[37] Law enforcement agencies like the Philadelphia Police Department and San Jose PD, which boast of being structured as "a paramilitary organization," actively seek military veterans by awarding preferential treatment.[38] Many police departments across the country have added increased incentives and benefits, including the acceptance of military active duty time towards retirement, to acquire veterans.

An October 2013 edition of the Army Times reports that "more than seven in 10 (local law enforcement agencies) said they attend military-specific job fairs, and three quarters reported developing relationships with the Labor Department's local veterans employment representatives." Also, "Half said they work with military transition assistance programs, and half also said they develop relationships with local National Guard and reserve units."[39] Most local departments also have some type of veterans hiring preference, and "more than 90 percent reported having at least one vet in a senior leadership position."

An example of this trend can be found in Hillsborough County, Florida, where the Sheriff's department is seeking to hire "200 law enforcement deputies and another 130 detention deputies," and Major Alan Hill has set his sights on veterans of Iraq and Afghanistan to fill these roles. Ironically, Hill points to "coping skills" as a main reason. "A lot of them know how to operate under stress. All of them know how to take orders," Hill said. "We want to get the best of the best, and bring them in here, and give them a home, and allow them to continue to serve."[40] Other departments across the country - such as the City of Austin Police Department and the Webb County Sheriff's Office, both in Texas; the Denver Police Department in Colorado; the Hillsborough County and Orange County sheriff's offices in Florida; and the Tucson Police Department in Arizona - have initiated similar efforts.

The correlation between the mental baggage of war, the increased hiring of military combat veterans as police officers, and an observable escalation of aggressive and violent police brutality is difficult to ignore. Police departments have screening processes, but many are lacking. The lingering effects from being in a war zone are unquestionable, and signs and symptoms which often are suppressed during "downtimes" tend to surface and intensify under distress - a common occurrence for police officers.

A 2006 study by the Centers for Disease Control and Prevention found that "19 percent of the 912 police officers surveyed in the New Orleans Police Department reported PTSD symptoms and 26 percent reported symptoms of major depression."[41] A 2008 report by the US Department of Justice concluded that "police who have unresolved mental health concerns - whether or not those concerns are associated with their combat-related experiences - are at risk of harming themselves or others because of the nature of their jobs." [42] Furthermore, the "mental health effects of combat deployment can manifest themselves in the daily activities of police work with more severity than perhaps other lines of work." Specifically, "Officers' combat experiences can affect how they use their weapons, their adherence to use-of-force policies, how they drive their police vehicles, and how they treat citizens with whom they come into contact." [43]

Despite the potential dangers of these mental health effects, police departments fail to adequately assess them during the evaluation and hiring process. And even in cases where they are considered, the presence of such conditions are either (1) intentionally hidden by candidates, (2) undetectable due to their impulsive nature, or (3) simply not considered a reasonable basis for disqualification.

Soldiers transitioning from military to civilian life will often mask the psychological effects of combat out of fears of being stigmatized or disqualified for employment. "Of those reporting a probable TBI, 57 percent had not been evaluated by a physician for brain injury."[44] In a recent study conducted at the Naval Center for Combat and Operational Stress Control (COCS), Kara Ballenger-Browning reported that "many of these soldiers are self-conscious about the diagnosis." In her findings, Ballenger-Browning cited a poll where "half of Iraq/Afghanistan combat veterans with suspected mental disorders believed that receiving treatment would harm their careers; and another 65% stated that they would be considered weak for seeking help and many were afraid that their peers would lose confidence in their abilities."[45]

The study also focused on military-sponsored "soldier-to-civilian" transition programs which sought to assist veterans with civilian job placement. Within such programs, "anonymous questions about PTSD treatment and future employment dominate online discussion forums, and many erroneously assume and advise that outside agencies embrace a 'don't ask, don't tell' policy." Consequently, "these findings give reason to believe that veterans may not seek treatment for PTSD, fearing automatic disqualification from employment based on the diagnosis."[46]

Since the transition from soldier to police officer has become commonplace, the COCS study included an assessment of the typical candidate evaluation process used by police departments to determine how or if the lingering mental health effects of combat would influence hiring decisions. Information was gathered from a dozen random departments throughout the US. The study found that:

- In each case, a psychological evaluation of the applicant was required; however, a separate evaluation for PTSD was not typically administered.

- The vast majority stated that a history of PTSD would not result in automatic disqualification.

- Although screening tools, such as the Clinician Administered PTSD Scale (CAPS), exist to evaluate levels of PTSD severity, no law enforcement agencies reported using one.

- In cases where mental health diagnoses were known, "most agencies suggested that medication, including psychotropic medication, was evaluated to ensure that safe and efficient job performance would not be adversely affected."[47]

While many advocate groups view this lack of screening as a positive thing - because it's one less obstruction for veterans to face when seeking employment with law enforcement - it should be concerning to members of the communities that are subjected to the ill effects of officers who suffer from combat-related conditions like PTSD or TBI. "Despite the challenges faced by veterans leaving active-duty military service for new or existing police careers," lauds Clark, "the ranks of police forces are swelling with veterans of the wars in Iraq and Afghanistan." [48] Considering that one-third of all soldiers returning from deployment suffer from PTSD, TBI, some form of depressive disorder, or a combination of these, it's probable that many of these new recruits who are "swelling the ranks" are bringing significant mental baggage with them.

The combination of this development with the standard process of objectification and internalized oppression, as well as the ingrained mentality of "war culture," is a volatile one. Add the deliberate militarization of domestic police forces to the mix and we have an alarming trend - one that is highlighted by the near-daily occurrence of indiscriminate police violence across the country.

The Evolution of Domestic Militarism

The militarization of America's police forces has been a gradual process which began as blowback from the cultural revolution of the 1960s. Radley Balko, an investigative journalist for the Huffington Post, has spent much of the past decade following this alarmingly fascistic development. What Matt Taibbi is to the mortgage banking scandal, and Jeremy Scahill is to US imperialism, Balko is to the militarization of domestic law enforcement agencies. Likening modern police forces to a "standing army," Balko has made compelling arguments - using constitutional law and the 13th amendment, as well as deploying an historical analysis extending back to old English law - that the mere existence of these forces are unconstitutional.[49]

"We got here by way of a number of political decisions and policies passed over 40 years," explains Balko. "There was never a single law or policy that militarized our police departments - so there was never really a public debate over whether this was a good or bad thing."[50]Over the course of several decades, Balko points to three main developments that have led to this massive domestic militarization:

First, as a general response to the grassroots militancy of the Cultural Revolution - which sought greater degrees of liberty, freedom, and equality - police forces began borrowing from the "special forces" model of the military. "They were largely a reaction to riots, violent protest groups like the Black Panthers and Symbionese Liberation Army, and a couple mass shooting incidents, like the Texas clock tower massacre in 1966." This led to the development and proliferation of SWAT teams. "Darryl Gates started the first SWAT team in L.A. in 1969," explains Balko. "By 1975, there were 500 of them across the country."[51]

The second development was the "war on drugs," which "overlapped" and developed simultaneously with the reactive militarization of the late '60s. Balko captures the vibe: "Nixon was declaring an 'all-out war on drugs.' He was pushing policies like the no-knock raid, dehumanizing drug users and dealers, and sending federal agents to storm private homes on raids that were really more about headlines and photo-ops than diminishing the supply of illicit drugs." Shortly thereafter, with the arrival of Reagan, "the two trends converged, and we started to see SWAT teams used on an almost daily basis - mostly to serve drug warrants."[52]

Two decades later, domestic militarization reached new heights with the third development in this evolution: The World Trade Center attacks of 9/11 and the Patriot Act. Broadening the "war on drugs" to include an all-encompassing and often-times ambiguous "war on terror" opened the door for massive increases in "domestic security measures," which led to seemingly limitless funding of police forces, the creation of new "security" agencies such as Homeland Security, and the opportunity for millions of dollars of profit to be made through the privatization of these services.

Private corporations like G4S Secure Solutions (formerly "The Wackenhut Corporation"), mimicking their international counterparts like Academi (formerly "Xe Services" and originally " Blackwater"), jumped at the chance to secure government contracts (including US Customs and Border Protection) and boost revenue.[53] The creation of a "police industrial complex" has allowed companies like these to benefit from a "business to business global security market that is estimated to generate revenuesof up to $14.9 billion per year" while being heavily subsidized by government contracts.[54] As a complementary development, the privatization of prisons works hand in hand with this newly-found, multi-billion-dollar law enforcement industry by creating even more incentive to seek out arrests and incarcerations.

"Federal funding in the billions of dollars has allowed state and local police departments to gain access to weapons and tactics created for overseas combat theaters."[55] In an ongoing study by the ACLU, which is awaiting responses to "over 260 public records requests with law enforcement agencies in 25 states," enough discernable evidence has been gathered to determine that "the use of military machinery such as tanks and grenades, as well as counter-terrorism tactics, encourage overly aggressive policing - too often with devastating consequences." The study highlights random developments across the country:

- A county sheriff's department in South Carolina has an armored personnel carrier dubbed "The Peacemaker," which can shoot weapons that the U.S. military specifically refrains from using on people.

- New Hampshire police received federal funds for a counter-attack vehicle, asking "what red-blooded American cop isn't going to be excited about getting a toy like this?"

- Police in North Dakota borrowed a $154 million Predator drone from Homeland Security to arrest a family who refused to return six cows that wandered onto their farm.

- Two SWAT Teams shut down a neighborhood in Colorado for four hours to search for a man suspected of stealing a bicycle and merchandise from Wal-Mart.

- Police in Arkansas announced plans to patrol streets wearing full SWAT gear and carrying AR-15 assault rifles. [56]

Furthermore, during a 2007 House subcommittee hearing, Balko reported a "1,500% increase in the use of SWAT teams over the last two decades." Today, in America, "SWAT teams violently smash into private homes more than 100 times per day." [57]

The equipment and machinery regularly utilized by local police forces across the US now mimics that of a war zone. They possess everything from body armor to high-powered weaponry to tanks, armored vehicles, and even drones. But why? Are the duties of police officers really as dangerous as they're made out to be? Out of approximately 900,000 police officers in the US, there are roughly 150 fatalities per year. Nearly 100 of these fatalities are accidental; therefore, 50 out of 900,000 officers - or 1 out of every 18,000 (five hundred thousandths of one percent of the entire force) - are 'maliciously' killed each year.[58] The odds of being struck by lightning over the course of a lifetime are 1 in 3,000.[59] Yet police are armed to the teeth - a fact that suggests conscious shifts from "defense" to "offense" and "protecting and serving" to "confronting and repressing." Citizens - most notably poor, working class, and people of color - who are intended to be the beneficiaries of this "protective service" are now viewed and treated as enemy combatants on a battlefield.

Coming Home to Roost

"It was, as I saw it, a case of 'the chickens coming home to roost.' I said that the hate in white men had not stopped with the killing of defenseless black people, but that hate, allowed to spread unchecked, had finally struck down this country's Chief Magistrate."
          - Malcolm X, explaining his "chickens" quote[60]

America's culture of war and violence was bound to catch up to all of us. Over the past decade, yearly US military expenditures more than doubled from a little over $300 billion in 2001 to over $682 billion in 2013. [61] [62] US military spending represents 39% of global spending - more than the combined spending of China, Russia, United Kingdom, Japan, France, Saudi Arabia, Germany, India, Italy, Canada, and Australia. Since 1945, the US military has invaded, intervened in, or occupied at least 50 countries.[63] Currently, the US operates and/or controls between 700 and 800 military bases worldwide, a list that includes locations in 63 countries. In addition to these bases, there are 255, 065 US military personnel deployed in 156 countries worldwide.[64]

This global military presence has real and often disastrous consequences for human life. In the 2011 book, *The Deaths of Others: The Fate of Civilians in America's Wars*, author John Tirman estimates that "between six and seven million people died in Korea, Vietnam and Iraq alone, the majority of them civilians."[65] However, wartime casualties pale in comparison to the lingering effects, chaos, and disorder stemming from prolonged military occupations. "In the period 1950-2005, there have been 82 million avoidable deaths from deprivation (avoidable mortality, excess deaths, excess mortality , deaths that did not have to happen) associated with countries occupied by the US in the post-1945 era."[66] While it's difficult to gauge how much of a role the military occupations played in this devastation, it's safe to assume the instability created by such occupations factor significantly.

The violence that is perpetrated abroad mimics the violent culture at home. As of June 2013, it's estimated that there are up to 310 million guns in the US, which amounts to just about one gun per person (the US population is 314 million).[67] The next highest number of guns per capita by country is Serbia at 58% and Yemen at 55%, compared to the US at 90%.[68] Since 1968, there have been 1,384,171 gunfire deaths in the US - which amounts to more American deaths than from all of the US wars in the nation's history combined (1,171,177).[69] The US averages 10.2 "firearm-related deaths" per every 100,000 people. Americans are 10 times more likely to suffer gun-related deaths than people in Australia and Ireland; 15 times more likely than people in Turkey; 40 times more likely than those in England; and 170 times more likely than those in Japan. [70]

America's police forces also reflect this culture. And while law enforcement agencies across the US have delivered pain and devastation to poorer, inner-city communities for nearly a half-century, their militarization has only recently begun to attract national attention. Much of this attention can be pinpointed to the Occupy Wall Street movement and the response it received from police, which included unadulterated brutality against peaceful protesters, unnecessary use of force, and the negligent use of tasers and Oleoresin Capsicum (pepper) spray - a substance that has been proven to cause "adverse cardiac, respiratory, and neurologic effects, including arrhythmias and even sudden death" in some cases.[71] However, it was not merely these careless and sadistic actions which have attracted such attention, but rather the changing profile of the victims of this brutality - young, white, "middle-class" women and men.

"For 25 years, the primary 'beneficiaries' of police militarization have been poor people in high-crime areas - people who generally haven't had the power or platform to speak up," explains Balko. "The Occupy protesters were largely affluent, white, and deft at using cell phones and social media to document and publicize incidents of excessive force." Their public victimization, despite falling far short of the police brutality that has existed within communities of color for decades, inevitably struck a chord with a nation still inundated with white supremacist ideals that assign varying degrees of value to American lives - mainly based on the color of one's skin and their socioeconomic background. Ultimately, white members of the media, seeing reflections of their own sons and daughters being abused, suddenly chose to report en masse. White viewers, seeing reflections of their neighbors and relatives, suddenly expressed widespread disgust. This was no longer an episode of COPS, "glamorizing controversial police tactics" and perpetuating "implicit biases regarding race and class."[72] These were now *white, middle-class* lives being affected and brutalized.

Essentially, the hate that Malcolm X spoke of, historically reserved for "defenseless black people," is now developing into indiscriminate rage - targeting poor and working-class people of all colors throughout the US. Through this ongoing process, it is becoming apparent that even white privilege, in itself, is beginning to lose its immunity from this unaccountable wrath.

The 2011 beating of a homeless schizophrenic man, Kelly Thomas, in a transit parking lot in Fullerton, California confirmed this wrath. The incident was, unbeknown to officers, recorded by security cameras on the night of July 5, 2011, and later viewed by millions of Americans as the officers' trial was closely followed. Thomas was unarmed and posed no threat at the time of the beating. "The surveillance camera footage shows Thomas being beaten, clubbed and stunned with a Taser by police." [73]Thomas suffered a coma and died five days later in a hospital bed.

November of 2011 showcased yet another incident of blatant disregard as a police officer doused UC-Davis students with streams of pepper spray. At the time, the students were engaged in non-violent protest by sitting together with their arms locked. Video footage of the officer calmly and methodically walking up and down the line of students, spraying in and around their faces without pause, epitomized the sadistic nature of modern policing. [74]

On August 10, 2013, Tallahassee police officers, while conducting a field sobriety test on 44-year-oldChristina West, forcefully slammed her face-first into the road as one officer screamed in rage. While obviously inebriated, Ms. West was subjected to what City Commissioner Scott Maddox later described as "a disturbing use of force against a completely non-aggressive arrestee."[75]

In September of 2013, 20-year-old David Connor Castellani was arrested, beaten by police, and attacked by a K-9 unit after a verbal altercation outside of an Atlantic City casino. Castellani was unarmed.[76] The following month, after a disagreement with his father over cigarettes, 19-year-old Tyler Comstockfound himself the target of a police chase in Iowa. Despite being told to "back off" in order to defuse the situation, officers escalated the incident by pursuing Comstock, crashing into the truck he was driving, and shooting and killing him. He was unarmed. [77]

In January of 2014, a 2009 surveillance video from a Seabrook, New Hampshire police station was leaked, showing police slamming Mike Bergeron face-first into a concrete wall and dousing him with pepper spray while he was on the floor. Bergeron was arrested under suspicion of drunk driving and was unarmed, handcuffed, and relatively calm when one officer decided to violently slam his face into the wall, to the apparent joy of the other officers who could be seen laughing. [78]

Incidents like these and many others have signified the donning of a new age - one that is eerily reminiscent of authoritarian societies gone by, draped with violently oppressive, daily interactions between agents of government and the citizenry, and dripping of fascistic notions built upon a culture of militarism and war. A violence historically reserved for the most disenfranchised of the population - and ignored by most of the rest - is finally extending itself beyond the oppressive structures of old, transcending targeted demographics to include a working-class-wide assault.

Conclusion

An extensive 2006 report by the *United Nations Human Rights Committee* concluded that, in the United States, the "War on Terror" has "created a generalized climate of impunity for law enforcement officers, and contributed to the erosion of what few accountability mechanisms exist for civilian control over law enforcement agencies. As a result, police brutality and abuse persist unabated and undeterred across the country."[79] "For 30 years, politicians and public officials have been arming, training, and dressing cops as if they're fighting a war," explains Balko. "They've been dehumanizing drug offenders and criminal suspects as the enemy. And of course they've explicitly and repeatedly told them they're fighting a war. It shouldn't be all that surprising that a lot of cops have started to believe it."

This development, while unwanted, was inevitable for a nation that was built on a foundation of Native American genocide, African enslavement, the ruthlessness of capitalism, a culture of misogyny, and persistent strains of racism and classism. The process of objectification which has become pervasive for America's youth has served as an expedient catalyst to a culture of war and oppression; and the insidious victimization of America's working class has worked in tandem with the internalization of this oppressive culture, producing willing participants eager to earn a place in the master's good graces by brutalizing their working class peers.

As products of this conditioning, the mindset of the modern police officer in the US remains peculiar. As individuals, within the confines of their own lives - amongst their families, loved ones, children, and friends - they aren't much different than many of us. Ironically, despite being enforcers of government policy in their professional capacity, many do not hesitate to jump on the soapbox of anti-government rhetoric - often opposing things like Obamacare, welfare, gun control, open immigration policy, and even taxation - on their "personal time." Right-wing fringe groups like the Tea Party and Oath Keepershave actively recruited both military personnel and police officers, finding an abundance of narrow and impressionably ripe minds within these ranks. While claiming to "return to the basics" and "serve the US Constitution," their actions (even when serving their "public" duties) ultimately rely on literal interpretations of a highly-subjective, often vague, and antiquated document that was written by wealthy, white (some slave-owning) landowners nearly 250 years ago. [80]

Naturally, these interpretations are skewed by a myriad of privileges. Regardless of the officer's own ethnicity or socioeconomic background, it is the *role* that ultimately represents a virtual arm of white supremacy and class oppression. Regarding the racist dynamics of law enforcement in the US, "It's useful to understand this as an allegory about how white skin privilege works," explains Annalee Newitz. "The police uniform (and) the badge are like white skin, and the person who wears that skin is allowed to enforce laws which he doesn't himself intend to follow." [81] Within their roles as "officers of the law," they become the embodiment of the government-backed suppression they often despise in their private lives. Only the suppression they carry out is against a specific target population (people of color, the poor and disenfranchised, and the working class). And, despite coming from that very working class, they undoubtedly lose any and all sense of class consciousness in their roles as ruling class watchdogs.

Within this role, they take ownership of a wide array of hypocritical entitlements - a mindset that wholeheartedly believes the US Constitution protects **my rights** to own guns, and **my rights** to protect my privileged status in society, and **my rights** to protect my property, and so on. However, those rights don't apply to **you**. And they certainly don't apply to young men of color who happen to be walking home at night. Nor do they apply to striking workers demanding a living wage. Nor do they apply to Occupy protestors collectively sitting in protest of illegal wars, corporate greed, and corrupt banks. Nor do they apply to evicted homeowners who were exploited by deceitful mortgage schemes. Nor do they apply to homeless people who are simply trying to survive on the streets.

Rather than seeing themselves as public servants, police officers have increasingly embraced the "us vs. them" mentality - anyone who isn't a cop is a potential threat. In doing so, they have become "mindless drones" void of any conscience amidst a world that is becoming increasingly unconscionable - the ultimate tool on an ever-intensifying class-war landscape. The collective baggage they bring with them - products of objectification, war culture, militarism, and combat-induced mental illness - serve as positive attributes in the eyes of those who use them as tools of oppression, while representing erratic triggers of violence to everyone else. The war has come home. The chickens are here to roost.

References

[1] Martha C. Nussbaum, "Objectification", *Philosophy and Public Affairs*, 24 (4), pp. 279-83. OCLC 484757897

[2] Vasily Grossman. Life and Fate. New York Review of Books, 2012, p. 19.

[3] The Science of Evil. Simon Baron-Cohen. NY Times, 6/6/11.

[4] Jeriah Bowser, Horsemeat, Child Soldiers, and Tiaras: Breaking Down Social Constructs. The Hampton Institute, 6/21/13.

[5] Freire, Paulo. Pedagogy of the Oppressed: 30th Anniversary edition. Continuum: New York, pp. 45-46

[6] Abdul JanMohamed. 'The Internalization and Reproduction of Violence: Alice Walker's 'Third Life of Grange Copeland': A guest lecture at the University of Georgia. 10/2/13

[7] Trayvon Martin and bell hooks' Prophetic Words: A Lesson in 'Imperialist White Supremacist Capitalist Patriarchy.' Critical Theory, 6/18/13. http://www.critical-theory.com/george-zimmerman-twitter-imperialist-white-supremacist-capitalist-patriarchy/

[8] Robert A. Gibson. The Negro Holocaust: Lynching and Race Riots in the US, 1880-1950. Yale-New Haven Teachers Institute. http://www.yale.edu/ynhti/curriculum/units/1979/2/79.02.04.x.html

[9] Guzman, Jessie P., ed., 1952 Negro Yearbook (New York, 1952), pp. 275-279.

[10] DuBois, WEB. Black Reconstruction in America. Russell & Russell, New York: 1935. p.725

[11] Titania Kumeh. When Police Shoot and Kill Unarmed Men. Mother Jones, July 14, 2010.

[12] Operation Ghetto Storm. An April 2013 report by the Malcolm X Grassroots Foundation.

[13] Adam Hudson. One Black Man is Killed Every 28 Hours by Police or Vigilantes: America is Perpetually at War with its Own People. Alternet, May 18, 2013.

[14] Jenee Desmond-Harris. Beyond Trayvon: Black and Unarmed. The Root, June 8, 2013.

[15] Oscar Guzman, Autistic Boy Beaten By Chicago Police, Could Get Half Million Dollar Settlement From City. Huffington Post, January 18, 2012.

[16] Andy Kossak. Police Scuffled With Gilberto Powell, Who Has Down Syndrome, Over Bulge That Was 22-Year-Old's Colostomy Bag. Opposing Views: November 7, 2013.

[17] Andrew Lynch. Deaf Man says Police Beat him for disobeying orders he couldn't hear. Fox 14 News: January 13, 2014.

[18] California dad begged for his life as police beat him to death - witnesses. RT.com, 5/10/13.

[19] Mitch Weiss and Jeffrey Collins. Jonathan Ferrell, Unarmed Man Killed in North Carolina, Was Shot 10 Times by Officer: Police. Huffington Post, 9/16/13.

[20] Long Beach Police beating of unarmed man in street under investigation. NBC News, 1/17/14.

[21] Robin Wilkey. Police Shoot and Kill Andy Lopez, 13-year-old Boy Carrying Pellet Gun. Huffington Post, 10/23/13.

[22] http://www.hippy.com/modules.php?name=News&file=article&sid=76

[23] Joe Rogan. The American War Machine. Podcast transcript.

[24] Deborah Warden, MD. Military TBI During the Iraq and Afghanistan Wars. Report for the Defense and Veterans Brain Injury Center, Walter Reed Army Medical Center, Washington, DC. 2006

[25] Invisible Wounds of War: Psychological and Cognitive Injuries, Their Consequences, and Services to Assist Recovery. RAND Center for Military Health and Policy Research. 2008

[26] Anoopa Singh. Insomnia Can Worsen PTSD, Depression and Anxiety in Returning War Veterans. Medical Daily, 6/28/13.

[27] Gehrman P, Seelig AD, Jacobson IG, et al. Predeployment Sleep Duration and Insomnia Symptoms as Risk Factors for New-Onset Mental Health Disorders Following Military Deployment.SLEEP. 2013.

[28] Tom Watkins and Maggie Schneider. 325 Army Suicides in 2012 a Record. CNN.com, 2/2/13.

[29] Bob Dreyfuss. War Crimes in Iraq and Afghanistan. The Nation, 4/13/10.

[30] Hersh, Seymour M. (May 17, 2004). "Chain of Command." The New Yorker. "NBC News later quoted U.S. military officials as saying that the unreleased photographs showed American soldiers "severely beating an Iraqi prisoner nearly to death, having sex with a female Iraqi prisoner, and 'acting inappropriately with a dead body.' The officials said there also was a videotape, apparently shot by U.S. personnel, showing Iraqi guards raping young boys."

[31] Shooting by US Soldiers in Afghanistan Fuels Karzai's Anger. Josh

Partlow, The Washington Post, 4/13/10.

[32] Shooting by US Soldiers in Afghanistan Fuels Karzai's Anger. Josh Partlow, The Washington Post, 4/13/10.

[33] Civilians Killed as US Troops Fire on Afghan Bus. Richard Oppel and Taimor Shah, The New York Times, 4/12/10.

[34] Military investigating photos of Marines burning bodies in Fallujah, Iraq, in 2004. William Branigan, the Washington Post, 1/15/14.

[35] US Department of Veteran Affairs. What is PTSD. Accessed at http://www.ptsd.va.gov/public/PTSD-overview/basics/what-is-ptsd.asp

[36] Mayo Clinic. Information on Traumatic Brain Injury. Accessed at http://www.mayoclinic.org/diseases-conditions/traumatic-brain-injury/basics/definition/con-20029302

[37] Mark Clark. Military Vets Joining Law Enforcement. POLICE: The Law Enforcement Magazine, 1/30/14.

[38] Philadelphia Police Department recruiting information. Accessed on http://www.phillypolice.com /careers/military-experience

[39] George Altman. Best for Vets: Law Enforcement 2014. Army Times, 10/15/13.

[40] George Altman. Best for Vets: Law Enforcement 2014. Army Times, 10/15/13.

[41] Weisler, R. H., J.G. Barbee IV, and M.H. Townsend, "Mental Health and Recovery in the Gulf Coast After Hurricanes Katrina and Rita," *Journal of the American Medical Association* 296 (5) (2006), 585--588.

[42] Webster, Barbara. *Combat Deployment and the Returning Officer.* Washington, DC: U.S. Department of Justice Office of Community Oriented Policing Services, 2008. p. 25.

[43] Combat Deployment Affects Police Officers Returning to Work. Community Policing Dispatch. COPS Office at the US Department of Justice. November 2008.

[44] Invisible Wounds of War: Psychological and Cognitive Injuries, Their Consequences, and Services to Assist Recovery. RAND Center for Military Health and Policy Research. 2008

[45] Kara Ballenger-Browning. Can a Veteran go into Law Enforcement after a PTSD Diagnosis? Naval Center Combat and Operational Stress Control.
http://www.pdhealth.mil/clinicians/downloads/PTSD_COCS.pdf

[46] Kara Ballenger-Browning, COCS report.

[47] Kara Ballenger-Browning, COCS report.

[48] Mark Clark, POLICE Magazine.

[49] Radley Balko. How did America's Police become a Military force on

the streets? ABA Journal, 7/1/13.

[50] How Cops became Soldiers: An Interview with Police Militarization Expert Radley Balko. Michael Arria, Vice.com.

[51] Interview with Balko

[52] Interview with Balko

[53] The Bus No One Wants to Catch: The End of the Road for Illegal Immigrants. G4S Case Study on Customs and Border Protection. http://www.g4s.com/~/media/Files/USA/PDF-Case-Studies/Customs%20and%20Border%20 Patrol%20112311%20FINAL.ashx

[54] G4S Annual Report and Accounts for 2012. http://www.g4s.com/~/media/Files/Annual%20Reports/g4s _annual_report_2012.ashx

[55] The Militarization of Policing in America: Towns Don't Need Tanks. An ongoing study by the ACLU, accessed at https://www.aclu.org/militarization

[56] ACLU report

[57] Balko. How did America's Police become a Military force on the streets? ABA Journal

[58] Causes of Law Enforcement Deaths, 2003 to 2012. National Law Enforcement Officers Memorial Fund. Accessed at http://www.nleomf.org/facts/officer-fatalities-data/causes.html

[59] Flash Facts about Lightning. National Geographic News, 6/24/05. Accessed at http://news.nationalgeographic .com/news/2004/06/0623_040623_lightningfacts.html

[60] In The Autobiography of Malcolm X: As Told to Alex Haley (1964)

[61] World Military Spending. Anup Shah, Global Issues. 6/30/13.

[62] Stockholm International Peace Research Institute. Interactive data report. Accessed at http://portal.sipri.org/ publications/pages/expenditures/country-search

[63] Dr Zoltan Grossman, "From Wounded Knee to Libya: a century of U.S. military interventions."http://academic.evergreen.edu/g/grossmaz/interventions.html

[64] Jules Dufour, "The world-wide network of US military bases", Global Research:http://www.globalresearch.ca/the-worldwide-network-of-us-military-bases/5564

[65] John Tirman. The Deaths of Others: The Fate of Civilians in America's Wars. Oxford University Press, 2011.

[66] The US has invaded 70 Nations since 1776. Dr. Gideon Polya,

countercurrents.org, 7/5/13.

[67] Pew Research Center. A minority of Americans own guns, but just how many is unclear. 6/4/13

[68] Geneva Graduate Institute of International Studies. "Small Arms Survey 2007." Cambridge.

[69] PBS Commentator Mark Shields says more killed by guns since '68 than in all US wars. Politifact.com. Accessed at http://www.politifact.com/truth-o-meter/statements/2013/jan/18/mark-shields/pbs-commentator-mark-shields-says-more-killed-guns/

[70] US has more guns - and gun deaths - than any other country, study finds. Sydney Lupkin, ABC News. 9/19/13. Accessed at http://abcnews.go.com/blogs/health/2013/09/19/u-s-has-more-guns-and-gun-deaths-than-any-other-country-study-finds/

[71] Deborah Blum. About Pepper Spray. PLOS.org, 11/20/11.

[72] After 25 Years of Perpetuating Racist Stereotypes, Fox Cancels "COPS." Alternet, 5/9/13.

[73] Ex-cops acquitted in beating death of homeless man in California. Chuck Conder. CNN, 1/14/14.

[74] Video Shows Occupy Protestors Pepper Sprayed, Beaten. Alyssa Newcomb. ABC News, 11/19/11.

[75] Tallahassee Police Brutality: Slam Woman's Face into Pavement during Arrest. Lorri Anderson. Freedomoutpost.com, 9/11/13.

[76] Atlantic City Police Beat Unarmed Man, Use Dogs, 200 Stitches. Examiner.com, 9/30/13.

[77] Tyler Comstock Killing: Iowa Police Shoot Unarmed 19-year-old after Father calls Authorities to Report the Teen Stole his Truck. Barry Leibowitz. CBS News, 11/8/13.

[78] Video shows New Hampshire police brutally beating man after drunken driving arrest. Travis Gettys. Raw Story, 1/18/14.

[79] "In the Shadows of the War on Terror: Persistent Police Brutality and Abuse in the United States." United Nations Committee on Human Rights. June 2006.

[80] Who are the Oath Keepers? Dean Scoville. COPS: The Law Enforcement Magazine, 4/4/13.

[81] Annalee Newitz. On the Whiteness of Police. 1997. http://www.techsploitation.com/socrates/ whiteness_police.html

Spirituality & Religion
DEPARTMENT

Out of Empire and Into the Margins

Exploring the Gospel of Mark

Kevin Burgess

Inbreaking on the Margins (Mark 1:1-20)

As part of the formation of a community, it helps to have an anchor, so to speak, in the form of something tangible to get folks on the same page.

The way my own little community is doing this is to come together regularly for liturgy and book study. Currently, we are reading the book " _Say to This Mountain_ " by Ched Myers. The book focuses on the Gospel of Mark; the oldest, shortest, and perhaps most intense of the synoptic gospels.

I would like to note that I am not a scholar, only a very average fellow trying to follow Jesus. As such, this series of posts will often be a retelling of Myers' points, though certainly not in a way that is as complete nor as insightful as his.

Our church decided to 'start again' by going back to the basics of our faith through the exploration of the most simple and direct of the four gospels. So many of the basic teachings of Jesus are never truly heard by more casual church-goers, or perhaps they have been heard so many times that much of the meaning falls on deaf ears. It is my intention here to explore my own reactions to the gospel, as well as summarize what we are reading. To be honest, I am writing this for myself in order to clarify my own thoughts through a deeper exploration of the texts, as well as to be reminded that in the most basic teachings of Jesus we can find the inspiration and renewal to 'turn around,' and explore how those teachings can be embodied in our ordinary lives. I hope that others might be interested in hearing about this gospel that feels quite like a manifesto for repentance, resistance, and hope.

Mark 1:1-8

1 The beginning of the good news about Jesus Christ, God's Son, 2 happened just as it was written about in the prophecy of Isaiah:

Look, I am sending my messenger before you.
He will prepare your way,
3 a voice shouting in the wilderness:
"Prepare the way for the Lord;
make his paths straight."

4 John the Baptist was in the wilderness calling for people to be baptized to show that they were changing their hearts and lives and wanted God to forgive their sins. 5 Everyone in Judea and all the people of Jerusalem went out to the Jordan River and were being baptized by John as they confessed their sins. 6 John wore clothes made of camel's hair, with a leather belt around his waist. He ate locusts and wild honey. 7 He announced, "One stronger than I am is coming after me. I'm not even worthy to bend over and loosen the strap of his sandals. 8 I baptize you with water, but he will baptize you with the Holy Spirit."

The word 'gospel' is from the Old English godspel, meaning "good news." The word comes to us from the Latin evangelium, which in turn came from the Greek euangelion. It is associated with propaganda used by the Romans to announce the 'good news' of military victory or the acquisition of power of a new emperor. From the get-go, the lingo of the dominant power is being subverted, announcing the coming of a new 'king,' but one quite different from what was expected by the people of Israel. This one shows up on the margins, calls his first followers from the margins, and embodies a kingdom centered in the margins, without the dominance or expression of power that is expected of kings that command troops toward military victories.

Also what occurs here is a lot of tie-ins with the Hebrew scriptures, with quotes from Isaiah 40:3 ("A voice of one calling: 'In the wilderness prepare the way for the LORD; make straight in the desert a highway for our God.'"), Malachi 3:1 ("'I will send my messenger, who will prepare the way before me. Then suddenly the Lord you are seeking will come to his temple; the messenger of the covenant, whom you desire, will come,' says the LORD Almighty"), and Exodus 23:20 ("See, I am sending an angel ahead of you to guard you along the way and to bring you to the place I have prepared."). Something easily missed in the text of Malachi is the word suddenly, which is understood as conveying God will come swiftly and with a judgment against those who "...defraud laborers of their wages, who oppress the widows and the fatherless, and deprive the foreigners among you of justice (Malachi 1:5). Mark has John dressed as Elijah in 2 Kings 1:8 ("He had a garment of hair and had a leather belt around his waist."). Elijah was announced in Malachi 4:5 as the one that would return to call for the people to repent, to "turn their hearts around."

All of these tie-ins emphasize how very important it is to Mark to demonstrate that Jesus is the one that was promised, the messiah, breaking into history to inaugurate the Kingdom of God, to break the chains of those who have been enslaved and oppressed. He is the King that has come to displace all others, forever.

Mark 1:9-13

9 About that time, Jesus came from Nazareth of Galilee, and John baptized him in the Jordan River.10 While he was coming up out of the water, Jesus saw heaven splitting open and the Spirit, like a dove, coming down on him. 11 And there was a voice from heaven: "You are my Son, whom I dearly love; in you I find happiness." 12 At once the Spirit forced Jesus out into the wilderness. 13 He was in the wilderness for forty days, tempted by Satan. He was among the wild animals, and the angels took care of him.

Jesus comes from Nazareth, which in John's gospel is criticized as a place of nobodies ("What good can come from Nazareth?" - John 1:46). Heaven being 'torn open' has a decidedly apocalyptic (literally an 'unveiling') tone, with Jesus again revealed as the messiah. The dove imagery is from Isaiah 42:1 ("Here is my servant, whom I uphold, my chosen one in whom I delight; I will put my Spirit on him, and he will bring justice to the nations."). Myers writes that in the gospel story a key element is that the story of liberation moves from the center to the margins. Jesus doesn't come to Jerusalem, which was understood by Jews as being the center of the world. Instead, Jesus comes to the 'wilderness,' to the margins, bypassing the place where wealth and privilege have their strongholds. He comes to those who are often dominated and oppressed.

Mark 1:14-20

14 After John was arrested, Jesus came into Galilee announcing God's good news, 15 saying, "Now is the time! Here comes God's kingdom! Change your hearts and lives, and trust this good news!" 6 As Jesus passed alongside the Galilee Sea, he saw two brothers, Simon and Andrew, throwing fishing nets into the sea, for they were fishermen. 17 "Come, follow me," he said, "and I'll show you how to fish for people." 18 Right away, they left their nets and followed him. 19 After going a little farther, he saw James and John, Zebedee's sons, in their boat repairing the fishing nets. 20 At that very moment he called them. They followed him, leaving their father Zebedee in the boat with the hired workers.

This inbreaking, this unveiling of the sovereignty of God is here now. It is breaking into the margins of our world, as it always is. Jesus is calling us to repent, to 'turn around,' to follow him as he brings the justice spoken of in Isaiah 42:1. We are called to be imitators, followers doing all the things that he did. He calls his first followers out of the working class, bypassing the privileged and the learned. He visits the shores, calling for his disciples from the fishermen, which was a trade being taken over by those in power. This commercialization by those in power was dislocating the poor, increasing taxes, and putting the little guys out of business. These are people struggling to get by, and from these Jesus begins to build his kingdom. (see Crossan, Excavating Jesus: Prologue)

Much like his first followers, we are invited to "a new location and a new vocation" (STTM, Chap. 1). We are being called out of Empire, into a new exodus towards the margins, joining with those who have no power, waiting, watching, and working as the inbreaking of God's sovereignty is witnessed. We are asked to ferret out places where our privilege interferes with God's desire to redistribute the surplus of the world, so that all have enough. It is in this very basic understanding of the teachings of Jesus that Mark's good news has its foundation.

Thus, we are asked to consider these questions:

How does our own privilege, power, and access create a world where people can be dislocated; where folks can be abandoned? And how do we repent of that power?

Where do we recognize the places of 'center and margin' in our own world/community/self? And how do we move out of the places where power is used to coerce and dominate, and into places of communion with those who are dominated and oppressed?

How can we subvert the ways those in power use fear and force to keep that power, without resorting to force and power-over? How do we create a mirror for oppressors to see where they have gone astray from their calling to love their neighbors, even their enemies?

Expelling False Authority (Mark 1:21-2:12)

The next part of Mark's gospel demonstrates what Myers refers to as "the three essential characteristics of Jesus' mission: the healing and exorcism of marginalized people, the proclamation of God's sovereignty and call to discipleship, and the resulting confrontations with the authorities."

We are beginning to see what Jesus' ministry is going to look like, and so much of what Jesus is about can be found in the first 50 verses of this gospel. From the first 20 verses, we have Jesus showing up as the one announced by scripture to inaugurate a new kingdom that subverts and counters the existing one. He calls his first disciples from the 'nobodies' of the world, as well as calling them out of empire and into the margins to join with the powerless, dislocated, and exploited.

In the next part of the gospel, Jesus performs an exorcism in a synagogue. Whether or not one believes in the literalness of the story, one can still glean what is important here: Jesus is demonstrating his authority over the scribal establishment, referred to below as 'legal experts.'

Mark 1:21-28

21 Jesus and his followers went into Capernaum. Immediately on the Sabbath Jesus entered the synagogue and started teaching. 22 The people were amazed by his teaching, for he was teaching them with authority, not like the legal experts. 23 Suddenly, there in the synagogue, a person with an evil spirit screamed, 24 "What have you to do with us, Jesus of Nazareth? Have you come to destroy us? I know who you are. You are the holy one from God." 25 "Silence!" Jesus said, speaking harshly to the demon. "Come out of him!" 26 The unclean spirit shook him and screamed, then it came out. 27 Everyone was shaken and questioned among themselves, "What's this? A new teaching with authority! He even commands unclean spirits and they obey him!" 28 Right away the news about him spread throughout the entire region of Galilee.

It is no coincidence that the 'evil spirit' speaks through the man in the synagogue. Jesus' conflict with the scribes makes up a large amount of his ministry. Scribes are those who have authority to teach the Torah, and later in the gospel Jesus warns people to be wary of them, for "they like to walk around in flowing robes and be greeted with respect in the marketplaces, and have the most important seats in the synagogues and the places of honor at banquets. They devour widows' houses and, for a show, make lengthy prayers." (Mark 12:38-40)
Basically, Jesus is calling out those who teach the law from a place of pretension, ego, and ostentation. Jesus is invading the turf of the scribes, calling out the 'spirit' of scribal power, which Myers says "holds sway over the hearts and minds of the people." He also points out that the framing of the text suggests that, in verse 24, the word 'us' is being used by the evil spirit on behalf of the scribal class. The demon's voice represents the voice of the scribes themselves, first expressing defiance, and then fear. It should be noted that the true miracle of the exorcism lies not in the literal act of expelling an evil spirit, but in the symbolic act of Jesus as one who has true authority through God, an authority that challenges the very order of power.

Mark 1:29-39

29 After leaving the synagogue, Jesus, James, and John went home with Simon and Andrew.30 Simon's mother-in-law was in bed, sick with a fever, and they told Jesus about her at once. 31 He went to her, took her by the hand, and raised her up. The fever left her, and she served them. 32 That evening, at sunset, people brought to Jesus those who were sick or demon-possessed. 33 The whole town gathered near the door. 34 He healed many who were sick with all kinds of diseases, and he threw out many demons. But he didn't let the demons speak, because they recognized him. 35 Early in the morning, well before sunrise, Jesus rose and went to a deserted place where he could be alone in prayer. 36 Simon and those with him tracked him down. 37 When they found him, they told him, "Everyone's looking for you!" 38 He replied, "Let's head in the other direction, to the nearby villages, so that I can preach there too. That's why I've come." 39 He traveled throughout Galilee, preaching in their synagogues and throwing out demons.

A surface reading of the verses above might lead one to either remain in or adopt a patriarchal understanding of verse 31. Imagining that to 'serve them' meant that Simon's mom got up and made everybody a sandwich misses not only what the verse is actually saying, but betrays the very typical patriarchal theology that understandably turns so many intelligent people off to Christianity.

Myers demonstrates that the Greek verb 'to serve' (where we get the term 'deacon') appears only two other times in Mark, one being 10:45 "For even the Son of Man did not come to be served, but to serve..." which likely had little to do with matters of the kitchen. The other time is in 15:41 "In Galilee these women had followed him and cared for his needs. Many other women who had come up with him to Jerusalem were also there", which Myers claims was a "summary statement of discipleship: from beginning (Galilee) to end (Jerusalem) these women were true followers who, unlike the men (see 10:32-45) practiced servanthood." Through the healing of Simon's mother, and her subsequent discipleship, Mark is demonstrating another of Jesus' conflicts with authority, in that Jesus is making it quite clear that the diminished status of women and the continued degradation of them by a patriarchal theology is about to be turned on its head.

Jesus becomes much sought after, so much so that "the whole town gathered at the door." So begins a cycle of engagement and withdrawal, where we find Jesus balancing the needs of the poor and sick, with time to perhaps process and clarify his intent and focus.

Mark 1:40-45

40 A man with a skin disease approached Jesus, fell to his knees, and begged, "If you want, you can make me clean." 41 Incensed, Jesus reached out his hand, touched him, and said, "I do want to. Be clean."42 Instantly, the skin disease left him, and he was clean. 43 Sternly, Jesus sent him away, 44 saying,"Don't say anything to anyone. Instead, go and show yourself to the priest and offer the sacrifice for your cleansing that Moses commanded. This will be a testimony to them." 45 Instead, he went out and started talking freely and spreading the news so that Jesus wasn't able to enter a town openly. He remained outside in deserted places, but people came to him from everywhere.

Mark 2:1-12

2 After a few days, Jesus went back to Capernaum, and people heard that he was at home. 2 So many gathered that there was no longer space, not even near the door. Jesus was speaking the word to them. 3 Some people arrived, and four of them were bringing to him a man who was paralyzed. 4 They couldn't carry him through the crowd, so they tore off part of the roof above where Jesus was. When they had made an opening, they lowered the mat on which the paralyzed man was lying. 5 When Jesus saw their faith, he said to the paralytic, "Child, your sins are forgiven!" 6 Some legal experts were sitting there, muttering among themselves, 7 "Why does he speak this way? He's insulting God. Only the one God can forgive sins."
8 Jesus immediately recognized what they were discussing, and he said to them, "Why do you fill your minds with these questions? 9 Which is easier-to say to a paralyzed person, 'Your sins are forgiven,' or to say, 'Get up, take up your bed, and walk'? 10 But so you will know that the Human One has authority on the earth to forgive sins"-he said to the man who was paralyzed, 11 "Get up, take your mat, and go home." 12 Jesus raised him up, and right away he picked up his mat

and walked out in front of everybody. They were all amazed and praised God, saying, "We've never seen anything like this!"

In these final two parts of the gospel we are discussing, Jesus performs two healings. Regarding the first, Myers brings up two principles that are basic to Levitical regulations regarding the healing of the skin disease. First, the impurity was communicable, and second, a priest must preside over a ritual cleansing. To quote Myers, "Our modern worldview assumes that the gospel healing stories relate 'supernatural' cures of medical disorders. In the ancient Mediterranean world, however, illness was primarily perceived as a 'socially disvalued state,' an aberrant or defective condition that threatened communal integrity."

Healing a person meant that they could then be welcomed back into the community. But to do so in Jesus' culture meant that a 'sick' person would need to be confirmed as 'cleansed' by a priest. In the case of the first healing, the one involving the man with the skin disease, it needs to be understood that this was not leprosy (as many translations name it) as in what we term Hansen's Disease, but rather some kind of general skin disorder. Any healing of such an 'illness' would not be a cure, in that the disorder would disappear. Rather it would be, as Myers puts it, "covered over."

The man with the skin disease assumes Jesus has the authority to heal him. Jesus was not a priest, however, but a 'nobody' from Galilee, an itinerant preacher and healer, with no authority to pronounce that a person has been cleansed of an affliction. Jesus performs no ritual, but rather touches him and makes the declaration that he is cleansed. Another slap to those with authority: Jesus, by touch (remember, the 'impurity' of the man caused by the skin diseases is communicable) and by word, pronounces the man cleansed, and welcomed back into the community. Jesus does all this with an indignation, which Myers proposes is the key to the story; Jesus' mood throughout the episode "is one of protest, not cooperation." Jesus then sends the man to the priests, who he knows will not accept his authority to heal. Just as Jesus protested the scribal establishment as those cornering the market on the interpretation of Torah, he is also protesting priestly authority to cleanse those who are outcasts to the community.

In the second healing, not only does Jesus heal the physically disabled man by curing his inability to walk, he challenges the collective understanding of sin held by his culture. The social maps of Jesus' time consisted of two codes: purity and debt (the terms 'debt' and 'sin' meant mostly the same thing). As there was no distinction between sacred and secular in his culture, debt and sin were all under the purview of those ordained to interpret and enact the law. According to Myers, "The debt code, under the jurisdiction of the scribal class, regulated individual and social responsibilities, criminal behavior, and economic status. Its rules determined sins of commission and omission." The purity codes pronounced by the law, and interpreted by the scribes, reinforced what defined sin/debt. The codes decided who was in and who was out. It was only through 'proper' channels that those factors could be changed. So, the question comes down to who gets to diagnose or treat those on the margins of the community, or perhaps outside the walls altogether?

To the scribal establishment, the answer was easy; it was them and their cohorts. In the second healing, they accuse Jesus of blasphemy, and claim it is God alone who can forgive sins. Of course, this is convenient for them, as it is they who get to define sin. They are very interested in maintaining their authority, and to have Jesus make such pronouncements as 'Your sins are forgiven' just isn't going to fly. But Jesus bypasses their authority, acting in a manner intent on 'liberating the captives.'

So, demons? What, in this modern age, are we to do with that? They're real, and we see demons all the time: demons of poverty, racism, classism, drug addiction, violence, depression. We see purity and debt codes deeply ingrained in our institutions, cycling over and over, keeping people in debt and making sure they remain outcasts. Consider who you know that is too poor to get health insurance in the ACA, or why so many of the nation's soldiers come from the poorest communities.

Even mainstream news sources are confirming this institutionalized evil. According to a _study_ from the Kaiser Family Foundation, "In states that expand their Medicaid programs, millions of adults will gain Medicaid eligibility under the law. However, with many states opting not to implement the Medicaid expansion, millions of adults will remain outside the reach of the ACA and continue to have limited, if any, option for health coverage: most do not have access to employer-based coverage through a job, few can afford coverage on their own, and most are currently ineligible for public coverage in their state."

In a _report_ from the Associated Press in 2007 that "nearly three-fourths of [U.S. troops] killed in Iraq came from towns where the per capita income was below the national average. More than half came from towns where the percentage of people living in poverty topped the national average."

Institutional evil exists, just like it always has. Myers makes the case that "Jesus relentlessly critiqued the purity and debt systems of his day because they tended to segregate and exclude rather than integrate and restore." He still does.

Food Emancipation and (In)security (Mark 2:13-3:6)

So far we have had Jesus challenging the authority of both the priests and the scribes, those who control and interpret the purity system and the debt system, respectively. In both instances, Jesus makes it clear that there is a new teaching (which in fact isn't new at all, but rather the original intention of God), and it does not allow for those in power to use the law to further their own agendas, nor allow them to maintain their power over those seen as outcasts and nobodies.

Jesus now turns his attention to the Pharisees. The Pharisees had the goal of holding the common folk to a fairly rigorous observance of the law, but in a way that was focused more on the village life rather than the Temple. Myers points out three practices that were important to the Pharisees: restrictive table fellowship, public piety, and Sabbath observances; and also how Jesus challenges those examples.

Mark 2:13-22

13 Jesus went out beside the lake again. The whole crowd came to him, and he began to teach them.14 As he continued along, he saw Levi, Alphaeus' son, sitting at a kiosk for collecting taxes. Jesus said to him, "Follow me." Levi got up and followed him. 15 Jesus sat down to eat at Levi's house. Many tax collectors and sinners were eating with Jesus and his disciples. Indeed, many of them had become his followers. 16 When some of the legal experts from among the Pharisees saw that he was eating with sinners and tax collectors, they asked his disciples, "Why is he eating with sinners and tax collectors?" 17 When Jesus heard it, he said to them, "Healthy people don't need a doctor, but sick people do. I didn't come to call righteous people, but sinners." 18 John's disciples and the Pharisees had a habit of fasting. Some people asked Jesus, "Why do John's disciples and the Pharisees'

disciples fast, but yours don't?" 19 Jesus said, "The wedding guests can't fast while the groom is with them, can they? As long as they have the groom with them, they can't fast. 20 But the days will come when the groom will be taken away from them, and then they will fast. 21 "No one sews a piece of new, unshrunk cloth on old clothes; otherwise, the patch tears away from it, the new from the old, and makes a worse tear. 22 No one pours new wine into old leather wineskins; otherwise, the wine would burst the wineskins and the wine would be lost and the wineskins destroyed. But new wine is for new wineskins."

Tax collectors were often Jews employed by a foreigner who worked for Rome. They would collect taxes for the Empire, as well as a little for themselves. They were not a popular bunch, and served as living reminders for how Israel was in debt servitude to Rome. The calling of Levi out of such business is another example of Jesus calling his followers from those who are despised. Levi, as a tax collector would not have been a popular fellow, but Jesus calls him, and redeems him. Myers points out how the very next scene of Jesus eating at Levi's house with a mixture of those in debt (sinners) and those enforcing the debt obligation (tax collectors) was "extraordinary table fellowship indeed!"

Jesus has just challenged the first important practice of the Pharisees: restrictive table fellowship. Next, he will take on public piety in the form of fasting as well as Sabbath observances. Fasting was important to the Pharisees, and they did so rigorously, as well as publicly. Myers points out that "Jesus...wishes to cut through piety to the real issue: a society in which some can afford to fast while others truly go hungry", as well as reminding us that Jesus makes the point that this "'new' wine of the discipleship movement must not be co-opted by 'old' forms of cosmetic piety."

Being able to afford to eat well daily is something that not everyone enjoys. Many go to bed hungry. In my own state, over 17% of the population is "food insecure," meaning that those households may often have to make trade-offs between housing and medical bills versus eating nutritionally adequate food.

According to *Bread for the World* , a fairly mainstream charitable institution:

· Out of the world's 7 billion people, 1.2 billion still live in extreme poverty, on less than $1.25 per day.

· Each year, 2.6 million children die as a result of hunger-related causes
· In the United States, the world's wealthiest nation, 14.5% of households - nearly 49 million Americans, including 15.9 million children - struggle to put food on the table.
· More than one in four American children are at risk of hunger. More than one in five children live in households that struggle to put food on the table.
· In the United States, hunger is not caused by a scarcity of food, but rather the continued prevalence of poverty.

These statistics are a serious rebuke for us. As long as we live in ways that sustain these serious failings of humanity, we are not the 'city on a hill' that the politicians want us to believe America is. The fact that over 2.5 million children will die this year because of hunger stands as a prime example of our complete lack of anything even resembling following the one who said "I was hungry and you gave me food to eat. I was thirsty and you gave me a drink. I was a stranger and you welcomed me." (Matthew 25:35)

Mark 2:23-28

23 Jesus went through the wheat fields on the Sabbath. As the disciples made their way, they were picking the heads of wheat. 24 The Pharisees said to Jesus, "Look! Why are they breaking the Sabbath law?" 25 He said to them, "Haven't you ever read what David did when he was in need, when he and those with him were hungry? 26 During the time when Abiathar was high priest, David went into God's house and ate the bread of the presence, which only the priests were allowed to eat. He also gave bread to those who were with him." 27 Then he said, "The Sabbath was created for humans; humans weren't created for the Sabbath. 28 This is why the Human One is Lord even over the Sabbath.

The disciples are hungry, and as they walk along, they pick handfuls of wheat berries and eat them. The problem is they are doing so on the Sabbath, and the oral tradition of the Pharisees forbids harvesting on the Sabbath. The Pharisees are again placing the needs of the people beneath their own man-made laws regarding (as Myers says) who to eat with, when not to eat, and when and where they should eat.

Jesus basically says "Rules be damned, when somebody is hungry they have the right to food despite what 'the law' says."

Mark 3:1-6

3 Jesus returned to the synagogue. A man with a withered hand was there. 2 Wanting to bring charges against Jesus, they were watching Jesus closely to see if he would heal on the Sabbath. 3 He said to the man with the withered hand, "Step up where people can see you." 4 Then he said to them,"Is it legal on the Sabbath to do good or to do evil, to save life or to kill?" But they said nothing.5 Looking around at them with anger, deeply grieved at their unyielding hearts, he said to the man,"Stretch out your hand." So he did, and his hand was made healthy. 6 At that, the Pharisees got together with the supporters of Herod to plan how to destroy Jesus.

The Pharisees want Jesus to commit heresy. There are waiting, poised to 'take him down.' But Jesus turns the tables, and publicly calls out the Pharisees for their attachment to their own man-made laws. Jesus, in many ways the new Moses, reminds us that we have a choice of either following the commandments of God in order that we might live in harmony with ourselves, each other, and Creation, or else we can take the road of death and adversity. (_Deuteronomy 30:15-18_)

Jesus also becomes angry at the lack of response from the Pharisees to his challenge. Myers points out that the word translated as 'anger' here is "a strong one, usually associated with...the phrase 'the wrath of God'" Where Jesus chooses the path of life, the Pharisees have chosen death, and begin to plot against Jesus.

It stuns me every time my friends and I meet to share food with those experiencing homelessness. I am frustrated that this is even an issue in this day, but I am reminded that this is nothing new. The privileged have always maintained that privilege by exploiting others. I am guilty too, for I enjoy a certain privilege as well, as do all of those reading these words. We have chosen en masse a hardness of heart, and we suffer from this disease of the Pharisees. Jesus is showing us what God's intentions are, that all who are hungry are fed, that all who are sick are cared for, and that we have before us two paths: one of life and one of death. So often we have chosen the latter, Jesus invites us to make a big u-turn, and choose the better way.

Jesus and Yeshua

An Examination of Cultural Icons

Jeriah Bowser

His long, well-conditioned, light-brown hair glistens softly in the sun. His deep blue, penetrating eyes betray his Anglo-Saxon heritage. His well-manicured facial hair parts to reveal a gleaming set of perfectly straight, white teeth. His soft white skin and delicate fingers hint at a life free of manual labor and toil. The long, flowing white robe that wraps around his body must have been recently washed and bleached, as it radiates purity and divine goodness. The child in his lap and the crowds that have gathered around him with admiration and awe written all over their faces communicate that this man must be saying something incredibly important and inspirational.

He teaches such divine truths as "Blessed are those who make lots of money, for God loves money" and "For God so loved the world, he made a special place for you to burn and suffer forever if you don't follow his moral boundaries" as well as "When someone slaps you on the cheek, turn to him the other also; unless your government decides that a group of people is a threat to your country, then go ahead and slaughter them."

He is the patron saint of Capitalism. He is the author and originator of Manifest Destiny. He is a card-carrying member of the NRA and a proud

Conservative Republican. He is invoked whenever one of his flock needs a new bike, car, house, or business merger. He rides atop our fighter jets and cruise missiles, and blesses our troops as they head off to foreign conquests. He is the epitome of the American dream- born into poverty and obscurity, yet through hard work and dedication he became a great prophet and then sacrificed his life for our sins. He is a prophet boldly upholding and defending the ideals that our glorious country was founded on. He is…. say it with me now… Jesus.

If you were raised in an American Christian family, then you are probably very familiar with the person I just portrayed to you. He was emblazoned on the walls of the churches of our youth, smiling at us from the pages of our illustrated children's bible, and his ideas and teachings were heavily reinforced by our family.

If you were not raised in an American Christian family, then you probably experienced a lot of bigotry, ignorance, and sheer stupidity at the hands of the prior group. Regardless of your personal beliefs, experiences, or awareness of said Jesus, it's safe to say that your life has been greatly affected by the character I just painted.

I would like now to introduce you to another character, one you may not be so familiar with. As a first-century Hebrew male, born into a lower-class minority family under Roman occupation, he was thrust into the center of one of the most tumultuous time periods and areas in history. He was a refugee (also known as "illegal immigrant") for much of his life, gratefully living off of the generosity and kindness of foreigners[1], and was exposed to a variety of cultures, races, and religious practices from an early age. [2] He was fascinated with the concept of God and the ways that humans come to know him, studying many religious texts and manuscripts and engaging in dialogue with priests and other religious leaders with an astounding awareness and openness to the Great Mystery.[3]

As he grew into a young man, he was greatly influenced by the social and political climate around him. He saw the daily injustice and oppression that was enacted on his people by the Roman Empire, and yet witnessed incredibly hateful and oppressive acts carried out by his brothers on another social minority - the Samaritans.[4] [5] He probably was exposed to the Roman tradition of weekly public beatings and executions that perpetuated a culture of fear and violence, and watched it shape some of his childhood friends into cold, calloused vigilantes- the Zealots.[6] [7] He immersed himself in religious studies and engaged in discussions and heated debates with some of the most respected and revered teachers of the Torah, and yet was also stunned by the hypocrisy and moral emptiness of their teachings. He experienced the power of the God Mammon- the power that money had to destroy and corrupt individuals, as he watched members of his community betray, rob, and sell each other out for just a few pieces of metal. [8] [9]

Growing up in the middle of all this, our young Rabbi friend somehow managed to not become bitter or jaded, somehow managed to not get sucked into the corruption or pettiness or hypocrisy that offered him sanctuary from the madness. Something pushed him deeper into his love for humanity, something that gently whispered into his ear, "Another world is possible."

In his 30th year of being human, he decided that he could no longer keep his feelings and thoughts to himself and began teaching, telling the people that, "The kingdom of heaven is here, and it is within you, if you want it. This kingdom is completely contrary, antithetical and incompatible to every kingdom of this earth. You don't have to buy this kingdom, pay taxes to this kingdom, fight wars for this kingdom, or live a certain way for this kingdom. It is already here, if you want it."[10]

As far as appearance, you wouldn't be able to pick him out of a crowd of lower-class Middle-Eastern men, except that he probably looked a tad scruffier than most. He was dark-skinned, probably with dark brown or black eyes and a scraggly, unkempt beard. His hair was probably dark, thick, and matted (also known as an "afro"), or wrapped in the traditional turban of lower-class Jewish males. His wardrobe was probably sparse and simple, maybe a tunic or two and a blanket for cold nights.[11]

He attracted dangerous characters to him - brawlers, prostitutes, drunkards, and thieves.[12] [13] He traveled the country on foot, refusing to be paid or put up for his teaching but instead preferring to sleep under the stars, where there was no barrier between him and God (also known as "homeless").[14] He visited dangerous and forbidden places - once crashing a bestiality and child-sacrifice party to extend his message of love and redemption to the crowd. [15] [16] He broke nearly every Jewish law in the book, breaking down old rituals, social barriers, and stereotypes and starting to heal several century-old wounds and grudges. He taught incredibly dangerous and revolutionary ideas to anyone who would listen, with no regard for the huge target he was painting on his back for doing so. He spoke out in the open to crowds of anyone who would listen to him, intentionally going to lower-class, uneducated, and oppressed areas that no respectable teacher would ever go to. [17] He performed miracles.

Not only did he perform miracles, he performed miracles that healed people, miracles that met people where they were at and gave them what they needed. He restored sight, strengthened withered limbs, healed diseases, fed hungry mouths, extended the life of a child taken too early, and healed wounded hearts with his compassion, validation, and love.

He turned the world upside down by claiming that we should not resist evil people or actions, but instead defeat them with the power of our soul and our love. If someone attacks you or wrongs you, do not seek revenge or compensation, but instead offer that brother or sister the full measure of your love for them and your willingness to suffer for them.[18] [19] He shattered centuries of tradition by claiming that it is not so much our actions that matter, but our words and intentions that birth those actions. [20][21] He boldly taught that patriotism has no place in this Kingdom, as we are all members of humanity.[22] He defended the marginalized, the poor, the oppressed, and the sick, exposing the ways that religious and political leaders exploited and victimized them.[23] He taught that joy is found in simplicity, contemplation, and community.[24] He completely devalued the currencies of the Empire by introducing a new form of exchange - relationship.[25] [26]

As it is with those who love dangerously, he was eventually killed for his ideas and actions. Yet even in his brutal and humiliating death he stood by his message, challenging the notions of justice and loving his executioners up to his final breath.[27]

He had lived an incredibly revolutionary, meaningful, and powerful life, introducing the world to a new way of being and creating a dedicated group of followers in just three years; his life was indeed complete. Yet he had one more trick to pull. He suddenly reappeared to his disciples, urging them on and inspiring to them to act on his teachings, reminding them yet again that another world is here and it is within them, if they want it. He stuck around for a few weeks, just long enough to lift his followers' spirits and start a chain of events that would end up impacting the geo-political and religious climate of the world in immeasurable ways for the next several thousand years.

His name was Yeshua.[28]

Unfortunately, the world was not ready for him or his teachings, and his message was quickly watered down into one that was much less disruptive to the established powers. Less than 300 years after his death, his followers were quickly either converted to the socially acceptable version of his teachings or subsequently executed.[29] [30] [31] The written accounts of his teachings were gathered together, submitted to a government committee for review of dangerous ideas, and then nicely packaged into a book which was given to the official State church, for the purpose of organizing and controlling the populace.[32] [33] Any offending accounts or stories were methodically destroyed and banned.[34] The Empire, under the influence of Constantine, artfully wove together the various Pagan, Roman, and Greek religious holidays, festivals, and traditions with this new religion, put a pretty bow on the whole thing, and called it: "Christianity."[35] [36]

This new religion survived the dramatic fall and dispersion of the Roman Empire and was forcefully launched into the rest of the world like a virus bursting from within, expelling its contents in all directions. Finding extremely fertile ground to the Northwest, in Europe, this religion planted deep roots, establishing such revered and powerful institutions as the Roman Catholic Church and the Church of England.

In the early sixteenth century, a small group of idealistic rabble-rousers somehow found buried deep within these old and dusty religious caverns a seed. They discovered the words of a young Rabbi who lived a long time ago and who dreamed of a better world. They created a wave of disturbances known collectively as the Protestant Reformation, as they were doing just that - protesting and demanding reform. [37] [38]

A few of these disgruntled disciples heard a rumor of a land across the sea, a land completely unsettled and uncivilized, a country with no fear of persecution or restraints of religious practice, a new frontier for those bold and brave enough to face the long journey and untold hardships and mysteries that such a land promised to offer. With hearts full of hope and courage, they answered the perceived call of destiny and sailed across the ocean to claim this land for themselves and their children.

On that fateful November morning when the great ship "The Mayflower" expelled its contents on the shore of this strange country and the first members of Christendom stepped foot in North America, their grand idealism was quickly dashed upon the rocks of hunger and fear, as their first encounters with the natives were hallmarked with theft, gravesite desecration, and murder.[39] It would seem that the peaceful, egalitarian principles which drove them to this land were quickly abandoned in favor of militarism and conquest, and Yeshua's message was once again buried deep under the soil, sharing a grave with the Indigenous peoples of North America. The pious pilgrims continued on their conquest- fearlessly and boldly "civilizing" this new land and finding that the inhabitants were simply too generous, peaceful, and primitive to put up any real resistance to the tidal wave of Western culture that crashed violently upon their shores. This new breed of Christians was emboldened by the perceived "blessing" of God upon their actions, as they exterminated tribe after tribe of Natives and reaped the bounty that their newly "acquired" lands had to offer them. [40]

Their sense of Divine guidance was greatly heightened when they came to a war with the country that birthed them, the child that had grown stronger than his father and wasn't going to take beatings anymore. When England decided that her resources were better spent killing Frenchmen instead of disenfranchised Englishmen[41], the final step in the dance between America and Christianity was completed. This new country, emboldened by their seeming "victory" over the most powerful nation in the world, was convinced that they were destined for conquest and power, and the continued "blessing" of God in the form of Jesus would carry them there.

A small group of men gathered in a courthouse in Philadelphia to draft the legal framework for their new country, so famously starting the document off with the words, "We the people of the United States of America..." It would prove to be incredibly prophetic and ironic, however, that among this group of brilliant minds sat not a single woman, slave, indigenous person, or working class person. It would appear that, "We the people..." was never really about the people, but about the interests and ideas of a few rich white Christian men.[42]

The next 200+ years of this countries legacy will need to be discussed at another time under another theme, yet we will summarize with the words: Conquest, Exploitation, Ecocide, and Genocide - all under the holy banner of Christendom.

Somehow, a poor, homeless, marginalized, and oppressed Semitic man who taught people how to live a more peaceful and a simple life ended up having his name splayed across the banner of one of the most violent, destructive forces the world has ever experienced.

As a culture, we have created a mythical Messiah, an imaginary figure who not only advocates for our economic and military exploitation, but who has created another world, a "heaven" if you will, that we will all retire to once our earthly duties are done. By fabricating a prophet who was mostly concerned with "saving souls" and populating an afterlife utopia, we have effectively absolved ourselves of any responsibility to actually protect and nurture this world and its inhabitants.

We have liberated ourselves of his life by celebrating his death - his crucifixion has become synonymous with his identity. Our delusion has even manifested itself in our physical representations of our beloved Christ, as it is virtually impossible to find a characterization of him that is even remotely close to reality. Do we actually think that a poor first-century ascetic Hebrew male would be white-skinned, have long smooth brown hair, blue eyes, and a clean white tunic?

But we have to believe this; we have to have this absurd representation to justify our grossly misguided beliefs about who he was and what he taught. Just think of the consequences if this were not so!

What if every self-professed Christian was to actually follow their Prophets teachings? What if the world's 2.1 billion adherents of this religion [43] were to actually be exposed to the homeless dissident whose symbol of death they adorn their houses and bodies with?

It would be absolute madness.

Imagine with me for a minute, what would happen if 31% of the world, that's almost 1 out of every three people, decided to adopt a lifestyle of non-violence, simplicity, tolerance, civil disobedience, communal living, and a rejection of material possessions. What kind of world would this be if the imaginary lines we call "countries" were erased and all of humanity embraced each other as brothers and sisters? What if war and violence became a thing of the past, a story told by old people around the dying light of campfires to bright-eyed children who couldn't imagine why people used to kill and hurt each other? What if we began to respect each other, our animal friends, and the earth that sustains us all, actively working towards sustainability and living in harmony with our environment? What if money became not so important, as people began to create economies of community and relationship? What if people began to live simply, so that others could simply live?

Absolute madness.

This is precisely why Yeshua must become Jesus. We have to take him to the spa and bleach his skin, straighten his hair, give him a shower, trim his beard, change his eye color, give him a new pair of clothes and some expensive shoes, and tell him very sternly, "Now, JESUS, listen carefully. No more of that controversial talk, ok? We are all just trying to live comfortable, happy lives around here, and you tend to make that difficult with all your talk about non-violence, simplicity, and your dislike of patriotism. I would much rather have you talk about loving me and blessing me and enlarging my territory and things like that. Got it? Great!" As we smile and pat him on the head.

If we want to keep enjoying the comforts, conveniences, and delusions that we have inherited from our birthright as American citizens, then we cannot accept the teachings and lifestyle of Yeshua. It is incompatible with nearly every facet and function of our culture.

The Narrative

I have just presented an alternative narrative to the dominant story that most of us know. The narrative I just presented you was formed after much research, many conversations, and no small amount of deliberation on my part due to my own life experiences and dissatisfaction with the dominant narrative.

I want to be very clear that, ultimately, we are all just making educated (and uneducated) guesses as to who this person really was and what his intentions were. I wasn't there, and neither was anybody else who is alive today. The important thing is that we are aware that there are many different narratives to every story and ultimately, we choose which one to believe. Whatever story you choose to believe is the story that you will perpetuate, and every story has incredible consequences attached to it.

So choose carefully, my friend, because this story is not yet finished.

Notes

[1] The narrative of Matthew 2: 13-23 , First Infancy Gospel of Christ, chapter 4
[2] "*Egypt: A Country Study*" - Helen Chapin Metz (1990)

[3] *"The Gospel According to Jesus"* - Stephen Mitchell (1991)

[4] http://www.everyculture.com/Africa-Middle-East/Samaritans.html

[5] *"Introducing the New Testament: A Historical, Literary, and Theological Survey "* - Mark A. (2009)

[6] http://www.britannica.com/EBchecked/topic/656131/Zealot

[7] http://www.thorncrownjournal.com/timeofchrist/zealots.html

[8] http://www.bible-history.com/sketches/ancient/tax-collector.html

[9] http://www.jewishencyclopedia.com/articles/10339-mamon-mammon

[10] *"The Kingdom of God is within you"* - Leo Tolstoy (1894)

[11] http://www.uhl.ac/files/7413/5005/2964/Clothing.pdf

[12] *"Disciples"* - Michael J Wilkins (1992)

[13] http://michaeljon.hubpages.com/hub/TwelveDisciplesofCrist

[14] The narrative of Luke 9:58, the narrative of Matthew 8:20

[15] http://www.fishingtheabyss.com/archives/44

[16] The narrative of Mark 8:27 - 38, The narrative of Matthew 16: 17-18

[17] *"Jesus & the Rise of Early Christianity: A History of New Testament Times"* by Paul Barnett (2002)

[18] *"Jesus and non-violence"* - Walter Wink (2003)

[19] The narrative of Matthew 5:38-46 & 50-53, The narrative of Luke 3:14 & 3:27-37, The narrative of John 18:36,

[20] http://www.religion-online.org/showarticle.asp?title=3102

[21] The narrative of Matthew chapters 5,6,and 7, the narrative of Luke 11:33-44

[22] *"Myth of a Christian Nation"* - Gregory Boyd (2005)

[23] The narrative of Matthew, chapters 5,6, and 7

[24] The narrative of Matthew, chapters 5,6, and 7

[25] *"Sacred Economics"* - Charles Eisenstein (2011)

[26] The narrative of Mathew 6:19-33 & 13:22, the narrative of Luke 12:15-24 & 16:13-15 & 6:38, The narrative of Thomas verse 54, 95, 63, and 100

[27] The narrative of Luke 23:34

[28] http://jesusisajew.org/YESHUA.php

[29] *"The early church "* - Henry Chadwick (1993)

[30] *"A Peculiar People"* - Rodney Clapp (1996).

[31] https://posttomorrow.wordpress.com/2012/09/29/constantinian-shift-part-1/

[32] http://www.bible-researcher.com/voorwinde1.html

[33] *"The Canon of Scripture"* - F.F. Bruce (1996)

[34] *"Lost Scriptures"* - Bart D. Ehrman (2003)

[35] *"The Making of a Christian Aristocracy: Social and Religious Change in the Western Roman Empire"* - Michele Salzman (2004)

[36] http://academia.edu/448782/From_Paganism_to_Christianity

[37] http://www.history.com/topics/reformation

[38] *"Christianity's Dangerous Idea: The Protestant Revolution"* -Alister Mcgrath (2008)

[39] *"A Peoples History of the United States"* - Howard Zinn (1980)

[40] *"A Peoples History of the United States"* - Howard Zinn (1980)

[41] http://www.smithsonianmag.com/history-archaeology/Myths-of-the-American-Revolution.html?c=y&story=fullstory

[42] http://hercules.gcsu.edu/~hedmonds/U.S.%20Constitution/Constitution%20signers.htm

[43] http://www.adherents.com/Religions_By_Adherents.html

Urban Issues
DEPARTMENT

America's Fastest Shrinking City

The Story of Youngstown, Ohio

Sean Posey

Only a few weeks ago, the U.S. Census Bureau released its findings on cities that have lost the most population since the 2010 decennial census. At the top of the list, the beleaguered City of Youngstown, Ohio, the only city to lose more than two percent of its population in two years. Less than two years before that, the Brookings Institute revealed that out of the top 100 metropolitan areas in the country, Youngstown registered the highest percentage of its citizens living in concentrated poverty. Youngstown, along with cities like Camden, New Jersey and Gary, Indiana, is often the poster child for the horrible ravages of deindustrialization. When traveling to the poorest areas in the country as part of book project, radical journalist Chris Hedges described the city he saw in 2010: "Youngstown, like many postindustrial pockets in America, is a deserted wreck plagued by crime and the attendant psychological and criminal problems that come when communities physically break down." [1]

This was not always the story. The fall of Youngstown, Ohio is among the most important devolutions in American urban history. And what ultimately happens to Youngstown, and to other post-industrial cities like it, portends either promise or peril for this country's future.

Nearly one hundred years ago, the steel city of Youngstown, Ohio was on the rise. Like many cities and towns in what was the "Industrial Heartland of North America," Youngstown steadily boomed with the rise of manufacturing. The population of the city rose from 33,000 in 1890 to 170,000 in 1930. Youngstown became the center of Mahoning Valley, better known as the "Steel Valley." Steel mills lined the Mahoning River for miles. Enormous industrial concerns like Republic Steel (founded in Youngstown) the U.S. Steel Ohio Works and Youngstown Sheet and Tube's Brier Hill Works operated day and night, dominating the city's skyline and encasing the heavens around Youngstown in a leaden haze. Few seemed to mind though, for as one steelworker put it, "Everybody breathing dirt, eating dirt-they call it 'pay dirt,' for Youngstown clean would be Youngstown out of work." [2] Youngstown grew as an economic monoculture. Steel dominated every aspect of life.

By the 1930s, Youngstown ranked fifth in the nation in terms of home ownership; the city became known as "The city of homes." [3] Amazingly enough, the city even suffered from a housing shortage during the 1930s. This led to the building of Westlake Terrace-the first housing project in the nation authorized by the U.S. Housing Act of 1937. [4] As early as 1940 though, the city faced a declining population. Between 1930 and 1940, the city experienced a slight population loss, making it the only city west of the Appalachian Mountains with a population over 100,000 to lose residents. [5]

The 1940s and 1950s represented another boom era for the city. Youngstown's mills proved so important to the war effort in Korea that when a steel strike loomed in 1952, Truman ordered the Sheet and Tube mills in Chicago and Youngstown seized. This led to the famous Youngstown Sheet and Tube Co. v. Sawyer case, which dealt with executive overreach. The 1950s ended however with what was to be the beginning of a long decline.

In 1959, the media dubbed Youngstown "Steel's Sick City," as the economy slowed and a national steel strike paralyzed the industry. By 1960, after several decades of African American migration into the city, Youngstown had become more segregated than ever. The west side of the city, which was almost entirely white due to redlining, became known as "west side white." Meanwhile, disastrous urban renewal and highway programs bulldozed black neighborhoods and created ghettoes. At no time during the urban renewal campaign did African Americans make up more than a quarter of the city's population; yet, 75 percent of those forcibly relocated were black.[6] The growth of ghettoes and neighborhood racial turnover accelerated after the urban riots on   Youngstown's South Side during 1968, and on the south and east sides in 1969.

Fear of a "Black Youngstown" also accompanied the rise of Black Power in the city, largely led by Dr. Ron Daniels. Days before the Martin Luther King riots in 1968, Daniels led hundreds of African Americans across the Market Street Bridge to downtown and proclaimed, "If we need a burger, we will build our own. If we need a country club, we will build our own. If we unite we can get anything we want." [7] After the riots and the increase in black economic power, more whites fled. Youngstown lost 16 percent of its population during the 1960s, a much larger percentage than most other industrial cities. Years before the first steel mill closed, the stage for the city's downward spiral was set.

Today, nearly one hundred years after the city's quick rise, the grime and soot from the mills are long gone; indeed, the mills themselves are long gone. Only a few rusty remnants still cling to the riverside. The once seemingly permanent mini-cities of men and machines are now fields. Industrial disinvestment, foreign competition, and globalization eliminated Youngstown's steel industry in the late 1970s and early 1980s-and with it the city's place in the world. The mafia, long a cancer on the local community, took over many aspects of the city and county government. Only an aggressive campaign by the FBI ended the mob's reign in the late 1990s.

Even with the mafia gone, Youngstown is known nationally for its violent crime rate, which remained among the very worst in the nation at the turn of the century. Much of the crime could be connected to the drug trade, the lack of inner-city employment opportunities, and the fact that Youngstown's African American community had become the poorest concentrated black population in the nation by the mid-1990s.[8] More people fled in the wake of increased crime in the 90s and Youngstown's population stood at only 82,000 at the beginning of the century.

In 2002, the city unveiled the Youngstown 2010 Plan. The 2010 plan was a unique attempt at "smart shrinkage," that is targeting investment, and even seeking to relocate people from areas of the city with high numbers of vacancies, to more viable neighborhoods. The national media focused on the 2010 plan as a blueprint for rebuilding post-industrial cities. Mayor Jay Williams, elected in 2005, even toured the country, touting the plan in places like Gary, Indiana. Yet, the 2010 plan proved to be illusory. The city did not follow through with the outreach needed for relocating citizens in low occupancy areas. Youngstown failed to even properly carry out a targeted demolition plan.

The spread of blight accelerates three years after 2010. According to GIS mapping by urban planner Tom Hetrick, there are now 6,000 vacant buildings in a city with an area of 34 square miles. The poorest and most blighted parts of the city are still predominately black; the most prosperous and stable areas are still white. The city planner's position is still vacant after five years. The downtown is actually growing, after spending nearly thirty years as a ghost town, due in large part to grants and suburban dollars. Block watches and neighborhood groups are filling the gap left by an absentee local government. Urban farms are popping up among the vast tracts of vacant land in the city. And despite the utterly bleak situation, community and cultural groups still struggle to effect change.

In his seminal 1992 book on the former steel town of Homestead, Pennsylvania, William Serrin wrote, "America uses things-people, resources, cities-then discards them." [9] Like many of its steel cities, America discarded Youngstown. The middle class and the surrounding suburban townships discarded Youngstown as well. Now, fittingly, as the American Dream deserts wide swaths of the country, we can look to Youngstown for answers, or at least for questions. What does the existence of a place like Youngstown, nestled in the most prosperous society the world has ever seen, say about America? What kind of country creates a place like Youngstown, while also creating the largest number of millionaires and billionaires in the world? What does America owe, if anything, to the forgotten and hollowed out places that-quite literally-built what it is today?

Notes

[1] Chris Hedges, "Heroes for the Beaten, Foreclosed on, Imprisoned Masses," *truthdig.com,* October 18, 2010, "http://www.truthdig.com/report/item/heroes_for_the_down_and_out_20101018/ (accessed June 1, 2013).
[2] Dan O'Brien, "Seeing Decades of Life Through Lens of Youngstown." *Business Journal,* July 11, 2005, http://businessjournaldaily.com/seeing-life-decades-ago-through-

lens-youngstown-2005-7-11(accessed June 1, 2013).

[3] *Youngstown: The City of Homes* , brochure, ca. 1931

[4] Sean T. Posey, "Crossing to Westlake Terrace: Public Housing in Youngstown, Ohio" (seminar paper, Youngstown State University, 2010)

[5] Pace and Associates, *Comprehensive City Plan-Report Number Two: "The Economy of Youngstown"* (Chicago, Illinois: June, 1951), 10.

[6] Charles Etlinger, "Population Shifts Burden Horse and Buggy Governments," *Youngstown Vindicator*, December 26, 1971, A-5.

[7] 200 Youths Stage Quiet March Here," *Youngstown Vindicator*, April 4, 1968, A-1.

[8] Segregation Spells Disaster, Expert Says," *Vindicator,* December 1, 1995, A-1

[9] William Serrin, *Homestead: The Glory and Tragedy of a an American Steel Town*

(New York: Vintage Books, 1992), 25.

The Failure of the Futurists

Picturing the Cities of Tomorrow

Sean Posey

"Today, the notion of progress in a single line without goal or limit seems perhaps the most parochial notion of a very parochial century."

- Lewis Mumford

America has long had a problematic relationship with the city. A country weaned on romantic notions of Jeffersonian agrarianism and rugged individualism didn't take well to the rapid urbanization of the nation in the late nineteenth and early twentieth centuries. Yet it was urbanization that turned America into the industrial colossus of the world. Still, American futurists alternatively have rejected the city as the habitat of tomorrow and dreamed of a future urbanism couched in the idea of continued technological progress-and ultimately, utopianism.

"Cities of the future" became the centerpiece of numerous world's fairs. Publications from *Popular Mechanics* (a serial offender) to the *New York Times* painted fanciful scenarios for future cities. Of course, the futurism of the past is often ripe fodder for ridicule: flying commuters, domed cities, terraced skyscrapers with aircraft landing fields, or even endless sprawl and commercial homebuilding, where the bubble would never burst.

Black Swan author Nassim Nicholas Taleb aptly describes the problem: "We also represent society according to our utopia of the moment, largely driven by our wishes - except for a few people called doomsayers, the future will be largely inhabited by our desires. So we will tend to over-technologize it and underestimate the might of the equivalent of these small wheels on suitcases that will be staring at us for the next millennia." [1]

However, urban futurism today discounts this notion, and is instead drifting into a dangerous world of self-deception and make-believe. We are limping into the future, while too many of our public intellectuals see us flying into tomorrow, often with little more than wishful thinking fueling our jetpacks.

The 20th Century City that Was and Wasn't

As the nineteenth century waned, the people of Chicago and America were wowed by the "White City" of the 1893 World's Fair (also known as the Columbian Exposition, in honor of 400th anniversary of Columbus' voyage.) Architect Daniel Burnham and famed landscape architect Frederick Law Olmstead unveiled their vision of a future metropolis to the City of the Big Shoulders. The exposition provided a powerful example of what American cities-mostly ugly, degraded, and industrial at the time-could look like in the near future: classically influenced, electrified, and filled with wonderful gadgets. Towering neoclassical architecture and the birth of modern city planning are often the most remembered legacies of the White City, but the technology displayed by the likes of Nikola Tesla and Elisha Grey ultimately had a larger impact on a society that would soon become increasingly in thrall to modern inventions and conveniences.

For a time, Beaux-Arts architecture, and the City Beautiful movement with which it was often connected, shaped the early "American Century." However this movement was ultimately eclipsed. The first principle of the City Beautiful was "the celebration of the idea of the city itself." [2] Unfortunately, early twentieth century cites were mostly industrial, dirty, overcrowded, and generally not very likable. And as the century progressed, Americans turned their backs on urbanism. Instead, they embraced the dream of the late Andrew Jackson Downing-the father of landscape architecture-that "there is a moral influence in the country home."[3]

Americans didn't get country homes, instead they got the suburban tract home. The flight from cities increased as the century went by. Futurists' predictions changed steadily during this time: sometimes recognizing trends as they happened, but often completely missing the whole picture. In 1925, *Popular Science Monthly* pictured 1950 New York as a towering city of skyscrapers (the skyscraper craze was still fresh in 1925 but on pause by 1950) with an enormously large population that required multiple city "levels" of transportation. Yet by 1950, the population of the city had tapered off (it actually declined in 1960) and the zeppelins flying overhead had vanished from the scene-understandably, considering the Hindenburg disaster in New Jersey in 1937. Harvey Corbett, the architect featured in the article, even predicted that cities would not decentralize in the future. [4] Exactly the opposite happened.

Americans moving to suburbia got something closer to a version of Frank Lloyd's Wright's "Broadacre City" plan. First described in his 1932 book, "The Disappearing City," the plan for Broadacre called for sprawling, decentralized cities that were to replace the industrial metropolises Wright despised. [5]Though fundamentally different from suburbs, which are by their very nature attached to central cities, Broadacre proved to be closer to post-war America than most predictions made by futurists in the early part of the century.

It's odd that futurists picturing cities of tomorrow remained so positive and utopian right up through the 1960s, considering America's then increasingly ambivalent feelings about urban living. The 1964 World's Fair, unlike the New York World's Fair of 1939, trafficked in a George Jetson-styled future: flying cars; raised, moving sidewalks; and jet packs. General Motor's 'Futurama' exhibit portrayed underwater living. Isaac Asimov even foresaw those underwater cities being featured at the 2014 World's Fair. Today, many Americans aren't even aware that world's fairs are still held.

Techno Futurism

Even as Americans soured on urban living in the second half of the twentieth century, the country's collective obsession with technological utopianism only grew. Movies dabbled in urban dystopian themes that often more honestly echoed America's fear of the city-producing nightmarish visions of future urbanity in the 1980s, like *Escape from New York, Blade Runner,* and *Robocop.* These dark artistic visions, though, were entirely absent from the gathering techno-theology that emerged in full bloom in the 1990s. The idea that technological innovation will solve future problems-many resulting from the increasing complexity of technological systems themselves-is of course not new. However, the blooming of television, and the world of computing, brought this kind of thinking to new heights. Its roots sprang from the work of futurist Marshall McLuhan.

An erudite student of the media, advertising, and technology, McLuhan foresaw such future evolutions as the coming of the Internet and the idea of a technological "singularity." In 1967, he stated that, "The city no longer exists, except as a cultural ghost for tourists. Any highway eatery with its TV set, newspaper, and magazine, is as cosmopolitan as New York or Paris.'"[6] In his characteristically obtuse way, he misjudged the importance of place, social space, urban design, and even economics. But McLuhan's writings would-rightly or wrongly-greatly influence the denizens of the computer age and the singularian futurists, who claim that the problems of a rapidly urbanizing planet will be solved by a coming "age of abundance."

The Magic of the Microchip

The enormously influential computer culture that came out of Silicon Valley in the 1980s and 1990s is, in many ways, a product of the futurism of McLuhan. With the magic of the microchip (and the economic boom era of the 1990s) the "Californian Ideology" was born. A strange mix of 1960s liberalism and 1990s libertarianism, the Californian Ideology took individualism and techno-theocracy to a new level. This suburban phenomenon-hatched in Silicon Valley-is part of what became the cult of Moore's Law and the extreme utopianism of futurists like Michio Kaku and Ray Kurzweil.

In his 2011 book, "Physics of the Future," complete with a cover featuring the ever wished for flying cars and Logan's Run look-alike cities, Michio Kaku describes a tomorrow when "land, capital, natural resources, no longer matter."[7] He touches on the current enormous problem of resource scarcity, but Kaku more or less brushes those aside; instead he simply skips to the part where we magically have a hydrogen and solar-based economy by the middle of the century.[8] He doesn't adequately address the enormous problems with hydrogen, which is actually not a fuel source.

Among its many issues, hydrogen is a net energy loser. It takes more energy (usually burning natural gas) to produce the hydrogen than what you would get out of a typical fuel cell. Much of the energy is lost as heat. In other words, the energy return-on energy-invested is unacceptable, especially when you consider scaling hydrogen to fuel hundreds of millions of vehicles in the United States alone.[9]

Kaku also makes similar questionable statements regarding Chinese urbanism. He claims the Middle Kingdom has learned from the mistakes of the building of American cities.[10] Instead the Chinese are replicating the same missteps Americans made-making the car the locus of transportation policy. The country is now, in the words of David Owen, embarking on the "fastest motorization in history." [11]

And are they really building cities of tomorrow? Kaku sees a future where millions of chips are stored in the road, communicating information to prevent accidents or traffic jams. But the Chinese are building their mega-cities right now using enormous amounts of concrete and steel that, steel especially, have large carbon footprints. The roads snaking through rapidly growing cities are spawning enormous traffic problems-and the attendant pollution-including a 100 kilometer-long traffic jam that lasted for ten days in 2010.

It's Ray Kurzweil, however, who has taken the cult of Moore's Law and Marshall McLuhan's idea of "the extension of the nervous system in the electrical age" to its logical (or illogical) conclusion. Kurzweil is mostly known for his proselytizing about the coming of the technological "singularity." According to Kurzweil, "As we gradually learn to harness the optimal computing capacity of matter, our intelligence will spread through the universe at (or exceeding) the speed of light, eventually leading to a sublime, universe wide awakening." Kurzweil's imagining of the eventual melding of humans and machines is based on Moore's Law, which states that computing power doubles about every two years. This exponential growth is what Kurzweil sees leading to the eventual singularity.

He has taken that idea and extrapolated it to things outside of computer hardware, like the medical field and nanotechnology. Kurzweil sees a post-scarcity future, one in which solar energy powers all of our needs within fifteen years. Flying cars will be with us by 2026. More pertinent here, he predicts cities will be obsolete in a few short decades-due to full-immersion virtual reality-because of this, populations will radically decentralize. [12]

No Magic Wand

Kurzweil's views on solar partially reflect what many left-leaning environmental groups are advocating: Solar and other renewables are the obvious answer to fossil fuels. For many years, solar energy has accounted for less than one percent of the world's total energy. And solar panels that convert the sun's energy into electricity using the photovoltaic effect contain a tremendous amount of embodied energy. This includes everything from the diesel-powered vehicles needed to mine minerals, to the cost and scarcity of the 'rare earth elements' needed to produce many thin solar panels, including tellurium, which is a key element in the construction of some of the most efficient solar cells available.[13]

Oddly enough, many environmentalists combine silver bullet utopian fantasies about solar power, electric cars, hydropower, et cetera, with problematic anti-urban notions.[14] Urban theorist James Howard Kunstler tackled this head on when he described his two visits to the Aspen Environmental Forum: "...I listened to the cream of the Green movement rhapsodize over all the cool new 'green' ways you can run cars other than on gasoline. They didn't once mention walkable communities or public transit. They're just not into it. I consider their position utterly disgraceful."[15]

Lewis Muford's comments about the problems of "progress" apply - so far - just as much to this century as they did to the twentieth century. The planet is reminding us that we do not live in a boundless age. "Progress" without limits will prove to be as problematic for the Chinese, the sheiks of Dubai, and the tech industry in Mumbai as it has been for us. On the whole, we are idly texting toward a *Dark Age Ahead*, as Jane Jacobs put it. Environmental daydreams and Age of Aquarius solutions wrapped in solar panels and lithium-ion batteries will not suffice. Common sense solutions are staring us in the face, even as we stare at our smart phones.

Fortunately, the Millennial Generation is embracing non-automobile oriented lifestyles and moving to walkable, mixed-use communities. If anyone is going to build the sustainable city of the future, it will be the Millennials. It remains to be seen, however, if they will lead effectively on energy and environmental issues when their turn to do so comes.

The near future will be much more about changing the way we live: sustainable design; curbing sprawl; planning for climate change scenarios; deemphasizing the automobile; and preparing for a low-carbon economy will be key elements. None of that will be easy, especially for Americans.

The futurists of today who see a clear path to a post-scarcity utopia are going to be in for as big of a surprise as all those who waited in vain for automated roads and commuter spaceships. Cities of tomorrow will have to be guided by the principles of our more sustainable recent past, rather than the fantastic futurism of Buck Rogers-inspired daydreaming.

Notes

[1] Nassim Nicholas Taleb, *Antifragile: Things That Gain from Disorder* (New York: Random House, 2012) 314.

[2] Robert Freestone, *Urban Planning in a Changing World: The Twentieth Century Experience* (Oxford: Taylor and Francis, 2000) 115.

[3] Andrew Jackson Downing, *The Architecture of Country Houses* (1850; repr., Mineola: Dover Publishing, 1969), xx.

[4] "The Wonder City You May Live to See" *Popular Science Monthly*, August 1925.

[5] See Frank Lloyd Wright, *The Disappearing City* (New York: William Farquhar Payson, 1932).

[6] Priscilla Boniface, *Dynamic Tourism: Journeying Through Change* (London: Cromwell Press, 2001), 8.

[7] Michio Kaku, *Physics of the Future: How Science Will Shape Human Destiny and Our Daily Lives by the Year 2100* (Norwell: Anchor Press, 2011), 320.

[8] Ibid., 234.

[9] For more on the problems with the "hydrogen economy" see Joseph J. Romm,*The Hype About Hydrogen: Fact and Fiction in the Race to Save the Climate* and Matthew L. Wald, and "Questions about a Hydrogen Economy" *Scientific American,* May 2004.

[10] Kaku, 321.

[11] David Owen, *Green Metropolis: Why Living Smaller, Living Closer, and Driving Less are the Keys to Sustainability* (New York: Riverhead Trade, 2009), 218.

[12] See Ray Kurzweil, *The Singularity is Near: When Humans Transcend*

Biology (New York: Viking Publishing, 2005).

[13] See Nicola Jones, *A Scarcity of Rare Metals is Hindering Green Technologies* (Yale School of Forestry and Environmental Studies: Yale Environment 360, 2013).http://e360.yale.edu/feature/a_scarcity_of_rare_metals_is_hindering_green_technologies/2711/ and Fthenakis, Vasilis M.; Kim, Hyung Chul; Alsema, Erik (2008). "Emissions from Photovoltaic Life Cycles". *Environmental Science & Technology* 42.

[14] See Andrew Light, "The Urban Blind Spot in Environmental Ethics," *Environmental Politics* Volume 10, Issue 1 (2001): 7-35; and Angie Schmitt, "When Will the Environmental Movement Embrace Cities?" *Streetsblog*, August 10, 2011. http://streetsblog.net/2011/08/10/when-will-the-environmental-movement-embrace-cities/

[15] "Straight Talk with James Howard Kunstler: 'The World is Going to Get Rounder and Bigger Again," ChrisMartenson.com, www.chrismartenson.com

Planning Without Precedent

The Fate of Neighborhoods in America's Fastest Shrinking City

Sean Posey

A trip down Glenwood Avenue from the Township of Boardman to the south side of Youngstown, Ohio, is a dizzying journey replete with mid-century ranch houses, handsome colonials and leafy suburban parcels, eventually giving way to vacant lots and collapsing trash-filled duplexes—their broken doors and windows thrown open to the world in a manner that strikes one as both tragic and indecent.

Not much further down the road, an intersection in the midst of a slow revitalization paints a picture of a neighborhood and a city undergoing an uncertain transition.

"A lot of the changes that have come are recent changes," said Kyle Gilchrist, co-owner of Ryan's Chair, a barbershop/salon and mainstay of the Glenwood/Indianola corridor. "It's taken me some time to adapt."

A grocery store (in an area that was once one of the worst food deserts in the city) a new restaurant, community art and murals are putting a fresh shine on a corridor near the tipping point. Only a few years ago the neighborhoods around Glenwood and Canfield Road were rapidly tumbling downward into a spiral of crime and vacancy. However, renewed investment, and the revival of the country's first shrinking cities initiative has given many in the area a new hope.

Youngstown is the country's fastest shrinking city. But at one time it symbolized the awesome power of America's industrial might. Industrial concerns like Youngstown Sheet and Tube, Republic Steel and U.S. Steel built otherworldly mills along the banks of the Mahoning River in the early twentieth century. At night, the hellish process of steelmaking lit up the city's skyline. By day, immigrants arrived in droves, looking for work in the Dantesque maws of the immense plants. In the early 1920s, Youngstown's steel production was second only Pittsburgh's, and by 1930, 170,000 souls called the city home.

Even as deindustrialization and suburbanization gradually unraveled 'Steel City' in the decades following World War II, thousands of African Americans arrived looking for a new start. The Gilchrist family, with young Kyle and Ryan in tow, came to the south side as the last of that migration in the early 1980s. Kyle's older brother developed a knack for barbering, thus launching what would become a family business: "He started cutting hair at an early age—twelve, thirteen years old," said Kyle.

From that modest start, Ryan rented a succession of slightly larger spaces on the south side, eventually buying a former vet's office on busy Glenwood Avenue that he transformed into Ryan's Chair.

Since opening in 1998, Ryan's Chair has occupied a tenuous space amidst neighborhoods undergoing immense physical and economic changes. The wave of crime and abandonment that hit so many neighborhoods in the 1990s eventually made its way to the area around the store. Kyle Gilchrist saw it all.

"We've seen the neighborhoods go down. A lot of people were leaving. A lot of the businesses that made it through, their names kept them going. Reputation means a lot in this area—A LOT in this area."

The recent history of Almyra Avenue, which runs adjacent to Ryan's Chair, is indicative of what happened to some of the neighborhoods around Glenwood. Almyra today is heavily dotted with derelict houses and vacant lots that blend together into a kind of urban prairie. A quick examination of local newspaper archives gives some clues as to why:

"Both were gunned down in the 400 block of Almyra Avenue."

"A 7-month-old Almyra Avenue girl was in serious condition Saturday night at Akron Children's Hospital after being left unattended in a bathtub."

"Fire Chief John O'Neill stood outside 620 Almyra Ave. on Thursday morning watching the 12th vacant building burn in less than 24 hours..."

This spreading urban crisis pushed Youngstown into the ranks of the most violent cities in the nation. Even as crime slowly waned during the first decade of the century, the population continued to decline. By 2000, Youngstown's population had decreased by over half to 82,000 people (65,000 live in the city today.) Yet Youngstown hadn't changed its comprehensive city plan since 1974—three years before the first steel mill closed. In response to continued shrinkage and the need for a new plan, the city took drastic steps. Youngstown implemented a strategy that violated basic rules of urban planning: it would accept and plan for shrinkage.

The genesis of what became the most talked about planning initiative in the country dates back to December 2002, when 1,400 people attended a "public vision" meeting held by the city. By the next year, volunteer committees and sub-committees were working on neighborhood property surveys and various aspects of what the city called the 'Youngstown 2010 Plan.'

Much of the impetus behind Youngstown 2010 came from then Community Development Agency Director Jay Williams. A former banker, Williams had helped Ryan Gilchrist obtain loans for the expansion of Ryan's Chair. As a public servant he recognized that Youngstown needed to change its thinking in regards to planning and development. In 2005, running on the strength of his connection with Youngstown 2010, Williams was elected as the city's youngest and first black mayor.

That same year Youngstown 2010 debuted. The American Planning Association recognized the plan in 2006 with the 'National Planning Excellence Award for Community Outreach,' and Youngstown 2010 made The New York Time's 'Sixth Annual Year in Ideas' list. Media outlets from as far away as Japan descended on Youngstown to see what the shrinking city might do next.

Youngstown 2010 hinged not only on accepting that the city was smaller—and likely to continue to shrink—but also that vacancy, economic diversification and racism must be adequately addressed. Unfortunately, the local government lacked the funding and perhaps the willingness to carry the plan much further than paper.

Progress stalled as early as 2007, when then the homicide rate reached a nine-year high. The city planner resigned in 2009, was not replaced, and Mayor Jay Williams moved to Washington in 2011 to join the Obama administration.

In 2013, the city signed a contract with the Youngstown Neighborhood Development Corporation to take over neighborhood planning responsibilities. For five years the YNDC has rehabilitated houses, installed community gardens and helped to expand homeownership in the city. The fifteen-month planning process is a kind-of continuation of the 2010 plan; however, people like Kyle Gilchrist are worried about more than just planning:

"The people here are struggling. They're not just struggling financially; they're struggling mentally and emotionally. And that's where it takes a toll on the area.... So, the people are my concern. I don't know how these different projects are going to help build the people so they can help build the community. But we have to make sure we get some plans in mind for the people."

No place in Youngstown is struggling more than the Oak Hill neighborhood. Located within clear view of downtown, this lower-south neighborhood has lost approximately half of its population since 1990. The average home sale is $6,455. Despite talk about infill housing in Youngstown 2010, many believe the area might be slated for gradual abandonment and 'greening.' No overt statements about deactivating neighborhoods have been made by the city—not with the legacy of the disastrous urban renewal schemes of the 1960s and 1970s still lingering. Nevertheless, many residents fear that outcome all the same.

Despite an uncertain future, an unassuming building recently reclaimed from abandonment is slowly but surely becoming the center of a local revival.

Several years ago former lawyer Patrick Kerrigan began a quest to start a non-profit organization called the Oak Hill Collaborative— dedicated to reviving the beleaguered neighborhood around his parish, St. Patrick's Church. He and a group of backers bought an old icehouse building on Oak Hill Avenue scheduled for demolition. After a thorough renovation, a once bombed-out shell became, in the words of Kerrigan, "a neighborhood revitalization center."

"My partners felt we should buy this to show what you can do rather than tear stuff down and create another empty lot."

According to Kerrigan, their mission is very straightforward. "We are really doing three things here: cleaning up the neighborhood; providing a neighborhood center for public meetings; and the third thing, which probably takes up most of our time now, is we are a business incubator."

He believes that "surface level" revitalization is not enough: "In this area, it's more than just cleaning up and putting a paint job on a building. You have to give people jobs. You have to give people hope."

A variety of local entrepreneurs have descended on the space. Among them is an urban farmer—who is growing food in a neighboring vacant lot— a group of local university students building 3D printers and a seamstress/fashion designer doing the Lord's work.

Corinne DeCesare's story is indicative of the many different paths that bring people to Youngstown. She spends most of her days now doing alterations and designing clothes in a space inside of the Oak Hill Collaborative. It's something she never imagined as a young girl with dreams of New York City.

Having grown up in nearby rural Mineral Ridge, DeCesare was cautioned to avoid the city at all costs: "I never spent any time in Youngstown. Where I grew up, people were afraid of Youngstown."

Her talents as a costume designer eventually took her to the Big Apple. After several years of hard but rewarding work, she decided to return home to a simpler lifestyle. She went back to work as a seamstress in her hometown of Mineral Ridge. After a zoning problem emerged with the building housing her workspace, she was forced to leave. With nowhere to go, DeCesare attended a local art show to sell off the last pieces in her collection.

At the show, she was introduced to Pat Kerrigan. Instead of leaving that day with nowhere to continue her business, DeCesare was offered a spot at the Collaborative. "I knew God brought me here, so I just went with it."

Her first time travelling down the broken artery of Oak Hill Avenue, DeCesare commented, "There was houses people were living in that no one should be living in. Something needed to be done."

She quickly came to know the neighborhood, joining a local prayer circle and doing work for the proprietor of an African clothing and bookstore. Inspired by her religious beliefs and a desire to continue designing clothes, DeCesare created 'Jesus Speak,' a business centered on custom designs and alterations. Each piece of custom clothing comes with a tag containing a message from one of the gospels.

A local university student who lives in the neighborhood soon joined her as an intern. Ciara Penny comes from a long line of south-siders, including her uncle Charles Penny Sr., who once headed the local Marcus Garvey Association. Penny's lifelong love of fashion led her to the Collaborative, and her enthusiasm for this new community resource is obvious and contagious. "I think it's really amazing to have something like this in the neighborhood," Penny said.

"I have to tell you about Ciara," DeCesare explained. "Most of the time people don't want to give. They want the benefits, but they don't want to put forth the effort. Ciara just blew me away. She called me and said, 'I'm not a fashion major. I just want to learn.' That's amazing..."

Collaborations like this are key to the organization's mission, according to Pat Kerrigan. "Our vision is to go forward with young enthusiastic people and give them opportunities to work together and to help themselves and the neighborhood."

Recently, the Oak Hill Collaborative hosted a fashion show to promote Jesus Speak. Outside, a cool spring sun illuminated the nearby downtown skyline. Inside, an eclectic mix of residents, business leaders, the young and the old, the black and the white, mingled among the comely outfits on display. For a neighborhood that has suffered so much disinvestment and whose challenging racial past has so dominated its decline, this was no minor event.

Many eyes will be fixed on the lower south side as the planning process goes on. However, despite whatever ideas planners might have for the neighborhood, it's clear that the Oak Hill Collaborative, and the residents themselves, have plans of their own.

As you drive down Oak Hill Avenue into the very heart of the city, you intersect with Mahoning Avenue, which takes you into the west side. For decades the neighborhoods there seemed immune to the concentrated poverty and deprivation that plagued much of the rest of the city. A highly redlined section of Youngstown, realtors knew it as 'West Side White.'

Driving over I-680, a lonely former gas station painted with a mural of the city's skyline silently announces, "You can change Youngstown" to the cars roaring furiously by. The growing number of abandoned and crumbling storefronts nearby suggest that much needs changing.

Over the past fifteen years or so the lower west side has begun to erode. Vacancy is growing on the side streets. The decay that ate away at so much of the city's fabric has come to the west side with a vengeance. The residents of the west side Rocky Ridge Neighborhood, a stable community in the midst of a growing crisis, are watching all of this closely.

A plethora of cars crowded the parking lot at the Shrine of Our Lady Comforter of the Afflicted on a cold February night in early 2014. Founded in 1964 by Franciscan Monks fleeing communist Hungary, the church symbolizes the rich trove of ethnic culture still ingrained in the west side's fabric. Inside, members of the Rocky Ridge Neighborhood Association gathered around the cookie table—a Youngstown favorite—as they waited for a city planning meeting to begin.

Before any neighborhood plans are proposed, input is gathered from the residents. The Rocky Ridge meeting was the first of many slated for neighborhoods on all sides of the city.

Planners first went through statistics that seemed to surprise no one. The census tract containing Rocky Ridge lost 17 percent of its populations between 1990 and 2010. Poverty increased twofold in the same period. Conversely, the housing stock is still in good shape, and the majority of residents are homeowners.

When it came time to solicit feedback from the crowd, a raucous discussion commenced. Many lamented the loss of young residents, the increase in renters and the spread of slumlords. One man vociferously denounced any plan to stabilize the area by claiming, "You can't build a fence around Rocky Ridge."

Amidst the lively discussion sat one of the visibly younger members in the crowd. A web developer and homeowner with a penchant for community service, Nicholas Serra is a regular at neighborhood meetings, and at age twenty-six, he represents the future of Youngstown.

Serra is one of many who first came to experience the city through its lively local music scene. For years, places like the South High Field House, Reed's Arena and the Youngstown Agora played host to national acts ranging from the Allman Brothers to James Brown. Even as downtown faded out during the eighties and nineties, Youngstown's lively punk rock/underground scene thrived—attracting acts like the Dead Boys and GG Allin.

This rich musical heritage drew Serra, raised in the suburbs, to the city. "I would either sneak into Cedars or go to Tuesday open mic night at the Bad Apple…. I don't even think I knew Youngstown existed until I had a license."

Six years ago he bought a house on the west side and soon discovered the 'I Will Shout Youngstown!' blog, written by local luminary John Slanina, who lives on Serra's block. According to Serra, "I ended up at a Rocky Ridge meeting. Grabbed a sign, grabbed a shirt and decided to get involved."

At first, he was the neighborhood bad boy—having parties and playing drums late into the night. But gradually Serra's older neighbors came to accept him.

"It's a very community oriented neighborhood. I know all my neighbors," he said.

"I go outside and it's like *King of the Hill*. We walk outside in the backyard and talk, me and my neighbors from like four houses down."

Serra's activities are not constrained to just his west side neighborhood. He can often be found thundering down the abandoned streets of Youngstown in search of discarded tires and fires. After noticing the explosion of illegal dumping that plagues the area, he began gathering hundreds of tires from vacant lots. When it came time for the city tire recycling drive, Serra maxed out at six hundred.

It's another unfortunate symptom of Youngstown's decline that has attracted his artistic side. Beginning in 1978, arson became a mainstay of life in the city. The wave of abandonment that accompanied the closing of the steel mills left Youngstown with a glut of unwanted housing. What the wrecking ball was unable to take down local arsonists would take care of. Armed with a police scanner and video camera, Serra routinely ventures out at all hours to document the torching of the city's dead housing stock.

"There's this huge arson problem, and there's many ways to look at it," he said. "I wanted to look at vacancy from different angles."

Cities like Youngstown are clamoring to attract and retain Millennials, especially those in the so-called Creative Class. When asked what the city and planners could do to attract younger people, Serra responded: "I feel young people are an easier demographic to get into this town. Housing is cheap. There's a cheap university that's good right next door."

Serra, and more and more like him, are bullish on Youngstown.

"I don't see any downside to moving into the city if you're a young person. I don't understand why anybody has an apartment anywhere outside of the city."

Crossing over from Mahoning to Glenwood Avenue feels like a

journey through Youngstown's recent past. Lower Glenwood is littered with the detritus of homes and businesses swept away by the economic maelstrom of the past few decades. Passing the corner of Breaden and Glenwood, the parting trees reveal the last skeletal remains of The Fort—a gutted post-war era diner, its forlorn sign forever reminding us of the burgers and ribs that once sizzled on the now cobweb covered grills.

Further down is the Youngstown Playhouse, one of the oldest community theaters in the country. Eventually Glenwood takes you to what used to be called Fosterville, an early mining community incorporated into the city after the Park and Falls Trolley line helped open up the area for settlement at the beginning of the twentieth century.

Fosterville represented one of the most thriving nodes of commercial activity in Youngstown. Idora Park, one of the longest operating urban amusement parks in the country when it closed in 1984, was a stone's throw from Fosterville. The neighborhoods surrounding it had population densities on par with Baltimore for much of the twentieth century. By 2009, nothing of the residue of Fosterville remained. The neighborhood's famous businesses—Parker's Frozen Custard, Mr. Paul's Bakery, Isaly's Dairy, Empire Club, etc. have all vanished from the landscape.

The new Glenwood Park sits only blocks from Ryan's Chair in the heart of old Fosterville. It's located where the famous Crystal Tavern and Spaghetti House once stood at the corner of Glenwood and Sherwood. On the other side of Sherwood, now a green space, was JB's Lounge, which once attracted rock acts like Ace Frehley from Kiss.

The park, which opened in 2013, now acts a gathering spot for local youths. As recently as last year, this part of the city lacked so much as a basketball court to play on.

It hasn't being easy for the young in Youngstown. Often feared, the past few generations of city youth grew up in some of the toughest neighborhoods in America. At the height of the inner city meltdown in 1995, Youngstown suffered more total homicides than Pittsburgh, despite having 274,000 less people.

James Grant grew up in that world. Casually shooting hoops at Glenwood Park, he can recall all of the businesses that once lined Glenwood Avenue, especially Parker's Frozen Custard, now just a slab of concrete a few blocks down: "I told myself I'd open something like that back up again someday."

Grant causally eyed his children on the nearby playground as he shot. "I bring my kids here in the morning. The teenagers have already taken this place over, and it isn't safe for the young kids in the afternoon... This place was supposed to be for little kids too."

With school out for the summer, the first of the basketball players started arriving by two. Grant packed up his children and headed out, and by five, the courts were packed. After hours of competitive but peaceful play, the large groups headed home into the spectacular orange haze of the June sun.

A week later, the little kids got their chance. The young children of the area streamed into Glenwood Park just days after school let out—their braids bouncing and eyes aglow. The city's summer day-camp program had begun. Children playing where gang corner boys once stood are just one sign of the small but growing changes happening on Glenwood.

This summer the Glenwood farmer's market began its first season. While this might be a garden-variety occurrence in many communities, it represents a small miracle in this part of the south side.

On a balmy July evening residents and visitors started arriving to procure fresh fruits and produce from a variety of vendors. Just five years ago, this corner symbolized the crime and chaos that led the *Vindicator* newspaper to call it " one of the meanest commercial corridors in the city."

The streets of Laclede, Sherwood, Parkview and Princeton—which all intersect with Glenwood—were once notorious for their association with the LSP gang. LSP executed much of the murder and drug trafficking in the area. Thanks to the actions of the local neighborhood association, most of the gang's members are in prison today.

Urban farmer Sophia Buggs didn't live through that side of Youngstown. At age ten, her mother moved Buggs to Orlando to look for work and to be closer to her aunt. In 2010, Buggs returned to the city. Her grandmother had stayed behind, weathering some of the worst years of decline on the south side, but she didn't live to see the recent revitalization efforts.

"One of the things my grandmother hoped for was to see Youngstown be a place for her children to come back home to, to have a hometown that they were proud of," said Buggs.

"She would often feel as if the city had forgotten about the residents on the south side because of all the pot holes and cracked side walks, dumping and blighted properties. Regardless of the conditions, she loved her home and would never move away. When I returned home in

2010, I was happy to see that my grandmother's hopes of a city that appeared to care about its residents was coming to reality."

This summer Buggs will represent her urban farm—Lady Bugg's Farm—at the Glenwood farmer's market. She only wishes her grandmother were alive to see it.

"Our street was finally paved, and Glenwood was finally turning into a descent passage. And even though there are tons of vacant lots, there is room for vacant land projects and urban farming and city gardens. The city may need to shrink in order for it to regain its truest connection the land…. There are enough skilled people here to be able to make this a great city."

As the fight to save Youngstown's neighborhoods goes on, people like Buggs will be critical. The hope is that 'boomerangs'—and newcomers—will grow from a trickle to a flood.

Despite long odds, the downtown and now some of the neighborhoods are slowly revitalizing. Crime, which derailed efforts to save the uptown district in the nineties, seems to have crested. However, it would be a mistake to think that the city is not fighting for its life.

The promise of Youngstown 2010 never really materialized. A widespread demolition plan cleared many of the vacant buildings, but very little followed. The recent indictment of Mayor John McNally resurrected Youngstown's well-deserved reputation for corruption. And any kind of planning, no matter how visionary, will be futile in a place with no respect for the rule of law. Youngstown's city government is lagging far behind the efforts of the citizens and non-profits that are leading the fight to save what remains of the 'Buckle on the Rust Belt.'

It's unclear whether the new planning process can succeed where so many other revitalization efforts have failed. In the meantime the fate the city—and the whole of Mahoning Valley—hangs in the balance. A quick drive through the now deteriorating inner-ring suburbs should be enough to convince anyone that the destiny of Youngstown will ultimately be the destiny of every township and village surrounding it. |

If a comeback is to happen, it will happen in the city—guided by sensible planning, competent government, economic development and the creation of small businesses in the neighborhoods. Yet a plan without precedent will have to be followed by mutual cooperation between the city and the suburbs if the Steel Valley is to survive and thrive in the new century.

Women's Issues
DEPARTMENT

Millennium Development Goals
A Focus on Women

Cherise Charleswell

Empowerment of women -- from the women's suffrage movements, to the marked increase of women working outside of the home, to the legal access to birth control and other reproductive rights-- has been one of the strongest drivers of social evolution over the past century, and continued empowerment is essential for addressing the current global challenges facing humanity. The condition of women helps to define the condition and rate of development of a nation, and this should be readily understood when taking into consideration, the fact that women make up a slight majority (52%) of the world's population. Therefore, if nation's are not willing to allow such a large percentage of their population to develop to their full potential, then they are also delaying or off-setting the nation's overall development.

The empowerment of women (and girls) is intrinsically linked to gender equality, and gender equality means both the equality of treatment under the law, as well as equality of opportunity. Thus, empowered women collectively work towards and advocate for gender equality, or they may become empowered when given various opportunities, such as the opportunities to delay marriage and pregnancy, receive an education, or earn (and control) their own income.

In understanding that the development and progress of any nation, is dependent upon the condition of its women, the United Nations issued the Millennium Declaration [A/RES/55/2]. The Millennium Declaration was the result of the gathering of 189 governments, from across the world, in September 2000, who met to make an initial commitment to take collective responsibility for halving world poverty by 2015. Yes, as in next year. More on the successes and failures later, but I'm sure that one can figure out, based on recent reports and the rise of social movements, such as the "Occupy" gatherings, which condemn the growing prevalence of global income inequity; whether or not these goals were actually achieved.

What are Millennium Development Goals?

The Millennium Declaration transformed into the Millennium Development Goals (MDGs), which set out to achieve 8 key development goals and 18 targets, which were framed to reflect its fundamental values by 2015. The MDGs are inter-dependent, and along with the initial goal of the reduction of poverty, commitments were also made for the reduction of poverty, the promotion of human development, environmental sustainability, and development partnership. Further, in the acknowledgement of the critical role of women in a nation's development, the MDGs have an explicit commitment to gender equality. This commitment to gender equality largely appears in the MDGs in relation to health and education. Actually, health (which again is much more than the mere absence of disease) influences all of the MDGs, and this makes sense, since a key component of a nation's "development" should be raising the standard of living and overall health of its population.

Examples of this interrelationship between gender equality, health, and the MDGs are as follows:

- Securing maternal health, allows for a decrease in infant mortality and the improved health of infants; and this better health enables children to learn, while having an education allows that child to become an adult who will be able to earn more over their lifetime.

· Being able to earn more, acquire living wages, and control their own income, allows women to live in better housing, avoid residences plagued by environmental hazards, afford more nutritious food, and ultimately maintain better health and well-being.

So, what are were the specific Millennium Development Goals?

GOAL	TARGET	INDICATORS
1.Eradicate extreme poverty and hunger	Reduce by half the proportion of people living on less than a dollar a day	1. *Proportion of population below $1 (1993 PPP) per day (World Bank) a** 2. *Poverty gap ratio [incidence x depth of poverty] (World Bank)* 3. *Share of poorest quintile in national consumption (World Bank)*
	Reduce by half the proportion of people who suffer from hunger	4. Prevalence of underweight children under five years of age (UNICEF-WHO) 5. Proportion of population below minimum level of dietary energy consumption (FAO)
2. Achieve universal primary education	Ensure that all boys and girls complete a full course of primary schooling	6. *Net enrollment ratio in primary education (UNESCO)* 7. *Proportion of pupils starting grade 1 who reach grade 5 (UNESCO) b** 8. *Literacy rate of 15-24 year-olds (UNESCO)*

3. Promote gender equality and empower women	Eliminate gender disparity in primary and secondary education preferably by 2005, and at all levels by 2015	*9. Ratio of girls to boys in primary, secondary and tertiary education (UNESCO)* *10. Ratio of literate women to men, 15-24 years old (UNESCO)* *11. Share of women in wage employment in the non-agricultural sector (ILO)* *12. Proportion of seats held by women in national parliament (IPU)*
4. Reduce child mortality	Reduce by two thirds the mortality rate among children under five	*13. Under-five mortality rate (UNICEF-WHO)* *14. Infant mortality rate (UNICEF-WHO)* *15. Proportion of 1 year-old children immunized against measles (UNICEF-WHO)*
5. Improve maternal health	Reduce by three quarters the maternal mortality ratio	*16. Maternal mortality ratio (UNICEF-WHO)* *17. Proportion of births attended by skilled health personnel (UNICEF-WHO)*
6. Combat HIV/AIDS, malaria and other diseases	Halt and begin to reverse the spread of HIV/AIDS	*18. HIV prevalence among pregnant women aged 15-24 years (UNAIDS-WHO-UNICEF)* *19. Condom use rate of the contraceptive prevalence rate (UN Population Division) c** *19a. Condom use at last high-risk sex (UNICEF-WHO)* *19b. Percentage of population aged 15-24 years with comprehensive correct knowledge of HIV/AIDS (UNICEF-WHO) d** *19c. Contraceptive prevalence rate (UN Population Division)* *20. Ratio of school attendance of orphans to school attendance of non-orphans aged 10-14 years (UNICEF-UNAIDS-WHO)*

		Halt and begin to reverse the incidence of malaria and other major diseases	21. Prevalence and death rates associated with malaria (WHO) 22. Proportion of population in malaria-risk areas using effective malaria prevention and treatment measures (UNICEF-WHO) e* 23. Prevalence and death rates associated with tuberculosis (WHO) 24. Proportion of tuberculosis cases detected and cured under DOTS (internationally recommended TB control strategy) (WHO)
7. Ensure environmental sustainability		Integrate the principles of sustainable development into country policies and programs; reverse loss of environmental resources	25. Proportion of land area covered by forest (FAO) 26. Ratio of area protected to maintain biological diversity to surface area (UNEP-WCMC) 27. Energy use (kg oil equivalent) per $1 GDP (PPP) (IEA, World Bank) 28. Carbon dioxide emissions per capita (UNFCCC, UNSD) and consumption of ozone-depleting CFCs (ODP tons) (UNEP-Ozone Secretariat) 29. Proportion of population using solid fuels (WHO)
		Reduce by half the proportion of people without sustainable access to safe drinking water	30. sustainable access to an improved water source, urban and rural (UNICEF-WHO) 31. Proportion of population with access to improved sanitation, urban and rural (UNICEF-WHO)
		Achieve significant improvement in lives of at least 100 million slum dwellers, by 2020	32. Proportion of households with access to secure tenure (UN-HABITAT)

| 8. Develop a global partnership for development | Develop further an open trading and financial system that is rule-based, predictable and non-discriminatory. Includes a commitment to good governance, development and poverty reduction - nationally and internationally | **Official development assistance (ODA)**
33. Net ODA, total and to LDCs, as percentage of OECD/Development Assistance Committee (DAC) donors' gross national income (GNI)(OECD)
34. Proportion of total bilateral, sector-allocable ODA of OECD/DAC donors to basic social services (basic education, primary health care, nutrition, safe water and sanitation) (OECD)
35. Proportion of bilateral ODA of OECD/DAC donors that is untied (OECD)
36. ODA received in landlocked developing countries as a proportion of their GNIs (OECD)
37. ODA received in small island developing States as proportion of their GNIs (OECD) |

	Address the special needs of the Least Developed Countries (includes tariff- and quota-free access for Least Developed Countries? exports, enhanced program of debt relief for heavily indebted poor countries [HIPCs] and cancellation of official bilateral debt, and more generous official development assistance for countries committed to poverty reduction)	**Market access** 38. Proportion of total developed country imports (by value and excluding arms) from developing countries and from LDCs, admitted free of duty (UNCTAD, WTO, WB) 39. Average tariffs imposed by developed countries on agricultural products and textiles and clothing from developing countries (UNCTAD, WTO, WB) 40. Agricultural support estimate for OECD countries as percentage of their GDP (OECD) 41. Proportion of ODA provided to help build trade capacity (OECD, WTO) Debt sustainability 42. Total number of countries that have reached their Heavily Indebted Poor Countries Initiative (HIPC) decision points and number that have reached their HIPC completion points (cumulative) (IMF - World Bank) 43. Debt relief committed under HIPC initiative (IMF-World Bank) 44. Debt service as a percentage of exports of goods and services (IMF-World Bank) Some of the indicators listed below are monitored separately for the least developed countries, Africa, landlocked developing countries, and small island developing states

		Address the special needs of landlocked developing countries and small island developing states (through the Program of Action for the Sustainable Development of Small Island Developing States and 22nd General Assembly provisions)	
		Deal comprehensively with the debt problems of developing countries through national and international measures in order to make debt sustainable in the long term	
		In cooperation with developing countries, develop and implement strategies for decent and productive work for youth	45. Unemployment rate of young people aged 15-24 years, each sex and total (ILO) f*
		In cooperation with pharmaceutical companies, provide access to affordable essential drugs in developing countries	46. Proportion of population with access to affordable essential drugs on a sustainable basis (WHO)
		In cooperation with the private sector, make available the benefits of new technologies, especially information and communications technologies	47. Telephone lines and cellular subscribers per 100 population (ITU) 48. Personal computers in use per 100 population and Internet users per 100 population (ITU)

Table 1: Millennium Development Goals, Targets, & IndicatorsSource: UN Millennium Project http://www.unmillenniumproject.org/goals/gti.htm

MDGs Relation to Women's Empowerment & Feminism

In its most basic definition feminism is a theory of political, economic, and social equality of the sexes.[1 (Merriam)] Thus, its primary function is to address and combat oppression and discrimination in all its forms: racism, sexism, ageism, ethnocentrism, discrimination based on sexual orientation, etc. In essence, feminism focuses on removing the barriers to global development, particularly gender inequity, that are outlined in the Millennium Development Goals. This is apparent, when looking at the first five goals: (1)eradicate extreme poverty and hunger, (2) achieve universal primary education, (3) promote gender equality and empower women, (4) reduce child mortality, (5) improve maternal health, which focus specifically on women and children's health and well-being. These goals focus on what are known as the social determinants of health, and they have a greater influence on health outcomes than genetic and biological determinants of health. Improving health outcomes, overall well-being, and the standard of living within a nation, through improving the status of women and girls, puts that nation on a path of development and progress. In other words, a nation benefits from having a healthy (having access to quality food, needed vaccinations, health care, etc.) and educated workforce, able to effectively compete in the global market.

Still, looking at a broader definition of feminism provides another viewpoint which must be considered when speaking about the goal of women's empowerment. Feminism is also defined as the "the analysis of unequal power relationships between woman and man and efforts to change them, and it constitutes the political expressions of the concerns and interests of women from different regions, classes, nationalities and ethnic backgrounds." [2 (Mahajan 2012)] Therefore, it must be understood that the great diversity in race, ethnicity, nationalities, class, sexuality, and experiences of women requires diversity in feminisms, which can be responsive to the different needs and concerns of women, defined by them for themselves. This is true empowerment. In other words, the only way that the MDGs can be achieved, is through the empowerment of women, and allowing them to take part, and have an active role in bringing about the needed transformations within communities and nations.

Being motivated, having-and-exercising choices are related to the central concept of empowerment, which is Agency. Agency itself is the processes by which choices are made and put into effect. [3 Kabeer] While, the other closely interrelated dimensions of empowerment are resources and achievement. Resources are the medium through which agency is exercised, and achievements refer to the outcomes of agency.

Thus, a feminist framework, which seeks changes on behalf of women by focusing on promoting and understanding women as a distinctive group amongst many within any society, who are identified as having different needs, desires, values, and priorities, due to their role and position within these societies; is the most applicable to helping women achieve empowerment, through self agency. Accordingly, the role of the various global organizations – governmental, non-governmental, private, etc. who are committed to the achievement of the MDGs, is to act as or provide the needed resources, through which agency can be exercised. Finally, if the MDGs are met, and whatever successes are measured, they would represent the outcomes of agency.

An example of the various stakeholders will have to work in order to meet the desired outcomes is as follows: If a woman's primary form of access to resources is as a dependent member of the family, her capacity to make strategic choices is likely to be limited. [3 Kabeer] For this reason, the primary mechanisms for transformative change would involve the removal of barriers and the availability and access to resources. Therefore, legislative policy is a critical first-step in the eradication of barriers to social mobility, and these policies can be very varied (policies that address the gender income gap, laws against child marriage, legislation that protects reproductive rights, laws that mandate equitable primary education, etc.) depending upon the needs of a society.

In her farewell remarks as Secretary of State, Hillary Clinton noted that "gender equality is the unfinished business of the 21st century," [(Chang, 2013)] and during her tenure the White House institutionalized a commitment to global gender equality in three areas: diplomacy, development, and national security, and cited that "promoting gender equality and advancing the status of all women and girls around the world….is vital to achieving our overall foreign policy objectives.([Chang, 2013)] Thus, making the case that progress and the security of developed nations is tied to the condition of women in developing nations. Prior to leaving office, Secretary Clinton created the Office of Global Women

Issues, and the position of Senior Coordinator for Gender Equality and Women's Empowerment, which also acts as an advisor to the USAID Administrator. Both the Office and position are permanent additions to the State.

Will the Millennium Development Goals Be Achieved By 2015?

Apologies in advance if this may come as a shock to you, but the answer is NO. When looking at the measures of the listed key indicators (see Table: 1), as well as the human development index, it becomes quite clear that the Millennium Development Goals cannot be met by the 2015 deadline. The Human Development Index (HDI) is based on a composite of life expectancy, infant mortality and educational attainment, and offers an alternative measure of development progress to GNP. [3 (Kabeer)]

The Obvious Failures

If a critical objective of the MDGs was the mitigation of social inequities, which impact health and wellbeing of the world's population, particularly women and children, then failure is the only way to describe the outcomes; whether discussing post-industrial nations or developing nations in the Global South. Further, this inequity most greatly affects women who are already marginalized (by race, ethnicity, sexuality, class, etc.) For instance, Table: 2, provides an overview of the economic status of women of color in the United States, and it is clear that there are great and continued disparities:

Table 2. Ratio of Women's Median Annual Earnings to White Men's by Education Level for Full-Time, Year-Round Workers Aged 25 and Older in the United States, by Race and Ethnicity, 2005

	All	White	African American	Asian American	Native American	Hispanic
All	68.8%	72.9%	62.5%	79.2%	60.0%	52.1%
Less than a High School Diploma	59.5%	66.3%	62.6%	62.6%	56.3%	53.1%
High School Diploma/GED	67.8%	70.3%	62.4%	65.2%	62.5%	59.8%
Some College	67.2%	71.2%	66.8%	70.1%	62.2%	66.8%
Associate's Degree	74.5%	76.6%	70.1%	76.6%	68.1%	66.0%
Bachelor's Degree	70.9%	72.5%	64.4%	73.9%	61.3%	64.4%
Graduate Degree	64.7%	65.8%	61.2%	73.0%	54.1%	58.8%

Notes: Racial categories white, African American, and Asian American do not include Hispanics. Hispanics may be of any race. The category Asian American includes Native Hawaiians/Pacific Islanders.
Source: US Department of Commerce, Bureau of the Census, 2005 American Community Survey. Tabulated by the Urban Institute for Women's Policy Research.

Income equality is imperative, and is tied to all of the MDGs, especially MDG-1, which is the "eradication of extreme poverty and hunger". In attempting to fulfill this objective, it must be understood that women, as a result of a growing Feminization of Poverty, experience higher rates of extreme poverty and hunger. Poverty is 'gendered" because women and men experience poverty differently unequally- and become poor through different, though related, processes. 3 (Kabeer) The fact that 70% of people currently living in poverty are women, mostly in rural areas,[5] Millennium Project again stands as evidence of the failure of MDGs.

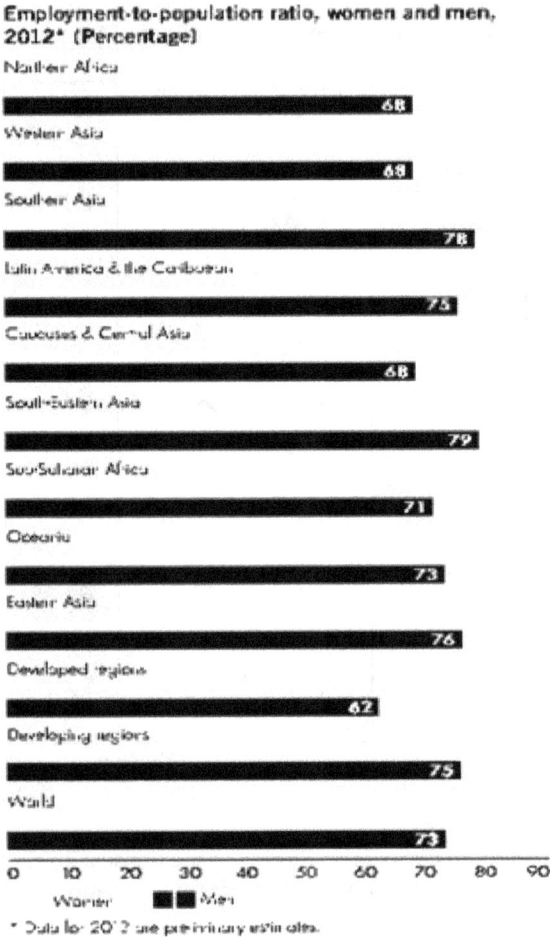

Employment-to-population ratio, women and men, 2012* (Percentage)

Northern Africa	68
Western Asia	68
Southern Asia	78
Latin America & the Caribbean	75
Caucuses & Central Asia	68
South-Eastern Asia	79
Sub-Saharan Africa	71
Oceania	73
Eastern Asia	76
Developed regions	62
Developing regions	75
World	73

Women ■ Men

* Data for 2012 are preliminary estimates.

Source: The Millennium Development Goals Report 2013 p. 8 - See more at: http://www.unwomen.org/en/news/stories/2013/7/the-gender-dimension-of-the-millennium-development-goals-report-2013/#sthash.PXvyEyaV.dpuf

620

Further, as illustrated above, the gender gap in employment persists, with a 24.8 percentage point difference between men and women in employment-to-population ratio in 2012. The employment-to-population ratio measures the proportion of a country's working-age population (ages 15 to 64 in most OECD countries) that is actually employed. While another example of gender inequity, is that as of January 31, 2013, the average share of women members in parliaments worldwide was just over 20%, [5 Millennium Project] and of course, the United States, continues to view itself as being a world leaders and a bastion for equality and progress; even though, a woman President has yet to be elected and women only make up 18.5%% of the 535 seats in the 113th U.S. Congress.[6 Rutgers]

Last, another blaring example of the failure of the MDGs, in regards to empowering, as well as improving the health and well-being of women is reflected by the fact that Violence against women is the largest war today, when one measures the number of death and casulties per year. [5 Millennium Project] Strongly connected to the status of women, is the status of children, and preliminary assessments of the MDGs have shown that the goals also fail to safeguard progress and development in this population, as well. Among the 75 countries with the highest number of preventable child deaths, just 17 are poised to actually meet their targets by 2015, and UNICEF estimates that all countries, if continuing at the current pace, will not reach MDG 4 until 2028. [7WHO] When considering the failure to address gender inequity and the continued barriers placed before women, the unfavorable statistics regarding children, particularly their health and life expectancy should be expected. For, a malnourished woman produces children, who will be faced with a host of medical issues, which will likely shorten their life span. Also, women remain the primary caregivers for children worldwide, and if they are without access to needed resources, then children to will also go without. The health outcomes of women and children are inexplicitly linked, and it is for this reason that Public Health often focuses on Maternal and Child Health.

Some Signs of Success?

As dire as the reports seem, child survival stands out as the success story, and much of that is due to the fact that much of the approach to achieving MDGs, is by the use of pharmaceutical drugs and technologies that can address the immediate biological determinants of health; although this approach does not help to bring about and sustain transformative change. As a result of these efforts, according to a UNICEF report, The number of children who die before their fifth birthday declined by nearly 50 percent between 1990 and 2012, from more than 12 million to 6.6 million.[7 UNICEF] Although not actually reaching the MDG of a 2/3 reduction, this does represent a great achievement.

What Was Missing From the MDGs?

The MDGs are criticized for excluding a number of factors that greatly impact health, well-being, and development, and for focusing on strategies that are not sustainable or rely on empowerment of target populations. In terms of the status of women, the MDGs remain silent on reproductive rights, violence against women, and other unjust laws and social norms that uphold patriarchal structures. Additionally, the MDGs encourage narrow approaches to meeting the targeted objectives, particularly those that rely heavily on technological solutions, and thus neglecting the need for broader social change and the strengthening of national institutions. Another problem with these approaches is that they attempt to address many social issues that impact women, outside of a feminist framework, and thus apply a "one size fits all" policy, which excludes the input of women who work in the countries and communities where these interventions are to be applied. For example, although policy is critical for national development, strategies under the MDGs do not focus any great deal of effort on political organizing and voter advocacy at the grassroots level; and doing so would empower community members, and would help to ensure that elected officials enact policies that reflect their needs and values. One can only hope that the recent Republican-led decision to not extend unemployment benefits, made at the close of 2013, would only inspire a concerted effort between various organizations (non-governmental, non-profit, professional, etc.) to get voters out to the polls, to remove the politicians who support policies that negatively impact the working class, especially women and children. Such an effort would be a great strategy to help achieve MDG-1 "eradicate extreme poverty and hunger". In other words, advocating for and having politicians who are willing to support and implement legislation that supports the social safety net, champion living wages, and are willing to actually tax corporate interest to ensure that they are paying their fair share, is a necessary approach for the eradication of poverty and hunger, that also allows for empowerment, self agency, and dignity.

Last, previous to the development of the MDGs, more holistic approaches were used to combat social problems, such as with the case of low birth weight babies and malnourished children. While the former approach took into account a mother's education and social, and was thus more sustainable, in that the mothers could readily transmit this information to their own children, and educational attainment could help ensure access to higher paying jobs and quality food. The current approach is short-sighted and dependent on technology, and would thus offer the distribution of nutritional supplements as the solution.

Conclusion

Despite their obvious failures, short-sightedness, and unwillingness to address critical components of a global patriarchial system that negatively impacts women and girls, the crafting of the Millennium Development Goals represents the first common framework for promoting global development. They are a necessary first-step to addressing the most dire socioeconomic disparities that negatively impact populations around the globe, particularly developing nations, and their most marginalized groups (women and children). While the Millennium Declaration itself, reflects widespread international acknowledgement that empowerment of women and the achievement of gender equality are matters of human rights and social justice, which can no longer be ignored, and are ultimately tied to a nation's development.

As we draw closer to the expiration date of the Millennium Development Goals, proposals for a post-2015 global agenda are beginning to be put forward, and they too will fall short, if the proposed efforts are still not conducted within a feminist framework, which seeks out and addresses discrimination and all forms of "isms" of oppression, as well as failing to acknowledge diversity and the need for appropriate approaches to meeting any of the objectives.

References

Merriam Webster Dictionary. Feminism. Retrieved from http://www.merriam-webster.com/dictionary/feminism. Accessed on January 22, 2014.

Mahajan V. Women empowerment and social justice: A socialist feminist social work approach. International Conference on Humanity, History, and Society. IPEDR. 2012; 34:69-73.

Kabeer N. (2005) Gender equality and women's empowerment: A critical analysis of the third millennium development goal 1, Gender & Development, 2005; 13(1):13-24

Chang AE. US Global leadership coalition: Smart empowerment-elevating women and girls in foreign policy. 2013; Retrieved from http://www.usglc.org/2013/02/22/smart-empowerment-elevating-women-and-girls-in-foreign-policy/. Accessed on January 23, 2014.

The Millennium Project. Global challenges facing humanity. Retrieved from http://www.millennium-project.org/millennium/Global_Challenges/chall-11.html Accessed on January 23, 2014.

Rutgers Center for American Women and Politics. Eagleton Institute of Politics. Women in Congress 2013. Retrieved from http://www.cawp.rutgers.edu/fast_facts/levels_of_office/Congress-CurrentFacts.php   . Accessed on January 23, 2014.

UNICEF. Committing to child survival: A promise renewed progress report 2013. Retrieved from http://www.unicef.org/publications/files/APR_Progress_Report_2013_9_Sept_2013.pdf Accessed on January 23, 2014.

Feminism is Not Just for Academics
Overcoming Disconnect and Division

Cherise Charleswell

In the most simplistic terms, a feminist is anyone who thinks about gender, access, and equality. In broader terms, feminism may be defined as the theory of the political, economic, and social equality of the sexes.[1] However, despite language that seems inclusive, feminism has always been plagued by division and disconnect, which has led various groups to feel marginalized, silenced, and as of recent, unrepresented by feminism. In short, there is an undeniable and understandable (if one considers historical events and circumstances) development that has led to a rift between academics and non-academics, scholars and practitioners, critics and activists, feminists and those who may not know that they are feminists, in every sense of the word, but are unable or unwilling to claim the term.

From a historical standpoint, feminism has been identified with the West, and each era has been seen as successive waves; with its origins steeped in social criticism (including the work of abolitionist), advocacy, and activism. These waves are characterized as distinct moments in history in which the face of feminism was, for some irrevocable reason, altered. First Wave feminists of the early 20th century were the

Suffragettes, fighting for voting, property rights, and the autonomy of women. These feminists were primarily white, middle-class, propertied, and well-educated, with the exception of noted women of color such as Sojourner Truth and Mary Church Terrell. From the onset, the focus of women organizing in the U.S. and West, neglected the important work and efforts of other women's rights workers. For example, the "First Wave" of Feminism took place in Japan, beginning in 1868 during the Meiji Restoration, which was a period of rapid transformation from a feudal shogunate to a modern nation.[2] It was during this time when women's consciousness began to raise and the term "good wife, wise mother" was coined. This term meant that, in order to become good citizens, women had to become educated and take part in pubic affairs.[2] Japan's Second Wave of feminism was in full-swing by the 1910s when, in 1911, Hiratsuka Haruko (pen name Raicho) founded the feminist magazine, Seito (Bluestocking).[2]

By the time of the Second Wave, the inherent racism and classism within feminism was being called out; along with other societal inequities. Other issues were explored, such as the unequal and inequitable distribution of labor (and today women still earn $0.77 for every $1.00 earned by men)[3] and middle-class ideals. However, another important change in dynamics was taking place, and that was the institutionalization of feminism within academia; with the earliest objectives being to counteract the rampant sexism and discrimination women academics faced.

The result of all of this is that, despite its grassroots origins and focus on social activism and transformative change, feminism has become the property of academics; which has led to open discussions about whether feminism is still relevant, needed, or useful. When considering the issues that continue to impact the lives and well-being of women and families - the gender income gap, feminization of poverty, street harassment, human/sex trafficking, attacks on reproductive rights, and a pervasive rape culture that leads to actual discussion of "legitimate" rape - it is clear that feminism is still quite relevant. However, the realization that there are so many issues which still need to be addressed contributes to the widening of the rift. Third Wave feminists who brought forth the concerns of the marginalized, such as lesbians, transgendered women, and women of color during the 1990s have taken it upon themselves to attempt to address the widening disconnect.

Academia

By the 1960s, the efforts of the women's liberation movement had helped to increase awareness that university education often lacked a woman's perspective. In 1970, the first Women's Studies department was found at San Diego State College (now San Diego State University), with the second department found at Cornell University in the same year, thus marking the beginning of academic feminism. Academic feminism has its roots in the women's liberation movement, and its initial critical objective was the interpretation of women's experience, in order to change women's condition. These programs attempted to and continue to serve an important role in re-examining history, literature, anthropology, psychology, communications and media, and more recently pop culture, as well as other subjects; as well as exploring the "missing women's" perspective.

Thus, academic feminism can rightfully be considered an extension of the women's liberation/feminist movement, but should not be viewed as the only form of feminism. These departments underwent rapid development and expansion, and the National Women's Studies Association was founded in 1977. However, it may have been inevitable that these departments, existing within the realm of an academic institution, would themselves become institutionalized. Women's studies have since continued to deal with this challenge, and have attempted to balance curriculum in an attempt to enact social change. In fact, the 2013 theme of the National Women's Studies Association Conference - largely attended by academics, established scholars, junior scholars, post-docs, and graduate students - was Negotiating Points of Encounter, while the sub-themes included Practices of Effecting Change." Nevertheless, the tension between feminism and women's studies remains, simply because there is an inherent difference between them. While women's studies function strictly in academia, as an institutionalized discipline, feminism is able to take place within academic culture while also remaining deeply rooted in the larger sociocultural arena outside of academia.

In the article, "The Relationship of Feminism and Women's Studies," columnist Melissa Miles McCarter expressed the differences between women's studies and feminism, and provided examples on how they intersect:

These different sites meant that women's studies practice of working within a methodology and institution that often differed from feminism in general meant that women's studies could be seen as inherently patriarchal, or at least as a study which didn't successfully subvert or undermine the institution. In fact, feminism could involve practices that were completely different than what went on in academia while although women's studies might critique and challenge its institutional site, it was also shaped by academic culture and epistemology, ultimately legitimizing academia's role in the larger culture.[4]

Despite academic feminism's awareness of intersectionality, it typically ignores and/or dismisses the classist and lingering racist underpinnings of its behavior. The following passages from the poem, **A Slam on Feminism in Academia**, by feminist poet, writer, artist and arts-educator, Shaunga Tagore, provides the greatest indictment of this behavior.

why did you let me through the doors in the first place
if you were just gonna turn around and force me out?
why did you let me in this ivory tower
filled with hippie feel-good activist academics
debating about feminist organizing in high theory discourse
while barely-paid migrant workers prepare lunches
for seminars, conferences, forums
and get deported the next day
an award winning tenured professor once told me
the only way i will succeed at graduate school
is if i read 300 pages of theory per work per class
and if i'm not capable
my writing must be of low quality
my intellect must be incredibly juvenile

Her indictment continues with...

your ideal graduate student is
someone who can't talk about personality or privilege
without referencing some article

your ideal graduate student is
rich enough
white enough
straight enough
able-bodied and minded-enough
to be given luxury of enjoying sitting in a corner reading 900 pages a
week
(with their fair trade starbucks coffee in hand and their lulu lemon track
pants on ass)

And then she draws to social activism...

some of us are not here to one day
soullessly recite the entire cannon of queer theory development
with our hearts and minds closed
some of us do not wish to compete to be the
newest biggest baddest radical faculty-hire
some of us need to engage with feminist theory
so we can ground it in our community activist work
our creative works
our personal relationships
for our families, communities and histories
for our own fucking deserved peace of minds

In the article, Disciplining feminism: From social activism to academic discourse, author Ellen-Messer-Davidow argues that any further separation of feminist activists and women's studies scholars damages both sides; however, it is her contention that academics have accepted this damage in exchange for the benefits of institutional acceptance.[5] Certainly being part of the institutional and patriarchal system of academia takes its toll on feminist expression and activism in women's studies. Effecting change becomes a secondary or tertiary concern, outside of being pre-occupied with numerous books and articles written with the perspective of other privileged academics (in a sense upholding a glass tower and preaching to the choir, as these scholarly works are from academic feminists who have/had-when-writing institutional backing and power; which means that their work largely remains inaccessible[5]), collecting more letters behind one's last name, becoming tenured, being sure that one is not signaled out as too 'political', and being perceived as not meeting some agreed upon political/intellectual standard. In understanding this, a valid question remains: Is the rift widening because academic feminists are now imprisoned by institutional structures and isolated from large-scale social feminist movements?

Everyday Feminism

The reality is that there are many women worldwide who are doing feminist work, have feminist beliefs, and are dedicated to the empowerment of women, but do not refer to themselves as feminists, or do not find feminism as welcoming and inclusive of their perspectives, immediate concerns, and life experiences. In her book, Full Frontal Feminism: A Young Woman's Guide To Why Feminism Matters, Jessica Valenti,[6] noted that it was her mother who introduced her to feminism but, when speaking about feminist issues, discussions about theory and rhetoric did not occur between them. Valenti's mother, like many other women who are not part of the academy, did not have a need for or desire to discuss and argue about mundane matters such as theory. Instead, they are concerned with Everyday Feminism. They are the field feminists and practitioners, women's rights activists, social justice activists, artists who work to challenge sexist images, public health specialists, clinicians, and research scientist advocating for women's health, lawyers and political activists working to safeguard legislation that will improve the lives of women and families, as well as the women who simply teach their daughters that they are equal to men, and should not accept societal inequities, whether based on race or gender.

These are the women who do not have the luxury to donate many hours to discussing theories, such as intersectionality, and instead have to cope with those very intersections on a daily basis; whether it is racial profiling, residential segregation which result in various health disparities, lack of access to healthcare, or poor housing. These are the women, and male allies, who may apply feminism to work through social issues, take collective action, make transformative cultural changes, and find their own voice and truth.

Digital Feminism: A Gateway for Fourth-Wave Feminists?

Online feminism involves the harnessing of online media to discuss, uplift, and activate gender equality and social justice.[8] Feminist thought is often met with hostility by women of color, who may not feel represented by women's studies, and many of whom are unaware of socialist feminism and womanism and how these schools address the intersectionality of race, class, and gender as drivers of oppression. Thus, social media and other online platforms provide an opportunity to interact with, educate, and increase awareness among audiences of color. Due to the fact that they provide personal perspectives on issues and communities that are outside of the realm, and thus off the radar of traditional and scholarly feminist discourse, grassroots social media sites have become an important source for breaking developments, as well as a source of stories and events that are often overlooked by mainstream media and established feminist organizations.

These viewpoints are shared on various social media pages and especially blogs and websites that are dedicated to different feminists' perspectives and groups, including the musings of those who, again, do not readily accept the label of 'feminist'. Unlike academic journal articles, this information is accessible and not tied to bias and competition that is pervasive in academia. In a sense, any person who has some form of access to digital media technologies, including limited service, has the potential to engage in the various feminist communities that exist today. In fact, one group, the Feminist Network[9], had undergone a global campaign to identify and link feminists from across the globe, and have begun doing so by building a directory and database.

Instead of dedicating many pages to discussions on theory, digital feminists are those who provide personal insight and analysis on their real-life experiences and observations. Thus, digital feminism can act as an entry point for feminist thought and actions, and provide a meeting space for non-academic feminists who may not have the means to attend women's studies conferences or afford exclusive, feminist, scholarly journal subscriptions.

Those who may have a problem with a digital platform being representative face for feminist discourse and activism, due to it not being rooted in academia, need to remember that the feminist movement in the U.S. picked up steam and gained its position of prestige *because* discontented housewives - including working-class women of color - stopped believing they were merely neurotic, grew tired of second-class citizen status, and began to organize on a grassroots level to address societal issues that negatively impacted their lives, health, and well-being.

Ultimately, the overwhelming variety of perspectives, viewpoints, and schools of thoughts found within online feminist communities represent the new face of feminism; and, for this reason, those engaged in digital feminism are being referred to as Fourth Wave feminists. Does the future of feminism lie in a non-academic, non-disciplinary path or an inter-disciplinary field feminism path? Regardless, in order for feminism to resist declarations that it is dead or irrelevant, it needs to repair the disconnect between academic feminism and non-academic feminists, and support the expansion of feminism outside of the walls of academia.

Conclusion

Truth is feminism is a Big Tent, with room for everybody, and needs to move marginalized groups into the center and make them an integral part of the movement. This can be done through focusing on inclusion, beyond academia and its contested women's studies courses whose curriculum still present the scholarly work of women of color as if they remain the exotic "Other." One does not have to be perfectly acquainted with every academic idea or truly understand the term 'feminist pedagogy', or possess the ability to recite various feminist academic theories, in order to effectively discuss feminist issues or self-identify as a feminist. If one is against all systems of oppression, particularly global patriarchy, and believes in women's freedom, gender equality, and equal opportunity in all spheres of life, then they are essentially feminists, whether they claim the label or not.

To be fair, it needs to be reiterated that academic feminism serves it purpose and is simply one avenue of feminism which one may choose to travel down. Overall, feminism is an empowering framework from which a person may understand, critique, and change the world, while defining their place in it. Central to the tenets of feminism is the matter of choice. Feminists should be free to self-identify as feminists, and should also be allowed to carve out their own path within feminism, whether it is in an academic career in women's studies or working within the realm of social justice activism and women's rights organizing. Feminism must remain inclusive and should not be dominated by any sub-group.

An oversimplification of the words of Antonio Gramsci, an Italian writer, politician, political theorist, philosopher, sociologist, linguist, and founding member of the Communist Party of Italy, in which he called for "traditional intellectuals," who are representative of today's academics, to join with the "organic intellectuals" from the working class to effect social change, best describes the path forward that feminism should choose.

References

1. Merriam-Webster Dictionary. Retrieved on December 29, 2013 from http://www.merriam-webster.com/dictionary/feminism
2. Reese L. Gender Difference in History. Teaching About Women in China and Japan. Social Education, NCSS, March 2003. Retrieved on December 19, 2013 fromhttp://www.womeninworldhistory.com/essay-04.html
3. The Institute for Women's Policy Research. Pay Equity & Discrimination.http://www.iwpr.org/initiatives/pay-equity-and-discrimination
4. McCarter MM. (2010). The Relationship of Feminism and Women's Studies Notes on Composition Studies. Retrieved on December 23, 2013 from http://voices.yahoo.com/the-relationship-feminism-womens-studies-5846764.html
5. Messer-Davidow E. Disciplining feminism: From social activism to academic discourse. Durham, NC: Duke University Press, 2002.
6. Valenti J. Full frontal feminism : a young woman's guide to why feminism matters. Emeryville, CA : Seal Press, 2007.
7. Feminist academics seem to have failed us. What now? Shadow's Crescent. Retrieved on December 23, 2013 from shadowscrescent.wordpress.com/2013/01/30/feminist-academics-seemed-to-have-failed-us-what-now/
8. Martin CE, Valenti V. FemFuture: Online revolution. New Feminist Solutions, Barnard Center for Research on Women. 2012; 8:1-34.
9. Feminist Network. http://feministnetworkproject.wordpress.com/

The Built Environment

The Source of Inequities in Health, Well-Being, and Feminist Activism in Communities of Color

Cherise Charleswell

Public health specialists and other social scientists would describe the built environment as a human-made space, where people live, work, and recreate, that consists of buildings, structures, and other products created or modified by people. Thus, it includes but refers to much more than a geographic location. The built environment includes one's neighborhood and all of its available resources - parks, bike lanes, libraries, schools, clinics/hospitals, full service grocery markets, etc., one's home and family unit, as well as their place of employment.

Traditionally, research and interventions carried out by public health specialists working in conjunction with legislators, city planners, engineers, and architects have primarily focused on housing, transportation, and physical neighborhood characteristics. However, there is a growing body of evidence that is emerging which suggests that physical and mental health problems -anxiety, depression, attention deficit disorder, substance abuse, aggressive behavior, asthma, heart disease, diabetes, and obesity - are linked to an unsupportive built environment, particularly to poor urban planning and inadequate housing.

A critical point when considering the built environment is the impact that it has on resident's health, particularly when keeping in mind that health comprises far more than the absence of disease and injury. Health also encompasses one's wellbeing. Thus, the circumstances within a built environment can greatly contribute to inequities in health outcomes, as well as diminish opportunities to become involved in feminist activism and any other activity that would require the commitment of valuable time and resources. Communities of color are those where the built environment is more likely to be plagued with barriers to health and wellbeing; and, for that reason, they also have the highest rates of social inequity and health disparities. Helping to mitigate these barriers may aid in increasing the number of women directly involved in feminist and social activism. The assumption is that concerns surrounding the procurement of food and housing, along with the burden of a reduced health status, will ultimately monopolize the time of women of color living within these socially constructed environments. Therefore, feminist organizing and analytics must include a focus on the role of the built environment in the lives of women, along with its affect on their physical and mental health.

Intersectionality and the Built Environment

Intersectionality, a term coined by feminist legal scholar, Kimberle Crenshaw, is a feminist sociological theory which takes a critical look at varying and multiple dimensions of social relationships. The theory essentially describes the ways in which oppressive institutions are interconnected and thus cannot be examined separately from one another. It has become an accepted and well respected research and policy paradigm.[1] The central tenets of intersectionality include: (1) that human experiences cannot be accurately understood by prioritizing any one single factor or constellation of factors, (2) that social categories/locations, such as race, ethnicity, gender, class, sexuality, and ability are socially constructed, fluid and flexible, and (3) that promotion of social justice and equity are paramount.[2,3] The theory of intersectionality serves as a tool for analyzing the ways dimensions of difference - e.g. race, gender, ethnicity, class, sexuality, ability, age - can form interlocking inequalities and must, therefore, be simultaneously considered if we are to understand accurately how people shape their environments and negotiate their everyday lives within the contexts of ideological, political, and economic systems of power.[4]

The built environment may be viewed as a sum of all of these various intersections, or as a site where they all convene. The built environment itself is socially constructed and has historically been formed and maintained through residential segregation. Racial segregation may be defined as the physical separation of the races by enforced residence in certain areas, which serves as an institutional mechanism of racism, which was initially designed to protect whites from social interactions with blacks and other populations of color.[4] When discussing societal oppressive institutions, it must be made clear that, racial segregation has long been identified as the central determinant of the creation and perpetuation of racial inequalities in America.[4] The Spatial Mismatch theory, first proposed in 1960 by John F. Kain, explains the correlation between residential segregation and economic performance for residents living in these socially excluded communities of color: "Black enclaves are often physically separated from employment opportunities. As a result, residents of these neighborhoods face high commuting costs and may lack information about new job openings, or the means to actually get to those jobs."[5]

Racial segregation is the keenest form of social exclusion, and concentrates poverty and excludes and isolates communities of color from the mainstream resources needed for success.[6] The problem of social exclusion remains a clear and present reality for communities of color. In fact, poor African Americans were 7.3 times as likely to live in high poverty neighborhoods as poor white Americans in 2000, followed by Latinos, who were 5.7 times more likely.[7] These rates of exclusive poverty actually doubled since 1960. Moreover, in understanding the relationship between intersectionality and the built environment, it is important to realize that factors which act as focal points in intersectionality include those that are multi-level forces. These external and often distant forces, such as policies and legislation, shape the built environment by acting upon it and influencing those who live within its boundaries. Thus, there is a realization that policies do not simply 'impact' people, instead they 'create' people." [8] In other words discriminatory, unjust, and unethical policies help to create marginalize populations and low income wage earners, or the working poor. Furthermore, these external forces take primacy in making the lives of women unequal.

This speaks to the fact that women of color are directly impacted by the racial wealth divide and women's wealth divide. A 2010 report by the Insight Center for Community and Economic Development revealed that single Black and Hispanic women have one penny of wealth for every dollar of wealth owned by their male counterparts and a fraction of a penny for every dollar of wealth owned by single white women.[9] This race and gender wage gap that compounds the lives of women of color is attributed to the fact that women of color are less likely to benefit from the "wealth escalator", as they represent the group that is most often without the intangible items that translate into wealth, such as workplace fringe benefits. In addition, women of color are excluded from fringe benefits because they work in larger numbers in service industries, which do not offer these benefits. The Insight Report also provided data to substantiate this claim. It reported that 28% of Black women and 31% of Latinas, compared to 12% of white men and 19% of white women, work in service jobs.[9]

For African American, Latina, and indigenous women, gender is a part of a large pattern of unequal social relations, but how it is experienced depends on their race and how it interjects with other inequalities.[10] Further, the intersections experienced within the built environment promote or constrain opportunities for health, socioeconomic advancement, and social/feminist activism. In terms of looking at gaps in educational achievement, residential segregation has led to highly segregated schools and may be viewed as the fundamental cause of racial differences in the quality of education.[4] This disparity is attributed to the fact that physical residence determines which public schools one can attend, and those living within a built environment with a deficit in resources will predictably receive less support. For older women of color, institutional discrimination grounded in residential segregation severely restricts employment opportunities and income levels. Thus, for women of color, the critical intersection of race in the built environment is a prominent concern due to the direct impact on health. Racism, primarily through racial segregation, influences how people are treated, what resources are available to them, how they live, how the world perceives them, what environmental exposures they are exposed to, and what opportunities they have in order to thrive and reach their full potential.[6]

Ultimately, a feminist and interdisciplinary approach to health inequities must include the consideration of all of the intersections within the various spaces that women occupy, which negatively impact their livelihood. Therefore, this approach must identify and examine the connections between disadvantage and health, and the distribution of power. [11] Additionally, in creating these disadvantages, the roles of race and gender must be closely scrutinized, particularly when considering how these circumstances act as barriers to the engagement and mobilization of women of color in feminist organizing.

Barriers and Realities

Barriers, whether they are cultural, physical, economic, or social - including discriminatory practices and circumstances - make it difficult for women of color to successfully navigate themselves towards a feminist ideology that is robust and able to embrace all aspects of their experiences. Cultural norms and how they dictate the way in which women are treated within families and communities helps to determine our understanding of womanhood, and the place of women in the world. [12] Further, cultural norms and practices are a significant part of the built environment, and represent an intersection that greatly influences the lives of women. Also, culture can directly, as well as negatively, impact the health and wellbeing of women, and thus consequently acts a as barrier to feminist discourse. An example of how cultural norms can act as a barrier to both health and feminist activism is provided when looking at female illiteracy in culture's that disvalue or do not allow women to actively pursue education, especially a higher education. This lack of education translates into the inability to assume employment outside of a service industry or outside of a household, and thus locks one into lower wages and ensures that they will be segregated into residential areas that have low resources, particularly in regards to health care. Researchers have already identified socioeconomic status as a fundamental cause of observed social inequalities in health. [13,14,15] The culminate effect is reduced health outcomes and a lowering of quality of life and well-being, which involves working many hours or multiple jobs, and thus having little time or ability to be actively involved in women's and social justice movements or political activism.

The sentiments shared by anthropologist, Patricia Williams Lessane, in her report on the panel discussions and roundtables referred to as the Women's "F" Series, which was a collaborative effort developed by the Chicago Foundation for Women and the Columbia College Center for the Study of Gender in the Media and Arts, helps to add credence to the argument that barriers in the built environment, the intersections that influence the lives of women - particularly women of color - diminishes their efforts and involvement in feminist organizing and discourse: "The experience of struggle was the core of many of the speaker's experiences. For some, the day-to-day struggle to get an education, find a job, and raise a family left no space for participating within an organized feminist movement."[12]

There is indeed a centrality of race to the formation of the North American built environment, as well as others in which societies are made up of diverse racial and ethnic populations, and it is imperative that we use feminist analytics, including the theory of intersectionality, to study these relationships and put forth efforts to address blatant inequities in built environments that reduce the quality of life and well-being for women of color, as well as act as a barrier to their engagement in feminist discourse and organizing. In short, when women are faced with the mounting challenges within their built environment, they are unable to readily identify time to take part in efforts that will help to improve their social conditions.

The Built Environment's Impact on Health

In terms of organizing and advocacy, health and well being will always remain the priority. Consequently, the higher rates of health disparities resulting from realities within the built environment unfairly help to diminish the involvement, advancement, and prominence of women of color in feminist discourse. The following rhetorical question posed by anthropologist William Dressler exemplifies the importance of taking into account non-biological or genetic factors role in health outcomes and mortality rates:

"So many medical conditions are differently distributed to African Americans - heart disease, diabetes, hypertension, low birth weight babies - are we to believe that Black people were so evolutionary unlucky that they got all the genes that predisposed them to every malady?"[6]

Of course, we are not to believe that all of these maladies and health disparities are attributed to biological differences in African Americans.

Instead, we must look at the factors - those intersections in the built environment that contributes to a lower status of health and well-being. Again social exclusion and residential segregation greatly influences the day-to-day realities of the built environment. In this case, they greatly constrained the choices that people have the selection of healthy and nutritional foods. A 2002 study revealed that African Americans were actually five times less likely to live in census tracts with supermarkets than white Americans.[16] Public health specialists have long been aware of the direct correlation between zip code, the availability of nutrient-rich products, and health.[17] Even when the nutritional and subsequently more expensive food options are available, women of color may face a barrier of not having the needed purchasing power to afford to buy and consume the healthier options. This lack of access to nutritious food products has translated into the increased risk or manifestation of chronic diseases in communities of color.

Championing the access to healthy foods and safe spaces should be a topic of monumental and mutual concern for women, public health specialists, and those engaged in feminist discourse; in that the topics highlight an area where women have traditionally held agency and a degree of influence, with their traditional roles as care givers and custodians of health and well-being within families. In this role women meditate activities concerning dietary habits, personal hygiene, and childhood activities. The buildings and structures within the built environment also largely impact health, and housing concerns are prominent for women of color and single women, especially single mothers. The quality of housing is also likely to be poorer in racially segregated areas. [18] Housing concerns, particularly crowded and substandard housing, which impact health and wellbeing are numerous and include: elevated noise, inadequate or extreme heat depending on the season, as well as exposure to environmental hazards, such as carcinogens, toxic compounds, allergens and lead paint. A number of empirical studies, conducted over 40 years have determined that low-income communities and communities of color are more likely to be exposed to environmental hazards.[19] Thus; women of color are burdened with the struggle to survive and thrive amidst environmental health risks.

Feminist organizing that addresses these issues would prove to be more attractive, inclusive, and beneficial to women of color. The final condition within the built environment that affects women's health and wellbeing is the level of crime and/or violence. Violence affects health by increasing the risk for injury and death, and of particular concern to women is domestic or intimate partner violence. Women of color experience high rates of domestic violence, and studies have found that African American women have the highest rates, followed by Latina women.[20] Despite these alarming statistics, discussions on rape culture are not openly discussed in communities of color, and rape itself often goes unreported, particularly within the African American community.

Conclusion

Feminism must be rooted in liberation and self-agency, and agency should be looked upon as a mode of action and site of intervention. In other words, feminist ideology must identify, address, and help to mitigate or remove barriers and oppressive institutions that impede gender equity. Therefore, feminist organizing and analytics must include a focus on the role of the built environment in the lives of women, due to its ability to directly and often negatively impact women's health and wellbeing, and thus decrease the likelihood that they would become involved in women's and social movements. If feminism ideology is truly rooted in liberation, it must willingly address the various social issues - violence, poverty, poor education, unemployment and underemployment, and the lack of access to health care - which disproportionately impact women, particularly women of color.

In conclusion, collaborative efforts between public health specialists and feminists will provide a needed interdisciplinary approach that can critically examine the varying intersections and barriers to health, wellbeing and equity in the built environment. Those working in the field of public health have expertise in addressing the health effects of poverty, material disadvantage, and inequity, while feminists are quite familiar with addressing the less tangible aspects of inequity, which include lack of power, discrimination, and oppression.

References

1. Ange-Marie Hancock, "When multiplication doesn't equal quick addition: Examining the intersectionality as a research paradigm", Perspectives on Politics, 5, no. 1 (2007b):63-78

2. Olena Hankivsky and Renee Cormier, " Intersectionality: Moving women's health research and policy forward", Vancouver: Women's Health Research Network. 2009. Retrieved fromhttp://www.bccewh.bc.ca/publicationsresources/documents/IntersectionaliyMovingwomenshealthresearchandpolicyforward.pdf(accessed June 30, 2013)

3. Olena Hankivsky, Daniel Grace , Gemma Hunting et al., ". Intersectionality-based policy analysis", This Volume (2012), Retrieved from: http://www.sfu.ca/iirp/ibpa.html (accessed July 4, 2013)

4. Dill Bonnie Thornton Dill and Saundra Murray Nettles, "What do we mean by Intersections?" Connections (2001); www.crge.umd.edu (accessed March 15, 2014); Lynn Weber, Understanding Race, Class, Gender, and Sexuality: A Conceptual Framework (New York: McGraw-Hill, 2001).

5.David Williams and Chiquita Collins , "Racial residential segregation: A fundamental cause of racial disparities in health", Public Health Reports, 116 (September-October 2011): 404-416.

6. John Kain, "Housing segregation, negro employment, and metropolitan decentralization". Quarterly Journal of Economics, 82 , no.2 (1968):175-197.

7. Brian Smedley , Michale Jeffries , Larry Adelman , Jean Cheng, "Race, racial inequality and health inequities: Separating myth from fact", Retrieved from:http://www.emfp.org/MainMenuCategory/Library/ResearchResourceLinks/RaceRacialInequalityandHealthInequitiespdf.aspx(accessed June 28, 2013)

8. Nancy Denson, Bridgit Anderson," Poverty and race research: Action Council analysis of U.S. Census Bureau data", The Opportunity Agenda, 2005, Retrieved fromhttps://www.opportunityagenda.org (accessed July 1, 2013)

9. Carol Bacchi and Joan Eveline, Mainstreaming and neoliberalism: A contested relationship. Mainstreaming politics: Gendering practices and feminist theory. 2010: 39-60. Adelaide: University of Adeliade Press.

10. Insight Center for Community Economic Development, "Lifting as we climb: Women of color, wealth, and America's future", http://www.insightcced.org/uploads/CRWG/LiftingAsWeClimb-ExecutiveSummary-embargoed-0303.pdf (accessed July 1, 2013).

11. Maxine Zinn and Bonnie Dill, eds., "Differences and Domination", Chap.1, In Women of color in U.S. society. Philidelphia: Temple University Press, (Dec 1993): 3-12

12. Rogers WA, "Feminism and public health ethics", Journal of Medical Ethics. 32, (July 2006): 351-354.

13. Patricia Lessane, "Women of color facing feminism-Creating our space at liberation's table: A report on the Chicago Foundation for women's "F" series", The Journal of Pan African Studies, 1 no. 7 (March 2007):3-10.

14. James House, Ronald Kessler, A. Regula Herzog, Kessler RC, et al., "Age, socioeconomic status and health", Millabank Quarterly. 68 (1990) 383-341.

15. Bruce Link and Jo Phelan," Social conditions as fundamental causes of disease". Journal of Health Sociology Behavior. Extra Issue, (1995): 80-94.

16. David Williams, " Socioeconomic differentials in health: a review and redirection" Social Psychology Quarterly ,53, no. 2 Special Issue: Social Structure and the Individual, (June 1990):81-99.

17. Kimberly Morland, Steve Wing, Anna Diez Roux K, "The contextual effect of the local food environment on resident's diets: the atherosclerosis risk in communities study" American Journal of Public Health, 92, (January 2002):1761-1767.

18. Cheadle A, Psaty BM, Curry S, Wagner E, Diehr P, Koepsell T, Kristal A. Community-level comparisons between the grocery store environment and individual dietary practices. Preventative Medicine. 1991; 20:250-261.

19. Gary Evans and Susan Saegert, "Residential crowding in the context of inner city poverty". In: Wapner S, Demick J. Yamamoto T, et al., ed. Theoretical perspectives in environment-behavior research, (New York: Kluwer Academic/Plenum Publishers, 2000), 247-267.

20. Luke Cole and Sheila Foster. From the ground up: Environmental racism and the rise of the environmental justice movement. (New York University Press, 2001), 167-183.

21. Sonia Frias and Ronald Angel, "The risk of partner violence among low- income Hispanic subgroups", Journal of Marriage and Family Therapy, 67 (August 2005): 552-564.

The Hampton Institute is a working-class think tank
providing commentary, analysis, research and
theory on a wide range of social, political, economic
and cultural topics. Visit us on the web at
www.hamptoninstitution.org.

www.ingramcontent.com/pod-product-compliance
Lightning Source LLC
Chambersburg PA
CBHW050327270326
41926CB00016B/3341